T0230164

Bernhard Nebel
Leonie Dreschler-Fischer (Eds.)

KI-94: Advances in Artificial Intelligence

18th German Annual Conference
on Artificial Intelligence
Saarbrücken, Germany, September 18-23, 1994
Proceedings

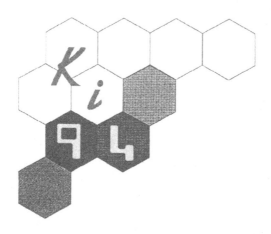

Springer-Verlag

Berlin Heidelberg New York
London Paris Tokyo
Hong Kong Barcelona
Budapest

Series Editors

Jaime G. Carbonell
School of Computer Science, Carnegie Mellon University
Schenley Park, Pittsburgh, PA 15213-3890, USA

Jörg Siekmann
University of Saarland
German Research Center for Artificial Intelligence (DFKI)
Stuhlsatzenhausweg 3, D-66123 Saarbrücken, Germany

Volume Editors

Bernhard Nebel
Fakultät für Informatik, Universität Ulm
D-89069 Ulm, Germany

Leonie Dreschler-Fischer
Fachbereich Informatik, Universität Hamburg
Vogt-Kölln-Straße 30, D-22527 Hamburg

CR Subject Classification (1991): I.2, F.4.1

ISBN 3-540-58467-6 Springer-Verlag Berlin Heidelberg New York

CIP data applied for

Typesetting: Camera ready by author
SPIN: 10479065   45/3140-543210 - Printed on acid-free paper

Foreword

Gathered in this volume are the 33 papers and 12 posters that were accepted for publication and presentation at the scientific program of the 18th Annual German Conference on Artificial Intelligence KI-94. Additionally, this volume contains the manuscript of the invited talk *"AI Approaches towards Sensor-Based Driver Support in Road Vehicles"* by H.-H. Nagel.

Because of the many excellent contributions – we received 98 contributions with almost half of them from abroad (e.g., Australia, China, France, Great Britain, India, Russia, The Netherlands) – the selection of papers was difficult and the program committee had to be very selective. Rather to our surprise the majority of the papers were on knowledge representation and logical foundations of artificial intelligence, so some members of the program committee had much more review work to do than they had bargained for.

The *KI-94 best paper award* was given by the program committee to the paper

Representing Concurrent Actions and Solving Conflicts

Congratulations to the authors *Sven-Erik Bornscheuer* and *Michael Thielscher!* Many thanks to our colleagues on the program committee for their hard and execellent work:

F. Baader (RWTH Aachen), W. Benn (TU Chemnitz-Zwickau), W. Bibel (TH Darmstadt), S. Biundo (DFKI, Saarbrücken), L. Bonsiepen (Univ. Bremen), G. Brewka (GMD, St. Augustin), H.-D. Burkhard (Humboldt-Univ., Berlin), H. Dörner (Halle), W. Förstner (Univ. Bonn), G. Görz (Univ. Erlangen), G. Gottlob (TU Wien), H. Kamp (Univ. Stuttgart), O. Kübler (ETH Zentrum, Zürich), B. Mertsching (GH Paderborn), K. Morik (Univ. Dortmund), W. Nejdl (RWTH Aachen), K. Noekel (Siemens, München), H. Novak (IBM, Böblingen), S. Pribbenow (Univ. Hamburg), B. Radig (TU München), U. Rembold (Univ. Karlsruhe), H. Ritter (Univ. Bielefeld), D. Roesner (FAW, Ulm), A. Voss (GMD, St. Augustin).

In addition, also many thanks to the additional reviewers:

K.-D. Althoff, M. Baaz, J. Bachmayer, P. Baumgartner, C. Beckstein, B. Beckert, S. Bell, S. Brüning, H.-J. Bürckert, J. Buhmann, J. Dix, A. Dold, T. Eiter, C. Eschenbach, K.-H. Erhard, Ch. Fermueller, E. Franconi, Ch. Freska, U. Furbach, J. Gamper, P. Getfert, S. Göser, G. Große, St. Hahndel, J. Heinsohn, W. Heitsch, B. Hollunder, D. Hutter, F. Jacquemard, S. Jockusch, U. Junker, W. Klein, V. Klingspor, S. Kockskämper, D. Korn, Ch. Kreitz, F. Kurfess, G. Lakemeyer, S. Lau, A. Leitsch, M. Lenz, N. Leone, E. Littmann, Ch. Löckenhoff, L. Martignon, F. Maurer, R. Möller, W. Müller, T. Noll, W. Nutt, H.-J. Ohlbach, G. Paul, H. Popp, T. Rath, A. Rieger, R. Röhrig, K. Rohr, H. Rott, H. Ruess, M. Rusinowitch, M. Schmidt-Schauss, A. Schopp, K. U. Schulz, U. Sigmund,

VI

W. Snyder, W. Stephan, P. Struss, M. Stumptner, M. Thielscher,
Ch. Walther, S. Weber, T. Wengerek, S. Wess, E. Weydert, L. Wieske,
C. Witteveen, R. Zach, K. Zimmermann.

Many thanks also to the local organization committee and to our secretaries at Hamburg, Saarbrücken and Ulm for their support.

Last but not least, many thanks to the authors, who somehow managed to send in their manuscripts before the deadline in spite of the postal strike.

Ulm
Hamburg
July 1994

Bernhard Nebel
Leonie Dreschler-Fischer

Contents

Machine Learning

Knowledge Representation

Non-monotonic Reasoning

Reasoning

Posters

AI Approaches towards Sensor-Based Driver Support in Road Vehicles

H.-H. Nagel [1, 2]

[1] Fraunhofer-Institut für Informations- und Datenverarbeitung (IITB)
Fraunhoferstr. 1, D-76131 Karlsruhe
[2] Institut für Algorithmen und Kognitive Systeme
Fakultät für Informatik der Universität Karlsruhe (TH)

Abstract. The concept of a sensor-based support system for drivers of road vehicles is outlined and subsequently refined step by step. The refinement steps emphasize the necessity to treat this problem on a conceptual rather than on a signal processing level. Moreover, this approach emphasizes the systems aspect. As a consequence, the challenge to AI is seen at the systems level. Various recent developments are pointed out which support the hypothesis that a combination of recent progress in formal logic, natural language processing, knowledge representation, and image sequence understanding can contribute substantially to experimental as well as theortical work in the design of driver support systems.

1 Introduction

Modern road vehicles have reached a level of reliability, ease of handling, and comfort which allows a driver to concentrate on finding his way, on keeping his vehicle along the desired trajectory, and on avoiding obstacles. This progress, however, may have contributed to the built-up of new pressures for a driver. The apparent ease, freedom, and low cost of travelling by motorvehicles have induced a still increasing number of people to consider driving a road vehicle not only as an occasionally used option, but to accept it as a necessity. Since there are large regions where it is no longer possible to substantially increase the network of public roads, traffic density increases. As a consequence, driving can still become taxing, despite the quality of modern road vehicles.

An analogous development can be observed with respect to highway systems which provide an environment with deliberately reduced complexity in order to facilitate long distance travel at higher speeds. Again, this option has turned into a necessity for a significant fraction of drivers, raising the following questions:

- How to reduce the danger of loosing alertness while driving along monotonous, straight highway sections as they can be found, e.g., in the Midwest of the United States?
- How to increase the throughput of traffic arteries by enabling the flexible formation of truck convoys travelling at close distance without danger of run-up accidents? This aspect might become relevant in heavily built-up areas

without sufficient space reserves to construct additional highway capacities, for example in Central Europe.

In all examples, the same basic question arises: can recent advances in sensing technology, signal processing, and computer technology be exploited in order to further reduce stress for a driver, thereby contributing to a reduction of the number as well as the severity of traffic accidents, and simultaneously increasing the efficiency of use of available road facilities ?

Today, it is technically and possibly even economically feasible to install special devices which facilitate a 'stimulus-response' type of action such as automatic lane keeping on well marked, not congested highway lanes, distance keeping during stop-and-go traffic, or tracking a preceding car. If the number and diversity of such support installations within a vehicle increase, however, a more balanced approach towards the totality of traffic situations and the required responses may become desirable. Pursueing this line of thought results in the concept of an 'Encompassing Driver Support System (EDSS)'.

The EDSS concept starts from the high standard of mechanics and dynamics of modern cars, and strives to supplement them with a kind of electronic 'seventh sense' for the security and comfort of the driver and his passengers. The EDSS implies the study of an automatic driving facility as an optional subsystem, for example based on machine vision. The design of such a subsystem is likely to start by exploiting the comparative simplicity of a highway environment and may become of particular interest for long-haul trucking.

Before the question is addressed what AI may contribute to the potential realization of an EDSS, the scope of the problem area should be assessed. In order to be truely useful, the EDSS should support a driver from the start through the actual driving period(s) until he reaches his final goal. The spatial scale over which a driver thus may expect support extends, for example, from a day's travel distance—say, 500 km—down to preventing an inadvertent bump into the car in front of him while creeping along in stop-and-go traffic. The relevant distance in the latter case is of the order of a meter. The ratio of 1:500,000 corresponds to more than five orders of magnitude. If this appears to be an accidental result, the following consideration lets one pause again. Planning a day's travel may easily cover a period of about ten hours or 36,000 seconds. Every driver knows that a traffic situation may become dangerous within fractions of a second, for example if some previously hidden or unnoticed car suddenly appears to be on a collision course. If we assume 0.3 second—a car may travel easily 10 m during this time—as a critical time scale, we again find a ratio corresponding to five orders of magnitude.

2 Towards a Model of an 'Encompassing Driver Support System (EDSS)'

The surprisingly large range of spatial and temporal scales which has been outlined in the preceding paragraph may serve as a quantitative indicator for the diversity of problems to be handled by an EDSS. Obviously, one has to structure the entire problem area in order to even get a chance of success for an attempt to design an EDSS. The decomposition of the problem area into a hierarchy of abstractions is the usual approach offered as a remedy. Given the diversity of the problem area, it should not come as a surprise if different people offer different decompositions, depending on the perspective from which they approach the problem. In many examples, moreover, only a partial decomposition will be attempted.

These considerations result in the following postulates for attempts to design an EDSS:

- It appears unreasonable to expect that a hierarchical decomposition based on a single specialisation relation will be able to capture all relevant aspects.
- Partial decompositions should be admitted unless they can immediately be subsumed into an already existing (sub-)hierarchy.
- Different representational methods have to be taken into account in order to facilitate selecting that representation which most easily allows to describe and analyse the problem aspect in question.
- Different decompositions should be mapped explicitly onto each other to the extent they attempt to describe the same part(s) of reality, albeit from different points of view.
- Each problem representation should be convertible into a form which allows analysis by formal methods such as logic.
- There should be algorithmic methods which transform an admitted level of problem representation into an executable form.

In essence, then, the goal consists in designing a model of an EDSS which can be formally analyzed as well as converted into an executable form for testing.

Such an ambitious goal can not be reached during a single attempt. Unless, however, this challenge is accepted right from the start and then systematically pursued in iterative design cycles, the result is likely to be less complete or reliable and the total expenses could easily turn out to be higher. If more than a single design cycle is planned for, it becomes advisable to start with explicitly mentioned restrictions during the early design cycles in order to be able to check whether the partial goals for the current design cycle have been met or not.

Subsequent sections sketch such a design process in order to indicate where AI approaches can play a role and how they interact with approaches from other disciplines. This latter aspect is important because each discipline, in particular a younger one, is in danger to overestimate the range of applicability of its methodological approaches and thus runs the risk to devalue its true contributions by overblown claims.

3 Outline of a Stepwise Specification for an EDSS

Although driving fully automatically is not the design goal of an EDSS, the capability to drive a road vehicle automatically is considered to be a precondition for substantial support in critical traffic situations. How could one believe a system which can not even in principle do itself what it recommends to others? In order to indicate the restrictions of subsequent considerations, we start by specifying a 'Single Agent Driving System (SADS)' which emphasizes a sensor-based capability for automatic guidance of a road vehicle.

3.1 A Single Agent Driving System (SADS)

The SADS should operate under conditions where activities of other traffic participants develop slowly enough to consider them as static aspects of the current traffic situation to be sensed by the SADS. Moreover, only standard road vehicles will be admitted as traffic participants, i.e. pedestrians, bicycle riders, animals, and special purpose vehicles will initially be excluded as traffic participants. This set of conditions will be referred to under the notion of 'quasi-static traffic'. This notion emphasizes the SADS activities as distinguished from those of other road vehicles. The SADS thus represents an attempt to study a capability for sensing and assessing the traffic environment in order to extract the information required for fully automatic control of a road vehicle. Within this task framework, a human has a supervisory function, not that of a regular driver and, therefore, will be referred to as the 'human operator'.

The interaction between a SADS and its human operator will be restricted to the following possibilities:

– The SADS receives the mission specification from the human operator.
– The SADS reports the successful completion of its mission.
– It transfers control back to the human operator in case of failure to handle a traffic situation automatically. Note that this implies the capability of an SADS to recognize its own limits.

It is implied that an SADS records its intermediate results in sufficient detail such that all decisions by the SADS can be traced back to check their root causes. As an initial substep, one could start with traffic on unidirectional highways since highway traffic is more formalized both with respect to the number and complexity of admitted maneuvers as well as with respect to the static road environment. The specifications for an SADS will be outlined in a subsequent section.

3.2 A Multiple Agent Driving System (MADS)

The next step consists in extending the SADS into one where more than a single traffic participant is *explicitly modelled*. For this purpose, the knowledge about automatically handling quasi-static traffic is exploited in order to provide a generic representation of the behavior of a road vehicle as an agent in road traffic. This generic representation has to be restricted in such a manner that only activities of a vehicle as an agent which can be sensed from outside the vehicle—like that recorded, for example, by a video camera configuration in another appropriately equipped agent vehicle—will be admitted for analysis. The SADS will then be augmented into a 'Multiple Agent Driving System (MADS)' by combining the core SADS capabilities with the capability (i) to determine the motion of other vehicles relative to their lane and road as well as (ii) relative to the core SADS vehicle. In addition, a MADS will be able to exploit the generic knowledge about handling quasi-static traffic in order to interpret the trajectory of another vehicle agent relative to itself in terms of 'intentions' which the observed agent vehicle pursues regarding its impending driving maneuvers. The—suitably restricted—knowledge base of an SADS thus is turned into a schema for the interpretation of other agent's behavior to the extent it can be inferred from video input. This should be seen as an analogy to the way a human driver observes his traffic environment in order to infer potential activities of neighboring traffic participants and to plan his next maneuvers, based on the instance of the current traffic situation around him obtained by his visual perception.

3.3 Incorporating the Driver into the Modelling Framework

The MADS concept models an agent which can control a vehicle for road traffic under somewhat restricted conditions such as, e.g., the exclusion of pedestrians. It comprises the capability to sense the presence and motion of other admitted traffic participants and to take an interpretation of the trajectory of other vehicles into account when selecting its next maneuver. In order to make such capabilities available as an unobtrusive support for the human driver of a suitably equipped vehicle, the MADS is extended via an intermediate step—the Driver's Activities Monitoring System (DAMS)—into an EDSS by incorporating facilities to *model the human driver himself.* This latter model will provide the basis to control the EDSS aspects of the interaction between a driver and the vehicle. The driver-vehicle interaction is here understood to comprise not only the manipulation of the standard controls available to the driver of a road vehicle, but in addition the interaction between the driver and the EDSS.

To simplify the presentation, the concept of a Driver's Activities Monitoring System is introduced. It comprises facilities to model the driver, but not yet the means to interact with the driver. It could be seen as a passive observer who carefully monitors the driver's activities and records them for later scrutiny. It may well turn out that this concept acquires its own raison d'être by becoming a tool which facilitates the systematic investigation of the relation between a particular traffic situation and (re-)actions of a human driver. The basic idea consists in taking the knowledge base underlying the MADS and to consider it as a schema which can be instantiated in order to build—within the DAMS— an estimated representation of the current state and intentions of the vehicle's driver:

- The 'Generic Driver Description (GDD)' represents a schema of what a human driver *could* do. It comprises the representational schemata developed for a MADS and in addition schemata describing how a driver manipulates the controls of a vehicle, such as the steering wheel, gas, brake, and direction indicators.

- The 'Current Driver Model (CDM)' refers to the actual DAMS-internal representation of the driver's current state and intentions. This representation will have been obtained as an instance of the GDD, appropriate for the actual moment, which implies that the CDM is continuously updated.

The idea of a DAMS can possibly be put to use even beyond being a tool during the EDSS development process. Given the facilities for recording all relevant aspects of a traffic situation and the associated reactions of a driver, the assessment process does not always need to run in real-time. One could consider the recording facilities as a kind of road vehicle analogy to a flight recorder. Data would only be evaluated if a situation needs to be clarified in detail. It is conceivable that such a 'driving recorder' becomes a legally required accessory of every vehicle equipped with an *interfering* EDSS in order to facilitate a decision whether the EDSS may have been causally involved in an accident.

3.4 Modelling the Driver-Vehicle Interaction

In order to clarify the subsequent discussion, we adopt the convention that the EDSS is a synonym for a road vehicle equipped with such an encompassing driver support system. Moreover, the EDSS is simultaneously used as the synonym for such a system *acting as an agent* which is considered to be able to control the vehicle in road traffic. The EDSS can thus be seen as an analogy to a copilot in a commercial airplane who carefully monitors the activities of the pilot—the DAMS aspect—and could take over control of the plane at any time if so asked by the pilot himself. The latter alternative relates to the MADS aspect. In order to realize a pilot–copilot analogy between the driver and the EDSS, it is assumed that there will be a need to establish a continuous communication between the driver and his support system, just as a pilot continually communicates either explicitly or implicitly with his copilot. Since a pilot can not spend all his attention to such a pilot–copilot communication, both partners carefully assess which communication channel (speech, pointing acts, face expressions, etc.) appears to be the most appropriate at any one moment. This includes the alternative to temporarily refrain from any communication at all if the partner appears to have no spare capacity for it.

These considerations suggest to introduce the following additional concepts:

- The 'Driver-Vehicle-Communication Resources Description (DVCRD)' denotes a schema which describes all relevant aspects of communication channels between a driver and his support system. These include speech I/O as well as a noise assessment process in order to determine whether the actual environmental noise level could jeopardize acoustic communication with the driver. Display devices, an assessment of current lighting conditions, and tactile communication facilities will have to be taken into account.

- The 'Driver-Vehicle-Communication Resources Model (DVCRM)': This is an instance of the DVCRD, representing the current best estimate which the EDSS can derive for the actual communication capacity of the driver.
- The 'Normative Driver Description (NDD)' represents a schema of what a human driver *should* do. Differences between the CDM and the NDD represent hints towards where and when a warning could be considered helpful by the driver (or at least appropriate by others).

The transition from a passively monitoring DAMS to an EDSS implies that the latter evaluates not only its internal assessment of the traffic situation, but in addition its Current Driver Model (CDM) and its DVCRM in order to decide whether and when it should become active, for example by issuing a warning to the driver. The decision will comprise not only the point in time when to issue a warning, but has to evaluate the DVCRM in order to select the momentarily most appropriate communication channel between the EDSS and the driver.

3.5 Intermediate Summary

A 'middle-out' approach has been chosen in order to present the concept of an encompassing driver support system: it has been hypothesized that an automatic agent—the MADS—can sense and assess suitably restricted real-world traffic situations and exploit this assessment for automatic lateral and longitudinal control of a road vehicle. This hypothetical capability has then been stepwise extended into the capabilities required for a truely useful driver support system. The need remains to show that the SADS underlying the MADS indeed constitutes a viable system concept. Eventually, the MADS and hence the GDD will have to be upgraded by dropping the restrictions regarding other traffic participants. This will have obvious consequences for the CDM, the NDD, and the EDSS.

4 Top-Down Exposition of a Single Agent Driving System

The preceding section introduced the concept of a SADS as an intermediate stage for the design of an EDSS. The SADS to be outlined here depends on having access to a digital road map which provides the 'long term knowledge' about the static aspects of the environment in which the SADS has to act. The 'short term knowledge' about the actual state of the environment, particularly in front of the SADS vehicle, has to be obtained by the evaluation of sensor input about the environment, predominantly by the evaluation of video sequences recorded by one or more video cameras mounted on the SADS vehicle.

4.1 Hierarchical Task Decomposition within the SADS

The principal components of a SADS, organized into a four level hierarchy,

- the Mission Master Level (MML),

- the Navigation Level (NL),
- the Maneuver Level (ML), and
- the Control Level (CL),

will be sketched here, based on Nagel and Enkelmann (1991), see also (Nagel et al. 1994).

The Mission Master Level, the highest in a SADS, communicates with the human operator. After having received the input about the current start and the desired goal location, a digital road map is used by the MML in order to search a route from start to goal. The result of this planning step is presented to the operator who may demand modifications and eventually has to confirm the final version of the route. This route is subsequently transmitted to the next lower level, the Navigation Level, which decomposes the route into a concatenation of route segments: each segment follows a road from a major connection, where this road is entered by the selected route, to the location where the route switches to another road. The digital road map is again used for this purpose.

The Navigation Level transmits each route segment in turn to the next lower level, the Maneuver Level, which further decomposes a segment into a sequence of driving maneuvers required to move the SADS vehicle safely from the start point to the end point of a segment. Each maneuver is transferred to the lowest level, the Control Level, which actually performs the lateral and longitudinal control steps required to execute a maneuver. In parallel, the Navigation Level will track the current vehicle position with respect to the digital road map. The NL, therefore, will know when a route segment ends and information about the next route segment has to be transmitted to the ML.

In case the 'short term' knowledge indicates that a certain maneuver can not be executed—for example due to an obstacle—control is returned to the ML which may select an evasion maneuver. If this turns out to provide no help, the ML reports back to the NL which would attempt to replan the route in order to find a detour around the blocked road section. In case no such detour can be found which is compatible with the boundary conditions set by the human operator during the initial specification phase of the entire mission, the NL would return control to the Mission Master Level which in turn would have to report the failure to the human operator and wait for further commands.

4.2   A Set of Driving Maneuvers as a Basis for SADS Actions

In order to perform the task assigned to the Maneuver Level, the ML needs to know which maneuvers can possibly be performed by the Control Level and what represents an admissible sequence of maneuvers. Nagel and Enkelmann (1991) suggested a set of 17 basic driving maneuvers in order to provide a tentative answer to the first question. In the course of attempts to implement this set, Tölle (1993) regrouped the maneuvers into three groups, depending on whether a maneuver refers, in addition to the motion verb itself, only to the road (Group 1), or to another object (Group 2), or to a special set of maneuvers for parking (Group 3). As will be discussed in a subsequent section, an analogous distinction came up independently during research efforts to associate motion verbs with vehicle trajectories which have been extracted automatically from image sequences recorded by a stationary video camera from road traffic scenes.

- Group 1 (maneuvers referring only to the road):
  Start_and_continue, Follow_a_road, Cross_intersection, Merge_to_{left_lane / right_lane}, Turn_{left / right}, Slowdown_to_right_road_edge_and_stop, Back_up, U_turn_to_the{left / right}, Reverse_direction.
- Group 2 (maneuvers referring to another object):
  Approach_obstacle_ahead, Overtake, Stop_in_front_of_obstacle, Pass_obstacle_to_the{left / right}, Start_after_preceding_car, Follow_preceding_car.
- Group 3 (parking maneuvers):
  Enter_parking_slot, Leave_parking_slot.

At the level of abstraction of the ML, each of these maneuvers constitutes a primitive—possibly generic, i.e. with free parameters such as the direction (left or right)—which is to be realized by the Control Level. The discussion whether, for example, emergency situations like stops in front of a suddenly appearing obstacle should be handled by switching back to the maneuver level and by selecting an appropriate reaction or by special approaches within each maneuver is still open.

4.3 Rules for the Concatenation of Maneuvers

In order to continue the exposition in a systematic manner, let us assume that the set of basic maneuvers is complete in the sense that all maneuvers are available which could possibly be required by the SADS. Let us assume further that all of them have been implemented and, therefore, can be activated by the ML at the CL. This still leaves the question open how the ML copes with the enormous search space defined by all combinatorically possible sequences of maneuvers during an attempt to determine the next maneuver while negotiating the current route segment. Once this problem has been recognized, one could argue that the evaluation of the video input, for example, should allow to quickly determine which maneuver has to be executed next. In emergency situations, this can sometimes be the case indeed, since only an immediate stop or an evasion maneuver to the right or left will be reasonable. But such an approach does not offer a completely satisfactory answer in general, since the evaluation of the sensorial input itself may need guidance by reasonable expectations about how to interpret the input.

It thus appears preferable to provide the SADS with an additional kind of 'long term knowledge' about sequences of maneuvers. This does not imply, however, that maneuver sequences have to be absolutely predetermined. It suffices if the ML has access to knowledge about which sequences of maneuvers are admissible. Nagel (1991) described the use of a cascade of finite state automata to represent sequences of driving actions which are admissible in visiting a petrol station, see also (Nagel et al. 1994). Essentially the same approach has been employed to define a significant part of admissible sequences of driving activities which may occur while driving along a highway, see Nagel (1994).

4.4 Summary of the Exposition of the SADS concept

As has been shown in the earlier section treating a coarse stepwise specification of an EDSS, the knowledge about how to perform lateral as well as longitudinal control in order to safely guide a road vehicle constitutes the backbone of an EDSS. This section represents an attempt to decompose this knowledge step by step into elementary driving maneuvers which are considered to be conceptual primitives, denoting activities which are executed by a control process at the Control Level. The combination of the SADS outline from this section with its use to construct an EDSS as outlined in the preceding section represents a conceptual framework for an encompassing driver support system.

5 The EDSS Framework and Research Results

At this point, time and space do not permit an extensive review of the widespread research activities on sensor-based autonomous road vehicle systems or investigations into driver-vehicle-interactions. Following a few pointers to the recent literature about these topics, it will be shown that considerable components of the framework outlined in the preceding sections have already been implemented and tested, albeit under simplified boundary conditions.

A good introduction to the recent literature has been given by Enkelmann (1993). More recent contributions can be found in the proceedings of the Intelligent Vehicles Symposium (1993) and its successor in 1994. The presentation of the development of autonomous as well as assisting road vehicle systems at the IITB in Nagel et al. (1994) provides additional references to the recent literature.

Recently, two systems have been announced as commercial products which offer—based on comprehensive digital road maps—route planning and navigation support for drivers of road vehicles. An earlier version of the Travelpilot[3] has been used in an experimental arrangement in order to demonstrate the combination of route planning and navigation based on a digital road map with automatic lateral and longitudinal control of a road vehicle based on machine vision, see Siegle et al. (1992) and Struck et al. (1993).

Numerous experiments have been pursued within the EUREKA-project PROMETHEUS (PROgraMme for a European Traffic with Highest Efficiency and Unprecedented Safety), see Glathe (1993) regarding PROMETHEUS. The final report about the activities of German research groups which investigated the application of AI approaches towards improvements of road traffic, in particular automatic guidance of road vehicles based on machine vision and the exploitation of such efforts for the design of driver support systems, will appear

---

[3] Travelpilot is a symbol registered for Robert Bosch GmbH of Stuttgart / Germany

shortly, see Nagel (1994b). In this context, Dickmanns et al. (1993) reported about extended automatic driving experiments in regular traffic on Autobahnen as well as on other roads. Similar extended automatic driving experiments have been performed by a research group at Daimler–Benz AG, Stuttgart, see, e.g., Ulmer (1992).

To my current knowledge, all among the primitive driving maneuvers from group 1 mentioned above, except Back_up, U_turn, and Reverse_direction, have already been executed automatically, most of them by several research groups with different automatic road vehicles. Similarly, all maneuvers from group 2 mentioned above, except Start_after_preceding_car, have to my knowledge already been executed automatically. As a consequence, it can be stated that a SADS—a Single Agent Driving System—has become already an *experimental* reality. The system realized by the research group around Dickmanns at the Universität der Bundeswehr München may already be considered as an example for a MADS, see Dickmanns (1993).

Given such a state, it could be considered surprising that progress appears so fast provided the human driver is taken out of the loop rather than keeping him in the control loop. Such an argument overlooks the fact that a human driver in the loop can not easily be brought to conform exactly to some particular conditions which appear necessary in order to successfully execute a sequence of driving maneuvers by an automatic setup. The diversity of human (re-)actions usually swart such attempts. On the other hand, it is exactly this diversity which enables the human driver to drive under most conditions and not only under restricted conditions which still have to be stipulated for automatic driving experiments.

Nevertheless, the growing capabilities of automatic systems can be and are exploited in order to push investigations into driver–vehicle interactions. Once it becomes possible to extract significant aspects of a traffic situation automatically from sensor data, (re-)actions of a human driver can be assessed in much more detail. As a consequence, subtle relations between aspects of a traffic situation and a driver activity can be separated more easily from irrelevant associations. The Driver's Activities Monitoring System (DAMS) begins to become a research tool.

A good access to research about driver support systems within PROME-THEUS is provided by the study of Reichart et al. (1993). Nirschl and Geiser (1993) investigated how the point in time, at which a warning will be issued to a driver, has to be chosen in order to maximize safety and simultaneously minimize potential inconveniences for the driver. This concept has been used by the authors to study the time at which warnings should be issued to a driver approaching an intersection where he does not have the right-of-way. This approach has been implemented and tested within a vehicle equipped with a video camera and image sequence evaluation so that the intersection could be detected in real-time based on machine vision (Enkelmann et al. 1993).

It thus appears justified to claim that even the apparently difficult transition from a Multiple Agent Driving System (MADS) via the Driver's Activities Monitoring System (DAMS) to an Encompassing Driver Support System (EDSS) comes within grasping distance for substantial experimental research.

6 Sensor-Based Warning Versus Sensor-Based Intervention

At this point, a comment appears appropriate regarding two—non-technical—questions which are very likely to pop up. Will a warning without automatic intervention provide sufficient progress in safety and comfort that its generation appears worthwhile? This immediately leads to the second question, touching an even more problematic and hence controversial topic: should an EDSS be authorized to interfere with the driver in case its criteria indicate that without immediate action a traffic accident can no longer be avoided?

Before attempting to answer these questions, the reader is reminded that an overwhelming majority of people—at least in areas where road vehicles are routinely used—has no problem to enter an automatic elevator and to let themselves be lifted to the tenth floor or higher. An accidental fall from that height is generally considered to be lethal! Even more surprising, once one begins to think about it, is the observation that apparently no airline passenger feels uneasy about the fact that most of the time during transatlantic flights an automatic pilot controls the airplane. Admittedly, this state of affairs constitutes the end of a long technical development and an accompanying technical licencing activity.

Taking these considerations into account, the answer to the second question must be: it appears premature to discuss about a facility which first has to prove its reliability. Once one can demonstrate that an EDSS reacts ten times as reliable as the average driver, it may be time to come back to this question. And the answer to the first question then may be somewhat along the following lines: unless detailed experience is gathered with the ways a driver could be supported before a system begins to interfere, one shall not know how reliable an EDSS may have become already. The true problem consists in finding intermediate stages of a development in the direction outlined here which allow to market them in order to begin early enough to defray already part of the development costs and to gather experience about larger scale use of component equipment.

7 AI and Driver Support Systems

So far, very little has been mentioned about contributions of AI research to the investigation, design, implementation, and evaluation of sensor-based driver support systems for road vehicles. The treatment deliberately emphasized the overall framework rather than investigations into detail problems. It should have become obvious by now that research into driver support systems like those discussed here under the acronym EDSS have passed from the stage of isolated investigations into detail problems to the stage of experimenting with entire systems. For the characteristics of Systems Engineering aspects for computer-based systems, the reader is referred to White et al. (1993). The question, then, becomes: what can AI offer for multi-disciplinary research on entire system structures of non-trivial size? Four major aspects come to the mind.

One consists in the decades of experience with the frustrating attempts to formalize predominantly qualitative aspects of everyday life. The methodological approach to insist on explicating the knowledge brought to bear for a solution attempt rather than hiding it away in heuristics appears to me to be of prime importance. In this context, various approaches to represent knowledge, to study the inherent complexity of their use and to evaluate the comparative advantages and disadvantages will play an increasing role.

A second aspect is the clarification about the role which first order predicate logic as well as extensions of it begin to play for knowledge representation—see, e.g., Bibel (1993). In particular, Terminological Logic Systems are likely to become very important during a systematic characterization of the extreme number of different traffic situations. Unless these are categorized systematically, based on a formal system which facilitates to continuously update and maintain the 'zoo of categorized traffic situations', it will be very difficult to prove that every one will be treated properly by a particular support system. Naturally, automatic proof systems will have to be explored in this context.

A third aspect refers to the work in natural language text and speech understanding. It has been very illuminating to experience the first touches between three initially unrelated research areas, see (Nagel 1994):

- The attempt to define a set of generic maneuvers as a basis to be provided by the Control Level of an SADS.
- The introduction of 'Metasymbols' as a representation for intermediate concepts during the attempts to establish a formal basis for the definition of admissible sequences of maneuvers.
- Research into the association of trajectory segments, which have been extracted automatically from image sequences of traffic scenes, with natural language motion verbs, see Kollnig and Nagel (1993), Kollnig et al. (1994).

The more one moves away from processing close at the signal level, the more the properties of natural language to cope with naturally occurring complexity will be felt as an advantage. One could be tempted to postulate that specifications for an EDSS will eventually be written in—somewhat restrained—natural language and translated into formal systems by means of natural language processing. The advantages of understanding natural language by an automaton for the optimization of driver-vehicle interactions need not be emphasized here separately.

The last aspect refers to the exposition of 'Discourse Representation Theory' by Kamp and Reyle (1993). The investigations discussed in this book represent a direct link between natural language, logic, and the requirements of a systematic approach towards the design of driver support systems as emphasized in this contribution, provided one accepts the premise that the problem of driver-vehicle communication will eventually necessitate the treatment of driver support systems at a conceptual level corresponding to natural language understanding.

8 Conclusion

Research into sensor-based driver support systems has passed the stage of isolated investigations. It has to be pursued on a systems level, combining many disciplines such as human-machine interaction, psychology, traffic science, control theory, image sequence evaluation, natural language understanding, formal logic, knowledge representation, just to name the most important. The challenge for AI consists in accepting that it has to contribute at the systems level. It appears that AI has developed the conceptual and programming tools to stand up to this challenge.

References

Bibel, W., zusammen mit Hölldobler, S., Schaub, T.: Wissensrepräsentation und Inferenz, Eine grundlegende Einführung. Friedrich Vieweg & Sohn Verlagsgesellschaft mbH, Braunschweig Wiesbaden 1993

Dickmanns, E.D., Behringer, R., Brüdigam, C., Dickmanns, D., Thomanek, F., v. Holt, V.: An All-Transputer Visual Autobahn-Autopilot/Copilot. Proc. Fourth International Conference on Computer Vision ICCV '93, 11-14 May 1993, Berlin / Germany, 608–615

Enkelmann, W.: Konzeption und Nutzung von Wissensrepräsentationen bei videogestützten Assistenzsystemen für die Straßenfahrzeugführung. In: O. Herzog, Th. Christaller, D. Schütt (Hrsg.), *Grundlagen und Anwendungen der Künstlichen Intelligenz*. 17. Fachtagung für Künstliche Intelligenz, Humboldt-Universität zu Berlin, 13.-16. Sept. 1993; Informatik aktuell, Springer-Verlag Berlin Heidelberg New York/NY etc. 1993, 74–89

Enkelmann, W., Nirschl, G., Gengenbach, V., Krüger, W., Rössle, S., Tölle, W.: Realization of a Driver's Warning Assistant for Intersections. Proc. Intelligent Vehicles '93 Symposium, 14-16 July 1993, Tokyo / Japan, IEEE Industrial Electronics Society, ISBN 0-7803-1370-4, 1993, 72–77

Glathe, H.-P.: PROMETHEUS – mobil in die Zukunft ? Mikroelektronik, Mobilität und Verkehr: Alternativen – Chancen – Grenzen. Mikroelektronik, Basis für innovative Verkehrskonzepte. Vorträge der GME-Fachtagung vom 21. bis 22. Januar 1993 in Berlin, GME-Fachberichte 10, vde-verlag gmbh Berlin Offenbach 1993, 13-19

Proc. Intelligent Vehicles '93 Symposium, 14-16 July 1993, Tokyo / Japan, IEEE Industrial Electronics Society, ISBN 0-7803-1370-4, 1993

Proc. Intelligent Vehicles '94 Symposium, 24-26 October 1994, Paris / France, in press

Kamp, H., Reyle, U.: From Discourse to Logic – Introduction to Modeltheoretic Semantics of Natural Language, Formal Logic and Discourse Representation Theory. Kluwer Academic Publishers, Dordrecht/NL Boston/MA London/UK 1993

Kollnig, H., Nagel, H.-H.: Ermittlung von begrifflichen Beschreibungen von Geschehen in Straßenverkehrsszenen mit Hilfe unscharfer Mengen. Informatik Forschung und Entwicklung 8 (1993) 186–196

Kollnig, H., Nagel, H.-H., Otte, M.: Association of Motion Verbs with Vehicle Movements Extracted from Dense Optical Flow Fields. Proc. Third European Conference on Computer Vision ECCV '94, Vol. II, Stockholm / Sweden, 2–6 May 1994, Eklundh, J.-O. (ed.), Lecture Notes in Computer Science 801, Springer-Verlag Berlin Heidelberg New York/NY 1994, 338–347

Nagel, H.-H.: The Representation of Situations and Their Recognition from Image Sequences. Proc. AFCET 8e Congrès Reconnaissance des Formes et Intelligence Artificielle, Lyon-Villeurbanne / France, 25-29 November 1991, 1221–1229

Nagel, H.-H.: A Vision of 'Vision and Language' Comprises Action: An Example from Road Traffic. Artificial Intelligence Review (1994), Special Issue on Integration of Natural Language and Vision, P. Mc Kevitt (guest ed.), in press

Nagel, H.-H.: infix, Sankt Augustin/Germany 1994 (in german, in preparation)

Nagel, H.-H., Enkelmann, W.: Generic Road Traffic Situations and Driver Support Systems. Proc. 5th PROMETHEUS Workshop, Munich/Germany, 15-16 October 1991, 76–85

Nagel, H.-H., Enkelmann, W., Struck, G.: FhG-Co-Driver: From Map-Guided Automatic Driving by Machine Vision to a Cooperative Driver Support. Computers & Mathematics with Applications (1994), Special Issue on "Network, Control, Communication and Computing Technologies for Intelligent Vehicle Highway Systems" (in press)

Nirschl, G., Geiser, G.: Zeitbudgetanalyse der Fahrer-Fahrzeug-Interaktion als Werkzeug für die Entwicklung von Fahrerassistenzsystemen. 2. VDI-BMW Gemeinschaftstagung "Sicherheit im Straßenverkehr", München, 25.–26. März 1993, VDI-Berichte 1046, VDI-Verlag Düsseldorf 1993, 219–239

Reichart, G., Haller, R., Naab, K.: Zur Entwicklung künftiger Fahrerassistenzsysteme. Mikroelektronik, Basis für innovative Verkehrskonzepte. Vorträge der GME-Fachtagung vom 21. bis 22. Januar 1993 in Berlin, GME-Fachberichte 10, vde-verlag gmbh Berlin Offenbach 1993, 47–57

Siegle, G., Geisler, J., Laubenstein, F., Nagel, H.-H., Struck, G.: Autonomous Driving on a Road Network. Proc. Intelligent Vehicles '92 Symposium, 29 June - 1 July 1992, Detroit / MI, 403–408

Struck, G., Geisler, J., Laubenstein, F., Nagel, H.-H., Siegle, G.: Interaction between Digital Road Map Systems and Trinocular Autonomous Driving. Proc. Intelligent Vehicles '93 Symposium, 14-16 July 1993, Tokyo / Japan, IEEE Industrial Electronics Society, ISBN 0-7803-1370-4, 1993, 461–466

Tölle, W.: Hierarchisches Regelungskonzept für die Fahrzeugführung. Interner Bericht (in German, preliminary version); Fraunhofer-Institut für Informations- und Datenverarbeitung (IITB), Karlsruhe / Germany, 1993

Ullmer, B.: VITA – An Autonomous Road Vehicle (ARV) for Colission Avoidance in Traffic. Proc. Intelligent Vehicles '92 Symposium, 29 June - 1 July 1992, Detroit / MI, 36–41

White, S., Alford, M., Holtzman, J., Kuehl, S., McCay, B., Oliver, D., Owens, D., Tully, C., Willey, A.: Systems Engineering of Computer-Based Systems. IEEE Computer 26:11 (November 1993) 54–65

Representing Concurrent Actions and Solving Conflicts*

Sven-Erik Bornscheuer   Michael Thielscher

FG Intellektik, FB Informatik, Technische Hochschule Darmstadt
Alexanderstraße 10, D–64283 Darmstadt (Germany)
E-mail: {sven,mit}@intellektik.informatik.th-darmstadt.de

Abstract. As an extension of the well–known *Action Description language* $\mathcal{A}$ introduced by M. Gelfond and V. Lifschitz [7], C. Baral and M. Gelfond recently defined the dialect $\mathcal{A}_C$ which allows the description of concurrent actions [1]. Also, a sound but incomplete encoding of $\mathcal{A}_C$ by means of an extended logic program was presented there. In this paper, we work on interpretations of contradictory inferences from partial action descriptions. Employing an interpretation different from the one implicitly used in $\mathcal{A}_C$, we present a new dialect $\mathcal{A}_C^+$, which allows to infer non-contradictory information from contradictory descriptions and to describe nondeterminism and uncertainty. Furthermore, we give the first sound and complete encoding of $\mathcal{A}_C$, using equational logic programming, and extend it to $\mathcal{A}_C^+$ as well.

1 Introduction

Intelligent beings are able to treat contradictory information more or less appropriately. For instance, imagine yourself asking two passers-by for the shortest way to the train station. The first one answers: "Turn right, and you will get there in five minutes." while the second one answers: "Turn right, and you will get there in ten minutes." Reasoning about these answers you find out that they are contradictory, i.e. the provided information is inconsistent and cannot be true. However, since both passers-by are in agreement with their recommendation to turn right, you would assume this part of the information to be true; you are only left in uncertainty about the time it takes to reach the station.

One should be aware of the difference between uncertain information explicitly stated as such like "you will arrive in five or in ten minutes" and contradictory information like the answers above. Contradictory information cannot be true; so, it has to be interpreted appropriately if you nonetheless want to derive some benefit from it.

When machines are used to reason about some complex information, it makes no sense to assume this information to be consistent in general; we know,i.a., from

* The second author was supported in part by ESPRIT within basic research action MEDLAR-II under grant no. 6471 and by the Deutsche Forschungsgemeinschaft (DFG) within project KONNEKTIONSBEWEISER under grant no. Bi 228/6-1.

Software Engineering that in general formalizations of something non-trivial are incorrect. Therefore, if a machine detects the incorrectness of the information it reasons about, this only gives certainty about circumstances which had to be assumed anyway. But it still has to be decided how this machine has to act in such a situation.

A typical field where the detection of the inconsistence of the used information has to be expected, is the one of reasoning about the execution of concurrent actions in dynamic systems.

Most complex dynamic systems include concurrent actions. Therefore, the ability for describing concurrent actions is of central interest in AI. For instance, to open a door locked by an electric door opener an autonomous robot has to press a button and to push the door concurrently. Hence, only knowing the effects of the seperate execution of each action, will not enable to open the door.

Since it is of course impractical to define the effects of the concurrent execution of each possible tuple of actions explicitly, it is preferable to infer most of these effects from the various descriptions of the involved individual actions. In certain cases, some of these descriptions may propose contradictory effects. The crucial question is again how to interpret such contradictions.

We discuss this question in the first part of this paper, and, for that, use a formalism $\mathcal{A}_C$ introduced by C. Baral and M. Gelfond. $\mathcal{A}_C$ allows the description of concurrent actions and was developed in [1] as an extension of the *Action Description Language* $\mathcal{A}$ [7] which was introduced in 1992 and became very popular since. Both $\mathcal{A}$ and $\mathcal{A}_C$ attract by the simple, elegant, and natural way in which the effects of actions are described. The execution of actions adds or removes elements from a particular set of facts representing some situation in the world; all non-affected facts continue to hold in the resulting situation due to the common assumption of persistence. The language $\mathcal{A}_C$ is defined in Section 2.

In Section 3 we examine the possibilities of interpreting contradictory inferences from partial action descriptions. Coming from a different point of view than the one implicitly underlying $\mathcal{A}_C$, we present an extension of $\mathcal{A}_C$ which we call $\mathcal{A}_C^+$. This new dialect allows to infer the non-contradicted information from contradictory descriptions, while such inference is not possible in $\mathcal{A}$ nor in $\mathcal{A}_C$. Moreover, $\mathcal{A}_C^+$ allows the describtion of nondeterministic actions with randomized effects and uncertain knowledge.

In the second part of this paper, we present the first sound and complete translation from $\mathcal{A}_C$ into a logic program with an underlying equational theory and, by modifying this translation in an appropriate way, an encoding of $\mathcal{A}_C^+$ as well. This translation allows to automate reasoning about dynamic systems following the concepts determined by $\mathcal{A}_C^+$ (and $\mathcal{A}_C$, respectively). Moreover, the translation of such high-level languages into different approaches designed for reasoning about dynamic systems, actions, and change, allows to compare the possibilities and limitations of these approaches in a precise and uniform way, which is in favorable contrast to the traditional way of explaining new approaches with reference to a few standard examples, such as some in the blocksworld or the famous "Yale Shooting Scenario" and its enhancements [7, 16, 17].

To this end, $\mathcal{A}$ was translated into several formalisms [7, 5, 14, 4, 19]. In [1], a sound but, unfortunately, incomplete encoding of $\mathcal{A}_C$ using extended logic programs following the lines of [7] was presented. In this paper, we extend the work [19] and show how an approach based on *equational logic programming* (ELP) [10, 9] can be used as a sound and even complete method for encoding $\mathcal{A}_C$ and $\mathcal{A}_C^+$.

ELP is a deductive approach using first-order-logic for describing actions. Similar to $\mathcal{A}$ and $\mathcal{A}_C$, the effects of actions are described by adding or removing resources from a single term representing a complete situation in the world (see also [2]). ELP is introduced in Section 4, and the translations encoding $\mathcal{A}_C$ and $\mathcal{A}_C^+$, respectively, are evolved in Section 5. Finally, our results are summarized in Section 6.

2 $\mathcal{A}_C$

We briefly review the concepts underlying the language $\mathcal{A}_C$ as defined in [1].

A *domain description* D in $\mathcal{A}_C$ consists of two disjoint sets of symbols, namely a set F_D of *fluent names* and a set A_D of *unit action names*, along with a set of *value propositions* (v-propositions) — each denoting the value of a single fluent in a particular state — and a set of *effect propositions* (e-propositions) denoting the effects of *actions*. A (compound) *action* is a non-empty subset of A_D with the intended meaning that all of its elements are executed concurrently. A v-proposition is of the form

$$f \text{ after } [a_1, \ldots, a_m] \tag{1}$$

where $a_1, \ldots, a_m$ ($m \geq 0$) are (compound) actions and f is a *fluent literal*, i.e. a fluent name possibly preceded by $\neg$. Such a v-proposition should be interpreted as: f has been observed to hold after having executed the sequence of actions $[a_1, \ldots, a_m]$. In case $m = 0$, (1) is written as initially f.

An e-proposition is of the form

$$a \text{ causes } f \text{ if } c_1, \ldots, c_n \tag{2}$$

where a is an action and f as well as $c_1, \ldots, c_n$ ($n \geq 0$) are fluent literals. (2) should be read as: Executing action a causes f to hold in the resulting state provided the conditions $c_1, \ldots, c_n$ hold in the actual state.

Example. You can open a door by running into it if at the same time you activate the electric door opener; otherwise, you will hurt yourself by doing this. The dog sleeping beside the door will wake up when the door opener is activated. You can close the door by pulling it. To formalize this scenario in $\mathcal{A}_C$, consider the two sets $A_{D_1} = \{activate, pull, run\_into\}$ and $F_{D_1} = \{open, sleeps, hurt\}$. The initial situation is partially described by the v-proposition initially *sleeps*, and the effects of the actions can be described by the e-propositions

$\{activate\}$	causes	$\neg sleeps$
$\{run\_into\}$	causes	$hurt$ if $\neg open$
$\{pull\}$	causes	$\neg open$
$\{activate, run\_into\}$	causes	$open$
$\{activate, run\_into\}$	causes	$\neg hurt$ if $\neg hurt$

Informally, the last e-proposition is needed to restrict the application of the second one (which we call to *overrule* an e-proposition). Let D_1 denote the domain description given by these propositions.

Given a domain description D, a *state* σ is simply a subset of the set of fluent names F_D. For any $f \in F_D$, if $f \in \sigma$ then f is said to *hold* in σ, otherwise $\neg f$ holds. For instance, *sleeps* and $\neg open$ hold in $\{sleeps, hurt\}$. A *structure* M is a pair (σ_0, Φ) where σ_0 is a state — called the *initial* state — and Φ is a partially defined mapping — called a *transition function* — from pairs consisting of an action and a state into the set of states. If $\Phi(a, \sigma)$ is defined then its value is interpreted as the result of executing a in σ.

Let $M^{(a_1,\ldots,a_k)}$ be an abbreviation of $\Phi(a_k, \Phi(a_{k-1}, \ldots, \Phi(a_1, \sigma_0)\ldots))$ where $M = (\sigma_0, \Phi)$, then a v-proposition like (1) is *true* in M iff

$$\forall 1 \leq k \leq m .\ M^{(a_1\ldots a_k)} \text{ is defined and}$$
$$f \text{ holds in } M^{(a_1,\ldots,a_m)}.$$

The given set of e-propositions determines how a transition function should be designed which is suitable for a domain description. If a is an action, f a fluent literal, and σ a state then we say (executing) a *causes* f *in* σ iff there is an action b such that a causes f by b in σ. We say that a causes f by b in σ iff

1. $b \subseteq a$,

2. there is an e-proposition b **causes** f **if** $c_1, \ldots, c_n$ such that each $c_1, \ldots, c_n$ holds in σ. $\hspace{2cm}$ (3)

3. there is no action c such that $b \subset c \subseteq a$ and a causes $\neg f$ by c in σ.

If 3. does not hold then action b is called to be *overruled* (by action c).

Using the two sets

$$\begin{aligned} B_f(a, \sigma) &:= \{f \in F_D \,|\, a \text{ causes } f \text{ in } \sigma\} \\ B'_f(a, \sigma) &:= \{f \in F_D \,|\, a \text{ causes } \neg f \text{ in } \sigma\}, \end{aligned} \hspace{1cm} (4)$$

a structure $M = (\sigma_0, \Phi)$ is called a *model* of a domain description iff

1. every v-proposition is true in M and

2. for every action a and every state σ, $\Phi(a, \sigma)$ is only defined in case $B_f(a, \sigma) \cap B'_f(a, \sigma) = \{\}$. $\hspace{2cm}$ (5)
   If it is defined then $\Phi(a, \sigma) = \sigma \cup B_f(a, \sigma) \setminus B'_f(a, \sigma)$.

A domain description admitting at least one model is said to be *consistent*. A v-proposition ν like (1) is *entailed* by a domain description D, written $D \models \nu$, if ν is true in every model of D.

Example (continued). The transition function determined by the e-propositions in our domain description D_1 is defined as follows. Let σ be an arbitrary state then

$$\begin{aligned} \Phi(\{\}, \sigma) &= \sigma \\ \Phi(\{run\_into\}, \sigma \cup \{open\}) &= \sigma \cup \{open\} \\ \Phi(\{run\_into\}, \sigma \setminus \{open\}) &= \sigma \setminus \{open\} \cup \{hurt\} \\ \Phi(\{pull\}, \sigma) &= \sigma \setminus \{open\} \\ \Phi(\{activate\}, \sigma) &= \sigma \setminus \{sleeps\} \\ \Phi(\{activate, pull\}, \sigma) &= \sigma \setminus \{sleeps, open\} \\ \Phi(\{run\_into, pull\}, \sigma \cup \{open\}) &= \sigma \setminus \{open\} \end{aligned}$$

$$\Phi(\{run\_into, pull\}, \sigma \setminus \{open\}) = \sigma \setminus \{open\} \cup \{hurt\}$$
$$\Phi(\{activate, run\_into\}, \sigma) \quad = \sigma \cup \{open\}$$
$$\Phi(\{activate, run\_into, pull\}, \sigma) \quad \text{is undefined}$$

D_1 has four models, viz.

$$(\{sleeps\}, \Phi) \qquad (\{open, sleeps\}, \Phi) \qquad (6)$$
$$(\{sleeps, hurt\}, \Phi) \quad (\{open, sleeps, hurt\}, \Phi)$$

If, for instance, the v-proposition $\neg hurt$ **after** $\{run\_into\}$ is added to D_1 then the only remaining model is $(\{open, sleeps\}, \Phi)$ since for all other structures in (6) we find that $hurt \in \Phi(\{run\_into\}, \sigma_0)$. Hence, the v-proposition initially $open$, say, is entailed by this extended domain.

3 Interpreting and handling contradictions and a robust language $\mathcal{A}_C^+$

In this section, we present different ways of interpreting descriptions of actions which may be executed concurrently. To illustrate our exposition, we use the terms of $\mathcal{A}_C$; nevertheless, the differences we work out classify other languages describing possibly concurrent actions as well.

Suppose a rather complex description of a part of the world has to be constructed. Because of the combinatorial explosion it obviously is impractible to describe the effects of all possible combinations of unit actions. Therefore, the effects of compound actions have to be inferred from the descriptions given seperately for the various involved actions. Combining these action descriptions might yield a contradiction among their effects.[2] In terms of $\mathcal{A}_C$ this means that $B_f \cap B'_f \neq \{\}$ and, hence, the particular compound action is not executable (see (5)). For instance, recall our domain description D_1. The e-propositions describing the effects of the elements of $\{activate, pull, run\_into\}$ propose both $open$ and $\neg open$.

There are several different ways of inferring the effects of a compound action from such contradictory partial descriptions. Therefore, languages describing actions can be classified according to the explicit resp. implicit methods they use to draw these conclusions.

Explicit methods provide further information about the effects of certain compound actions. In terms of $\mathcal{A}_C$, additional e-propositions may

1. add a fluent to B_f or B'_f : obviously, the set $B_f \cap B'_f$ will remain nonempty, i.e., no conflicts will be solved;

2. remove a fluent from B_f or B'_f : this allows to remove predicted conflicts, but not to redefine facts not mentioned by the unit action descriptions (the approach [15] uses this method)

3. add or remove a fluent from B_f or B'_f : this allows to give a complete new definition of B_f and B'_f (used in $\mathcal{A}_C$, $\mathcal{A}_C^+$, and in the State Event Logic [8]).

---

[2] Of course, this prolem might even occur without concurrency involved, i.e. if several descriptions of the same unit action are used to infer the effects of this single action. If such an inference yields a contradiction, the semantics of $\mathcal{A}$, for instance, define the whole domain description to be inconsistent.

Example (continued). The e-proposition $\{activate, run\_into\}$ causes $open$ adds the fluent $open$ to the set $B_f(\{activate, run\_into\}, \sigma)$ [3] while the e-proposition $\{activate, run\_into\}$ causes $\neg hurt$ if $\neg hurt$ removes the fluent $hurt$ [4] from $B_f(\{activate, run\_into\}, \sigma)$ by overruling the unit action description. Our example can only be modelled by using both addition and cancellation of effects.

Suppose the effects are not defined explicitly for all possible compound actions. In this case, it can happen that certain actions still are proposed to have contradictory effects. This might indicate that these actions are not executable in the world.[5] On the other hand, if such actions are observed then they indicate that the descriptions of their effects are wrong, uncertain or include nondeterministic actions.[6] In this case, depending on the chosen interpretation and the extent of certainty required one has to regard

1. the whole domain description (State Event Logic [8]),
2. the whole situation ($\mathcal{A}_C$ and [15]),
3. the effects of the conflicting actions, or
4. the contradictory fluents ($\mathcal{A}_C^+$).

as unreliable.

Example (continued). Recall our example. Of course, it is conceivable that the door opener is activated, the door is pulled, and somebody runs into it at the same moment. The domain description D_1 proposes both $open$ and $\neg open$ to be an effect of this compound action. Hence, D_1 is incomplete with respect to the world it describes. In fact, without further information we cannot say wether the door will be closed after executing this action or not.

However, we are sure that the dog will not sleep afterwards since we know that $\{activate\}$ causes $\neg sleeps$, and there is no proposition contradicting this.

In our example, by using the semantics of $\mathcal{A}_C$ it cannot be inferred that the dog does not sleep after executing $\{activate, pull, run\_into\}$. As an extreme case, imagine an agent in Saarbrücken executing this action and, concurrently, another agent in Franfurt switching off a light. Again, by $\mathcal{A}_C$ it cannot be inferred that the light is switched off in Frankfurt because the description used proposes contradictory states of a door in Saarbrücken. Nonetheless it seems to be reasonable to draw some conclusions about the resulting state instead of declaring it to be totally undefined, as it is done in $\mathcal{A}_C$.

We therefore weaken the basic assumption which says that $\Phi(a, \sigma)$ is undefined whenever the corresponding sets $B_f(a, \sigma)$ and $B_f'(a, \sigma)$ share one or more elements. To this end, we adopt a concept which has been introduced in [19]

---

[3] Note that the fluent $open$ is not mentioned by the unit action descriptions $\{activate\}$ causes $\neg sleeps$ and $\{run\_into\}$ causes $hurt$ if $\neg open$, respectively.

[4] postulated by $\{run\_into\}$ causes $hurt$ if $\neg open$

[5] For instance, closing and opening the same door concurrently is not possible; these actions themselves are contradictory with respect to concurrent execution.

[6] In our example, running into the door, activating the door opener, and pulling the door concurrently might be regarded as a nondeterministic action wrt. the truth value of $open$. Also, D_1 could be intended to express uncertain knowledge about the effect of this action.

where $\mathcal{A}$ has been extended by integrating nondeterministic actions. The crucial idea is to drop the notion of a single resulting state determined by an action and a state, and to define a collection of possible resulting states instead. We use a ternary transition *relation* Φ such that an action a and two states σ, σ' are related if the execution of a in σ *possibly* yields σ'. Informally, if no conflicts occur wrt. a and σ then there is only one possible resulting state which should be exactly as in $\mathcal{A}_C$. If, on the other hand, there are conflicts, i.e. if the corresponding set $B_f(a,\sigma) \cap B'_f(a,\sigma)$ is not empty, then each combination of the truth values of the controversial fluent names determines one possible result.

By using this transition relation Φ, it becomes necessary to define which action names occuring in different v-propositions denote one and the same execution of actions (having distinct effects) and which do not. To this end, as in [19] we premise each two sequences of actions $a_1,\ldots,a_k,a_{k+1},\ldots,a_m$ and $a_1,\ldots,a_k,a_{m+1},\ldots,a_n$ occuring in the same domain description to refer to one and the same execution of $a_1,\ldots,a_k$ and, consequently, augment each structure by a function φ which maps each sequence $[a_1,\ldots,a_m]$ to a distinct resulting state $M^{(a_1,\ldots,a_m)}$ wrt. Φ and this premise.

The following definition of the dialect $\mathcal{A}_C^+$ makes these ideas manifest.

Definition 1. $\mathcal{A}_C^+$ is defined by the syntax and semantics of $\mathcal{A}_C$, but where
- a structure is a tripel $(\sigma_0, \Phi, \varphi)$
- a structure $(\sigma_0, \Phi, \varphi)$ is a model of a domain description D iff

$$\varphi([\,]) = \sigma_0,$$
$$\left(\varphi([a_1,\ldots,a_{m-1}]) \,,\, a_m \,,\, \varphi([a_1,\ldots,a_m]) \right) \in \Phi,$$
$$(\sigma, a, \sigma') \in \Phi \text{ iff } \sigma' = ((\sigma \cup B_f) \setminus B'_f) \cup B^{\natural} \text{ for some } B^{\natural} \subseteq B_f \cap B'_f,$$

and for all v − propositions (1) in D, f holds in $\varphi([a_1,\ldots,a_m])$.

$\mathcal{A}_C^+$ is a proper extension of $\mathcal{A}_C$ in so far as whenever a v-proposition is entailed by a consistent domain description in $\mathcal{A}_C$ then it is also entailed wrt. the semantics of $\mathcal{A}_C^+$.

Example (continued). If our domain description D_1 is augmented by either the v-proposition *open* **after** $\{activate, pull, run\_into\}$ or the contrary proposition $\neg open$ **after** $\{activate, pull, run\_into\}$ then both extended domains have models (with different functions φ) according to the semantics of $\mathcal{A}_C^+$. On the other hand, if D_1 is augmented by *sleeps* **after** $\{activate, pull, run\_into\}$ then there is no model wrt. $\mathcal{A}_C^+$. Hence, as intended we can conclude that $D_1 \models_{\mathcal{A}_C^+} \neg sleeps$ **after** $\{activate, pull, run\_into\}$'.

Note that $\mathcal{A}_C^+$ does not distinguish between intentionally expressed non-determinism of actions and the interpretation of contradictory defined actions as to have uncertain effects. For instance, D_1 could be augmented by the e-propositions *activate* **causes** $\{bark\}$ and *activate* **causes** $\{\neg bark\}$ for describing that the dog possibly starts or stops barking when the door opener is activated. In fact, for someone or something reasoning about a domain description it makes no difference, whether the producer of this domain description was conscious of the uncertainty of the described effects of an action or not.

4 The ELP Approach

The equational logic programming approach to reasoning about actions and change [10, 11] is based on using reification to represent a complete situation by a single term $t_1 \circ \cdots \circ t_n$ where $t_1, \ldots, t_n$ are the facts holding in this situation. Since the order in such terms should be irrelevant, the connection function $\circ$ is required to be associative (A) and commutative (C). In addition, it admits a unit element (1), viz. the constant $\emptyset$ denoting the empty situation.

Actions are defined and executed in a STRIPS-like fashion [6] using a ternary predicate[7]

$$action \, (V \circ c_1 \circ \cdots \circ c_l \,, \, a_1 \circ \cdots \circ a_m \,, \, V \circ e_1 \circ \cdots \circ e_n \,) \qquad (7)$$

meaning that the compound action[8] $a_1 \circ \cdots \circ a_m$ transfers every situation $V \circ c_1 \circ \cdots \circ c_l$ [9] into the situation $V \circ e_1 \circ \cdots \circ e_n$ (in other words, if $a_1 \circ \cdots \circ a_m$ is executed in a situation in which the *conditions* $c_1 \circ \cdots \circ c_l$ hold, it removes these conditions and adds the *effects* $e_1 \circ \cdots \circ e_n$). Thus, all facts which are not amongst the conditions hold after the application of (7) if they did so before. Therefore, no additional axioms for solving the frame problem are needed although dealing with a purely deductive method.

The result of executing a sequence of actions is then defined by the two clauses (12) (see further below) which conform to the semantics of $\mathcal{A}_C$.

Based on similar ideas, a logic program associated with the equational theory (AC1) was presented in [19] which forms a sound and complete encoding of the original Action Description Language $\mathcal{A}$. In the following section we evolve an analogous program encoding of domain descriptions given in $\mathcal{A}_C$ or $\mathcal{A}_C^+$, respectively. Due to the large number of compound actions implicitly described by a domain description in $\mathcal{A}_C$, it seems impractical to describe all of them explicitly in ELP. Therefore, definitions (7) are represented implicitly by clause (8) in the translations defined in the following section.

5 Translating $\mathcal{A}_C$ and $\mathcal{A}_C^+$ into ELP

In $\mathcal{A}_C$, classical negation of fluent symbols determines these fluents to be false. Since in the ELP based method fluents are reified and, hence, cannot be negated in this way we represent negated fluent symbols by defining a new complementary symbol for each fluent name. Let $\overline{F_D}^{\varphi}$ denote a set of symbols such that $F_D \cap \overline{F_D}^{\varphi} = \{\}$ then we define a bijective mapping φ over $F_D \cap \overline{F_D}^{\varphi}$ such that $x \in F_D \Leftrightarrow \varphi(x) \in \overline{F_D}^{\varphi}$ and $\varphi(\varphi(x)) = x$. For instance, if $F_D = \{open, sleeps, hurt\}$ then we might use $\overline{F_D}^{\varphi} = \{closed, awake, safe\}$,

---

[7] Throughout this paper, we use a PROLOG-like syntax, ie. constants and predicates are in lower cases whereas variables are denoted by upper case letters. Moreover, free variables are assumed to be universally quantified and, as usual, the term $[h \,|\, t]$ denotes a list with head h and tail t.

[8] In [12] the concurrent execution of actions is not taken into consideration; this extension is obviously necessary for encoding $\mathcal{A}_C$.

[9] i.e. every situation unifiable with $V \circ c_1 \circ \cdots \circ c_l$ wrt. to the underlying equational theory (AC1)

say, along with $\varphi(open) = closed$, $\varphi(sleeps) = awake$, $\varphi(hurt) = safe$, and vice versa.

Now, we are able to map sequences of fluent literals using a function τ_{φ_D} into a single term based on the (AC1)–function $\circ$:

$$\tau_{\varphi_D}(f_1, \ldots, f_m, \neg f_{m+1}, \ldots, \neg f_n) := f_1 \circ \cdots \circ f_m \circ \varphi_D(f_{m+1}) \circ \ldots \circ \varphi_D(f_n)$$

where $f_i \in F_D$.

In $\mathcal{A}_C$, a state in the world is described as a set σ of fluent symbols f_i implying that the fluent literals f_i are true and the fluent literals corresponding to $F_D \setminus \sigma$ are false in this state. Therefore, a state σ is represented by an (AC1)–term corresponding to $\sigma \cup \{\varphi(f) \mid f \notin \sigma\}$:

$$\gamma_{\varphi_D}(\{f_1, \ldots, f_m\}) := f_1 \circ \ldots \circ f_m \circ \varphi_D(f_{m+1}) \circ \ldots \circ \varphi_D(f_n),$$

where $\{f_1, \ldots, f_n\} = F_D$.

Finally, we represent compound actions by simply connecting the unit action names using again our (AC1)–function:

$$\mu_{\varphi_D}(\{a_1, \ldots, a_k\}) := a_1 \circ \cdots \circ a_k$$

where $\{a_1, \ldots, a_k\} \subseteq A_D$.

Using the definitions above, we are now prepared for translating $\mathcal{A}_C$ domain descriptions into an equational logic program. For each fluent name, we use a unit clause to relate it to its counterpart in the set $\overline{F_D}^\varphi$:

$$\varphi_D^{ELP} := \{complement(f \circ \varphi_D(f)). \mid f \in F_D\}$$

For each e-proposition we use a unit clause stating its conditions, its action name, and its effect:

$$EPROP_{\varphi_D} := \{eprop(\tau_{\varphi_D}(c_1, \ldots, c_n), \mu_{\varphi_D}(a), \tau_{\varphi_D}(f)). \mid$$
$$a \text{ causes } f \text{ if } c_1, \ldots, c_n \in D\}$$

To encode the semantics of $\mathcal{A}_C$ we use a ternary predicate $action(i, a, h)$ intending that executing action a in state i yields state h. It is defined as follows.

$$action(I, A, H) \leftarrow \neg overruled(H, I, \emptyset, A),$$
$$\neg non\_inertial(H, I, A), \qquad (8)$$
$$\neg inconsistent(H).$$

where the resulting state h is required

1. not to be *overruled*, i.e. there is no non-overruled e-proposition applicable to i and postulating the complement of a fluent literal in h.
2. not to be *non-inertial*, i.e. there is no resource in h but not in i which is not postulated by an applicable e-proposition, and
3. not to be *inconsistent*, i.e. h contains exactly one element of each pair of complementary resources and, thus, is of the form $\tau_{\varphi_D}(\sigma)$ for some σ.

The predicates *overruled*, *non_inertial*, and *inconsistent* are defined by

$$overruled(F \circ H, C \circ J, A, A \circ B \circ D)$$
$$\leftarrow eprop(C, A \circ B, G),$$
$$F \neq_{AC1} \emptyset,$$
$$B \neq_{AC1} \emptyset, \qquad (9)$$
$$complement(F \circ G),$$
$$\neg overruled(G, C \circ J, A \circ B, A \circ B \circ D).$$

In words, the effect F of an action A is overruled by an *eprop* postulating the effect $G = \varphi_D(F)$ of an action $B \supset A$ if B is not overruled with respect to G. The termination of the decision about $overruled(H, I, B, B \circ A)$ for all H, I, B, A can be shown by induction over the strictly increasing third argument, if a fair selection rule is used.

$$non\_inertial(F \circ G, H \circ J, A) \leftarrow complement(F \circ H), \\ \neg overruled(H, H \circ J, \emptyset, A). \tag{10}$$

In words, the truth value of a fluent literal F of the initial state $H \circ J$ is changed although no non-overruled e-proposition postulates this change.

$$\begin{aligned} inconsistent(G \circ G \circ H) &\leftarrow G \neq_{AC1} \emptyset. \\ inconsistent(F \circ G) &\leftarrow complement(F). \\ inconsistent(H) &\leftarrow complement(F \circ G), \\ & \quad F \neq_{AC1} \emptyset, \ G \neq_{AC1} \emptyset, \\ & \quad \neg holds(F, H), \ \neg holds(G, H). \\ holds(F, H \circ F). \end{aligned} \tag{11}$$

In words, a situation term is inconsistent if it contains a resource twice or if it contains a resource along with its counterpart $\varphi(f)$ or if it neither contains f nor $\varphi(f)$ for some $f \in F_D$.

The transition of σ_0 into the state $M^{(a_1,\ldots,a_m)}$ (the result G of executing $[a_1, \ldots, a_m]$ in the initial state I) is modelled by

$$\begin{aligned} result(I, [], G) &\leftarrow I =_{AC1} G. \\ result(I, [A \mid P], G) &\leftarrow action(I, A, H), \\ & \quad result(H, P, G). \end{aligned} \tag{12}$$

The termination of the decision about $result(H, P, G)$ for all H, P, G can be shown by induction over the strictly decreasing second argument.

Finally, let n be the number of v-propositions of the form (1) then these are translated into the clause

$$\begin{aligned} model(I) \leftarrow \ & \neg inconsistent(I), \\ & result(I, [\mu_{\varphi_D}(a_{11}), \ldots, \mu_{\varphi_D}(a_{1m_1})], \tau_{\varphi_D}(f_1) \circ G_1), \\ & \qquad\qquad\qquad \vdots \\ & result(I, [\mu_{\varphi_D}(a_{n1}), \ldots, \mu_{\varphi_D}(a_{nm_n})], \tau_{\varphi_D}(f_n) \circ G_n). \end{aligned} \tag{13}$$

with the intended meaning that $model(i)$ is true if i represents a consistent initial state such that all v-propositions are satisfied.

To summarize, a domain description D in $\mathcal{A}_C$ is translated into the set of clauses $P = \varphi_D^{ELP} \cup EPROP_{\varphi_D} \cup \{(8)\text{--}(13)\}$. As we have negative literals in the body of some clauses, the adequate computational mechanism for P is SLDNF–resolution where, due to our equational theory (AC1), standard unification is replaced by a theory unification procedure. Following [18], the semantics of our program is then given by its *completion* (cf. [3]) $(P_D^*, AC1^*)$ where $AC1^*$ denotes a *unification complete* theory wrt. AC1 (see [13] or [18]).

The following theorem forms the basis of our soundness and completeness result regarding the completion of our constructed equational logic program.

Theorem 2. *Let D be a domain description in $\mathcal{A}_C$ determining a transition function Φ; then, there exists a σ_0 such that the structure (σ_0, Φ) is a model of D and some $I = \gamma_{\varphi_D}(\sigma_0)$ iff*

$$(P_D^*, AC1^*) \models model(I).$$

Example (continued) Let φ_{D_1} be defined by

$$\varphi_{D_1}(sleeps) = \overline{sleeps}, \quad \varphi_{D_1}(hurt) = \overline{hurt}, \quad \varphi_{D_1}(open) = \overline{open}$$

Then $P_{D_1} =$

$\quad complement(sleeps \circ \overline{sleeps})$.
$\quad complement(hurt \circ \overline{hurt})$.
$\quad complement(open \circ \overline{open})$.
$\quad eprop(\emptyset, activate, \overline{sleeps})$.
$\quad eprop(\overline{open}, run\_into, hurt)$.
$\quad eprop(\emptyset, pull, \overline{open})$.
$\quad eprop(\emptyset, activate \circ run\_into, open)$.
$\quad eprop(\overline{hurt}, activate \circ run\_into, \overline{hurt})$.
$\quad model(I) \qquad\qquad\qquad\quad \leftarrow \neg inconsistent(I),$
$\qquad\qquad\qquad\qquad\qquad\qquad\quad result(I, \emptyset, sleeps \circ G_1)$.

$\cup (8) - (12)$

The equational logic program developed above can be easily modified to simulate the semantics defined by $\mathcal{A}_C^+$. We use the very same translation, but the literal $\neg overruled(H, I, \emptyset, A)$ in the body of (8) is replaced by $\neg impossible(H, I, A)$ and the following clause is added.

$$impossible(F \circ H, I, A) \leftarrow overruled(F, I, \emptyset, A),$$
$$complement(F \circ G),$$
$$\neg overruled(G, I, \emptyset, A).$$

In words, *a causes $\neg f$ in σ* and $\neg(a \text{ causes } f \text{ in } \sigma)$ where $I = \gamma_{\varphi_D}(\sigma)$ Also, according to Definition 1, the head of (8) is replaced by $action(I, A(H), H)$ and the action names in (9) have to be labeled similarly with variables such that two action names are labeled with the same variable iff they denote one and the same execution of an action (see also [19]).

6 Summary

We investigated possible interpretations of partially contradictory descriptions of the effects of concurrently executed actions. Our analysis lead to a new language $\mathcal{A}_C^+$ describing concurrent actions which extends the work of C. Baral and M. Gelfond: $\mathcal{A}_C^+$ allows to infer all the non-contradicted information from contradictory descriptions, whereas $\mathcal{A}$ and $\mathcal{A}_C$ does not. Moreover, $\mathcal{A}_C^+$ enables one to describe nondeterministic actions and uncertain knowledge.

Furthermore, we presented sound and complete encodings of the languages $\mathcal{A}_C$ and (by a simple modification) $\mathcal{A}_C^+$ by means of equational logic programs.

Acknowledgements. The authors would like to thank Wolfgang Bibel, Gerd Große and Wulf Röhnert for valuable discussions and comments on an earlier version of this paper.

References

1. C. Baral and M. Gelfond. Representing Concurrent Actions in Extended Logic Programming. In R. Bajcsy, ed., *Proc. of IJCAI*, p. 866–871, Chambéry, August 1993. Morgan Kaufmann.

2. W. Bibel. A Deductive Solution for Plan Generation. *New Generation Computing*, 4:115–132, 1986

3. K. L. Clark. Negation as Failure. In H. Gallaire and J. Minker, ed.'s, *Workshop Logic and Data Bases*, p. 293–322. Plenum Press, 1978.

4. M. Denecker and D. de Schreye. Representing Incomplete Knowledge in Abductive Logic Programming. In D. Miller, ed., *Proc. of ILPS*, p. 147–163, Vancouver, October 1993. MIT Press.

5. P. M. Dung. Representing Actions in Logic Programming and its Applications in Database Updates. In D. S. Warren, ed., *Proc. of ICLP*, p. 222–238, Budapest, June 1993. MIT Press.

6. R. E. Fikes and N. J. Nilsson. STRIPS: A new approach to the application of theorem proving to problem solving. *Artificial Intelligence*, 5(2):189–208, 1971.

7. M. Gelfond and V. Lifschitz. Representing Action and Change by Logic Programs. *Journal of Logic Programming*, 17:301–321, 1993.

8. G. Große. Propositional State-Event Logic. To appear JELIA'94, Springer LNAI.

9. G. Große, S. Hölldobler, J. Schneeberger, U. Sigmund, and M. Thielscher. Equational Logic Programming, Actions, and Change. In K. Apt, ed., *Proc. of IJCSLP*, p. 177–191, Washington, 1992. MIT Press.

10. S. Hölldobler and J. Schneeberger. A New Deductive Approach to Planning. *New Generation Computing*, 8:225–244, 1990.

11. S. Hölldobler and M. Thielscher. Actions and Specificity. In D. Miller, ed., *Proc. of ILPS*, p. 164–180, Vancouver, October 1993. MIT Press.

12. S. Hölldobler and M. Thielscher. Computing Change and Specificity with Equational Logic Programs. *Annals of Mathematics and Artificial Intelligence*, special issue on Processing of Declarative Knowledge, 1994. (To appear).

13. J. Jaffar, J.-L. Lassez, and M. J. Maher. A theory of complete logic programs with equality. *Journal of Logic Programming*, 1(3):211–223, 1984.

14. G. N. Kartha. Soundness and Completeness Theorems for Three Formalizations of Actions. In R. Bajcsy, ed., *Proc. of IJCAI*, p. 724–729, Chambéry, France, August 1993. Morgan Kaufmann.

15. F. Lin and Y. Shoham. Concurrent Actions in the Situation Calculus. In *Proc. of AAAI*, p. 590–595, South Lake Tahoe, California, 1992.

16. E. Sandewall. Features and Fluents. Technical Report LiTH-IDA-R-92-30, Institutionen för datavetenskap, Technical University Linköping, Schweden, 1992.

17. E. Sandewall. The range of applicability of nonmonotonic logics for the inertia problem. In R. Bajcsy, ed., *Proc. of IJCAI*, p. 738–743, Chambéry, France, August 1993. Morgan Kaufmann.

18. J. C. Shepherdson. SLDNF-Resolution with Equality. *Journal of Automated Reasoning*, 8:297–306, 1992.

19. M. Thielscher. Representing Actions in Equational Logic Programming. In P. Van Hentenryck, ed., *Proc. of ICLP*, p. 207–224, Santa Margherita Ligure, Italy, 1994. MIT Press.

Preselection Strategies for Case Based Classification

Klaus Goos

Lehrstuhl für Informatik VI
Universität Würzburg
Allesgrundweg 12
D-97218 Gerbrunn
e-mail: goos@informatik.uni-wuerzburg.de

Abstract. In the field of case based classification little research has so far been done into the step of preselecting possible candidate solutions from a given set of cases. Such a preselection becomes increasingly necessary and profitable as the casebases examined grow larger. This paper contains a description of various preselection strategies and their theoretical comparison as to applicability, pre-computation effort, running time, and error rate (completeness). The approaches are then evaluated in the case based classification shell CcC+, using a practical application on plant classification with appr. 3000 cases. The evaluation also studies these approaches in relation to changes in casebase size.

1 Introduction

When selecting a case similar to the case in question from a large casebase, it is useful to integrate existing domain knowledge in the similarity match. In complex domains, however, this renders the individual steps in the similarity match very expensive. For practical use of large casebases, an examination of all cases would cost much effort. Therefore an essential step within the paradigm of case based reasoning consists in the preselection of potentially similar cases. This step aims at reducing as far as possible the number of cases to be examined in a subsequent similarity match without eliminating any relevant cases.

To our knowledge, practical handling of large casebases in case based reasoning has hardly been dealt with in relevant publications. The evaluation by CASEY [2], for example, was limited to a casebase of 240 cases. It revealed, for one thing, that a much larger variation (number) of cases was required to yield good results. Furthermore, in spite of a selection based on indexation in the hierarchically organised case memory [6] the search effort for these 240 cases was relatively high and increased in an linear fashion with the number of cases. A problem which often arises in evaluating smaller casebases consists in the difference between a preselection and a complete comparison not being noticeable at all.

The difficulties in such a practical evaluation lie with the fact that for a prototype application only very few cases exist and case acquisition involves much effort. In order to evaluate the methods described here on a suitably extensive casebase, appr. 3000 cases were generated from domain knowledge for a heuristic problem solver and random checked for plausibility by an expert.

There are several approaches trying to tackle the problem of preselection. Almost all of them develop selection criteria - sometimes simple ones, sometimes sophisticated ones - which allow for an efficient similarity-based search in the casebase by supplying suitable access structures. For reasons of efficiency, these selection criteria must, of course, be less specific than the subsequent similarity criteria. The difficulty in making use of such less specific though more efficient selection criteria is to ensure that the most similar cases in terms of the similarity measure are amongst the preselected cases.

This problem does not arise with approaches which are built on massive parallel processes (e.g. [7]) and which, in similarity matches, employ a processor for each case in the casebase. Strictly speaking, however, such methods do not select cases at all but carry out a complete similarity match facilitated by extensive hardware facilities. These approaches are therefore not dealt with in the following.

Criteria for efficient preselection depend strongly on the type of similarity measure chosen. Two classes of similarity measures can be distinguished:

1. Hierarchical similarity measures: Supported by a knowledge intensive model of the application domain, hypothetical explanations of the problem are inferred. The various explanation paths inferred are compared to those stored with the cases in the casebase. The better the explanation paths of a compared case tally with those of the new case, the more similar the stored case and the new case are. Similarity measures of this kind are used e.g. by CASEY [8], PROTOS [3], and CREEK [1].

2. Numerical similarity measures: By means of data abstraction, systems belonging to this category such as PATDEX [14] and CcC^+ ([11], [5]) also expand the problem by reliably inferrable links. However, no further explanations are inferred. Instead, for all features appearing in the expanded problem partial similarity is computed in relation to the features of the existing cases used for comparison. The similarity measure for two cases is then computed from the partial similarities of the features occurring in the cases.

In terms of preselection, the inference of explanation paths also is an indexation on the casebase; due to the knowledge intensive model it is, however, very expensive and very difficult to implement with large casebases. Comparing the explanation paths includes a numerical similarity measure but takes place on an abstract level.

Our target being an efficient case comparison based problem solution, the approach presented below appears more promising. It directly defines a numerical similarity measure for the features. Cases may here be considered as vectors in an M-dimensional search space, with M equalling the number of features existing in the domain. The case based approach aims at finding the vector closest to the search vector given by the problem.

The vectors in the search space thus opened must subsequently be compared to the search vector in a detailed similarity match. With the help of various preselection stategies, the size of the search space may be reduced. Several such methods applicable in the field of case based classification are depicted in the following. The conditions of the individual methods are presented irrespective of the underlying numerical similarity measure, and problems arising in case of non-fulfilment of these conditions are discussed. The strategies implemented in the case based classification shell CcC^+ are then evaluated by using them in a plant classification application.

2 Major Preselection Strategies for Case Based Classification

This chapter presents the functioning of the most prominent preselection strategies for case based classification, including standard procedures such as the preselection of weighted features (generalisation of database indices), K-D-trees, hierarchical organisation of the casebase, and domain-specific methods (e.g. other problem solvers). A comparatively new method is called hill-climbing via case neighbours. The description of these procedures pinpoints, in particular, the required access structures:

2.1 Preselection by Means of Weighted Features

In this fairly simple method a certain number of relevant features are picked from the new case, the relevance of a feature increasing with its value-dependent weight as defined by the similarity measure. Around these relevant features m_i a similarity interval $[m_u, m_o]$ is created so that $\forall\, m_k \in [m_u, m_o] : sim(m_k, m_i) \geq X$ applies for a given minimum similarity X. For preselection, all cases found within these similarity intervals are picked from the casebase. The weights of all features where minimum similarity exists are then added up and the selected cases are sorted according to the total sum of weights. A certain number of best cases are subsequently returned as potential candidate solutions. For N cases, the effort of this methods amounts to $O(N)$ value comparisons for searching and $O(N' * \log(N'))$ value comparisons for sorting, with N' being the number of cases returned. This number depends on the predefined minimum similarity. N' normally being considerably smaller than N, the increase in effort is roughly linear to that in the number of cases in the casebase. This method can be improved by feature values indices contained in the database in which the cases are stored. However, when working with database indices, it is not possible to use any further domain-specific knowledge. The advantage of this method lies with the fact that no pre-computation is necessary.

2.2 Preselection by Means of Hillclimbing via Case Neighbours

For this variant, a certain number of most similar cases in the casebase are pre-computed and stored for each case. Neighbours may be fully pre-computed which leads to an effort of $N * (N-1)$ case comparisons for initial computation of all neighbours and to an effort of $2 * (N - 1)$ case comparisons for incremental insertion of a case. The incremental insertion effort, however, may be reduced by means of a simplified heuristic method which computes the neighbours of the new case and enters the new case with the neighbours if it features stronger similarity than the existing neighbours. Case comparison effort is thus reduced by half. If case insertion is preceded by a case similarity match anyway, the results may be re-used, thus avoiding additional effort altogether. To keep the error rate low, occasional exact re-computation may be useful.

For problem solving itself, a start case is picked from the casebase. From the set of its pre-computed nearest neighbours the case most similar to the search case is selected. The case thus found is then considered the new start case. This process is repeated until no case in the neighbourhood can be found to feature stronger similarity to the search case. Thus, metaphorically speaking, you approach the search case by hillclimbing from one neighbour to the next.

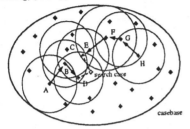

Search via case neighbours of size 3. (The similarity measure corresponds to the distance in the plane). The process is started from the cases A and H.
From A, the path runs to the nearest neighbour B and moves on to D which is considered the case most similar to the search case and is hence returned as the solution. The path starting at case H arrives at case E accordingly.

Fig. 1. Example of a search via case neighbours in 2-dimensional space

Two problems may arise when this searching procedure is applied. For one thing, the search may get caught in a cycle. To overcome this problem once a cycle has been detected, the second nearest neighbour is selected as the next start case instead of the nearest one. Secondly there is a certain risk of ending up in a local extremum. This problem can be lessened though not fully eliminated by starting the search from several start cases, thus approaching the search case via several paths and reducing the probability of getting stuck in such an extremum.

The effort of this method is contingent upon the size of the neighbour and on the number of start cases. It also depends, of course, on how similar the start cases are to the search case. The closer the start cases are to the search case, the less searching effort is involved. It therefore makes sense not to pick the start cases at random but to position them carefully using a different, less specific criterion.

2.3 Preselection by Means of a K-D-Tree

This method was developed by Jon L. Bentley [4] (cf. [13], [15]). It consists in a generalisation of a one-dimensional binary tree used for sorting and searching. The fundamental idea is that of spreading out the casebase in the shape of a tree. In order to create such a tree, a feature value is determined in each node which partitions the set of cases opened by the node into two subsets (cf. Fig. 2). This partitioning step is repeated until the sets of cases opened by the nodes have reached a predefined minimum size (e.g. 1). These final sets of cases then represent the leaves of the tree.

As opposed to the decision tree generated by ID3/C4 [12] which splits the sets of cases into two subsets as homogeneously as possible, the K-D-tree tries to find the feature value that will split the set of cases into two sets of the strongest possible dissimilarity. The main effort of creating a K-D-tree therefore consists in computing optimized partitioning values. According to [9], the effort of computing an optimized partitioning value from a set of N cases with M features is $O(M * N)$. Since on each tree level exactly N cases are to be partitioned, the effort of computing even several partitioning values remains the same for each tree level. The overall effort involved in the creation of a K-D-tree with a tree depth of $log(N)$ (binary tree) thus amounts to $O(log(N) * M * N)$.

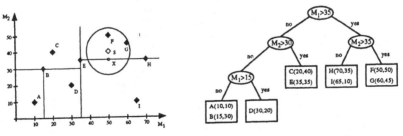

Fig. 2. Example of a K-D-tree for a 2-dimensional search space with Euclidian distance

In order to find cases similar to a search case you descend the tree according to the partitioning criteria until arriving at a leaf. There the search case is compared to the cases contained in the leaf.

Afterwards you mount in order to ensure that no cases of stronger similarity exist elsewhere in the tree. In mounting, a computation is carried out in every node checking whether the currently visited part of the tree may contain more similar cases. To this end, the space opened by the node is searched for a case more similar to the search case than the one already found. Taking, for example, the tree given in Fig. 2 and $S(50/40)$ as a search case, you descend the node on the right where the search case S is compared to the cases F and G. Afterwards you mount in the tree and check whether a case more similar to the search case S than case G may be contained in the left part of the tree. Graphically speaking, this means that you search the surroundings of S for cases which are more similar than G (i.e. a circle around S) and which at the same time belong to the set defined by $M_2 \leq 35$. For this check a case is invented that fulfils all partitioning values and is as similar as possible to the search case. The sole difference between this invented case and the search case is the feature M_2 since you now wish to descend the left part of the tree created by the node $M_2 > 35$. There you have to check whether a case exists with a partial similarity in the M_2 feature stronger than that of case G.

Such a case could be case $X(50, 35)$. To carry out this check you descend to the left and carry out detailed similarity comparisons with the cases H and I. They turn out, however, to be less similar to the search case than case G. Next you mount to the roots. There you check whether a case more similar than case G might be found in the tree spreading from the roots to the left, or, to put it differently, whether an invented case may be more similar to the search case than case G despite the move to the subset $M_1 \leq 35$ opened by the node M_1. The most similar possible invented case would be $Y(35, 40)$. The partial similarity in M_1 between Y and S is, however, lower than that between G and S. Thus this part of the tree does not contain any cases of stronger similarity than case G; the search may therefore be stopped.

The process comes to a close after finding that no more similar cases are contained in the tree, or, at worst, after checking all nodes.

At best, you have to descend to one leaf of the tree only during your searching process. If this occurs, and if the tree is a balanced one, the effort is tree depth $log(N)$ comparisons in descending, plus the number of detailed similarity computations according to the number of nodes found in the leaf, plus tree depth partial feature comparisons in mounting. This shows that it is of minor importance whether the tree is a balanced one. Good partitioning features are far more crucial since they minimize the number of detailed comparisons necessary.

Unfortunately, however, you may have to descend and mount several times within the tree, which considerably increases the effort. This occurs wherever cases contain values unknown or not recorded which make it impossible to decide into which part of the tree to descend. If this happens, both parts of the tree have to be searched.

The advantage of the K-D-tree method is its complete and correct searching. The assets of this method are most evident where the casebase is partitioned by rare, significant features since this reduces the probability of multiple descending and mounting. Even with large casebases the number of detailed comparisons will, in favourable conditions, be fairly limited. Most of the comparisons necessary are partial ones. However this holds true only if the cases are complete, i.e. if there are no values unknown or not recorded.

2.4 Preselection based on Hypotheses of Other Problem Solvers

As was mentioned in connection with systems using hierarchical similarity measures, other problem solvers may help in inferring more abstract features with which the casebase is indexed. One possible way is to compute solutions statistically by means of the Bayesian Theorem and to index the casebase via these solutions. Normally, however, the conditions for the Bayesian Theorem to be applied are not fulfilled, so that this method can be regarded as heuristic.

The probability $P(L)$ of each solution and the conditional probability $P(S/L)$ of each feature value assuming the selection of solution L from the casebase are, in this approach, established by pre-computation.

For preselection the most probable solutions are then computed according to the Bayesian Theorem and corresponding cases (possibly sample cases) are retrieved from the casebase. These cases are afterwards compared in detail by means of the similarity measure. Problems in the Bayesian Theorem may be caused by zero probabilities which may occur in particular with rare solutions. This difficulty can be eliminated by simplifying the computation, namely by adding the conditional probabilities instead of multiplying them.

Furthermore, of course, it is possible to replace statistical problem solvers with others (e.g. heuristic or causal problem solvers) and to use their suspected solutions which correspond to those statistically computed. When making use of other problem solvers, the effort involved in pre-computation is due to the acquisition of relevant knowledge. This strategy therefore appears particularly useful in cases where such knowledge has already been acquired.

2.5 Hierarchical Organisation of the Casebase

This procedure is not an autonomous one; it is most valuable when combined with another prese-lection strategy. In a pre-computation phase the casebase is divided into several so-called similarity clusters. To this end all cases are dealt with incrementally. The first case is the representative of the first cluster. Every further case is then checked to find out whether it features a predefined minimum similarity to a representative of a cluster and the same solution. If so, it is classified with the cluster of the corresponding representative. Otherwise it is made the representative of a new cluster. This procedure corresponds to the cluster analysis [10].

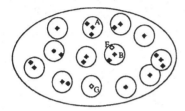

Computation of the hierarchical structure in the plane by means of the distance measure.
Starting point was A, the case A being the first clu-ster. Next the cluster around B was established. Now case F is to be classified. It is classified with the clu-ster around B since it lies within the maximum di-stance and has the same solution as B. For case G, on the other hand, a new cluster is created as the di-stances from G to A and from G to B both exceed the maximum distance.
The procedure is continued accordingly for all remai-ning cases of the casebase.

Fig. 3. Example of a hierarchical organisation of a casebase

Frequent cases (e.g. cases of influenza in a GP's database) are thus grouped in clusters, and many very similar cases have one common representative. Any of the preselection methods described above will now be able to work with the (normally still quite large) number of repre-sentatives, to preselect one or several representatives, and to return the cases stored with these representatives as the result of the combined preselection process.

3 Evaluation of the Individual Methods

This chapter evaluates the different procedures with a view to certain problem areas. The follo-wing aspects are dealt with in detail: (1) The question is discussed in how far pre-computation is necessary; and if it is, what costs are incurred by incremental addition of one case to the case-base and by the resulting improvement of the pre-computed structure? (2) We examine first the impact of a modification of the underlying similarity measure on the pre-computed structure and afterwards the requirements concerning the underlying similarity measure. (3) The question is discussed whether a solution-dependent similarity measure can or cannot be supported. (4) Fur-thermore we evaluate the impact of feature values unknown and/or not recorded on the different strategies.(5) Finally, we take a look at the search effort in relation to running time.

3.1 Pre-Computation Required?

With the exception of the method using weighted features all the approaches fall back on a pre-computed access structure. If the approach with indices is used these will also be pre-computed. The effort for the computation of these structures, however, varies. We can differentiate between the initial computation effort of such a structure and the incremental effort which arises with the creation of a structure via continuous incremental growth of the casebase through the addition of new cases.

With a number of N cases in the casebase and M features in the domain $O(M*N)$ tests are required for the initial computation of a complete index on the features. Every further case can be added incrementally with the effort $O(M)$.

For the initial computation of most similar neighbours $M*N*(N-1)$ feature comparisons are necessary. The effort for exact initial computation is therefore $O(M*N^2)$, increasing quadratically with the number of cases. A new case can be added at the effort of $2*(N-1)$ feature comparisons. As mentioned above, the effort can be reduced by using a simplified incremetal approach. In this case, the neighbours for a new case are computed each time with $O(M*(N-1))$ and it is assessed whether the new case has to be entered in the proximity of the neighbours. For exact addition as well as for simplified addition the effort for the computation of the neighbour of the new case can be taken over from a previous classification result. The incremental effort for a simplified setup of the structure is therefore 0, for the exact setup the effort is $M*(N-1)$ feature comparisons. For the simplified approach a reorganisation is sometimes required which corresponds to a new computation.

As already mentioned, the general effort to generate a balanced K-D-tree is $O(M * N * log(N))$. To fit a case incrementally in the tree takes $M * log(N)$ comparisons. After various incremental classifications in the tree, however, the separability in the tree cannot be guaranteed as the partitioning values are no longer ideal. To improve the separability, the tree has to be rebalanced which is equivalent to a new computation. This means that the incremental effort to set up the structure corresponds to the effort for initial computation $O(M * N * log(N))$.

For preselection via statistically determined hypotheses no comparisons on the basis of the similarity measure are needed. Instead, within the casebase the absolute occurence has to be counted. For this, there are M tests for N cases to determine whether a feature is contained in the solution of the case, and as many divisions ($O(N * M)$). The effort for initial computation is therefore $O(N * M)$. For every new case in the casebase there has to be a change in the occurences of M features under the condition of the solution and a change in the occurences of N solutions. The incremental insertion effort therefore amounts to $O(M + N)$.

The effort for the initial computation of a hierarchical case structure is dependent on the number H of the hierarchy levels. $O(H * M * N)$ feature comparisons occur during the setup of the structure. For sorting, H comparisons are necessary ($O(H * M)$). As with the approach for case neighbours, this effort has already been made in a previous problem-solving process and can then be used. Therefore, the incremental effort for this approach is 0.

3.2 Impact of Changes of the Similarity Measure?

Often the similarity measure is not a fixed default; instead, it can be adapted by the expert or via the help of a learning procedure in order to increase the problem-solving capacity of the case based system. This also leads to possible pre-computations which are based on this measure having to be adapted or newly computed respectively when the measure is changed.

For the different approaches it turns out that this applies to those three approaches which use the similarity measure for pre-computation (hillclimbing via case neighbours, K-D-tree, hierarchical case structure). For the other appraoches a change does not present any problems.

3.3 Solution-Dependent Modification?

Depending on the domain of application it can be useful to introduce a mechanism in the similarity measure with the help of which a certain feature is assigned different weights for various solutions. This signifies that the weighting of features for the similarity measure is changing dynamically depending on the solution of the comparative case, e.g. with an existing appendicitis a pain on pressure at the right side of the abdomen has to be diagnosed. This pain on pressure can, however, also be present with other diagnoses and is therefore only assigned medium weighting. In case of no pain on pressure, appendicitis has to be devaluated stronger than via the meaning of the pre-installed weight. Therefore the weight will be modified solution-dependently (i.e. only in cases with the solution appendicitis). This leads to the similarity measure not being symmetrical any longer as the comparison of two cases once requires the solution of one case and once the solution of the other case in order to set the weightings in the similarity measure.

In the approach with weighted features a solution-dependent modification leads to the situation where the relevant features for the creation of search intervals cannot be determined with certainty. This creates a less specific criterion.

For hillclimbing via case neighbours an asymmetric similarity measure results in greater errors occuring while classifying a new case in the neibour relations during the simplified approach for the incremental setup of the structure. This means that for a strongly asymmmetric similarity measure an exact setup of the structure requiring a greater effort has to be accepted. Otherwise, a solution-dependent modification of the similarity measure can be taken into account fully as the solutions of the cases are known.

While searching in the K-D-tree the similarity between the actual case and a case generated from search bounds is computed. This means that the solution for a possible solution-dependent modification is not present. This leads to a changed similarity measure during the search and thus to a possibly wrong path in the tree. The K-D-tree is therefore incompatible to such a similarity measure.

During hierarchical organisation of the case structure such a modification can be considered because the different clusters have a common known solution, which can be accessed for solution-dependent modification.

In the procedure via hypotheses of other problem solvers such knowledge does not explicitly enter during preselection. This knowledge, however, is not required as it is modelled in the knowledge of other problem solvers.

3.4 Impact of Unknown or Not Recorded Values?

Often in the classification the problem of knowing only a subset of the problem features occurs. It does not make any difference whether a value has not been entered or has been entered as unknown. These values correspond to the above mentioned representation, where a case represents a vector in a search space, a degree of freedom in a dimension. This problem has particularly negative effects on the approach with the K-D-tree. For the search in the K-D-tree the right and the left parts of the tree have to be examined further for any unknown value in the problem. This has strong negative effects on the search time.

For the other approaches this problem is irrelevant. For the preselection with weighted features the relevant features are used. Unknown or not recorded features are, however, irrelevant and will therefore not be used. For hillclimbing via case neighbours and the hierarchic case structure the unknown or not recorded values are entered into a similarity comparison and will therefore automatically be taken into account.

3.5 Search Effort in Relation to Problem-Solving Time?

The search effort during preselection via weighted features without additional database index amounts to $R * N$ comparisons with R being the number of relevant feature intervals to be searched. Additionally, there is a sorting of the weighted cases. With the use of a database index the effort is reduced to an average of $O(R * log(N))$ comparisons plus the effort to carry out the sorting $N' * log(N')$ with N' being equivalent to the number of cases found via the indices.

In the search via case neighbours the search effort is dependent on the number F of neighbours and on the number D of the neighbours to be searched. The result are $F * D$ case comparisons and thus $M * F * D$ feature comparisons for M features. The number D of the neighbours to be searched depends on the selection of a good start case. With a good selection of start cases it is hardly greater than 1, therefore $M * F$ feature comparisons are required. On average it is logarithmic $(M * F * log(N)$ feature comparisons), in the worst case it is linear to the number of cases (M*N feature comparisons).

	Weighted features	Hillclimbing via case neighbours	K-D-tree	Preselection with statistic problem solver	Preselection with heuristic problem solver
Effort for initial computing of the access structure	$O(M * N)$ index creation	$O(M * N^2)$	$O(M * N * log(N))$	$O(M * N)$	knowledge acquisition
Incremental effort for insertion into access structure	$O(M)$	none (simplified) $O(M * N)$ $O(M * N^2)$ reorganisation	$O(M * log(N))$ $O(M * N * log(N))$	$O(M + N)$	none
Effort for change of similarity measure	none	initial computation	initial computation	none	none
Problem with unknown and not recorded values	none	none	increased search effort	none	none
Solution-specific modification possible	yes, preselection is becoming less exact	yes, more elaborate pre-computation	incompatible	yes	yes
Performance (worst case)	$R*N$ comparisons $N * log(N)$ for sorting	$M * N$ comparisons	N tests $N + M * N$ comparisons	$L * M$ multiplications	# fired rules
Performance (best case)	$R * log(N)$ comparisons $N * log(N)$ for sorting	$M * P * log(N)$ comparisons	$log(N)$ tests $log(N) + M * V$ comparisons	$L * M$ multiplications	# fired rules

Table 1. Summarized comparison of the individual preselection strategies (N ... number of cases in the casebase, M ... number of features in the domain, R ... set number of most relevant features, I ... number of pre-computed neighbours, L ... number of solutions in the domain, V ... number of complete matches)

The effort for the K-D-tree is derived from tracking the tree, from the partial comparisons while mounting where it is tested whether further similar cases are present in the tree, and from the complete matches that are carried out in the leaves. The tree depth corresponds to $log(N)$. If no unknown values occur in the casebase, the average effort will be $log(N)$ tests, $log(N)$ feature comparisons and M feature comparisons for each complete match. The higher the number of unknown values in the search case, the greater the effort because in such a case one has to descend into the right and the left parts of the tree.

In the preselection via other problem solvers the search effort cannot be measured by the number of feature comparisons. In this case it is constituted by the computation of hypotheses. For the statistic approach for all solutions L the conditional feature probabilities M will be multiplied or added for the simplified statistic approach. The result will be $L * M$ multiplications or additions respectively. For a heuristic approach the effort is dependent on the number of fired rules.

For a better understanding of the relations one looks at a scenario to determine the effort in absolute figures. Following are the reflections and evaluations of the application for plant classification. The statistic values for this application were number of cases $N = 1500$, number of features $M = 40$ and number of solutions $L = 89$. A partial comparison between two features is computed in approximation as 4 operations.

For the preselection with relevant features with index $R * log(N)$ search comparisons and $N' * log(N')$ sorting comparisons are yielded for $R = 15$ relevant features. N' is estimated as $N' = 1/3 * N$, so that a total of appr. 4.650 operations are yielded. For hillclimbing via case neighbours it is assumed that for a correlative location of the start case $D = 3$ neighbours have to be tracked. With these values and 3 start cases the approach requires appr. 7.200 operations. For the K-D-tree it is estimated that due to the low separability one has to descend in three different parts of the tree. This results in appr. 7.200 operations. In order to compute the Bayesian Theorem appr. 3.600 multiplication or addition operations are required.

4 Combinations of Different Preselection Strategies

In the previous evaluation it was shown that the average search effort for extremely big casebases is still relatively high. Particularly for the preselection with hillclimbing via neighbours it was mentioned that the effort depends on the selection of favourable start cases.

For a further improvement of the individual procedures the preselection can be done step-by-step via a combination of two procedures. The approach for hierarchical organisation of the casebase is particularly well suited for this. This approach, which has not been dealt with as an approach of its own, allows for partitioning the casebase into many sets of very homogeneous cases, which are described each by a representative. The efficiency of the different procedures can now be improved by no longer working on the complete casebase but on the representatives of the individual clusters only.

A further useful combination is yielded through the link with the method of weighted features and hillclimbing via neighbours. With the help of a less specific criterion (few, relevant features) some cases can be selected which in a second step serve as start cases for the hillclimbing approach. Two combinations should furthermore be taken into account:

1. Combination of weighted features and hierarchical case structure
2. Combination of weighted features to determine start cases for hillclimbing and hierarchical case structure.

Undoubtedly, other useful combinations are possible. The evaluation in this work will be limited to the individual procedures and the two combinations mentioned.

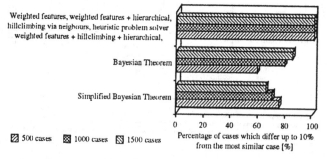

Fig. 4. What was the percentage of cases detected that deviated up to 10% from the most similar case? Apart from the statistic approaches the most similar case was always detected. As already mentioned, the preselection with the K-D-tree is a complete search. It is therefore not surprising that it detects 100% of most similar cases. In preselection with heuristic problem solvers the result was also to be expected as the cases have been generated via heuristic knowledge.

5 Evaluation

The strategies and their combinations mentioned above are integrated into the case-comparing classification Shell CcC+. For the evaluation a practical application for plant classification with appr. 3000 cases was taken. The application domain contains 40 different features with each appr. 5-7 feature values and 89 plants as solutions. The solution of the cases each consisted of exactly one solution. The problem in the cases was given at 29 features on average, 16% of the values were given as unknown. There is no solutions-dependent in the application domain. The cases were divided into different casebases with 500, 100 and 1500 cases. For testing purposes a set of 50 search cases was used that are not contained in the individual casebases.

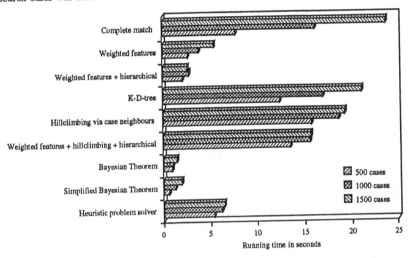

Fig. 5. Comparison of the running time of the individual approaches. This table shows the running time of the approaches while evaluating the above mentioned criterion. The measurements were made on a Macintosh Quadra 950 under Macintosh Common Lisp 2.0.1.

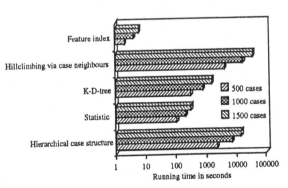

Fig. 6. Computation effort for the different structures

On the one hand the efficiency of the different approaches in dependence on the size of the casebase was evaluated (Fig. 5). Furthermore, the quality of the solution of the preselection step was assessed (Fig. 4). The criteria were: (1) Whether the most similar case in the casebase in relation to the search case was among the preselected cases. (2) The percentage of the cases deviating by up to 10% from the most similar case among the preselected cases. The scale was always the complete match on the full casebase. Finally, the pre-computation effort for the individual approaches was measured (Fig. 6, Fig. 7).

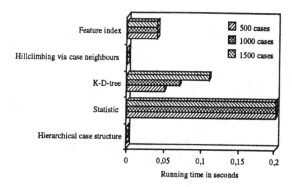

Fig. 7. Costs for incremental insertion of a new case after preliminary classification

6 Discussion of the Results

With the exception of statistic approaches all the approaches have fulfilled the criterion to find the best case for 100%. Even the hardest criterion, to find all the cases with a 10% deviation to the most similar case, was virtually achieved by these approaches. For the preselection via the K-D-tree this was evident as this approach is complete. One reason for the minimal error is the low separability of the similarity knowledge of the domain, i.e. there are hardly any feature values that would clearly indicate a certain solution. The exactitude can, however, be improved via an increased effort during preselection.

For the following description of the running times of the individual approaches not only the absolute running time but mainly the trend for an increased number of cases has to be taken into account. Despite the fact that the preselection with weighted features had excellent results in the absolute measurings for running time as well as for the exactitude of the preselection the trend is rather unfavourable. The opposite is true for hillclimbing via neighbours, particularly in the combined form. It requires a high base effort but shows no relevant increase in running time with an increase in the number of cases. The advantage of the approach with weighted features lies mainly in the low pre-computation effort as compared to the other approaches (see Fig. 4).

The weaknesses of the preselection with the Bayesian Theorem as regards to the exactitude can be accounted for in two ways. From the clear increase in quality using 500 and 1500 cases it can be assumed that too small a number of cases have been used for a statistic application. Due to many unknown values in the casebases there have been statistically unfavourable preconditions. There seem to be no advantages of the simplified Bayesian Theorem. The running time is not substantially better than that of the complete Theorem and the quality is rather getting worse with an increase in the number of cases.

The heuristic preselection shows very good results. But the measurements as regards the exactitude of the preselection are only an additional confirmation of the fact that the cases taken here have been generated correctly from the heuristic knowledge base. The efficient running time of the approach is interesting. The application, however, requires a lot of heuristic background knowledge.

The preselection with K-D-trees shows longer running times as compared to the theoretically computed search effort. The reason for this being the considerable increase in the search effort due to appr. 16% of unknown values in the cases. With less or no unknown values the result would improve markedly.

By and large one can state that the approach with weighted features shows advantages during the setup phase of a casebased system (frequent adapting of the similarity measure and adding of new cases) due to the low pre-computation effort. Should there be a large casebase this approach will get increasingly inefficient. Then there are other approaches such as hillclimbing via neighbours or preselection with the help of a K-D-tree. These approaches will offer the more advantages the more stable the similarity knowledge and the casebase gets. As compared to the K-D-tree, hillclimbing via neighbours has the advantage that the efficiency is not influenced by many unknown values and that solution-specific modifications can be considered.

The quality of the evaluated approaches can partly be enhanced by adapting corresponding parameter values to the existing domain. Samples have shown that a better quality of the solution can be achieved with slightly modified parameter values of the approaches (the measurings presented here were not tuned). This means that there are further measurings to be conducted to find out at which set of parameters a given approach offers the best solution quality at a limited search time. Furthermore, an evaluation of the combination of the different approaches, which were mentioned in this work but not taken up, is due. Here, investigations in different domains and with considerably higher numbers of cases are required which will be at the focus of our future work.

Acknowledgements

I would like to thank Frank Puppe for the many fruitful discussions and valuable comments on earlier versions of this work. For advice concerning hillclimbing via neighbours I am indebted to Klaus Wagner.

References

1. Aamodt, Agnar: *A Knowledge-intensive, Integrated Approach to Problem Solving and Sustained Learning.* PhD thesis, University of Trondheim, 1991.
2. Aghassi, David S.: *Evaluating cased-based reasoning for heart failure diagnoses.* MIT/LCS/TR-478, Laboratory for Computer Science, Massachusetts Institute of Technology, 1990.
3. Bareis, Ray: *PROTOS: A Unified Approach to Concept Representation, Classification and Learning.* PhD thesis, University of Texas, 1988.
4. Bentley, John L.: *Multidimensionale binary search trees used for associative searching.* Commun ACM, 18:509–517, 1975.
5. Goos, Klaus and Schewe, Stefan: *Case-based reasoning in clinical evaluation.* In Andreassen, S., Engelbrecht, R., and Wyatt, J. (editors): *Proc. of AIME-93, 4th Conference on Artificial Intelligence in Medicine Europe,* pages 445–448, Munich, 1993.
6. Kolodner, Janet L.: *Maintaining organisation in a dynamic long-term memory.* Cognitive Science, 4(7):243–280, 1983.
7. Kolodner, Janet L.: *Retrieving events from a case memory: A parallel implementation.* In Kolodner, Janet L. (editor): *Proceedings: Case-Based Reasoning Workshop, San Mateo, California,* Morgan Kaufmann Publishers, Clearwater Beach, Florida, USA, 1988. DARPA.
8. Koton, Phyllis: *Using Experience in Learning and Problem Solving.* PhD thesis, Department of Electrical Engineering and Computer Science, MIT, 1988.
9. Mehlhorn, K.: *Data Structures and Algorithms 1: Sorting and Searching.* Springer, 1984.
10. Nagel, H.-H.: *Digitisierung und Klassifikation von Signalen.* Ausarbeitung einer Vorlesung an der Fakultät für Informatik der Universität Karlsruhe. 1984.
11. Puppe, Frank und Goos, Klaus: *Improving Case-Based Classification with Expert Knowledge.* In Christaller, Th. (Herausgeber): *Informatik-Fachberichte 28,* 15. Fachtagung für Künstliche Intelligenz, GWAI-91, Seiten 196–205. Springer, 1991.
12. Quinlan, J. Ross: *Probabilistic Decision Trees,* chapter 5, pages 140–152. Machine Learning, An Artificial Intelligence Approach III. Morgan Kaufmann, 1990.
13. Steinert, Dagmar: *Effiziente Zugriffsstrukturen für die ähnlichkeitsbasierte Vorauswahl von Fällen.* Diplomarbeit am Lehrstuhl für Informatik VI (Künstliche Intelligenz), Universität Würzburg, 1993.
14. Weß, Stefan: *PATDEX - Ein Ansatz zur wissensbasierten und inkrementellen Verbesserung von Ähnlichkeitsbewertungen in der fallbasierten Diagnostik.* In Puppe, Frank und Günther, Andreas (Herausgeber): *Expertensysteme 93,* 2. Deutsche Tagung Expertensysteme (XPS-93), Seiten 42–55, Hamburg, 1993.
15. Weß, Stefan, Althoff, Klaus-Dieter, and Derwand, Guido: *Improving the retrieval step in case-based reasoning.* In Richter, M. M., Weß, S., Althoff, K.-D., and Maurer, F. (editors): *First European Workshop on Case-Based Reasoning EWCBR,* pages 83–88, Kaiserslautern, 1993.

Utilizing Spatial Relations for Natural Language Access to an Autonomous Mobile Robot

Eva Stopp[1], Klaus-Peter Gapp[1], Gerd Herzog[1], Thomas Laengle[2], Tim C. Lueth[2]

[1] SFB 314 – Project VITRA, FB 14 Informatik
Universität des Saarlandes, D-66041 Saarbrücken
email: vitra@cs.uni-sb.de
[2] Institute for Real-Time Computer Systems and Robotics
Prof. Dr.-Ing. U. Rembold and Prof. Dr.-Ing. R. Dillmann
Universität Karlsruhe, D-76128 Karlsruhe
email: t.lueth@ieee.org

Abstract. Natural language, a primary communication medium for humans, facilitates better human-machine interaction and could be an efficient means to use intelligent robots in a more flexible manner. In this paper, we report on our joint efforts at providing natural language access to the autonomous mobile two-arm robot KAMRO. The robot is able to perform complex assembly tasks. To achieve autonomous behaviour, several camera systems are used for the perception of the environment during task execution. Since natural language utterances must be interpreted with respect to the robot's current environment the processing must be based on a referential semantics that is perceptually anchored. Considering localization expressions, we demonstrate how, on the one hand, verbal descriptions, and on the other hand, knowledge about the physical environment, i.e., visual and geometric information, can be connected to each other.

1 Introduction

The great flexibility of autonomous mobile robots offers interesting possibilities for more advanced applications in dynamic environments. If, however, the capabilities of intelligent robots are to be fully exploited, flexible human-machine interaction becomes an important issue.

We argue that natural language is an appropriate means of making advanced robot systems more easily accessible and more responsive to their human partners. A practical advantage of a natural language interface is that information can be conveyed with changing accuracy and on different levels of abstraction. In [4, p. 52] it is claimed that the kind of flexibility needed for the instruction of autonomous agents requires a *"representation that embodies the same conceptualization of tasks and action as natural language itself."*

Tactile, acoustic, and vision sensors provide robots with perceptual capabilities, enabling them to explore and analyze their environment in order to behave more intelligently. Communicating about spatio-temporal aspects of the environment, like the spatial arrangement of objects, plays an important role for human-robot interaction. Thus, a natural language interface must not only consider the relationship between expressions of a knowledge representation language and natural language expressions, but must also rely on the definition of a referential semantics that is perceptually anchored.

Although both technical fields constitute major research areas within AI, there has been little emphasis on natural language interaction with intelligent robot systems (see, e.g., [15, 19, 22]). Other approaches have been concerned with natural language control of autonomous agents within simulated 2D or 3D environments (cf. [4, 6, 23]) or with natural language access to visual data (cf. [5, 11, 18, 25]).

The aim of our joint effort is the integration of the Karlsruhe autonomous mobile robot KAMRO [17] and the natural language component VITRA (VIsual TRAnslator) developed in Saarbrücken [11]. Focused on here is the problem of spatial reference. The specific need for generating and understanding localization expressions will be shown. In addition, we will describe how such natural language utterances can be processed taking into account information provided by vision sensors and the environment model.

2 Natural Language Access to the Robot System KAMRO

The anthropomorphic robot KAMRO (Karlsruhe Autonomous Mobile Robot) is a two-arm robot system that is being developed to take on service tasks in an industrial environment. It consists of a mobile platform with an omnidirectional drive (3 DoF) on which there are mounted two PUMA-type manipulators (6 DoF) in a hanging configuration. Further mounted on this platform are several different sensor systems for CCD-cameras, ultrasonic range sensors, laser scanner and force-torque sensors.

KAMRO is capable of autonomously performing service tasks as transportation, maintenance and assembly. The tasks or robot operations can be described on different levels: assembly precedence graphs, implicit elementary operations (pick, place) and explicit elementary operations (grasp, transfer, fine motion, join, exchange, etc.). Given a complex task, it is transformed by the control architecture from assembly precendence graph level to explicit elementary operation level (cf. Fig. 1). The generation of suitable sequences of elementary operations depends on position and orientation of the assembly parts on the worktable while execution is controlled by the real-time robot control system. Status and sensor data returned to the planning-system enable KAMRO to control the execution of the plan and if necessary correct it. Different strategies are used to avoid error situations that can occur by uncertainties. On the other hand, the robot is also able to recover from error situations.

To use natural language just as a sophisticated command-language for the operator of a robot system would be an insufficient proposal. Flexible human-machine interaction only becomes possible if intelligent robots are made more responsive, i.e., a robot needs the capability to describe and explain its tasks and behaviour as well as the current situation. In a dialog-based approach, which is our choice, further queries can always be utilized to resolve ambiguities or misunderstandings. Four main situations of human-machine interaction can be distinguished in the context of natural language access to the KAMRO system (cf. [16]):

- *Task specification:*
  Operations and tasks to be performed by the robot can be specified on various levels of abstraction. Natural language instructions can refer to elementary operations, like *pick* and *place*, and even to explicit elementary operations, if fine control is required.

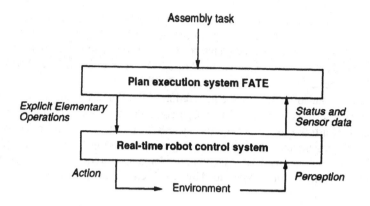

Fig. 1. Control Architecture of the KAMRO System

On a higher level, the operator could specify a suitable assembly sequence, in order to perform a designated task. The most abstract specification would only provide a qualitative description of the desired state, i.e., the final positions of the different assembly parts.

– *Execution monitoring:*
During the execution of a task the robot could generate a simultaneous report concerning its actions. Depending on the demands formulated by the user, descriptions and explanations can be given in more or less detail.

– *Explanation of error recovery:*
The capability of recovering from error situations leads to dynamic adjustment of assembly plans during execution. This feature makes it more difficult for the operator to predict and understand the behaviour of the robot. Natural language explanations and descriptions of why and how a specific plan was changed would increase cooperativeness of the intelligent robot. Similar descriptions are even more important in error situations that can not be handled by the robot autonomously.

– *Updating the environment representation:*
Because of the dynamic nature of the environment, geometric and visual information can never be complete, even for an autonomous robot equipped with several sensors. In a natural-language dialog, user and robot aid each other by exchanging additional information about the environment and world model.

In any case it is crucial to be able to refer to spatial aspects of the complex environment. Spatial configurations need to be described and specific locations must be refered to. In addition, spatial prepositions can be utilized to refer to assembly parts and other objects; in general one can not rely on unique object identifiers. This leads to the question of how such natural language expressions (e.g. *"Take the spacer on the left and put it into the nearest hole of the sideplate."*) can be related to visual and geometric information about the environment.

3 Evaluation of Spatial Relations

The prepositions in their spatial meanings (cf. [20]) combined with descriptions of placement, an *object to be localized* (LO) and a *reference object* (REFO), build the class of *localization expressions* [10]. The semantic analysis of spatial prepositions leads to the term *spatial relation* as a target-language independent meaning concept. Conversely, the definition and representation of the semantics of spatial relations is an essential condition for the synthesis of spatial reference expressions in natural language. Spatial relations can be defined by specifying conditions for object configurations, such as the distance between objects or the relative position of objects. In this sense, a spatial relation characterizes a class of object configurations (cf. [3]).

3.1 Computing the Elementary Spatial Relations

The perceptual information available to the robot system is encoded in a 3-dimensional geometric model (cf. Fig. 2), which can be accessed by the natural language component. The basic meanings of spatial relations are defined with respect to this geometrical representation. Following [14], people do not account for every detail of the objects involved when they apply spatial relations. Hence, an *approximative* algorithm can be utilized for the computation of spatial relations, considering only essential shape properties of an object. For instance, in most cases the center of gravity is sufficient to approximate the object to be localized because the object position is the only information that counts for the applicability of the specific spatial relation. The following idealizations are currently provided in our implementation:

- *Center of gravity*
- *Bounding rectangle* (BR)
  The bounding rectangle of an object with respect to a direction vector v, is the minimum rectangle aligned to v and containing the object's 2D representation.
- *2D representation*
- *Bounding right parallelepiped* (BRP)
- *3D representation*

Three distinct classes of static spatial relations are considered: The topological relations (e.g., *at* and *near*), the projective relations (e.g., *in front of*, *behind*, *right*, *left*, *above*, *below*, and *beside*), and the relation *between*, which takes an exceptional position in the group of spatial relations.

The algorithm for the computation of applicability of the topological relation's, *at* and *near*, basic meaning considers only the distance between the LO and the REFO scaled by the REFO's extension in each of the three dimensions, i.e., the *local distance*. The computation of projective relations also has to include the scaled (*local*) deviation angle of the LO from the canonical direction implied by the relation. The dependency of the local distance and the local angle from the REFO extension ensures for a bigger REFO in a dynamic enlargement of a relation's region of applicability (cf. [7]). The evaluation of the applicability of a spatial relation differs from one person to another (cf. [13]). Because of this we map the local distance and the local angle to user adjustable *cubic spline functions* $Spline_{Rel}$, which enable a cognitively plausible continuous gradation of the relation's applicability. The product of both spline values determines the *degree of applicability* DA_{Rel} of an elementary projective spatial relation.

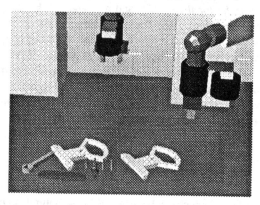

Fig. 2. A snapshot from KAMRO's environment

The evaluation process can be applied to 2-dimensional, e.g., maps, as well as to 3-dimensional environments. In the latter case, we get a 3-dimensional extented region of applicability for spatial relations. This seems reasonable when we look at Fig. 3, because *"the LO in front of the REFO"* is an adequate application of the spatial relation *in front of* although there is a vertical difference between the LO and the REFO.

To get an idea of a region's applicability structure we extend the so-called *potential fields* presentation of a spatial relation (cf. [21]) into the third dimension. For instance, Fig. 4 is a visual example of the 3D applicability structure of *above* (a) and *right* (b) using a building as REFO.

3.2 Compositional Use of Spatial Prepositions

If it is necessary to give a more specific localization of objects it is usual to use more than one spatial preposition. Normally not more than two prepositions are combined, e.g., the LO is *in front of* and *to the right of* the REFO. Therefore we also need to consider

Spatial prepositions	at,near	in front of,behind	right,left	above,below
at,near				
in front of,behind	X		X	X
right,left	X	X		X
above,below				

Table 1. Ordered 2-place compositions of some German spatial prepositions

the composite use of spatial relations and additionally which relations are combinable.

The relations we take into account are the topological *at* and *near* and the projective *in front of*, *behind*, *right*, *left*, *above*, and *below*. Table 1 gives an overview of the possible ordered two-place compositions of the spatial prepositions (in German use). According to the table, the prepositions *in front of*, *behind*, *right*, and *left* are reflexive in their compositional use, however *at*, *near*, *above*, and *below* are not. The latter always occupies the second position in the composition.

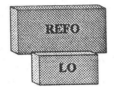

Fig. 3. LO *in front of* the REFO

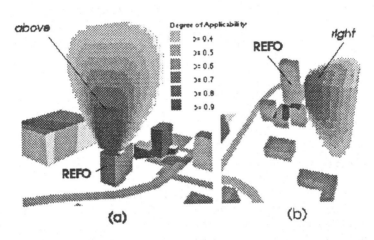

Fig. 4. Cross-sections of the 3D applicability structure of *above* and *right*

3.3 Computation of Compositional Spatial Relations

For the computation of compositional spatial relations we are able to neglect the problem of which relation occupies the first position. We define two classes of 2-place composite spatial relations, the *2-place composite projective projective* (Rel_{cpp}^{2p}), a composition of two elementary projective relations, and the *2-place composite projective topological* (Rel_{cpt}^{2p}), which is a combination of a projective and a topological.

The applicability of Rel_{cpp}^{2p} as well as Rel_{cpt}^{2p} requires positive evidence from both elementary spatial relations involved. Taking into account the general structure of the region of applicability (cf. Fig. 5 and Fig. 6) an important difference between the two classes of compositions becomes obvious. In the case of the Rel_{cpp}^{2p} the combination of both degrees of applicability yields a higher degree of applicability for the composition, i.e., the two elementary relations intensify each other. The Rel_{cpt}^{2p} grounds on two elementary relations which are independent from each other. The composition can be seen as a conjunction of two elementary conditions, i.e., the weakness of one relation can not be compensated by the other.

For the computation of the Rel_{cpp}^{2p} we use the following evidence combination calculus (cf. [24]), which guarantees a degree of applicability not higher than 1:

$$EV_{1 \wedge 2} := EV_1 + EV_2 - EV_1 \cdot EV_2, \quad EV_1, EV_2 > 0$$

The degree of applicability $DA_{Rel_{cpp}^{2p}}$ can than be defined as:

$$DA_{Rel_{cpp}} := \begin{cases} DA_{Rel1} + DA_{Rel2} - |DA_{Rel1} \cdot DA_{Rel2}| & :DA_{Rel1}, DA_{Rel2} > 0 \\ 0 & :else \end{cases}$$

with $Rel1 \in \{in\ front\ of, right, above\}$, $Rel2 \in \{behind, left, below\}$

or $Rel1 \in \{behind, left, below\}$, $Rel2 \in \{in\ front\ of, right, above\}$

For the Rel_{cpt}^{2p}, the degree of applicability, $DA_{Rel_{cpt}^{2p}}$, is determined by the minimal degree of the single relations:

$$DA_{Rel_{cpt}} := Min\{DA_{Rel1}, DA_{Rel2}\}$$

with $Rel1 \in \{in\ front\ of, behind, right, left\}$, $Rel2 \in \{at, near\}$

3.4 Interpreting Relation Tuples

In many cases, the interpretation of a proposition containing a spatial relation can be thought of as verifying the given relation tuple with respect to the geometric model. Depending on the arguments, possible instantiations of the relation tuple are computed and the most plausible interpretation will be selected. Sometimes, however, this kind of query is not possible, e.g., if the operator refered to a part of the environment the robot can not currently perceive. Thus, a referential semantics for spatial relations remains uncomplete, if it only defines how a relation tuple can be computed from the underlying sensory data. Similar issues arise in the field of text understanding and have extensivly been dealt with, e.g., within the LILOG project (cf. [12])

In [21], we show how a plausible imagination, i.e., a coherent geometric model, can be generated from a set of propositions. An adequate interpretation is constructed by searching for a maximally typical representation of the situation described by the given propositions. The typicality distribution corresponding to a certain proposition is encoded in a so-called *Typicality Potential Field* (TyPoF), which is a function mapping locations to typicality values. TyPoFs are instances of typicality schemas associated with the spatial relations. Each TyPoF takes into account the dimensionality, size, and shape of the objects involved. A typicality value associated with a spatial expression corresponds to the (degree of) applicability of a spatial relation for a given object configuration. If several propositions impose restrictions on an object, the corresponding

TyPoFs are combined through superimposition. Hillclimbing is employed in order to find an interpretation with maximal typicality.

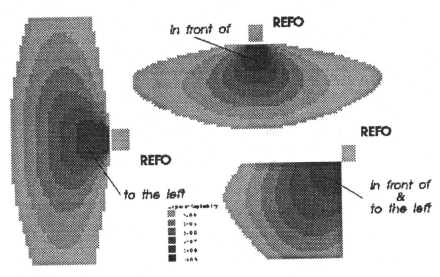

Fig. 5. Potential fields of: *to the left, in front of, and their composition*

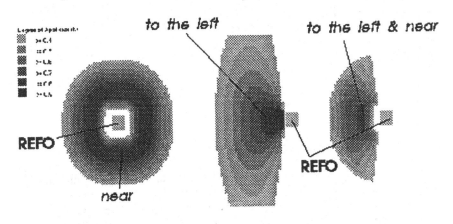

Fig. 6. Potential fields of: *to the left, near, and the composition*

4 Towards a Natural Language Dialog

A simple natural language front-end does not provide enough flexibility for communicating with an autonomous robot, which is situated in a complex dynamic environment. Thus, the natural language interface should have access to all processed information and the environment representation inside the intelligent agent (cf. [16]).

The architecture for such an integrated system is depicted in Fig. 7. Natural language commands and queries from the user form the input for the natural language access system. The linguistic analysis is carried out by a syntactic-semantic parser and translates the natural language expressions into propositions. The parser we use is a modified version of SB-PATR [8] which is based on a unification grammar with semantic information. The propositions are further interpreted in the evaluation component, which is also responsible for the reference semantic interpretation. The evaluation component realizes the interface to the robot and the shared knowledge sources. It is also responsible for the appropriate reactions and responses of the system. The generation component is responsible for translating selected propositions into natural language descriptions, explanations, and queries. An incremental generator, which is based on *Tree Adjoining Grammars* (cf. [9]), generates the surface structures.

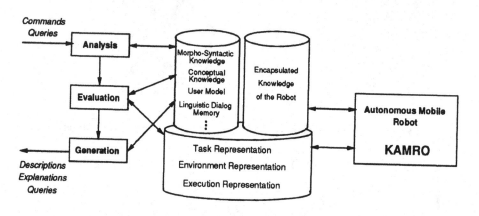

Fig. 7. Architecture of KAMRO's natural language interface

4.1 Interpreting Localization Expressions

In general, a proposition corresponding to the linguistic analysis of a localization expression can not provide a fully instantiated relation tupel. Consider a phrase like *"the spacer on the left"*, which is employed to denote a specific object. The spatial relation (*left*) and a type restriction for the LO (*spacer*) are specified. Neither the REFO, nor the frame of reference are given. A reference system is required since projective relations, as well as the corresponding prepositions, depend on an orientation. The following uses can be distinguished (cf. [2, 20]):

1. *Intrinsic use*

   Orientation is given by an inherent organization of the REFO, e.g., by perceptual organs (humans, animals), by the characteristic direction of movement (vehicles, etc.), or by functional properties (position of the robot's manipulators, etc.). Depending on whether the REFO is thought of as being seen from the outside (e.g., buildings, desks, mirrors, etc.), or from the inside (e.g., chairs, clothing, etc.) the back-front-vector and the left-right-vector form either an orthogonal right-handed-system (*mirror principle*), or left-handed-system (*coincidence principle*).

2. *Extrinsic use*

Orientation is determined by the position of a possible imaginary observer, i.e., it is given by contextual factors, such as the accessibility of the reference objects or objects in its vicinity (e.g., *"Looking though the window, the lever is behind the spacerreservoir"*). If the REFO and the observer coincide, the orientation of the observer is transferred to the REFO. If the observer and the REFO are spatially separated, the orientation follows from the mirror principle.

3. *Deictic use*

A specific case of extrinsic use where the observer coincides with the speaker or listener.

In our example, the deictic use seems to be plausible and the robot would play both the role of the observer and of the REFO. Depending on the context a different interpretation of the utterance could be more appropriate.

During the referential analysis a type of visual search is being carried out in order to generate and test candidates for the uninstantiated arguments of the relation tuple. The most plausible instantiation, with respect to the degree of applicability and focus values in the dialog memory, will be considered as the correct interpretation. Note that even the REFO could be uninstantiated, e.g., if there are several assembly parts of the same type (*"the spacer beside the lever"*). Even in this example, the interpretation may be specific if there is exactly one spatial configuration involving two objects of the appropriate types, i.e., LO and REFO are both identified by the spatial relation.

If the LO or the REFO are not inside the visual field of the robot (e.g., *"the lever behind you"*) a plausible imagination has to be constructed and added to the environment representation. Revisions or adjustments might be necessary later on if the interpretation is falsified by sensory data. The mechanism of generating an imagination is also required if an utterance refers to a hypothetical or future situation (e.g., *"put the lever behind you"*).

4.2 Synthesis of Spatial Reference Expressions

For the synthesis and for the analysis of an localization expression similar aspects must be considered:

- *Selection of the reference objects*
  The following criteria guide the selection:
  1. Distance between LO and REFO, i.e., prefer objects which are closer to LO.
  2. Salience of the REFO, depends on factors like shape, size, color, etc.
  3. Linguistic context, i.e., prefer objects which have been previously mentioned and which are in focus.
- *Selection of spatial relations*
  Not only the degree of applicability of a relation tuple, but also the size of the corresponding region of applicability must be taken into account, e.g., a composite

projective relation could enable a more specific spatial reference than a binary topological relation like *"in"* or *"on"*.

– *Selection of the frame of reference*
In the case of projective relations, the system must choose an orientation. This selection depends on the properties of the REFO and on the situational context.

A detailed description of the generation of localization expressions within our system is given in [1].

5 Summary

Advances in both technical fields during the last decade form a promising basis for the design and construction of integrated natural language interfaces for autonomous mobile robots. Such a natural language access could provide better human-machine interaction for the flexible use of intelligent robots. The required communicative capabilities can only be achieved if the natural language interface has access to the robot's perceptual information and if that knowledge about the environment is accounted for in the interpretation and generation of utterances. Thus, a referential semantics that is perceptually anchored must be defined.

In this contribution we have focused on the problem of spatial reference. We propose to utilize spatial relations as an intermediate representation between the linguistic level and the sensory level. These conceptual structures bridge the gap between geometric data and natural language concepts, such as spatial prepositions. Our computational model is based on a continuous gradation of the applicability of a spatial relation and supports both, the synthesis and the analysis of propositions containing spatial relations. The current implementation copes with elementary topological and projective relations as well as compositional spatial relations. Important aspects of the analysis and generation of localization expressions, such as determination of the frame of reference and the selection of reference objects, have been considered. The ideas presented here, however, still need to be integrated into a fully operable prototype of a natural language interface for the autonomous mobile robot KAMRO.

References

1. E. André. *Generierung natürlichsprachlicher Äußerungen zur simultanen Beschreibung von zeitveränderlichen Szenen: Das System SOCCER.* Memo 26, Universität des Saarlandes, SFB 314 (VITRA), 1988.
2. E. André, G. Bosch, G. Herzog, and T. Rist. *Coping with the Intrinsic and the Deictic Uses of Spatial Prepositions.* In: K. Jorrand and L. Sgurev (eds.), Artificial Intelligence II: Methodology, Systems, Applications, pp. 375–382. Amsterdam: North-Holland, 1987.
3. E. André, G. Herzog, and T. Rist. *Natural Language Access to Visual Data: Dealing with Space and Movement.* Report 63, Universität des Saarlandes, SFB 314 (VITRA), Saarbrücken, 1989. Presented at the 1st Workshop on Logical Semantics of Time, Space and Movement in Natural Language, Toulouse, France.

4. N. I. **Badler**, B. L. **Webber**, J. **Kalita**, and J. **Esakov**. *Animation from Instructions*. In: N. I. Badler, B. A. Barsky, and D. Zeltzer (eds.), Making Them Move: Mechanics, Control, and Animation of Articulaited Figures, pp. 51–93. San Mateo, CA: Kaufmann, 1991.

5. R. **Bajcsy**, A. **Joshi**, E. **Krotkov**, and A. **Zwarico**. *LandScan: A Natural Language and Computer Vision System for Analyzing Aerial Images*. In: Proc. of the 9th IJCAI, pp. 919–921, Los Angeles, CA, 1985.

6. D. **Chapman**. *Vision, Instruction, and Action*. Cambridge, MA: MIT Press, 1991.

7. K.-P. **Gapp**. *Basic Meanings of Spatial Relations: Computation and Evaluation in 3D Space*. In: Proc. of AAAI-94, Seattle, WA, 1994.

8. K. **Harbusch**. *A First Snapshot of XTRAGRAM, A Unification Grammar for German Based on PATR*. Memo 14, Universität des Saarlandes, SFB 314 (XTRA), 1986.

9. K. **Harbusch**, W. **Finkler**, and A. **Schauder**. *Incremental Syntax Generation with Tree Adjoining Grammars*. In: W. Brauer and D. Hernandez (eds.), Verteilte Künstliche Intelligenz und kooperatives Arbeiten: 4. Int. GI-Kongreß Wissensbasierte Systeme, pp. 363–374. Berlin, Heidelberg: Springer, 1991.

10. A. **Herskovits**. *Language and Spatial Cognition. An Interdisciplinary Study of the Prepositions in English*. Cambridge, London: Cambridge University Press, 1986.

11. G. **Herzog** and P. **Wazinski**. *VIsual TRAnslator: Linking Perceptions and Natural Language Descriptions*. Artificial Intelligence Review Journal, 8(2), 1994.

12. O. **Herzog** and C.-R. **Rollinger** (eds.). *Text Understanding in LILOG: Integrating Computational Linguistics and Artificial Intelligence. Final Report on the IBM Germany LILOG-Project*. Berlin, Heidelberg: Springer, 1991.

13. M. **Kochen**. *Representations and Algorithms for Cognitive Learning*. Artificial Intelligence, 5:199–216, 1974.

14. B. **Landau** and R. **Jackendoff**. *"What" and "Where" in Spatial Language and Spatial Cognition*. Behavioral and Brain Sciences, 16:217–265, 1993.

15. H. **Lobin**. *Situierte Agenten als natürlichsprachliche Schnittstellen*. Arbeitsberichte Computerlinguistik 3-92, Univ. Bielefeld, Germany, 1992.

16. T. C. **Lüth**, Th. **Längle**, G. **Herzog**, E. **Stopp**, and U. **Rembold**. *KANTRA: Human-Machine Interaction for Intelligent Robots using Natural Language*. In: 3rd IEEE Int. Workshop on Robot and Human Communication, RO-MAN'94, Nagoya, Japan, 1994.

17. T. C. **Lüth** and U. **Rembold**. *Extensive Manipulation Capabilities and Reliable Behaviour at Autonomous Robot Assembly*. In: Proc. of IEEE Int. Conf. on Robotics and Automation, San Diego, CA, 1994.

18. B. **Neumann**. *Natural Language Description of Time-Varying Scenes*. In: D. L. Waltz (ed.), Semantic Structures, pp. 167–207. Hillsdale, NJ: Lawrence Erlbaum, 1989.

19. N. J. **Nilsson**. *Shakey the Robot*. Technical Note 323, Artificial Intelligence Center, SRI International, Menlo Park, CA, 1984.

20. G. **Retz-Schmidt**. *Various Views on Spatial Prepositions*. AI Magazine, 9(2):95–105, 1988.

21. J. R. J. **Schirra** and Eva **Stopp**. *ANTLIMA – A Listener Model with Mental Images*. In: Proc. of the 13th IJCAI, pp. 175–180, Chambery, France, 1993.

22. M. C. **Torrance**. *Natural Communication with Robots*. Master's thesis, MIT, Department of Electrical Engineering and Computer Science, Cambridge, MA, 1994.

23. S. **Vere** and T. **Bickmore**. *A Basic Agent*. Computational Intelligence, 6(1):41–60, 1990.

24. W. **Wahlster**. *Natürlichsprachliche Argumentation in Dialogsystemen*. Berlin, Heidelberg: Springer, 1981.

25. W. **Wahlster**, H. **Marburger**, A. **Jameson**, and S. **Busemann**. *Over-answering Yes-No Questions: Extended Responses in a NL Interface to a Vision System*. In: Proc. of the 8th IJCAI, pp. 643–646, Karlsruhe, FRG, 1983.

Cardinality Restrictions on Concepts[*]

Franz Baader[1], Martin Buchheit[2], Bernhard Hollunder[2]

[1] Lehr- und Forschungsgebiet Theoretische Informatik, RWTH Aachen
Ahornstraße 55, 52074 Aachen, Germany
e-mail: baader@informatik.rwth-aachen.de

[2] Deutsches Forschungszentrum für KI (DFKI)
Stuhlsatzenhausweg 3, 66123 Saarbrücken, Germany
e-mail: ⟨last name⟩@dfki.uni-sb.de

Abstract. The concept description formalisms of existing terminological systems allow the user to express local cardinality restrictions on the fillers of a particular role. It is not possible, however, to introduce global restrictions on the number of instances of a given concept. This paper argues that such cardinality restrictions on concepts are of importance in applications such as configuration of technical systems, an application domain of terminological systems that is currently gaining in interest. It shows that including such restrictions into the description language leaves the important inference problems such as instance testing decidable. The algorithm combines and simplifies the ideas developed for the treatment of qualifying number restrictions and of general terminological axioms.

1 Introduction

Terminological representation systems can be used to represent the conceptual and taxonomic knowledge of an application domain in a structured and semantically well-understood way. To describe this kind of knowledge one starts with atomic concepts (unary predicates) and roles (binary predicates), and employs the concept description formalism provided by the system to define more complex concepts. In addition to this terminological component (TBox), most systems also have an assertional component (ABox), in which concepts and roles can be instantiated by individual names (constant symbols) representing particular elements of the problem domain.

The reasoning services of terminological systems allow the user to retrieve not only the knowledge that is explicitly stored in a TBox and an ABox, but to access implicitly represented knowledge as well. For a given TBox, the system automatically computes the concept hierarchy according to subconcept-superconcept relationships (subsumption relationships) induced by the structure of the concepts. In addition, it can determine the consistency of the knowledge base (consisting of

---

[*] This work was partly supported by the German Ministry of Research and Technology under grant ITW 92-01 (TACOS).

a TBox and an ABox), and it answers queries regarding the existence of instance relationships between individuals and concepts.

To make these inference services feasible, the description formalism of a terminological system must be of limited expressive power. On the other hand, a too severely restricted formalism may turn out to be too weak for certain applications. For this reason, several extensions of "core" concept languages have been investigated in the literature (see, e.g., [4, 10, 1]). In the present paper, we shall consider an extension that is motivated by the use of terminological systems for solving configuration tasks, which is an application domain that is currently gaining more and more importance (see, e.g., [13, 6, 11, 17, 12]). Technical domains such as configuration seem to be well suited for terminological systems since they usually rely on a large number of terminological conventions, which are in most cases precisely defined. In contrast, more traditional AI applications of terminological systems, such as natural language processing [8], often rely on vague notions and incomplete knowledge, which require the representation of beliefs, as well as probabilistic and default information.

In contrast to these very demanding, and not yet well-understood extensions of terminological representation languages, the additional language construct we shall introduce in this paper is more or less along the lines of traditional constructs, albeit of a rather expressive and thus algorithmically hard to handle nature. It allows one to express restrictions on the number of elements a concept may have: $(\geq m\ C)$ and $(\leq n\ C)$ respectively express that the (possibly complex) concept C has at least m elements and at most n elements, thus restricting the possible models of the knowledge base.

The traditional language constructs that most closely resemble this new one are the so-called number restrictions, which are present in almost all existing systems. Number restrictions allow one to specify the number of possible role-fillers of a particular role. Such a restriction can, for example, express that an admissible PC may have at most 17 parts, by restricting the number of role-fillers of the has-part role to less or equal 17. If one allows for qualifying number restrictions [10] (which are not available in most systems), one can also express that the PC must have exactly one CPU and at most four 1MB memory chips, where CPU and 1MB-memory-chip may be complex concepts. But these cardinality restrictions are still localized to the fillers of one particular role. In contrast, the cardinality restrictions on concepts we propose here are global in the sense that they restrict the number of objects belonging to a given concept for the whole domain of interest (e.g., the whole technical system that is configured). For example, one can express that (in a computer) there must be exactly one electrical power supply unit, which supplies all the devices with electrical power. With a conventional concept description language, even one including qualifying number restrictions, one can only express that every device must have a power supply, but not that all must have the same (or one out of a specified number n).

The expressive power of the new construct is also demonstrated by the fact that it can be used to express terminological axioms of the form $C \doteq D$ (see Section 2 below), which express that the (possibly complex) concepts C and D have exactly the same instances. Such axioms are known to be algorithmically hard to handle (satisfiability is EXP-TIME hard) [15]. In a very restricted setting, cardinality restrictions have already been considered by van der Hoek and de Rijke [16]. However, their language is far less expressive than ours (satisfiability is in PSPACE).

Like number restrictions and several other concept constructors, cardinality restrictions on concepts can be seen as specific generalized quantifiers [7]. In [14], J. Quantz proposes an integration of various generalized quantifiers into terminological formalisms in order to cope with problems related to bound anaphora resolution. However, like most of the research on generalized quantifiers in the area of linguistics and philosophical logics, Quantz's article is only concerned with expressibility issues and not with computability. In fact, for his representation language the important inference problems turn out to be undecidable. The main goal of the present paper is to design sound and complete inference algorithms for the language we propose.

In the following, we shall first formally introduce the terminological formalism considered in this paper, which contains both cardinality restrictions on concepts and qualifying number restrictions. Section 2 also defines the relevant reasoning services for terminological knowledge bases consisting of a terminological and an assertional component. In Section 3 we shortly sketch how these services can be utilized in a configuration application. Then we shall develop an algorithm that tests a knowledge base for consistency. This is sufficient since all the other interesting inference services can easily be reduced to this task [5]. The consistency algorithm combines the ideas developed in [3, 9] for handling inclusion axioms (in a language with number restrictions), and in [10] for handling qualifying number restrictions.

2   The Terminological Formalism

The expressive power of a terminological system is determined by the constructs available for building concept descriptions, and by the way these descriptions can be used in the terminological (TBox) and the assertional (ABox) component of the system. The description language $\mathcal{ALCQ}$ defined below coincides with the one introduced in [10]. The new expressivity lies in the TBox, where the usual terminological axioms are replaced by cardinality restrictions on concepts. The assertional component is the standard one.

The description language

The *concept descriptions* (for short, concepts) of the language $\mathcal{ALCQ}$ are built from *concept names* and *role names* using the constructors *conjunction* ($C \sqcap D$), *disjunction* ($C \sqcup D$), *negation* ($\neg C$), and *qualifying number restrictions* (($\geq n\ R\ C$) and ($\leq n\ R\ C$)), where C, D stand for concepts, R for a role name, and n for a nonnegative integer.

Note that (unqualifying) number restrictions, value restrictions ($\forall R.C$) and existential restrictions ($\exists R.C$) are not explicitly included in the language since they can all be expressed with the help of qualifying number restrictions [10].

To define the semantics of concept descriptions, we interpret concepts as subsets of a domain of interest and roles as binary relations over this domain. More precisely, an *interpretation* $\mathcal{I}$ consists of a set $\Delta^{\mathcal{I}}$ (the *domain* of $\mathcal{I}$) and a function $\cdot^{\mathcal{I}}$ (the *interpretation function* of $\mathcal{I}$). The interpretation function maps every concept name A to a subset $A^{\mathcal{I}}$ of $\Delta^{\mathcal{I}}$, and every role name R to a subset $R^{\mathcal{I}}$ of $\Delta^{\mathcal{I}} \times \Delta^{\mathcal{I}}$.

The interpretation function is extended to arbitrary concept descriptions as follows. Let C, D be concept descriptions, R be a role name, n be a nonnegative integer, and assume that $C^{\mathcal{I}}$ and $D^{\mathcal{I}}$ are already defined. Then

$$(C \sqcap D)^{\mathcal{I}} = C^{\mathcal{I}} \cap D^{\mathcal{I}},$$
$$(C \sqcup D)^{\mathcal{I}} = C^{\mathcal{I}} \cup D^{\mathcal{I}},$$
$$(\neg C)^{\mathcal{I}} = \Delta^{\mathcal{I}} \setminus C^{\mathcal{I}},$$
$$(\geq n\ R\ C)^{\mathcal{I}} = \{a \in \Delta^{\mathcal{I}} \mid \sharp\{b \in \Delta^{\mathcal{I}} \mid (a,b) \in R^{\mathcal{I}} \wedge b \in C^{\mathcal{I}}\} \geq n\},$$
$$(\leq n\ R\ C)^{\mathcal{I}} = \{a \in \Delta^{\mathcal{I}} \mid \sharp\{b \in \Delta^{\mathcal{I}} \mid (a,b) \in R^{\mathcal{I}} \wedge b \in C^{\mathcal{I}}\} \leq n\},$$

where $\sharp X$ denotes the cardinality of a set X.

The terminological component

A *terminological axiom* is an expression of the form $C \doteq D$, where C and D are (possibly complex) concept descriptions. A finite set of such axioms is called a *TBox*. The semantics of a TBox is quite obvious: an interpretation $\mathcal{I}$ *satisfies* an axiom $C \doteq D$ iff $C^{\mathcal{I}} = D^{\mathcal{I}}$, and it is a *model* of a TBox $\mathcal{T}$ iff it satisfies all axioms in $\mathcal{T}$.

Most systems impose severe restrictions on admissible TBoxes: *(1)* The concepts on the left-hand sides of axioms must be concept names, *(2)* concept names occur at most once as left-hand side of an axiom, and *(3)* there are no cyclic definitions. The effect of these restrictions is that terminological axioms are just macro definitions (introducing names for large descriptions), which can simply be expanded before starting the reasoning process. Unrestricted terminological axioms are a lot harder to handle algorithmically [15, 3, 9], but they are very useful in expressing important constraints on admissible configurations (see Section 3 below).

Now we introduce a new type of axioms, which we call cardinality restrictions on concepts, and which are even more expressive than unrestricted terminological axioms of the form $C \doteq D$. Such a *cardinality restriction* is an expression of the form $(\geq n\ C)$ or $(\leq n\ C)$, where C is a concept description and n a nonnegative integer. An interpretation $\mathcal{I}$ *satisfies* the restriction $(\geq n\ C)$ iff $\sharp C^{\mathcal{I}} \geq n$ and $(\leq n\ C)$ iff $\sharp C^{\mathcal{I}} \leq n$.

Obviously, saying that C and D have the same instances is equivalent to stating that the concept $(C \sqcap \neg D) \sqcup (\neg C \sqcap D)$ is empty, i.e., contains at most zero elements. This demonstrates that terminological axioms can be expressed by cardinality restrictions. For this reason, a *TBox* will from now on simply be a finite set of cardinality restrictions. The interpretation $\mathcal{I}$ is a *model* of such a TBox iff it satisfies each of its restrictions.

The assertional component

In this component, facts concerning particular objects in the application domain can be expressed as follows. The objects are referred to by *individual names*, and these names may be used in two types of *assertional axioms:* concept assertions $C(a)$ and role assertions $R(a, b)$, where C is a concept description, R is a role name, and a, b are individual names. A finite set of assertions is called *ABox*.

In order to give a semantics to assertions we extend the interpretation function to individuals. Each individual name a is interpreted as an element $a^{\mathcal{I}}$ of the domain such that the mapping from individual names to $\Delta^{\mathcal{I}}$ is 1-1. This restriction is usually called unique name assumption (UNA). The interpretation $\mathcal{I}$ *satisfies* the assertion $C(a)$ iff $a^{\mathcal{I}} \in C^{\mathcal{I}}$ and the assertion $R(a, b)$ iff $(a^{\mathcal{I}}, b^{\mathcal{I}}) \in R^{\mathcal{I}}$. We say that an interpretation $\mathcal{I}$ is a *model* of an ABox $\mathcal{A}$ iff $\mathcal{I}$ satisfies every assertion in $\mathcal{A}$.

The reasoning services

A terminological *knowledge base* $\Sigma = \langle \mathcal{A}, \mathcal{T} \rangle$ consists of an ABox $\mathcal{A}$ and a TBox $\mathcal{T}$. After representing the relevant knowledge of an application domain in such a KB, one can not just retrieve the information that is explicitly stored. Terminological systems also provide their users with services that allow to access knowledge that is only implicitly represented in the KB. For example, these reasoning services provide answers to the following queries:

1. *KB-consistency*: Is the given KB consistent? That is, does there exist a model of the KB (i.e., a model of both the ABox and the TBox)?
2. *Concept Satisfiability*: Given a KB and a concept C, does there exist a model of the KB in which C is interpreted as a nonempty set?
3. *Subsumption*: Given a KB and two concepts C and D, is $C^{\mathcal{I}} \subseteq D^{\mathcal{I}}$ in any model $\mathcal{I}$ of the KB? Subsumption detects implicit dependencies among the concepts in the KB.
4. *Instance Checking*: Given a KB, an individual a and a concept C, is $a^{\mathcal{I}} \in C^{\mathcal{I}}$ for all models $\mathcal{I}$ of the KB?

Since concept satisfiability, subsumption, and instance checking can be reduced to KB-consistency or inconsistency in linear time (see, e.g., [5]), it is sufficient to devise an algorithm for this problem. Before describing such an algorithm for KBs with cardinality restrictions, we give some ideas of how such an algorithm can be employed to solve configuration tasks.

3 Application in Configuration

Figure 1 contains some parts of the description of a SPARCstation 2 in our terminological formalism. The first three axioms of the TBox are traditional concept definitions, which (in a top-down manner) introduce names for complex descriptions. A SPARCstation 2 is defined to have four obligatory parts, namely system unit, monitor, keyboard, and mouse and pad. In addition, it may have as optional parts terminals and printers, but no other parts are admissible. The concepts

---

The terminology:

SPARCstation_2 $\doteq$
 (= 1 has-part System_Unit) $\sqcap$ (= 1 has-part Monitor) $\sqcap$
 (= 1 has-part Keyboard) $\sqcap$ (= 1 has-part Mouse&Pad) $\sqcap$
 $\forall$has-part.(System_Unit $\sqcup$ Monitor $\sqcup$ Keyboard $\sqcup$ Mouse&Pad $\sqcup$ Terminal $\sqcup$ Printer)

System_Unit $\doteq$
 (= 1 has-part Main_Logic_Board) $\sqcap$
 (= 1 has-part Power_Supply) $\sqcap$
 (= 2 has-part Hard_Drive) $\sqcap$
 (= 1 has-part Diskette_Drive)

Main_Logic_Board $\doteq$
 (= 1 has-part CPU) $\sqcap$
 (= 16 has-part SIMM_slots) $\sqcap$
 (= 3 has-part SBUS_slots)

Main_Logic_Board	$\sqsubseteq$	(= 1 is-supplied-by Power_Supply)
Hard_Drive	$\sqsubseteq$	(= 1 is-supplied-by Power_Supply)
Diskette_Drive	$\sqsubseteq$	(= 1 is-supplied-by Power_Supply)
Terminal $\sqcap$ ($\geq$ 1 has-type VT100)	$\sqsubseteq$	($\geq$ 1 has-part Female-male_null_modem_cable)
Terminal $\sqcap$ ($\geq$ 1 has-type WY-50)	$\sqsubseteq$	($\geq$ 1 has-part Male-male_null_modem_cable)

($\leq$ 1 Power_Supply)

The ABox:

SPARCstation_2(sparci), has-part(sparci, term), Terminal(term), has-type(term, vt100), VT100(vt100)

Fig. 1. A SPARCstation 2

standing for the parts are again defined by descriptions. In the example, we have just given the (simplified) descriptions of the system unit, and of the main logic board, which is a part of this unit. Note that $(= n\ R\ C)$ is an abbreviation for $(\geq n\ R\ C) \sqcap (\leq n\ R\ C)$.

 The next five axioms are inclusion axioms of the form $C \sqsubseteq D$, which should be read as abbreviations of the corresponding cardinality restrictions $(\leq 0\ C \sqcap \neg D)$. The (complex) concepts main logic board, hard drive, and diskette drive are required to have a power supply, and certain types of terminals need specific cables. The qualifying number restrictions in these inclusion axioms express that each part has exactly one power supply, but different parts could still have different power supplies. The last terminological axiom, which is a cardinality restriction on the concept power supply, makes sure that all parts use the same power supply. It seems to be impossible to express such a constraint in a traditional terminological formalism unless one allows for role-value maps (which would, however, cause undecidability).

Configuration checking
The instance test of a terminological system can be employed to check whether a computer configuration is admissible (this idea has, for example, been used in an application of the CLASSIC system [17]). In the TBox, one defines a concept that describes admissible computer systems, and in the ABox one describes

the actual configuration of a computer system. The instance test then checks whether the individual corresponding to the configuration is an instance of the concept "admissible computer system." The description of the actual configuration can be done on different levels of abstraction. For example, we can describe a SPARCstation 2 by saying that it has four fillers of the has-part role that are respectively in the concepts System_Unit, Monitor, Keyboard, and Mouse&Pad. On a lower level of abstraction, the realization that the parts belong to these concepts is also left to the instance test.

In addition, one can also define concepts that describe the most frequent errors made when configuring such a system (e.g., forgetting some cables). When the instance test finds out that the configuration belongs to such an error concept then one knows the reason why the configuration was not admissible, and can take appropriate action.

Configuration generation

The configuration domain is again modeled in the TBox, and the ABox contains a (high level) description of what should be configured. The consistency algorithm we shall describe below has the property that it not only answers with "consistent" or "inconsistent." If the KB is consistent, it also yields a finite model (see the definition of the canonical model in Section 4), in which all the implicit information contained in the TBox and ABox is made explicit. In principle, this model describes an admissible configuration.

In Figure 1, the ABox describes that we want to have a SPARCstation 2 with an additional VT100 terminal. If we invoke the consistency algorithm of Section 4, it will generate the obligatory parts like system unit, etc. It also makes sure that the integrity constraints expressed by the inclusion axioms and the cardinality restriction are satisfied (more information on this idea of configuration by model generation can be found in [12]).

4   The Consistency Algorithm

The method for deciding consistency of a KB presented below is rule-based in the sense that it starts with the original KB (consisting of an ABox $\mathcal{A}_0$ and a TBox $\mathcal{T}_0$), and applies certain consistency preserving transformation rules to the ABox until no more rules apply. If the "complete" KB thus obtained contains an obvious contradiction (called clash) then the original KB $\langle \mathcal{A}_0, \mathcal{T}_0 \rangle$ was inconsistent. Otherwise, $\langle \mathcal{A}_0, \mathcal{T}_0 \rangle$ was consistent since the complete KB can be used to construct a finite model.

The transformation rule that handles number restrictions of the form ($\geq n\ R\ C$) will generate n new ABox individuals $x_1, \ldots, x_n$ that stand for the role-fillers required by the restriction. Unlike the individuals present in the original ABox (called "old" individuals in the following) these "new" individual names should not be subjected to the unique name assumption. In fact, in a model they may well be interpreted identical to an old individual or a new individual introduced by another rule application. What must be ensured, however, is that

$x_1, \ldots, x_n$ are interpreted by different objects. In order to express this we need a new type of assertions, called *inequality assertions*. Such an assertion is of the form $s \neq t$ for individuals s, t, and it has the obvious semantics, i.e., an interpretation $\mathcal{I}$ satisfies $s \neq t$ iff $s^{\mathcal{I}} \neq t^{\mathcal{I}}$. These assertions are considered as being symmetric, i.e., saying that $s \neq t \in \mathcal{A}$ is the same as saying that $t \neq s \in \mathcal{A}$.

In the following, we assume that the set of individual names is partitioned into a set I_{old} of old individual names (subjected to the UNA) and a set I_{new} of new individual names. The elements of I_{old} are just the individuals present in the original ABox, which means that I_{old} is finite. We assume that I_{new} is infinite to allow for an arbitrary number of rule applications. We denote individuals of I_{old} by the letters a, b, of I_{new} by x, y, and of $I = I_{\text{old}} \cup I_{\text{new}}$ by s, t (all possibly with index).

The transformation rule that handles disjunction (as well as the rules concerned with at-most restrictions) is *nondeterministic* in the sense that a given ABox is transformed into two (or finitely many) new ABoxes such that the original ABox is consistent with the TBox iff *one of* the new ABoxes is so. For this reason we will consider *generalized* KBs of the form $\langle \mathcal{M}, \mathcal{T} \rangle$, where $\mathcal{M} = \{\mathcal{A}_1, \ldots, \mathcal{A}_l\}$ is a finite set of ABoxes. This generalized KB is called *consistent* iff there is some i, $1 \leq i \leq l$, such that $\langle \mathcal{A}_i, \mathcal{T} \rangle$ is consistent.

Treatment of cardinality restrictions

So far, all that has been said also applies to rule-based consistency algorithms for less expressive languages (see, e.g., [5]). Now we shall point out two new problems that are due to the presence of cardinality restrictions.

To see the *first problem*, assume that the TBox contains the restriction $(\leq n\ C)$, and that all individuals contained in the ABox are either asserted to be in C or in its complement. If the number m of individuals in C is larger than n then we know that we must take action, whereas $m \leq n$ shows that no action is required. In general, however, the ABox will also contain individuals for which no assertions relating them to C or $\neg C$ are present. For these individuals, we do not know a priori whether a model of the TBox and ABox will interpret them as elements of C or of $\neg C$. Thus we are not necessarily able to decide whether action is required or not.

To make sure that in the end all such indeterminate situations are resolved, we introduce a rule (called choose-rule below) that makes sure that at some stage of the transformation process each individual will either be asserted to be in C or its complement. (The choice is "don't know" nondeterministic, i.e., both cases have to be considered.) In a slightly modified way the idea of such a choose-rule was already presented in [10] since qualifying number-restriction of the form $(\leq n\ R\ C)$ cause a similar problem.

The *second problem* is that, due to the choose-rule, the transformation process need no longer terminate, unless one takes specific precautions to detect cyclic computations. In fact, if the concept C from above is of the form $(\geq m\ R\ D)$ (for $m \geq 1$), then asserting C for an individual s_0 causes the introduction of a new individual s_1. Because of the choose-rule, at some stage of the transformation we must consider an ABox were s_1 is asserted to be in C, which causes the introduction of a new individual s_2, etc.

In order to regain the termination property, we restrict the applicability of transformation rules that generate new individuals. The idea is that the application of such rules is blocked for a new individual x if there is another individual s in the ABox that has all concept assertions that x has. Termination is then due to the fact that there are only finitely many different concepts D that can occur in such assertions. To prevent cyclic blocking, which would destroy the correctness of the algorithm, we consider an enumeration $t_0, t_1, t_2, \ldots$ of I in which all elements of I_{old} come before all elements of I_{new}. We write $t < t'$ iff t comes before t' in this enumeration.

Now blocking can formally be defined as follows: An individual $x \in I_{\text{new}}$ is *blocked* by an individual $s \in I$ in an ABox $\mathcal{A}$ iff $\{D \mid D(x) \in \mathcal{A}\} \subseteq \{D' \mid D'(s) \in \mathcal{A}\}$ and $s < x$. Note that only new individuals can be blocked.

Similar termination problems are already caused by terminological axioms of the form $C \doteq D$. For this reason, the idea of blocking is already present in [9]. The main difference between the two notions of blocking is that in [9] equality of sets is required whereas we are satisfied with set inclusion. It turns out that our notion of blocking facilitates the termination proof. In addition, termination can be shown for arbitrary sequences of rule applications. It no longer depends on the use of a specific strategy (as required in [9]).

Preprocessing

In order to facilitate the description of the transformation rules, we start with a preprocessing step that transforms the original KB into a simplified form.

As usual, all concepts occurring in the KB are transformed into negation normal form, where negation occurs only immediately in front of concept names. Negation normal forms can be computed in linear time by pushing negation signs into the descriptions (see, e.g., [5]). The expression $\sim C$ will denote the negation normal form of the concept $\neg C$.

In addition, we assume that the TBox contains only restrictions of the form $(\leq n\ C)$. In fact, a restriction $(\geq n\ C)$ can be expressed in the ABox by adding assertions $C(x_i)$ and $x_i \neq x_j$ (for $1 \leq i, j \leq n, i \neq j$), where the x_i are new individuals that did not occur in the original KB.

Finally, the UNA for old individuals is made explicit in the ABox by adding the assertions $a \neq b$ for each pair of distinct elements $a, b \in I_{\text{old}}$.

The transformation rules

As a result of the preprocessing steps, the input of the consistency algorithm is a generalized KB $\langle \{\mathcal{A}_0\}, \mathcal{T}_0 \rangle$ where $\mathcal{A}_0$ and $\mathcal{T}_0$ are in the simplified form described above. Starting with $\langle \{\mathcal{A}_0\}, \mathcal{T}_0 \rangle$, the algorithm applies the *transformation rules* of Figure 2 as long as possible.

The rules should be read as follows. They are applied to a generalized KB $\langle \mathcal{M}, \mathcal{T}_0 \rangle$ (where $\mathcal{M}$ is a set of ABoxes). The rules take an element $\mathcal{A}$ of $\mathcal{M}$, and replace it by one ABox $\mathcal{A}'$, by two ABoxes $\mathcal{A}'$ and $\mathcal{A}''$, or by finitely many ABoxes $\mathcal{A}_{i,j}$. The TBox $\mathcal{T}_0$ of the input is left unchanged.

The $\to_\sqcap$-rule
Precondition: $\mathcal{A}$ contains $(C_1 \sqcap C_2)(s)$, but it does not contain both $C_1(s)$ and $C_2(s)$.
Postcondition: $\mathcal{A}'$ is obtained from $\mathcal{A}$ by adding $C_1(s)$ and $C_2(s)$.

The $\to_\sqcup$-rule
Precondition: $\mathcal{A}$ contains $(C_1 \sqcup C_2)(s)$, but neither $C_1(s)$ nor $C_2(s)$.
Postcondition: $\mathcal{A}'$ is obtained from $\mathcal{A}$ by adding $C_1(s)$, and $\mathcal{A}''$ is obtained from $\mathcal{A}$ by adding $C_2(s)$.

The $\to_\geq$-rule
Precondition: $\mathcal{A}$ contains $(\geq n\ R\ C)(s)$, s is not blocked in $\mathcal{A}$, and there are no individual names $s_1, \ldots, s_n$ such that $R(s, s_i)$, $C(s_i)$, and $s_i \neq s_j$ $(1 \leq i,j \leq n, i \neq j)$ are contained in $\mathcal{A}$.
Postcondition: $\mathcal{A}'$ is obtained from $\mathcal{A}$ by adding $R(s, t_i)$, $C(t_i)$, and $t_i \neq t_j$ $(1 \leq i,j \leq n, i \neq j)$, where $t_1, \ldots, t_n \in I_{\text{new}}$ are such that $t_i > s'$ for all individual names s' occurring in $\mathcal{A}$.

The $\to_{\text{choose}}$-rule
Precondition: $\mathcal{A}$ contains an individual t such that either
 1. $(\leq n\ R\ C)(s)$ and $R(s, t)$ are in $\mathcal{A}$, or
 2. $(\leq n\ C)$ is in $\mathcal{T}_0$,
and $\mathcal{A}$ does not contain $(C \sqcup {\sim}C)(t)$.
Postcondition: $\mathcal{A}'$ is obtained from $\mathcal{A}$ by adding $(C \sqcup {\sim}C)(t)$.

The $\to_\leq$-rule
Precondition: $\mathcal{A}$ contains distinct individuals $t_1, \ldots, t_{n+1}$ such that either
 1. $(\leq n\ R\ C)(s)$ and $R(s, t_1), \ldots, R(s, t_{n+1})$ are in $\mathcal{A}$, or
 2. $(\leq n\ C)$ is in $\mathcal{T}_0$,
and $C(t_1), \ldots, C(t_{n+1})$ are in $\mathcal{A}$, and $t_i \neq t_j$ is not in $\mathcal{A}$ for some $i \neq j$.
Postcondition: For each pair t_i, t_j such that $t_j < t_i$ and $t_i \neq t_j$ is not in $\mathcal{A}$ the ABox $\mathcal{A}_{i,j} := [t_i/t_j]\mathcal{A}$ is obtained from $\mathcal{A}$ by replacing each occurrence of t_i by t_j.

Fig. 2. Completion rules of the consistency algorithm.

The transformation rules are *sound* in the sense that the ABox $\mathcal{A}$ is consistent iff one of the ABoxes it is replaced by is so (see [2] for the proof). Thus, if $\langle \mathcal{M}, \mathcal{T}_0 \rangle$ is obtained from $\langle \{\mathcal{A}_0\}, \mathcal{T}_0 \rangle$ by a sequence of rule applications then $\langle \mathcal{A}_0, \mathcal{T}_0 \rangle$ is consistent iff $\langle \mathcal{M}, \mathcal{T}_0 \rangle$ is consistent.

The second important property of the set of transformation rules is that the transformation process always terminates, i.e., there cannot be an infinite sequence of rule application (see [2] for the proof). Thus, after finitely many transformation steps we obtain a generalized KB to which no more rules apply. We call such a generalized KB *complete*. Consistency of a complete (generalized) KB $\langle \{\mathcal{A}_1, \ldots, \mathcal{A}_n\}, \mathcal{T}_0 \rangle$ can be decided by looking for obvious contradictions, so-called clashes, in the KBs $\langle \mathcal{A}_i, \mathcal{T}_0 \rangle$.

A KB $\langle \mathcal{A}, \mathcal{T} \rangle$ contains a *clash* iff one of the following three situations occurs:

1. $\{B(s), \neg B(s)\} \subseteq \mathcal{A}$ for some individual s and some concept name B.
2. $\{(\leq n \; R \; C)(s), R(s, t_i), C(t_i), t_i \neq t_j \mid 1 \leq i, j \leq n+1, i \neq j\} \subseteq \mathcal{A}$ for individuals $s, t_1, \ldots, t_{n+1}$, a nonnegative integer n, a concept C, and a role name R.
3. $(\leq n \; C) \in \mathcal{T}$ and $\{C(s_i), s_i \neq s_j \mid 1 \leq i, j \leq n+1, i \neq j\} \subseteq \mathcal{A}$ for individuals $s_1, \ldots, s_{n+1}$, a nonnegative integer n, and a concept C.

Obviously, a KB that contains a clash cannot be consistent. Consequently, if all KBs $\langle \mathcal{A}_i, \mathcal{T}_0 \rangle$ contain a clash, then $\langle \{\mathcal{A}_1, \ldots, \mathcal{A}_n\}, \mathcal{T}_0 \rangle$ is inconsistent, which by soundness of the rules implies that the original KB $\langle \mathcal{A}_0, \mathcal{T}_0 \rangle$ was inconsistent.

If, however, one of the KBs $\Sigma_i = \langle \mathcal{A}_i, \mathcal{T}_0 \rangle$ is clash-free then the corresponding canonical interpretation $\mathcal{I}_{\Sigma_i}$ (as defined below) can be used to construct a model of the original KB $\langle \mathcal{A}_0, \mathcal{T}_0 \rangle$ (see [2] for the proof).

Let $\Sigma = \langle \mathcal{A}, \mathcal{T} \rangle$ be a KB. The *canonical interpretation* $\mathcal{I}_\Sigma$ induced by Σ is defined as follows:

- The domain $\Delta^{\mathcal{I}_\Sigma}$ of $\mathcal{I}_\Sigma$ consists of all the individuals occurring in $\mathcal{A}$.
- For all concept names A we define $A^{\mathcal{I}_\Sigma} = \{s \mid A(s) \in \mathcal{A}\}$.
- For a role name R we define $R^{\mathcal{I}_\Sigma}$ inductively with respect to the total ordering $<$ on the individual names. If s_0 is the least element in $\Delta^{\mathcal{I}_\Sigma}$ then $(s_0, t) \in R^{\mathcal{I}_\Sigma}$ iff $R(s_0, t) \in \mathcal{A}$. Now let $s \in \Delta^{\mathcal{I}_\Sigma}$ be different from s_0.
  - If s is not blocked in $\mathcal{A}$ then we define $(s, t) \in R^{\mathcal{I}_\Sigma}$ iff $R(s, t) \in \mathcal{A}$.
  - If s is blocked in $\mathcal{A}$ then let s' be the least (with respect to the ordering $<$) individual name in $\Delta^{\mathcal{I}_\Sigma}$ that blocks s. By the definition of blocking, $s' < s$, and thus we can assume that the set $\{t \mid (s', t) \in R^{\mathcal{I}_\Sigma}\}$ is already defined, and we define $(s, t) \in R^{\mathcal{I}_\Sigma}$ iff $(s', t) \in R^{\mathcal{I}_\Sigma}$.
- For an individual s occurring in $\mathcal{A}$ we set $s^{\mathcal{I}_\Sigma} := s$.

To sum up, we have seen that the transformation rules of Figure 2 reduce consistency of a KB $\langle \mathcal{A}_0, \mathcal{T}_0 \rangle$ to consistency of a complete generalized KB $\langle \mathcal{M}, \mathcal{T}_0 \rangle$. In addition, consistency of this complete KB can be decided by looking for obvious contradictions (clashes). This shows the main result of the paper:

Theorem 1. *It is decidable whether or not a KB $\langle \mathcal{A}_0, \mathcal{T}_0 \rangle$ is consistent.*

5 Conclusion

We have shown how to extend a terminological KR formalism by a construct that can express global restrictions on the cardinality of concepts. The usefulness of these cardinality restrictions on concepts was demonstrated by an example from a configuration application. Unlike role-value maps (which could be used to model similar situations), our new construct leaves all the important inference problems decidable. The consistency algorithm combines and simplifies the ideas developed for the treatment of qualifying number restrictions and of terminological axioms.

References

1. F. Baader. Augmenting concept languages by transitive closure of roles: An alternative to terminological cycles. In *Proceedings of the 12th International Joint Conference on Artificial Intelligence*, Sydney, Australia, 1991.

2. F. Baader, M. Buchheit, and B. Hollunder. Cardinality restrictions on concepts. Research Report RR-93-48, DFKI Saarbrücken, 1993.

3. F. Baader, H.-J. Bürckert, B. Hollunder, W. Nutt, and J. H. Siekmann. Concept logics. In *Proceedings of the Symposium on Computational Logics*, Brüssel, Belgium, 1990.

4. F. Baader and P. Hanschke. A scheme for integrating concrete domains into concept languages. In *Proceedings of the 12th International Joint Conference on Artificial Intelligence*, Sydney, Australia, 1991.

5. F. Baader and B. Hollunder. A terminological knowledge representation system with complete inference algorithms. In M. Richter and H. Boley, editors, *International Workshop on Processing Declarative Knowledge*, volume 567. Springer, 1991.

6. C. Bagnasco, P. Petrin, and L. Spampinato. Taxonomic reasoning in configuration tasks. Technical Report QR-91-1, Quinary SpA, 1991.

7. J. Barwise and R. Cooper. Generalized quantifiers and natural language. *Linguistics and Philosophy*, 4:159–219, 1981.

8. R. J. Brachman, R. J. Bobrow, P. R. Cohen, J. W. Klovstad, B. L. Webber, and W. A. Woods. *Research in natural language understanding, annual report*. Technical Report No. 4274. Bolt, Beranek and Newman, Cambridge, Mass., 1979.

9. M. Buchheit, F. M. Donini, and A. Schaerf. Decidable reasoning in terminological knowledge representation systems. *Journal of Artificial Intelligence Research*, 1:109–138, 1993.

10. B. Hollunder and F. Baader. Qualifying number restrictions in concept languages. In *Proceedings of the 2nd International Conference on Principles of Knowledge Representation and Reasoning*, Cambridge, Mass., 1991.

11. R. Klein. Model representation and taxonomic reasoning in configuration problem solving. In *Proceedings of the German Workshop on Artificial Intelligence, GWAI-91*, 1991.

12. R. Klein, M. Buchheit, and W. Nutt. Configuration as model construction: The constructive problem solving approach. In *Proceedings of the Third International Conference on Artificial Intelligence in Design*, Lausanne, Switzerland, 1994.

13. B. Owsnicki-Klewe. Configuration as a consistency maintenance task. In *Proceedings of the German Workshop on Artificial Intelligence, GWAI-88*, 1988.

14. J. Quantz. How to fit generalized quantifiers into terminological logics. In *Proceedings of the 10th European Conference on Artificial Intelligence*, pages 543–547, Vienna, Austria, 1992.

15. K. Schild. Terminological cycles and the propositional μ-calculus. In *Proceedings of the 4th International Conference on Principles of Knowledge Representation and Reasoning*, Bonn, Germany, 1994.

16. W. van der Hoek and M. de Rijke. Generalized quantifiers and modal logic. *Journal of logic, language and information*, 2:19–58, 1993.

17. J. R. Wright, E. S. Weixelbaum, K. Brown, G. T. Vesonder, S. R. Palmer, J. I. Berman, and H. H. Moore. A knowledge-based configurator that supports sales, engineering, and manufacturing at AT&T network systems. *AI Magazine*, 14(3):69–80, 1993.

An Artificial Neural Network for High Precision Eye Movement Tracking

Marc Pomplun, Boris Velichkovsky, Helge Ritter

Department of Information Science
Bielefeld University, D-33615 Bielefeld, FRG
email: impomplu@techfak.uni-bielefeld.de

Abstract. Research of visual cognition often suffers from very inexact methods of eye movement recording. A so-called *eye tracker*, fastened to the test person's head, yields information about pupil position and facing direction related to a computer monitor in front of the subject. It is now a software task to calculate the coordinates of the screen point the person is looking at. Conventional algorithms are not able to realize the required non-linear projection very precisely. Especially if the test person is wearing spectacles, the deviation may exceed 3 degrees of visual angle. In this paper a new approach is presented, solving the problem with a *parametrized self-organizing map* (PSOM). After a short calibration it reduces the average error to approximately 30 percent of its initial value. Due to its high efficiency (less than 150 μs per computation on a PC with a 486DX2-66 processor) it is perfectly suited for real-time application.

1 Introduction

High precision recording of eye movements in real time is of considerable importance in many fields, ranging from research in visual cognition, over commercial studies, to the creation of future, more powerful man-machine interfaces that use eye movement information to control the interaction with a computer or with virtual reality.

A sufficiently flexible approach for achieving this goal is to rely on the evaluation of camera images of the human eye, together with additional sensors from which the head position can be inferred. A recent system of that kind has been developed by Stampe and Reingold at the University of Toronto [6] and is in use in our lab for visual cognition research.

In this system two tiny cameras, fastened to a head set, monitor the eye of the test person and four reference marks in his or her view field (see figure 1). Suitable image processing software then extracts the required coordinate information from the two camera images (the first providing the gaze direction in head centered coordinates, the second yielding the orientation of the head relative to the scene). While this approach yields satisfactory results for normal-sighted persons, the accuracy decreases with gaze eccentricity and drops significantly when subjects wear spectacles.

This motivated the research reported in the present paper, namely the use of adaptive neural networks that can be trained to compensate (at least part of) the (systematic) measurement errors made by the current system. Since the characteristics of these errors vary with the test person, it is essential to use an adaptive network that can be retrained for each different test person. Furthermore, practical considerations dictate that such retraining be fast and possible on the basis of a small number of training examples (for which the test person has to fixate known positions on a computer screen).

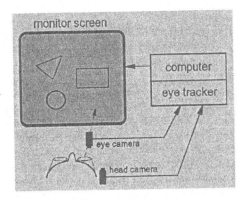

Figure 1: Scheme of the system developed by Stampe and Reingold

In the present paper we report an approach that solves this problem with a *parametrized self-organizing map* ("PSOM") [3, 4, 5], a recently proposed variant of Kohonen's self-organizing map [1, 2]. An attractive property of the PSOM is that it can be trained with an extremely small number of training examples (this does, in fact, lead to restrictions on the representable mappings, but they are of no consequence in the present context). We have implemented and tested this approach on a PC with a 486DX2-66 processor and applied it to correcting data subsequently to an experiment. However, the computation of a single position takes less than 150 μs, which is negligible considering the system's temporal resolution. The method can therefore be applied in real time as well. We found that by this approach the average error of the system can be reduced to approximately 30 percent of its previous value. This improvement is achieved with only 16 training examples, gathered during a short calibration session where the subject has to fixate known points of a 4×4 grid. As a result, we can now track eye movements for subjects wearing spectacles at a higher precision than the system could achieve for normal sighted subjects before. For normal sighted subjects very high precision eye tracking (error $< 0.4°$) has become possible.

In the next section we first describe the PSOM-network in the context of the present application (for a more general description, see e.g. [4, 5]). In Sec.3 we describe a method to speed up the basic approach, Sec.4 concludes with results from experimental measurements and a discussion.

2 How to Construct a PSOM

The basic computational task to be solved by the network is to transform the output data (a two-dimensional vector specifying the gaze direction of the subject) in such a way that the systematic measurement errors become compensated. Since the errors vary with gaze direction, the required mapping f must be nonlinear, and it must be rapidly constructable for a new subject.

For the representation of nonlinear mappings, in particular to two-dimensional spaces, the Kohonen *self-organizing map* (SOM) has during recent years turned out to be a very favorable method [2]. However, the basic approach is restricted to a discrete lattice, and, while showing very favorable convergence properties in many situations, would still require more training examples than would be convenient for the present purpose.

Exactly these two aspects, continuity and the fact that only a very small number of training examples are required, are among the favorable properties of PSOMs. In a PSOM, the "localist" representation of the SOM is built from a set of *basis* or *prototype manifolds*. The contribution of each basis manifold to the map is controlled by a weight vector that can be viewed as a member of a very coarse SOM with only very few nodes. As a result, smooth mappings can be constructed from very few data samples.

However, as a price to pay, the usual "bestmatch-step" of the SOM has to be replaced by an iterative scheme for the continuous manifold (see eq. (6) below). In neural terms, this iterative scheme can be interpreted as a recurrent dynamics that assigns a point on the manifold to each input vector as the associated output. Therefore, a PSOM can be viewed as a recurrent network which realizes a continuous attractor manifold that represents the graph of the desired non-linear mapping (for additional details, see [4, 5]).

In the present context, this mapping **f** shall be constructed on the basis of a set of 4×4 input-output pairs $\mathbf{w_r} \in I\!\!R^4$. Each reference vector is associated with a fixation point $\mathbf{r} \in \mathbf{A}$, where $\mathbf{A} = \{\mathbf{r}_{ij} \mid \mathbf{r}_{ij} = i\hat{\mathbf{e}}_x + j\hat{\mathbf{e}}_y; \ i,j = 0\dots3\}$ is a two-dimensional 4×4 grid of 16 fixation points shown to the subject during the calibration phase. The 4×4 set of reference vectors $\mathbf{w_r}$ could be regarded as a (very coarse) SOM which would represent the desired transformation, however, at a very low resolution that would be unacceptable for the present purpose. The PSOM now extends this SOM by providing a smooth, parametrized manifold that passes through the points $\mathbf{w_r}$ of the coarse SOM.

The PSOM represents the desired interpolating function $\mathbf{f(s)}$ that is a superposition of a suitable number of simpler basis functions $H(.,.)$ in the following way:

$$\mathbf{f(s)} = \sum_{\mathbf{r} \in \mathbf{A}} H(\mathbf{s}, \mathbf{r})\mathbf{w_r} \quad , \tag{1}$$

Here the basis functions $H\colon I\!\!R^2 \times \mathbf{A} \to I\!\!R$, have to comply with the requirement

$$H(\mathbf{s}, \mathbf{r}) = \delta_{\mathbf{s}, \mathbf{r}} \quad \forall \ \mathbf{s}, \mathbf{r} \in \mathbf{A} \quad , \tag{2}$$

where δ represents the Kronecker symbol. This ensures that $\mathbf{f(s)} = \mathbf{w_s} \ \forall \ \mathbf{s} \in \mathbf{A}$, i.e., the constructed function passes through the given points. The final question that remains is

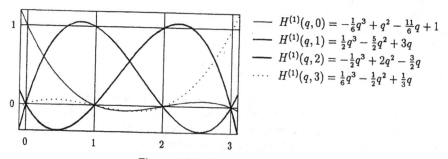

$$H^{(1)}(q,0) = -\tfrac{1}{6}q^3 + q^2 - \tfrac{11}{6}q + 1$$
$$H^{(1)}(q,1) = \tfrac{1}{2}q^3 - \tfrac{5}{2}q^2 + 3q$$
$$H^{(1)}(q,2) = -\tfrac{1}{2}q^3 + 2q^2 - \tfrac{3}{2}q$$
$$H^{(1)}(q,3) = \tfrac{1}{6}q^3 - \tfrac{1}{2}q^2 + \tfrac{1}{3}q$$

Figure 2: The four basis functions

how can we choose suitable functions H, that obey (2) and that are smooth and simple to handle? One convenient choice is first to make a product ansatz

$$H(s_x\hat{\mathbf{e}}_x + s_y\hat{\mathbf{e}}_y, \ \mathbf{r}_{ij}) = H^{(1)}(s_x, i) \cdot H^{(1)}(s_y, j) \tag{3}$$

The new, simpler function $H^{(1)}: \mathbb{R} \times \{0,1,2,3\} \to \mathbb{R}$ must then have the property

$$H^{(1)}(q,n) = \delta_{q,n} \quad \forall \quad q \in \mathbb{R}, \; n \in \{0,1,2,3\} \tag{4}$$

to constitute a valid function H. Due to the discrete parameter n it is possible to use a set of 4 basis functions $\mathbb{R} \to \mathbb{R}$, and a convenient choice are cubic polynomials (see figure 2). (We also tried trigonometric functions, however the cubic polynomials gave slightly better results.)

Now we have built a function f, but it is not what we finally desire. f is a projection from the "correct" orthogonal lattice to an "error lattice" distorted by the system's inaccuracy. Our intention is, however, to deduct the correct coordinates from the distorted ones! Therefore, we must calculate the inverse function f^{-1}, and the non-linearity of f forces us to apply a numerical procedure. To invert $f(s)$, we minimize the error function $E(s)$, given by the equation

$$E(\mathbf{s}) = \frac{1}{2}(\mathbf{f}(\mathbf{s}) - \mathbf{f}_{et})^2 \quad , \tag{5}$$

where $\mathbf{f}_{et}$ is the output vector of the eye tracker with respect to $\mathbf{s}$. Starting with an estimate value $\mathbf{s}_0 = \mathbf{s}(t = 0)$, we use a gradient descent in the variables $\mathbf{s}$:

$$\mathbf{s}(t+1) = \mathbf{s}(t) - \epsilon \cdot \frac{\partial E(\mathbf{s})}{\partial \mathbf{s}} \tag{6}$$

with the positive step size parameter ϵ. Equation (6) has to be iterated until $E(\mathbf{s}(t))$ falls below a prespecified threshold value, which we should set according to the screen solution. In neural terms, the iteration of (6) can be viewed as a recurrent network dynamics driving the "state vectors" towards an optimum value that is constrained to lie on the (here) two-dimensional PSOM-manifold embedded in the four-dimensional "feature

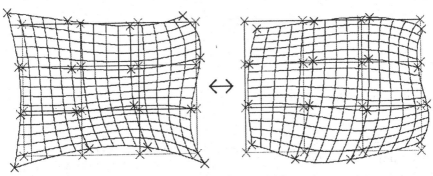

Figure 3: Left: PSOM-Interpolation $f(s)$ for eye tracker errors, constructed from 16 measurements at the positions of the underlying 4×4 "calibration grid". Right: Inverse mapping $f^{-1}(s)$ that, when applied to the eye tracker output, will compensate the errors. This mapping is constructed via equation (6).

space" of input-output pairs. The resulting final value $\mathbf{s}(t)$ represents the output vector $\mathbf{s}_{out}$ of the PSOM. As a result of the polynomial structure of $\mathbf{f}$, the implementation of this iteration is not problematic at all. Figure 3 demonstrates the very natural and topology-conserving interpolation capabilities of our just completed PSOM by illustrating the distortion effects of $\mathbf{f}$ and its inverse $\mathbf{f}^{-1}$ for a typical situation.

3 Speeding up the Neural Net

The calculation speed of the PSOM mainly depends on the efficiency of its iteration procedure. For that reason, the parameters s_0 and ϵ need a careful investigation. A good choice for s_0 seems to be the input vector f_{et}, because it will be in the range of the result s_{out}, unless we use a strange distortion like mirroring the whole vector plane. The average amount of iterations needed by this straight forward method is shown in figure 4, yielding best results at $\epsilon \approx 0.79$. At this point it must be explained that all measured values in this section vary slightly with the underlying function f and the test person's eye movement characteristics. But the differences do not exceed a few percent and have no qualitative effects.

How can we increase the PSOM's calculation speed further? The following idea is based on the fact that we are interested in correcting many coordinates in succession, and not in dealing with single data. Successive fixations are very likely to be located in the same area of the screen. Therefore, the *local deviation* $f_{et} - s_{out}$ does not vary essentially between successive PSOM computations. For the first calculation we set $s_0 := f_{et}$ as we did before. But this time we store the vectors f_{et} and s_{out} as $f_{et,stored}$ and $s_{out,stored}$ to get

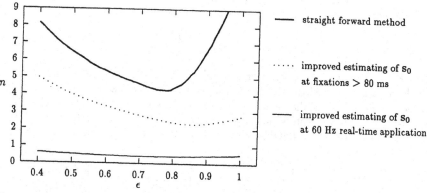

Figure 4: The average number n of performed iterations as a function of the step size parameter ϵ

a better estimate value s_0 for the next iteration:

$$s_0 = s_{out,stored} + f_{et} - f_{et,stored} \tag{7}$$

The improvement of efficiency by using this estimating method is shown in figure 4. Its effect increases with the data frequency, because the shift between successive input vectors becomes smaller on the average. At 60 Hz use, the number n of iteration steps per computation remains under the value 1, because in most cases the estimate s_0 already constitutes a valid output s_{out}! Here we achieve an improvement factor of approximately 10, since the efficiency of the standard method remains invariable at different frequencies.

4 Results and Discussion

We implemented the PSOM on a PC with a 486DX2-66 processor, using a screen solution of 640×480 pixels. The tolerance of f^{-1} was set to 0.5 pixels to get optimum accuracy. Table 1 shows the average delay caused by a single calculation of the neural net in various applications.

In our experiments the eye tracker system already used a built in conventional algorithm (see [6]), based on a calibration procedure involving 9 lattice points. Our goal was to improve the outputs of this system further by doing a suitable post-processing of the data with the PSOM. For this purpose an additional calibration matrix was presented to get information for the subsequent data processing. After the experiments the neural net was used to correct a list of all fixations that took longer than 80 ms, received as the eye tracking result. But how is it possible to compare the accuracy of the original coordinates and the corrected ones?

For that purpose the test person was shown a further 6×6-lattice, which was entirely different from the calibration lattice. Then we took the standard deviations σ_{orig} and

	single data	fixations > 80 ms	60 Hz use
straight forward method	1480 μs	1480 μs	1480 μs
improved method	1480 μs	725 μs	143 μs

Table 1: Average delay

	σ_{orig}	α_{orig}	σ_{PSOM}	α_{PSOM}	remaining error
spectacles	65.5 pixels	2.92°	19.3 pixels	0.82°	28.1%
no spectacles	25.4 pixels	1.13°	8.9 pixels	0.39°	34.5%

Table 2: Effects on the cartesian standard deviation σ and its corresponding visual angle α

σ_{PSOM} of the original output coordinates and the PSOM-corrected output respectively. One group of test persons had to be investigated separately, namely the people wearing spectacles. Table 2 demonstrates the average improving effect of our neural net for each of these groups.

The whole calibration procedure takes less than 20 seconds, so it is an acceptable effort considering the significant increase of data accuracy. The new method allows us also to carry out investigations on subjects wearing spectacles. For normal sighted subjects, the very high precision eye tracking that has now become possible allows us to envisage a range of new experiments and ways to evaluate data from the existing experiments that would not have been meaningful before.

Indeed, this is not the first approach of this kind. Baluja and Pomerleau [7] have recently reported on an eye tracker system in which the entire processing, i.e. including the evaluation of the camera images, was achieved by a neural network. However, training of this network required on the order of several thousand training examples, and the final accuracy of the system is about 1.5°, which compares well to the accuracy of Stampe's system. While the work by Baluja and Pomerleau is a very impressive demonstration of what can be achieved on the basis of neural networks alone, it is difficult to compare with the present study, since the authors solve a much more general estimation problem. The motivation of the present study was somewhat different, namely to improve the accuracy of an existing system, and to achieve this on the basis of a number of training examples that is sufficiently small to be compatible with the daily use of the system in laboratory experiments.

In the future, we intend to integrate the neural component in the eye tracker software, so that real time use becomes possible. On a broader perspective, we view the present work as one demonstration of the many potential uses of neural networks to contribute to the creation of better and more powerful, multi-modal man-machine interfaces that can adapt to their user in real time. This is a challenging area of research, in which the vigorously developing fields of virtual reality, robotics, neural networks and vision research can converge in a potentially very fruitful manner for shaping the computers of tomorrow to the needs of humans and not vice versa, as it is still very much the case today.

Acknowledgements: We would like to thank Dave Stampe and Eyal Reingold for providing the eye tracker system, Thomas Clermont for his help with the eye tracker hardware, and Peter Munsche for carrying out the experiments for collecting the test data. This work was supported by a grant of the German Science Foundation (SFB 360).

References

[1] Kohonen, T. (1984), *Self-Organization and Associative Memory*, Springer Series in Information Sciences 8, Springer, Heidelberg.

[2] Kohonen, T. (1990), *The Self-Organizing Map*, in *Proc. IEEE* 78, pp. 1464–1480.

[3] Ritter, H., Martinetz, T., Schulten, K. (1992), *Neural Computation and Self-Organizing Maps*, Addison-Wesley, Reading, MA.

[4] Ritter, H. (1993), Parametrized Self-Organizing Maps. *ICANN93-Proceedings* (S. Gielen and B. Kappen eds.), pp. 568–577, Springer Verlag, Berlin.

[5] Ritter, H. (1994), Parametrized Self-Organizing Maps for Vision Learning Tasks. *ICANN94-Proceedings*, Springer Verlag (to appear).

[6] Stampe, D. (1993), Heuristic filtering and reliable calibration methods for video-based pupil-tracking systems. *Behaviour Research Methods, Instruments, & Computers 1993*, 25 (2), pp. 137–142.

[7] Baluja, S., Pomerleau, D. (1994), Non-Intrusive Gaze Tracking using Artificial Neural Networks. *Neural Information Processing Systems 6*, Morgan Kaufmann Publishers.

A Kripke-Kleene Logic
over General Logic Programs

Vladimir Kuznetsov*

Moscow Power Institute, P.O. Box 46, Moscow 129164, Russia

e-mail: appmat@univax.free.net

Abstract

We propose a logic for partial reasoning over all general logic programs in a certain first-order language L. We need such a logic to express statements like *it is impossible that a ground atom is both true and false in any program*. To construct this logic we start with Kleene's three-valued logic. Then we extend L to a metalanguage L^* by including a new system of connectives. Basing upon Kripke's approach we introduce the notion of truth for formulas of L^*. Comparison with classical logic and intuitionistic one is given. We prove that every intuitionistic theorem is true in our logic. We also show how classical tautologies are mapped onto true formulas.

Keywords: Logic Programming, Kleene's Logic, Kripke Semantics.

1 Introduction

Since 1985 when Fitting proposed a 3-valued semantics for general logic programs [4] several other approaches of that kind have been presented [9, 10, 15]. Although being different in details all these approaches either explicitly or implicitly use Kleene's three-valued logic (see, for example, [4]). It leads to the notion of a *partial model* instead of a total (or 2-valued classical) model and so formulas of the first-order language associated with a general logic program may be true, false or undefined.

Attempts have been made to "save" 2-valued classical logic [1, 3, 12] — the most powerful example of that sort gives the stable model semantics [5]. A stable model is defined as one that is able to reproduce itself in a certain sense; a program may have zero, one, or many stable models. The stable model semantics extends the perfect model semantics [12] from the class of locally stratified logic programs to a much broader class of programs. However, the stable model semantics does not always exist. For example, the one-rule program $R(a) \leftarrow \sim R(a)$ has no stable model (here $\sim$ stands for negation).

*Research supported by Russian Fund for Fundamental Research Grant 93-012-590.

Since 2-valued semantics does not always exist we believe that the 3-valued approach is unavoidable if we aim to have a suitable semantics *for all* logic programs. But if we accept a 3-valued semantics for general logic programs and partial reasoning as a result, then we have to reconsider the logic foundations we use.

In fact, the situation is the following. Given a general logic program P and a 3-valued semantics for P we can assign truth values to ground literals. Then by means of conventional saturation procedure [4] we extend this evaluation to formulas of the first-order language L_P associated with P. The problem is how to define "logic laws", i.e. formulas that are true in every general logic program?

As the excluded middle law formula

$$R(a) \vee \sim R(a)$$

shows the 2-valued logic is no more acceptable — this formula is true in every 2-valued model, but it is not the case under 3-valued consideration. To show it consider again the one-rule program $R(a) \leftarrow \sim R(a)$. Given the well-founded semantics for this program we conclude that both $R(a)$ and $\sim R(a)$ are undefined. Hence the excluded middle law formula is undefined in this program.

On the other hand, the statement *it is impossible that a ground atom is both true and false in any program*[1] gives an example of "logic law" over all general logic programs. Another example of that sort gives the statement *if a ground atom is false in a general logic program it is impossible that it is true in the same program*. Since the 2-valued logic is no more acceptable the question arises what kind of logic we shall use to express the above statements?

In this paper we aim to propose a logic that provides us with true formulas over general logic programs. The paper is organized as follows. In the next Section 2 we introduce the basic notation and terminology. In Section 3 following Fitting [4] we define the notion of *truth in a general logic program* for formulas of the first-order language in Kleene's three-valued logic. In Section 4 we show that the the first-order language (associated with general logic programs) is not sufficient to formulate "logic laws". We extend this language to a certain metalanguage. In Section 5 basing upon Kripke's approach we propose a semantics for formulas of this metalanguage. In Section 6 several examples are considered. In Section 7 our approach is compared with classical logic and intuitionistic one.

2 General Logic Programs

We use a first-order language L in which we have the propositional connectives $\wedge$ (conjunction) and $\sim$ (negation) as primitive. We also allow universal quantifier $\forall$, taking it as primitive. Other connectives can be introduced via the usual definitions. A formula formed by a predicate symbol with terms as arguments is called an *atomic formula* (or just an *atom*). An atom A is a *positive literal*, its negation $\sim A$ is a *negative literal*.

---

[1]Provided that we use a consistent semantics for general logic programs. Further we will use the well-founded semantics.

We consider *general program clauses* with a single atomic formula in the conclusion of the form

$$A \leftarrow L_1, \ldots, L_n,$$

where A is a positive literal and $L_1, \ldots, L_n$ are (not necessarily positive) literals $(n \geq 0)$. A *general logic program* (or just a *program*) is a finite set of general program clauses.

Given a program P, we denote by $ground(P)$ the set of all ground (i.e. "variable-free") instances of clauses in P. For a given program P, we consider only ground literals whose atoms actually appear in $ground(P)$, *and no others*.

Definition 2.1 Let M be a set of ground literals of L. M is *consistent* if not both A, $\sim A$ are in M for any ground atom A.

In further consideration we will use the well-founded semantics for general logic programs. The following is based upon the definitions of [13, 15].

Definition 2.2 Let P be a general logic program and M be a consistent set of ground literals of L. Let $Pos(M)$ and $Neg(M)$ be the following sets.

(a) $A \in Pos(M)$ iff there is a clause $A \leftarrow L_1, \ldots, L_n$ in $ground(P)$ such that, for all $i \leq n$, $L_i \in M$.

(b) $Neg(M)$ is the largest set of negative literals $\sim A$ with the property that for every clause $A \leftarrow L_1, \ldots, L_n$ in $ground(P)$ there is an $i \leq n$ such that either L_i is false in M or $L_i = B_i$ is an atom and $\sim B_i \in Neg(M)$.

We define the transformation W_P of Van Gelder, Ross and Schlipf [15] as follows.

$$W_P(M) = Pos(M) \cup Neg(M).$$

The smallest fixed point of W_P is called a *well-founded partial model* for P.

Definition 2.3 Given a program P, its well-founded partial model M_P, and a ground atom A we say that:

A is *true* in P iff $A \in M_P$;

A is *false* in P iff $\sim A \in M_P$;

A is *undefined* in P iff $A \notin M_P$ and $\sim A \notin M_P$.

We will use the standard notion of definability [2, 11, 14].

Definition 2.4 We say that a general program P *defines* an n-ary predicate r using an n-ary relation R if, for all ground terms $t_1, \ldots, t_n$,

$$(t_1, \ldots, t_n) \in r \text{ iff } R(t_1, \ldots, t_n) \text{ is true in } P.$$

Definition 2.5 A predicate is called a *GLP predicate* if it can be defined in a general logic program.

Now we introduce the class of programs that have a *well-founded model*.

Definition 2.6 A general logic program is said to be *complete* if its well-founded partial model is two-valued.

Definition 2.7 A predicate is *complete* if it can be defined in a complete program.

3 Kleene's Three-Valued Logic

Although connective $\land$ and quantifier $\forall$ will not be used in actual writing of programs, the following shows that they can be defined implicitly in general logic programs[2].

Definition 3.1 Let R and S be predicates defined in a program P. $R \land S$, the *conjunction* of R and S, is defined using W in the program Q which is obtained by taking the clauses of P and the new clause

$$W(x_1, \ldots, x_n) \leftarrow R(x_1, \ldots, x_n), S(x_1, \ldots, x_n).$$

To justify this definition of conjunction we show that W is true in Q iff R is true in P and S is true in P (in the sense of the well founded semantics). Let M_P and M_Q be the well-founded models for P and Q respectively. Let A (resp. B) be a ground instantiation of R (resp. S) and C be the ground instantiation of W corresponding to $A \land B$. It is immediate by Definition 2.2 that $A \in M_P$ and $B \in M_P$ iff $C \in M_Q$. Moreover, just like 2-valued logic W is false in Q iff R or S is false in P.

Definition 3.2 Let R be a predicate defined in a program P. $\sim R$, the *negation* of R, is defined using W in the program Q which is obtained by taking the clauses of P and the new clause

$$W(x_1, \ldots, x_n) \leftarrow \sim R(x_1, \ldots, x_n).$$

By Definition 2.2 W is true in Q iff R is false in P. Moreover, W is false in Q iff R is true in P.

Definition 3.3 Let R be a predicate defined in a program P. Let $n > 0$. For an $i \le n$, $(\forall x_i) R(x_1, \ldots, x_n)$, the *universal quantification* of R, is defined using W in the program Q which is obtained by taking the clauses of P and the new clauses

$$W(x_1, \ldots, x_{i-1}, x_{i+1}, \ldots, x_n) \leftarrow \sim H(x_1, \ldots, x_{i-1}, x_{i+1}, \ldots, x_n),$$
$$H(x_1, \ldots, x_{i-1}, x_{i+1}, \ldots, x_n) \leftarrow \sim R(x_1, \ldots, x_n).$$

---

[2]In fact, all the machinery from [14] is directly available for conjunction, disjunction and existential quantification. What remains is to show how to define negation and universal quantification.

By Definition 2.2 W is true in Q iff, for all x_i, R is true in P. Moreover, W is false in Q iff there is an x_i such that R is false in P.

Now notice that the above definitions of negation, conjunction and universal quantifier lead to Kleene's 3-valued logic [6]. The idea behind Kleene's logic is explained by Fitting [4] as follows. Given a logic program P let A and B be ground atoms. Since these atoms may be true, false or undefined in P we have to use a logic with truth values **t** (true), **f** (false), and **u** (undefined) to mirror the situation. Now consider how to assign truth values to $A \wedge B$. Certainly in cases not involving **u** truth values behave classically. Now say A has value **f** but B is **u**. Still B "has" a truth value; because of incompleteness of program P we just don't know what it is. Since A is **f**, $A \wedge B$ will be **f** no matter whether B turns out to be **t** or **f**. Consequently $A \wedge B$ is given value **f** in this case. On the other hand, say A has value **t** but B is **u**. If we eventually discover that B is **t**, $A \wedge B$ will turn out to have value **t**. But if we discover B is **f**, $A \wedge B$ will be **f**. Given no further information then, we must say the value of $A \wedge B$ is **u**.

Then a table for connective $\wedge$ is as follows:

$\wedge$	t	f	u
t	t	f	u
f	f	f	f
u	u	f	u

It is easy to see that this table corresponds to Definition 3.1. In the same manner we can show that a table for negation

	$\sim$
t	f
f	t
u	u

corresponds to Definition 3.2. Considering the universal quantifier $\forall$ as a conjunction (maybe infinite) we conclude that, in accordance with Definition 3.3, for every formula $A(x)$:

(a) $(\forall x)A(x)$ is **t** iff, for all x, $A(x)$ is **t**;

(b) $(\forall x)A(x)$ is **f** iff there is x such that $A(x)$ is **f**;

(c) $(\forall x)A(x)$ is **u** iff it is neither **t** nor **f**.

To assign truth values to formulas of L we can use saturated sets or valuations in the Kleene 3-valued sense (see for details [4]). But we prefer an approach based upon the notion of definability.

Proposition 3.1 *The class of GLP predicates is closed under conjunction, disjunction, negation, and quantification (existensial and universal).*

PROOF. Immediate from Definitions 3.1, 3.2, and 3.3. □

Definition 3.4 Let $R_1, R_2, \ldots, R_n$ be predicates defined in a program P. Let F be a formula composed of these predicates by using connectives $\wedge$, $\sim$ and universal quantifier $\forall$. Due to Proposition 3.1 formula F can be defined in a general logic program Q via a certain predicate W_F, provided that, for all $i \leq n$, R_i is true in Q iff R_i is true in P (i.e. in Q we use the same definition of R_i). We will say that F is *true in P* iff W_F is true in Q.

Example 3.1 Let R be a binary predicate defined in a program P. Let F be the formula

$$\sim(\sim R(x, y) \wedge \sim R(y, x)).$$

Then F can be defined using W_F in the program Q which is obtained by taking the clauses of P and the new clauses

$$
\begin{aligned}
W_1(x, y) &\leftarrow \sim R(x, y) \\
W_2(x, y) &\leftarrow \sim R(y, x) \\
W_3(x, y) &\leftarrow W_1(x, y), W_2(x, y) \\
W_F(x, y) &\leftarrow \sim W_3(x, y)
\end{aligned}
$$

4 Metalanguage

Definition 3.4 introduces the notion of *truth in a given program*. Now we aim to extend it to the *truth* over all programs. In other words, we would like to have formulas that are true in all general logic programs, and so do not depend on the definitions of predicates they are composed of. However, on the contrary to the classical logic it is not clear now, in the 3-valued logic, how to make this extension. To understand the problem better let us "return" for a while to classical 2-valued logic and restrict our consideration to the class of complete programs. How to introduce true formulas then? First notice that the following 2-valued counterpart of Proposition 3.1 holds [10].

Proposition 4.1 *The class of complete predicates is closed under conjunction, disjunction, negation, and quantification (existensial and universal).*

PROOF. The details of verifying completeness are straightforward, and omitted here. □

¿From Proposition 4.1 immediately follows that complete predicates correspond to classical two-valued logic. Thus true formulas of classical predicate calculus represent "logic laws" over complete general logic programs. Any such formula will be true in every complete program. For example, formula $R(a) \vee \sim R(a)$ is true regardless of definition of predicate R (provided that this definition is complete). So, it turns out that the language L is sufficient to formulate "logic laws" over complete programs.

The situation is quite different in the class of GLP predicates. The following shows that *truth* over general logic programs cannot be formulated in the language L.

Proposition 4.2 *Let F be a formula of L. There is a general logic program P in which F is undefined.*

PROOF. Straightforward, and omitted here. □

To solve the problem we extend L to a metalanguage L^* as follows.

Definition 4.1 (a) If A is a formula of L then it is a formula of L^*.

(b) If A, B are formulas of L^*, then $(\neg A)$, $(A \wedge B)$, $(A \vee B)$, $(A \to B)$, $(\forall A)$, and $(\exists A)$ are formulas of L^*.

Notice that in the language L^* we have, in fact, the two systems of connectives. The first one is composed of connectives $\sim$, $\wedge$, and $\forall$ of the language L. The second one — of connectives $\neg$, $\wedge$, $\vee$, $\to$, $\forall$, and $\exists$ of L^* introduced in Definition 4.1. The first system of connectives can be applied to any formula of L, the second one — to any formula of L^*.

Also notice that although the connectives $\wedge$ and $\forall$ belong to both systems their meaning depends on context — either they are applied to formulas of L or to ones of L^*. In general, it would cause the collision between the two meanings when these connectives are applied to formulas of L because by Definition 4.1(a) formulas of L are at the same time formulas of L^*. However, we will show below in Section 5 that the two meanings coincide for formulas of L.

As for negation, we have in L^* *two* sorts of negation: $\sim$ and $\neg$. The first one can be applied *only* to formulas of L, the second one — to any formula of L^*.

Example 4.1 If A, B are formulas of L^*, then

$$\neg(A \vee B)$$

is a formula of L^*. On the other hand,

$$\sim(A \vee B)$$

is not a formula of L^* because $A \vee B$ is not a formula of L (although $A \vee B$ is a formula of L^*).

5 Kripke Semantics

The set of all general logic programs associated with L will be denoted by U. In terms of Kripke's approach [7, 8] a subset of U is said to be a *possible world* and the power set $\mathcal{P}(U)$ is a *universum* of possible worlds. Given possible worlds X, Y we say that the world Y is *accessible* from the world X iff $Y \subseteq X$. True formulas of L^* are defined inductively in three steps. First we define the relation "a possible world X *forces* a formula A of L" denoted by $X \Vdash A$. Roughly, this relation means that a formula A is true or is a "logic law" *in the whole* possible world X. Then we extend forcing relation to formulas of L^* by assigning the possible world semantics to connectives $\neg$, $\wedge$, $\vee$, $\to$, $\forall$, and $\exists$ (negation $\sim$ not included). And finally we define *truth* — a formula of L^* is true if it is forced in the world of all logic programs. What follows is a straightforward adaptation of Kripke's approach [7, 8] to the problem under consideration.

Definition 5.1 Let $X, Y \subseteq U$.

(1) Let A be a formula of L. $X \Vdash A$ iff A is true in every program $P \in X$.

(2) Let A, B be formulas of L^*.

    (a) $X \Vdash A \wedge B$ iff $X \Vdash A$ and $X \Vdash B$.
    (b) $X \Vdash A \vee B$ iff $X \Vdash A$ or $X \Vdash B$.
    (c) $X \Vdash A \rightarrow B$ iff, for all $Y \subseteq X$, if $Y \Vdash A$ then $Y \Vdash B$.
    (d) $X \Vdash \neg A$ iff $Y \not\Vdash A$ for every nonempty $Y \subseteq X$.
    (e) $X \Vdash (\forall x)A(x)$ iff, for all x, $X \Vdash A(x)$.
    (f) $X \Vdash (\exists x)A(x)$ iff   there is an x such that $X \Vdash A(x)$.

(3) A formula of L^* is said to be *true* iff $U \Vdash A$.

Notice that we use connective $\wedge$ and quantifier $\forall$ in both L and L^*. For example, if A, B are formulas of L then the connective $\wedge$ in $A \wedge B$ can be considered either as an element of L or as an element of 'L^*'. It turns out, however, that the meaning of $X \Vdash A \wedge B$ does not depend on the choice. In the first case $X \Vdash A \wedge B$ means that $A \wedge B$ is true in P for every $P \in X$. In the second — that $X \Vdash A$ and $X \Vdash B$. Since A, B are formulas of L by Definition 5.1(1) both meanings coincide. It is straightforward to show that the same holds for quantifier $\forall$ — if $A(x)$ is a formula of L then both meanings of $X \Vdash (\forall x)A(x)$ coincide.

6   Examples

We give several examples to illustrate the machinery introduced above. The following example shows the difference between negations $\sim$ and $\neg$.

Example 6.1 Let A be a ground atom and X_A be the set of all general logic programs P such that A is true in P. Then by Definition 5.1(1) $X_A \Vdash A$. Since A is true in the one-rule program

$$A \leftarrow$$

the set X_A in not empty. Now let $X_{\sim A}$ be the set of all programs P such that $\sim A$ is true in P. Then by Definition 5.1(1) $X_{\sim A} \Vdash \sim A$. Since in the one-rule program

$$A \leftarrow \sim A$$

atom A is undefined

$$X_A \cup X_{\sim A} \neq U.$$

On the other hand, let $X_{\neg A}$ be the set of all general logic programs P such that A is not true in P. Then by Definition 5.1(2d) $X_{\neg A} \Vdash \neg A$. Since in every program each ground atom is either true or not[3],

$$X_A \cup X_{\neg A} = U.$$

---

[3] A ground atom is not true if it is false or undefined.

Thus

$$X_{\sim A} \subset X_{\neg A}.$$

Now we show the existence of true formulas.

Example 6.2 Let A be a formula of L^*. It is obvious that, for all $X \subseteq U$, if $X \Vdash A$ then $X \Vdash A$. Thus by Definition 5.1(2c)

$$U \Vdash A \rightarrow A$$

and so by Definition 5.1(3) the formula

$$A \rightarrow A$$

is true.

The following gives an example of true formula containing both kinds of negation: $\sim$ and $\neg$.

Example 6.3 Let A be a formula of L. Since the formula of L

$$A \wedge \sim A$$

is not true in any program the formula

$$\neg(A \wedge \sim A)$$

is true by Definition 5.1(2d).

This formula states that "contradiction in the sence of negation $\sim$" is impossible in general logic programs.

And here is another example of "logic law" over all general logic programs.

Example 6.4 Let A be a formula of L. Then, for all $X \subseteq U$, if $X \Vdash \sim A$ then $X \Vdash \neg A$. Thus by Definition 5.1(2c)

$$U \Vdash \sim A \rightarrow \neg A$$

and so by Definition 5.1(3) the formula

$$\sim A \rightarrow \neg A$$

is true.

This formula states that "if a fact is false in a general logic program the fact cannot be true". Notice that the converse of this formula does not hold — the formula

$$\neg A \rightarrow \sim A$$

is not true in our logic because if a fact is not true in a program it is not necessarily false.

Here is a more complex example of true formula using double negation $\neg\neg$.

Example 6.5 Let A be a ground atom. Notice that the expression $X_A \cup X_{\neg A} = U$ from Example 6.1 is reminiscent of the excluded middle law. However, we have to be care — the formula

$$A \vee \neg A$$

is not true. It is the double negation that saves the situation — we show that the formula

$$\neg\neg(A \vee \neg A)$$

is true[4]. By Definition 5.1(2b)

$$X_A \Vdash A \vee \neg A$$

and

$$X_{\neg A} \Vdash A \vee \neg A.$$

Now let $X \subseteq U$ and $X \neq \emptyset$. Since $X_A \cup X_{\neg A} = U$ there is a nonempty subset $Y \subseteq X$ such that

$$Y \Vdash A \vee \neg A.$$

Then by Definition 5.1(2d)

$$X \nVdash \neg(A \vee \neg A).$$

Since it holds for all $X \subseteq U$ by Definition 5.1(2d)

$$U \Vdash \neg\neg(A \vee \neg A)$$

and so $\neg\neg(A \vee \neg A)$ is true formula. This formula express the idea that each ground atom in every program have **to be or not to be** true.

7 Comparison with other Logics

The above examples show that our logic has a flavour of intuitionism. And the following explains why it is so.

Definition 7.1 If a formula of L^* does not contain the symbol $\sim$ it is called an *intuitionistic formula*.

Proposition 7.1 *An intuitionistic formula of L^* is true iff it is a theorem[5] of intuitionistic calculus.*

PROOF. Since our accessibility relation $\subseteq$ is reflexive and transitive it is immediate from the results of [7, 8]. □

Roughly, we can say that our logic is an extension of intuitionistic one by including formulas of L in addition to intuitionistic ones. Moreover, Proposition 7.1 can be improved as follows.

---

[4] In Section 7 we will show that this formula is true for every formula A of I^*

[5] A formula is a theorem of a calculus if it can be derived in it.

Proposition 7.2 *Given an intuitionistic theorem, any result of replacing of all predicate letters by formulas of L^* is true (in our sense).*

PROOF. The above replacing can be done in two steps. First replace predicate letters by intuitionistic formulas — it leads to an intuitionistic formula and so the new formula is true by Proposition 7.1. Then replace predicate letters by formulas of L. By Proposition 3.1 it is equivalent to replacing by corresponding predicate letters which leads to an intuitionistic formula as well and so we obtain a true formula. □

The following shows a close relationship between our logic and classical one.

Proposition 7.3 *Let A be a formula of L. The formula $\neg A$ is true iff $\sim A$ is a tautology.*

PROOF. Let A be a formula of L. $\neg A$ is true iff $U \Vdash \neg A$ iff, for all nonempty $X \subseteq U$, $X \nvdash A$ iff A is not true in any program iff A is a contradiction iff $\sim A$ is a tautology. □

Corollary 7.4 *Let A be a formula of L. A is a tautology iff $\neg \sim A$ is true.*

PROOF. Immediate from Proposition 7.3. □

Roughly, it means that our logic contains each tautology prefixed by double negation $\neg\sim$.

8 Conclusions

We have shown that although the first-order language L (associated with general logic programs) can be used to define *truth in a program* it is not sufficient to formulate "global" truth over all programs. To make it possible we have extended this language to a certain metalanguage L^*. Basing upon Kripke's possible world semantics we have defined *truth* for formulas of this extension.

We have shown that our logic can be considered as an extension of intuitionistic one by including formulas of Kleene's three-valued logic. In other words, our logic is an application of intuitionistic one to reasoning about formulas of Kleene's one. So, given an intuitionistic theorem, if we replace all predicate letters by formulas of L we obtain a true formula of L^*.

Another class of true formulas is given by formulas of the form $\neg A$, where A is a classical contradiction (i.e. $\sim A$ is a tautology). These formulas state *impossibility of contradiction in any program.*

References

[1] Apt, K.R., Blair, H., and Walker, A. Towards a theory of declarative knowledge. In J.Minker, ed. *Foundations of Deductive Databases and Logic Programming.* Morgan-Kaufmann, Sun Mateo, Calif., 1988, pp. 89–148.

[2] Apt, K.R., Logic Programming. In: J. van Leeuwen, ed. *Handbook of Theoretical Computer Science*, Elsevier Science Publishers B.V., 1990, pp. 495–574.

[3] Clark, K.L. Negation as Failure. In: H.Gallaire and J.Minker (eds.), *Logic and Databases*, Plenum, New York, 1978, pp. 293-322.

[4] Fitting, M. A Kripke-Kleene Semantics for Logic Programs, *J. Logic Prog.*, 2:295-312 (1985).

[5] Gelfond, M., and Lifschitz, V. The stable model semantics for logic programming. In *Proceedings of the 5th International Conference and Symposium on Logic Programming* (Seattle, Wash.). IEEE, New York, 1988, pp.1070-1080.

[6] Kleene, S.C., *Introduction to Metamathematics*, Van Nostrand, New York, 1952.

[7] Kripke, S.A. Semantical Analysis of Intuitionistic Logic I, In *Formal Systems and Recursive Functions*, Amsterdam, 1965, pp.92-129.

[8] Kripke, S.A. Semantical Consideration on Model Logic. In L.Linsky, ed. *Reference and Modality*, Oxford University Press, London, pp.63-72, 1971.

[9] Kunen, K. Negation in Logic Programming, *J. Logic Prog.*, 4:289-308 (1987).

[10] Kuznetsov, V. Negation as Exception. In B.Neumann, ed. *Proceedings of the 10th European Conference on Artificial Intelligence* (Vienna). John Wiley and Sons, 1992, pp.107-108.

[11] Martin-Löf, P. Notes on Constructive Mathematics. Almqvist & Wiksell, Stockholm, 1970.

[12] Przymusinski, T.C. On the declarative semantics of deductive databases and logic programs. In J.Minker, ed. *Foundations of Deductive Databases and Logic Programming*. Morgan-Kaufmann, Sun Mateo, Calif., 1988, pp. 193-216.

[13] Przymusinski, T.C. The Well-Founded Semantics Coincides with the Three-Valued Stable Model Semantics, *Fundamenta Informaticae*, 13:445-464 (1990).

[14] Smullyan, R.M. *Theory of Formal Systems*, revised edition, Princeton U.P., Princeton, 1961.

[15] Van Gelder, A., Ross, K.A., and Schlipf J.S. The Well-Founded Semantics for General Logic Programs, *J. ACM*, 38:620-650 (1991).

The Stable Semantics and its Variants: A Comparison of Recent Approaches

Jürgen Dix[1] and Martin Müller[2]

[1] University of Koblenz, Dept. of Computer Science, Rheinau 1,
D-56075 Koblenz, Germany dix@informatik.uni-koblenz.de
[2] Graduiertenkolleg Kognition and German Research Center for AI (DFKI),
Stuhlsatzenhausweg 3, D-66123 Saarbrücken mmueller@dfki.uni-sb.de

Abstract. The stable and the well-founded semantics are among the leading semantics for logic programs. While stable models do not always exist (and therefore no meaningful inferences can be drawn), the (three-valued) well-founded model is always defined. A weakness of WFS on the other hand is its inability to allow for *reasoning-by-cases*.

We claim that - besides the inconsistency problem - the reason of the anomalous behavior of STABLE is the failure of *Relevance* – a principle introduced in previous work of the first author.

We define, discuss and compare various extensions of STABLE and WFS under both aspects. In particular, we determine the relationship with the approach recently introduced by J. Schlipf. We use our own approach to show that Schlipf's semantics WFS_C coincides with Dix' WFS^+.

1 Introduction and Motivation

The well-founded semantics and the stable semantics are undoubtedly the most influential semantics for normal logic programs. One may almost speak about two schools of how to give meaning to programs with negation, observing the frequent and vehement discussions between followers of both semantics, be it users or developers. Our impression is that both sides often miss to clarify their general intent in using a particular semantics, which is the reason for a number of misunderstandings.

A semantics like the stable model semantics STABLE [GL88], associating a set of classical models with a given program, may serve three purposes: It may

1. answer the question of what is necessarily true (true in *all* models), or
2. answer the question of what is possibly true (true in *at least one* model), or
3. offer every model as *one complete scenario* satisfying the constraints imposed by the program.

The first two are usually called the *sceptical* and *credulous* view of a semantics. The third may be called *nondeterministic* as by Torres [Tor93], who makes the same distinction. We prefer to talk, more intuitively, about *scenario* semantics.

The well-founded semantics WFS [vGRS91] associates a single three-valued model with any normal program. Therefore WFS is inherently sceptical and all three views sketched above coincide. This means that a formal comparison between STABLE and WFS can only be performed using the sceptical semantics induced by STABLE. The program begun by Dix [Dix91, Dix92] follows this path.

That STABLE *may* be used as a scenario semantics is often pointed out as a major advantage of STABLE over WFS (see e.g. [Tor93]), and illustrated by the following example:

Example 1 Cafeteria-Lounge Scenario.
Imagine a network of hotels buildings $a, b, c, \ldots$, defined by a set of facts of the form *adjacent(a,b)*. The problem is how to supply every building with either a cafeteria or a lounge, but not both, such that: *i)* every building without a cafeteria is adjacent to a building with one, and *ii)* no two adjacent buildings have a cafeteria. This may be captured by the following program, supplemented by the definition of adjacency:

$$P_{lounge}: \quad lounge(X) \leftarrow adjacent(X, Y), cafeteria(Y)$$
$$cafeteria(X) \leftarrow \neg lounge(X)$$

The stable models of this program are exactly the solutions of the problem, namely the possible scenarios under the given constraints.

WFS essentially returns the adjacency facts. This weakness, together with the inability to express case-based reasoning, is the major objection against the well-founded semantics:

Example 2 Case-Splitting.
$$P_{splitting}: a \leftarrow \neg b$$
$$b \leftarrow \neg a$$
$$p \leftarrow a$$
$$p \leftarrow b$$

Although neither a nor b can be "derived" in a semantics based on two-valued models the disjunction $a \vee b$, hence also p, is true. STABLE as well as completion semantics handle this program accordingly. WFS, however, leaves p undefined.

On the other hand WFS is defined on *all* normal programs, while STABLE may turn out to be inconsistent: in Example 1, we just have to add the trivial negative loop $p \leftarrow \neg p$ to P_{lounge}.

STABLE suffers from the *brute force* inconsistency handling known from first order logic: Just a *small inconsistency* in a possibly large set of axioms makes *everything* classically derivable from them, which is as good as nothing. This makes pure first order logic essentially unusable for practical purposes in knowledge representation and logic programming, and we claim that the same holds for the *pure* version of STABLE. This does not affect, however, the success of the stable semantics in establishing links between nonmonotonic reasoning and logic programming [MS89] and its fertilizing effect on abstract investigations into logic program semantics.

An important objection may be that it sometimes *is* intended that a program have no models if certain integrity constraints are not satisfied. In the particular case of STABLE, integrity constraints even belong to the essence of the semantics [FLMS93]. Yet, also integrity constraints are usually relevant only to a part of the program and failure of one constraint should not lead the whole thing astray; for instance, in order to support localization of errors. Furthermore, we feel that integrity constraints add a level of complexity to a semantics and should be understood independently.

In the sequel we define, discuss, and compare a number of extensions of STABLE that avoid the mentioned shortcomings. We also show that the somewhat anomalous behavior of STABLE is due to the failure of *Relevance* which cannot be repaired in an obvious or straightforward manner.

The plan of the paper is as follows: In Section 2 below we give some notation and briefly review the stable and the wellfounded semantics. Section 3 recalls the abstract approach to what we call a *well-behaved* semantics and lays ground for the subsequent sections. Section 4 applies our abstract approach to define elegantly various extensions of STABLE and WFS. We show that the semantics proposed by Schlipf recently ([Sch92]) are instances in our framework. We also discuss the most important variants of STABLE recently proposed and determine their interrelationships. Section 5 addresses related attempts and concludes.

In a companion paper ([DM94]), we employ our approach to define STABLE^{rel}, a version of STABLE satisfying the *Relevance* condition while staying close to STABLE in spirit. There, we also discuss different versions of the *unfolding* property used in logic programming.

2 Notation

A program clause or a *rule* is a formula $a \leftarrow b_1, \ldots, b_m, \neg c_1, \ldots \neg c_l$, where $n \geq 1$ and $m, l \geq 0$. As usual, the comma represents conjunction. A *rule* is called *positive* or *definite* rule if $l = 0$. a is said to be the *head* of the rule, $b_1, \ldots, b_m, \neg c_1, \ldots \neg c_l$ its *body*. A *program* P is a finite set of rules and it straightforwardly inherits the typology of clauses. The *Herbrand base* induced by a program P is denoted B_P. In general the a, b_j, c_l are arbitrary atomic formulæ. But to make our point here we join the community which restricts itself to fully grounded programs. If we have no function symbols, i.e., deal only with so-called *datalog* programs, and at least one constant symbol, then the grounded program is finite iff the original program is. In the sequel *program* will mean *fully grounded program* (which may be infinite).

A program P induces a notion of *dependency* between atoms from B_P. We will say a depends immediately on b if b appears in the body of a clause in P, such that a appears in its head. The two place relation *depends on* is defined as the transitive closure of *depends immediately on*. We will need the notions *dependencies of* and *rules relevant for an atom x*:

- $dependencies\_of(x) := \{a : x \text{ depends on } a\}$,
- $rel\_rul(P, x)$ is the set of *relevant rules* of P with respect to x, i.e., the set of rules that contain an $a \in dependencies\_of(x)$ in their heads,

These definitions extend straightforwardly to arbitrary literals by setting $dependencies\_of(\neg x) := dependencies\_of(x)$ and $rel\_rul(P, \neg x) := rel\_rul(P, x)$.
Our notion of a semantics is very general ([Dix91]):

Definition 1 SEM.
A semantics SEM is a mapping from the class of all programs into the powerset of the set of all 3-valued Herbrand structures. SEM assigns to every program P a set of 3-valued Herbrand models of P:

$$\mathrm{SEM}_P \subseteq \mathrm{MOD}_{3-val}^{Herb_\mathcal{L}P}(P).$$

We associate with any semantics SEM a sceptical entailment relation SEM^{scept}:

Definition 2 Sceptical entailment relation $\vdash_P$.
Let P be a program and U a set of atoms. Any semantics SEM induces a sceptical entailment relation SEM_P^{scept} as follows:

$$\mathrm{SEM}_P^{scept}(U) := \bigcap_{\mathcal{M} \in \mathrm{SEM}_P(U)} \{L : L \text{ is a pos. or neg. literal with: } \mathcal{M} \models L\}$$

Since our main emphasis lies on the sceptical semantics, we will henceforth use SEM instead of SEM^{scept}.

We have to distinguish between two different notions of one semantics being an *extension* of another one:

- SEM $\leq_k$ SEM': this means that SEM' classifies more atoms as true or false than SEM, or
- SEM' is defined for a class of programs that includes the class of programs for which SEM is defined, and for all programs of the smaller class *SEM* and *SEM'* coincide.

For instance, STABLE extends WFS in the former sense while both STABLE and WFS extend the supported semantics M_P^{supp} ([ABW88]) in the latter sense.

2.1 Stable Semantics vs. Well-founded Semantics

One of the central ideas of the stable semantics is that any atom in a potential model should have a definite reason to be true or false. This idea was made explicit by Bidoit and Froidevaux [BF91] and, independently, by Gelfond and Lifschitz [GL88] as follows: for a program P and a model $N \subseteq B_P$ we define

$$P^N := \{rule^N : rule \in P\}, \qquad \text{where}$$

$$(a \leftarrow b_1, \ldots, b_n, \neg c_1, \ldots \neg c_m)^N := \begin{cases} a \leftarrow b_1, \ldots, b_n, & \text{if } \forall j : c_j \notin N, \\ \mathbf{t}, & \text{otherwise.} \end{cases}$$

P^N is called the *Gelfond-Lifschitz transform*. P^N is always a *definite* program. Therefore, we can compute its least Herbrand model M_{P^N} and check whether it coincides with the model N with which we started:

Definition 3 STABLE.
N is called a *stable* model of P, if $M_{PN} = N$. The stable semantics $STABLE(P)$ is given by the set of (classical or two-valued) stable models of P.

WFS maps a program into one of its three-valued Herbrand Models (due to lack of space we cannot give the full definition of WFS here). WFS relates to STABLE as follows [vGRS91]:

- Every stable model $\mathcal{N}$ of P is an extension of WFS(P): $WFS(P) \leq_k \mathcal{N}$.
- If WFS(P) is two-valued, WFS(P) is the unique stable model.

Our earlier statement that STABLE extends WFS with respect to $\leq_k$ depends on the interpretation of $STABLE(P)$ if P has no stable models. If in analogy to classical logic we define $STABLE(P) = B_P \cup \neg B_P$ if P has no stable models, then we have $WFS \leq_k STABLE$. If we consider STABLE undefined in that case, WFS and STABLE are incomparable:

Example 3 Adding irrelevant clauses.

$P_{stratified} : a \leftarrow \neg b$ $\quad$ $P_{no\_stable\_model} : a \leftarrow \neg b$
$$p \leftarrow \neg p$$

Both WFS and STABLE coincide with the supported model on $P_{stratified}$: therefore, a is derivable. WFS also derives a from $P_{no\_stable\_model}$ which equals $P_{stratified}$ plus the clause $p \leftarrow \neg p$. In contrast, $P_{no\_stable\_model}$ does not have stable models.

3 Abstract Approach to Reasonable Semantics

All examples (1, 2, and 3) mentioned so far contain a negative cycle, the main crux of the whole enterprise of giving meaning to programs with negation. In order to cope with this problem, but not to argue on arbitrary example programs, the first author formulated abstract properties which a semantics should have.

It is possible to define the notion of a *well-behaved* semantics (see [Dix94]) as a sceptical semantics with certain such properties. Some of them state the equality between the semantics on programs which may be transformed into each other by arguably *meaning-preserving* steps. We will not review this definition here: instead, we illustrate the properties which we need here on some examples.

Look for instance at the following two (closely related) intuitive properties, which we require any reasonable semantics SEM to have:

C_1: If $a \leftarrow l_1, \ldots, l_k \in P$ and SEM(P)$\models l_1 \wedge \ldots \wedge l_k$ then SEM(P)$\models a$,
Cut: If SEM(P)$\models a$ and SEM($P \cup \{a\}$) $\models x$ then SEM(P)$\models x$.

The most important principle for our present goal is the *Principle of Relevance*, which may be motivated by looking at the way a program is written down. A program as a set of clauses expresses a set of implicational dependencies between literals. While there may be mutual dependencies, the *basic structure* of a program is of a hierarchical nature. The developer of a program will deliberately choose this structure when writing the program and will most probably write down the (recursive) definition of some literals before proceeding to literals which may or may not use the program written so far.

The formalization of this idea needs to list those rules, which could ever contribute to l's derivation (or to its nonderivability by negation as failure). This is captured by the set of *relevant rules of a program P with respect to a literal l* (see Section 2). In general, l may depend on a large set of atoms. But rules that do not contain these atoms in their heads should not affect the meaning of l in P: these rules are therefore *not relevant for l*.

The *Principle of Relevance* states exactly that it is reasonable for the truth-value of a literal l only to depend on the subprogram formed from the *relevant rules* of P with respect to l.

Definition 4 Relevance.
For all literals l: $\mathrm{SEM}(P)(l) = \mathrm{SEM}(rel\_rul(P, l))(l)$.

STABLE does not satisfy this principle (see Example 3) due to the nonexistence of stable models. As to the well-founded semantics, *Relevance* holds. Equally important and intimately related is the following principle:

Definition 5 Modularity.
Let $P = P_1 \cup P_2$ and for every $a \in B_{P_2}$: $rel\_rul(P, a) \subseteq P_2$.
The principle of Modularity is: $\mathrm{SEM}(P) = \mathrm{SEM}(P_1^{\,SEM(P_2)} \cup P_2)$.

P_1 can be seen "to make calls to the subprogram P_2". The assumption says that all necessary information about $a \in B_{P_2}$ is contained in P_2. Therefore, we can *reduce* the program P_1 with all literals that are already decided in P_2: $P_1^{\,SEM(P_2)}$. The formal definition of *reducing a program P with a set M of literals* cannot be given here for lack of space. Intuitively though, every occurrence in P of a literal from M is evaluated to true and false and the program P is simplified accordingly [Dix94]. This idea is present also in the context of truth maintenance systems [Wit91]. Note that *Modularity* is satisfied for STABLE.

Recently, Alferes et al. ([ADP94]) used these properties to define a *Top-Down Query Evaluation* method for an extension of WFS. Clearly, if a semantics does not satisfy *Relevance* it is not amenable to any form of Top-Down computation, simply because a query Q does not only depend from the atoms below it (i.e., from *dependencies_of(Q)*).

The property of *Rationality* will be needed for a lemma to follow:

Rationality: If $\mathrm{SEM}(P) \not\models \neg a$ and $\mathrm{SEM}(P) \models x$ then $\mathrm{SEM}(P \cup \{a\}) \models x$.

The lemma presents a general construction of extending a (rational) semantics that does not satisfy *Cut* to one where the *Cut* holds.

Lemma 6 SEM$^+$.

Let SEM be a rational semantics and define an increasing sequence of sets of atoms M_i by $M_0 := \emptyset$, $M_{i+1} := SEM(P \cup M_i)$. We have

$$SEM(P \cup M_i) \leq_k SEM(P \cup M_{i+1}).$$

There exists therefore a γ such that $M_\gamma = M_{\gamma+1}$. We define

$$SEM^+(P) := SEM(P \cup M_\gamma).$$

SEM$^+$ is the weakest extension of SEM satisfying Cut. *In addition, SEM$^+$ is also rational.*

The proof is obvious: we only add those atoms that have to be added in order to satisfy *Cut*. We need *Rationality* to prove inductively SEM($P \cup M_i$) $\leq_k$ SEM($P \cup M_{i+1}$)[3] and to reach a limit M_γ. Otherwise, the sequence M_i could be oscillating.

The last abstract property we need is that *Supraclassicality*, well-known in the context of general nonmonotonic reasoning. Schlipf used it to overcome both the weakness of the well-founded semantics (see Example 2) and the inconsistency of the stable semantics by looking for extensions satisfying the following property:

Supraclassicality[4]: $P \models a$ implies $a \in SEM(P)$ for atoms a.

Supraclassicality solves some of the case splitting problems and also removes in many examples the inconsistency (e.g. in Examples 2 and 3).

4 Variants of STABLE

4.1 Two First Attempts

One might think that the inconsistency problem of STABLE can simply be solved by redefinition if no stable models exist. Taking the relation $WFS \leq_k STABLE$ as evidence, the following definition is the easiest such definition:

$$STABLE^*(P) := \begin{cases} WFS(P), & \text{if no stable model exists,} \\ STABLE(P), & \text{otherwise.} \end{cases}$$

This definition has also be used in [SNV92], albeit implicitly: There, STABLE models are computed as extensions of WFS, and WFS remains as an approximation if this extension fails. STABLE* is obviously comparable to WFS. In combination with what was said earlier we have WFS $\leq_k$ STABLE* $\leq_k$ STABLE.

Unfortunately, STABLE* only solves some of the toy problems. Slightly more complex programs (e.g., $P_{splitting} \cup \{p \leftarrow \neg p\}$) show that STABLE* does not satisfy *Relevance*. Consider the following example:

---

[3] The definition of M_{i+1} ensures that if $x \in M_{i+1}$ then $\neg x \notin$ SEM($P \cup M_i$) so that *Rationality* can be applied.

[4] Schlipf calls this property *classical completeness* in [Sch92].

Example 4 (Non-) Existence of Stable Models.

$P_{\neg \exists \, stab.}$: $a \leftarrow \neg b$	P_{stable} : $a \leftarrow \neg b$	$P_{stable} \cup \{p\}$: $a \leftarrow \neg b$
$b \leftarrow \neg a$	$b \leftarrow \neg a$	$b \leftarrow \neg a$
$p \leftarrow \neg p$	$p \leftarrow \neg p$	$p \leftarrow \neg p$
	$p \leftarrow a$	$p \leftarrow a$
		p

While P_{stable} has the unique stable model $\{p, a\}$, $P_{\neg \exists \, stab.}$ fails to have any stable model. P_{stable} has the unique stable model $\{p, a\}$ and $P_{stable} \cup \{p\}$ has two stable models: $\{p, a\}$ and $\{p, b\}$.

P_{stable} has exactly the stable model $\{p, a\}$, so that a is derivable. This seems to be very strange because the relevant part of P with respect to a is just the program consisting of the first two clauses, from which nothing can be derived.[5]

Note that the supraclassicality condition already avoids the problem in Example 4: since p is derivable in P_{stable}, supraclassical semantics (like STABLE$_C$ and STABLE$^+$ to be introduced below) make no difference between P_{stable} and $P_{stable} \cup \{p\}$. But more complex programs can be constructed to show the failure of *Relevance*. In addition, even if we define a semantics by *explicitly focussing on the relevant part of the program*[6] we can show that such a semantics does not satisfy the condition C_1 (nor the *Cut*) which makes it useless. We refer the reader to [DM94] for a full discussion.

4.2 Schlipf's Approach Revisited

In [Sch92] John Schlipf also noticed a serious drawback of STABLE besides the inconsistency. He defines the notion of a *stratified pair* which, interestingly enough, coincides with the condition used in *Modularity* (Definition 5):

(P_2, P_1) is a stratified pair if for $P = P_1 \cup P_2$ the following holds: for every $A \in B_{P_2}$: $rel\_rul(P, A) \subseteq P_2$.

Based on this notion he define a principle of *weak stratification*:

Definition 7 (Schlipf) Weak Stratification.
Let (P_2, P_1) be a stratified pair of logic programs. The principle of *Weak Stratification* states: If a relation R appears in P_2, then $R(t) \in SEM(P_1 \cup P_2)$ iff $R(t) \in SEM(P_2)$.

Modularity is weaker than *Weak Stratification*. While he requires that $R(t) \in SEM(P_1 \cup P_2)$ iff $R(t) \in SEM(P_2)$ (*not* true for STABLE) we require that $SEM(P) = SEM(P_1{}^{SEM(P_2)} \cup P_2)$ (satisfied by STABLE). Again *Relevance* is crucial:

Lemma 8 Modularity and Relevance imply Weak Stratification.
Any semantics satisfying Modularity and Relevance also satisfies Weak Stratification.

---

[5] We have two stable models: $\{a, \neg b\}$ and $\{\neg a, b\}$.
[6] Which means that *Relevance* is automatically built-in.

Therefore we think that Schlipf's notion of weak stratification is overloaded and should be split into *Modularity* and *Relevance*: The latter being the proper reason why weak stratification is not satisfied.

Schlipf introduces two semantics WFS_C (wellfounded-by-case) and $STABLE_C$ (stable-by-case) using *derived rules*. His definitions are very technical and far from being elegant. We do not repeat his definitions here; instead, we give an elegant and useful definition of a semantics equivalent to WFS_C. The definition is based on Lemma 6 and considerably simplifies the original one from [Dix92]:

Definition 9 WFS$^+$.
Let P be a normal program, and define

$$SEM(P) := WFS(P) \cup \{a : a \text{ an atom with: } P \models a\}.$$

The assumptions of Lemma 6 are satisfied and we get a rational semantics WFS$^+$.

Theorem 10 WFS$^+$ as $\leq_k$-weakest extension of WFS.
WFS$^+$ is the weakest extension of WFS that satisfies Cut *and* Supraclassicality. *In addition WFS$^+$ is rational and satisfies the following property (stronger than Supraclassicality):*

$$\text{If } P \cup WFS^+(P) \models a \text{ then } a \in WFS^+(P).$$

Using the last theorem it is easy to prove that Schlipf's WFS_C essentially coincides with WFS$^+$ for all programs. A straightforward attempt to incorporate Supraclassicality explicitly into the definition of STABLE gives the following:

Definition 11 STABLE$^\#$.

$$STABLE^\#(P) := \begin{cases} STABLE(P \cup \{a : P \models a\}), & \text{if stable models exist,} \\ WFS^+(P), & \text{otherwise.} \end{cases}$$

STABLE$^\#$ is supraclassical and satisfies *Cut*. It does not satisfy the strong version of Supraclassicality.[7]

Iterating the construction of STABLE$^\#$ gives us a semantics STABLE$^+$ which is strongly related to $STABLE_C$:

Definition 12 STABLE$^+$.
Let P be a normal program. If $P \cup \{a : (P \cup WFS^+(P)) \models a\}$ has no stable models, set $STABLE^+(P) := WFS^+(P)$. Otherwise, define a decreasing sequence M_i of sets by $M_0 := STABLE(P \cup \{a : (P \cup WFS^+(P)) \models a\})$ and

$$M_{i+1} := STABLE(P \cup \{a : (P \cup M_i) \models a)\}.$$

We define $\qquad\qquad STABLE^+(P) := \bigcap_i M_i.$

---

[7] I.e., the appropriate instance of "If $P \cup SEM(P) \models a$ then $a \in SEM(P)$

Lemma 13 STABLE$^+$ $\leq_k$ STABLE.

STABLE$^+$ is a semantics below STABLE$^\#$ (and therefore also below STABLE) satisfying Cut *and* Strong Supraclassicality. *On all programs where STABLE$_C(P)$ is consistent, STABLE$_C(P)$ =STABLE$^+(P)$.*

The next example shows that all these semantics are no solutions to *Relevance*. In addition they are strict extensions with respect to $\leq_k$:

Example 5 Properties of STABLE$_C$, STABLE$^+$, STABLE$^\#$.

$P_{Schlipf1} : p \leftarrow \neg q$ $P_{Schlipf2} : a \leftarrow \neg b$

$\quad\quad\quad\quad q \leftarrow \neg p$ $c \leftarrow a, \neg d$

$\quad\quad\quad\quad a \leftarrow p, \neg b$ $d \leftarrow a, \neg c$

$\quad\quad\quad\quad b \leftarrow p, \neg c$ $e \leftarrow a, \neg e$

$\quad\quad\quad\quad c \leftarrow p, \neg a$ $e \leftarrow a, c$

$P_{Schlipf1}$ has only one stable-by-case model: $\{\neg p, q, \neg a, \neg b, \neg c\}$. But $rel\_rul(P_{Schlipf1}, p) = rel\_rul(P_{Schlipf1}, q) = \{p \leftarrow \neg q, \; q \leftarrow \neg p\}$. Concerning $P_{Schlipf2}$: no atoms can be derived classically. Hence, STABLE$^\#$ coincides with STABLE and derives $\{a, c, e, \neg b, \neg d\}$. STABLE$_C$ only derives a and e.

We therefore have: WFS$^+$ $\leq_k$ STABLE$^+$ $\leq_k$ STABLE$^\#$ $\leq_k$ STABLE.

4.3 Other Variants

Closely related to STABLE is REG-SEM [YY93], the semantics based on regular models. You and Yuan showed [YY93] that REG-SEM is equivalent to

- Sacca and Zaniolo's *partial models* ([SZ91]),
- Przymusinski's $\leq_k$-*maximal 3-valued stable models* ([Prz90]), and
- Dung's *preferred extensions* ([Dun91]).

These semantics satisfy *Relevance, Modularity, Cut* but not *Rationality* ([DM94]) and therefore can also be seen as interesting *well-behaved* approximations of STABLE. In addition, REG-SEM is stronger than WFS$^+$:

Example 6 REG-SEM vs. WFS$^+$.

$P_{splitting} : a \leftarrow \neg b$ $P'_{splitting} : a \leftarrow \neg b$

$\quad\quad\quad\quad b \leftarrow \neg a$ $b \leftarrow \neg a$

$\quad\quad\quad\quad p \leftarrow a$ $p \leftarrow \neg b$

$\quad\quad\quad\quad p \leftarrow b$ $p \leftarrow \neg a$

The second program results from the first by evaluating a (by $\neg b$) and b (by $\neg a$). While WFS$^+$ derives p from $P_{splitting}$, it does not derive p from $P'_{splitting}$. REG-SEM derives p from both programs!

Note that REG-SEM is not supraclassical: for $"p \leftarrow \neg p"$, the atom p is assigned undefined. Thus, REG-SEM is incomparable with WFS$^+$. But it is possible to define (in much the same way as WFS$^+$) a semantics WFS' that shares all nice properties with WFS$^+$, except the supraclassicality. These semantics are related as follows:

$$\text{WFS}' \leq_k \text{REG-SEM} \leq_k \text{STABLE}$$

In [DM94] we show how REG-SEM is related to *unfolding*.

5 Conclusion and related attempts

We have shown that a major reason of certain anomalies of the STABLE semantics is its failure of *Relevance*. This property is strongly related to Schlipf's notion of *weak stratification* and essential for Top-Down Query Evaluation methods. This has also been observed in [ADP94], where our abstract approach is used to implement an extension of WFS containing explicit negation. Lifschitz and Turner [LT94] investigate a notion closely related to *Relevance*: *splitting a program*. A set U is a *splitting set*, if U contains with every atom a also all literals of $rel\_rul(P, a)$. Brewka [Bre93] approached the anomalies of STABLE by considering abduction but his proposal did not completely capture negation as failure. In his framework it is possible that atoms occuring in no head are assigned *undefined* instead of *false*.

In addition, we discussed extensions of WFS which allow for reasoning-by-cases and can be seen as *well-behaved* approximations and improvements of STABLE. Our approach enabled us to give an elegant definition of Dix' WFS$^+$ and to show that it coincides with Schlipf's WFS$_C$. We also noted that REG-SEM is a relevant approximation of STABLE.

6 Acknowledgements

The authors would like to thank John Schlipf for very helpful remarks and clarifying examples. His suggestions helped to improve the paper a lot. Two anonymous referees also provided us with useful suggestions which, along with the space restrictions, led us to a major rewriting of this paper.

References

[ABW88] K. Apt, H. Blair, and A. Walker. Towards a theory of declarative knowledge. In Jack Minker, editor, *Foundations of Deductive Databases*, chapter 2, pages 89–148. Morgan Kaufmann, 1988.

[ADP94] J. J. Alferes, Carlos Viegas Damasio, and L. M. Pereira. Top-down query evaluation for well-founded semantics with explicit negation. In *Proceedings ECAI*. John Wiley & Sons, 1994.

[BF91] Nicole Bidoit and Christine Froidevaux. General logical Databases and Programs: Default Logic Semantics and Stratification. *Information and Computation*, 91:15–54, 1991.

[Bre93] Gerhard Brewka. An Abductive Framework for Generalized Logic Programs. In *Logic Programming and Non-Monotonic Reasoning, Proc. 2nd Int. Workshop*, MIT Press, July 1993.

[Dix91]   Jürgen Dix. Classifying Semantics of Logic Programs. In *Logic Programming and Non-Monotonic Reasoning, Proc. 1st Int. Workshop*, pages 166–180. MIT Press, July 1991.

[Dix92]   Jürgen Dix. A Framework for Representing and Characterizing Semantics of Logic Programs. In *Principles of Knowledge Representation and Reasoning: Proc. 3rd Int. Conf.*, pages 591–602. Morgan Kaufmann, 1992.

[Dix94]   Jürgen Dix. Semantics of Logic Programs: Their Intuitions and Formal Properties. An Overview. In *Logic, Action and Information. Proc. Konstanz Colloquium in Logic and Information (LogIn '92)*. DeGruyter, 1994.

[DM94]   Jürgen Dix and Martin Müller. Extensions and Improvements of the Stable Semantics. In *Proc. 8th Int. Symp. on Methodologies for Intelligent Systems*. Springer, LNAI, to appear, 1994.

[Dun91]   P. M. Dung. Negation as Hypotheses: An Abductive Foundation for Logic Programming. In *Proc. 8th Int. Conf. on Logic Programming*. MIT Press, June 1991.

[FLMS93]   J. A. Fernandez, J. Lobo, J. Minker, and V. S. Subrahmanian. Disjunctive LP + Integrity Constraints = Stable Model Semantics. *Annals of Mathematics and Artificial Intelligence*, 8(3-4), 1993.

[GL88]   Michael Gelfond and Vladimir Lifschitz. The Stable Model Semantics for Logic Programming. In *5th Int. Conf. on Logic Programming*, pages 1070–1080. MIT Press, 1988.

[LT94]   Vladimir Lifschitz and Hudson Turner. Splitting a Logic Program. This volume.

[MS89]   Wiktor Marek and V.S. Subrahmanian. The Relationship between Logic Program Semantics and Nonmonotonic Reasoning. In *Proc. 6. Int. Conf on Logic Programming*, pages 600–617. MIT Press, July 1989.

[Prz90]   Teodor Przymusinski. Well-founded Semantics Coincides With Three-Valued Stable Semantics. *Fundamenta Informaticae*, XIII:445–463, 1990.

[Sch92]   John S. Schlipf. Formalizing a Logic for Logic Programming. *Annals of Mathematics and Artificial Intelligence*, 5:279–302, 1992.

[SNV92]   V.S. Subrahmanian, Nau, and Vago. WFS + Branch and Bound = Stable Models. Technical Report CS-TR-2935, Univ. of Maryland, July 1992. To be published with *IEEE Transactions on Knowledge and Data Engineering*

[SZ91]   D. Sacca and C. Zaniolo. Partial models and Three-Valued Models in Logic Programs with Negation. In *Logic Programming and Non-Monotonic Reasoning, Proc. 1st Int. Workshop*, pages 87–104. MIT Press, July 1991.

[Tor93]   Alberto Torres. Negation as Failure to Support. In *Logic Programming and Non-Monotonic Reasoning, Proc. 2nd Int. Workshop*, pages 223–243. MIT Press, July 1993.

[vGRS91]   Allen van Gelder, Kenneth Ross, and John S. Schlipf. The well-founded semantics for general logic programs. *Journal of the ACM*, 38:620–650, 1991.

[Wit91]   Cees Witteveen. Partial Semantics for Truth Maintenance. In *Logics in AI*. Springer, LNAI 478, 1991.

[YY93]   Jia-Huai You and Li-Yan Yuan. On the Equivalence of Semantics for Normal Logic Programs. In *Proc. Workshop on Logic Programming with Incomplete Information, following ILPS' 93*, pages 161–176, 1993.

TabVer
A Case Study in Table Verbalization

Ingo Glöckner, Andrea Grieszl, Martin Müller and Marc Ronthaler

Institut für Semantische Informationsverarbeitung,
Universität Osnabrück,
D – 49069 Osnabrück

Abstract. The purpose of this paper is to give a brief overview of Tab-Ver, a front–end component that verbalizes large tables generated by a commercial expert system.
TabVer's aim is to highlight the essential information that is contained in possibly very large tables by generating a small text. This text gives a short summary of appropriate communicative and pragmatic acceptability, supresses all unneccessary information and also provides some additional information, which is not directly expressed in the table. The output text is generated from basic templates by a 'planner' which operates on a special plan language according to the A*–algorithm. All basic and higher order templates are encoded in this language, which is a cost-based version of Prolog. Using all these plans (including control plans), the planner searches for the best way to verbalize the input table and (via A*) finds the optimal method first.

1 Introduction

TabVer[1] was developed in the context of the existing commercial expert system EXCEPT (EXpert system for Computer-aided Environmental Planning Tasks, see [1], [2]).[2] EXCEPT's primary aim is to support the evaluation and documentation of environmental impact assessments (EIA).[3] EIA's are examinations of environmental actions and projects (e.g. building projects) and their consequences to environment. In order to prevent damage to the ecological balance, EIA's are prescribed for larger projects by the ministries of each federal state in Germany. There are predefined standards which prescribe how to evaluate the results of these tests and how to represent all results and evaluations to the reader. Therefore an EIA is a very complex procedure (examination of environment and the results of interfering with environment) followed by the complex task of documenting this examination to communicate the results of an EIA to the public (like law–courts, unions of public utility and the individual person).

While carrying out such an investigation, huge sets of data must be processed and evaluated (e.g. according to threshold values by law) which in part will be

---

[1] TabVer is an acronym for 'TabellenVerbalisierung' (table verbalization).
[2] EXCEPT was originally implemented by Dr. Martin Hübner at the Technical University of Hamburg–Harburg.
[3] "Umweltverträglichkeitsprüfung" (UVP) in German.

presented in tables. A detailed examination of nature is very extensive due to a large number of measuring values according to many measuring methods, measuring points and times resulting in ratings due to different evaluation methods and aggregation methods. So the final result is lots of very large tables. Large tables pose two problems: On the one hand these tables have to be constructed out of large sets of data (mostly by experts) and on the other hand all information has to be extracted and interpreted by the reader (mostly no experts).

EXCEPT was planned to support referees in the (often monotonous) work of carrying out and documenting EIA's. In 1993, IBM Germany started to enhance EXCEPT in course of the eXu–project.[4] One project partner was the University of Osnabrück, where TabVer was developed.[5] The aim of TabVer is to verbalize and summarize tables of measurements, e.g. measured values and corresponding evaluations, in order to simplify the process of reading and interpreting of such tables.

Hidden information may be relatively frequent occurences of values that are distributed among the whole table, and which do not seem to be interesting as singularities but are relevant as accumulation of entities. Another kind of information loss is caused by the fact that values that are close enough to a certain threshold still may be classified as one of minor importance. In particular the combination of the two phenomena above reveals, that tables are not always the best method of representing large sets of data: First, one cannot simply annotate additional information to entries, and secondly reading and interpreting such tables takes more time and attention than one might expect. A short summary, by contrast, provides all important information, ignores quite a lot of uninteresting details, and it may also give some additional information that is not well expressed numerically in a table.

2 TabVer: An Overview

Since our prototype system should work as part of a commercially available expert system, we had to take into consideration the constraints that arise within an existing system. The demands on TabVer were to produce readable texts of ecological acceptability (wrt. the relation between the facts and the text produced), and furthermore these texts should be generated quickly. Obvious problems that occur while we address these demands are e.g. the almost complete lack of nearly any linguistic information in EXCEPT, which makes it hard to produce "readable" sentences. On the other hand, additional information has to be retrieved from the database of EXCEPT. But both problems, of course, had to be solved in order to produce texts that could be understood by laypeople. The original EXCEPT (which was written in Lisp) was enhanced and ported to

---

[4] The aim of eXu was to enhance the EXCEPT kernel in order to achieve a more general planning and evelution expert system, whose domain is not restricted to environmental investigations.

[5] TabVer was implemented by the authors, together with Uwe Hauck and Frank Kolhosser, under the guidance of Prof. Dr. C.-R. Rollinger.

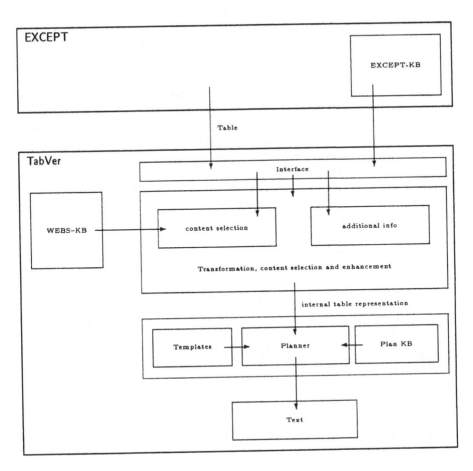

Fig. 1. A sketch of the TabVer architecture

BIM–Prolog (running under AIX on IBM RS/6000 machines) at the German Software Development Laboratory (GSDL) of IBM. Simultaneously TabVer was coded in BIM–Prolog and C in cooperation with GSDL. The original EXCEPT (which was written in Lisp) was enhanced and ported to BIM–Prolog (running under AIX on IBM RS/6000 machines) at the German Software Development Laboratory (GSDL) of IBM. Simultaneously TabVer was coded in BIM–Prolog and C in cooperation with GSDL.

The data that EXCEPT hands over to TabVer are tables encoded in a description language, which, to begin with, is transformed into a TabVer–internal representation. Then each item in the table is tagged by labels that contain information about its relevance of being verbalized. All relevance information is encoded in a seperate knowledge base (WEBS-KB). Besides an elaboration of relations between rows and columns (like causal or descriptive relations), the total amount of information is now reduced to a smaller set, and additional information is attached to items which provides information about e.g. a value close to a boundary between evaluations. Relations between rows and columns can be extracted from the incoming table data using additional ("meta–table"–) knowledge of EXCEPT–KB. Additional information, like thresholds, also have to be retrieved from the EXCEPT–internal knowledge base.

On this enlarged table representation, a general–purpose planner operates, which constructs paragraphs of text based on small textual building blocks (templates). The planner tries to find the cheapest (that is: the best) complex plan that consists of given elementary plans (Plan KB) by controlling Prolog's prove procedure. In fact, the whole process of text planning and verbalization is covered by the elementary plans which are encoded in a special plan language, L_{TabVer}, and which are compiled to Prolog clauses. So TabVer divides into two parts: (1) The interface and content selection modules are (highly) application dependent. They can be seen as a kind of preprocessing in order to achieve a data structure, on which our planner can work. (2) The planner, which is the kernel of TabVer, is independent from the application that calls TabVer and is therefore embeddable into any other application which produces tables.

Due to the power of our internal representation and our planner, the output is a piece of coherent text containing quantified NP's, pronouns (in some cases) and certain pragmatic hints, like the particle 'even'. Furthermore, all additional information we extracted and the relations between rows or columns will be expressed. The process of verbalizing average tables (see chapter 3) takes 2–5 seconds (on IBM RS/6000 220 Workstations).

2.1 TabVer in Context of existing NL–Generation Systems

In AI, text generation is a planning process. Since [11] the generation process is usually divided into two parts: (1) content selection (*What to say*) (2) verbalization (*How to say it*).

In most systems this dichotomy has given rise to the same sequential architecture as in TabVer (e.g. TEXT [3], MUMBLE [4], and SUTRA [5]). More sophisticated systems like PAULINE [6] or KAMP [7] make use of interacting or integrated architectures, but such systems are not suitable for applications that have to be efficient. The crucial disadvantage of sequential generation is that occasionally selected content cannot be verbalized. This problem does not occur within TabVer: Content selection (which finally is directed by the ecologist) is much too important to be influenced by considerations concerning text structures. Moreover, the set of relevant text schemes (these are high order templates in the plan KB) for verbalizing tables is clearly enumerable and is entirely covered by plans.

In a sense, TabVer's generating sentences comes down to gap filling, and so belongs to the group of "canned–text" generators like SHRDLU [8]. However, on the other hand, our planner is capable of "parallel proving"[6] and is therefore more sophisticated than planners which simply perform linear scheme instantiation. Furthermore our planning module is completely domain independent,

---

[6] This means parallel unfolding of the proof tree with cost–based pruning.

an advantage it shares with MUMBLE-86[9]. Another feature, which the system has in common with SUTRA is that TabVer is also capable of generating pronouns, elliptic constructions, quantified NPs and pragmatic particles.

To sum up, TabVer is ecclectic in a sense that it adopts more sophisticated techniques if neccessary and resorts to more basic solutions whenever possible.

3 TabVer in Action

3.1 What's in a Table?

We had to extract the encoded information of a table in a very detailed way in order to 'explain' it to the program. Thus the following description of our terminology might seem to be a bit redundant. But the reader may take into account that a system has no a priori knowledge about the characteristic features of tables. Every table is characterized by *columns* and *rows*. We say that different relations hold between these, i.e. we can *compare* the rows while the columns *describe* or *supply* each other. The upper-most row and the left-most column possess a particular feature: They represent the *basic dimensions* of an evaluation whereas the remaining 'inner' entries contain the corresponding *evaluation results*. Our sample table includes three evaluation dimensions: location, applied method, and time of evaluation.[7] Each result is related to all of these. Sometimes there is a variation within the dimensions and sometimes there is not. Distinguishing between variant and invariant dimensions is necessary for a separate formulation of *basic-* and *result-dependent* templates, which are required for condensed text. The frame of a text is the *invariant* dimension(s) of the table described. If several tests have been made at e.g. one location, it is generally sufficient to name that location only once. The *variant* elements are named in relation to the relevant results. Some instances of variant dimensions might become summarized by a quantified expression, others will be mentioned by name, according to criteria, which will be discussed below.

3.2 What's the 'Point' in a Table?

Having analyzed a table's entire structure we had to find a way of presenting the global message that is meant to be conveyed. We decided to verbalize only information, which is relevant according to some given *point of view*.[8] Every result name like e.g. 'polluted' belongs to an ordered set of evaluation values, which must be classified with respect to the relevance of the elements for the user. Such a scale might look as follows: (a) <'not polluted', 'slightly polluted', 'polluted', 'strongly polluted'>. If we had a set like: (b) <'very bad', 'bad', 'good', 'very good'>, the scale reflects the opposite idea of relevance for the same kind of user. For several reasons we were not able to assign a semantics

---

[7] We find the evaluation method in a separate line above the table. The actual column-labels describe three kinds of results that arise from applying this *one* method.

[8] In the EXCEPT context, every *critical* or *dangerous* result counts as relevant.

Benzo(a)pyren value of suspended particles (long period) with regard to endangering health (precaution and protection standard HEIDBREDER/WEILAND 1984)

Evaluation subject	Value/Reason	Evaluation result	Description
Temes–Station Reisholz 06.11.91	9.1 ng/cbm	polluted	detrimental health effects not excluded
Temes–Station Reisholz 10.11.91	12.3 ng/cbm	strongly polluted	detrimental health effects expected
Temes–Station Reisholz 17.11.91	6.8 ng/cbm	polluted	detrimental health effects not excluded
Temes–Station Reisholz 20.11.91	8.8 ng/cbm	polluted	detrimental health effects not excluded
Temes–Station Reisholz 28.11.91	4.4 ng/cbm	polluted	detrimental health effects not excluded

With respect to the evaluation method 'Benzo(a)pyren value of suspended particles (long period) with regard to endangering health (precaution and protection standard HEIDBREDER/WEILAND 1984)' in a series of measurements from 6/11/91 to 28/11/91 the evaluation subject 'Temes–Station Reisholz' has been evaluated at almost every point of time as at least **polluted**, at 10/11/91 even as **strongly polluted**. I.e. detrimental health effects cannot be excluded or are to be expected.
The evaluation result at 6/11/91 is very close to the threshold of **strongly polluted**.

Fig. 2. EXCEPT Sample Table and Corresponding TabVer Output[10]

to single elements,[9] instead we decided to assign a kind of *polarity* to the sets and to partition the elements of each set into three subsets. Verbalization of these sets is either *optional, interesting,* or *obligatory*. The polarity describes the order of the elements within the sets. We might say that relevance 'increases' in set (a) and 'decreases' in (b), i.e. in case (a) the final elements are obligatory, whereas in (b) the first elements have this value. The notion of polarity serves two purposes: On the one hand, we are able to make use of (pragmatic) particles like 'at least' and 'even' (see sample verbalization), on the other hand, we can easily adjust the system to the opposite point of view by only reversing the polarity of each set. This would turn 'obligatory' to 'optional' and vice versa. Of course, it may happen that no entry of a table corresponds with an obligatory result. Consequently, there would be nothing to verbalize. In order to avoid this, a special mechanism 'shifts' the scale. If necessary (the case that all entries of a table are only optional), this mechanism will shift the values twice.

---

[9] Some result names simply consist of numbers, which bear different meanings in different contexts.

[10] Table and text have been literally translated from the German output.

3.3 Quantification

Based on the threefold classification of evaluation sets, TabVer performs a selection of content in order to decrease the amount of information to be verbalized. A big table can result in a short text if it permits formulations that cover *groups* of entries. So the next step is to form groups of identical or inclusive results (e.g. the set of 'polluted' items includes the set of 'strongly polluted' items). In contrast to the relatively simple task of selecting quantified expressions (Qex) for groups of identical items, verbalization of inclusion groups is rather tricky. For simply identical results (homogeneous groups) the percentage of these results will be computed and assigned an appropriate Qex (e.g.: 9 out of 10 := 'almost every' , 5 out of 10 := 'half', 7 out of 10 := 'most of', etc.). For inclusion groups, a special algorithm coordinates the decision whether to quantify or enumerate groups of currently focussed table entries. Furthermore, it determines whether or not to insert the expressions 'at least' or 'even'.

The Quantifying Algorithm This algorithm has been constructed to deal with many potential combinations that arise from different inclusive structures. We had to consider several features of inclusion sets: the number of elements within such sets, the 'depth'[11] of inclusion, the distribution of elements between the different depth–levels, and finally the percentage of the inclusion set within the total amount of table–values under consideration. The main question to be solved is: when and how to *summarize* elements into groups and when to *enumerate* single elements. Without going into all the details about the algorithm, we will mention a few (crucial) operations. The following sketch of the algorithm deals with inclusion sets as in the above example ('polluted', etc.) in which the more critical expressions are included by the less critical ones (via 'at least'). So talking about *level 1* corresponds with e.g. 'polluted', while *level 2* would describe 'strongly polluted' etc. (if applied to our example). The levels 1 and 3 form the extremes of (inclusion) scale.

- Anything with 4 numbers or less is enumerated.
- You can enumerate single elements on different depth–levels.
- If the inclusion–depth is more than 2, only enumerate elements on the extremes of scale .
- In order to enumerate, choose that extreme of scale with the least number of elements and summarize the other levels.
- If both extremes have the same number of elements, always enumerate the higher–level (=most critical) elements (for enumerating means: mentioning the evalutions by name).
  Additionally, this rule allows for the insertion of the pragmatic particles 'at least' and 'even'. We would say, e.g.: 'Most of all results have been evaluated as *at least* polluted or strongly polluted, the result at location XY *even*

---

[11] i.e. how many different evaluation names belong to one set, like: 'very strongly polluted', 'strongly polluted', and 'polluted' form an inclusion set with the depth of 3

as very strongly polluted'. I.e. the system summarizes the elements of the first two levels by the Qex 'most of all' and names the single element of level 3. If it would sum up the levels 2 and 3 to name a single element at level 1, it would do without these particles (e.g.: 'Most of all results have been evaluated as strongly polluted or very strongly polluted, the result at location XY as polluted').

- In order to summarize the higher level elements, compute the corresponding Qex *minus* the low level element(s) (to be enumerated) in relation to the absolute number of table–results and, of course, do *not* make use of the expression 'at least' after the Qex.

- In order to enumerate the highest level element(s), compute the Qex for *all* elements of the inclusion set in relation to the total results, say 'at least' after the Qex, and 'even' before the most critical result.

The deeper the inclusion structure is, the more complicated are the calculations. We considered depths up to 5 (which are not very likely to occur) and solved many more specific problems that arose from the many different ways the elements can be distributed to the levels. The result of these processes is a balance between shortness and informative content of text. The text becomes more complex if the table contains several kinds of relevant information, especially if it is structured in an irregular way. Comprehensive verbalization is possible only for comparable entries. So in the example above, we can summarize columns and not rows, but we take care of the descriptive relation that holds within the rows by using expressions like 'i.e.'.

Our sample text also contains additional information that is not explicitly revealed by the table. Since we have access to the system's database, we can make such information available to the user. With a definition of 'close', TabVer recognizes values close to evaluation boundaries and makes these explicit by applying an adequate template. In the case of multiple occurences of such 'borderline cases' we can recursively apply our special algorithm on these to form quantified phrases. The result text consists of many small units (templates) which have been designed to be as general as possible. Of course, they have to fit in their domain, but as far as possible, we tried to avoid purely linguistic problems[12] by formulating the templates wisely. One 'trick' was to form nominal phrases (NP's) in which names of instances are preceded by the corresponding class name, e.g. *evaluation subject*^{class} *Temes–Station Reisholz*^{instance}. In German, the resulting complex NP inherits case, number, and gender from the class prefix. Therefore, attaching agreement information to a very small set of superconcepts (class names) was sufficient to achieve correct congruence although EXCEPT does not provide linguistic information at all.

---

[12] e.g. congruence in case, numerus, genus

4 TabVer in Detail

TabVer has to deal with heterogeneous tasks which should not be performed sequentially. Some decisions can be made globally (e.g. forming groups of comparable table entries), while others must be made on a rather local level, e.g. insertion of pragmatic particles like 'even' . While some of these decisions are context–independent, others depend on the preceding discourse (e.g. proper choice of pronomials, elliptic constructions), which suggests a left–to–right generation order. In view of these complex dependencies among verbalization decisions, existing methods of text generation were considered too inflexible for TabVer because of their rather specialized planning components. Therefore, we favoured a more general approach.

These considerations led us to using a 'proof trees as search trees' metaphor, making available the A* algorithm of heuristic search to control the planning process. Heuristic best–first search (as realized by A*) seemed to be a viable means for coordinating the interaction between decisions at varying levels of processing. Furthermore, it allows for selecting the 'best' verbalization by means of a cost assignment.

Consequently, TabVer was equipped with a plan language incorporating specifications of costs and heuristics. The language developed, L_{TabVer}, is syntactically very close to Prolog. However, it is interpreted differently: the Prolog control–strategy is replaced by a heuristic unfolding of proof trees, guided by A*. Information about costs and heuristics are mostly 'hidden' and handled automatically. So the lay–out of L_{TabVer} source code is not confused by cost information. This *cost hiding* is the key idea behind the L_{TabVer} language: it ensures a level of abstraction suitable for programming and avoids being drowned in too many cost details.

Let us now see how an implicit handling of cost information and an automatic computation of correct heuristics for L_{TabVer} knowledge bases are achieved.

4.1 Heuristic Proofs

If one tries to guide proofs by a heuristic search procedure, then of course the search tree is just the *proof* tree, labelled by cost information. In the TabVer case, the nodes of this tree are given by clauses, and the edges are given by resolution of the left–most goal in a clause with a matching rule or fact, or by execution of a 'foreign' plan (e.g. a Prolog predicate). The success criterion applies if a resulting node is the empty clause. Costs are handled additively, i.e. they are attached to the edges of the tree. The cost of a given node ν is computed by summing costs along the path starting at the root node. Hence, the cost of proving some goal is just the sum of all costs of proving the literals in the applied rule. In order to 'anchor' this recursive definition, it is required that both facts and 'external' plans (which are called directly) return a cost argument.

Due to the strictly additive treatment of cost within L_{TabVer}, the intended 'cost hiding' is easily achieved. Literals used in L_{TabVer} rules need not be assigned cost information, as they return costs anyway: the cost of proving them. And due to the fact that the method used for the aggregation of costs is *fixed*, it can be taken care of by the heuristic proof procedure itself and hence does not confuse source code written in the plan language.

An implicit handling of *heuristics* is possible as well. According to the 'admissibility theorem' [10], A* guarantees the best (cheapest) solution to be computed first, provided that for each node ν, the heuristic h(ν) is a lower–bound on the cost of the optimal solution reachable from ν.

In L$_{\mathsf{TabVer}}$, heuristic estimations h only need to be assigned to facts and linked–in Prolog predicates. Based on this 'anchor' of h in the facts and foreign plans, the heuristic can be extended to all complex plans P : $\varphi \leftarrow \pi_1, \ldots, \pi_n$ according to

$$h(P) = \sum_{i=1}^{n} \min \; \{h(Q) \mid \text{the head of plan Q matches } \pi_i \} .$$

Provided that facts and external plans are assigned correct heuristics (in the sense stated above), this recursive definition results in a correct assignment of heuristics to all *complex* plans (rules) as well. Since the admissibility theorem applies, the best solution (according to the cost criterion) is always returned first.

The assignment of heuristics to complex plans is performed at compile time, but can be further improved at run time once specific instantiations of arguments are known, which reduce the number of matching plans in evaluating the above min expressions, and thus improve the heuristic. For each goal γ to be expanded using some plan P : $\varphi \leftarrow \pi_1, \ldots, \pi_n$, the improved heuristic for P, call it h$'$(P), can be determined at linear time according to

$$h'(P) = \sum_{i=1}^{n} \min \; \{h(Q) \mid \text{the head of plan Q matches } \pi_i \, \sigma \} ,$$

where σ is the most general unifier of γ and φ.

4.2 Practical Aspects of L$_{\mathsf{TabVer}}$

Having extended Prolog with this A* control procedure, we can now write complex plans at a very high level. The plan language, L$_{\mathsf{TabVer}}$, supports specification of cost information, heuristics, and planner control commands. Prolog predicates and foreign C functions can be linked into the plan knowledge base as external plans. Programming in L$_{\mathsf{TabVer}}$ is easy since cost–information is mostly hidden (handled automatically) and only needs to be assigned to facts and external plans, not to complex plans.

In *TabVer, shortness of text and readability were taken as selection criteria. Formation of (inclusion) groups from table data, partitioning of the table for increased readability, choice of quantified expressions etc. have all been implemented in L$_{\mathsf{TabVer}}$. Especially the policy of 'cost hiding' and the automatic completion of the heuristic function based on an anchor have contributed very much to the success of this implementation.

Application of A* guarantees a very efficient processing of the verbalization knowledge in TabVer: the planner operates at considerable speed since about half of it has been coded in C. As a result, verbalization of tables, which envolves some hundreds of planning steps, takes only about 2–5 sec. for medium–sized tables.

5 TabVer in Perspective

IBM has presented TabVer to interested local governments as part of EXCEPT. The positive reactions of the civil servants as well as a successful demonstration of TabVer at the German Software Development Lab caused the IBM management to integrate the actual implementation of TabVer into the EXCEPT system. The *expanded* EXCEPT system will be delivered to the customers in the near future.

But what about future enhancements? TabVer is externally connected to EXCEPT through a clear–cut interface, while internally it is strictly divided into dependent and independent modules. Therefore, adapting the system to a new domain requires writing new (or additional) basic plans and templates in order to adapt terminology. In general, this task will be relatively easy, since the changes to be made are local while the data format may be retained.

On the other hand, it seems to us that some extensions of TabVer would be desirable. E.g. to detect wrong or extremely improbable values by means of encoding domain dependent background knowledge. This could prevent alarming system reactions based on arithmetic errors or impossible or highly implausible measurements (e.g. 1500g of Hg dissolved in 1l H_2O). TabVer shall of course not to silently ignore these cases but generate a more precise interactive reaction like context-sensitive help, which takes the user to a correct input specification.

Occasionally, graphical modes of presentation, e.g. statistical properties of time series like mean values, divergences, linear regression and trends could be investigated by some external statistics module and then displayed in diagrams. Again, this is not an attempt to restrict text generation by TabVer but a tribute to human perception: different kinds of facts are often best represented in different formats.

Furthermore, the mechanisms of content selection and group–formation, which we employed in the verbalization task, could support the division of horribly monolithic tables into smaller subtables. Embedded in, say, a small text which explains the overall structure of the presentation, this procedure would show the entire facets of the actual task, each specially emphasized but all together forming the problem. Finally EXCEPT and with it TabVer is challenged by the development of the European Community. Due to the ongoing process of a standardization of laws all over Europe and the example set by some German environmental protection laws, chances are that EXCEPT will be used in other European countries. In this case several language specific versions of TabVer must be provided.

In principle, TabVer can cooperate with applications other than EXCEPT. Besides modifications due to a change in domain, an adaptation of the component, which transforms tables from application data format to TabVer's own representation is the crucial prerequisite in this case.

Verbalization of tables might be of interest in a wide range of applications, such as spreadsheet, planning, and scheduling programs. The tables produced by such programs are often too large to be displayed perspicuously. Because of the often multidimensional outline especially of spreadsheets, verbalization of tables would be a very difficult task in such applications. But the advantages of a system, which is able to identify, analyze and handle the information within the output of such programs should be clear: the benefit could be a massive reduction of informational redundancy and an increasing intelligibility by making explicit critical values that are hidden between the lines. Although there are system enhancements required to enable TabVer to deal with considerably varying input, we regard the actually implemented system as a first step into this direction.

References

1. Hübner, M., von Luck, K., Weiland, U.: *Die Konzeption des EXCEPT–Systems. Ein Überblick*, IWBS–Report 130, 1990.
2. Weiland, U., Hübner, M.:*Das Projekt EXCEPT: Expert–System for Computer–Aided Environmental Planning Tasks*, IWBS–Report 114, 1990.
3. McKeown, K.R.: *Text Generation: Using Discourse Startegies and Focus Constraints to Generate Natural Language Text*, Cambridge University Press, Cambridge, 1985.
4. McDonald, D.D.: *Natural Language Generation as a Computational Problem: An Introduction*, in: Brady, M., Berwick, R.C. (eds.): *Computational Models of Discourse*, 209–265, MIT–Press, Cambridge MA, 1983.
5. Busemann, S.: *Surface Transformations During the Generation of Written German Sentences*, in: McDonald, D. D., Bolc, L. (eds.):*Natural Language Generation Systems*, 98–165, Springer, Berlin, New York, 1988.
6. Hovy, E.: *Generating Natural Language under Pragmatic Constraints*, Lawrence Erlbaum, Hillsdale, NJ, 1988.
7. Appelt, D. E.: *Planning English Sentences*, Cambridge University Press, 1985.
8. Winograd, T.:*Understanding Natural Language*, Academic Press, New York, 1972.
9. McDonald, D. D., Meteer, M. W.:*From Water to Wine: Generating Natural Language Text from Today's Applications Programs*, in: *Proceedings of the second Conference on Applied Natural Language Processing*, 41–48, Austin, Texas, 1988.
10. Hart, R.E., Nilsson, N.J., Raphael, B.:*A formal basis for heuristic determination of minimum cost paths* , in: *IEEE Transactions on System Sciences and Cybernetics (SSC)*, vol.4, no.2, 1968, p.100-107.
11. Thompson, H.: *Strategy and Tactics in Language Production*, in: Beach, W. A. , Fox, S. E., Philosoph, S. (eds.): *Papers from the Thirteenth Regional Meeting of the Chicago Linguistics Society*, Chicago, April 14–16, 1977.

Cooperating to Be Noncooperative:
The Dialog System PRACMA

A. Jameson, B. Kipper, A. Ndiaye, R. Schäfer, J. Simons, T. Weis, and D. Zimmermann

Department of Computer Science, University of Saarbrücken
PO Box 151150, D-66041 Saarbrücken, Federal Republic of Germany
{jameson, kipper, ndiaye, ralph, jsimons, tweis, detlev}@cs.uni-sb.de

Abstract. The modeling of noncooperative dialogs, as opposed to dialogs in which the goals of the participants coincide, presents novel challenges to a pragmatically oriented dialog system. PRACMA models noncooperative sales dialogs. In the role of the potential buyer of a used car, the system tries to arrive at a realistic evaluation of the unknown car in spite of biased information presentation on the part of the seller. In the role of the seller, PRACMA tries to form a usable model of the buyer even while using this model to manipulate the buyer's impressions. To realize this behavior, heterogeneous modules and representation formalisms cooperate within a multi-agent architecture.

1 Introduction

1.1 Issues

Almost all computational modeling of the pragmatic aspects of human dialogs has examined the ideal case of cooperative dialog partners. Typically, the system has taken the role of an information-provider whose sole motivation is to help a human information-seeker achieve the latter's goals. Research on the dialog system PRACMA[1] broadens this perspective by modeling noncooperative information-providing dialogs, in which the participants, though constrained by dialog conventions, pursue conflicting goals. In the specific example domain, the two participants are a person S who is trying to sell her used car and a potential buyer B.[2]

A long-term practical motivation of this research is the observation that the application of information-providing dialog systems will not always be restricted to purely cooperative situations. But the more immediate aim is to yield general insights into the pragmatics of dialog by investigating how several issues, which are in part familiar from research on cooperative dialogs, can be handled in the context of noncooperative motivation. As it is not possible within this paper to discuss all of the questions being

---

This research is being supported by the German Science Foundation (DFG) in its Special Collaborative Research Program on Artificial Intelligence and Knowledge-Based Systems (SFB 314), project N1, PRACMA. Substantial programming support has been provided by A. Fiedler, R. Knop, T. Wagner, A. Werner, and C. Wirtz.

[1] PRocessing Arguments Among Controversially-Minded Actors.

[2] We arbitrarily use feminine pronouns to refer to S and masculine pronouns for B.

investigated, we concentrate here on the following central issues. For concreteness, we formulate them in terms of the example domain introduced above.

1. How can an information-seeker elicit and interpret information from a non-cooperative information-provider and cope with the uncertainty inherent in the dialog situation? (Section 2.) Whereas a cooperative information-provider often offers *more* useful information than the information-seeker explicitly requests, the B in PRACMA's situation requires considerable sophistication to arrive at a well-founded decision in the face of the largely evasive and potentially misleading formulations of S.

2. How can a biased information-provider reconstruct, anticipate, and manipulate the inferences and evaluations of a largely unknown information-seeker? (Section 3.) Even the most sophisticated S is limited by her ignorance about the interests, general knowledge, and specific prior expectations of the specific B that she is dealing with—and B is not in general motivated to help her to solve this problem. So S must exploit her model of B with caution and continually try to improve it on the basis of largely unreliable evidence.

3. What are the benefits and costs of simulating two conflicting dialog roles? PRACMA has been designed to be *transmutable* (cf. [13]), i.e. to be able to simulate either B or S in the example domain. This allows us to investigate the extent to which components that appear to be primarily relevant to one role are also useful when the system assumes the other role. It also raises the issue of how to represent as much knowledge as possible in such a way that it can be used in both roles. One advantage of transmutability is that the system's behavior in each role can be explained and motivated in terms of an explicit model of how the dialog partner in the other role behaves.

4. What type of architecture best supports the necessary pragmatic processing? (Section 4.) A system that addresses the above issues requires an architecture that supports flexible interaction among modules which differ widely in their internal structure and representational techniques. In PRACMA, we evaluate the suitability of a new multi-agent architecture for these purposes.

Each of these issues will be discussed in one of the later sections of the paper, as indicated above (except for the third issue, which is touched on at various points). But first we present an example dialog and give an overview of PRACMA's agents, with special attention to the central task of dialog planning.

1.2 Example Dialog and Overview

Figure 1 shows an example dialog typical of those that PRACMA can conduct in the role of either S or B (cf. Sect. 5). Although the other role is always taken by a human user, we will describe the processing of both S and B as they are simulated by the system. Figure 2 shows the agents of PRACMA and the nature of the communication that takes place between them.

The agent NATURAL LANGUAGE ANALYZER translates German-language input strings into semantic representations in the language $\mathcal{NLL}$ ([7]; cf. 4.2), sending these representations to the PRAGMATIC DIALOG MEMORY, in which descriptions of all utterances of the two dialog partners are stored. The main control over dialog processing is exerted by the DIALOG PLANNER (1.3), which may attempt to execute any of various dialog plans, depending on the current context; the context is determined in part by the simple

B: Hello! How much gas does this car consume?

B begins by asking a question about an aspect of the car that is likely to have a major impact on his evaluation.

S: Hello. It consumes 7 liters per 100 km.

S has now answered B's question; but since she interpreted the question as a sign of interest in environmental-friendliness, she takes the opportunity to volunteer the following additional information, which ought to make a good impression:

S: It has a catalytic converter.

To be sure, this fact has somewhat negative implications for the dimension "sportiness"; but these implications are not known to everyone, and besides S has no evidence that B is especially interested in sportiness.

B: That's too bad.

Explicit reactions like this are usually associated with negative evaluation shifts. So S now suspects that B is in fact interested in sportiness and probably also fairly knowledgeable about aspects of cars relevant to that dimension.

B: What are the chances that the car will pass the next inspection?

B switches to another aspect that is important to his evaluation.

S: It ought to pass the inspection.

S actually judges the car's chances to be only about 55%. She figures that saying this explicitly would have an unfavorable impact on B; but on the other hand, to give a definitely optimistic characterization of the car's chances would be too untruthful. As a compromise, S chooses a vague, positive formulation, with which she expects at least to prevent B's evaluation from becoming much less favorable.

B: Good.

B's evaluation of the car with respect to this aspect has apparently improved, contrary to S's expectation. S explains this mainly by postulating that B's initial impression of the car's chances of passing the inspection was unusually pessimistic.

Fig. 1. *Initial portion of an example dialog with* PRACMA.

agent EGO, which stores information on which role the system is playing and what its motivational parameters are.

Most of the pragmatic-level inferences are performed by the COMMENT AND QUESTION HANDLER and the EVALUATION HANDLER. The former agent is invoked by the DIALOG PLANNER when the system needs to generate or interpret a comment or a question about the car (cf. Sect. 2 and Sect. 3). When PRACMA takes the role of S, this agent needs specific information about the car; it gets this from the DOMAIN BELIEFS (4.2), where S's knowledge about the car is represented with the knowledge representation system MOTEL (see, e.g., [2]). When the system takes the role of B (Sect. 2) the EVALUATION HANDLER is responsible for forming evaluative impressions of the car; when the system takes the role of S, the EVALUATION HANDLER engages in meta-level reasoning about this evaluation process of B. The EVALUATION HANDLER calls upon the EVALUATION EXPRESSION HANDLER to help determine the evaluative implications of natural language formulations (e.g., "That's not bad"). The NATURAL LANGUAGE GENERATOR (currently under development) is responsible for verbalizing the $\mathcal{NLL}$ expressions produced by other agents.

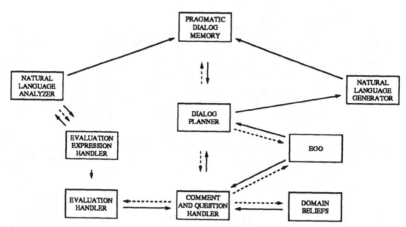

Fig. 2. *Overview of* PRACMA*'s agents. (Dashed arrows correspond to requests for information, solid arrows to the provision of information.)*

1.3 Dialog Planning

The Dialog Planner. As Fig. 2 shows, the DIALOG PLANNER plays a central role, invoking either directly or indirectly the help of other agents and using their replies in the construction and execution of a dialog strategy. The planner is realised in the planning system VIPER[3], a hierarchical (cf. [8]) incremental planner extended with dependency-directed backtracking and a nonlinear plan expansion strategy. Planning structures for open (sub)goals are built up with generic schemes for problem decomposition, called *plan operators*. For each subgoal stated in a plan operator, a separate subplanner is created which tries to achieve that subgoal. The order in which subgoals are pursued is a priori undetermined; it is controlled by heuristics or by explicit constraints (as illustrated in Fig. 3). This nonlinear plan strategy, augmented with declarative constraints on operator selection and subgoals, supports flexible planning strategies. Plan generation is intertwined with plan execution so that the requirements of a dynamic dialog environment can be met. The execution of (sub)plans obeys the linearization dictated by the left-to-right-bottom-up strategy of the generated global plan structure. Backtracking is adapted to this incremental planning strategy in that it takes into account the execution state of subplans.

Dialog strategies. The main dialog strategies implemented so far for S and B result in the sort of sequence illustrated in Fig. 1: B asks a question about some aspect of the car; S answers the question and then perhaps volunteers some comments on related aspects of the car; after each of S's utterances, B may express an evaluation verbally. With a view to expanding PRACMA's repertoire of dialog strategies, various knowledge elicitation techniques are now being applied with professional car salespersons. Initial results show, for example, that such an S not only presents facts about the car but also emphasizes the positive *consequences* of these facts with respect to B's evaluation standards—in some cases, even when it seems likely that B is already aware of these

---

[3] Verteilter Inkrementeller PlanER ("distributed incremental planner"), see [14].

```
(define-viper-operator
:NAME ANSWER-QUESTIONS-AND-TRY-TO-VOLUNTEER-COMMENTS
:POSTCONDITIONS    (...)
:APPLICABILITY-CONDITIONS                                  ; For this operator to be usable, there has to be a
   ((PDM (:find-recent (:func is-from-partner-and-class question  ; question from the dialog partner in the
              (whole topic-of-question)) (?ask ?topic) 1)))       ; Pragmatic Dialog Memory.

:SUBGOALS
  (...
   (CQH (:answer-question ?ask ?answer) :after :linear)    ; This is a request to the Comment and Question Hand-
                                                           ; ler to answer the question from the dialog partner.
   (NLG-PDM (verbalise ?answer) :after :linear)            ; Here the answer is sent to the Natural Language
                                                           ; Generator and to the Pragmatic Dialog Memory.
   (ABS (volunteer-comments ?topic ?remarks ?buyer ?seller) ; This abstract goal triggers operators that will
        :after :linear)                                    ; try to volunteer some extra comments, if the
                                                           ; Comment and Question Handler can supply some.
   (ABS (advertise ?handling-of-topic-next ?buyer ?seller) ; This abstract goal calls plan operators which try to
        :after :linear)                                    ; answer another question from the dialog partner.
   ... )
:ABSTRACT-TRIGGERS                                         ; This slot contains the trigger which has to match for
   ((advertise ?handling-of-topic ?buyer ?seller))         ; this operator to be taken into consideration.
:SELECTION-HEURISTICS                                      ; This slot states that this operator should be tried
   ((:before STOP-ADVERTISING)))                           ; before the operator named STOP-ADVERTISING.
```

Fig. 3. *An example of a dialog plan operator.*

consequences. Also, S often engages in diagnostic question-asking, to determine B's interests and knowledge and (especially toward the end of the dialog) to find out what reservations B has about the specific car in question.

To illustrate the main principles realized in PRACMA to date, the system's processing in the roles of B and S, respectively, will now be discussed in the context of the central dialog strategy mentioned above.

2   PRACMA as Buyer: Evaluation Under Uncertainty

2.1   Representation of Beliefs and Evaluations

B starts the dialog with little definite information about the car. He has mainly uncertain *impressions* based on the information in the advertisement and on general knowledge about cars. Furthermore, since S is not especially motivated to make B's impressions as definite as possible (but rather to invoke favorable evaluations), S often makes vague comments that serve only to replace one indefinite impression with another slightly different one.

Accordingly, when PRACMA takes the role of B it represents B's beliefs and evaluations probabilistically in the form of a Bayesian belief network (see, e.g., [10]), which will be referred to as B's *evaluation network* (cf. Fig. 4).

Beliefs about the car. Each *factual node* in this network includes a probability distribution representing some *aspect* of the car. For example, the node INSPECTION CHANCES in Fig. 4 might store the fact that B is a priori quite uncertain, and rather pessimistic, about the car's chances of passing the next inspection.[4]

---
[4] For aspects (like this one) that involve an infinite number of possible states, a finite set of *possibilities* is distinguished (cf. [4] and [9]).

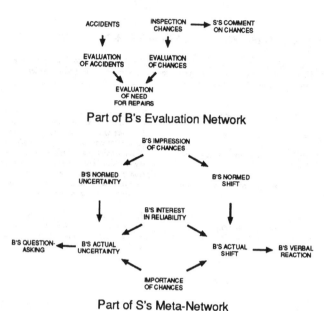

Part of B's Evaluation Network

Part of S's Meta-Network

Fig. 4. *Parts of the Bayesian networks used by B and S.*

Evaluations. The model of how B evaluates the car is based on the metaphor of an *evaluation form* (cf. [3]). For each aspect, if B knew exactly which possibility was realized, B would assign to the car some number of points for that aspect (cf. the first two columns in Fig. 5).[5] He could then add up the points assigned so as to arrive at an overall evaluation, or an evaluation of some more general aspect such as *need for repairs*. Since B in fact usually has only an impression of most aspects, he likewise has only impressions of the evaluation to be assigned to most aspects. These latter impressions are represented by *evaluation nodes* in his network. An evaluation node corresponding to a specific aspect (e.g., EVALUATION OF CHANCES) is a *child* of the corresponding factual node, i.e., the evaluation is treated as dependent on the factual belief. A node representing a more global evaluation (e.g., EVALUATION OF NEED FOR REPAIRS) is a child of several more specific evaluation nodes.

2.2 Role of the Evaluation Network in the Dialog

Selection of questions. B's principal motivation is to reduce the uncertainty in his evaluation nodes to the point where he can confidently make a decision as to whether to buy the car. He can only do this by eliciting information from S, mainly by asking questions. To determine which questions are likely to yield the most valuable information, B compares the evaluation nodes with respect to the amount of *uncertainty*

---

[5] Many aspects of a car are relevant to two or more *evaluation dimensions*, e.g., for the existence of a catalytic converter, "Environmental Friendliness" and "Sportiness" (cf. Fig. 1 and [4]). To simplify exposition, we consider here only an example where a single evaluation dimension, "Reliability", is involved.

Chances of passing inspection	Evaluation according to	
	B's actual evaluation form	S's normed evaluation form
95%	+1.4	+2.5
85%	+0.9	+2.0
75%	+0.6	+1.5
65%	+0.4	+1.0
55%	+0.2	+0.5
45%	−0.2	−0.5
35%	−0.4	−1.0
25%	−0.6	−1.5
15%	−0.9	−2.0
05%	−1.4	−2.5

Fig. 5. *Actual and normed evaluation forms used by B and S, respectively.*

they exhibit (operationalized as the standard deviation of the probability distribution). For example, the fact that EVALUATION OF CHANCES has a broad distribution is responsible for B's decision in Fig. 1 to ask about the inspection chances.

Interpretation of comments. When a comment by S specifies unambiguously which of the possibilities for a given aspect is realized (e.g., "The chances are 55%"), it is straightforward for B to update the belief for the corresponding factual node, assigning a probability of 1.0 to the realized possibility. This change propagates from parent to child in the network, affecting some of the evaluation nodes. But for interpreting vague comments, B needs a more general method: For each comment by S concerning a factual node, a *dummy node* (cf. [10], p. 170) is linked to that factual node in B's network—as the factual node's child, because the comment can be viewed as having been probabilistically "caused" by the truth about the corresponding aspect of the car. The conditional probabilities linking the comment node to the factual node are determined by the meaning of the comment. The meaning can be represented by a *membership function* in the sense of fuzzy set theory. For German-language adverbs and modal verbs expressing judgments of the chances of a given event, we obtained experimental data on the membership functions of German speakers (see [6]). For example, for the modal verb *dürfte* (*ought to*, as in "The car ought to pass the inspection"), the average membership curve is monotonically increasing and sigmoid, with a steep rise at 50%. These membership values are not probabilities, but within a given pragmatic context they can serve as the basis for probability assessments (cf. [6]). One reasonable assumption is that, all other things being equal, the higher the membership value of a possibility for a given comment, the greater the likelihood that S will make that comment. B applies this assumption when interpreting S's comment in our example dialog.[6] The resulting child-to-parent propagation in B's network causes the more positive possibilities in INSPECTION CHANCES to be judged more probable. In turn, by parent-to-child propagation,

---

[6] A more sophisticated approach to comment interpretation, which takes into account the alternative comments that S might have made but did not, was introduced in the system IMP (see [3]) and is presently being adapted for use within PRACMA. This approach also involves an assessment by B of aspects of S's dialog motivation, such as bias.

the evaluative impression in EVALUATION OF CHANCES is shifted upward.

Generation of reactions to comments. This sort of shift in an evaluation impression is often reflected in an overt verbal reaction, as shown by an unpublished empirical study conducted in the PRACMA context (cf. [4]). When simulating B, PRACMA selects such verbal reactions in a fashion consistent with the results of that study.

3 PRACMA as Seller: Forming and Exploiting Meta-Level Impressions

S's main task is to reconstruct, anticipate and manipulate the processing by B described in the previous section. When deciding what to say, her goal is not to reduce the uncertainty in B's evaluation nodes (as a cooperative speaker would do), but rather to shift the evaluation impressions upward. To do this effectively, S must try to derive a reasonably accurate model of B's network, making use of any clues in B's behavior that reflect properties of that network. It might at first be thought that S could use a model of B's network that was isomorphic to it. But in fact, to deal adequately with all of S's uncertainty about various aspects of B's network, a more complex type of model is required, which we call a *meta-network* (cf. the lower half of Fig. 4).

The first complication arises when S tries to take into account the various initial impressions that B might have in each of his factual nodes. In INSPECTION CHANCES, for example, B might have any of a potentially infinite number of impressions; S can in general only have an impression of B's impression. In the meta-network, a node like B'S IMPRESSION OF CHANCES distinguishes 16 classes of possible impressions, which differ in terms of both their expected value and their uncertainty. In our example, the meta-level impression in B'S IMPRESSION OF CHANCES represents the belief that it is most probable that B will expect the car's inspection chances to be around 75% and that B will have only a moderate amount of uncertainty about this. The type of initial impression that is in fact initially present in B's network in our example—centered around 35% with a high degree of uncertainty—is considered by S to be a priori unlikely.

S's second complication arises when she tries to predict the content of B's evaluation nodes: S of course doesn't know exactly what the content of B's evaluation form is, mainly because S doesn't know how much interest B has in the evaluation dimension "Reliability". A solution is to (a) use a *normed evaluation form* that is presumably typical of a B with a *moderate* level of interest in this dimension (cf. the right-hand column in Fig. 5), and (b) take into account separately (as described below) the possibility that B's interest might be quite different, or that the numbers in the form might be systematically inaccurate even for B's who do have a moderate level of interest.

For each of the factual impressions that B might have in INSPECTION CHANCES, S can use the normed evaluation form to determine the corresponding evaluation impression, and in particular to assess the uncertainty in B's evaluation. In this way, the normed evaluation form constitutes the basis for the conditional probabilities that link B'S IMPRESSION OF CHANCES to its child node B'S NORMED UNCERTAINTY, which represents the uncertainty in B's node EVALUATION OF CHANCES under the assumption that B has a moderate level of interest in "Reliability".

In a similar way, whenever S considers making a particular comment, she can predict what sort of evaluation shift it might evoke in B: For each of the possible impressions that B might have, S simulates the process of comment interpretation that was described above for B, using the normed evaluation form, and calculates the extent to which B's relevant evaluation node would shift upward or downward. The results are summarized in S's node B'S NORMED SHIFT.

The remaining nodes in S's meta-network will be explained in terms of how S uses the meta-network to interpret B's behavior and to select comments.

Interpretation of B's question-asking. B'S ACTUAL UNCERTAINTY can be predicted as a multiplicative function of B'S NORMED UNCERTAINTY, B'S INTEREST IN RELIABILITY and IMPORTANCE OF CHANCES. In turn, B'S ACTUAL UNCERTAINTY influences the assessment of B'S QUESTION-ASKING, a two-valued variable representing whether B asks or does not ask a question about the car's chances of passing the inspection. The utility of defining these nodes can be seen in the case where B does ask such a question, as in Fig. 1: By child-to-parent propagation, S gets the impression that B's has more evaluative uncertainty about the inspection chances than S originally thought. Further child-to-parent propagation represents an attempt by S to "explain" this unexpected shift in terms of one or more underlying variables: Perhaps B is especially interested in the dimension "Reliability" (B'S INTEREST IN RELIABILITY), perhaps the aspect "chances of passing the inspection" is especially important (IMPORTANCE OF CHANCES), or perhaps B's a priori impression of this car's chances is different from what S thought—in particular, B may have a much less definite impression than S would have expected (B'S IMPRESSION OF CHANCES). These adjustments in S's meta-network will influence S's further inferences and decisions with respect to this particular B (and in the case of IMPORTANCE OF CHANCES, with respect to future potential buyers as well).

Judging the desirability of a comment. Prediction of the evaluative shift that a given comment would evoke in B is important when S is considering whether to make that comment, either as an answer to a direct question or as a piece of unsolicited information. Analogously to the case with B'S ACTUAL UNCERTAINTY, for example, B'S ACTUAL SHIFT can be predicted as a multiplicative function of B'S NORMED SHIFT, B'S INTEREST IN RELIABILITY, and IMPORTANCE OF CHANCES. Although producing positive evaluation shifts is S's primary goal, her judgment of the desirability of a given comment also takes into account general dialog conventions. In particular, there is some danger in using a comment whose truthfulness is questionable, e.g. "The car will definitely pass the inspection", for which the actually realized possibility of 55% chances would have only approximately .3 as a membership value. S therefore assigns to each comment a *penalty* that is a positive function of the extent to which the relevant membership value is lower than 1.0. The result of this policy is that S avoids outrightly lying, but she is willing to apply a vague expression in a marginally acceptable way (e.g., *ought to* for chances of 55%) if she can thereby evoke a more favorable impression.

Interpreting B's verbal reactions to comments. As noted in Sect. 2, B's verbal reaction to a comment by S can be viewed as a probabilistic function of the shift in B's relevant evaluation node. This probabilistic relationship (derived from the empirical study mentioned above) links B'S ACTUAL SHIFT to the node B'S VERBAL REACTION. So any observed reaction by B constitutes an observation whose effects are subject to child-to-parent propagation and ultimately affect the same nodes that can be affected by the asking of a question. In our present example, the explicitly positive reaction by B is unexpected: All S really expected to achieve with her vague comment was to prevent B from being disappointed. The fact that B's evaluation apparently does change for the better is hard to explain in terms of a high level of B'S INTEREST IN RELIABILITY or IMPORTANCE OF CHANCES; more likely is that B's initial impression was more pessimistic than S originally expected (B'S IMPRESSION OF CHANCES).

4 A Cooperative Architecture

4.1 Overall Multi-Agent Architecture

Processing such as that described in the previous sections requires flexible communication among the system modules, because it is largely unpredictable when particular types of information will be required or become available. To this end, the architecture CHANNELS[7] was developed, integrating techniques from distributed artificial intelligence and the concurrent object-oriented paradigm.

The modules within the system are realized as (semi-)autonomous specialized problem solvers, called *agents*, which interact cooperatively. In CHANNELS, communication and interaction among the agents are achieved through a *communication-act-based protocol* which governs the exchange of messages. Each message is characterized by attributes including: the sender, the recipient(s), the type of communication act, the mode of communication (*synchronous* or *asynchronous*), the actual content of the message, and optionally the history of the message and the agents to whom the answer to the message's query should be forwarded. The communication acts supported at present are *ask*, *reply*, and *inform*. An *ask* message requests the recipient(s) to send back information in a *reply* to the originator of the message, while an *inform* message sends unsolicited information.

With the three basic communication acts and the two modes of communication, we attain some of the flexibility of concurrent object-oriented languages, e.g., ABCL (see [15]). Approaches similar to that of CHANNELS can be found in CARAMEL (see [11]) and TALISMAN (see [12]). They differ with respect to the nature of the communication supported and the mechanism for controlling the interaction among the agents (cf. [9]).

4.2 Interlocking of Heterogeneous Architectures

CHANNELS supports agents with complex internal structures which may be quite different from that of the overall multi-agent architecture. In this way, one can exploit the advantages of alternative languages and architectures for specific purposes, or make use of modules that were developed previously in another context. This interlocking approach is illustrated by the following two examples.

A blackboard for natural language analysis. The agent NATURAL LANGUAGE ANALYZER itself comprises six heterogeneous and relatively independent modules. Direct communication among these modules according to the principles embodied in CHANNELS would be problematic in that a module in this set does not always know which

---

[7] Cooperating Heterogeneous Agents for a Natural-Language System, see [9].

other modules can give it the information it needs or which modules can make use of the results it generates (cf. [5]). In accordance with the criteria proposed, e.g., in [1], a blackboard architecture was chosen for the internal structure of the agent NATURAL LANGUAGE ANALYZER. The following modules have been realized as knowledge sources which use the blackboard (cf. [5]): An HPSG-based chart parser; a module that constructs semantic representations in $\mathcal{NLL}$ (cf. 4.2) on the basis of the parser's output; a rudimentary speech act recognizer; an anaphora resolution module that handles personal pronouns; a component for the disambiguation of modal verbs; and an external communicator that writes input strings onto the blackboard and sends results to other PRACMA agents.

A modal logic representation for domain beliefs. A further example of heterogeneous representation concerns the system's beliefs about (the dialog partner's beliefs about) cars in general and the specific car being discussed. Although these beliefs are in part implicitly reflected in the Bayesian (meta-)networks described in Sect. 2 and Sect. 3, there is also a need for an explicit, declarative representation—for example, to enable PRACMA, when modeling S, to determine the truth value of possible comments. These beliefs are therefore represented within the agent DOMAIN BELIEFS in MOTEL, a multi-agent logic-based knowledge representation system (see, e.g., [2]). MOTEL's belief contexts enable the system to reason using its own specific and general domain beliefs, the corresponding beliefs which it ascribes (tentatively) to the dialog partner, and generally shared conceptual knowledge. Messages to DOMAIN BELIEFS are formulated using the logical semantic representation language $\mathcal{NLL}$ (see, e.g., [7]) which serves as the output language of the NATURAL LANGUAGE ANALYZER and the input language of the NATURAL LANGUAGE GENERATOR. To process *ask* and *inform* messages coded using $\mathcal{NLL}$, the agent DOMAIN BELIEFS has an $\mathcal{NLL}$-query-answerer and a corresponding updating procedure.

5   Further Research

A PRACMA prototype now exists which can simulate a dialog similar to the one in Fig. 1, taking the role of either S or B. Some of the more recently developed parts of the system have been tested and demonstrated in separate modules and are at the time of this writing being integrated into the main prototype.

Some of the further issues being investigated have been mentioned in passing above, e.g., the expansion of S's repertoire of dialog strategies and the problem of how B can assess and take into account S's dialog motivation. The work done so far on these extensions suggests that the basic mechanisms described in this paper have sufficient generality to accommodate them. For example, when modeling B, the system can form impressions of the motivational parameters of S using the same probabilistic techniques currently used by S to assess B's interests and knowledgeability.

More generally, the ideas introduced here should be of some use, on an abstract or concrete level, for modeling or analyzing information-providing dialogs where at least one of the participants forms impressions of general dispositions and internal states of the other participant, and/or where the goals of the participants partly conflict.

References

1. Cawsey, A., Galliers, J. R., Reece, S., & Sparck Jones, K. (1992). A comparison of architectures for autonomous multi-agent communication. *Proceedings of the Tenth ECAI*, Vienna, 249–251.

2. Hustadt, U., & Nonnengart, A. (1993). Modalities in knowledge representation. *Proceedings of the Sixth Australian Joint Conference on Artificial Intelligence*, Sydney, 249–254.

3. Jameson, A. (1989). But what will the listener think? Belief ascription and image maintenance in dialog. In A. Kobsa & W. Wahlster (Eds.), *User models in dialog systems* (pp. 255–312). Berlin: Springer.

4. Jameson, A., & Schäfer, R. (1993). Probabilistische Einschätzung von Wissen und Interessen. Die Anwendung der intuitiven Psychometrik im Dialogsystem PRACMA. *Arbeitspapiere des Workshops Adaptivität und Benutzermodellierung in interaktiven Softwaresystemen*, 100–117. Report 30/93, Project BGP-MS, Dept. of Information Science, University of Konstanz, Germany.

5. Kipper, B. (1994). A blackboard architecture for natural language analysis. *Proceedings of the Seventh Florida AI Research Symposium*, Pensacola Beach, FL.

6. Kipper, B., & Jameson, A. (1994). Semantics and pragmatics of vague probability expressions. *Proceedings of the Sixteenth Annual Conference of the Cognitive Science Society*, Atlanta.

7. Laubsch, J., & Nerbonne, J. (1991). *An overview of NCL*. Technical report, Hewlett Packard Laboratories, Palo Alto, CA.

8. Moore, J. D., & Paris, C. L. (1989). Planning text for advisory dialogues. *Proceedings of the Twenty-Seventh Annual Meeting of the ACL*, Vancouver, 203–211.

9. Ndiaye, A., & Jameson, A. (1994). Supporting flexibility and transmutability: Multi-agent processing and role-switching in a pragmatically oriented dialog system. *Proceedings of the Sixth International Conference on Artificial Intelligence: Methodology, Systems, Applications*, Sofia, Bulgaria.

10. Pearl, J. (1991). *Probabilistic reasoning in intelligent systems: Networks of plausible inference*. San Mateo, CA: Morgan Kaufmann. (Revised second printing).

11. Sabah, G., & Briffault, X. (1993). CARAMEL: A step towards reflection in natural language understanding systems. *Proceedings of the Fifth IEEE International Conference on Tools with AI*, Boston.

12. Stefanini, M.-H., Berrendonner, A., Lallich, G., & Oquendo, F. (1992). TALISMAN: Un système multi-agents gouverné par des lois linguistiques pour le traitement de la langue naturelle. *Proceedings of the Fourteenth COLING*, Nantes.

13. Wahlster, W., & Kobsa, A. (1989). User models in dialog systems. In A. Kobsa & W. Wahlster (Eds.), *User models in dialog systems* (pp. 4–34). Berlin: Springer.

14. Weis, T. (1994). *VIPER: Ein verteilter inkrementeller Dialogplaner für eine Multi-Agenten-Umgebung*. Master's thesis, Dept. of Computer Science, University of Saarbrücken.

15. A. Yonezawa (Ed.) (1990). *ABCL: An object-oriented concurrent system*. Cambridge, MA: MIT Press.

Robust Constructive Induction

Bernhard Pfahringer

Austrian Research Institute for Artificial Intelligence *
Schottengasse 3, A-1010 Vienna, Austria
E-mail: bernhard@ai.univie.ac.at

Abstract. We describe how CiPF 2.0, a propositional constructive learner, can cope with both noise and representation mismatch in training examples simultaneously. CiPF 2.0 abilities stem from coupling the robust selective learner C4.5 with a sophisticated constructive induction component. An important new constructive operator incorporated into CiPF 2.0 is the *simplified Kramer operator* abstracting combinations of two attributes into a single new boolean attribute. The so-called *Minimum Description Length* (MDL) principle acts as a powerful control heuristic guiding search in the representation space through the abundance of opportunities for constructively adding new attributes. Claims are confirmed empirically by experiments in two artificial domains.

1 Introduction

When learning concept descriptions from preclassified examples, simple concept learners typically make strong assumptions about the way these examples are represented. For effectively learning a concept its examples must populate one or a few regions of the hypothesis space expressible in the description language. For example, decision trees encode axis-parallel nested hyper-rectangles. Two different problems may cause irregular distributions of learning examples in the original representation space: *noise* and/or an *inadequate description language*.

As a remedy for the latter problem constructive induction has been introduced, e.g. in [4]. The basic idea is to somehow transform the original representation space into a space where the learning examples exhibit (more) regularities. Usually this is done by introducing new attributes and forgetting old ones. So constructive induction is searching for an adequate representation language for the learning task at hand.

Just like when learning from noisy examples, constructive induction must be controlled properly. Otherwise its application may yield too complex, convoluted induced concept descriptions which may be hard to understand and may perform poorly at predicting concept membership of unclassified examples. This phenomenon can be called *overfitting the representation language* in analogy to

* Financial support for the Austrian Research Institute for Artificial Intelligence is provided by the Austrian Federal Ministry of Science and Research. I would like to thank Gerhard Widmer for constructive discussion and help with this paper, and Johannes Fürnkranz for providing the king-rook-king position generator.

fitting the noise. The presence of both noise and an inadequate language obviously increases the possibilities for *overfitting* even further.

In [10] we reported on our constructive learner CIPF and its relative success in noise-free domains due to rigid control applying the *Minimum Description Length* principle. This paper will concentrate on how the improvements found in the newest version CIPF 2.0 allow for *robust constructive induction* handling both noise and inadequate language. The main improvements over CIPF 1.0 are incorporating as the basic induction module a well-known sophisticated decision tree learner, namely C4.5 [12]; and including a new general operator for constructive induction, a simplified, more efficient version of the operator described in [7].

Section 2 briefly describes the architecture of CIPF 2.0. In section 3 we will focus on how the problem of controlling search for useful changes of representation is solved in CIPF 2.0 by means of the powerful *Minimum Description Length (MDL) Principle* [13]. Section 4 describes the simplified *Kramer* operator. Experiments in two artificial domains - the *Monk's Problems* [14] and illegal king-rook-king chess positions [5] - are summarized in section 5. Section 6 draws conclusions, relates to various other approaches of constructive induction and talks about further research directions we are pursuing within CIPF.

2 Design Rationales and CIPF's Architecture

This section will briefly discuss some important design rationales of CIPF. Then we will describe CIPF's architecture.

The main goal in building CIPF is designing a practical system for constructive induction that minimizes the number of user-settable parameters. So we try to identify principled choices or automated ways of choosing good values for necessary decisions where other systems rely on user-specified parameter values. This was one reason for choosing the *Minimum Description Length Principle* as an evaluator. This will be described in more detail in the next section.

CIPF borrows heavily from existing systems in that we have tried to collect useful features of known machine learning systems. We try to combine these in a synergetic fashion in CIPF. Most implemented constructive induction systems can be described in terms of three different modules working together: a CI module, a selective learner, and an evaluator. These three main components of CIPF will be detailed in the following.

2.1 Constructive Induction in CIPF (the CI Module)

Just like the multi-strategy system AQ17-MCI [2], CIPF takes an operator-based approach to constructive induction. It supplies a (still growing) list of generally useful CI operators plus an interface allowing for user-supplied special operators. For instance, these operators might encode possibly relevant background knowledge. We have currently implemented the following generally useful CI operators in CIPF 2.0:

- Compare attributes of the same type: is attribute **A1** *Equal to/Different from* attribute **A2**.
- Conjoin possible values of nominal attributes occuring in good rules into a subset of *useful* values for the respective attribute.
- Conjoin two attributes occuring in a good rule [8]. We use the simplified *Kramer* operator for this task as will be described in Section 4.
- For the set of positive examples covered by a good rule: compute subsets for the respective base-level attributes, so that these subsets exactly cover these positive examples.
- Drop attributes not used by any of the good rules. [2]

Recursive application of these operators may yield complex new attributes.

2.2 CiPF's Selective Learner

CiPF 1.0 used a simple propositional FOIL-like learner [11], i.e. an original implementation of a simplified FOIL dealing with propositional horn clauses only. We preferred direct induction of rules over induction of decision trees mostly for two important reasons:

- Unknown values can be dealt with pragmatically: never incorporate tests for *unknown* in a rule.
- Induction focuses on one class at a time. At least in relational learning this approach seems to be superior to decision trees [15] and we suspect that the same might be true for propositional learning.

Due to pitfalls regarding CiPF 1.0's disabilities handling noise CiPF 2.0 now incorporates C4.5 [12] as its selective learner, a sophisticated decision tree algorithm well able to deal with noise. Fortunately C4.5 also includes a rule-generator transforming decision trees into sets of production rules. These rules are then processed and analyzed by CiPF 2.0's module for constructive induction. We use default settings for C4.5 in all experiments, so CiPF's selective learner essentially still is a parameter-less module, thus fulfilling one of our design criteria. Regarding the above-mentioned preference for production rules, reason a) is still true when using the output of C4.5RULES and reason b) is achieved by artificially turning an N-class learning task into N 2-class learning tasks.

3 Using MDL to Control Constructive Induction (the Evaluator Module)

CiPF takes a rather eager approach to constructive induction: at every step all possible new attributes are added. This over-abundance in the representa-

---

[2] One might argue whether *dropping an attribute* really is a *constructive induction* operator or not. Anyway it being a very useful operator we have chosen to include it in the above list. Furthermore the terminology used in [2] defines the *set of constructive induction operators* as the union of *constructors* and *destructors*.

tion space may quickly results in unwieldy, overly complex induced rule sets or attributes when learning without appropriate control. Such rule sets can be difficult to comprehend for the user and may yield mediocre results when classifying unseen examples. In analogy to *noise fitting* [1] this phenomenon can be called *language fitting*. Typical examples of such behaviour are published in the section on AQ17-HCI in the *Monk report* [14], which describes three artificial learning problems for evaluating and comparing different algorithms. We have made similar experiences with early versions of CIPF lacking sophisticated control.

To prevent CIPF from *language* or *noise fitting* we have devised the following simple, yet effective control regime:

- Every time the CI module is called, it is allowed to construct a (possibly large) number of new attributes.
- These attributes will be input to the next learning step. There they will *compete* with each other for being used in induced rules.
- Only the *fittest* attributes will be allowed to survive.

So how are the *fittest* attributes determined in CIPF? We pragmatically equate these with the set of attributes being used by *good* rules. Right now *good* rules is pragmatically defined as just the rule-set returned by C4.5RULES as C4.5's rule generator does a good job of generalizing/pruning both single rules and complete rule-sets constructed out a decision tree. So one basic step in CIPF consists of the following actions:

- Express the training examples in terms of the currently active attributes, not distinguishing between base-level or constructed attributes).
- Call C4.5 on this training set, and call C4.5RULES to generate production rules out of the decision tree.
- Analyze the set of production rules to a) determine surviving *old* attributes and b) constructing new attributes via some CI-operator.

How does overall control work, how many such basic steps are taken? CIPF at the moment just iterates as long as new attributes are introduced. It keeps track of dropped attributes and never introduces an attribute twice, so this criterion leads to termination in between a few and a few dozen cycles, depending on both the amount of noise and the mismatch of the representation language.

Now we can answer the question of which rule set will be chosen as the final result of induction. Instead of using some ad-hoc measures of accuracy and quality or some user-supplied evaluation functions we have identified the so-called *Minimum Description Length Principle* [13] as a very well-performing evaluator when it comes to choosing the one *best* rule-set from all the induced rule-sets.

In a nutshell, MDL is a concept from information theory that takes into account both a theory's simplicity and a theory's predictive accuracy simultaneously. Concept membership of each training example is to be communicated from a sender to a receiver. Both know all examples and all attributes used to describe the examples. Now what is being transmitted is a theory (set of rules) describing the concept and, if necessary, explicitly all positive examples not covered by the theory (the false-negative examples) and all negative examples erroneously covered by the theory (the false-positive examples). Now the cost of a transmission is equivalent to the number of bits needed to encode a theory plus its exceptions in a sensible scheme. The MDL Principle states that the best theory derivable from the training data will be the one requiring the minimum number of bits.

So for any set of rules generated by the selective learner a *cost* can be computed. The rule-set with minimum cost is supposed to be (and in the experiments reported below most often really is) the best theory for the training data. The precise formula used to apply the MDL Principle in CiPF is the same one as used by C4.5 [12] for simplifying rule sets:

$$Cost = TheoryCost + log_2 \left(\binom{C}{FP} \right) + log_2 \left(\binom{NC}{FN} \right)$$

In this formula `TheoryCost` is an estimate for the number of bits needed to encode the theory. `C` is the total number of training examples covered by the theory, `FP` is the number of false-positive examples, `NC` is the total number of training examples not covered by the theory, and `FN` is the number of false-negative examples. So the second and the third term of the formula estimate the number of bits needed to encode all false-positive and all false-negative examples respectively. In summary this formula approximates the total cost in number of bits for transmitting a theory and its exceptions. As in C4.5 the actual implementation uses a weighted sum of both the theory and the exception cost. These weights have been hard-wired into CiPF after some initial experiments and are set to one and three for theory and exceptions respectively.

It is of course necessary to also assess and include cost for constructed attributes into the total cost of theories. Otherwise CiPF would successively create more and more complex attributes probably only stopping at a theory of exactly two rules testing a single boolean attribute: if true we conclude class A, if false we conclude class B. This way the complexity would solely be shifted from the rules into the structure of the attributes (and would be hidden there at zero cost).

To prevent this from happening, CiPF assesses cost of constructed attributes by estimating the cost of encoding such constructions (expressed in numbers of bits). For example a subset test (attribute A's value is one of the following values) needs to encode the kind of attribute (subset test), the underlying attribute being involved (A), the set of values (possibly as a bitmask for the total set of possible values for attribute A), and an additional bit to represent whether we test for truth or falsity Thus using a *constructed* attribute entails a kind of penalty or cost, which can be amortized either if this attribute offers superior compression or if it is used in more than one rule.

Empirically, this simple strategy produces good results, as indicated by the experiments reported in section 5 and it is effectively computable. Also, to repeat its two main advantages, the strategy includes no user-settable parameters, and it also does not require a secondary training set (*train-test set*) to evaluate the quality of constructed attributes, like e.g. AQ17-MCI does.

4 The Simplified Kramer Operator

In [7] a new, general constructive induction operator is introduced, which essentially abstracts the extensional product of the set of possible values of two given attributes to a new boolean attribute. For example two attributes A1 with possible values a or b and A2 with possible values 1, 2, or 3 could be abstracted to C(A1,A2) as:

```
C(A1,A2) = t iff A1 = a and A2 is 1 or 2
C(A1,A2) = f iff A1 = b and A2 is 3
```

When applied to two boolean attributes, the result can of course be any binary boolean function (including e.g. xor or nand). We take care of immediately rejecting trivial constructions like tautologies or projections.

CIPF 2.0 introduces the following simplifications. In [7] a heuristic chooses a few good rules and from these rules a few pairs of co-occuring attributes are taken as input for a involved A*-search for the best split according to another heuristic estimating split values. On the contrary, CIPF uses all pairs of co-occuring attributes, estimates for each such pair its info-gain on the original training set, and introduces the single (non-trivial) abstraction with the highest info-gain. Info-gain and binarization for abstraction are computed greedily as follows:

- For each pair of values of the two attributes determine the number of positive and negative examples covered by these two tests.
- Sort all pairs according to the ratio of positive versus all examples covered.
- Compute info-gain for all split-points in this sorted list of pairs.
- Finally choose the split yielding the maximal info-gain.

So this operator can also be partially described as compiling limited look-ahead information for decision tree induction into new attributes. Our simplifications allow for efficient implementation with tightly limited search (linear in the number of pairs of values), but still seems to yield useful abstractions. This operator can also be seen as a generalization of the technique described in [3] for computing optimal binary splits for *single* attributes: we handle combinations of two attributes. The usefulness of this operator is also evident in the results of the experiments reported on below.

5 Experiments

In the following experiments, CIPF 2.0's performance was usually averaged over ten runs randomly choosing the appropriate number of training examples and randomly reversing the class attribute (from *yes* to *no* or vice versa) for N% of the these examples, when the noise level was set to N. We always report testing accuracy of the initially induced rule-set (which is of course identical to the result of just calling C4.5 followed by C4.5RULES) and the accuracy of the *best* set according to the MDL-heuristic used. Typically this *best* accuracy as selected by the MDL principle is also the absolute best value of any of the induced rule-sets. Occasionally though, for combinations of higher noise levels with a low percentage of examples selected for training CiPF 2.0 failes to choose the best possible candidate rule-set. Nonetheless the final result is most often better than the initial result, and for the rare cases where it is not, differences are marginal, e.g. an accuracy of 80% instead of 82%.

5.1 Monk's Problems

The *Monk's problems* [14] are three artificially constructed problems in a space formed by six nominal attributes having from two to four possible values. There is a total of 432 different possible examples. The three problems are abbreviated to Monk1, Monk2, and Monk3 in the following. CiPF 2.0 results for the Monk's problems very encouraging. The original Monk's Problems' definition explicitly specifies a training set for each of the three problems and measures accuracy on the total set of possible examples. From table 1 we see that CiPF 2.0 solves all three problems satisfactorily.

Monk1 was solved without problems. CiPF finds the correct theory:

```
true <= (jacket_color = red)
true <= (head_shape = body_shape)
```

This is no surprise as this example is simple and CiPF has the necessary constructive operator *compare attributes of the same type* at its disposal. Furthermore, regarding solely accuracy, even the initial rule-set is a 100% accurate; but when (implicitly) rewritten by constructive induction to the above given concept definition, it is much more concise and therefore it correctly gets assigned a lower MDL estimate.

Performance on Monk2 shows how effective constructive induction can be. Starting from an accuracy of only 67.1% CiPF 2.0 manages to induce an almost correct concept definition giving an accuracy of 95.6%. This success can be attributed to the addition of the simplified *Kramer* operator as described in section 4. This general constructive operator is (after repeated application in 11 cycles of induction and construction) able to compute a very good approximation of the correct theory.

Results for Monk3 are quite good, shoowing that CiPF 2.0 has overcome its initial problems regarding noise. This is of course the result of incorporating such a robust induction algorithm like C4.5 into CiPF. Actually C4.5 alone is able to solve this problem to full 100% accuracy when called with the -s flag to force subsetting of nominal attributes. But this flag is not set as a default because it can cause large computational overheads and it is speculated, that a more focussed way of introducing subsets of possible values might be more useful. At least for Monk3 CiPF 2.0 seems to prove this speculation, as its constructive operators allow for the introduction of the right subsets necessary to improve accuracy from the intial 96.3% to the final 100%.

Additionally we would like to mention that some other learning systems also exhibit very good performance on the original *Monk's problems*, e.g. AQ17-HCI achieves 100%, 93.1%, and 100% on Monk1, Monk2, and Monk3 respectively, [3] and a specialized form of Backpropagation yields 100%, 100%, and 97.2% respectively.

Table 1. Monk's Problems: accuracies (percentages) for CiPF after the first and after the best cycle of induction.

	CiPF first	CiPF best
Monk1	100.0	100.0
Monk2	67.1	95.6
Monk3	96.3	100.0

As there are fixed, prespecified training and test sets for the Monk's problems, there is of course always the danger lurking that one tunes one's system to good performance on these sets. To prevent us from this pitfall and to a larger degree to study *CiPF 2.0*'s abilities regarding noise and inadequate representations simultaneously, we designed the following series of experiments.

For Monk1 we randomly chose 30, 40, 50, or 60% of all examples for training, chose a noise level of 0, 5, 10, 15, 20, or 25% respectively and for every combination did ten test-runs of CiPF to average results. These averages are given in table 2.

Interpreting table 2 we can notice a few interesting facts regarding Monk1: certainly results get more flakey when both noise is high and the number of training examples is small. Still in the worst case of 25% noise and only 30% percent training examples CiPF 2.0 still on average achieves an accuracy of 81.5%. Furthermore, on average the final result is never worse than the initial accuracy, and if both values are equal, then these values are also high. C4.5 alone proves to be quite a robust learner given medium or smaller levels of noise and adequate numbers of examples: the initial runs for these cases always yield accuracies around $(100 - Noise/2)\%$ or better. Still in almost all cases constructive induction significantly improves the final result.

For Monk2 we deliberatly left columns for 30 and 40% training set size empty, because results looked more or less like for the 50% experiments: final accuracies are rarely significantly better than the average initial 65%. For constructive

---

[3] AQ17-HCI has at its disposal a very special Cl operator which perfectly fits the Monk2 problem, thus explaining its impressive performance on this problem.

Table 2. Monk's Problems: accuracies (percentages) for CIPF 2.0 after the first and after the best cycle of induction for various levels of noise and various sizes of the training set for Monk1, Monk2, and Monk3.

TrainEx%	Noise%	Monk1		Monk2		Monk3	
		first	best	first	best	first	best
30	0	99.1	100.0			99.9	100.0
	5	97.4	100.0			98.7	99.1
	10	93.7	99.4			97.0	98.4
	15	87.4	96.6			93.8	93.4
	20	80.4	89.2			90.0	90.4
	25	77.8	81.5			84.3	85.7
40	0	99.4	100.0			100.0	100.0
	5	98.8	99.9			99.4	100.0
	10	97.8	99.4			97.0	98.3
	15	92.7	97.7			95.5	98.3
	20	89.5	97.9			89.0	95.4
	25	78.9	88.9			84.4	91.9
50	0	100.0	100.0	68.2	79.8	100.0	100.0
	5	99.7	100.0	66.5	87.1	99.3	99.8
	10	96.9	99.7	67.8	84.8	97.3	99.8
	15	92.9	99.0	63.7	64.1	95.1	98.0
	20	88.0	96.3	63.2	63.4	93.3	97.8
	25	83.8	95.8	60.2	60.9	87.7	94.1
60	0	100.0	100.0	64.5	97.3	100.0	100.0
	5	99.8	99.8	66.1	83.6	99.6	99.9
	10	96.7	99.6	63.7	81.7	97.6	99.2
	15	93.1	98.8	64.1	65.2	95.9	99.1
	20	91.1	97.9	63.6	63.6	90.5	97.5
	25	85.2	99.0	60.7	65.4	87.3	94.7

induction to reliably push overall accuracy to levels above 90% we need both an adequate number of training examples and a moderate noise level. This is due to the rather complicated target concept definition: it is a kind of an xor including *all* base-level attributes testing if exactly two of these six attributes have as their respective value the first possible value given in their domains. But given sufficient information CIPF 2.0 is able to achieve impressive improvements. Other approaches seem to achieve such improvements only by incorporating specialized CI operators fitting well this special kind of target concept.

For Monk3 we can more or less repeat the facts found for Monk1, with overall final accuracies being even better: with the exception of the 25% noise and 30% training examples case every final accuracy is above 90%.

This test series empirically proves the utility of constructive induction even when "only" dealing with noise. Constructive induction seems to shift the representation language towards appropriate, more concise definitions allowing the learner to distinguish more easily between variety and noise.

5.2 Illegal King-Rook-King Chess Positions

This domain is a very valuable testbed for experiments involving various amounts of noise and varying sizes of training sets. As such it has been used intensivly in inductive logic programming. There are a few hundred thousand different possible examples. [5] is a theoretical study including various approximate theories and showing a test-set size of 5000 to be sufficient for estimating accurracies of induced theories.

KRK is very easily represented for CiPF. The original example tupels of the relation `illegal/6` have six arguments encoding rank and file of all three pieces. Background knowledge in the original formulation consists of definitions for `=/2`, `less_than/2` and `adjacent/2`. Taking into regard predicate modes, symmetries, and the fact that in CiPF with a boolean attribute both a test and its negation can be represented, every original `illegal/6` example was transformed into a tuple of 18 boolean attributes encoding all possible body literals.

Induced theories (with no noise present) usually resemble the approximate theories given in [5]. A sample theory derived by CiPF from 100 training examples looks as follows:

```
[1] illegal <= (BLACK-KING-FILE = WHITE-ROOK-FILE)
[2] illegal <= (BLACK-KING-RANK = WHITE-ROOK-RANK)
[3] illegal <= (adjacent BLACK-KING-FILE WHITE-KING-FILE) and
               (adjacent BLACK-KING-RANK WHITE-KING-RANK)
[4] illegal <= (adjacent BLACK-KING-FILE WHITE-KING-FILE) and
               (BLACK-KING-RANK = WHITE-KING-RANK)
```

This approximate theory was tested with 5000 test examples yielding an accuracy of 98.4%. This is consistent with [5] which proves a theory consisting of the first three clauses 1,2,3 to be 98.451% correct.

To get a better picture of the relationship between class noise, training set size, and testing accuracy, we ran experiments using training sets of 100, 250, and 500 examples, choosing noise levels of 0, 10 and 20% each and randomly iterating five times for each pair of settings. Averaged accuracies are given in table 3.

Using only 100 training examples at a noise level of 10%, CiPF 2.0 significantly outperforms all approaches compared in [6]. When using 250 training examples, it performs slightly worse than the best approach (incremental reduced error pruning - IREP) cited in [6]. For 500 training example CiPF 2.0 in turn outperforms IREP by an even smaller margin: 98.48% vs. 98.9%. These small differences for training set sizes of 250 or 500 examples may not be statistically significant, though.

On the overall the expected effect - larger absolute error - can be found when dealing with small example sets at higher noise levels. The absolute differences are rather small, though. Generally, for this domain the selective learner on its

Table 3. Illegal KRK: accuracies (percentages) for CiPF 2.0 after the first and after the best cycle of induction for various levels of noise and various sizes of the training set in the King-Rook-King domain.

Noise%	100 Ex		250 Ex		500 Ex	
	first	best	first	best	first	best
0	98.6	98.6	98.5	98.6	99.1	99.3
10	95.0	95.7	97.1	97.5	98.5	98.9
20	92.4	93.2	96.2	96.5	97.2	97.8

own produces almost perfect theories. Therefore constructive induction is only occasionally able to improve the scores marginally. But in every test-run the initially induced theory was rewritten into a concise and easily comprehensible form like exemplified by the above given sample rule-set.

6 Conclusions, Related Work, and Further Research

We have shown empirically, that interfacing a robust selective learner to strong constructive operators under a rigid control schema can result in a robust constructive induction system being able to deal with both noise and inadequate representation language simultanously. Incorporating the MDL Principle into CiPF as the single, uniform heuristic for evaluating theories and thereby implicitly guiding constructive induction proved valuable. The MDL Principle combines both accuracy and complexity of a theory into a single uniform measure. Thus CiPF does not require any ad-hoc measurements or user-defined evaluation functions of possibly questionable quality and can nonetheless use *all* of the available training data for induction. Other approaches (e.g. AQ17-MCI) have to resort to splitting the training data into two or more sub-parts performing some sort of cross-validation on these sub-parts. Such an approach may be more expensive computationally and may miss regularities in the data for reasons intrinsic to this approach. Still, on a systems level, CiPF certainly is most closely related to and influenced by the multi-strategy system AQ17-MCI. The main differences are the underlying inductive learner and the way control is imposed on constructive induction. CiPF eagerly uses every opportunity for constructive induction applying the MDL principle to choose the best result. AQ17-MCI takes a different approach: relying on a set of meta-rules, it tries to identify the need (*when*) and the directions (*how*) for a change in the representation space.

The problem of *language fitting* is also mentioned and discussed in [9] in the context of the CITRE system. Their approach uses additional background knowledge to construct new attributes. Though these ideas do not currently fit directly into CiPF's schema for constructive induction, they might still point to valuable further improvements possible for CiPF.

Our further research directions for CiPF 2.0 include adding again support for numerical attributes (as was already present in CiPF 1.0), application to especially medical databases, and the definition of constructive operators dealing with structured objects.

References

1. Angluin D., Laird P.: Learning from Noisy Examples, Machine Learning, 2(4), 343-370, 1987.
2. Bloedorn E., Wnek J., Michalski R.S.: Multistrategy Constructive Induction: AQ17-MCI, in Michalski R.S. and Tecuci G.(eds.), Proceedings of the Second International Workshop on Multistrategy Learning (MSL-93), Harpers Ferry, W.VA., pp.188-206, 1993.
3. Breiman L., Friedman J.H., Olshen R.A., Stone C.J.: Classification and Regression Trees, Wadsworth International Group, Belmont, CA, The Wadsworth Statistics/Probability Series, 1984.
4. Dietterich T.G., Michalski R.S.: Inductive Learning of Structural Descriptions: Evaluation Criteria and Comparative Review of Selected Methods, Artificial Intelligence, 16(3), 257-294, 1981.
5. Fürnkranz J.: A numerical analysis of the KRK domain. Working Note, 1993. Available upon request.
6. Fürnkranz J., Widmer G.: Incremental Reduced Error Pruning. Proceedings of the Eleventh International Conference on Machine Learning (ML-94), New Brunswick, N.J., 1994.
7. Kramer S.: CN2-MCI: Ein zweistufiges Verfahren für konstruktive Induktion, Master's thesis in preparation, Vienna, 1993.
8. Matheus C.J., Rendell L.A.: Constructive Induction On Decision Trees, in Proceedings of the Eleventh International Joint Conference on Artificial Intelligence (IJCAI-89), Morgan Kaufmann, Los Altos, CA, 645-650, 1989.
9. Matheus C.J.: Adding Domain Knowledge to SBL Through Feature Construction, in Proceedings of the Eighth National Conference on Artificial Intelligence (AAAI -90), AAAI Press/MIT Press, Menlo Park, CA, pp.803-808, 1990.
10. Pfahringer B.: Controlling Constructive Induction in CiPF: An MDL Approach, in Proceedings of the European Conference on Machine Learning (ECML94), 1994.
11. Quinlan J.R., Cameron-Jones R.M.: FOIL: A Midterm Report, in Brazdil P.B.(ed.), Machine Learning: ECML-93, Springer, Berlin, pp.3-20, 1993.
12. Quinlan J.R.: C4.5: Programs for Machine Learning, Morgan Kaufmann, San Mateo, CA, 1993.
13. Rissanen J.: Modeling by Shortest Data Description, in Automatica, 14:465-471, 1978.
14. Thrun S.B., et.al.: The MONK's Problems: A Performance Comparison of Different Learning Algorithms, CMU Tech Report, CMU-CS-91-197, 1991.
15. Watanabe L., Rendell L.: Learning Structural Decision Trees from Examples, in Proceedings of the 12th International Conference on Artificial Intelligence, Morgan Kaufmann, San Mateo, CA, pp.770-776, 1991.

Enriching a Semantic Network Language by Integrating Qualitative Reasoning Techniques

T. Fuhr, F. Kummert, G. Sagerer*

Technische Fakultät, Angewandte Informatik
Universität Bielefeld, Postfach 100131, 33501 Bielefeld, Germany
e-mail: fuhr@techfak.uni-bielefeld.de

Abstract. To interpret sensor signals like images, image sequences, or continuous speech the representation and use of task-specific knowledge is necessary. The paper scetches a framework for the representation and utilization of declarative and procedural knowledge using a suitable definition of a semantic network. To meet the needs of machine-human interaction we extend this framework in two ways. A temporal model similar to Bruce is incorporated and representational structures are integrated to formulate qualitative (relational) knowledge. The problem-independent inference rules are extended to allow for the temporal prediction and the dynamic refinement of this knowledge. Our integration of relational knowledge exemplarily shows how semantic network representations can benefit from developments in qualitative reasoning research.

1 Introduction

The KL-ONE-like semantic network language ERNEST [14, 18] has been especially designed for the purpose of knowledge–based signal understanding and has proven successfully in different larger scale applications in the area of image and speech understanding. Because of this quality, this semantic network language shall now also be used to model the domain–specific knowledge needed by a knowledge–based system that communicates with a human user via continuous speech and disposes of a camera input. However, this extended task domain introduces a new issue: the communication with a human user makes it essential to allow for the use of qualitative terms in this communication.

A lot of expertise on the modeling and utilization of qualitative knowledge has been evolved from qualitative reasoning (QR) research. Beside the research in qualitative temporal [3, 1, 8] and spatial reasoning [10, 11, 4] a lot of progress has been achieved in the field of qualitative physics and qualitative simulation [19, 4]. Also, QR research addressed issues regarding the interaction of numerical data and qualitative models [12, 7, 5].

In this paper, we present an extension of the semantic network language ERNEST that fulfills the above mentioned needs and is designed in awareness of the approaches developed in QR research. Our extension allows the formulation of qualitative knowledge in the semantic network model in a way, that firstly, supports the construction of qualitative interpretations from numerical input sensor

* This work has been supported by the German Research Foundation (DFG) in the project SFB 360.

data on the basis of this model. Secondly, it allows to use qualitative expectations (e.g. some spatial position of an object qualitatively described in a sentence uttered by the human user) to infer focused expectations on the numerical input (e.g. excluding parts of an image frame, where this object need not be searched).

We furthermore outline how a notion of time can be settled into the formalism, that accounts for both, the sampledness of the analyzed data and the necessity to formulate complex temporal relations between concepts. Temporal prediction is introduced as a new inference rule.

In the next section, the paper describes a subset of the ERNEST language. In section 3 we present the new representational structures to represent qualitative knowledge together with the adapted inference rules. Section 4 outlines our integration of an explicit notion of time into the network. A small example is explained in section 5 that illuminates one aspect of our extension of ERNEST by especially focusing on the interaction of qualitative and numerical data. Finally, we give some conclusions and an outlook on further work.

2 The Semantic Network Language

ERNEST is a semantic network language that has been designed to meet the specific needs of pattern interpretation and understanding tasks. In this section we describe only that subset of its representational vocabulary that is essential to understand the rest of this paper. Beside other details, we particularly omit how specialization hierarchies can be formulated, in which way inheritance is bound to this hierarchy and how knowledge can be organized in different levels of abstractions w.r.t. the signal level. The reader will find descriptions of the complete ERNEST language in [16, 18, 14].

As usual in semantic networks, **concept** nodes are the central representational entities to model notions of the task domain. In ERNEST a **concept** is an intensional description of some notion and can be specified by establishing **links** to other concepts as well as by annotating it with **attributes** and **relations**. Finally, the definition of a concept must be completed by defining a **judgment function** that allows to estimate the correspondence of some area of the sensor signal to the notion represented by the concept. This correspondence cannot simply be characterized as being true or false due to the different certainty, quality, and reliability of the input sensor data. The judgment calculus underlying the judgment functions can be determined by the modeler. A concept can be specified as the composition of other concepts by establishing **part** links to other concepts (e.g. Car $\xrightarrow{part}$ Wheel). **Attributes** (e.g. color, size) can be used to represent features characterizing the notion modeled by the concept. For every attribute A of a concept C a function f for the **computation of values** (of A) must be defined. Attributes of C and attributes of its parts may be used as parameters of f. Also a function for the **inverse computation of values** (w.r.t. f) can be bound to A. This allows to express in which way attributes of a concept can restrict the attributes of its parts. The possibility to bind procedural knowledge to attributes allows the modeler to integrate domain-specific algorithms (e.g. for signal filtering, segmentation) appropriate for handling the kind of the domain-specific

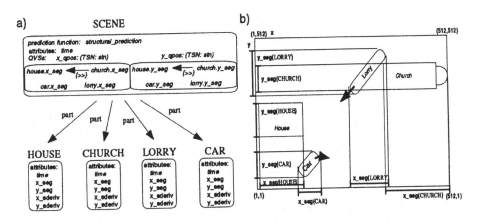

Fig. 1 Simple semantic network model of some image scene

sensor data. Finally, a **judgment function** for an attribute may be specified. However, a concept is usually not definable as simply *any* combination of its parts and also not *any* combination of values of the concept's attributes will correctly characterize it. Hence, a concept may be annotated by **relations** (e.g. "height < length") to constrain such combinations. A relation is defined by a **judgment function** that can take attributes of the concept and its parts as parameters. That relations are being *judged* rather than being *tested* on being true or false is a concequence of the fact that attributes and parts are judged. Again, an inverse function (**inverse judgment of relation**) can also be supplied to model the restrictions imposed on attributes of parts due to the semantics of the relation.

Fig. 1-a) shows a very small ERNEST network to model simple scenes that contain a church, a house and the two moving objects car and lorry (Fig. 1-b)). All objects are attributed by bounding rectangles, given as the two projection segments w.r.t. to the x and y axis (x_seg, y_seg). Furthermore, their velocity is qualitatively described through the signs of the derivatives of the segments' bounds (x_sderiv, y_sderiv). All network entries printed in italics, belong to the extended network language and will be explained later.

To allow the utilization of the modeled knowledge the ERNEST system embodies a set of problem–independent inference rules. The basic idea behind these rules is, that the interpretation of some signal area is established by connecting it to some notion (i.e. concept) in the knowledge base. Such connections are represented by **instance** nodes. An instance describes an extension of the corresponding concept. The concept's parts are replaced by instances of parts, concrete **values** are given for all its attributes, and also judgments for attributes, relations and the instance itself. The latter judgment expresses the certainty (and/or validity, quality etc.) of the assumption that the corresponding signal area is correctly interpreted by the related concept. In an intermediate state of the analysis it may occur that for some concepts instances cannot be computed due to missing parts. Nevertheless, the available partial information can be used to constrain an uninstantiated concept, i.e. derive restrictions for its attributes. The third node type **modified concept** allows to represent constrained but uninstantiated con-

---

IF   for a concept A or a modified concept $M_j(A)$ instances exist for all parts

THEN create instances $I_k(A)$ as follows:

- create for $I_k(A)$ an empty instance,
- connect $I_k(A)$ with those instances referred to by the premise,
- activate the attached functions for $I_k(A)$ in the sequence: judgment of links, computation of attributes, *computation of QVSs, extraction of QVSs from members, qualitative propagation on QVSs, member-centered propagation for each attribute of A which is a member of a QVS of A*, judgment of attributes, judgment of relations, judgment of the concept A

Fig. 2 Rule for the creation of instances

cepts. In modified concepts only **restrictions** (i.e. sets of values that are still admissible) are given for attributes, and only some parts (given as instances or modified concepts) may be bound.

The rule for **the creation of instances** (see Fig. 2) shows how instances are constructed by the ERNEST system. It reflects the idea that the recognition of some complex object in the data needs the detection of all its parts as a prerequisite. It can also be seen that due to this rule concepts with no parts can be directly instantiated on the basis of the sensor data, and that increasingly complex concepts can be constructed in a data–driven fashion. Furthermore, a rule for the **data-driven modification of concepts** is defined that looks very similar to the instantiation rule. The important difference is that not all parts must be bound to a given concept (or modified concept) and only restrictions may be given for attributes. So, this rule formulates a data–driven propagation based on *partial information*. Contrarily to instances, a **model-driven modification of concepts** is also possible (see Fig. 3). Here the inverse functions come into play. The ERNEST system includes a problem–independent algorithm that controls the activation of the inference rules to construct interpretations for the input data. Due to the noise inherent in sensor data several competing interpretations may be inferred for identical signal areas. Hence, the most adequate interpretation must be searched for. The control algorithm manages this in an A*-based fashion. For details see [16, 14].

The successful application in different task–domains indicates the quality of the ERNEST language. The applications cover the detection of a roboter hand in complex scenes [13], the diagnostic interpretation of image sequences of the heart [17], and the understanding of spoken language in a speaker–independent dialog system [18]. The obtained results show that the network language and the problem-independent control algorithm are able to handle totally different applications in an efficient manner.

3   Incorporating Qualitative Knowledge

The incorporation of qualitative knowledge must account for its *dynamic* nature. Spatial relations between objects in a frame t are usually not (totally) known in advance and hence, cannot be modeled by static relations. The spatial structure

IF   for a concept A or a modified concept $M_j(A)$ a new instance $I(B)$ or a new modified concept $M(B)$ exists and there is a link $B \overset{part}{\rightharpoonup} A$

THEN create new modified concepts $M_k(A)$ as follows:

- create for $M_k(A)$ a new empty modified concept,
- connect $M_k(A)$ to all instances and modified concepts referred to by $M_j(A)$,
- activate for $M_k(A)$ the attached functions of A and B in the following sequence:
  - inverse computation of attributes of B, which have an attribute of A as an argument,
  - *inverse computation of QVSs of B, which have an QVS of A as an argument,*
  - *member–centered propagation for each attribute of A which is a member of a QVS of B*
  - inverse judgment of relations of B, which have an attribute of A as an argument,
  - inverse judgment of links of B, which have A as the goal node,
  - functions of A like for the creation of instances

Fig. 3 Rule for the **model–driven modification of concepts**

of the objects in frame t may be different from their relations in frame $t+1$ and might even constrain the latter. Furthermore, some spatial description extracted from an utterance could constrain the image positions (pixel areas) for the mentioned objects. Consequently, relational knowledge should be extractable from numerical or other lower level data (data-driven usage). Additionally, it should be able to constrain lower-level numerical and qualitative data (model-driven usage), and also should be usable to derive temporal expectations (predictive usage). However, in the ERNEST system only *static* expectations on attributes can be modeled via the **relation** entry in concepts. Those relations may constrain attribute values (model-driven usage) but their fulfillment can only be judged (data-driven usage). Hence, an extension of the ERNEST system is necessary.

3.1 New Representational Structures

To formulate dynamic qualitative knowledge we introduce **base relation sets** (BRSs) and **temporally structured neighborhoods** (TSNs) as representational entities that have network-wide validity. Their content can be used to specify the **qualitative value spaces** (QVSs) that can additionally be formulated in each concept.

Base relation sets. The user can define sets of binary base relations for any type of attributes he uses in the semantic network. So e.g. point relations may be introduced, Cohn's 2D relations ([4]), etc. A **base relation** r is described by two procedures. The first procedure tests for the fulfillment of the relation using the restrictions/values of two attributes. In this way the relations can be numerically defined. The second procedure propagates the restriction/value of one attribute to another according to r. Finally, for each set of base relations a procedure implementing its composition table must be given. Fig. 4-a shows the base relation set **segmentrels**. The relations are adaptations of Allen's relations to

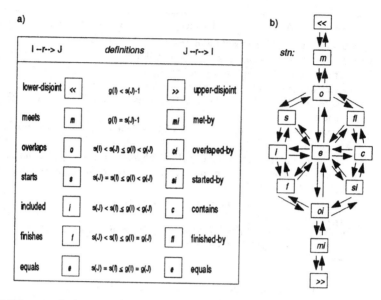

Fig. 4 Binary relations on 1D spatial segments and their TSN

one-dimensional (spatial) segments. A *segment* I is a chain of consecutive discrete points with smallest point $s(I)$ and greatest point $g(I)$. In our case, the points correspond to pixel positions w.r.t. a single image axis, and consecutive points have difference 1. The corresponding composition function implements Allen's transitivity table.

Temporally structured neighborhoods. On sets of relations often continuity structures, called *neighborhoods* (Freksa) can be imposed ([8, 11, 4]), that reflect and depend on the possible valid transformations on the related attributes. Furthermore, neighborhoods support the qualitative prediction of relations ([4, 9]). We incorporated a special version of neighborhoods into the semantic network, called **temporally structured neighborhood**. They enable a qualitative temporal characterization of changes analogous to Forbus' *equality change law*. Consequently, a temporally more precise qualitative prediction is achievable when simultaneous changes may happen (see [9]). Fig. 4-b shows the TSN stn we imposed on segmentrels. Its structure reflects that projections of image regions scale *and* translate at simultaneously. Furthermore, due to the discreteness of segments all transitions between relations must be regarded as being of non-zero duration (solid arcs).

Qualitative value spaces. In each concept an arbitrary number of relational networks, called **qualitative value spaces**, can be formulated. A QVS q of a concept C has an entry referencing a single TSN. QVS nodes, called *members*, are identified with attributes of C or of its parts. Arcs may be labeled by disjunctions of base relations of the referenced TSN. If any relation of the base relation set may hold between two members, no arc is established. A QVSs **restriction** or **value** is given by some refined version of its relational network. Finally, two user procedures may be associated with a QVS q. The **QVS computation function** can take QVSs of C or QVSs of C's parts to compute a refined restriction or a value of q. The **inverse computation function of a QVS** supports the refinement of QVSs of C's parts. Both functions directly counterpart the functions bound to attributes and allow e.g. the incorporation of transformations like Metric-to-Allen and Allen-to-Metric [12].

Fig. 6-a shows the QVSs represented in the concept SCENE. In the extended ERNEST version. They express the a priori known spatial relation between the stable landmark objects Church and House in a Guesgen-like fashion [10]. They also express that a Car and a Lorry with unknown qualitative position are expected in the scene. Restrictions and values of these QVSs that were computed during an example analysis process can be seen in Fig. 6-b,c,d,e (see section 5).

3.2 Adapted Inference Rules

Three general system procedures are implemented and incorporated into the semantic networks' inference rules (see Figs. 2, 3). Our extensions of the rules are printed in italics: **computation** and **inverse computation of QVSs** (see section 3.1), **extraction of a QVS** from its members, **qualitative propagation** on QVSs, and **member-centered propagation**. In this way, the utilization of the dynamic qualitative knowledge within QVSs is ensured. This is also demonstrated in our small example in section 5.

Extraction of a QVS. This routine applies the test routines bound to base relations in the following way to refine QVSs. For each pair of members **a** and b of some QVS q determine the base relations that may hold between them by testing for all base relations of the corresponding BRS. Intersect this set with the current label between a and b to yield the new label. In this way QVSs can be computed bottom-up from (numerical) attribute data and numerical data can be checked for accordance with QVSs.

Qualitative propagation. This is a slightly modified Allen-like propagation ([1]) algorithm that works on QVSs: the initial queue contains *all* QVS arcs that were changed during the last extraction process. So, the extraction phase is clearly seperated from the propagation. This system routine uses the composition functions bound to base relation sets. The qualitative propagation is always activated directly after the extraction phase (see Fig. 2). So data-driven extracted QVSs can be refined, due to the semantics of the underlying BRS.

Member-centered propagation. The refined qualitative constraints in a QVS can be used to further restrict attribute restrictions of the modified concept or instance or to propagate numerical restrictions top-down to parts. The new restriction for a member attribute A is calculated simply, by intersecting all numerical restrictions propagated along each arc leading to A with the actual restriction for A. The restriction obtained along an arc is given by the union of the restrictions returned by the propagation procedures bound to the base relations labeling this arc (see description of BRSs). This kind of propagation is a simplified numerical propagation [15] in the sense that information is transfered to a member from its direct QVS neighbors only and resulting changes are not further propagated to other members. Although being computationally less expensive, this propagation doesn't yield the most restrictive result for the regarded member. However, most often the less refined attribute restrictions already allow to sufficiently focus expectations on lower level concepts.

4 Introducing Time into the Semantic Network

We decided to introduce a model of time similar to Bruce [3] since in opposite to [1, 8] it accounts for both, the sampledness of the data and the need to formulate complex temporal relationships. Bruce regards time as a set of time-points. Gapless chains of linearly ordered time-points are called **time-segments**. Binary relations, similar to Allen [1], are defined on time-segments that allow the formulation of qualitative temporal knowledge. Consequently, we annotate each concept with an attribute time that can take a time-segment as value. As a standard semantics we incorporate computation and inverse computation functions for time that ensure, that each concept's time value expresses which subsequence of the signal data it interpretes. The attributes time can be treated by the modeler like any other attribute. So, qualitative relations between time-segments can be introduced and used like other qualitative knowledge according to section 3.

An adequate tool for the analysis of image/utterance sequences needs the capability to express expectations on future frames due to the (intermediate) analysis results of the previous images/utterances. This expectations have a highly dynamic character and do not only affect attribute values, but might also affect the bindings between modified concepts that interpret subsequent data. For this purpose we introduce a new inference rule that allows for inferring expectations along the time axis: **rule for the creation of corresponding modified concepts** (see Fig. 5). This rule is not directly executed by the problem–independent control algorithm [14]. It rather must be activated by a user prediction function. These user functions may be bound to concepts via the newly introduced optional slot **prediction function**. In contrast to the attribute and QVS functions (see section 3), they can use information of the whole subgraph underneath the concept they belong to. This together with the optionality of the prediction function entry in concepts allows for the implementation of centralized temporal predictions: only one high-level concept (e.g. SCENE) embodies a prediction function, whenever it is instantiated for some time-segment $[t, t]$, this function uses the full scene description (i.e. including all instantiated subconcepts) to derive expectations for the scene in the next frame. On the other hand, there might just as well concept specific prediction functions be defined in each concept. In this way, a decentralized local temporal prediction can be formulated.

The modeler is offered a **qualitative prediction** routine as a tool to support him in realizing temporal prediction functions. Given a set of QVSs and qualitative derivative values for their members the algorithm determines new arc labels for each given QVS on the basis of their TSNs, assuming that all changes occur simultaneously. The new label sets express which relations are principally admissible between the connected members in any temporally directly subsequent qualitative state. If the *simplest action assumption* ([6]) can be applied to the signal data the new labels express the qualitative expectations on the data of the subsequent sample point (for further details see [9]). The prediction algorithm is

```
IF      for a concept A an instance $I_j(A)$ or a modified concept $M_j(A)$ exists
THEN create new modified concepts $M_k(A)$ as follows:
          • create for $M_k(A)$ a new empty modified concept,
          • insert restrictions for all attributes and all QVSs due to the prediction func-
            tion of A,
          • connect $M_k(A)$ to instances and modified concepts selected by the prediction
            function,
          • connect $M_k(A)$ to $I_j(A)$ or $M_j(A)$, respectively, via the correspondence link,
          • activate the attached functions for $M_k(A)$ like in the rule for the creation of
            instances (see Fig. 2)
```

Fig. 5 Rule for **creation of corresponding modified concepts**

offered to the user as a tool he may use to implement user prediction functions (see previous section). We are well aware, that Forbus' assumption will often not be fulfilled by image sequence data. Furthermore, in contrast to [5] we are not able to compute a total envisionment of the observed system prior to the analysis to be able to fill observation gaps during the analysis. The possible behavior of the scene objects captured in images are usually to manyfold. Hence, what is needed is an adapted qualitative prediction algorithm that also predicts the relations of non-directly successive states that could match the next image frame. So far, we have no solution for this.

In connection with this new inference the new link type **correspondence** between modified concepts and/or instances is introduced. It expresses that the connected modifications or instances refer to the ontologically same object in the world, although they interpret it with respect to different time-segments.

5   A Small Example

The example analysis process we scetch in this section is based on the very simple semantic network model of some image scene shown in Fig. 1-a) (including the parts printed in italics) and no real image data was used. However, it is sufficient to describe, how the interaction between numerical attribute data and qualitative knowledge works due to our adapted inference rules.

We omit to regard any competing modified concepts or instances, hence we can ignore judgment computation. To visualize the effects of the inference rules we depict the bounding boxes that characterize the modified concepts and instances that are currently computed for the objects. Since the concept SCENE contains QVSs only but no attribute or relation entries, the application of the modification rules as well as the instantiation of the concept SCENE merely consist of the activation of the newly introduced functions (cf. section 3.2). So, their effect can purely be demonstrated. Our example analysis starts at a point where the content of the image frame (scetched in Fig. 1-b)) taken at time point t is fully interpreted by the construction of $I_1(SCENE)$. The bounding boxes in Fig. 6-a) capture the objects' positions and the QVSs x_qpos and y_qpos exactly represent their spatial relations seperately for the x and y axis (cf. [10]). The little

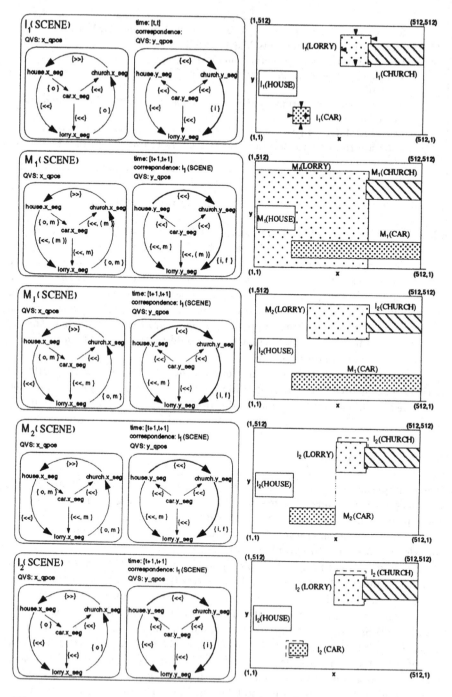

Fig. 6 The SCENE concept and some analysis states

arrows at the rectangle for CAR and LORRY represent their qualitative velocity. By activating the prediction function structural_prediction of SCENE concept-local predictions w.r.t. time point $t + 1$ are computed for each instance of time segment$[t, t]$. The new QVSs in Fig. 6-b) including the meets relations in round brackets result from applying our qualitative prediction algorithm to the QVSs of $I_1(SCENE)$ (Forbus' simplest action assumption is assumed to hold.). The subsequent qualitative propagation eliminates these meets. The restrictions for the objects at time-point $t+1$ are computed using the qualitative velocity information only. Church and house are regarded as immovable. It should also be noted that the prediction rule connects the modified concept $M_1(SCENE)$ with $I_1(SCENE)$. Next, a model-driven modification of LORRY takes place yielding the refined box of $M_2(LORRY)$ in Fig. 6-c). This box is computed by the member–centered propagation function. Subsequently, LORRY is instantiated directly from the data (its old position is illustrated by the dashed box), SCENE, is modified data-driven (the QVSs don't change), and CAR is modified model-driven. The result of these three steps shows Fig. 6-d). CAR's bounding rectangle is substantially refined. After activating the instantiation of CAR all prerequisites are given to instantiate SCENE to $I_2(SCENE)$. As part of the instantiation rule the QVS extraction function restricts all arc labels to a single relation. Fig. 6-e) shows the resulting interpretation for the frame at time segment $[t + 1, t + 1]$.

This example shows that our extension of the network formalism allows to

- focus the search space for instances by allowing to convert qualitative knowledge top-down to numerical expectations (this is an important aspect also, when a human user verbally describes the position of some object to be identified by the image analysis system),
- extract qualitive knowledge from the numerical sensor data, and
- derive qualitative expectations on temporally successive sensor data.

We further want to point out, that this example is not a claim for a Guesgen-like ([10]) representation for modeling spatial properties of complex scenes. This representation was only chosen in this paper, because it is easy to understand without much explanation.

6 Conclusion and Outlook

We scetched the semantic network language ERNEST that has already proven its quality for the knowledge–based understanding of sensor data, like images and speech. The incorporation of a notion of time is described. Furthermore, representational structures are introduced to model qualitative (relational) knowledge. The problem–independent inference rules of ERNEST are extended to allow for the dynamic refinement of this knowledge and its interaction with numerical data. We believe that our extension is a further example of a beneficial integration of qualitative reasoning into another reasoning framework, namely a semantic network language. With our extension arbitrary domain-specific relations between concepts can be modeled in a systematic way without violating the demands e.g. put forward in [2]: they have a well-defined domain-specific semantics and can be utilized by domain-independent algorithms.

In our future work we will focus on the integration of judgments for QVSs and their labeling relations. This is necessary since relations that have continuous domains in the world have to be modeled on the basis of sampled input data. Also an adaptation of our prediction algorithm is of great interest, that is based on restrictions less strong than Forbus' *simplest action assumption* .

Literatur

1. J. F. Allen. Maintaining knowledge about temporal intervals. *CACM*, 26(11):832–843, November 1983.
2. R. J. Brachman. On the epistemological status of semantic networks. In N. V. Findler, editor, *Associative Networks*, p. 3–50. Academic Press, New York, 1979.
3. B. C. Bruce. A model for temporal references and its application in a question answering program. *Artificial Intelligence*, 3:1–25, 1972.
4. Z. Cui, A.G. Cohn, and D.A. Randell. Qualitative simulation based on a logic of space and time. In *Proc. of QR92*, Heriott Watt University, 1992.
5. Dennis DeCoste. Dynamic across-time measurement interpretation. *Artificial Intelligence*, 51:273–341, 1991.
6. K. D. Forbus. Qualitative process theory. *Artificial Intelligence*, p. 85–168, 1984.
7. K. D. Forbus. Interpreting measurements of physical systems. In *Proceedings of AAAI-86*, p. 113–117, 1986.
8. Christian Freksa. Temporal reasoning based on semi-intervals. *Artificial Intelligence*, 54:199–227, 1992.
9. T. Fuhr, F. Kummert, S. Posch, and G. Sagerer. An approach for qualitatively predicting relations from relations. In Erik Sandewall and Carl Gustav Jansson, editors, *Proc. of the Scandinavian Conference on Artificial Intelligence*, p. 38–49, Amsterdam, 1993. IOS Press.
10. H. W. Guesgen. Spatial reasoning based on allen's temporal logic. Techn. Report TR-89-049, Int. Computer Science Institute, Berkeley, August 1989.
11. Daniel Hernandez. *Qualitative Representation of Spatial Knowledge*. PhD thesis, Technical University of Munich, 1992.
12. Henry A. Kautz and Peter B. Ladkin. Intergrating metric and qualitative temporal reasoning. In *Proceedings of AAAI-91*, p. 241–246, 1991.
13. F. Kummert, E. Littmann, A. Meyering, S. Posch, H. Ritter, and G. Sagerer. A Hybrid Approach to Signal Interpretation Using Neural and Semantic Networks. In *Mustererkennung 93, 15. DAGM-Symposium*, p. 245–252. Springer, Berlin, 1993.
14. F. Kummert, H. Niemann, R. Prechtel, and G. Sagerer. Control and Explanation in a Signal Understanding Environment. *Signal Processing, special issue on 'Intelligent Systems for Signal and Image Understanding'*, 32:111–145, 1993.
15. Alan K. Mackworth and Eugene C. Freuder. The complexity of some polynomial network consistency algorithms for constraint satisfaction problems. *Artificial Intelligence*, 25:65–74, 1985.
16. H. Niemann, G. Sagerer, S. Schröder, and F. Kummert. ERNEST: A Semantic Network System for Pattern Understanding. *IEEE Transactions on Pattern Analysis and Machine Intelligence*, 12(9):883–905, 1990.
17. G. Sagerer. Automatic interpretation of medical image sequences. *Pattern Recognition Letters*, 8:87–102, 1988. Special Issue on Expert Systems in Medical Imaging, Elsevier Science Publisher, Amsterdam.
18. G. Sagerer. *Automatisches Verstehen gesprochener Sprache*, volume 74 of *Reihe Informatik*. Bibliographisches Institut, Mannheim, 1990.
19. Daniel S. Weld and Johan de Kleer, editors. *Readings in Qualitative Reasoning about Physical Systems*. Morgan Kaufmann, San Mateo, California, 1990.

Combining Spatial and Terminological Reasoning

Volker Haarslev, Ralf Möller, and Carsten Schröder

University of Hamburg, Computer Science Department,
Vogt-Kölln-Str. 30, D-22527 Hamburg, Germany
{haarslev,moeller,schroed}@informatik.uni-hamburg.de

Abstract The paper presents a method for terminological reasoning about spatial objects on the basis of a KL-ONE-like framework (LOOM). We apply this method to the domain of deductive geographic information systems and parsing of visual languages. In contrast to existing work, which mainly focusses on reasoning about qualitative spatial relations, we integrate quantitative information with conceptual or terminological reasoning by the use of "generative" qualitative relations. These relations allow a modularization of systems for terminological reasoning and domain-specific storage and indexing of, e.g., spatial data. Qualitative relations are computed on demand from quantitative data during forward-chaining assertional reasoning.

1 Introduction

A lot of inference processes of knowledge-based systems are based on different kinds of spatial reasoning. In this paper we present an inference scheme which combines terminological reasoning with inferences about spatial data. This scheme is useful for interpreting spatial data in different application domains. In terms of terminological reasoning an *interpretation* is defined as the most specialized classification of the objects of the domain. Here, classification of spatial objects depends on the specific relations found in a concrete spatial "constellation".

1.1 Spatio-Terminological Inferences

Current research about spatial reasoning mostly concentrates on inference processes about qualitative spatial relations and how they can be combined to model spatial reasoning [10, 22]. Calculi for qualitative relations are proposed to represent intrinsic properties of space (like neighborhood). Two-level representations have been proposed to integrate logical representations for qualitative spatial relations (like upon, over, above) and coordinate-oriented, i.e., quantitative information [6, 20].

However, since qualitative relations are considered as the basis for reasoning processes, in current proposals there is no adequate transition from quantitative information to terminological or conceptual reasoning via, e.g., qualitative relations. Thus, terminological reasoning is not integrated with spatial reasoning in a well-formalized way. Besides concept classification (in the TBox), we are especially interested in using spatial information during forward-chaining object classification processes (ABox reasoning). We would like to propose the term "spatio-terminological inferences" for a three-level view of inference processes combining quantitative, qualitative and conceptual representations.

1.2 Overview

In order to demonstrate how spatial reasoning can be efficiently combined with terminological reasoning, Sect. 2 presents two examples from two different domains: image interpretation and parsing of visual programming languages. Section 3 compares our appoach with a proposal for combining propositional and analogical representations and the work concerning deductive databases for Geographic Information Systems. After discussing open problems we conclude with a summary.

2 Spatio-Terminological Reasoning for Interpretation Tasks

In the first example, which deals with aerial image interpretation, object classification is used to model recognition of meaningful "constellations" of concrete spatial objects. With this example we discuss what patterns of inferences are useful for modeling spatio-terminological reasoning. The second example extends this work and uses a complete set of spatial relations for declaratively specifying knowledge for parsing "constellations" of graphical objects (rectangles, lines, etc.) as part of a visual programming language.

In our examples, the basic representation of spatial objects is quantitative in nature. For simplification purposes we use a two-dimensional representation where objects are represented by bounding boxes. Furthermore, we assume that these spatial data are stored in a special database that provides adequate indexing mechanisms for the retrieval of geometric objects (e.g., R-Trees [11], see also [2]). These databases are called spatial databases from now on. Spatial databases have been developed for Geographic Information Systems (GIS). Similar systems have also been implemented to support spatial reasoning for diagnostic purposes [23]. However, none of these systems implements models that combine spatial reasoning with terminological reasoning. The examples in this paper show how this can be exploited for interpretation tasks.

Each of the examples we would like to discuss introduces problems that have to be dealt with when terminological reasoning is to be used in practical applications:

- How can the assertional knowledge base (ABox) be coupled with a spatial database?
- How to deal with a huge number of spatial objects?
- How to control the computation of qualitative spatial relations during forward-chaining?

2.1 Image Interpretation by Object Classification

In the context of an aerial image interpretation system we assume that there exists a two-dimensional model of a geographic scene stored in a GIS. In this system multi-spectral images are interpreted, for example, in order to detect changes in the scene. To speak of an *interpretation* of an image, e.g. a change has to be described not only at the geometrical level but also at the conceptual level. For a description of an aerial image interpretation project where reconstructions of, e.g., airports are to be recognized see [8].

We use the terminological knowledge representation system LOOM (actually LOOM 2.1, [19]) to represent a model of an example world. Types of spatial objects are

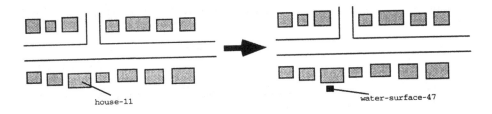

Figure1. A configuration of houses in a village.

represented by concepts using the TBox of LOOM. For illustration purposes we consider a small example where houses, villas, water surfaces and swimming pools are represented:[1]

    spatial-object ⊑_C ⊤
    spatial-relation ⊑_R spatial-object × spatial-object
        water-surface ⊑_C spatial-object
                house ⊑_C spatial-object
    swimming-pool ≐_C water-surface ⊓ (≥1 near : house)
                villa ≐_C house ⊓ (≥1 near : swimming-pool)

In our application, concepts like house and water-surface can be adequately defined as primitive concepts, because we assume that a rectangle can definitely be asserted to be a water surface or a house. Our example presupposes that the underlying image interpretation process is not only able to detect rectangular areas but will also determine the material of any object found in an image (e.g., by using spectral analysis).

The definitions can be paraphrased using natural language. A swimming-pool is a water-surface with at least one house in the neighborhood (relation near). A villa is a special house with at least one swimming-pool in the neighborhood. The definitions of villa and swimming-pool use *defined* relations (i.e., relations with sufficient as well as necessary conditions) with value and range restrictions for near.

Figure 1 provides a sketch of a village where an initial scene with several houses (light-gray rectangles) is shown in the left part. The objects are assumed to be asserted using LOOM's tell facility. Furthermore, we assume that houses are stored in a spatial database with appropriately defined coordinates.

When interpreting an image of this scene, a new object might be found in the neigborhood of a certain house (house-11). The image interpretation process detects a water surface (water-surface-47, small dark-gray rectangle in the right part of Fig. 1) which is then asserted as an instance in LOOM's ABox. For "interpreting" the image the following deductions are needed. When a water-surface is found near a house, this water-surface will be considered as a swimming-pool.[2] However, when

---

[1] Whenever possible, we use the common abstract syntax instead of the concrete LOOM syntax. See [3] for a definition of the syntax and semantics of the complete abstract language.

[2] In a full-size knowledge-base there might also be a garden pond concept, but this is another topic.

it is known to be a `swimming-pool`, the house will have to be classified (or recognized) as a `villa`.

Note, that we are interested in the most specialized classification of any object visible in the scene, so the object classification must be performed in a forward-chaining manner. However, the recognition of every relation holding between any pair of objects might not necessarily be of interest. It therefore suffices to compute them in a backward-chaining way only when needed for classifying an object.

How can this simple pattern of inference be modeled using a KL-ONE system and what extensions are advantageous? Consider the following declaration of `near` as a defined relation:[3]

```
(defrelation near
 :is (:and spatial-relation (:satisfies (?x ?y) ...)))
```

According to our definition of `spatial-relation`, `near` can only hold between spatial objects.

There are several problems with this declaration. First, the definition of `near` requires every pair of spatial objects to be explicitly declared as a member of `spatial-relation` because `spatial-relation` is primitive. Second, in order to determine for a given object whether there exists any other object in the relation `near` to it, a standard ABox inference system (like LOOM) would have to check the predicate specified in the `:satisfies`-form for every other spatial object. In a real application there will be far too many objects for this complex operation to be efficient. Even worse, when forward-chaining is not only used for object classification but for the recognition of defined relations as well, this has to be done for each pair of spatial objects.

However, in our example application, spatial indexing mechanisms can be used which provide quick access to the objects in the neighborhood of, for instance, `water-surface-47`. It would be unfortunate if the services of a spatial database could not be made available to the reasoning system.

We propose the following view. The spatial database can be interpreted as a surrogate for a set of ABox terms (or assertions) for spatial relations. In LOOM terminology, this can be paraphrased as a set of implicit assertions like (`tell` (`near water-surface-47 house-11`)). Thus, during the forward-chaining process of object classification we need a mechanism that accesses these statements on demand and makes them available to the ABox inference processes. Or, put in another way, while considering object specialization possibilities, the ABox reasoner must be able to use an efficient *candidate generator*.

The necessary integration of the ABox reasoning mechanisms with the functionality of a spatial database can be achieved by a special LOOM feature called *functional relation*. The following definition shows the use of a function as a generator for the tuples of the relation `near`.

```
(defrelation near
 :function ((x) (compute-nearby-objects *spatial-database* x))
 :characteristics (:multiple-values :symmetric))
```

---

[3] The `:satisfies`-form allows a concept to be defined using a query formula.

The function is used as follows. LOOM specializes an instance if there still exists a *defined* subconcept and the sufficient conditions for this subconcept can be proven to hold (process of forward-chaining). Since we defined `swimming-pool` as a subconcept of `water-surface` with at least one house in the near-relation, the ABox inference engine tries to find a corresponding tuple of `near` with `water-surface-47` in the domain. The function `compute-nearby-objects` will be evaluated.[4] In our example from Fig. 1 the function returns `house-11`. This house can, in turn, be specialized when there is a `swimming-pool` found to be in the near-relation. Thus, `compute-nearby-objects` is evaluated again,[5] now with `house-11` as an input parameter. In this case, `swimming-pool-47` is returned and `house-11` is specialized to a `villa`.

This example shows that spatio-terminological domain-level inferences can be carried out using the definitions of a terminological knowledge base. Furthermore, qualitative spatial relations can be computed on demand and with access to efficient storage and computation systems. If generative relations (via functions) were not available in terminological description languages, we had to define relations like `near` as given in our first `defrelation`-form. During forward-chaining object classification, e.g. of `water-surface-47`, the ABox inferencer will have to use backward-chaining to prove whether a corresponding object is found to exist in the range of the `near`-relation. Thus, `near` had to be a *defined* relation using the query-defining term `:satisfies`. The disadvantage is that the ABox inferencer can hardly exploit domain knowledge to preselect candidates. In the worst case the inferencer tries to prove whether the predicate `near` holds for every spatial object in the knowledge base.

In this example we used the relation `near`. The same problems occur with other spatial relations. The next section introduces the definition of other qualitative spatial relations and demonstrates how the same pattern of inference can be applied to other domains.

2.2 Visual Parsing by Object Classification

This section presents the application of spatio-terminological reasoning to parsing of visual programming languages. These languages are represented by (at least 2D) graphics instead of text. Syntax and semantics of "pure" visual languages are mostly expressed by pictorial relationships between (graphical) language elements[6]. Programs expressed in a visual language are graphically represented and are defined as meaningful "constellations" of *abstract* spatial objects. Therefore, we consider parsing of visual languages as an image interpretation or object classification process.

Pictorial Janus as Example Domain. The example described in this section has been fully implemented using LOOM. It is based on a full treatment of the visual programming language Pictorial Janus (PJ) [16]. PJ is a language for the domain of flat guarded horn

---

[4] In this paper we do not consider the details of this function.
[5] Since `near` is declared to be symmetric a cache might also be used. Note however, that a linguistic analysis reveals that in general the relation `near` is not symmetric [21].
[6] Also simply referred to as *objects*.

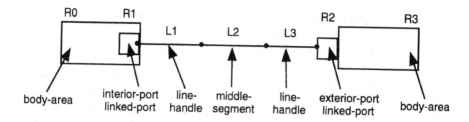

Figure2. Linking situation in a Pictorial Janus program.

clauses. PJ's syntax and semantics are defined through topological relations which have to hold between language elements. Nearly all basic language elements (agents, rules, ports, primitive functions, constraints, constants, arrays, bags) are represented as closed contours, others are represented as (directed) lines (links, channels, call arrows). We refer to Haarslev [12] for more details about this approach.

In the following we assume the existence of a spatial database storing information about elements of visual programs. Programs might be entered into the database by using appropriate techniques (e.g. via graphic editors, by scanning (hand)drawings, etc.) For sake of simplicity we ignore any low-level vision processes and assume an object-oriented representation based on rectangles, straight line segments, and arrows. Figure 2 gives an example for a typical subpart of PJ programs. This subpart consists of four rectangles R0, ... , R3 and three line segments L1, ... , L3. The rectangles R1 and R2 are connected via a chain of line segments.

A Small Knowledge Base. We present a simplified subpart of a knowledge base developed for Pictorial Janus. A lot of (more complex) concept, relation and rule definitions are left out for sake of simplicity. The concept definitions make use of primitive generative relations that model qualitative, topological relationships between language elements. Due to space limitations, however, we left out many explanations for number and value restrictions of roles.

We define two concepts line-segment and area as a spatial-object with dimension 1 or 2, respectively. Dim is a primitive generative relation which associates spatial objects with their geometric dimension.

```
(defrelation dim
  :function ((x) (compute-dimension-of x)))
```

$$\text{line-segment} \doteq_C \text{spatial-object} \sqcap (\text{dim}:1)$$
$$\text{area} \doteq_C \text{spatial-object} \sqcap (\text{dim}:2)$$

Areas—either classified as *port* or *body-area*—are basic building blocks of PJ programs. Ports are used for denoting data-item handles, for connecting list elements, and as arguments of other entities. A body area is used to represent PJ language elements such as messages, rules, and agents.

empty-area $\doteq_C$ area $\sqcap$ (≤ 0 containing) $\sqcap$ (≤ 0 covering)

    port $\doteq_C$ empty-area $\sqcap$ (≤ 3 touching) $\sqcap$ (≤ 1 touching : area) $\sqcap$

        (≤ 2 touching : line-segment)

body-area $\doteq_C$ area $\sqcap$ (≤ 0 covered-by) $\sqcap$ ($\forall$ touching : empty-area) $\sqcap$

        (≤ 0 touching : line-segment)

A port can be further classified as *interior* (R1) or *exterior* (R2), *empty* or *linked* (R1,R2). An interior port (R1) denotes the object (R0) that covers this port. Ports usually serve as "docking place" for connecting lines. See Fig. 2 for the examples.

interior-port $\doteq_C$ port $\sqcap$ (1 covered-by) $\sqcap$ ($\forall$ covered-by : body-area) $\sqcap$

        (≤ 1 touching) $\sqcap$ ($\exists$ touching : line-handle) $\sqcap$

        (≤ 1 touching : segment) $\sqcap$ (≤ 0 touching : area)

exterior-port $\doteq_C$ port $\sqcap$ ($\exists$ touching : body-area) $\sqcap$ (≤ 0 covered-by)

  empty-port $\doteq_C$ port $\sqcap$ (1 touching : body-area) $\sqcap$ (≤ 0 touching : segment)

  linked-port $\doteq_C$ port $\sqcap$ ($\exists$ touching : line-handle)

A true-segment is defined as a line-segment which satisfies some restrictions on the number of objects touching it. The concepts end-segment and middle-segment are specializations of true-segment and specify corresponding geometric situations.

  true-segment $\doteq_C$ line-segment $\sqcap$ (≥ 1 touching) $\sqcap$ (≤ 4 touching)

  end-segment $\doteq_C$ true-segment $\sqcap$ (≤ 3 touching) $\sqcap$

        (≤ 1 touching : line-segment) $\sqcap$ (≥ 1 touching : (dim : $\{1, 2\}$))

middle-segment $\doteq_C$ true-segment $\sqcap$ ($\forall$ touching : (dim : $\{0, 1\}$)) $\sqcap$

        (2 touching : line-segment)

Touching is defined as a primitive generative relation which associates touching objects. The other relations crossing, covering, covered-by are analogously defined.

```
(defrelation touching
  :function ((x) (compute-touching-of x))
  :characteristics :multiple-values)
```

Touching as well as the other basic topological relations are defined as generative relations in the same way as near in the introductory example. The formal definition of these relations is based on a proposal by Clementini et al. [7]. The advantage of their approach compared to similar proposals (e.g. see [9]) is its ability to deal with intersections of lines *and* regions. It is also important to note that their relations are complete and mutually exclusive.

    There are several constraints on the types of geometric objects: Areas have to be convex, connected and without holes, lines must not be self-intersecting, are either circular or directed, and have exactly two end points.

The possible relationships are defined by the dimension of intersections between mathematical point-sets representing the geometric objects mentioned above. Every object is composed of a *boundary* and an *interior*. The boundary of a region is a circular line. The boundary of a line is either an empty point-set (circular line) or a point-set consisting of two end points (non-circular line), the boundary of a point is an empty point-set. The interior of an object is the object without its boundary. In case of circular lines and points the interior is identical to the object itself.

Using these definitions six binary topological relations can be defined (see also [7]). The boundary of λ_n is formally denoted by $\partial\lambda_n$, its interior by λ_n^o.

- **touching:** $touching(\lambda_1, \lambda_2) \Leftrightarrow (\lambda_1 \cap \lambda_2 \neq \emptyset) \wedge (\lambda_1^o \cap \lambda_2^o = \emptyset)$
  Only the boundaries are intersecting; touching is symmetric and applies to every situation except point/point.

- **overlapping:** $overlapping(\lambda_1, \lambda_2) \Leftrightarrow (\lambda_1 \cap \lambda_2 \neq \lambda_1) \wedge (\lambda_1 \cap \lambda_2 \neq \lambda_2) \wedge (\dim(\lambda_1^o \cap \lambda_2^o) = \dim(\lambda_1^o) = \dim(\lambda_2^o))$
  The intersection is either a line or a point which has to be different to both objects; overlapping is symmetric and applies only to area/area and line/line situations.

- **crossing:** $crossing(\lambda_1, \lambda_2) \Leftrightarrow (\lambda_1 \cap \lambda_2 \neq \lambda_1) \wedge (\lambda_1 \cap \lambda_2 \neq \lambda_2) \wedge \dim(\lambda_1^o \cap \lambda_2^o) = (\max(\dim(\lambda_1^o), \dim(\lambda_2^o)) - 1)$
  Two lines are crossing if their intersection is an internal point. A line crosses a region if the line is partly inside and outside of this region; crossing is symmetric and applies only to line/line and line/area situations.

- **containing/inside:** $containing(\lambda_1, \lambda_2) \Leftrightarrow (\lambda_1 \cap \lambda_2 = \lambda_2) \wedge (\lambda_1^o \cap \lambda_2^o \neq \emptyset)$
  An object λ_1 contains an object λ_2 if the intersection between λ_1's and λ_2's regions is equal to λ_2 and the interiors of their regions intersect; the inverse containing is inside. They are transitive and apply to every situation.

- **equal:** $equal(\lambda_1, \lambda_2) \Leftrightarrow \lambda_1 \cap \lambda_2 = \lambda_1 = \lambda_2$
  The intersection is equal to both objects; equal is symmetric, transitive and applies to every situation.

- **disjoint:** $disjoint(\lambda_1, \lambda_2) \Leftrightarrow \lambda_1 \cap \lambda_2 = \emptyset$
  The intersection is empty; disjoint is symmetric and applies to every situation.

With respect to our application domain, we defined a seventh relation which is a specialization of 'containing' and 'inside':

- **covering/covered-by:** $covering(\lambda_1, \lambda_2) \Leftrightarrow containing(\lambda_1, \lambda_2) \wedge \dim(\partial\lambda_1 \cap \partial\lambda_2) = \dim(\partial\lambda_2)$
  An object λ_1 covers an object λ_2 if λ_1's region contains λ_2's region and the intersection of their boundaries has a dimension equal to the dimension of λ_2's boundary; the inverse of covering is covered-by. They apply to every situation except point/point.

These seven relations may hold between geometric objects *and* their boundary and interior. Additionally, we defined a relation *dimension* (also called dim) which applies to any object.

Parsing PJ Programs. Rectangles and line segments as presented in Fig. 2 define the input to the assertional reasoning process. For example, as the result of this reasoning, a rectangle like R1 is specialized to an `interior-port` since it is an `empty-area` and can be proven to be in the `covered-by`-relation to R0 which, in turn, is a `body-region`.

Similar deductions will be performed for other graphical objects. Figure 2 illustrates the complete result of this reasoning process (denoted by arrows).

2.3 Summary of the Examples

The last example shows how spatio-terminological reasoning can be applied to parsing problems. A complete set of topological spatial relations together with appropriately defined concepts is used for interpreting constellations of geometrical objects. A subset of visual languages is completely specifiable by terminological definitions, and parsing is reduced to assertional reasoning. Thus, spatio-terminological reasoning is applicable not only to toy problems but scales up to be the basic reasoning mechanism for various applications.

3 Related Work

In the AI literature representations with domain-specific indexing mechanisms are also discussed in the context of "analogical" representations. In the project "LILOG" there have been attempts to couple a propositional representation and reasoning system with a special system for representing spatial information ("depictional system", [13, 5]) using cell matrices. The depictional system supports special "imagination" and "inspection" processes in the sense of Kosslyn [18]. The propositional representation system of LILOG integrates some aspects of terminological description languages with a theorem prover for a sorted logic. The connection to the depictional (non-logical) component is done by explicit switching statements declared inside of LILOG rules (see [17], p. 38). In LILOG, the spatial (depictional) representation system is not used for object classfication.

Recently, research in spatial databases has concentrated on providing databases with deductive capabilities. Especially, work in geographic data handling proposes the use of extended Prolog systems to describe domain knowledge on the basis of primitive spatial relations [1]. In our group, we used CLP(R) [15] to model spatial domain knowledge using Horn clauses and constraints. The results were that adequate indexing mechanisms for spatial data beyond the standard Prolog (and CLP(R)) resolution mechanisms are necessary due to severe performance problems. However, the main problem with Prolog-like backward-chaining systems is that in order to drive inference processes, goals have to be set up. Therefore, in our first image interpretation example, we have to directly ask whether a given house is a villa. Unfortunately, in an image interpretation domain the "right" questions (or queries) are almost never known in advance. In addition to object classification by forward-chaining, terminological description systems (like LOOM) also support backward-chaining inferences as a by-product.

4 Open Problems and Future Work

In the examples of Sect. 2 we have shown how a generator function using a proper indexing mechanism can be used for classifying objects in a forward-chaining manner based on quantitative spatial information. However, this approach has some problems with the revision of information.

4.1 Reason Maintenance

What happens when the quantitative spatial information is revised? Consider the case were water-surface-47 near house-11 is removed. Then, the condition (≥ 1 near : swimming-pool) for house-11 being a villa is no longer fulfilled, and the classification as a villa must be retracted. Unfortunately, by using a function generating the tuples of the near-relation in an extra-logical way, the ABox reasoning mechanism has no information about the dependencies and, therefore, an automatic retraction is not possible. In order to allow for reason maintenance of the near-relation a mechanism must be provided for declaring the information the relation depends on.

What is the information a relation tuple depends on? In our case the near-relation of a house and a water-surface depends on the existence of both the house and the water-surface and on their respective location. In general, all the ABox-objects and all the relation-tuples used in a generator function must be "marked" to allow for a correct reason maintenance.

However, the use of generator functions in combination with a means for marking the information a relation depends on, has one major disadvantage: the user is responsible for consistently and correctly using these mechanisms. More desirable would be an intra-logical, declarative construct for defining spatial relations were the information needed for reason maintenance could be acquired automatically. This would require a means for declaring *defined* relations and powerful, expressive constructs for declaring spatial contraints. Recently, Baader & Hanschke [4, 14] proposed a very general scheme for integrating special domains with their own reasoning mechanisms into a description logic. However, their language $\mathcal{ALCFP(D)}$ does not allow for the declaration of defined roles and, therefore, cannot be directly used for our purposes. Whether this approach can be appropriately extended, has to be explored in the future.

4.2 Intrinsic Properties of the Domain

We have shown how terminological inferences can be drawn on the basis of certain spatial relations and concepts. Other inferences, however, most notably those which are based on intrinsic properties of space, are still missing. For example, non-penetrable objects cannot overlap in space. This fact can be used for ABox- as well as TBox-reasoning. Trying to assert two different objects located at the same place must result in an inconsistency, and a concept requiring at least 2 different spatial objects at overlapping locations must be detected as being inconsistent.

For another example, assume that the spatial region under consideration in an application is completely covered or filled by non-penetrable objects. This might give rise to another line of reasoning: asserting an object as being a villa and assuming there is only one object near to it which is classified as a spatial-object, then this spatial-object would have to be specialized to a swimming-pool.

For these kinds of reasoning the intrinsic properties of the domain must be axiomatisized in a description logic. When the reasoning services of a real system are based on a consistency or satisfiability test as proposed by Schmidt-Schauß & Smolka [24] this might be done by extending the rule sets of the satisfiability test by certain rules realizing the spatial axioms. Again, this has to be explored by future work.

5 Conclusion

Our proposal shows that non-logical representations can directly and consistently be combined with the ABox resoning services of a KL-ONE-like description logic. The examples indicate that for an interesting subset of problem domains this hybrid combination is sufficient to realize the necessary inference processes. We discussed an augmentation of the ABox of LOOM with a system that provides efficient access functions for spatial data. We also showed that (distributed) *explicit* switching statements (placed in rules like in LILOG) are not necessary if we use the concept of functional or generative relations. In our proposal the services of the external database system can even be described in terms of ABox (tell) statements. Furthermore, for our applications, the discussion of a canonical analogical representation system (in the context of the "imagery debate") is not important. Our point of view is that we want to provide the most suitable representation for application-specific computational processes. Terminological description languages are suitable for deductive reasoning involving classification while, e.g., R-Trees are suitable for efficiently accessing spatial data. Both systems are coupled in a well-formalized way. However, our current approach requires the reasoning to be monotonous.

Acknowledgements

We thank our colleague Ralf Röhrig for thoughtful comments and interesting discussions.

References

1. A. I. Abdelmoty, M. H. Williams, and N. W. Paton. Deduction and Deductive Databases for Geographic Data Handling. In Abel and Ooi [2], pages 443–464.
2. D. Abel and B. C. Ooi, editors. *Advances in Spatial Databases*, Singapore, June 23–25 1993, volume 692 of *Lecture Notes in Computer Science*. Springer-Verlag, Berlin – Heidelberg – New York, 1993.
3. F. Baader et al. Terminological Knowledge Representation: A Proposal for a Terminological Logic. In Bernhard Nebel, Christof Peltason, and Kai von Luck, editors, *International Workshop on Terminological Logics*, Schloß Dagstuhl, Germany, May 6–8, 1991, KIT-Report 89, pages 120–128. TU Berlin, Fachbereich Informatik.
4. F. Baader and Ph. Hanschke. A Scheme for Integrating Concrete Domains into Concept Languages. In John Mylopoulos and Ray Reiter, editors, *Proceedings of the Twelfth International Joint Conference on Artificial Intelligence IJCAI-91*, Sydney, Australia, August 24–30, 1991, pages 452–457. Morgan Kaufmann Publ. Inc., San Mateo, CA, 1991. Extended version published as DFKI Research Report RR-91-10, Kaiserslautern.
5. T. Bollinger and U. Pletat. The LILOG Knowledge Representation System. IWBS Report 156, IBM Wissenschaftliches Zentrum, Institut für Wissensbasierte Systeme, Stuttgart, 1991.
6. P. Breuer and J. Müller. A Two Level Representation for Spatial Relations, Part I. DFKI Research Report RR-91-14, Deutsches Forschungszentrum für Künstliche Intelligenz, Kaiserslautern, July 1991.
7. E. Clementini, P. Di Felice, and P. van Oesterom. A Small Set of Formal Topological Relationships Suitable for End-User Interaction. In Abel and Ooi [2], pages 277–295.

8. L. Dreschler-Fischer, Ch. Drewniok, H. Lange, and C. Schröder. A Knowledge-Based Approach to the Detection and Interpretation of Changes in Aerial Images. In Sadao Fujimura, editor, *1993 International Geoscience and Remote Sensing Symposium (IGARSS'93)*, Tokyo, August 1993, volume I, pages 159–161. Institute of Electrical and Electronics Engineers, 1993.

9. M. J. Egenhofer. Reasoning about Binary Topological Relations. In Oliver Günther and H.-J. Scheck, editors, *Advances in Spatial Databases*, Zürich, August 28–30 1991, volume 525 of *Lecture Notes in Computer Science*, pages 143–160. Springer-Verlag, Berlin – Heidelberg – New York, 1991.

10. Ch. Freksa. Qualitative Spatial Reasoning. In David M. Mark and Andrew U. Frank, editors, *Cognitive and Linguistic Aspects of Geographic Space*, NATO ASI Series. Kluwer Academic Publ., Boston – Dortrecht – Lancaster, 1991.

11. A. Guttman. R-Trees: A Dynamic Index Structure for Spatial Searching. In *Proc. ACM SIGMOD International Conference on Management of Data*, page 47ff, 1984.

12. V. Haarslev. Knowledge-based Parsing and Formal Specification of Visual Languages. Bericht, Fachbereich Informatik, Universität Hamburg, 1994. in preparation.

13. Ch. Habel. Repräsentation räumlichen Wissens. Mitteilung FBI-HH-M-153/87, Fachbereich Informatik, Universität Hamburg, 1987.

14. Ph. Hanschke. Specifying Role Interactions in Concept Languages. In Bernhard Nebel, Charles Rich, and William Swartout, editors, *Principles of Knowledge Representation and Reasoning – Proc. of the Third International Conference KR'92*, Cambridge, Mass., October 25–29, 1992, pages 318–329. Morgan Kaufmann Publ. Inc., San Mateo, CA, 1992.

15. J. Jaffar, S. Michaylov, P. J. Stuckey, and R. H. C. Yap. The CLP(R) Language and System. *ACM Trans. on Programming Languages and Systems* **14** (3), 339–395, 1992.

16. K. M. Kahn, V. A. Saraswat, and V. Haarslev. Pictorial Janus: Eine vollständig visuelle Programmiersprache und ihre Umgebung. In J. Encarnacao, editor, *GI-Fachgespräch Programmieren multimedialer Anwendungen der GI-Jahrestagung 1991*, Darmstadt, Oktober 1991, pages 427–436. Springer-Verlag.

17. K. Klabunde. Erweiterung der Wissensrepräsentationssprache L-LILOG um Konstrukte zu Spezifikation von Kontrollinformation. IWBS Report 92, IBM Wissenschaftliches Zentrum, Institut für Wissensbasierte Systeme, Stuttgart, 1989.

18. S. Kosslyn. *Image and Mind*. Harvard University Press, 1980.

19. R. M. MacGregor. The Evolving Technology of Classification-Based Knowledge Representation Systems. In John F. Sowa, editor, *Principles of Semantic Networks – Explorations in the Representation of Knowledge*, chapter 13, pages 385–400. Morgan Kaufmann Publ. Inc., San Mateo, CA, 1991.

20. J.-P. Mohren and J. Müller. Representing Spatial Relations (Part II): The Geometrical Approach. DFKI Research Report RR-92-21, Deutsches Forschungszentrum für Künstliche Intelligenz, Kaiserslautern, April 1992.

21. S. Pribbenow. *Räumliche Konzepte in Wissens- und Sprachverarbeitung – Hybride Verarbeitung von Lokalisierung*. Deutscher Universitäts Verlag, Wiesbaden, 1993.

22. R. Röhrig. A Theory for Qualitative Spatial Reasoning Based on Order Relations. In *Proceedings of the Twelfth National Conference on Artificial Intelligence AAAI-94*, Seattle, Washington, July 31 – August 4, 1994. AAAI-Press/The MIT Press, Menlo Park – Cambridge – London, 1994.

23. M. Schick, S. Kockskämper, and B. Neumann. Konstellationserkennung auf Basis einer hybriden Raumrepräsentation. Behavior Memo 03-93, Fachbereich Informatik, Universität Hamburg, 1993.

24. M. Schmidt-Schauß and G. Smolka. Attributive concept descriptions with complements. *Artificial Intelligence* **48** (1), 1–26, 1991.

Detecting gestalts in CAD-plans to be used as indices for case-retrieval in architecture

Jörg Walter Schaaf

Artificial Intelligence Research Division
German National Research Center for Computer Science (GMD)
P.O. Box 1316 D-53757, Sankt Augustin, Germany

Abstract. Design and construction of buildings is one of the most expensive enterprises. CAD plans in the domain of architecture contain thousands of design fragments (cases) which could be helpful for later use. In FABEL[1] we try to find those fragments which are useful for a problem, to evaluate them and adapt them to the current context. The present approach helps to support a CAD system with case based reasoning. As usual in CBR we reduce the notion of *usefulness* of cases to the one of *similarity*. We describe a similarity criterion that is based on detection of "gestalts". "Gestalts" try to catch the main topological properties and spatial relations of an object constellation. To detect them, focused object groups of a CAD plan are represented as sketches and compared with a set of sketches of predefined gestalts. Comparison yields an index for the determination of similarity between a plan to be elaborated and a plan stored in a conventional case base. In this paper we focus on the aspects of "gestalt" acquisition, representation and recognition.

1 Problem and idea

1.1 The problem to find reusable cases in CAD-plans in architecture

Architecture is a rewarding research area. The design and construction of buildings is one of the most expensive enterprises. The plans are of extraordinary complexity (tenthousands of parts in a CAD-plan) and the lifetime of a building lasts a generation or longer. The present approach helps to support a CAD system with case based reasoning. This CAD system is called A4 [4] and is built up on the design methodology ARMILLA [2]. Objects called "containers" are placed in the three spatial dimensions. They are presented as ellipses or rectangles. In this context a "problem" is a section of an A4-plan that is to be refined or augmented. In their work, architects often encounter problems that remind them at similar situations in previous designs. Adapting the former solution may be

---

[1] This research was supported by the German Ministry for Research and Technology (BMFT) within the joint project FABEL under contract no. 01IW104. Project partners in FABEL are German National Research Center for Computer Science (GMD), Sankt Augustin, BSR Consulting GmbH, München, Technical University of Dresden, HTWK Leipzig, University of Freiburg, and University of Karlsruhe.

easier than solving their problem from scratch. However, searching for the old cases in all the old plans may be very time consuming. It would be great help if the retrieval for similar problems could be done automatically and solutions could be made available in seconds.

So our first task is how we can find cases in a case base which are similar to our actual problem.

The retrieval of reusable, similar sections of CAD plans is a new and interesting research problem. In the FABEL[2] project different approaches to this have been developed. Some of them ignore geometry and calculate similarity using the type of objects and their number. These approaches calculate results fast but the precision is low. Others focus on the topology of the objects in detail, but are to slow to deal with bigger case bases.

1.2 The idea to use gestalts as indices

In this paper we will introduce a new method of how to catch the main topological properties of a case in very short time. It is most important to us to focus on the constellations that "jump out and grab the architect" instead of examining all relationships between all objects. Often constellations of objects remind experts of things out of their everyday lives e.g. "'combs", "fish-bones" or "quadrangles". Naturally the combs or the fish-bones are never included in the plans. Because these constellations are only patterns in our mind, we chose the term *gestalt* to refer to them. In cooperation with architects, we learned that experts use such "gestalts" to remember similar problems and their solutions. This is the reason why the gestalts shall be used in FABEL to retrieve similar cases. We try to recognize gestalts fastly and use them in quick-time retrieval methods like associative memories.

Although knowing how useful gestalt indexes would be, it is not realistic to ask architects to index the plans by hand because there are sometimes more than hundreds of cases in the plans of a building. We have to ask how we can index cases automatically which means how we can automatically recognize gestalts. So, the problem of how to find reusable cases specializes to the problem of how to find gestalts in A4-plans.

2 Define and recognize gestalts

2.1 Defining relevant gestalts

In working with experts, we identified a set of gestalts. We gave the architect sections of A4-plans, which he should attribute with gestalts given on cards.

---
[2] This research was supported by the German Ministry for Research and Technology (BMFT) within the joint project FABEL under contract no. 01IW104. Project partners in FABEL are German National Research Center for Computer Science (GMD), Sankt Augustin, BSR Consulting GmbH, München, Technical University of Dresden, HTWK Leipzig, University of Freiburg, and University of Karlsruhe.

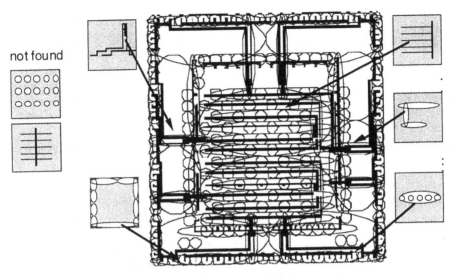

not found

Fig. 1. An A4-Plan with "gestalt indices"

Besides these gestalts, he had empty cards on which he could draw some new ones. From all the gestalts we finally had, only those which were really used are included in figure 2.

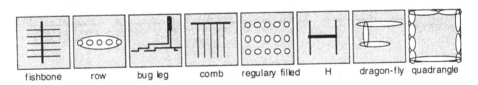

fishbone   row   bug leg   comb   regulary filled   H   dragon-fly   quadrangle

Fig. 2. The current set of predefined gestalts

2.2 How to recognize gestalts automatically

The question arises how to search for gestalts in A4-plans.

First possibility: For each gestalt an algorithm is given that searches for the gestalt within the plan. In the worst case, this approach must check the position and constellation of hundreds of A4-objects. If a feature for a gestalt is found, the search for others may become necessary. Because the feature tests have to be done redundantly for each gestalt, in the worst case we need time depending on the product out of the number of predefined gestalts, the number of features of each gestalt and the number of objects in the whole group.

Another way: On the other hand, we may find an abstract representation of object groups which matches the equivalent representations of gestalt examples[3]. In this manner, each object would only be examined once. The identification of an object group is then only a comparison of abstract representations. We have to be careful that this comparison will not become too expensive. Because architects only accept response times below a few seconds, it is important to keep the time for representation and comparison as short as possible. For this reason we decided on the second method.

The questions are now, what must be represented, what can be neglected and what representations are easy to compare?

2.3 Gestalts can be represented as sketches.

The main idea is to sketch a group of A4-objects in the same manner as we sketch a stick person; the constellation of head, body, arms and legs of a human. Perhaps the challenge of this approach is to find sketches that represent groups of the same gestalt equally and those of different gestalt unequally.

Figure 3 shows the origin of the idea and how it was developed.

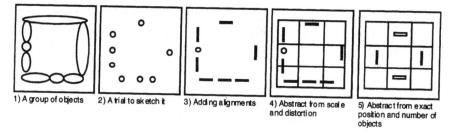

1) A group of objects   2) A trial to sketch it   3) Adding alignments   4) Abstract from scale and distortion   5) Abstract from exact position and number of objects

Fig. 3. How a group of objects can be sketched

Object group: Part 1 of figure 3 shows an occurrence of an object group that is often found in A4-plans. It may represent a way to divide the boundaries of a building into rooms and floors. Architects sometimes call this constellation a "quadrangle". Each ellipse stands for the bounding box – here a room.

Trial to sketch it: The second subfigure shows how a sketch would look if only the centers of objects were represented. The problems are that on the one hand, too much information would get lost while on the other hand, this way we would get different sketches for constellations of the same gestalt. (E.g. if two quadrangles differ in size.)

Adding alignments: To avoid too much loss of structure, we decided to take the alignment of an object into account. The alignment is represented as a short line

---

[3] You find the idea that humans transform pictures for a comparison into an abstract form e.g. in [5]

of the same orientation. A small circle indicates a missing alignment. (Subfigure 3 in fig. 3)

Abstract from scale and distortion: If the scale and the distortion of a gestalt were considered, it would be impossible to classify gestalts correctly. Humans also neglect these attributes while sketching things and in recognizing gestalts. Subfigure 4 shows a sketch which abstracts from scale (by scaling a grid) and abstracts from distortion (by distorting the grid the same way).

Neglect exact position and number of objects: In the previous sketches, the exact number of objects is noticed. To abstract from similarly aligned objects, we defined a way to merge objects into one element. Subfigure 5 shows the result of this merging.

Thus we constructed a sketch that may be developed out of many occurrences of the gestalt "quadrangle".

Fig. 4. Possible elements of a sketch

These considerations, gave rise to the set of sketch elements shown in fig. 4. It is not reasonable for the architecture domain under A4 to consider other description elements than horizontal or vertical alignments because the designs contain only orthogonally arranged elements. As the dimension of an object is to remain unconsidered, there is no reasonable interpretation for possible concepts such as "corner" or "T-connection" when "corner" and "T-connection" describe the point where the ends of objects meet.

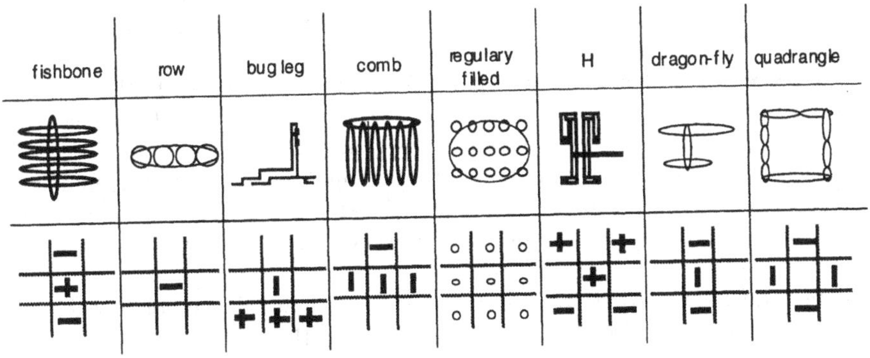

fishbone	row	bug leg	comb	regulary filled	H	dragon-fly	quadrangle

Fig. 5. Examples of object groups and their sketches

2.4 Sketching algorithm

This section describes the steps of the sketching algorithm.
Input: A group of A4-Objects and a name for its gestalt.

- **Create a reference set:** To recognize gestalts we have to create a reference set for each gestalt. *In this set we insert any representative sketches for the gestalt.*
- **Bounding box:** Set a bounding box around the given object group. *This serves to place the grid.*
- **Grid:** Scale a grid of 3*3 equal sized fields so that it fills out the bounding box. *Scaling and distorting the grid we abstract from scale and distortion of the object group.*
- **Alignments:** Sketch each object in its center as a line with the alignment of the object. If the object has no detectable orientation we represent it as a circle. *This keeps information needed to distinguish the gestalts.*
- **Inner merge:** Merge equally oriented objects within the same grid field. (Cf. 6) *This reduces the number of sketch elements and abstracts from the exact position of each.*

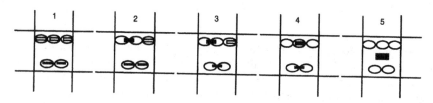

Fig. 6. Snapshots from an "inner merge"

- **Objects without orientation:** If there are only objects without orientation within one field, compute the orientation of the whole group. *We currently develop an algorithm to do that.*
- **First entry to the reference set:** Center all symbols of one field. *So we get only one of the elements shown in fig. 4 in each grid field.* Put the resulting sketch into the representative set of the gestalt.
- **Outer merge** Try to apply the rules of the inner merge to objects in neighboring grid fields. *The outer merge is crucial because it abstracts very much from the exact position of objects.* We are currently testing rules for the outer merge.
- **Second entry to the reference set:** Center again all symbols of one field and make a second entry in the reference set with the specified name.

A first implementation of the sketching algorithm (in C++ on a SUN 4) shows that groups of one hundred objects can be sketched in less than a second. Gestalts are normally made up of a few dozen objects. According to true examples, we currently experiment with strategies for merging.

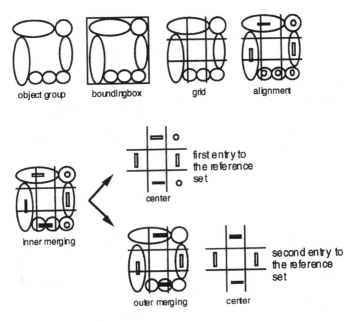

object group   boundingbox   grid   alignment

first entry to
the reference
set

center

inner merging

outer merging   center

second entry to
the reference
set

Fig. 7. Steps of the sketching algorithm illustrated by means of the gestalt "quadrangle".

2.5 Problems

The algorithm lets down if two object groups are represented by the same sketch. We call this failure *collision*. (See the lightning-bolt line in figure 8) If the number of collisions increases too much, we have to refine the classification. This can be accomplished as follows:

- Through expansion of the alphabet. (See fig. 4)
- Through refinement of the grid, e.g. from 3*3 to 5*5 fields.
- Through changing the layout of the grid (e.g. like a honeycomb).
- Through statistical methods during the calculation of a "balanced bounding box"
- Through changing the merging rules.
- Through renunciation of the grid, using a sort of compass card to locate the elements.

Even though it is desirable to distinguish the gestalts carefully, we have to take into account that it does not matter to FABEL if an object group – in question – is annotated with all possible interpretations. Even humans do not always manage to make a clear classification. Instead, they say that something almost looks like X but at the same time has similarities to Y.

2.6 How to choose the reference sets

Although ideal, it is not realistic to have one sketch for each gestalt. Therefore
we allow different representations in the reference set of the same gestalt. Some
examples must be chosen carefully, to ensure that as many occurrences as possible of a gestalt can be recognized and that no ambiguous sketches are in the
reference set. The reference sets can be extended dynamically. The architect can
give a new constellation as an example of a new gestalt at anytime (without the
help of a knowledge engineer).

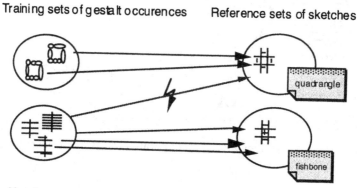

Fig. 8. Sketches are associated as representatives of gestalts (here quadrangle
and fish-bone)

3 Gestalts as indices

For retrieval the case base (in a preprocessing phase) and the current problem situation (during runtime) have to be indexed by gestalt names. For this purpose,
the sketching is applied to the current problem (that means to an incomplete
plan) as well as to the cases. Because the same mechanism (sketching) is used
to represent groups of objects in cases and in problems, the recognition of the
gestalts is insensitive toward the quality of the representation through the sketching.

The new question is now, how these groups of objects that possibly constitute
a gestalt can be focused? This question is deferred to section 3.1. For the time
being, we assume that an interesting object group has already been chosen and
describe the indexing of a problem situation.

- **First, try to find the gestalt after completing the inner merge.**
  We first sketch the object group (as in 2.4) until the inner merge is completed.

We now try to find[4] the generated sketch in one of the reference sets. If a sketch is found, the name of the gestalt is one of the indices for the retrieval. According to our intuition, sketches are representations which make similar things equal. If these sketches are reduced too much, dissimilar things may possibly be equally represented. To prevent this, we check if the gestalt can already be found prior to a further abstraction during outer merging.

– **Second, try to recognize a gestalt after the outer merge.**

If an identification after inner merging fails, we merge between neighboring grid fields (outer merging) and check again to see if the sketch under consideration is contained in the reference set of any gestalt. Otherwise, two explanations are possible: The sketched group of objects does not contain any of the predefined gestalts (this should lead to ignoring the group, or to defining a new gestalt[5]), or the group of objects is a distorted, uncommon representation of a gestalt. Then it pays off to "repair" the sketch,

– **Third, try to repair the generated sketch.**

As a last resort, repairing the sketch may be tried in order to correct too far or wrongly abstracted sketches. For that purpose we have to find that sketch within all the reference sets which is most similar to the one we generated. For each difference between the generated sketch and the most similar gestalt sketch, we have to find a justification to eliminate it. We find arguments for this in early stages of the merging process or in the object group itself by answering questions like: *Is it possible to find an object close to field 5, which was only by chance represented in field 4? Is there a good reason to represent it alternatively in field 5? Can this object be represented by a horizontal line? When yes, then this was the sketch of an abnormal "comb".*
The example in fig. 9 shows how we can repair a misbuilt sketch of the gestalt "comb".

In repairing the sketch, the point of view changes. During sketching, objects are abstracted from. During repair, the original objects are examined to find justification for demanded changes of sketches. In this way, the repair is a form of "expectation driven recognition". The expectation is that the focused and sketched object group is a representative of a predefined gestalt. Accordingly, the conditions positioning an object in certain boundaries can be relaxed without leading to an insufficient discrimination. So the recognition of gestalts is supported by a repairing that couples the data driven representation with an expectation driven interpretation.

If one of the three attempts was successful, a gestalt within a group of objects was recognized and the A4-plan can be indexed by its name. We are currently extending two retrieval methods in FABEL to gestalt indices. (See [12]) The question remains, how those groups, for which the test for a gestalt is worthwhile, can be found.

---

[4] This search is not a major problem because a sketch is only made up of 9 fields and each field can only contain one of 8 possible elements.

[5] Sketches not identified during retrieval are proposed as new.

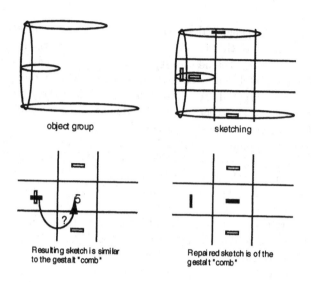

Fig. 9. An object is interpreted as a "comb tooth"

3.1 Focusing

Focusing is only relevant for the sketching of the cases and the actual problem. For the reference sets, the expert has isolated any relevant object groups.

First, we try to focus on neighboring objects that are similar in one of their attributes (e.g. type, scale or use) so that one group may be built e.g. out of these fresh-air-objects that are close together. The research of Treisman [9] und [10] confirms the cognitive relevance of this approach.

Maybe focusing can be guided by additional knowledge about interesting constellations and perception rules. (See the results of gestalt psychology in [3] or [13].) Currently, we are examining whether the MAX system ([7] and [8]) developed at GMD within the TASSO project can be used to focus on object groups. MAX realizes a grouping according to perception laws of gestalt psychology .

In addition, focusing could be controlled by the objects. In accordance with the model of pattern recognition in the visual cortex, specific regularities in the image could lead to a "synchronization" of the related objects (cf. [6])

On the other hand, we discuss using sketching itself for the focusing. The idea is to sketch the whole case or problem and to examine only those parts in more detail, where "structure" strikes.

4 Summary and outlook

Although largely tailored to the requirements of FABEL the present approach can certainly be used beyond this domain. It indexes plans in accordance with the gestalts contained in a plan. In FABEL, these indices are used to determine

similarity and finally for case selection. In other domains gestalts could be used e.g. for focusing attention or recursive image reduction.
In order to determine the scope of the approach, input and sketching algorithm are to be examined.

– The input should be an image. The image should be composed of objects since the central idea of producing a sketch depends on the alignment and topology of objects. If the image consists of pixels, an appropriate preprocessing is to be performed. Several realistic examples of the gestalts to be recognized should be available to generate powerful reference sets.
– The suggested representation algorithm sketches object groups in A4-CAD plans in the domain of architecture. If two object groups are of similar gestalt they are sketched equally (or at least as sketches of the same reference set). The comparison of sketches is fast. If gestalts should be recognized in other domains, the set of the representation elements may have to be modified.

The presented approach should not be mixed up with the tasks of pattern, image feature or character recognition. It is more comparable with watching the stars on firmament, finding the constellation[6] "scorpion" than finding which one of the 2965 japanese kanji characters (e.g. [1]) can be identified. We try to name characteristic constellations that were never created as items. Nevertheless we use some common techniques of pattern recognition such as finding a bounding box, scaling grids or representing alignments.
In the future we will work out the sketching of gestalts. Sketches shall not only represent the data, but also a model of what is represented and the way sketching is usually done.

Acknowledgment
I would like to thank the FABEL team, especially Barbara Schmidt-Belz and M. Nowak for their support in knowledge acquisition and in programming. Special thanks also to Angi Voš for the great support she gave editing this paper.

References

1. A.Kawamura, T.Minamikawa, K.Yura, A.Tanaka, T. Hayama, S. Masuda, and Y. Hidai. On-line Recognition of Freely Handwritten Japanese Characters Using Directional Feature Densities. In *Pattern Recognition Methodology and Systems*, volume II, pages 183–186, Los Alamitos, California, September 1992. 11th IAPR International Conference on Pattern Recognition, IEEE Computer Society Press.
2. Fritz Haller. Armilla – Ein Installationsmodell. Technical report, Institut für industrielle Bauproduktion, Universität Karlsruhe, Germany, 1985.
3. H.H. Helson. The Fundmental Propositions of Gestaltpsychologie. *Psychological Review*, 40:13–32, 1933.

---

[6] The most similar approach we found was [11]

4. L. Hovestadt. *A4 - Digitales Bauen - ein Modell für weitgehenden Computerein-satz im Bauen.* PhD thesis, Institut für Industrielle Bauproduktion, Universität Karlsruhe (TU), Germany, 1993.

5. D. Marr. *Vision - A Computational Investigation into the Human Representation and Processing of Visual Information.* W.H. Freeman and Company, New York (NY), 1982.

6. H. J. Reitböck. Mechanismen der Mustererkennung im Sehsystem. In O. Herzog, Th. Christaller, and D. Schütt, editors, *Grundlagen und Anwendungen der Künst-lichen Intelligenz,* pages 90–106, Berlin, 1993. 17. Fachtagung für Künstliche Intelligenz, Springer-Verlag.

7. Erich Rome. Wahrnehmungspsychologie, Bilderkennung und der Grafikdesigner. Technical Report TASSO 36, GMD, Februar 1992.

8. Erich Rome. Max, ein maschinelles Gestalt-Erkennungssystem. *KI - Künstliche Intelligenz,* 7(Sonderheft):70–71, 1993.

9. A. Treisman. Perceptual Grouping and Attention in Visual Search for Features and for Objects. *Journal of Experimental Psychology: Human Perception and Per-formance,* 8(2):194–214, 1982.

10. A. Treisman. Preattentive Processing in Vision. *Computer Vision, Graphics and Image Processing,* (31):156–177, 1985.

11. M. Tuceryan, A.K. Jain, and N. Ahuja. Supervised Classification of Early Percep-tual Structure in Dot Patterns. In *Pattern Recognition Methodology and Systems,* volume II, pages 88–91, Los Alamitos, California, September 1992. 11th IAPR International Conference on Pattern Recognition, IEEE Computer Society Press.

12. A. Voß et. al. Approaches to similarity in FABEL. FABEL-Report 13, GMD I3.KI, GMD, Sankt Augustin, Germany, 1993.

13. L. Zusne. *Visual Perception of Form.* Academic Press, Inc., New York (NY), 1970.

The NeuDB-System: Towards the Integration of Neural Networks and Database Systems

Erich Schikuta

Institute of Applied Computer Science and Information Systems, Dept. of Data Engineering, University of Vienna, Rathausstr. 19/4, A-1010, Vienna, Austria

Abstract. In this paper the NeuDB system is presented, which accomplishes the physical and conceptual integration of neural networks with an object-oriented database system. In the context of the database system neural networks are seen as basic objects and are administrated via the conventional and handy interface of the system. The network paradigm of a neural network object is defined by the respective sub type according to the type hierarchy of the general neural net database type. The structural information is stored using a data oriented approach. The dynamic components of the neural networks are triggered by conventional database operations (insertion, update, etc.) and are processed by an independent neural network server.
Overall a conceptual framework for the embedding of neural networks into database systems and an embedding classification is given.

Keywords. Neural networks, database systems, object-orientation, integrational aspects, data modeling

1. Introduction

Object oriented database systems have proven very valuable at handling and administrating complex objects. Guidelines for embedding neural networks into such systems are presented. It is our objective to consider neural networks as conventional data in the database system. From the logical point of view a neural network is a complex data value and can be stored as a normal data object.

Until now little research has been done both in the area of database systems and neural networks to integrate these two areas. This is surprising, because neural networks can be seen as representation of intensional knowledge of intelligent database systems [1] and the area of knowledge based and rule based database systems is growing dramatically.

It is generally accepted that rule-based reasoning will play an important role in future database applications. Basically the knowledge base consists of facts and rules, which are both stored and handled by the underlying database system.

Therefore they can be part of a rule based knowledge pool and can be used like conventional rules. The user has a unified view about his knowledge base regardless of the origin of the unique rules.

2. Objectives

The proposed framework allows the definition of a single network up to a family of similar networks. These are networks with similar properties, like network paradigm and structure. The adjective 'similar' is not restricted to network properties only, but covers also networks, which accomplish special tasks. The characteristics of these networks can be totally different, but the data base input (the task description) is the same. The data manipulation facilities of the system are exploited to handle the networks and their tasks within the same framework.

The object-oriented approach seams (and in our opinion has proven) the most comfortable and natural design model for neural networks [2]. In the context of object-oriented database systems neural networks are treated generally as complex objects. These systems showed very valuable at handling and administrating such objects in different areas, as computer aided design, geographic databases, administration of component structures, etc.

2.1 Advantages

The usage of a database system as an environment for neural networks provides both quantitative and qualitative advantages.

Quantitative Advantages. Modern database systems allow an efficient administration of objects. This is provided by a 'smart' internal level of the system, which exploits well studied and well known data structures, access paths, etc. A whole bunch of further concepts is inherent to these systems, like models for transaction handling, recovery, multi-user capability, concurrent access etc. This places an unchallenged platform in speed and security for the definition and manipulation of large data sets at the users disposal.

Qualitative Advantages. The user has powerful tools and models at hand, like data definition and manipulation languages, report generators or transaction processing. These tools provide a unified framework for handling neural networks and the input or output data streams of these networks. The user is confronted with one general user interface only. This spares him awkward tricks to analyze the data of his database with a separate network simulator system.

A second very important aspect (which is beyond the scope of this paper) is the usage of neural networks as part of the rule component of a knowledge base data base system [3]. Neural networks represent inherently knowledge by the processing in the nodes [4]. Trained neural networks are similar to rules in the conventional symbolic sense. A very promising approach is therefore the embedding of neural networks directly into the generalized knowledge framework of a knowledge based database system.

3. Embedding of neural networks into database systems

In the last few years many different systems for the easy and software supported creation and administration of neural networks were presented. Some of the system tackle only special types of neural networks as for example Aspirin/MIGRAINES [5] or SOM-PAK [6]. Other try to give a comprehensive tool as AXON [7], SNNS [8], Xerion [9] or NeurDS [10]. In general all systems provide the user with a proprietary software environment, which reaches from highly sophisticated interactive systems to programming language extensions by special libraries.

All these approaches confront the user with the problem to cope with a new and sometimes quite complex tool. Further most of these systems deliver a stand alone environment, which is not capable to interconnect to other software systems. A further problem of all these systems is the lack of a generalized framework for handling data sets connected with neural networks. During the training phase and the evaluation phase of a neural net the user has to support the net with large amount of data. Conventionally data sets are often supported via sequential files only and the definition of the input stream, output or target stream into a neural net is often extremely clumsy, static and complex.

In the following we show how to solve these problems by a direct embedding of neural networks as a basic data type of a data base system and we give a generalized model for the definition, usage and administration of neural networks in object oriented systems.

3.1 Levels of Embedding

With the embedding of neural networks into database systems different levels of embedding can be distinguished according to the functionality presented to the user. These levels are obviously highly dependent on the characteristics and properties of the underlying database system. If the database system doesn't support a certain functionality, the neural network embedding has to consider it and is restricted accordingly.

The levels of embedding can be defined by the control of the user of the static and dynamic properties of neural network objects. Control means the possibility to change or adapt the properties in question.

Static properties describe the structure of the processing elements (PE), the connections (C) or the overall network structure (NS). The dynamic property defines the evaluation and the training methodology. Depending on the user's control of the one, the other or both, we basically classify 3 levels (0 to 2) of embedding. The following table gives a level classification. 'Y' res. 'N' (Yes/No) denotes user controllable res. not user controllable.

level	static property		dyn. prop.
	NS	PE & C	
0	N	N	N
1 a	Y	N	N
1 b	Y	Y	N
2	Y	Y	Y

Tab. 1. embedding level classification according to user control

An embedding of level 0 characterizes a system, which allows to use predefined neural networks as conventional evaluation rules similar to mathematical functions. These neural networks are pretrained outside of the system and accessible by the user as executable functions only. This situation is useful where neural network are part of the algorithmic or mathematical library, which the user can employ to solve his application problems.

If the user can administrate neural networks as normal objects in the database systems and can to some extent control the static structure of a network, then a level 1 embedding is provided by the system. We distinguish between a level 1a and 1b embedding, depending on the control of the processing element structure or not. Obviously controlling the processing element structure without controlling the dynamic component (which uses the adapted structure) is of minor interest. Therefore if we consider level 1 embedding, we normally have the level 1a in mind.

Level 1 embedding is the typical situation, where the user can choose from a set of predefined network paradigms and can define his own special network object. He has the possibility to train and to evaluate the neural network. A level 1 embedding represents a very powerful and rather flexible instrument. How flexible it is in practice depends heavily on the network paradigms provided by the system. Therefore a weak implementation can restrict the user to a limited range of applications only. On the other hand a level 1 embedding can have the advantage of high performance, if the system uses specialized hardware in its implementation.

A level 2 embedding gives the most comprehensive flexibility to the user. He can define his own network and element structures and can also describe the methods for evaluation and training. This level makes high demands on the underlying database system functionality.

3.2   The NeuDB system

The NeuDB system represents a level 1 embedding according to the presented framework.

The NeuDB basis. Basis for the development of the NeuDB system were two free available systems, the Postgres database system [12] and the NeurDS neural network simulator [10].

Postgres: It is a highly extensible database system with object oriented features, like type inheritance. The data model of Postgres consists of classes (relations) containing tuples, which represent real-world entities. A class has attributes of a fixed type that represent properties of the objects stored in the class.

We chose Postgres because of its capability to define user functions written in a high programming language [11] (like C). This allowed the development of a function library, which establishes the connection and communication to the neural network simulator. Using the rule system a data-driven request-action strategy was established. The insertion or update of neural network objects causes requests to the NN simulator. Its actions represent the dynamic component of the system. Finally the type inheritance features made possible a natural and comfortable modeling of the neural network data type according to our embedding framework.

NeurDS: The NeurDS system (Neural Design and Simulation system) is a general purpose tool for building , running and analyzing neural network models. Its main advantages are

- generic model definition capability and
- machine independence.

We adapted the source code to our needs and developed a library of functions for a number of common network paradigms.

The NeuDB system architecture. A neural network class is embedded into the Postgres class system and the rule system of Postgres is heavily exploited to emulate the dynamic neural network component.

The Neural network simulator runs as an independent server process (NNserver) in parallel to the database system and performs the actual network evaluation and training. It provides a user interface, which allows to monitor the state of the simulator. This proved extremely useful for the training phase of a network. The user can create trace files, which can be used for the definition of consecutive training phases. The following figure shows the structure of the NeuDB system.

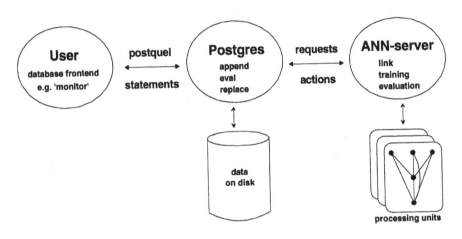

Fig. 1. NeuDB structure

The Postgres database server administrates the data on disk and requests actions of the ANN-server (artificial neural network server) corresponding to database commands (append, replace, eval). The ANN-server creates an artificial neural network according to the data description, performs the requested actions and updates the database accordingly. The user at the computer console directs both processes and controls interactively the system status.

The distribution of the tasks to 2 separate and independently running servers gives the advantage of exploiting the inherent parallelism of the system. While the ANN-server is processing the neural networks (training or evaluation), the database server is providing the input data streams in parallel. Generally it can be seen as a pipelined process structure. Postgres is designed to support the database server paradigm, where an independent database server runs on a dedicated machine and communicates with the front-end processes via the network.

We exploit this paradigm by a 'request - action' strategy. The user connects to the database via a front-end process (this can be the usual Postgres 'monitor' or any other available front-end program). User inputs trigger actions (e.g. the insertion of a training object triggers a training phase), which are resolved by a call to the ANN-server. The server processes the requests (e.g. the training phase) and performs dependent data actions (e.g. the insertion of link weights).

The ANN-server can physically distribute its tasks among available processing units of the underlying network. So it can exploit idle workstations of the network to perform the very time consuming neural network actions. This increases the performance of the whole system not only in multi-user mode operation, but also if the user chose the non-blocking operation mode. Using this mode he has not to wait for the accomplishment his requested actions; he just initiates it and continues with his work.. This allows the user to parallelizes his requests, for example multiple training phases.

The whole system presents a comfortable and customary interface to the user. A typical screen shot is given by the next figure. It shows the system running on an HP 9000 workstation. The pictured task consists of the creation, training and evaluation of a neural network to solve the well known XOR problem (see the example at the end of the paper). The screen consists of 3 windows, one (inactive) postgres server window, the ANN-server window tracing the neural network actions and the postgres monitor window (user window) requesting the actions by object insertions.

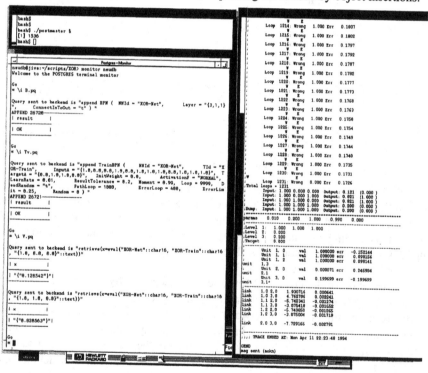

Fig. 2. NeuDB screen

The following section presents an in-depth definition of the data model of the neural network class in the Postgres database system.

Data types. The 'NeuralNet' type is a subtype of the general object type of the database system. Subtypes of this NeuralNet type can be differentiated into specialized neural network types according to their network paradigm. It is also possible that a network paradigm is the supertype of another more specialized paradigm. In the NeuDB system a neural network is generally defined by the 'NeuralNet' class, which provides a unique identifier for referencing the neural network object. It also describes the basic structure of the network by a Layer attribute. This contains a sequence (basically an array) of integer values, which defines the number of processing elements in each layer. (In the following we give the Postquel statement for the respective class creation.)

```
create NeuralNet (
    NNId = char16,
    Layer = int4[]
)
```

At this definition level nothing is said about the network paradigm. This is defined via a specialization, a subtype of 'NeuralNet'. This subtype (which inherits all characteristics of its supertype) provides the specific and necessary attributes dependent on the network paradigm. Connected with the definition of the paradigm is the dynamic behavior of the network. For example, a feedforward network paradigm with backpropagation training algorithm is provided by the system,

```
create BPN (
    ConnectInToOutput = bool
) inherits (NeuralNet)
```

The boolean 'ConnectInToOutput' attribute controls the automatic generation of connecting links (a full connection) between the processing elements. If it is set to 'true', a rule triggers a 'create links' action, which is performed by the ANN-server. After completion of this action, corresponding links can be found in a 'Links' class, which defines the network interconnections. The user can by-pass the automatic link generation and can insert appropriate Links object into the 'Links' class by hand. This allows the creation of arbitrary network topologies.

The characteristics of a trained network is defined by the 'Train' class. This class provides all attributes for the training phase of the referenced neural network object. It is organized as a hierarchical type structure similar to the basic neural network class. Generally a 'Train' class consists of the neural object reference (NNId), a unique 'Train' object identifier (TId) and a definition of the input and target data stream.

```
create Train (
    TId = char16,
    NNId = char16,
    InputA = float8[],
    TargetA = float8[],
    InputF = char16,
    TargetF = char16
)
```

The data values can be defined explicitly by a value sequence or implicitly via a Postquel statement (see the following section).
A 'Train' sub-class provides object characteristics dependent on the network paradigm.

```
create TrainBPN (
   InitWeight = float8,
   ActivationF = char16,
   ...
   LogFile = char16
) inherits (Train)
```

This class defines all describing attributes for the training phase respective to the network paradigm. The training action is started by the insertion of a training object into the specialized class. The action is processed in similar way as the link action. A request is sent to the ANN-server, which performs the training and inserts calculated link weight values back into a 'weight'-class of the database. After a completed training phase the user can use the 'trained' neural network object to analyze his data sets. This can be done via two mechanisms, the creation of an 'Eval' (evaluate) object or the use of the 'eval'-function.

The 'eval' function allows the user to evaluate a neural network object according to the training characteristics responding to an input data stream. This function can be seen as an embedded operator and can be used in any Postquel statements.

The second possibility is the insertion of an 'Eval' object into the respective class. The insertion triggers an eval action, which is resolved by the ANN-server. The result is inserted into a result class. The user can directly access this class or via a composed 'Output' attribute (a Postquel function) defined on 'Eval'.

The creation of an 'Eval' object has the advantage that the result of the neural network evaluation is stored in the database and has not to be calculated again. It can easily be accessed via the conventional database operations.

We have to look more closely at two topics, which arose in the preceding discussion,

- functional data stream definition
- blocking versus non-blocking requests

Both topic have important effects on the overall system behavior.

Functional data stream definition. There are two advantages with the definition of the data streams via functions:

A homogenous working environment: This method allows the user to specify the data sets in a comfortable way. He has the well known apparatus of the Postquel database manipulation language at hand. He can use the same tool either for administrating or analyzing his stored information. So it is easily possible for him both to use his 'real world' data sets as training set for neural networks and to analyze other (or the same) data with trained networks.

The handling of a neural network has to be simple. That means that there has not to be a complex or artificial procedure to use it, in contrary the environment has to supply functions to manipulate neural network in a natural and (more important) commonly known way.

In the formalism of the database system both types of information (the 'real-world' data and the neural networks) are 'just' data. These data objects are therefore administrated and handled homogeneously within the same framework.

Increased system performance: To perform a useful training phase the user has to provide certain training phase controlling parameters. The type and the number of parameters are highly dependent on the network paradigm. All paradigms expect input and target data. In an increasing number of neural network applications these data sets show tremendous sizes, like in cluster analysis, pattern recognition, etc.. Therefore the access costs are not neglectable and have to be considered in the processing times.

In these cases the database facilities of the NeuDB system can improve the performance of the data analysis process tremendously. Besides the mentioned data pipelining of the independent processes, the access mechanisms of the database system provide a powerful tool for the handling of these large data sets.

Blocking versus non-blocking requests. The resolution of a requested action can be a rather time consuming process (e.g. the training phase). This leads to an obvious discrepancy in completion time of the database server triggering operation (the insertion), which has (beneath) no delay, and the ANN-server operations, which can last from minutes to hours (depending on the problem). Two possibilities were implemented:

- blocking request
- non-blocking request

Blocking suspends the request is until the completion of the requested action. This leads to an obvious response delay of the system for the user. The user has to wait for the completion of the action before he has further access to the system. This keeps a very simple consistency property:

- If an action triggering object exists in the database (i.e. is accessible for all users), the corresponding action has completed and the dependent information is available in the database system.

That means in the context of the insertion of a training object a completed 'append', the respective training phase has finished and the link values and their respective update values can be found in the 'weight' class.

In contrary a non-blocking request initiates the action only and gives back control to the user. The user has immediate access to the system, but has to deal with a sever consistency problem. For example, the append to the 'Train' class creates a training object without respective trained network information (like link weights).

This problem is solved by a transaction protocol with object hiding. It allows a triggering object (TO) insertion, but keeps the inserted object invisible for the database until the training phase completed. An additional request class (RC) is be necessary, where TOs are only inserted temporarily. The method can be described by the following simple algorithm.

```
User inserts TO into the RC
Initiation of the triggered action
Wait for completion of the action
Store action specific dependent information (e.g. link weights)
Transfer TO from RC into the original class
```

It is the responsibility of the user to target the original class for the 'arrival' of the object. Via the request class he is always informed about the pending actions.

In the current NeuDB the user can choose via a 'Control' object between both possibilities.

3.3 An example: The XOR problem

The following section gives an example of the creation, training and usage of a neural network object which solves the well known XOR-problem [13].

All user inputs are marked by a preceding '>' prompt. The shown examples represent actual screen dumps. The sometimes intricate format is a 'specialty' of the Postgres monitor program.

Creation and administration. To solve the XOR-problem we use a feedforward multi-layer network with the backpropagation training algorithm [14].

First we have to create a neural network object within the database system. This is easily done by an append to the back-propagation network class BPN. We define the network identifier (for future references to this object) and the number of layers and number of processing elements for each layer.

```
> append BPN (
      NNId = "XOR-Net",
      Layer = "{ 3, 1, 1 }",
      ConnectInToOutput = "t"
  )
```

The user doesn't have to insert the links between the processing nodes. In this case it is done automatically by setting the 'ConnectInToOutput' flag to true. This triggers a Postgres rule, which appends the correct links to the Link class automatically. (Actually a request is sent to the ANN-server, which performs the insertions.)

The status of the new neural network object is untrained. Via the network identifier NNId the object can be referenced and conventional database tasks can be performed, like updating

```
> replace BPN (Layer = "{ 3, 5, 1 }") where BPN.NNId = "XOR-Net"
```

or deleting.

```
> delete BPN where BPN.NNId = "XOR-Net"
```

During the update and the delete operation the consistency is kept in the database system in accordance to the status or properties of the neural network. Both operations trigger rules, which change accordingly to the operation dependent objects. This can be an update of the connections of the processing elements represented by entries in the Link class (see replace example) or the deletion of training characteristics connected with neural network object, which was deleted (see delete example). All these consistency keeping operations are performed automatically without a forced activity by the user.

Besides the typical database tasks the user has to have the possibility to express specialized neural network operations, like training and evaluation.

Training. The training phase is started by the insertion of a training object. This object contains the necessary training parameter as attribute values. Besides the neural network identifier, the training identifier and the Input and Target data stream the other values are set to default values. So it is not necessary to specify all values explicitly (, but it is good programming practice).

```
> append TrainBPN (
      NNId = "XOR-Net,
      TId = "Train1",
      InputA = "{
```

```
        1.0, 0.0, 0.0,
        1.0, 0.0, 1.0,
        1.0, 1.0, 0.0,
        1.0, 1.0, 1.0
    }"
    TargetA = "{ 0.0, 1.0, 1.0, 0.0 }"
    ...
)
```

The above example uses input res. target values explicitly. But as mentioned above, it is also possible to use Input res. Target functions. These functions are conventional Postquel statements. The result of these statements is a sequential data stream with the same position property as the respective explicit value definition.

A training object with a functional data definition is therefore inserted by

```
> append TrainingBPN (
    NNId = "XOR-Net,
    TId = "Train2",
    InputF = "retrieve(A.x, A.y) from A in InputValues",
    TargetF = "retrieve(B.z) from B in TargetValues",
    ...
)
```

The result of the completed training phase is a new object in the 'weight' class. This object can be checked by the following retrieve statement

```
> retrieve (weight.all) where NNId = "XOR-Net" and TID = "Train2"
```

which produces as result

```
--------------------------------------------------------
| NNId       | TId        | Weights      | cWeights      |
--------------------------------------------------------
| XOR-Net    | Train2     | {"1.93072","4.76279","-5.74234","-
3.07542","-5.74085","-3.075","-7.72916"}|
{"0.000641426","0.00224068","-0.00127401","-0.00165155","-
0.00126514","-0.00171889","-0.00279093"}|
--------------------------------------------------------
```

Usage. As mentioned above, neural networks can be used to analyze test data via the insertion of an 'Eval' object, e.g.

```
> append Eval (
    EId = "E1",
    NNId = "XOR-Net",
    TId = "Train1",
    InputA = "{ 1.0, 1.0, 1.0 }"
}
```

or via the 'eval' function,

```
> retrieve(x = eval("XOR-Net"::char16, "Train1"::char16, "{ 1.0,
1.0, 1.0 }"::text)
```

which produces

```
----------------
| x             |
----------------
| "{"0.199699"}"|
----------------
```

We have the possibility to use a Postquel function instead of explicit input values, too.

The result of the 'eval' function is (because of type restriction of the Postgres system) a general text string. This string can be transferred via cast operations easily into the wished data type (normally an array of floating point numbers).

3.4 Temporary results and future work

We used the NeuDB system now for a short period and it proved amazingly well with practical applications. We tested it with the administration and analysis of medical data sets and it reached a high degree of acceptance throughout the group of test user. The homogeneity of the database and neural network simulator interface found general acceptance and a high attraction.

A slight performance gain was notable because of the data pipeline parallelism with very large data sets during the training phase. The non-blocking requests were generally preferred by the users to the blocking requests. It proved very useful for the parallel execution of multiple training phases in a single user session.

The next step will be a replacement and general new development of the neural network simulator. We aim for a highly parallel system design, which can employ an underlying parallel shared nothing hardware architecture.

4. References

1. Parsaye K., Chignell M., Khoshafian S., Wong H., *Intelligent data base and automatic discovery*, In Neural and Intelligent Systems Integration, (ed. B. Soucek), John Wiley Inc., pp. 615 - 629, 1991
2. Heileman G., et al., *A general framework for concurrent simulation of neural networks models*, IEEE Trans. Software Engineering, 18, 7, pp. 551-562, 1992
3. Schikuta E., *The role of neural networks in knowledge based systems*, Proc. Int. Symp. on nonlinear theory and applications, Hawaii, 1993
4. Pao Y.-H., Sobajic D.J., *Neural networks and Knowledge Engineering*, IEEE Knowledge and Data Engineering, 3, 2, pp. 185 - 192, June 1991
5. Leighton R., *The Aspirin/MIGRAINES Neural Network Software*, user manual, MITRE Corp., 1992
6. SOM Prog. Team, *SOM-PAK, The Self-Organizing Map Program Package*, user guide, Helsinki, 1992
7. Hecht-Nielsen R., *Neurocomputing*, Addison/Wesley, 1989
8. Zell A. et al., *SNNS, Stuttgart Neural Network Simulator*, User Manual, Tech.Rep.No. 3/92, Univ. Stuttgart, 1992
9. Camp D.v., *Xerion Neural Network Simulator*, user guide, Univ. Toronto, 1992
10. Wecker D.B., *The Neural Design and Simulation System (NeurDS)*, Digital Tech. Rep. 589, May 1989
11. Stonebraker M., et. al., *Extending a Database system with Procedures*, ACM Transactions on Database Systems, Sept. 1987
12. Rowe L., Stonebraker M., *The POSTGRES data model*, Proc. 1987 Conference on Very Large Database Systems, Brighton, 1987
13. Beale R., *Neural Computing: an introduction*, Hilger, 1990
14. Rumelhardt, D.E. et al., *Learning internal Representation by Error Propagation*, in Rumelhardt D.E. et al., Parallel Distributed Processing: Explorations in the Microstructure of Cognition, Vol 1, MIT Press, 1986

Weighted Defaults in Description Logics: Formal Properties and Proof Theory [*]

J. Joachim Quantz and Sven Suska

Technische Universität Berlin, Projekt KIT-VM11
FR 5-12, Franklinstr. 28/29, D-10587 Berlin
{jjq,svs}@cs.tu-berlin.de

Abstract. We present a Preferential Default Description Logic (PDDL) based on weighted defaults and show that the preferential entailment relation $\approx_\Sigma$ satisfies all properties of system **P** and Rational Monotonicity. The main characteristics of this PDDL is that it uses an ordering between multisets of defaults for priorization, treats defaults similar to material implications, and adheres strictly to the principle of exception minimization.

We furthermore show how maximization of default applications can be consistently combined with $\approx_\Sigma$ without violating exception minimization. Furthermore, the resulting entailment relation $\approx_\Sigma^F$ still satisfies all properties of system **P**.

We then develop a proof theory for $\approx_\Sigma$ based on default spaces, which shows that $\approx_\Sigma$ is decidable if the underlying DL is. $\approx_\Sigma$ can be syntactically characterized by strict entailment from all maximal default spaces and can thus be computed by an exponential algorithm.

1 Introduction

In this paper we present an integration of *weighted defaults* into Description Logics (DL). The general framework of this integration has first been proposed in [13], where specificity wrt strict subsumption determines a priority ordering on defaults. The weighted defaults used in this paper, however, not only order individual defaults, but also multisets of defaults. Such a fine-grained priorization is motivated by an application in Natural Language Processing, more precisely by the task of disambiguation. The approach of preferential interpretation, which is used in the project KIT-VM11[2], is described, for example, in [12, 15]. Here we will concentrate on the formal aspects of weighted defaults and take the motivation for their integration into DL for granted.

In Section 2 we define a Preferential Default Description Logic (PDDL) based on weighted defaults by using standard model-theoretic techniques from Nonmonotonic Reasoning [7, 9]. One benefit of using these techniques is that the resulting preferential entailment relation $\approx_\Sigma$ satisifies a number of desirable formal properties, i.e. it is logically well-behaved. We prove some of these properties and refer the interested

---

[*] The project KIT-VM11 is supported by the German Federal Minister of Research and Technology (BMFT) under contract 01 IV 101Q8.

[2] KIT-VM11 is part of the German Machine Translation project VERBMOBIL.

reader to [14], where all properties are proved in detail and where $\mathrel{\vdash\!\!\!\sim}_\Sigma$ is compared with other PDDLs.[3]

In a second step we then develop a proof theory for $\mathrel{\vdash\!\!\!\sim}_\Sigma$, show that it is decidable if the underlying DL is, and that it can be computed by an exponential algorithm based on default spaces.

It should be noted that the general framework of PDDL allows the definition of various different preferential entailment relations. The following list contains the most interesting parameters of variation:

1. Minimization of exceptions can be based on either the domain D or a set of object names $\mathcal{O}$, yielding different behavior wrt implicit objects.
2. Priorization between defaults can be realized, for example, by ordering individual defaults or by ordering multisets of defaults.
3. In addition to exception minimization, maximization of default application can be considered.
4. Defaults can behave as forward-chaining trigger rules or as material implications.

The logic $^D\!\mathrel{\vdash\!\!\!\sim}_\prec$ presented in [13] and $\mathrel{\vdash\!\!\!\sim}_\Sigma$ are thus two different instantiations of the general framework, differing wrt the particular choices made for the above parameters. When defining $\mathrel{\vdash\!\!\!\sim}_\Sigma$ in the following section, we will indicate how definitions have to be changed to obtain different choices for the respective parameters. In particular we will point out the differences between $\mathrel{\vdash\!\!\!\sim}_\Sigma$ and $^D\!\mathrel{\vdash\!\!\!\sim}_\prec$. Interestingly, $\mathrel{\vdash\!\!\!\sim}_\Sigma$, which is motivated by application-oriented considerations, is also preferable from a logical point of view—in contrast to $^D\!\mathrel{\vdash\!\!\!\sim}_\prec$ it satisfies Rational Monotonicity and preserves formal properties when combined with a maximization of default applications.

Finally, it should be noted that the results presented in this paper are not specific to PDDL but are of general interest for Nonmonotonic Reasoning. In particular, the fact that weighted defaults allow a fine-grained priorization and satisfy Rational Monotonicity could be straightforwardly applied to Circumscription [10] or to Ordered Theory Presentations [17]. Furthermore, the distinction between minimizing exceptions and maximizing default applications is a general distinction between preferential-model approaches and Reiter-style approaches [16].

2 A PDDL Based on Weighted Defaults

Due to page limitations we will not give any introduction into DL in this paper. Results on complexity and decidability of different DL dialects can be found, for example, in [4]; a small application example illustrating the functionality provided by DL systems is given in [15].

In the following we assume a standard model-theoretic semantics for our DL, in which a model M is a pair $\langle D, [\![\cdot]\!]^{\mathcal{I}} \rangle$. D is a set, called the domain, and $[\![\cdot]\!]^{\mathcal{I}}$ is an interpretation function mapping concepts into subsets of D and object names from a finite set $\mathcal{O}$ injectively (Unique Name Assumption) into D. DL dialects differ wrt the

---

[3] Note that the presentation in [13] is based on Shoham's preferential-model approach [18] and does not address these formal properties.

concept-forming operators they contain. For the presentation in this paper we only need the boolean connectives $c_1 \sqcap c_2$, $c_1 \sqcup c_2$, and $\neg c$.[4]

We write $M \models \gamma$ to express that M is a model of a DL formula γ, which is defined by

$$M \models c_2 \sqsubseteq c_1 \text{ iff } [\![c_2]\!]^{\mathcal{I}} \subseteq [\![c_1]\!]^{\mathcal{I}}$$
$$M \models o :: c \text{ iff } [\![o]\!]^{\mathcal{I}} \in [\![c]\!]^{\mathcal{I}}$$

As usual, M is a model of a set of formulae Γ (written $M \models \Gamma$) iff it is a model of every formula in Γ. A formula γ is entailed by a set of formulae Γ (written $\Gamma \models \gamma$) iff every model of Γ is also a model of γ.

Given such a basic DL we now define a PDDL based on weighted defaults:

Definition 1. A **weighted default** δ has the form $c_1 \rightsquigarrow_n c_2$, where c_1 and c_2 are DL concepts and n is a natural number. We call c_1 the premise of δ (written δ_p), c_2 its conclusion (written δ_c) and n its weight (written $w(\delta)$).

The basic idea of PDDL is to use the information contained in a set of weighted defaults Δ to establish an ordering on models. Intuitively, we want to prefer models which have as few exceptions as possible. Obviously, an exception to a default δ is an object o which is an instance of δ_p but not of δ_c:

Definition 2. Let δ be a weighted default, $\mathcal{O}$ a finite set of object names, and M a model. The **exceptions** to δ in M are defined as

$$E_M(\delta) \overset{\text{def}}{=} \{o \in \mathcal{O} : [\![o]\!]^{\mathcal{I}} \in [\![\delta_p]\!]^{\mathcal{I}} \wedge [\![o]\!]^{\mathcal{I}} \notin [\![\delta_c]\!]^{\mathcal{I}}\}$$

Instead of taking $\mathcal{O}$ we could also take the domain D as exception base, as has been done in [13]. The main difference is the effect on implicit objects (see [14] for details). To let defaults behave like forward-chaining trigger rules instead of like material implications, the exceptions have to be defined wrt to instanceship of epistemic concepts defined with the k-operator from [5]. We are currently investigating such a logic.

When defining the preference ordering on models we have to take into account the respective relevance of an exception, which is given by the weight of the default:

Definition 3. Let M be a model and Δ a finite set of weighted defaults. The **negative score** of M is defined as

$$score^-(M) \overset{\text{def}}{=} \sum_{\delta \in \Delta} (|E_M(\delta)| \cdot w(\delta))$$

Note that it would be more accurate to speak of the negative score of a model wrt some sets Δ and $\mathcal{O}$. In the following, Δ and $\mathcal{O}$ are always assumed to be specified, and we will not mention them explicitly. Thus the ordering on models defined below is also relative to given sets Δ and $\mathcal{O}$:

---

[4] The results presented in this paper are valid for the integration of weighted defaults into arbitrary DL dialects. As we will show in Section 3 the resulting PDDL is decidable if the underlying DL is.

Definition 4. Let M, N be two models. Σ-**preference** is defined as

$$M \sqsubset_\Sigma N \text{ iff } score^-(M) > score^-(N)$$

Note that this definition reflects the chosen priorization and that alternative orderings can be defined to obtain alternative priorizations [14]. We will illustrate below the major difference between this ordering based on weighted defaults and the one based on specificity used in [13].

Given this ordering, we can use the standard technique to define a preferential entailment relation, e.g. [7, 9].

Definition 5. Let Γ be a set of DL formulae and M a model. M is a $\sqsubset_\Sigma$-**maximal** model of Γ iff M is a model of Γ and there is no model N of Γ such that $M \sqsubset_\Sigma N$.

In the definition of the preferential entailment relation $\models_\Sigma$ only $\sqsubset_\Sigma$-maximal models are taken into account:

Definition 6. Let Γ be a set of DL formulae, $\mathcal{O}$ a finite set of object names, Δ a finite set of weighted defaults, $\sqsubset_\Sigma$ the corresponding ordering on DL models, and γ a DL formula. γ is Σ-**entailed** by Γ and Δ (written $\Gamma; \Delta \models_\Sigma \gamma$) iff all $\sqsubset_\Sigma$-maximal models of Γ are models of γ.

In addition we define preferential entailment of default subsumption separately (a motivation is given in [14]).

Definition 7. Let Γ be a set of DL formulae, Δ a finite set of weighted defaults, and $c_1 \rightsquigarrow c_2$ a **default subsumption**. $\Gamma; \Delta \models_\Sigma c_1 \rightsquigarrow c_2$ iff for any object name o not occurring in Γ we have $\Gamma, o :: c_1; \Delta \models_\Sigma o :: c_2$.

It is straightforward to prove that $\models_\Sigma$ satisfies all the properties of system **P** [7] and *Rational Monotonicity* [9] as shown in Figure 1. The detailed proofs are given in [14]. Here we will just prove that $\sqsubset_\Sigma$ is *stoppered* (which implies that the properties of system **P** hold for $\models_\Sigma$ [9]), and that $\models_\Sigma$ satisfies Rational Monotonicity, a non-Horn condition not implied by system **P** and only seldomly satisfied by Nonmonotonic Logics.

Definition 8. Let $\sqsubset$ be an ordering on models. $\sqsubset$ is **stoppered** iff for each set of DL formulae Γ and for each model M of Γ

1. M is a $\sqsubset$-maximal model of Γ or
2. there is a $\sqsubset$-maximal model N of Γ such that $M \sqsubset N$.

To prove stopperedness of $\sqsubset_\Sigma$ we prove transitivity and co-well-foundedness of $\sqsubset_\Sigma$, which implies stopperedness:

Lemma 9. *Let $\sqsubset$ be an ordering on models. If $\sqsubset$ is transitive and co-well-founded, i.e. there is no infinite chain $M_1 \sqsubset M_2 \sqsubset \ldots$, then it is stoppered.*

Proof. We prove the converse, namely that transitive orderings which are not stoppered are not co-well-founded.

Property	Preferential Entailment	Default Subsumption
Reflexivity	$\Gamma, \gamma; \Delta \mathrel{|\!\approx}_\Sigma \gamma$	$\Gamma; \Delta \mathrel{|\!\approx}_\Sigma c \leadsto c$
Left Logical Equivalence	$\dfrac{\Gamma, \alpha \models \beta \quad \Gamma, \beta \models \alpha \quad \Gamma, \alpha; \Delta \mathrel{|\!\approx}_\Sigma \gamma}{\Gamma, \beta; \Delta \mathrel{|\!\approx}_\Sigma \gamma}$	$\dfrac{\Gamma \models c_1 \doteq c_2 \quad \Gamma; \Delta \mathrel{|\!\approx}_\Sigma c_1 \leadsto c_3}{\Gamma; \Delta \mathrel{|\!\approx}_\Sigma c_2 \leadsto c_3}$
Right Weakening	$\dfrac{\Gamma, \alpha \models \beta \quad \Gamma; \Delta \mathrel{|\!\approx}_\Sigma \alpha}{\Gamma; \Delta \mathrel{|\!\approx}_\Sigma \beta}$	$\dfrac{\Gamma \models c_1 \sqsubseteq c_2 \quad \Gamma; \Delta \mathrel{|\!\approx}_\Sigma c_3 \leadsto c_1}{\Gamma; \Delta \mathrel{|\!\approx}_\Sigma c_3 \leadsto c_2}$
Cut	$\dfrac{\Gamma, \alpha; \Delta \mathrel{|\!\approx}_\Sigma \gamma \quad \Gamma; \Delta \mathrel{|\!\approx}_\Sigma \alpha}{\Gamma; \Delta \mathrel{|\!\approx}_\Sigma \gamma}$	$\dfrac{\Gamma; \Delta \mathrel{|\!\approx}_\Sigma c_1 \sqcap c_2 \leadsto c_3 \quad \Gamma; \Delta \mathrel{|\!\approx}_\Sigma c_1 \leadsto c_2}{\Gamma; \Delta \mathrel{|\!\approx}_\Sigma c_1 \leadsto c_3}$
Cautious Monotonicity	$\dfrac{\Gamma; \Delta \mathrel{|\!\approx}_\Sigma \alpha \quad \Gamma; \Delta \mathrel{|\!\approx}_\Sigma \gamma}{\Gamma, \alpha; \Delta \mathrel{|\!\approx}_\Sigma \gamma}$	$\dfrac{\Gamma; \Delta \mathrel{|\!\approx}_\Sigma c_1 \leadsto c_2 \quad \Gamma; \Delta \mathrel{|\!\approx}_\Sigma c_1 \leadsto c_3}{\Gamma; \Delta \mathrel{|\!\approx}_\Sigma c_1 \sqcap c_2 \leadsto c_3}$
Or		$\dfrac{\Gamma; \Delta \mathrel{|\!\approx}_\Sigma c_1 \leadsto c_3 \quad \Gamma; \Delta \mathrel{|\!\approx}_\Sigma c_2 \leadsto c_3}{\Gamma; \Delta \mathrel{|\!\approx}_\Sigma c_1 \sqcup c_2 \leadsto c_3}$
Rational Monotonicity		$\dfrac{\Gamma; \Delta \mathrel{|\!\not\approx}_\Sigma c_1 \sqcap c_2 \leadsto c_3 \quad \Gamma; \Delta \mathrel{|\!\approx}_\Sigma c_1 \leadsto c_3}{\Gamma; \Delta \mathrel{|\!\approx}_\Sigma c_1 \leadsto \neg c_2}$

Fig. 1. Formal properties of system **P** from [7] and Rational Monotonicity [9] for preferential entailment and default subsumption.

Assume that $\sqsubset$ is not stoppered, i.e. there is a set of DL formulae Γ and a model M_1 of Γ such that M_1 is not a $\sqsubset$-maximal model of Γ and there exists no $\sqsubset$-maximal model M_2 of Γ with $M_1 \sqsubset M_2$.

Since M_1 is not a $\sqsubset$-maximal model of Γ there must be a model M_2 of Γ with $M_1 \sqsubset M_2$. Since M_2 is not a $\sqsubset$-maximal model of Γ either, there must be a model M_3 of Γ with $M_2 \sqsubset M_3$. Since $\sqsubset$ is transitive we also have $M_1 \sqsubset M_3$, hence M_3 is not a $\sqsubset$-maximal model of Γ. We thus have constructed an infinite chain $M_1 \sqsubset M_2 \cdots$.

Proposition 10. $\sqsubset_\Sigma$ *is transitive, co-well-founded, and stoppered.*

Proof. Transitivity follows immediately from transitivity of $>$. For co-well-foundedness note that in the "worst" model all members of $\mathcal{O}$ are exceptions to all defaults in Δ, such that its score is $\sum_{\delta \in \Delta}(|\mathcal{O}| \cdot w(\delta))$. The "best" model, on the other hand, has no exception to any default and the score therefore is 0. Clearly, since $\mathcal{O}$ and Δ are finite there are only finitely many natural numbers between 0 and $\sum_{\delta \in \Delta}(|\mathcal{O}| \cdot w(\delta))$. Stopperedness then follows from Lemma 9.

To prove Rational Monotonicity we need the following Lemma:

Lemma 11. *Let Γ be a set of DL formulae and M, N two models of Γ. If N is a $\sqsubset_\Sigma$-maximal model of Γ and M is not, then $M \sqsubset_\Sigma N$.*

Proof. M is not a $\sqsubseteq_\Sigma$-maximal model of Γ, i.e. we have a model M_2 of Γ with $M \sqsubseteq_\Sigma M_2$. Either we have $M_2 \sqsubseteq_\Sigma N$, which gives $M \sqsubseteq_\Sigma N$ by transitivity, or M_2 and N have the same score. But then also $M \sqsubseteq_\Sigma N$.

Given Makinson's terminology, $\sqsubseteq_\Sigma$ is *modular* or *ranked* [9].

Proposition 12 (Rational Monotonicity).

If $\Gamma; \Delta \not\models_\Sigma c_1 \sqcap c_2 \leadsto c_3$ *and* $\Gamma; \Delta \models_\Sigma c_1 \leadsto c_3$ *then* $\Gamma; \Delta \models_\Sigma c_1 \leadsto \neg c_2$.

Proof. The first premise means that we have a $\sqsubseteq_\Sigma$-maximal model M_1 of $\Gamma \cup \{o :: c_1 \sqcap c_2\}$ which is not a model of $o :: c_3$. Because of the second premise M_1 cannot be a $\sqsubseteq_\Sigma$-maximal model of $\Gamma \cup \{o :: c_1\}$, thus we must have a $\sqsubseteq_\Sigma$-maximal model M_2 of $\Gamma \cup \{o :: c_1\}$ with $M_1 \sqsubseteq_\Sigma M_2$ (stopperedness). Due to Lemma 11 we have $M_1 \sqsubseteq_\Sigma M_i$ for all $\sqsubseteq_\Sigma$-maximal models M_i of $\Gamma \cup \{o :: c_1\}$.

Since all the M_i are models of $\Gamma \cup \{o :: c_1\}$ and M_1 is a $\sqsubseteq_\Sigma$-maximal model of $\Gamma \cup \{o :: c_1 \sqcap c_2\}$, no M_i can be a model of $o :: c_2$, i.e. they are all models of $o :: \neg c_2$.

Note that there are three important characteristics of $\models_\Sigma$. First, weighted defaults behave more like material implications than like forward-chaining trigger rules. This is due to the definitions of exceptions and Σ-preference, which imply that a default $c_1 \leadsto_n c_2$ is equivalent to the default $\top \leadsto_n \neg c_1 \sqcup c_2$ (both have identical exceptions). Thus this PDDL is closer in spirit to Circumscription [10] or Ordered Theory Presentations [17] than to Reiter's Default Logic [16] or its application to DL [1].

Second, most approaches to priorization in Nonmononotic Logics are based on *lexicographic priorizations* in which a stronger default can cancel an arbitrary number of weaker defaults. Given the *numerical priorization* underlying $\models_\Sigma$, however, weak defaults can accumulate to overwrite a stronger default, as illustrated by the following example:

$$\Gamma = \{o_1 :: c_1 \sqcap c_2, o_2 :: c_1 \sqcap c_3, o_3 :: c_1 \sqcap c_2 \sqcap c_3\}$$
$$\Delta = \{c_1 \leadsto_{10} c_4, c_2 \leadsto_7 \neg c_4, c_3 \leadsto_8 \neg c_4\}$$
$$\Gamma; \Delta \models_\Sigma \{o_1 :: c_4, o_2 :: c_4, o_3 :: \neg c_4\}$$

Thus instead of having only priorities between individual defaults, $\models_\Sigma$ is based on priorities between *multisets* of defaults. In this respect $\models_\Sigma$ differs considerably from priorized Nonmonotonic Logics like [2, 3, 8, 13, 17].

It is this property which is essential in the NLP application described in [12, 15]. It would thus be interesting to apply the framework of weighted defaults and the numerical priorization to Reiter-style Default Logics. In doing so, we would treat weighted defaults as forward chaining trigger rules instead of material implications, which might lead to more efficient algorithms (see below). There is, however, a third characteristic of $\models_\Sigma$, which also distinguishes it from Reiter-style Default Logics.

Third, $\models_\Sigma$ adheres strictly to the principle of exception minimization (as do Circumscription and Ordered Theory Presentations). In contrast, Reiter's Default Logic mixes minimization of exceptions with maximization of default applications. To illustrate this distinction, consider the weighted defaults $c_1 \leadsto_m c_2$, $c_2 \leadsto_n c_3$ and the description $o :: c_1 \sqcap \neg c_3$. Clearly, o will be an exception to either the first or the second default.

If we adhere to the principle of exception minimization, $o :: c_2$ is Σ-entailed only if $m > n$. Thus the entailment depends solely on the weights m and n. In Reiter's framework, however, there is a built-in priorization of defaults occurring "earlier in a default chain". This priorization is caused by Reiter's definition of extensions (if the premise of a default is in an extension and the conclusion is consistent, it has to be in the extension as well). Since $o :: c_2$ is consistent, it will be contained in every extension. Thus simply applying our approach to Reiter's Default Logic by scoring and ordering extensions would violate the principle of exception minimization. We would infer $o :: c_2$ even if $m < n$.

There is, however, some justification in maximizing applications of defaults. But in our approach, minimization of exceptions has priority over maximization of default application. This intuition can be formalized by combining the $\sqsubseteq_\Sigma$-ordering with an $\sqsubseteq^F$-ordering.

Definition 13. Let δ be a weighted default, $\mathcal{O}$ a finite set of object names and M a model. The **fulfillers** to δ in M are defined as

$$F_M(\delta) \stackrel{\text{def}}{=} \{o \in \mathcal{O} : [\![o]\!]^{\mathcal{I}} \in [\![\delta_p]\!]^{\mathcal{I}} \wedge [\![o]\!]^{\mathcal{I}} \in [\![\delta_c]\!]^{\mathcal{I}}\}$$

We then define fulfillment preference as follows:[5]

Definition 14. Let Δ be a finite set of weighted defaults, and M, N two models. N is **fulfillment preferred** to M (written $M \sqsubseteq^F N$) iff

1. $\exists \delta \in \Delta \ F_N(\delta) \cap E_M(\delta) \neq \emptyset$ and
2. $\forall \delta \in \Delta \ F_M(\delta) \subseteq F_N(\delta)$ and
3. $\forall \delta \in \Delta \ F_N(\delta) \setminus F_M(\delta) \subseteq E_M(\delta)$

The third condition guarantees that fulfillment preference does not yield ungrounded default applications.

We will use $\sqsubseteq^F$-preference only to order models which are *not* ordered by $\sqsubseteq_\Sigma$. Thus only when minimization of exceptions does not distinguish between two models, maximization of fulfillers is used.

Definition 15. Let M, N be two models. N is Σ-**fulfillment-preferred** to M (written $M \sqsubseteq^F_\Sigma N$) iff

1. $M \sqsubseteq_\Sigma N$ or
2. $N \not\sqsubseteq_\Sigma M$ and $M \sqsubseteq^F N$.

In the above example we would thus get $\models_\Sigma o :: c_2$ if $m > n$ and $\models^F_\Sigma o :: c_2$ if $m \geq n$.

Interestingly, all properties of system **P** also hold for $\models^F_\Sigma$, whereas this is not the case for the corresponding specificity-based PDDL developed in [13]. This may seem surprising since $\sqsubseteq^F_\Sigma$ is neither transitive nor stoppered. We can show, however, that we obtain the same preferential entailment relation for $\sqsubseteq^F_\Sigma$ and its transitive closure $^*\sqsubseteq^F_\Sigma$. To prove this we need the following lemma:

---

[5] Note that the definition of fulfillment preference in [13] is not correct as pointed out to us first by Franz Baader.

Lemma 16. *Let M_1, M_2, and M_3 be models.*

1. *If $M_1 \sqsubseteq_\Sigma M_2$ and $M_2 \sqsubseteq_\Sigma^F M_3$ then $M_1 \sqsubseteq_\Sigma M_3$.*
2. *If $M_1 \sqsubseteq_\Sigma^F M_2$ and $M_2 \sqsubseteq_\Sigma M_3$ then $M_1 \sqsubseteq_\Sigma M_3$.*

Proof. (1) Assume we have $M_1 \sqsubseteq_\Sigma M_2$ and $M_2 \sqsubseteq_\Sigma^F M_3$. The second ordering is either due to $M_2 \sqsubseteq_\Sigma M_3$, which immediately gives $M_1 \sqsubseteq_\Sigma M_3$ because of transitivity of $\sqsubseteq_\Sigma$, or to $M_3 \not\sqsubseteq_\Sigma M_2$ and $M_2 \sqsubseteq^F M_3$. But since we assume $M_2 \not\sqsubseteq_\Sigma M_3$ in this case, M_2 and M_3 must have the same score. But then $M_1 \sqsubseteq_\Sigma M_2$ implies $M_1 \sqsubseteq_\Sigma M_3$.
    The proof for (2) is symmetric.

Proposition 17. *Let Γ be a set of DL formulae and M a model. M is a $\sqsubseteq_\Sigma^F$-maximal model of Γ iff M is a $^*\sqsubseteq_\Sigma^F$-maximal model of Γ.*

Proof. The 'if' part is trivial since $^*\sqsubseteq_\Sigma^F$ is the transitive closure of $\sqsubseteq_\Sigma^F$. For the 'only if' part we have to show that if M_1 is a $\sqsubseteq_\Sigma^F$-maximal model of Γ, then there is no model M_n of Γ with $M_1 \sqsubseteq_\Sigma^F \ldots \sqsubseteq_\Sigma^F M_n$.
    Since M_1 is a $\sqsubseteq_\Sigma^F$-maximal model of Γ, no model M_i with $1 < i < n$ is a model of Γ. (More precisely only M_2 is not a model of Γ, but if any other M_i is, we can take it instead of M_n in the proof.) Given Definition 4 each link in the chain is either resolvable to $M_i \sqsubseteq_\Sigma M_{i+1}$ or to $M_{i+1} {}^D\!\not\sqsubseteq_\Sigma M_i \wedge M_i \sqsubseteq^F M_{i+1}$. Due to Lemma 16 we can shorten links of the form $M_{i-1} \sqsubseteq_\Sigma M_i \sqsubseteq_\Sigma^F M_{i+1}$ or $M_{i-1} \sqsubseteq_\Sigma^F M_i \sqsubseteq_\Sigma M_{i+1}$ to a single link $M_{i-1} \sqsubseteq_\Sigma M_{i+1}$. Thus if there is at least one link $M_i \sqsubseteq_\Sigma M_{i+1}$ in the chain, the whole chain collapses and we have $M_1 \sqsubseteq_\Sigma M_n$ which concludes the proof.
    The chain must thus have the form $M_1 \sqsubseteq^F \ldots \sqsubseteq^F M_n$ (we can ignore the information $M_{i+1} {}^D\!\not\sqsubseteq_\Sigma M_i$ in the following). Since we have $M_1 \sqsubseteq^F M_2$ but do not have $M_1 \sqsubseteq^F M$ for any model M of Γ (M_1 is a $\sqsubseteq_\Sigma^F$-maximal model of Γ!), the fact that $M_1 \sqsubseteq^F M_2$ must be due to the fact that M_2 is not a model of Γ. Thus the fulfiller in M_2 responsible for $M_1 \sqsubseteq^F M_2$ must be inconsistent with Γ, i.e. $\Gamma \cup \{o :: \delta_p \sqcap \delta_c\}$ is inconsistent. But since we have $M_2 \sqsubseteq^F \ldots \sqsubseteq^F M_n$, this fulfiller must also be a fulfiller in M_n, which is a model of Γ.

Proposition 18. $\approx_\Sigma^F$ *satisfies all properties of system* **P**.

Proof. Since $^*\sqsubseteq_\Sigma^F$ and $\sqsubseteq_\Sigma^F$ have the same maximal models (Proposition 17), they also yield the same preferential entailment relation. $^*\sqsubseteq_\Sigma^F$ is trivially transitive and co-well-founded, and therefore stoppered. Thus $^*\!\approx_\Sigma^F$, and hence also $\approx_\Sigma^F$, satisfies all properties of system **P**.

3 Proof Theory

In this section we will develop a proof theory for $\approx_\Sigma$ and show that it is decidable if the underlying DL is. Our proof theory is based on the notion of *default spaces* as proposed in [13]:

Definition 19. Let $\mathcal{O}$ be a finite set of object names and Δ a finite set of weighted defaults. A **default space** S (over Δ) is any set of descriptions $o :: \neg \delta_p \sqcup \delta_c$ with $o \in \mathcal{O}$ and $\delta \in \Delta$.

Intuitively, a default space represents which defaults are applied at which objects. Thus default spaces can be consistent or inconsistent with a set of strict formulae Γ.

What we are interested in are the maximal default spaces given a particular Γ and Δ. Obviously, having the description $o :: \neg \delta_p \sqcup \delta_c$ in a default space S means that o is not an exception to δ. We can thus compute the negative score of a default space in complete analogy to the negative score of a model.

Definition 20. Let S be a default space.

$$score^-(S) \stackrel{\text{def}}{=} \sum_{\delta \in \Delta}(|\{o :: \neg \delta_p \sqcup \delta_c \notin S\}| \cdot w(\delta))$$

Given this definition a default space is maximal if it has minimal negative score:

Definition 21. S is maximal wrt Γ iff

1. S is consistent wrt Γ and
2. there is no default space S'
   (a) which is consistent wrt Γ and
   (b) $score^-(S') < score^-(S)$

Maximal default spaces give us a sound and complete syntactic characterization for $\approx_\Sigma$, as shown in Proposition 25. To prove this proposition, a couple of lemmata are useful.

We start with associating a default space with each model:

Definition 22. Let Δ be a finite set of weighted defaults and M a model. We define M's default space as

$$S_M \stackrel{\text{def}}{=} \{o :: \neg \delta_p \sqcup \delta_c : M \models o :: \neg \delta_p \sqcup \delta_c\}$$

Note that the negative score of a model and the negative score of its default space are the same, i.e. $score^-(M) = score^-(S_M)$.

We can then show an interesting correspondence between (maximal) default spaces and models:

Lemma 23. *Let Γ be a set of* DL *formulae, M a model of Γ, and S a default space.*

$$M \models \Gamma \cup S \text{ iff } S \subseteq S_M$$

If S is a maximal default space wrt Γ we even get

$$M \models \Gamma \cup S \text{ iff } S = S_M$$

Proof. We begin with the first equivalence:

$$M \models \Gamma \cup S \text{ iff } \forall o :: \neg \delta_p \sqcup \delta_c \in S \ M \models o :: \neg \delta_p \sqcup \delta_c$$
$$\text{iff } \forall o :: \neg \delta_p \sqcup \delta_c \in S \ o :: \neg \delta_p \sqcup \delta_c \in S_M$$
$$\text{iff } S \subseteq S_M$$

The second equivalence is easily proven by noting that $S \subset S_M$ would yield $score^-(S) > score^-(S_M)$ (all weights are *positive numbers*), which contradicts maximality of S.

Finally, we can prove a correspondence between $\sqsubseteq_\Sigma$-maximal models and maximal default spaces.

Lemma 24. *Let Γ be a set of DL formulae and M a model.*

M is a $\sqsubseteq_\Sigma$-maximal model of Γ iff S_M is a maximal default space wrt Γ

Proof. **(if)** We have to prove that M is a $\sqsubseteq_\Sigma$-maximal model of Γ, i.e. that for all models N of Γ we have $score^-(M) \leq score^-(N)$.

Since S_M is a maximal default space wrt Γ, we have $score^-(S_M) \leq score^-(S_N)$ and thus $score^-(M) \leq score^-(N)$.

(only if) We have to prove that S_M is a maximal default space wrt Γ, i.e. that $score^-(S_M) \leq score^-(S)$ for all default spaces S consistent wrt Γ.

Since S is consistent wrt Γ, there is a model N of $\Gamma \cup S$ and from Lemma 23 we get $S \subseteq S_N$. Since M is a $\sqsubseteq_\Sigma$-maximal model of Γ, we have $score^-(M) \leq score^-(N)$ and thus $score^-(S_M) \leq score^-(S_N)$. Since $S \subseteq S_N$ implies $score^-(S_N) \leq score^-(S)$ we also get $score^-(S_M) \leq score^-(S)$.

We can now finally prove the proposition showing that maximal default spaces provide a sound and complete syntactic characterization of $\approx_\Sigma$.

Proposition 25. *Let Γ be a set of DL formulae, Δ a finite set of weighted defaults, o an object and c a concept.*

$$\Gamma; \Delta \approx_\Sigma o :: c \text{ iff } \Gamma \cup S \models o :: c$$

for all maximal default spaces S over Δ

Proof. **(if)** We have to show that any $\sqsubseteq_\Sigma$-maximal model of Γ is a model of o :: c.

Due to Lemma 24 we know that S_M is a maximal default space wrt Γ and Lemma 23 implies that M is a model of $\Gamma \cup S_M$. But since we know that $\Gamma \cup S_M \models o :: c$ (premise), M must be a model of o :: c.

(only if) We have to show that if S is a maximal default space wrt Γ then $\Gamma \cup S \models o :: c$, i.e. that all models of $\Gamma \cup S$ must be models of o :: c.

Let M be such a model. Since S is a maximal default space wrt Γ and M is a model of $\Gamma \cup S$, we know that $S = S_M$ (Lemma 23). From Lemma 24 it follows that M is a $\sqsubseteq_\Sigma$-maximal model of Γ. From the premise $\Gamma; \Delta \approx_\Sigma o :: c$ we thus know that M is a model of o :: c.

A couple of remarks seem in order. First, this proposition shows that $\approx_\Sigma$ is decidable if the underlying DL is. Since both $\mathcal{O}$ and Δ are finite, there are only finitely many default spaces. To determine the maximal ones, we only have to check consistency in the underlying DL, more precisely, we have to enumerate all possible default spaces (subsets of $\{o :: \neg \delta_p \sqcup \delta_c : o \in \mathcal{O}, \delta \in \Delta\}$), and pick the consistent sets with lowest score.

It is easy to see, however, that the number of default spaces is exponential, namely $2^{|\mathcal{O}| \cdot |\Delta|}$. Not all default spaces have to be considered by the algorithm, but even the number of maximal ones can, in the worst case, be exponential. (Consider a case when all sets of cardinality $> (|\mathcal{O}| \cdot |\Delta|)/2$ are inconsistent, all the others are consistent.)

Since maximal default spaces cannot be subsets of each other, their number is bounded by $n!/(n \text{ DIV } 2)!$, where $n = |\mathcal{O}| \cdot |\Delta|$.

In [19] a class of algorithms to compute the maximal default spaces is studied. It results naturally from the approach of the proof theory—transferring all the logical work to the DL system, and only allowing to check consistency of default spaces. The crucial default spaces to be considered are those being maximal wrt consistency. But it could be shown that even if their number is polynomially bounded, no algorithm can guarantee computation in polynomial time.

It thus seems inevitable to compromize on the (very desirable) semantics of PDDL to achieve efficient computation, or to put severe restrictions on the input to enable a polynomial algorithm to be correct. In [19] a tractable subclass is given, characterized by small clash size, a *clash* being a minimal inconsistent default space. If all clashes contain at most k atoms, less than $(|\mathcal{O}| \cdot |\Delta|)^k$ consistency checks are sufficient to detect them all. This information can be used in a second stage to build the maximal default spaces. This can be done in polynomial time, if the total number of atoms contained in more than one clash is logarithmically bounded. In this case the complexity of preferential entailment is thus polynomially reducible to DL entailment.

Moreover, we are currently investigating a weaker semantics based on the k operator [5], in which contraposition and disjunctive application of defaults are not valid, i.e. defaults behave as forward-chaining trigger rules. Though the worst-case complexity for such a semantics is still exponential, computation might become much more efficient in realistic applications. Regarding formal properties it seems that Cautious Monotonicity is still valid for this weakened semantics, whereas Or and Rational Monotonicity are not.

Finally note that other numerical default systems supply very different answers to the problem of efficiency. In Goldszmith and Pearl's System-Z^+ a precomputed ranking function is used to allow deduction in linear time [6]. Pinkas shows that formulae of his real-valued *penalty calculus* can be transformed into symmetric neural networks, allowing to use classical connectionist techniques [11]. It might be worthwhile to investigate possible adaptations of these ideas into our PDDL framework.

4 Conclusion

We have presented a Preferential Default Description Logic (PDDL) based on weighted defaults and shown that the preferential entailment relation $\models_{\Sigma}$ satisfies all properties of system **P** [7] and Rational Monotonicity [9]. The main characteristics of this PDDL is that it uses an ordering between multisets of defaults for priorization, treats defaults similar to material implications, and adheres strictly to the principle of exception minimization.

In Reiter-style Default Logics a maximization of default application is built-in, sometimes violating the principle of exception minimization. We have shown how maximization of default applications can be consistently combined with $\models_{\Sigma}$ without violating exception minimization. Furthermore, the resulting entailment relation $\models_{\Sigma}^{F}$ still satisfies all properties of system **P**.

We have developed a proof theory for $\models_{\Sigma}$ based on default spaces, which shows that $\models_{\Sigma}$ is decidable if the underlying DL is. $\models_{\Sigma}$ can be syntactically characterized by strict entailment from all maximal default spaces and can thus be computed by an exponential algorithm.

Acknowledgements

We would like to thank two anonymous reviewers for helpful comments.

References

1. F. Baader, B. Hollunder, "Embedding Defaults into Terminological Knowledge Representation Formalisms", *KR-92*, 306–317
2. F. Baader, B. Hollunder, "How to Prefer More Specific Defaults in Terminological Default Logic", *IJCAI-93*, 669–674
3. G. Brewka, *Nonmonotonic Reasoning: Logical Foundations of Commonsense*, Cambridge: Cambridge University Press, 1991
4. F.M. Donini, M. Lenzerini, D. Nardi, W. Nutt, "Tractable Concept Languages" *IJCAI-91*, 458–463
5. F.M. Donini, M. Lenzerini, D. Nardi, A. Schaerf, W. Nutt, "Adding Epistemic Operators to Concept Languages", *KR-92*, 342–353
6. J. Goldsmith, J. Pearl, "System-Z^+: A Formalism for Reasoning with Variable-Strength Defaults", *AAAI-91*, 399–404
7. S. Kraus, D. Lehman, M. Magidor, "Nonmonotonic Reasoning, Preferential Models and Cumulative Logics", *Artificial Intelligence* 44, 167–207, 1990
8. V. Lifschitz, "Computing Circumscription", *IJCAI-85*, 121–127
9. D. Makinson, "General Patterns in Nonmonotonic Reasoning", in D. Gabbay, C. Hogger, J. Robinson (eds), *Handbook of Logic in Artificial Intelligence*, Oxford: Oxford University Press, in print
10. J. McCarthy, "Circumscription—A Form of Non-Monotonic Reasoning", *Artificial Intelligence* 13, 1980
11. G. Pinkas, "Propositional Non-Monotonic Reasoning and Inconsistency in Symmetric Neural Networks", *IJCAI-91*, 525–530
12. J.J. Quantz, "Interpretation as Exception Minimization", *IJCAI-93*, 1310–1315
13. J.J. Quantz, V. Royer, "A Preference Semantics for Defaults in Terminological Logics", *KR-92*, 294–305
14. J.J. Quantz, M. Ryan, *Preferential Default Description Logics*, KIT-Report 110, Technische Universität Berlin, 1993
15. J.J. Quantz, B. Schmitz, "Knowledge-Based Disambiguation for Machine Translation", *Minds and Machines* 4, 39–57, 1994
16. R. Reiter, "A Logic for Default Reasoning", *Artificial Intelligence* 13, 1980
17. M. Ryan, "Representing Defaults as Sentences with Reduced Priority", *KR-92*, 649–660
18. Y. Shoham, *Reasoning about Change: Time and Causation from the Standpoint of Artificial Intelligence*, Cambridge: MIT Press, 1988
19. S. Suska, *A Proof Theory for Preferential Default Description Logics*, KIT Report in Preparation

Epistemic Queries in Classic

Andreas Becker and Gerhard Lakemeyer

University of Bonn
Institute of Computer Science III
Römerstr. 164
53117 Bonn
becker@uran.informatik.uni-bonn.de
gerhard@cs.uni-bonn.de

Abstract. Levesque showed that the ability to formulate queries that refer explicitly to the knowledge of a knowledge base significantly increases the expressiveness of a query language. He demonstrated also that epistemic queries can be reduced to a sequence of non-epistemic, that is to say, conventional queries. However, this reduction technique relies on the very expressive language of full first-order logic with equality. In this paper we show that epistemic queries as expressions of an extension of the concept language Classic, which is severely limited in expressiveness compared to first-order logic, can nevertheless be reduced to non-epistemic queries in many cases.

1 Introduction

While query languages for knowledge bases (KBs) are usually well-suited to probe the application domain in question, they do not normally allow the user to refer explicitly to the *knowledge* of the KB. Levesque [9] showed that the ability to formulate queries about the knowledge of a knowledge base can be of great advantage in that it significantly increases the expressiveness of the query language. The following example illustrates this gain in expressiveness:

> Let us assume that the knowledge base knows that Susi has 2 sons. Questioned whether Susi only has sons, the knowledge base should return "don't know" as the correct answer, as it cannot rule out that Susi might have other children and, in particular, daughters. However, when asked whether all of Susi's children known to the knowledge base are sons, the KB should answer "yes."

Notice that the second query could not be formulated without the ability to refer explicitly to the knowledge of the knowledge base. An interesting result of Levesque's work is that epistemic queries to a given non-epistemic knowledge base can be evaluated by reducing them to a sequence of non-epistemic queries. More precisely, while a knowledge base in Levesque's paper consists of first-order sentences, queries to the knowledge base are formulated in a first-order modal logic and can be answered correctly by posing a sequence of queries formulated in the base language. The advantage, of course, is that there is no need for inference techniques based on modal logics.

On the other hand, Levesque's work is mainly of theoretical interest since FOL as the underlying representation language is still far too powerful to allow for efficient processing of queries. So-called concept languages or terminological logics [2] have proved to be a good compromise between expressiveness and efficient inference techniques. One example of this language family is Classic [11], which is rather restricted in expressiveness even in comparison with other concept languages, but allows for relatively efficient inferencing.[1]

Recently Donini et al. ([4]) applied Levesque's notion of an epistemic query language to concept languages. In particular, the authors sketch a technique in analogy to Levesque's approach for reducing an epistemic query to a sequence of non-epistemic queries. However, this reduction technique assumes a highly expressive base language containing, among others, disjunction and negation as operators.

In this paper we tackle the question of how to deal with an epistemic query language for Classic in the fashion of Levesque's approach. In particular, we will show that the reduction of epistemic Classic-queries to non-epistemic queries is possible in many cases, even though disjunction is available only in a restricted sense and negation is not available at all.

In the next section we introduce the syntax and semantics of K-Classic, an epistemic extension of Classic. In Section 3 we briefly introduce Levesque's logic $\mathcal{KL}$ and his reduction technique for epistemic queries. In Section 4 we elaborate a corresponding reduction technique for K-Classic and show which cases cannot be handled with this technique. Proofs are largely omitted due to space limitations. They can be found in [1].

2 Syntax and Semantics of K-Classic

2.1 The Syntax of K-Classic

The syntax of Classic is based on two alphabets, one for the so-called primitive concepts (one-place predicates) and another for primitive roles (two-place predicates). In the following A denotes a primitive concept and P a primitive role. Let Δ be a countably infinite set of standard names a_i which syntactically behave like constants.[2] Let n be a natural number, g and j natural numbers or strings. All concepts C and roles R occurring in Classic are constructed from the two alphabets together with Δ and the following rules:[3]

---

[1] see section 4.4

[2] We refer to standard names and therefore do not explicitly differentiate between semantic objects and syntactic identifiers for individuals. We use standard names as in [9].

[3] Apart from these, Classic also contains the test-predicates TEST-C and TEST-H representing interfaces to the host-language, as well as the primitive concepts THING and HOST-THING, which subsume the objects of the host-language, and the operator SAME-AS, which expresses the equality of the final elements of two attribute chains. For the sake of simplicity we do not consider these constructs.

$$C, C_i \longrightarrow A$$
$$\text{CLASSIC-THING}$$
$$(\text{AND } C_1 \ldots C_n)$$
$$(\text{ALL R C})$$
$$(\text{AT-LEAST n R})$$
$$(\text{AT-MOST n R})$$
$$(\text{PRIMITIVE C j})$$
$$(\text{DISJOINT-PRIMITIVE C g j})$$
$$(\text{ONE-OF } a_1 \ a_2 \ldots a_n)$$
$$(\text{FILLS R } a_1 \ a_2 \ldots a_n)$$
$$R \longrightarrow P$$

We extend Classic to K-Classic by adding the epistemic operator K. Informally, the meaning of (K C) is that the system knows which individuals (standard names) are instances of C. The syntax of K-Classic results from adding the following two rules to the syntax rules of Classic.

$$C \longrightarrow (\text{K C})$$
$$R \longrightarrow (\text{K P})$$

Concepts can be formed recursively and may contain several occurrences of the K-operator, which may also be nested.

In order to make assertions about the world, we introduce a countably infinite set of variables. A K-Classic *formula* has the form C (x), where C is a K-Classic concept and x is either a standard name or a variable. If x is a standard name, C (x) is also called a K-Classic *sentence* or simply sentence. A K-Classic formula is called *objective* if it does not contain the modal operator K. While Classic knowledge bases consist of objective K-Classic sentences only, the query language considered in this paper ranges over arbitrary K-Classic sentences.

2.2 The semantics of K-Classic

The semantics presented here is an adaptation of the one used in [4]. As K-Classic is an epistemic language, models consist of two parts, an interpretation $\mathcal{I}$ representing the real world and a set of interpretations $\mathcal{W}$ representing what the system knows or believes about the world. In short, the system knows precisely those sentences that are true in all interpretations in $\mathcal{W}$ (this corresponds to the possible-world semantics of the logic K45, see [5, 6, 7]). Formally, a pair $(\mathcal{I}, \mathcal{W})$ is called an epistemic interpretation if $\mathcal{I}$ is an interpretation and $\mathcal{W}$ a set of interpretations, where these interpretations are functions that map every concept into Δ and every role into a subset of $\Delta \times \Delta$ such that the following conditions are satisfied:

$$\text{CLASSIC-THING}^{\mathcal{I},\mathcal{W}} \qquad\qquad = \Delta$$

$$\text{A}^{\mathcal{I},\mathcal{W}} \qquad\qquad\qquad\quad = \text{A}^{\mathcal{I}}$$

$$\text{P}^{\mathcal{I},\mathcal{W}} \qquad\qquad\qquad\quad = \text{P}^{\mathcal{I}}$$

$$(\text{AND } C_1 \ldots C_n)^{\mathcal{I},\mathcal{W}} \qquad = C_1^{\mathcal{I},\mathcal{W}} \cap \ldots \cap C_n^{\mathcal{I},\mathcal{W}}$$

$$(\text{ALL R } C)^{\mathcal{I},\mathcal{W}} \qquad\quad = \{p_1 \in \Delta \mid \forall p_2 (p_1, p_2) \in R^{\mathcal{I},\mathcal{W}} \to p_2 \in C^{\mathcal{I},\mathcal{W}}\}$$

$$(\text{AT-LEAST n R})^{\mathcal{I},\mathcal{W}} \quad = \{p_1 \in \Delta \mid |\{p_2 \in \Delta \mid (p_1, p_2) \in R^{\mathcal{I},\mathcal{W}}\}| \geq n\}$$

$$(\text{AT-MOST n R})^{\mathcal{I},\mathcal{W}} \quad = \{p_1 \in \Delta \mid |\{p_2 \in \Delta \mid (p_1, p_2) \in R^{\mathcal{I},\mathcal{W}}\}| \leq n\}$$

$$(\text{PRIMITIVE C j})^{\mathcal{I},\mathcal{W}} \quad \subseteq C^{\mathcal{I},\mathcal{W}}$$

$$(\text{DISJOINT-PRIMITIVE C g j})^{\mathcal{I},\mathcal{W}} \subseteq C^{\mathcal{I},\mathcal{W}} \wedge$$

$$(\text{DISJOINT-PRIMITIVE C g j})^{\mathcal{I},\mathcal{W}} \cap$$

$$(\text{DISJOINT-PRIMITIVE C g j'})^{\mathcal{I},\mathcal{W}} = \emptyset,$$

$$\forall j, j' \ j \neq j'$$

$$(\text{ONE-OF } a_1 \ldots a_n)^{\mathcal{I},\mathcal{W}} \quad = \{a_1, \ldots, a_n\} \subseteq \Delta$$

$$(\text{FILLS R } a_1 \ldots a_n)^{\mathcal{I},\mathcal{W}} = \{p \in \Delta \mid \{(p, a_1), \ldots, (p, a_n)\} \subseteq R^{\mathcal{I},\mathcal{W}}\}$$

$$(\text{K } C)^{\mathcal{I},\mathcal{W}} \qquad\qquad\quad = \bigcap_{\mathcal{J} \in \mathcal{W}} (C^{\mathcal{J},\mathcal{W}})$$

$$(\text{K } P)^{\mathcal{I},\mathcal{W}} \qquad\qquad\quad = \bigcap_{\mathcal{J} \in \mathcal{W}} (P^{\mathcal{J},\mathcal{W}})$$

The semantics of the non-epistemic constructs is exclusively determined by the interpretation $\mathcal{I}$. The second parameter $\mathcal{W}$ is relevant only in the context of the meaning of a construct (K C) or (K P), i.e. those constructs that distinguish K-Classic from Classic. For example, (K C) is interpreted as the set of all standard names belonging to the extension of C in every interpretation contained in $\mathcal{W}$.

An interpretation $\mathcal{I}$ and a set of interpretations $\mathcal{W}$ satisfy a K-Classic sentence $C(a)$ for a standard name a (written $\mathcal{I}, \mathcal{W} \models C(a)$) iff. $a \in C^{\mathcal{I},\mathcal{W}}$. In the case of (K C) (a) we often write $\mathcal{W} \models (\text{K } C)(a)$, as the satisfiability does not depend on $\mathcal{I}$. Let Σ be a set of objective sentences. $\mathcal{I} \models \Sigma$ means that $\mathcal{I}$ every sentence in Σ and $\Sigma \models C(a)$ denotes that every model of Σ satisfies the sentence $C(a)$.

In the context of a Classic knowledge base Σ we are particularly interested in the set $\mathcal{M}(\Sigma)$ of all models of Σ as $\mathcal{W}$, because $\mathcal{M}(\Sigma)$ semantically denotes the knowledge of a system that knows *only* the sentences in Σ in the sense of [10]. Such an epistemic interpretation interprets (K C) as the set of all standard names that are instances of C in all models of Σ. In other words, (K C) consists of all standard names that are known in the KB to be instances of C ((K P) analogous).

3 Epistemic query evaluation in Levesque's logic $\mathcal{KL}$

We briefly sketch (a subset of) Levesque's logic $\mathcal{KL}$ [9, 10] including his technique to reduce epistemic queries to non-epistemic queries. Levesque's notation is modified slightly to suit the style of this paper.

3.1 The logic $\mathcal{KL}$

$\mathcal{KL}$ is a modal first-order logic with standard names and equality, but without function symbols. To simplify matters, we restrict the logic to one- and two-place predicates, since that is all we need for our purposes.

Terms are either variables and standard names. Atomic formulas are predicate symbols applied to terms or have the form $t_1 = t_2$, where t_1, t_2 are terms. Formulas are built in the usual fashion from atomic formulas $\neg$, $\vee$, $\exists$ and the modal operator K.[4] Formulas without free variables are sentences. Formulas without a modal operator are called objective. The sublanguage $\mathcal{L}$ denotes the set of all objective formulas. α_t^x denoted α with all occurrences of the free variable x replaced by t.

Just as in K-Classic, the semantics of $\mathcal{KL}$ is based on interpretations and sets of interpretations, which map every unary predicate into the set of standard names and every binary predicate into the set of pairs of standard names. Let $\mathcal{I}$ be such an interpretation, $\mathcal{M}$ a set of interpretations, P an atomic formula, $\mathbf{n}$ a vector of standard names, n and m standard names. Then the semantics of $\mathcal{KL}$ is as follows:

1. $\mathcal{I}, \mathcal{M} \models_{\mathcal{KL}} P(\mathbf{n}) \Longleftrightarrow \mathbf{n} \in P^{\mathcal{I}}$
2. $\mathcal{I}, \mathcal{M} \models_{\mathcal{KL}} (n = m) \Longleftrightarrow n$ and m are identical standard names
3. $\mathcal{I}, \mathcal{M} \models_{\mathcal{KL}} \neg\alpha \Longleftrightarrow \mathcal{I}, \mathcal{M} \not\models_{\mathcal{KL}} \alpha$
4. $\mathcal{I}, \mathcal{M} \models_{\mathcal{KL}} \alpha \vee \beta \Longleftrightarrow \mathcal{I}, \mathcal{M} \models_{\mathcal{KL}} \alpha$ or $\mathcal{I}, \mathcal{M} \models_{\mathcal{KL}} \beta$
5. $\mathcal{I}, \mathcal{M} \models_{\mathcal{KL}} \exists x\, \alpha \Longleftrightarrow \mathcal{I}, \mathcal{M} \models_{\mathcal{KL}} \alpha_i^x$ for some standard name i
6. $\mathcal{I}, \mathcal{M} \models_{\mathcal{KL}} K\alpha \Longleftrightarrow \forall \mathcal{J} \in \mathcal{M}\ \ \mathcal{J}, \mathcal{M} \models_{\mathcal{KL}} \alpha$

Notions like validity of a sentence α (written $\models_{\mathcal{KL}} \alpha$) are defined as usual. An axiomatization can be found in [10].

3.2 The semantics of the ASK-operator

Levesque defines an operation ASK, which allows us to query an objective knowledge base whether it knows an arbitrary sentence in $\mathcal{KL}$. Formally, let k be a set of objective sentences (the KB), $\mathcal{M}(k)$ the set of models of k, and α an arbitrary sentence in $\mathcal{KL}$.[5]

$$\text{ASK}[\mathcal{M}(k), \alpha] = \begin{cases} \text{yes} & \text{, if } \mathcal{M}(k) \models_{\mathcal{KL}} K\alpha \\ \text{no} & \text{else} \end{cases}$$

3.3 Reducing epistemic queries to non-epistemic queries

Levesque showed that every $\mathcal{KL}$ argument of an ASK-operation can be reduced to a first order formula of $\mathcal{L}$ depending on the state of an objective knowledge base k by applying the reduction function $|\ |_k$ to the argument.[6]

---

[4] $\wedge, \equiv, \forall$ are used as conventional abbreviations.
[5] The following definition of ASK is actually somewhat simpler than Levesque's and better suits the limited language of K-Classic, which does not allow for negation.
[6] The restriction of $\mathcal{KL}$ to one- and two-place predicate symbols is no problem in this context, because the reduction does not affect the arity of predicates.

The function $|\ |_k$ is defined as:

$$
\begin{aligned}
|\alpha|_k &= \alpha, \text{ if } \alpha \in \mathcal{L} \\
|\neg\alpha|_k &= \neg|\alpha|_k \\
|\alpha \vee \beta|_k &= (|\alpha|_k \vee |\beta|_k) \\
|\exists x \alpha|_k &= \exists x\, |\alpha|_k \\
|K\alpha|_k &= \mathrm{RES}[k, |\alpha|_k]
\end{aligned}
$$

The function RES is defined as follows:

RES $[k, \alpha] =$

> if α does not contain a free variable
>> then if $\models_{\mathcal{KL}} (k \supset \alpha)$
>>> then $\forall x\, (x = x)$ $/*true/*$
>>> else $\forall x\, (x \neq x)$ $/*false/*$

>> else (Let x be free in α and
>> $i_1, \ldots, i_n$ be the standard names occuring in k or α.
>> Let i^* be a standard name occurring neither in k nor in α.)
>> $$((x = i_1) \wedge \mathrm{RES}[k, \alpha_{i_1}^x]) \vee \ldots \vee ((x = i_n) \wedge \mathrm{RES}[k, \alpha_{i_n}^x])$$
>> $$\vee ((x \neq i_1) \wedge \ldots \wedge (x \neq i_n) \wedge \mathrm{RES}[k, \alpha_{i^*}^x]_x^{i^*})$$

In case there are no free variables in α a tautology (or true) is returned if $k \supset \alpha$ is a theorem of $\mathcal{L}$, i.e. α is known in k, and an inconsistency (or false) otherwise. Free variables in α are successively instantiated by recursive applications of RES so that in the end equality expressions specify those standard names that are known in k to be instances of α. We write $a \in k$ to express that a is a standard name known to k, i.e. a syntactically in k occurring standard name.

Epistemic ASK-operations can be reduced to non-epistemic operations with the help of the reduction function $|\ |_k$ ([9]):

Theorem 1. *Levesque's Representation Theorem*

$$
ASK[\mathcal{M}(k), \alpha] = \begin{cases} yes & , \text{if } \models_{\mathcal{KL}} (k \supset |\alpha|_k) \\ no & otherwise \end{cases}
$$

4 Epistemic queries in Classic

4.1 The semantics of the ASK-operator for Classic

Following Levesque we define the semantics of the ASK-operator for Classic as

$$
ASK[\mathcal{M}(\Sigma), C(a)] = \begin{cases} yes & , \text{if } \mathcal{M}(\Sigma) \models (KC)(a) \\ no & otherwise \end{cases}
$$

The question now is how this semantic specification of ASK can be realised syntactically. If $C(a)$ is objective we are done, since it can easily be shown that

$\mathcal{M}(\Sigma) \models (\text{K } C)(a)$ is equivalent to $\Sigma \models C(a)$ in this case, i.e. conventional Classic inference algorithms can be used to check whether C (a) follows from Σ.

The case where C (a) contains K-operators is handled in two parts. In the first part we look at the sublanguage of K-Classic where K is applied only to concepts in C (a). We call the the the resulting sublanguage K-Classic⁻. In the second part we look at the case in which K is also applied to roles.

4.2 Reduction of K-Classic⁻ queries to Classic queries

The reduction of an epistemic expression (K C) to a non-epistemic expression proceeds as follows.[7] If C itself is objective, then for a given knowledge base Σ, (K C) represents the set S of all individuals a such that $\Sigma \models C(a)$. This set can be determined by finitely many conventional Classic queries. Moreover, S is either finite, i.e. $S = \{ a_1, a_2, \ldots, a_n \}$, in which case it is representable as (ONE-OF $a_1 \ldots a_n$), or S is the set of all standard names, which can be represented by CLASSIC-THING. In the case of nested occurrences of K, this process is applied recursively starting bottom-up from the innermost K operators. For example, let $a_1, a_2, \ldots, a_n$ be the known instances of a concept C for a given knowledge base and let $b_1, b_2, \ldots, b_m$ be the known instances of the concept (ALL P (ONE-OF a_1 a_2 ... a_n)). Then the following transformations would result from a query (K (ALL P (K C))) (c):

$$(\text{K (ALL P (K } C))) \text{ (c)} \quad \text{->}$$
$$(\text{K (ALL P (ONE-OF } a_1 \ldots a_n))) \text{ (c)} \quad \text{->}$$
$$(\text{ONE-OF } b_1 \ldots b_m) \text{ (c)}$$

Note that each transformation results in a K-Classic expression and eventually in a Classic expression in a way that is quite similar to Levesque's reduction technique.

We exploit this similarity to prove the correctness of the technique. First we translate the problem from K-Classic to $\mathcal{KL}$, then we apply Levesque's reduction and finally translate the result back to Classic. The final step presents the real hurdle, since we need to make sure that the objective sentences generated by Levesque's reduction can always be represented in Classic.[8]

To formalize these ideas, we begin by defining the reduction technique for transforming epistemic K-Classic concepts into (objective) Classic concepts by using appropriate ONE-OF concepts. As always, let Σ be a Classic knowledge base.

Let the reduction function for K-Classic⁻,

$$| \ |_\Sigma : \text{K-CLASSIC}^- \longrightarrow \text{CLASSIC}$$

be defined as follows:

---

[7] The basic idea was already mentioned in [4].

[8] This is no problem in [4], since the underlying concept language is expressive enough to allow a straightforward representation of all reduction results produced by Levesque's technique.

$$
\begin{aligned}
|C|_\Sigma &= C, \text{ if } C \in \text{CLASSIC} \\
|(\text{AND } C_1 \dots C_n)|_\Sigma &= (\text{AND } |C_1|_\Sigma \dots |C_n|_\Sigma) \\
|(\text{ALL P } C)|_\Sigma) &= (\text{ALL P } |C|_\Sigma) \\
|(\text{PRIMITIVE } C \text{ j})|_\Sigma &= (\text{PRIMITIVE } |C|_\Sigma \text{ j}) \\
|(\text{DISJOINT-PRIMITIVE } C \text{ g j})|_\Sigma &= (\text{DISJOINT-PRIMITIVE } |C|_\Sigma \text{ g j})
\end{aligned}
$$

$$
|(\text{K } C)|_\Sigma = \begin{cases}
\text{CLASSIC-THING,} \\
\quad \text{if } \forall x \in \Delta \; \Sigma \models |C|_\Sigma(x) \\
(\text{ONE-OF } a_1 \dots a_n) \text{ o.w., where} \\
\quad \{a_1, \dots, a_n\} = \\
\quad \{a \mid \Sigma \models |C|_\Sigma(a), a \text{ occurring in } \Sigma \cup \{C\}\}
\end{cases}
$$

Notice that due to the restriction to K-Classic$^-$, $|\cdot|_\Sigma$ is defined for all occurring constructs. $|C|_\Sigma$ is objective, i.e. conventional (non-epistemic) algorithms for ASK $[\mathcal{M}(\Sigma), |C(a)|_\Sigma]$ can be used.

The following theorem is the analogue to Levesque's representation theorem for K-Classic$^-$.

Theorem 2. *Representation Theorem for K-Classic$^-$*
If Σ is a Classic knowledge base and $C(a)$ is a K-Classic$^-$ query, then

$$
ASK\ [\mathcal{M}(\Sigma), C(a)] = yes \ \ iff \ \ ASK\ [\mathcal{M}(\Sigma), |C(a)|_\Sigma] = yes.
$$

To prove this theorem we need to establish the correctness of the reduction $|C(a)|_\Sigma$, i.e. we need to show that a knowledge base Σ knows a sentence $C(a)$ if and only if it knows $|C(a)|_\Sigma$. As indicated above we prove this by exploiting Levesque's result. More precisely, the reduction of a K-Classic expression to a Classic expression takes place in the context of a Classic knowledge base Σ as depicted in Figure 1 by mapping a K-Classic expression into $\mathcal{KL}$, then reducing the result of this translation to $\mathcal{L}$ by Levesque's reduction function $|\ |_{kl(\Sigma)}$, and, finally, translating the result of this reduction back to Classic. The problem is to show that the result of the reduction by $|\ |_{kl(\Sigma)}$ can always be represented in Classic and coincides with $|C(a)|_\Sigma$. In other words, we need to prove that the diagram in Figure 1 commutes (Theorem 7 below), a task we now turn to and which eventually allows us to prove Theorem 2. We begin by showing how to embed K-Classic in $\mathcal{KL}$, which in fact is not hard since $\mathcal{KL}$ is more expressive than K-Classic. The following table defines the translation in a rather straightforward way. Concept and role names need to be mapped into unary and binary predicates in a unique way, which we indicate by using the same letters. Also, care must be taken that primitive and disjoint primitive concepts are mapped into predicates of $\mathcal{KL}$ in a unique way as well. x denotes both a variable and a standard name.

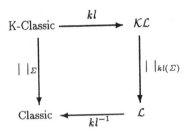

Fig. 1. Reduction of K-Classic formulas to Classic formulas by exploiting Levesque's reduction of $\mathcal{KL}$-formulas

K-Classic Formel	$\mathcal{KL}$-Formel
A (x)	$\mapsto A(x)$
CLASSIC-THING (x)	$\mapsto \forall x \, (x = x)$
(AND $C_1 \ldots C_n$) (x)	$\mapsto kl(C_1)(x) \wedge \ldots \wedge kl(C_n)(x)$
(ALL R C) (x)	$\mapsto (\forall y) \, R(x,y) \supset kl(C(y))$
(AT-LEAST n R) (x)	$\mapsto \exists \, y_1, \ldots, y_n$
	$R(x, y_1) \wedge \ldots \wedge R(x, y_n) \wedge \bigwedge_{i \neq j} y_i \neq y_j$
(AT-MOST n R) (x)	$\mapsto \neg \, (\exists \, y_1, \ldots, y_n, y_{n+1}$
	$R(x, y_1) \wedge \ldots \wedge R(x, y_{n+1}) \wedge \bigwedge_{i \neq j} y_i \neq y_j$
(PRIMITIVE C j) (x)	$\mapsto A_j(x) \wedge (\forall y) \, A_j(y) \supset kl(C(y))$
(DISJOINT-PRIMITIVE C g j) $(x) \mapsto A_{g,j}(x) \wedge$	
	$(\forall y) A_{g,j}(y) \supset (kl(C(y)) \wedge \neg A_{g,i}(y)) \wedge i \neq j$
(ONE-OF $a_1 \ldots a_n$) (x)	$\mapsto (x = a_1) \vee \ldots \vee (x = a_n)$
(ONE-OF) (x)	$\mapsto \forall x \, (x \neq x)$
(FILLS R $a_1 \ldots a_n$) (x)	$\mapsto R(x, a_1) \wedge \ldots \wedge R(x, a_n)$
(K C) (x)	$\mapsto K(kl(C)(x))$

The following lemma and corollaries show that kl indeed translates K-Classic sentences to logically equivalent sentences of $\mathcal{KL}$.

Lemma 3. *Let $C(a)$ be a K-Classic expression, $\mathcal{I}$ an interpretation, and $\mathcal{M}$ a set of interpretations. Then $\mathcal{I}, \mathcal{M} \models C(a)$ iff $\mathcal{I}, \mathcal{M} \models_{\mathcal{KL}} kl(C(a))$.*

Corollary 4. $\Sigma \models C(a)$ *iff* $kl(\Sigma) \models_{\mathcal{KL}} kl(C(a))$.

Corollary 5. $\mathcal{M}(\Sigma) = \mathcal{M}(kl(\Sigma))$.

The next lemma is a key result, since it guarantees that Levesque's reduction operator RES when applied to formulas of the form $kl((KC)(x))$ always returns results that can also be expressed in Classic.

Lemma 6. *If C is a Classic concept and Σ is a Classic knowledge base, then it follows*

$$|kl((KC)(x))|_{kl(\Sigma)} = \begin{cases} \forall x\,(x = x) & \text{iff } \forall x \in \Delta \ kl(\Sigma) \models_{\mathcal{KL}} kl(C(x)) \\ (x = a_1 \vee .. \vee x = a_n) & \text{iff } kl(\Sigma) \models_{\mathcal{KL}} kl(C(a_i)) \\ & \text{for all } i,\ 1 \leq i \leq n,\ \text{with} \\ & a_i \text{ occurring in } kl(\Sigma) \text{ or } kl(C) \\ \forall x\,(x \neq x) & \text{iff } \forall x \in \Delta \ kl(\Sigma) \not\models_{\mathcal{KL}} kl(C(x)) \end{cases}$$

This and the previous result enable us to prove that Figure 1 commutes.

Theorem 7.

1. $kl^{-1}(|kl(C(a))|_{kl(\Sigma)})$ is well defined.
2. $kl^{-1}(|kl(C(a))|_{kl(\Sigma)}) = |C(a)|_\Sigma$.

With these preliminary results we are now ready to prove Theorem 2, the representation theorem for K-Classic⁻.

Proof of Theorem 2: ASK $[\mathcal{M}(\Sigma), C(a)] = yes$, if $\mathcal{M}(\Sigma) \models (\text{K } C)(a)$

$\mathcal{M}(\Sigma) \models (\text{K } C)(a)$

iff $\mathcal{M}(kl(\Sigma)) \models_{\mathcal{KL}} \text{K}kl(C(a))$ Lemma 3 and Corollary 5

iff $\models_{\mathcal{KL}} kl(\Sigma) \supset |kl(C(a))|_{kl(\Sigma)}$ Theorem 1

iff $kl(\Sigma) \models_{\mathcal{KL}} |kl(C(a))|_{kl(\Sigma)}$ property of $\mathcal{KL}$

iff $\Sigma \models |C(a)|_\Sigma$ Corollary 4 and Theorem 7

iff ASK $[\mathcal{M}(\Sigma), |C(a)|_\Sigma] = yes$.   □

4.3 Constructs with epistemic roles

While epistemic concepts (K C) can always be represented as objective ONE-OF concepts, the reduction of epistemic roles (K P) is far more problematic. Intuitively, for a given Σ, (K P) represents all *pairs* of standard names (a_i, b_i) which are known by Σ to satisfy the role P. To represent such sets of pairs, Donini et al. [4] introduced a further ONE-OF construct which has pairs of standard names as its extension. As the concept language examined there also contains negation, it is easy to show that all equality expressions generated by Levesque's reduction technique can be represented in the language.

The question now is to what extent a reduction of epistemic roles is feasible in Classic bearing in mind that we have neither a ONE-OF construct for roles nor negation at our disposal.

Epistemic roles can occur in K-Classic in four constructs: (FILLS (K P) $a_1 \ldots a_n$), (AT-LEAST n (K P)), (AT-MOST n (K P)), (ALL (K P) C). We will see that the first two constructs can indeed be reduced to Classic, whereas this is not possible for the latter two.

(FILLS (K P) $a_1 \ldots a_n$):

The proof that (FILLS (K P) $a_1 \ldots a_n$) can be reduced is especially simple, because this construct is equivalent to (K (FILLS P $a_1 \ldots a_n$)) and therefore it lies within the scope of K-Classic⁻. To see this notice that (FILLS (K P) $a_1 \ldots a_n$)(x) is equivalent to the $\mathcal{KL}$ formula KP $(x, a_1) \wedge \ldots \wedge$ KP (x, a_n) which itself is equivalent to K $(P (x, a_1) \wedge \ldots \wedge P (x, a_n))$ which is again equivalent to (K (FILLS P $a_1 \ldots a_n$))(x).

(AT-LEAST n (K P)):

The case of (AT-LEAST n (K P)) constructs is more complicated. For lack of space we only define the reduction and state the main result, namely that Figure 1 still applies when K-Classic⁻ is extended by the epistemic roles within AT-LEAST constructs.

Definition 8. Reduction for epistemic AT-LEAST constructs
Given a Classic KB Σ, let

$|(\text{AT-LEAST n (K P)})|_\Sigma = (\text{ONE-OF } a_1 \ldots a_n)$, where $\{a_1, \ldots, a_n\} = \{a \in \Sigma \mid kl(\Sigma) \models_{\mathcal{KL}} P(a, b_1) \wedge \ldots \wedge P(a, b_n) \wedge \bigwedge_{i \neq j} b_i \neq b_j$ for $b_i \in \Sigma\}$

Theorem 9. *Let Σ be a Classic KB. If K-Classic⁻ is extended by allowing epistemic roles of the form (AT-LEAST n (K P)), then Figure 1 still commutes, that is*

1. $kl^{-1}(|kl(C(a))|_{kl(\Sigma)})$ *is well defined.*
2. $kl^{-1}(|kl(C(a))|_{kl(\Sigma)}) = |C(a)|_\Sigma$.

(AT-MOST n (K P)), (ALL (K P) C):

In contrast to (FILLS (K P) $a_1 \ldots a_n$) and (AT-LEAST n (K P)) the constructs (AT-MOST n (K P)) and (ALL (K P) C) cannot be reduced to a ONE-OF concept. In short, the problem is caused by the fact that in both cases the concepts at hand are satisfied by *infinitely* many standard names. In particular, every standard name not occurring in the KB trivially satisfies these concepts.

Lemma 10. *Let Σ be a consistent Classic knowledge base and $\mathcal{I}$ be an interpretation. Then*

1. $|\{a \in \Delta \mid a \in (\text{AT-MOST n (K P)})^{\mathcal{I}, \mathcal{M}(\Sigma)}\}| = \infty$
2. $|\{a \in \Delta \mid a \in (\text{ALL (K P) C})^{\mathcal{I}, \mathcal{M}(\Sigma)}\}| = \infty$

4.4 Discussion

Our work raises several issues. For one, a central motivation for using a restricted concept language like Classic has been the hope for efficient inference methods. However, as shown in [8], computing inferences in Classic is co-NP hard in the worst case, and the culprit are the ONE-OF concepts. For that reason, actual Classic implementations use incomplete but polynomial algorithms that treat ONE-OF in a non-standard way. It is not hard to see that using these fast algorithms for our reduction method may sometimes lead to *unsound* reasoning. Alternatively, one may choose to use complete Classic inference methods and risk high complexity. We tend to favor risking unsound reasoning, but the viability of such an approach needs further study.

Another issue raised by our results is the fact that not all epistemic constructs can be reduced to Classic. While this is a clear limitation, we would like to point out that the reduction method, as it stands, has interesting applications beyond querying. For example, it is possible to enforce a local closed world assumption on a concept C wrt a KB Σ by adding the ONE-OF concept $|(KC)|_\Sigma$ (the currently known individuals of C) to the definition of C. Furthermore it allows an elegant implementation of integrity constraints such as *all known instances of C are among the known instances of D*, which is also related to *trigger rules* in Classic [11, 4].

5 Summary

In this paper we presented a technique to evaluate epistemic queries in Classic knowledge bases. We adopted Levesque's ideas and reduced epistemic queries to a sequence of Classic queries which can be handled by conventional methods. In contrast to concept languages sufficiently powerful to represent Levesque's reduction technique completely, Classic cannot accommodate for all possible reductions. An important result of our work is that it is nevertheless possible to use this technique for a large class of epistemic queries in Classic.

Acknowledgements We thank Werner Nutt for discussions on this subject and an anonymous referee for helpful comments.

References

1. A. Becker, *Eine epistemische Erweiterung von Classic als Interaktionssprache für Classic-Wissensbasen*, Diploma Thesis (in German), University of Bonn, 1994.
2. F. Baader et al., *Terminologische Logiken*, in: Künstliche Intelligenz, 1992, 23–33.
3. R. J. Brachman, D. L McGuinness, P. F. Patel-Schneider, L. A. Resnick, *Living with Classic: When and How to Use a KL-ONE-Like Language*, in: J. Sowa (ed.), Principles of Semantic Networks, Morgan Kaufmann, San Mateo, 1990.
4. F. M. Donini et al., *Adding Epistemic Operators to Concept Languages*, in: Proceedings of the 3rd International Conference on Principles of Knowledge Representation and Reasoning, Morgan Kaufmann, San Mateo, 1992, 342-53.
5. J. Y. Halpern, Y. Moses, *A guide to completeness and complexity for modal logics of knowledge and belief*, in: Artificial Intelligence 54, 1992, 319–379.
6. J. Hintikka, *Knowledge and Belief: An Introduction to the Logic of the Two Notions*, Cornell University Press, Ithaka, NY, 1962.
7. S. A. Kripke, *Semantical considerations on modal logic*, in: Acta Philosophica Fennica 16, 1963, 83–94.
8. M. Lenzerini, A. Schaerf, *Querying Concept-Based Knowledge Bases*, in: H. Boley, M. M. Richter, (eds.), Processing Declarative Knowledge, Workshop-Proceedings PDK 91, Springer, 1991, 107–123.
9. H. J. Levesque, *Foundations of a functional approach to knowledge representation*, in: Artificial Intelligence 23, 1984, 155-212.
10. H. J. Levesque, *All I know: A Study in Autoepistemic Logic*, in: Artificial Intelligence 42, 1990, 263–309.
11. L. A. Resnick et al., *Classic Description and Reference Manual For the Common Lisp Implementation Version 1.2*, 1991.

Communicating Rational Agents

B. van Linder, W. van der Hoek, J.-J. Ch. Meyer

Utrecht University, Department of Computer Science
P.O. Box 80.089, 3508 TB Utrecht, The Netherlands

Abstract. We demonstrate how communication between agents can be incorporated in a dynamic/epistemic multi-agent system, in which the knowledge and ability of agents, and the opportunity for, and the result of their actions are formalized. We deal with two sorts of communication inside this system: one in which a didactic agent passes on its knowledge to every other agent, and one in which agents only send information upon request. The ability and opportunity to communicate depends on the knowledge and lack of knowledge of agents, and the trust and dependence relations that exist between them. The semantics of communication actions is given by means of the machinery of epistemic updates, which is a useful instrument when modelling knowledge-producing actions. Our approach allows the whole process of communication to be defined inside a Kripke model. We compare our communication system to other multi-agent epistemic notions, viz. belief dependence, and distributed and common knowledge.

1 Introduction

The construction of models for multi-agent systems has received a lot of attention in the theory of AI. An important aspect of any multi-agent system is the possibility of communication between agents. Agents can for instance communicate to advance their goals, to indicate their mental state, or to affect the mental state of others. Here we deal with the kind of communication in which knowledge of agents is passed on to other agents. In a planning system for rational agents, this kind of knowledge propagation makes agents more effective in their reasoning concerning the correctness and feasibility of their plans.

We show how communication and the transfer of knowledge between agents can be incorporated in a system in which knowledge, abilities, results, and opportunities are formalized. The system that we use here has previously been investigated in [6, 7, 11]; it contains elements from epistemic and dynamic logic, and furthermore provides for a consistent treatment of abilities.

The rest of the paper is organized as follows. In Sect. 2 we present the basic system in which we incorporate communication. In Sect. 3 two approaches towards communication are introduced. In the first approach didactic agents lavishly pass on their knowledge without anybody asking for it; in the second approach agents pass on knowledge on request only. In Sect. 4 we look at other multi-agent epistemic notions, viz. belief dependence and distributed and common knowledge. We round off in Sect. 5.

2 Knowledge, Abilities, Opportunities, and Results

Formalizing *knowledge* has been a subject of continuing research both in analytical philosophy and in AI (cf. [3, 4, 12]). In representing knowledge we follow, both from a syntactical and a semantic point of view, the approach common in epistemic logic: the formula $K_i\varphi$ denotes the fact that agent i knows φ, and the semantics of knowledge is given by means of a possible worlds semantics.

An important aspect of any investigation of (human) action is the relation that exists between *ability* and *opportunity*. In order to successfully complete an action, both the opportunity and the ability to perform the action are necessary. Although these notions are interconnected, they are surely not identical (cf. [10]): the abilities of agents can be seen as comprising mental and physical powers, moral capacities, and human and physical possibility, whereas the opportunity to perform actions is best described by the notion of circumstantial possibility. A nice example that illustrates the difference between ability and opportunity is that of a lion in a zoo (cf. [1]): although the lion will never have the opportunity to eat a zebra, it certainly has the ability to do so. We propose that in order to make the behaviour of rational agents, like for instance robots, as realistic as possible, abilities and opportunities need also be distinguished in AI environments. The abilities of the agents are formalized via the A_i operator; the formula $A_i\alpha$ denotes the fact that agent i has the ability to do α.

In defining the *result* of an action, we follow the ideas of [14], in which the state of affairs brought about by execution of the action is defined to be its result.

When using the definitions of opportunities and results as given above, the framework of (propositional) dynamic logic provides an excellent means to formalize these notions. If we use events $do_i(\alpha)$ to refer to the performance of the action α by the agent i, the formula $\langle do_i(\alpha)\rangle\varphi$ represents the fact that the agent i has the opportunity to do α and that doing α leads to φ. The formula $[do_i(\alpha)]\varphi$ is noncommittal about the opportunity of the agent to do α but states that should the opportunity arise, a state of affairs satisfying φ would result. Besides the possibility to formalize both opportunities and results when using dynamic logic, another advantage lies in the compatibility of epistemic and dynamic logic from a semantic point of view: the possible world semantics can be used to provide meaning both to epistemic and dynamic notions.

2.1 Epistemic updates

When formalizing the behaviour of rational agents, the treatment of *knowledge-producing*, or *informative*, actions should receive due attention, not only since these actions frequently occur in real life, but also because of the importance of these actions for planning. The distinguishing feature of knowledge-producing actions is that their effect is to change what is known about the current situation. As such, typical examples of informative actions are sensing and observing.

In [11] we show how the informative action that consists of testing (or observing) the real world can be formalized in our system. The semantics of the test action is based on the use of *epistemic updates*, a notion we introduced in [11]. The idea behind these epistemic updates is the following. Informative actions produce knowledge concerning some proposition φ. If the agent that performs the informative action does not have any *a priori* knowledge concerning φ, this action puts an end to its uncertainties concerning φ. As such, informative actions reduce the number of epistemic alternatives that an agent has.

The formalization of epistemic updates in the models of our system, which obeys an S5 axiomatization for knowledge, is based on the idea that an update with φ of the knowledge of an agent i in a state s removes all the possible worlds that contradict the newly acquired knowledge φ from the epistemic equivalence class of i in s. As a result of an epistemic update with φ, the original epistemic equivalence class of i in s is divided into two new equivalence classes: one containing the epistemic alternatives that support φ, the other containing those that do not support φ.

Given this intuitive meaning of epistemic updates, it is obvious that these actions cause transitions between pairs (Model, State), thus generalizing the usual actions from dynamic logic that cause inter-state transitions within a model. Our formalization of the transitions caused by actions is such that informative actions cause transitions in which the model under consideration differs while the state stays the same, whereas 'ordinary' actions cause transitions in which the state alters but the model remains the same.

It is already remarked in [11] that the machinery of epistemic updates is not applicable for epistemic formulae since it could give undesired results. We do not consider this a serious restriction since in general one is not interested in actions that produce knowledge concerning knowledge, but in actions that produce knowledge on aspects of the real world, on results, abilities, and opportunities.

2.2 The Formal Definitions

Definition 1 (Defining the language). Let a finite set $\{1,\ldots,n\}$ of agents, and some denumerable sets Π of propositional symbols, and At of atomic actions be given. The language $\mathcal{L}$ and the class of actions Ac are defined by mutual induction as follows.

1. $\mathcal{L}$ is the smallest superset of Π such that
   - if $\varphi, \psi \in \mathcal{L}$ then $\neg\varphi, \varphi \vee \psi \in \mathcal{L}$,
   - if $i \in \mathcal{A}$, $\alpha \in Ac$ and $\varphi \in \mathcal{L}$ then $K_i\varphi, \langle do_i(\alpha)\rangle\varphi, A_i\alpha \in \mathcal{L}$.
2. Ac is the smallest superset of At such that
   - if $\varphi \in \mathcal{L}$ then confirm $\varphi \in Ac$,
   - if $\alpha_1 \in Ac$ and $\alpha_2 \in Ac$ then $\alpha_1; \alpha_2 \in Ac$,
   - if $\varphi \in \mathcal{L}$ and $\alpha_1, \alpha_2 \in Ac$ then if φ then α_1 else α_2 fi $\in Ac$,
   - if $\varphi \in \mathcal{L}$ and $\alpha_1 \in Ac$ then while φ do α_1 od $\in Ac$.

An element of $\mathcal{L}$ that contains no K_i operator is called *K-free*. The meta-action that performs an epistemic update is for any K-free formula ϑ and agent j defined by ep_update (ϑ, j). The class of actions consisting of those of Ac united with the epistemic updates is denoted by Ac'.

Remark. The action ep_update (ϑ, j) is a primitive action, that is used in the implementation of more sophisticated actions like observations and communication actions. In itself the epistemic update action is not one to be executed by agents: it is a sort of meta-action, used to describe the semantics for knowledge-producing actions in a concise way. Note in particular that this action is never a part of a formula in the agent's language.

The constructs $\wedge, \to, \leftrightarrow, \text{tt}, \text{ff}, M_i\varphi$ and $[\text{do}_i(\alpha)]\varphi$ are defined in the usual way. Other additional constructs are introduced by definitional abbreviation: skip is confirm tt, α^0 is skip, and α^{n+1} is $\alpha; \alpha^n$.

Definition 2 (Defining the models). The class $\mathfrak{M}$ of Kripke models contains all tuples $M = < S, \pi, R, r, c >$ such that

1. S is a set of possible worlds, or states.
2. $\pi : \Pi \times S \to \text{bool}$ is a total function that assigns a truth value to propositional symbols in possible worlds.
3. $R : A \to \wp(S \times S)$ is a function that yields the epistemic accessibility relations for a given agent. Since we assume to deal with S5 models, it is demanded that $R(i)$ is an equivalence relation for all i. For reasons of practical convenience we define $[s]_{R(i)}$ to be $\{s' \in S \mid (s, s') \in R(i)\}$.
4. $r : A \times At \to S \to \wp(S)$ is such that $r(i, a)(s)$ yields the (possibly empty) state transition in s caused by the event $\text{do}_i(a)$. This function is such that for all atomic actions a it holds that $|r(i, a)(s)| \leq 1$ for all i and s, i.e., these events are *deterministic*.
5. $c : A \times At \to S \to \text{bool}$ is the capability function such that $c(i, a)(s)$ indicates whether the agent i is capable of performing the action a in s.

Definition 3. Let $M = < S, \pi, R, r, c >$ be some Kripke model, let $S' \subseteq S$, and φ be some formula. The set $\text{Cl}_{eq}(S')$ is defined as $S' \times S'$, and $\llbracket \varphi \rrbracket$ is defined to denote the worlds in which φ holds, i.e., $\llbracket \varphi \rrbracket = \{s \in S \mid M, s \models \varphi\}$.

Definition 4 (Defining $\models$). Let $M = < S, \pi, R, r, c >$ be some Kripke model from $\mathfrak{M}$. For propositional symbols, negated formulae, conjunctions, and epistemic formulae, $M, s \models \varphi$ is inductively defined as usual. For the other clauses $M, s \models \varphi$ is defined as follows:

$$M, s \models \langle \text{do}_i(\alpha) \rangle \varphi \quad \Leftrightarrow \exists M', s'[M', s' \in r(i, \alpha)(M, s) \,\&\, M', s' \models \varphi]$$
$$M, s \models A_i \alpha \quad \Leftrightarrow c(i, \alpha)(M, s) = 1$$

where r and c are defined by:

$$
\begin{aligned}
r \quad &: A \times Ac' \to (\mathfrak{M} \times S) \cup S \to \wp(\mathfrak{M} \times S) \\
r(i, a)(M, s) &= M, r(i, a)(s) \\
r(i, \text{confirm}\ \varphi)(M, s) &= \{(M, s)\} \text{ if } M, s \models \varphi \text{ and } \emptyset \text{ if } M, s \not\models \varphi \\
r(i, \alpha_1; \alpha_2)(M, s) &= r(i, \alpha_2)(r(i, \alpha_1)(M, s)) \\
r(i, \text{if}\ \varphi\ \text{then}\ \alpha_1 &= r(i, \alpha_1)(M, s) \text{ if } M, s \models \varphi \text{ and} \\
\quad \text{else}\ \alpha_2\ \text{fi})(M, s) &\quad r(i, \alpha_2)(M, s) \text{ if } M, s \not\models \varphi \\
r(i, \text{while}\ \varphi\ \text{do}\ \alpha_1\ \text{od})(M, s) &= \{(M', s') \mid \exists k \in \mathbb{N} \exists M_0, s_0 \ldots \exists M_k, s_k \\
&\quad [M_0, s_0 = M, s \,\&\, M_k, s_k = M', s' \,\&\, \forall j < k
\end{aligned}
$$

$$[\mathcal{M}_{j+1}, s_{j+1} = \mathbf{r}(i, \mathtt{confirm}\ \varphi; \alpha_1)(\mathcal{M}_j, s_j)]$$
$$\&\ \mathcal{M}', s' \models \neg\varphi]\}$$

and
$\mathbf{r}(i, \mathtt{ep\_update}\ (\vartheta, j))(\mathcal{M}, s) = \mathcal{M}', s$ where
$\mathcal{M}' = <\ \mathcal{S}, \pi, \mathrm{R}', \mathbf{r}, \mathbf{c} > \in \mathfrak{M}$ with
$\quad \mathrm{R}'(j') = \mathrm{R}(j')$ for $j' \neq j$,
$\quad \mathrm{R}'(j) = (\mathrm{R}(j) \setminus \mathrm{Cl_{eq}}([s]_{\mathrm{R}(j)})) \cup \mathrm{Cl_{eq}}([s] \cap \llbracket \vartheta \rrbracket) \cup \mathrm{Cl_{eq}}([s] \cap \llbracket \neg\vartheta \rrbracket)$
where $\mathbf{r}(i, \alpha)(\emptyset) \qquad = \emptyset$

and

$\mathbf{c}$	$: \mathcal{A} \times Ac \to (\mathfrak{M} \times \mathcal{S}) \cup \mathcal{S} \to \mathrm{bool}$
$\mathbf{c}(i, a)(\mathcal{M}, s)$	$= \mathbf{c}(i, a)(s)$
$\mathbf{c}(i, \mathtt{confirm}\ \varphi)(\mathcal{M}, s)$	$= 1$ if $\mathcal{M}, s \models \varphi$, and 0 if $\mathcal{M}, s \not\models \varphi$
$\mathbf{c}(i, \alpha_1; \alpha_2)(\mathcal{M}, s)$	$= \mathbf{c}(i, \alpha_1)(\mathcal{M}, s)\ \&\ \mathbf{c}(i, \alpha_2)(\mathbf{r}(i, \alpha_1)(\mathcal{M}, s))$
$\mathbf{c}(i, \mathtt{if}\ \varphi\ \mathtt{then}\ \alpha_1$	$= \mathbf{c}(i, \mathtt{confirm}\ \varphi; \alpha_1)(\mathcal{M}, s)$ or
$\qquad \mathtt{else}\ \alpha_2\ \mathtt{fi})(\mathcal{M}, s)$	$\mathbf{c}(i, \mathtt{confirm}\ \neg\varphi; \alpha_2)(\mathcal{M}, s)$
$\mathbf{c}(i, \mathtt{while}\ \varphi\ \mathtt{do}\ \alpha_1\ \mathtt{od})(\mathcal{M}, s)$	$= 1$ if $\exists k \in \mathbb{N}[\mathbf{c}(i, (\mathtt{confirm}\ \varphi; \alpha_1)^k;$
	$\mathtt{confirm}\ \neg\varphi)(\mathcal{M}, s) = 1]$
	and 0 otherwise
where $\mathbf{c}(i, \alpha)(\emptyset)$	$= 1$.

Satisfiability and validity are defined as usual.

Remark. With regard to the abilities of agents, the motivation for the choices made in Def. 4 is the following. The definition of $\mathbf{c}(i, \mathtt{confirm}\ \varphi)(s)$ expresses that an agent is able to get confirmation for a formula φ iff φ holds. Note that the definitions of $\mathbf{r}(i, \mathtt{confirm}\ \varphi)$ and $\mathbf{c}(i, \mathtt{confirm}\ \varphi)$ imply that in circumstances such that φ holds, the agents both have the opportunity and the ability to confirm φ. An agent is capable of performing a sequential composition $\alpha_1; \alpha_2$ iff it is capable of performing α_1 and it is capable of executing α_2 after it has performed α_1. An agent is capable of performing a conditional composition, if it is able to either get confirmation for the condition and thereafter perform the then-part, or it is able to confirm the negation of the condition and perform the else-part afterwards. An agent is capable of performing a repetitive composition $\mathtt{while}\ \varphi\ \mathtt{do}\ \alpha_1\ \mathtt{od}$ iff it is able to perform the action $(\mathtt{confirm}\ \varphi; \alpha_1)^k; \mathtt{confirm}\ \neg\varphi$ for some $k \in \mathbb{N}$. Note that no definition of the ability for the epistemic update function is given, since this action is used in the implementation of other actions only and is not available to the agent for execution.

3 The Transfer of Information

We want to deal with communication through which knowledge of agents is passed on to other agents. We are in particular interested in knowledge concerning abilities and results. For by passing on this kind of knowledge agents can inform each other on the correctness and feasibility of the plans that they might have.

Example 1. Consider the following scenario, involving three rational agents.

Agent 1 'My goal is to put on the light, but I do not know whether turning this switch will put on the light, neither do I know whether I am altogether able to turn the switch. Since I trust agent 2 as far as my abilities are concerned, I ask it whether I am able to do this.'

Agent 2 'Hm, agent 1 asks me whether it is able to turn the switch. I know that this is the case, so I tell this to agent 1.'

Agent 1 'Aha, a message from agent 2. It tells me that I am capable of turning the switch, and since I trust agent 2 on this subject, I know now that I am indeed capable of doing this. With regard to the opportunities and results of my actions I have faith in agent 3. Let's ask agent 3 whether it is possible for me to put on the light by turning the switch.'

Agent 3 'Agent 1 asks me whether it is possible to put on the light by turning the switch. I know that this is the case, and I tell this to agent 1.'

Agent 1 'Agent 3 tells me that it is possible for me to put on the light by turning the switch, and since I trust agent 3 on this subject, I now conclude that this is indeed the case.'

Note all the different aspects of the agents' behaviour that are part of this scenario: actions and their results, opportunities, abilities, (in)complete knowledge, requests for information, sending and incorporation of information, and dependence and trust relations. With regard to these latter relations we agree with Huang (cf. [8]) that in multi-agent systems the concept of trust and dependence relations deserves considerable attention. In our opinion this observation holds *a fortiori* when communication is involved: an agent i may or may not accept the information on φ that an agent j sends to it, depending on i's trust in j concerning φ.

3.1 The Didactic Agent

The first formalization of communication that we present is that of super-cooperative, didactic agents. These agents always have the opportunity to pass on all of their knowledge to every other agent. It is in particular not necessary that a request for some piece of information has been made to the agent in order for it to pass on its knowledge. The behaviour of these didactic agents bears some resemblance to that of the robots of Shoham ([13]), that can also inform anyone of the facts they know.

When agent i receives the information φ from the didactic agent j, it is checked whether i trusts j on φ. If this is the case, the information φ is used to expand the knowledge of agent i. Otherwise i lets the information pass without using it. We formalize the dependence relations between agents using the *dependent* operator $D_{i,j}$, introduced in [8]. We like to think of $D_{i,j}\varphi$ as expressing the fact that agent j is a *teacher* of agent i on the subject φ.

The actual formalization that we present here uses, besides the constructs already given in Sect. 2, two additional ones: apart from the dependent operator

$D_{i,j}$, we add an action constructor **send**. For a K-free formula ϑ, $\text{send}(\vartheta, i)$ corresponds to the action of sending the formula ϑ to the agent i.

With regard to the abilities for the send actions, we remark that for our aims it is sufficient to stipulate that each agent that has the knowledge that ϑ holds, both has the opportunity and ability to pass on this knowledge.

Definition 5 (Extending the syntax). We extend Def. 1 as follows:
- if $i, j \in \mathcal{A}$ and $\varphi \in \mathcal{L}$ then $D_{i,j}\varphi \in \mathcal{L}$,
- if $j \in \mathcal{A}$ and ϑ is a K-free formula then $\text{send}(\vartheta, j) \in Ac$.

Definition 6 (Extending the semantics). The Kripke models from Def. 2 are extended with a function $D : \mathcal{A} \times \mathcal{A} \times \mathcal{S} \to \wp(\mathcal{L})$. We define:
- $\mathcal{M}, s \models D_{i,j}\varphi$ iff $\varphi \in D(i, j, s)$,
- $r(i, \text{send}(\vartheta, j))(\mathcal{M}, s) = \emptyset$ if $\mathcal{M}, s \not\models K_i\vartheta$
- $r(i, \text{send}(\vartheta, j))(\mathcal{M}, s) = \mathcal{M}, s$ if $\mathcal{M}, s \models K_i\vartheta \wedge \neg D_{j,i}\vartheta$
- $r(i, \text{send}(\vartheta, j))(\mathcal{M}, s) = r(i, \text{ep\_update}\,(\vartheta, j))(\mathcal{M}, s)$ if $\mathcal{M}, s \models K_i\vartheta \wedge D_{j,i}\vartheta$
- $c(i, \text{send}(\vartheta, j))(\mathcal{M}, s) = c(i, \text{confirm } K_i\vartheta)(\mathcal{M}, s)$

It is not possible that agents can be forced to incorporate new facts that contradict their old knowledge. This is because we are modelling *knowledge*, and, in contrast with belief, knowledge is usually assumed to be veridical: it obeys the T-axiom $K_i\varphi \to \varphi$.

Lemma 7. *Let* $i, j \in \mathcal{A}$, $\alpha \in Ac$, $\varphi \in \mathcal{L}$, *and let* ϑ *be some K-free formula.*
1. $\models K_i\vartheta \leftrightarrow \langle \text{do}_i(\text{send}(\vartheta, j))\rangle\text{tt} \wedge A_i\text{send}(\vartheta, j)$, *for all* $j \in \mathcal{A}$
2. $\models K_i\vartheta \wedge D_{j,i}\vartheta \leftrightarrow \langle \text{do}_i(\text{send}(\vartheta, j))\rangle K_j\vartheta$
3. $\models \langle \text{do}_i(\alpha)\rangle\varphi \to [\text{do}_i(\alpha)]\varphi$

The first clause of Lemma 7 corresponds to the intuition that agents have both the opportunity and ability to pass on all the information that they possess, and that only the information that they possess can be passed on. The second clause formalizes the actual knowledge production that is a consequence of the transfer of information if done by a trusted agent: if some agent i has knowledge on ϑ, and is trusted by j on ϑ, then the sending of ϑ from i to j results in j knowing ϑ. The last clause states that events containing actions from the extended class Ac are still deterministic.

3.2 The Second Approach: Sending upon Request

The agents formalized in 3.1 have the opportunity to pass on their knowledge without anybody asking them to do so. Although this behaviour is not unrealistic even for human agents, another kind of communication is more common. In this kind of communication agents make requests for certain pieces of information. The agent to which the request is addressed, answers this by sending the requested information if this is in its possession; otherwise it lets the request pass.

The formalization of the actual request action is far from trivial, since it is necessary to register the fact that the agent actually made a request. The usual approaches towards communication in computer science (cf. [5]) use some form of channels through which requests and sends are transferred, but it is not straightforward to adopt this approach in a propositional possible worlds semantics. In order to register the requests that have been made we propose the use of an additional operator $C_{i,j}$, where the 'C' can be seen as referring to Channel, Communication, or Common memory. The intuitive interpretation of the formula $C_{i,j}\vartheta$ is that agent i has made a request on the subject ϑ, addressed to agent j. If the agent j knows ϑ, truth of $C_{i,j}\vartheta$ is a trigger to pass on its knowledge on ϑ to i for it to incorporate in its knowledge.

Semantically, the $C_{i,j}$ operator is interpreted through a cluster of possible worlds. Truth of a formula ϑ in all the worlds from this cluster then indicates that agent i is somehow interested in ϑ: the agent desires or prefers to know ϑ, and wants j to tell it. The recording of requests from i to j is now brought about by updating the cluster corresponding to $C_{i,j}$. In this way, the request from i to j on a formula ϑ results in $C_{i,j}\vartheta$ being true. Truth of $C_{i,j}\vartheta$ and $K_j\vartheta$ then provides the opportunity for agent j to transfer the knowledge on ϑ to i, which results in $K_i\vartheta$ being true.

With regard to the ability and opportunity to request and send information, the situation is even less clear in this case than it was for the didactic agent. The actual choices that we have made are the following. Agents have the *opportunity* to request any information that they do not already possess, from any other agent, but they are *capable* of requesting information only from agents that they trust. If an agent has some information that has been requested, it has the *opportunity* to pass on this information. However an agent is *capable* of sending information only to agents that trust the sending agent with regard to this information.

Definition 8 (Extending the syntax). We extend Def. 5 as follows:
- if $i, j \in A$ and $\varphi \in \mathcal{L}$ then $C_{i,j}\varphi \in \mathcal{L}$,
- if $j \in A$ and ϑ is a K-free formula then $\texttt{request}(\vartheta, j) \in Ac$.

Definition 9 (Modifying the semantics: Extending the models). The Kripke models from Def. 6 are extended with a function $C : A \times A \times S \to \wp(S)$. This function is such that $C(i, j, s) \subseteq [s]_{R(i)}$ for all i and j. It is furthermore demanded that initially, that is, when no request has been made, $C(i, j, s) = [s]_{R(i)}$.

Definition 10 (Modifying the semantics: Modifying $\models$). Let $\mathcal{M}$ be some Kripke model as given in Def. 9. We define:
- $\mathcal{M}, s \models C_{i,j}\vartheta \Leftrightarrow \forall t \in C(i, j, s)[\mathcal{M}, t \models \vartheta]$
- $r(i, \texttt{request}(\vartheta, j))(\mathcal{M}, s) =$
  $r(i, \texttt{confirm } \neg K_i\vartheta; \texttt{record\_req}(\vartheta, i, j))(\mathcal{M}, s)$ where
  $r(i, \texttt{record\_req}(\vartheta, i, j))(\mathcal{M}, s) = \mathcal{M}', s$ with $\mathcal{M}' = < S, \pi, R, D, C', r, c >$
  and
  $C'(i, j, s) = [s]_{R(i)} \cap [\![\vartheta]\!]$ and
  $C'(i', j', s') = C(i', j', s')$ for $(i', j', s') \neq (i, j, s)$

- $r(i, \mathtt{send}(\vartheta, j))(\mathcal{M}, s) = r(i, \mathtt{ep\_update}\ (\vartheta, j))(\mathcal{M}, s)$ if $\mathcal{M}, s \models K_i \vartheta \wedge C_{j,i} \vartheta$
- $r(i, \mathtt{send}(\vartheta, j))(\mathcal{M}, s) = \mathcal{M}, s$ otherwise.
- $c(i, \mathtt{request}(\vartheta, j))(\mathcal{M}, s) = c(i, \mathtt{confirm}\ D_{i,j} \vartheta)(\mathcal{M}, s)$
- $c(i, \mathtt{send}(\vartheta, j))(\mathcal{M}, s) = c(i, \mathtt{confirm}\ D_{j,i} \vartheta)(\mathcal{M}, s)$

Defining the semantics of the request action as we did above, has two important consequences which are very important in communication. Firstly, it is possible that agents make requests for contradictions. After such a request, the communication channel is empty and hence $C_{i,j}\mathrm{ff}$ holds. Secondly, the requests for contradictions do not propagate. That is, if one considers the request for a contradiction to be an error, the agents have the possibility to recover from these errors by making a request for another formula. Lemma 11 formalizes these desirable properties.

Lemma 11. *Let $i, j \in \mathcal{A}$ and let ϑ be some K-free formula.*

1. $\models \neg M_i \vartheta \rightarrow \langle \mathtt{do}_i(\mathtt{request}\ (\vartheta, j)) \rangle C_{i,j} \mathrm{ff}$
2. $\models M_i \vartheta \wedge \neg K_i \vartheta \rightarrow \langle \mathtt{do}_i(\mathtt{request}\ (\mathrm{ff}, j); \mathtt{request}\ (\vartheta, j)) \rangle (C_{i,j} \vartheta \wedge \neg C_{i,j} \mathrm{ff})$

Lemma 12. *Let $i, j \in \mathcal{A}$, $\alpha \in Ac$, $\varphi \in \mathcal{L}$, and let ϑ be some K-free formula.*

1. $\models [\mathtt{do}_i(\mathtt{request}\ (\vartheta, j))] C_{i,j} \vartheta$
2. $\models \neg K_i \vartheta \leftrightarrow \langle \mathtt{do}_i(\mathtt{request}\ (\vartheta, j)) \rangle C_{i,j} \vartheta$
3. $\models D_{i,j} \vartheta \leftrightarrow A_i \mathtt{request}\ (\vartheta, j)$
4. $\models K_j \vartheta \wedge C_{i,j} \vartheta \rightarrow \langle \mathtt{do}_j(\mathtt{send}(\vartheta, i)) \rangle K_i \vartheta$
5. $\models D_{i,j} \vartheta \leftrightarrow A_j \mathtt{send}(\vartheta, i)$
6. $\models \neg K_i \vartheta \wedge K_j \vartheta \wedge D_{i,j} \vartheta \rightarrow (A_i \mathtt{request}\ (\vartheta, j) \wedge \langle \mathtt{do}_i(\mathtt{request}\ (\vartheta, j)) \rangle ((\langle \mathtt{do}_j(\mathtt{send}(\vartheta, i)) \rangle K_i \vartheta) \wedge A_j \mathtt{send}(\vartheta, i))$
7. $\models \langle \mathtt{do}_i(\alpha) \rangle \varphi \rightarrow [\mathtt{do}_i(\alpha)] \varphi$

Lemma 12 shows that we indeed succeeded in formalizing communication in which information is transferred on request only. An agent has the opportunity to request any formulae that it does not know, and this request is recorded (clause 2). Clause 4 states that agents have the opportunity to send any information that they posses to any agent that has made a request for this information. Furthermore, if some agent j knows something that i does not, and i is willing to accept j's authority on this particular subject ϑ, then by a request from i to j and the subsequent sending of information from j to i, agent i can acquire knowledge concerning ϑ (clause 6). The last clause again states determinism of the events build from the extended class of actions.

Example 2. Let τ denote the action that consists of turning a light switch, and let l denote the fact that the light is on. The following Kripke model $\mathcal{M} = \langle \mathcal{S}, \pi, R, D, C, r, c \rangle$ formalizes the scenario of example 1.

- $\mathcal{S} = \{s_0, \ldots, s_4\}$,
- R is the set $\{s_0, s_1, s_2\}^2 \cup \{(s_3, s_3), (s_4, s_4)\}$,
- $D(1, 2, s_0) = \{A_1 \tau\}$, $D(1, 3, s_0) = \{\langle \mathtt{do}_1(\tau) \rangle l\}$,
- $C(i, j, s)$ is initially equal to $R(i)$,

- $r(1,\tau)(s_0 = \{s_3\}, r(1,\tau)(s_2) = \{s_4\}$
- $c(1,\tau)(s_0) = c(1,\tau)(s_1) = 1$, $c(1,\tau)(s) = 0$ otherwise.

Initially, agent 1 does not have any knowledge concerning correctness and feasibility of its plan to put on the light by turning the switch, neither has it made any requests concerning these subjects; agent 2 knows that agent 1 is able to turn the switch. After the first request of agent 1, the communication cluster of agents 1 and 2 indicates that 1 has requested information on its ability to turn the switch from agent 2. After agent 2 has passed on its knowledge on the ability of agent 1, agent 1 knows that it is able to turn the switch. Thereafter agent 1 makes a request to agent 3 on the opportunity and result of turning the switch. Finally, after agent 3 has passed on its knowledge, agent 1 knows that turning the switch is a correct plan to put on the light. Hence through communication agent 1 acquires the knowledge that turning the switch is a correct and feasible plan to put on the light. Formally, this amounts to the following being true:

- $\mathcal{M}, s_0 \models \neg K_1 \langle do_1(\tau) \rangle l \wedge \neg K_1 A_1 \tau$
- $\mathcal{M}, s_0 \models \langle do_1(\text{request } (A_1\tau, 2)) \rangle C_{1,2} A_1 \tau$
- $\mathcal{M}, s_0 \models \langle do_1(\text{request } (A_1\tau, 2)) \rangle \langle do_2(\text{send}(A_1\tau, 1)) \rangle K_1 A_1 \tau$

Let $\mathcal{M}', \mathcal{M}''$ be defined by:

- $\mathcal{M}', s_0 = r(2, \text{send}(A_1\tau, 1))(r(1, \text{request } (A_1\tau, 2))(\mathcal{M}, s_0))$
- $\mathcal{M}'', s_0 = r(3, \text{send}(\langle do_1(\tau) \rangle l, 1))(r(1, \text{request } (\langle do_1(\tau) \rangle l, 3))(\mathcal{M}', s_0))$

Then we have:

- $\mathcal{M}', s_0 \models \neg K_1 \langle do_1(\tau) \rangle l \wedge K_1 A_1 \tau$
- $\mathcal{M}', s_0 \models \langle do_1(\text{request } (\langle do_1(\tau) \rangle l, 3)) \rangle C_{1,3} \langle do_1(\tau) \rangle l$
- $\mathcal{M}', s_0 \models \langle do_1(\text{request }(\langle do_1(\tau) \rangle l, 3)) \rangle$
  $\langle do_3(\text{send}(\langle do_1(\tau) \rangle l, 1)) \rangle K_1 \langle do_1(\tau) \rangle l$
- $\mathcal{M}'', s_0 \models K_1 \langle do_1(\tau) \rangle l \wedge K_1 A_1 \tau$

4 Belief dependence, distributed and common knowledge

The logic of belief dependence is especially aimed at formalizing the various dependencies of belief in epistemic multi-agent environments (cf. [8]). In these environments agents may rely on other agents for their beliefs. Besides the dependent operator $D_{i,j}$, the logic of belief dependence furthermore contains the subbelief, or compartment, operator $B_{i,j}$, such that the intuitive interpretation of $B_{i,j}\varphi$ is that agent i believes φ due to agent j. Several classes of models are proposed to provide the semantics for the dependent and subbelief operator. In our opinion the most acceptable one is the class of so called D-models, in which the $D_{i,j}$ operator is interpreted by means of a $D(i,j,s)$ relation, and the compartment operator $B_{i,j}\varphi$ is defined to be $D_{i,j}\varphi \wedge B_j\varphi$.

The ultimate goal underlying the logic of belief dependence is the formalization of the process in which some of the subbeliefs of an agent, this is called the *compartmentalized information*, are used to update the actual, real beliefs of the agent and thus become *incorporated information*. In [9] several update strategies are given that can be used to guide the transformation of compartment beliefs into actual beliefs. The need for these strategies arises since it is possible that compartment beliefs contradict the actual beliefs of the agent: dependent on the trust relation that the agents bear either the compartment belief or the actual belief is rejected. However due to the non-existence of adequate belief revision algorithms, the actual change of belief that results from the incorporation of compartmentalized knowledge is not formalized. In our opinion there are two major points where the framework of the previous section could be of use. Firstly, the acquisition and incorporation of compartmentalized information is obviously a *dynamic* process. The modelling of this dynamic process requires the explicit representation of actions, which indeed is the case with our framework. Secondly, if one considers *knowledge* instead of belief, the need for revision of beliefs with its sophisticated strategies disappears, since it is not possible that different agents have contradicting knowledge in the same world.

In the situation where a group of agents is passing on its knowledge to one other agent, this receiving agent seems to be in the possession of the combined knowledge of the group of agents. From this point of view, the relation with the knowledge that is *distributed* over a group of agents seems to be obvious. This is not the knowledge of all the agents in the group, but the knowledge that would obtain if the agents could somehow 'combine' their knowledge (cf. [3]). Also the relation with *common* knowledge, the knowledge of which all the agents know that it is common to everyone of them, is worth looking at.

Without going into detail, we remark that it is not for all formulae possible to change the state of knowledge from distributed knowledge of a group to knowledge of one member of the group (this is called *fact discovery* in [2]) through communication as introduced in the previous sections. One reason underlying this impossibility is the fact that in a non-compact system as ours it could be possible that an infinite number of premises is necessary to conclude a formula. In situations where these premises are distributed knowledge, an infinite number of communication transactions would be necessary to go from distributed knowledge to knowledge of one of the agents. The exact relation between our kind of communication and distributed knowledge is subject of further research.

With regard to acquiring common knowledge from ordinary knowledge via communication (this is called *fact publication* in [2]), we encounter the usual problems due to the *Byzantine agreement*, or *coordinated attack*, problem (cf. [2]). That is, acquiring common knowledge requires in general an infinite number of communication events (if the medium of communication is faulty). If anything, this property would show that our formalization of communication is a realistic one, since real-life communication does in general not lead to common knowledge.

5 Discussion

In this paper we have shown how communication can be formalized in a multi-agent dynamic/epistemic framework. We defined two kinds of communication: one in which didactic agents lavish their knowledge, and one in which information is transferred on request only. Both kinds of communication are defined inside a Kripke model by combining epistemic updates with a new modal operator $C_{i,j}$ that records the request that agent i has addressed to agent j. We furthermore compared our system of communication to other multi-agent epistemic notions, namely belief dependence and distributed and common knowledge. As far as we know our approach is one of the first to present a genuine possible worlds semantics for communication.

Acknowledgements This research is partially supported by ESPRIT III BRA project No.6156 'DRUMS II', ESPRIT III BRWG project No.8319 'MODE-LAGE', and the Vrije Universiteit Amsterdam; the third author is furthermore partially supported by the Katholieke Universiteit Nijmegen. Thanks are also due to the referees for their comments which helped improve this paper.

References

1. D. Elgesem: Action Theory and Modal Logic. PhD thesis, Institute for Philosophy, University of Oslo, Oslo, Norway (1993)
2. J.Y. Halpern and Y. Moses: Knowledge and Common Knowledge in a Distributed Environment. Journal of the ACM **37** (1990) 549–587
3. J.Y. Halpern and Y. Moses: A guide to completeness and complexity for modal logics of knowledge and belief. Artificial Intelligence **54** (1992) 319–379
4. J. Hintikka: Knowledge and Belief. Cornell University Press, Ithaca NY (1962)
5. C.A.R. Hoare: Communicating Sequential Processes. Communications of the ACM **21** (1978) 666–677
6. W. van der Hoek, B. van Linder, and J.-J. Ch. Meyer: A logic of capabilities. Technical Report IR-330, Vrije Universiteit Amsterdam (An extended abstract is to appear in the Proceedings of LFCS'94)
7. W. van der Hoek, B. van Linder, and J.-J. Ch. Meyer: Unravelling nondeterminism: On having the ability to choose. Technical Report RUU-CS-93-30, Utrecht University (An extended abstract is to appear in the Proceedings of AIMSA'94)
8. Z. Huang: Logics for belief dependence. In E. Börger, H. Kleine Büning, M.M. Richter, and W. Schönfeld, editors, *Computer Science Logic, 4th Workshop CSL'90.* Lecture Notes in Computer Science **533** (1991) 274–288
9. Z. Huang and P. van Emde Boas: Belief dependence, revision and persistence. In P. Dekker and M. Stokhof, editors, Proceedings of the Eight Amsterdam Colloquium (1992) 271–281
10. A. Kenny: Will, Freedom and Power. Basil Blackwell, Oxford (1975)
11. B. van Linder, W. van der Hoek, and J.-J. Ch. Meyer: Tests as epistemic updates: Pursuit of knowledge. Technical Report UU-CS-1994-08, Utrecht University (An extended abstract is to appear in the Proceedings of ECAI'94)
12. R.C. Moore: Reasoning about knowledge and action. Technical Report 191, SRI International (1980)
13. Y. Shoham: Agent-oriented programming. Artificial Intelligence **60** (1993) 51–92
14. G. H. von Wright: Norm and Action. Routledge & Kegan Paul, London (1963)

Knowledge-Level Modularization of a Complex Knowledge Base

Josef Meyer-Fujara, Barbara Heller, Sonja Schlegelmilch, Ipke Wachsmuth

Faculty of Technology, University of Bielefeld, D-33501 Bielefeld

Abstract. An increasingly relevant theme for knowledge-based systems (KBS) is how to model and use a large and complex knowledge domain. On the one hand, this involves developing new ideas on a modular construction of a knowledge base and, on the other hand, an appropriate architecture of a KBS that takes account of such a modular knowledge base. In the HYPERCON project[1] we conceptualize a complex medical domain (hypertension) according to ideas of a knowledge-level modularization. In this paper, we give a brief account of our approach and describe how specific knowledge is structured and accomodated in a modular knowledge base. Using a specific case of a patient, we exemplify focussing procedures based on plan-and-tactics and on changing between different granularity levels in the course of a consultation.

1   Introduction

One of the severe limits for the application of knowledge-based systems still lies in the restricted size of manageable knowledge bases. Many fields of application, however, require the handling of complex – i.e., large and diverse – stocks of knowledge. This issue has been noticed for some time, e.g., [18, 10, 2, 21, 16, 13], and its actuality is witnessed by a growing number of activities at major AI conferences.

Complex domain knowledge can neither be acquired nor implemented and maintained by a single person. But division of labor necessitates that team members can restrict their attention to limited parts of the overall knowledge. Efficiency requires that the problem solver strictly focus on parts of knowledge relevant for the actual issue if the system is not to drown in memory search. Hence, a modularization of KBS seems necessary. This task cannot be addressed solely in a way that is convenient for software development. In our view, modularization must follow semantic borders of relevance and must be addressed at the *knowledge level* in the sense of Newell [14]. Such a modularization should entail three questions:

1. Which criteria guide modularization?
2. How is relevant knowledge actually retrieved?
3. How is access to the relevant knowledge organized?

---

[1] Our work is supported in part by the North-Rhine-Westphalian Ministry of Research and Technology (MWF grant IVA6-400 015 92). We thank the medical experts Prof. K. Kauffmann, Prof. H.-D. Faulhaber and Dr. U. Müller-Kolck for their patience in explaining medical facts as well as our students Ch. Dücker, J. Hamann, A. Möller, Ch. Scheering and J. Stoye for their assistance.

We deal with these questions in the context of the HYPERCON project which aims at supporting diagnosis and therapy of hypertension patients [20]. The interest of the system lies in helping the user to compare possible diagnostic procedures, diagnoses and therapies in the light of heuristic and deep knowledge automatically related and applied to his actual case.

A very large body of knowledge has to be represented pertaining to diverse fields of medicine such as laboratory tests, image generating procedures, epidemiology, and pathophysiological models. In addition, there is knowledge about reasonable courses of actions for finding a diagnosis that reduce strain and cost to the patient.

The knowledge is of diverse origin (from textbooks, expert interviews, case studies) and it is needed at different levels of detail: For dealing with standard cases, compiled instructions for action are sufficient. For taking care of, e.g., multimorbidity, however, and also for explanation, detailed knowledge is needed. Morphological knowledge is needed on size levels reaching from organs down to electron-microscopical structures.

Finally, the particular parts of knowledge may strongly interact: a heart murmur may be caused by high blood pressure originating from a kidney damage caused by diabetes, but may as well be a symptom of a primary heart disease. In total, our domain clearly illustrates the need for modularization.

In our current work, we concentrate on the highly relevant subfield of hypertension due to kidney diseases or hormonal dysfunctions, possibly complicated by diabetes. Our system is realized on top of the hybrid expert system shell Knowledge Craft.

After discussing related work, we will explain our approach to modularization with respect to knowledge partitioning, knowledge focussing, aspects of granularity, and system architecture. Then we will illustrate the concepts introduced by the example of an authentic medical case.

2   Previous Approaches

Known approaches to modularization of knowledge representations (as opposed to modularization of knowledge-based *systems*) have concentrated on several aspects. Since long, possibilities of syntactical rule grouping have been available, e.g., in variants of OPS such as RIME [18], and in major expert system tools. For frames, such tools often offer so-called contexts or worlds to restrict visibility of slots and values. On a more knowledge-related level, Davis [6] already suggested content-directed invocation of rules by means of meta-rules. Clancey [4] has proposed to differentiate knowledge according to its use (e.g., for problem solving or explanation), and to separate control knowledge from domain knowledge.

This latter separation is favored and refined in KADS [22] where several layers of control knowledge are distinguished in the acquisition-oriented *conceptual* model. Soloway et al. [18] suggest domain specific "buckets" (hierarchically organized *problem spaces*) that correspond to common purposes such as a variety of configuration functions. Purpose and content ("topic") are emphasized also by Clare [5]. In the "Knowledge Sharing Effort" – cf. [13, 15, 7] – a possibility to tackle the problem of realizing large knowledge bases is seen in the reuse of already existing knowledge bases; accordingly, efforts for standardization and for the establishment of libraries are made.

Finally, starting from the observation that any particular axiom (e.g., rule) will be irrelevant in many contexts, the incremental acquisition and representation of self-contained clusters of domain knowledge in a *partitioned knowledge base with dynamic access conditions* have been suggested. Their basic principles consider content and specificity of knowledge as structuring aspects and suggest to organize knowledge in layered, possibly overlapping *knowledge packets* [19].

3   Modules, Knowledge Packets and their Focussing

Our approach is led by the following motivations: the knowledge base should be partitioned into parts
- that are competent for definite task domains
- that may hold specific knowledge representations and control strategies
- that may hide their contents from other parts
- that, to a large extent, may be developed independently
- to which changes, debugging and consistency checks may be restricted
- that are manageable in themselves and allow the aggregation of more complex knowledge parts.

Our examination of the domain suggests to differentiate knowledge to be modularized by the following criteria:
- simultaneous use in the problem solving process
- cohesion of content
- similar granularity level (size, abstraction)
- specificity (applicability in particular circumstances, usability for particular goals).

knowledge about	knowledge about	criteria
resting electrocardiogram	exercise electrocardiogram	cohesion of content
findings that give hints at a disease	findings that confirm a disease	simultaneous use
macroscopic parts (e.g. renal calices)	microscopic parts (e.g. glomeruli)	granularity (size)
comparison of resting/exercise/	interpretation of resting/exercise/	specificity (usability)
long-term electrocardiogram	long-term electrocardiogram	
physiological parameters during	normal physiological parameters	specificity (applicability)
pregnancy		

Fig. 1. Separable knowledge parts (first and second column) according to differentiating criterion (third column).

For illustration, fig. 1 shows a table of knowledge parts that will be kept separate from each other, and indicates the relevant criterion. In the rest of the paper, further examples will be found.

3.1   Knowledge Modules and Knowledge Packets

By intensive discussion of diverse authentic cases with medical experts of different background (theorists, clinicists, and a practitioner), a general model of the diagnostic reasoning process was established (cf. fig. 2). The overall diagnostic plan suggested by this model includes different stages that ideally follow one another, although in reality often are subject to iteration. These processing steps were found to concern patient history, physical examination, laboratory tests, diagnostic procedures, hypothesis generation, hypothesis verification, and therapy. Correspondingly, *knowledge modules* were defined that are conceived to be highly independent and active one at a time. In a less chronologically separable way, knowledge about nosology and about physiological and anatomical models was found to be used.

All knowledge modules are characterized by self-contained specific knowledge and well-defined interfaces towards a coordination component. The interfaces hide the interior representation choices and the specific knowledge.

Altogether, these are the following modules:

acquisition modules: patient history, physical examination, laboratory tests, diagnostic procedures

diagnostic modules: hypothesis generation, hypothesis verification

therapy module: drug treatment, non-drug treatment, invasive treatment, operative treatment

library modules: nosology, anatomical and pathophysiological models

The knowledge modules are subdivided into *knowledge packets*, assembling collections of knowledge elements to be focussed simultaneously.

The packets may properly contain further packets as particular bodies of knowledge may branch to extend in competitive subbodies. Knowledge elements not in focus are invisible to the inference engine in order to exclude irrelevant knowledge from searching and matching. The set of packets is structured hierarchically according to their degree of specificity. For illustration, an extract of the packet structure "image generating procedures" in the module "diagnostic procedures" is shown in fig. 3. The overall knowledge base has approximately 250 knowledge packets.

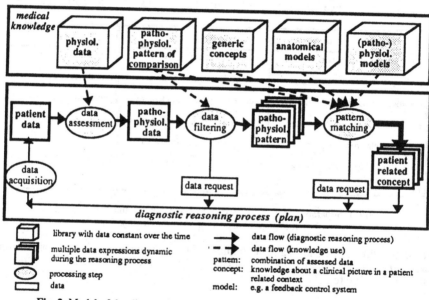

Fig. 2. Model of the diagnostic reasoning process (further explanation in text).

Packets shown side by side are competitive with each other. Competitive packets may represent alternative views or conflicting knowledge. Besides domain knowledge, modules (always) and packets (often) must contain *control knowledge*, describing, e.g., in which circumstances subpackets are focussed.

Similar to KADS the entire knowledge is organized in five levels, namely, strategic, task, tactics, inference, and domain level. This allows for smooth extension of packets in case the KBS must be enlarged for handling further tasks. Control knowledge, in our opinion, must be split along with domain knowledge. E.g., unless image generation procedures are considered at all, the choice among these procedures is irrelevant. Also, whether to proceed by establish-refine or generate-and-test depends on the local disease heterarchy. So packets have their own five-level control knowledge. In smaller packets, the three upper levels may be unimportant. We will explain the levels in section 3.3.

3.2 Partitioning Knowledge According to Granularity

In our opinion, *granularity* [9,3] must be taken into account as a special aspect of cohesion [23]. Reasoning most often occurs at a definite granularity level that is switched if necessary, and primarily to an adjacent level. Thus knowledge packets should contain knowledge at a comparable grain size. Two aspects of granularity seem particularly important for knowledge modularization.

Foundation concerns the bottom level of hierarchies used, that pertains to the objects taken for atomic, i.e., needing no further differentiation. For instance, the foundation of anatomic knowledge needed for the interpretation of sonographic findings about the kidney lies at macroscopic structures such as renal pelvis and artery; due to the restricted resolution of sonography, smaller ones (e.g., glomeruli) need not be considered. Only when this restriction turns out to be too strict, other levels are called in. Analogously, a finding of proteinuria gives a hint at a kidney disease as opposed to a heart disease, but with this finding alone, knowledge about differentiating kinds of specific kidney diseases are not relevant.

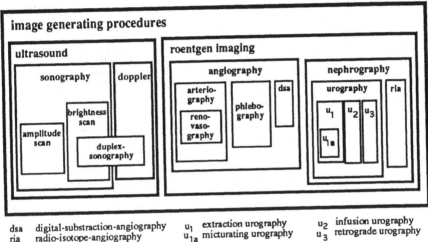

| dsa | digital-substraction-angiography | u_1 | extraction urography | u_2 | infusion urography |
| ria | radio-isotope-angiography | u_{1a} | micturating urography | u_3 | retrograde urography |

Fig. 3. Extract of the packet structure inside the module "Diagnostic Procedures".

The second aspect of granularity is the *field of view*, i.e., the region of physical or abstract entities that are focussed at the same time. It is a special kind of context as formalized, e.g., by McCarthy [11] and determines the interpretation of names of entities (e.g., leucocyte-count) and inferences associated with them (e.g., assessment of normality). As far as possible, our knowledge packets admit a well defined field of view to be automatically used when the packet is focussed. Technically, packets can be associated with Knowledge Craft contexts and contain context-dependent schemata and rules.

Defining packets according to granularity entails the need to link specific terms to more general ones at changes of packet focus. For example, the packet P "therapy of chronic kidney diseases" suggests protein-reduced dieting. A diagnosis of chronic-pyelonephritis cannot lead to this suggestion unless it is classified as chronic-kidney-disease. But this classification knowledge is contained neither in packet P nor in more general ones: P has incomplete knowledge about the hierarchy its entities belong to.

This dilemma is tackled by packet interfaces: By them, the diagnosis chronic-pyelo-nephritis suggested is linked there to the taxonomic hierarchy. The interfaces also deal with partonomic foundation and with view-dependent terms.

3.3 Global and Local Focussing of Knowledge

Focussing of knowledge is done at two abstraction levels: choosing among modules (*global focussing*) and choosing among packets inside a module (*local focussing*).

Global focussing (GF). During problem solving, the module to be activated next is determined by the global focussing component. It is structured in a way similar to KADS [22] (cf. fig. 4).
On the *strategic level*, in our case, the problem class is preset, succcessively to "diagnosis" and to "therapy", and the problem-solving method is preset, in our subsequent example, to "heuristic classification". Efficient focussing of knowledge is based on global strategies, which are described by global plans and different alternatives within the plans. They describe a global procedure of inferencing which corresponds to abstractions of our model of the diagnostic reasoning process shown in fig. 2.

Strategic Level	problem classes problem-solving methods global strategies global plans
Task Level	classes of tasks, partial tasks, subtasks
Tactics Level	default plans alternative plans competitive plans
Inference Level	rule-classes for description of inference steps during problem-solving process, rule-classes for plans
Domain Level	modules

Fig. 4. The levels of global focussing.

The *task level* describes the particular tasks for diagnosis (e.g., establish hypothesis) which are structured in different subtasks. These can be instantiated one at a time.
    To obtain a more specific focussing within the modular knowledge base, we introduced a further level – *the tactics level* – as an extension of the KADS-model. Tactics describe methods for situation-dependent application of inference steps according to the goal of the actual subtask. Default tactics may be abandoned for alternative tactics. E.g. the default tactics for generating a hypothesis is "patient-related". If the system cannot generate a hypothesis from the existing patient data, the alternative tactics of epidemiology-based hypothesis generation is used.
    In the REFLECT-project [17], a framework with a reactive planning task that makes strategic decisions about optimal sequences of problem solving actions is given. In contrast, in our approach, the tactics level serves as an integrated link between task and inference level and allows a situation-based preparation and use of problem solving actions (e.g. by loading and activating rule-classes).
    At the *inference level*, rule-classes implementing inference steps and tactics are to be found.
    At the bottom level (*domain level*) of the GF, the modules and their competence are described.
    In order to further focus domain-specific knowledge inside a module being focussed on the global level, a suitable interface must exist between the GF and the local focussing component (LF) of a packet. The interface is described by the following contents:
- global situation (consisting of the task, subtask and the suggested tactics)
- patient related concept (consisting of processed patient data and already obtained results, e.g., patterns, hypotheses, ...)
- chosen module.

Local focussing (LF). The local focussing component focusses part of the domain knowledge inside a module or a knowledge packet. In the following, for simplicity we will assume to be dealing with a module. There is a specific LF for each module. It uses the module's control knowledge and is subdivided into five levels similar to those of the GF. The local strategy and the task level of the LF correspond to a refinement of levels of the global focussing component depending on the particular content competence of a module. This means: If the GF focusses, e.g., the module "Diagnostic Procedures", the global subtask "Generate Hypothesis" becomes a local strategy in the LF of the module. Depending on this strategy and on the local plan, now the tasks to be executed by this module are determined. According to the associated task-specific tactics, the corresponding knowledge packets in this module are focussed and activated.

The contents of the different levels in the LF of the module "Diagnostic Procedures" look as in fig. 5 for the medical case described in section 4. There the reader will also find a more precise trace of focussing.

The domain level consists of descriptions of packets with respect to their specificity, degree of abstraction, etc. Normally, the LF chooses a packet just one step down the packet hierarchy.

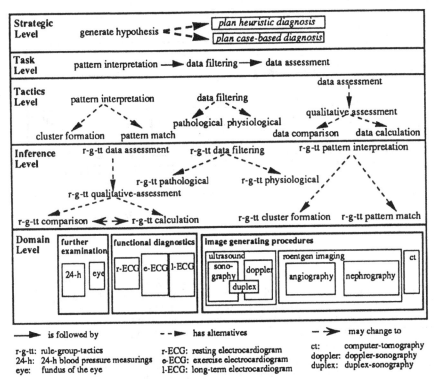

Fig. 5. LF of the module "Diagnostic procedures". On the domain level, for lack of space, only the packets needed to diagnose kidney artery stenosis are shown.

Rules may be focussed according to packets they belong to (static structure), but also according to object classes and attribute names occuring in the rules' premises or conclusions (dynamic structure). This possibility was created by associating a description schema to each rule.

3.4   System Architecture

The most important components of the system architecture are the global focussing
component (GF), the knowledge base component (KB) and the coordination
component (CO) (cf. fig. 6).

The global focussing component discussed above manages the knowledge-related
interaction of modules. It carries out the overall plan by successively activating
modules, examining their results and continuing or modifying the plan accordingly.
The knowledge base component consists of the knowledge modules as described in
section 3.1, where each module possesses its own local focussing component. Some of
the modules are shown in fig. 6.

The coordination component organizes the data transfer between the user and the
system. It contains descriptions of the actual situation and data and is responsible for
furnishing them to and obtaining them from the GF and thus to and from the modules.
Each transfer process is managed by a standardized communication structure [8, 12].
Thereby the independence of the knowledge-related components GF and KB from
technical specificities is supported.

In the following section the diagnostic reasoning process will be explained on the
basis of a patient case.

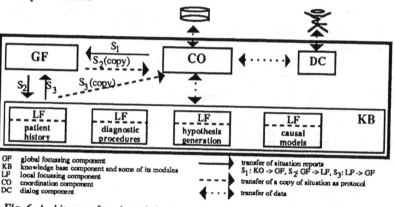

Fig. 6. Architecture for a knowledge-based system with modular knowledge bases.

4   Example

Now we present a trace of the focussing procedure during processing an authentic case
(obtained from one of our medical experts). The following background is given: A
middle-aged woman consults a physician (a general practitioner) who has not met her
before. From the physician's input concerning the patient data an adequate pathological patient concept is constructed. (Geneva font indicates system output to the user).

Pathological patient concept:

History: female, 52 years old, insulin-dependent diabetes mellitus
                  (IDDM) and frequent pyelitis in the past.
Physical exam.:   160 cm, 85 kg, blood pressure 160/90 mmHg.
Laboratory test: blood leucocyte count 13000/ml, haemoglobin 11 g/dl, glucose
                  200 mg/dl, blood-urea concentration 60 mg/dl, serum uric acid
                  8.2 mg/dl, creatinemia 3.6 mg/dl, creatinine clearance 25 ml/min,
                  urine leucocyte count 75.
This concept is transferrred to the GF.

(1) GF The GF must decide which module is suited best for the given status of the patient. The levels of the GF will be described by the following schema given that there is no hypothesis available yet:

global strategy: *\<heuristic classification\>*
global plan: *\<default plan\>*
main task: *\<specify diagnosis\>*
subtask: *\<generate hypothesis\>*

According to the ordinary plan and the subtask, the GF focusses the first module ("Patient History") and sends the patient history data to this module as part of the patient concept .

(2) LF The LF interprets the data obtained by the GF and this results in the LF having (cf. fig. 5):

local strategy: *\<generate hypothesis\>*
local plan: *\<data assessment, data filtering, pattern interpretation\>*

Considering the present task, the corresponding tactics and the related rule classes will be instantiated and activated. This leads to a condensation of information resulting in a more detailed focussing on specific packets inside the module. At first the patient history will be assessed. Depending on the underlying pathological and physiological knowledge about the patient, the obtained data will be filtered. Regarding the filtered data, a pathological pattern will be interpreted. The particular tasks will be processed step by step and the preliminary results will be transferred to the GF.

Output of the results of the module "Patient History":
> female, 52 years, insulin-dependent diabetes mellitus and frequent pyelitis
> explanation: possibly there is a dependency between diabetes and frequent
> pyelitis. Please check the status of the kidney.

The preliminary results of the module will be worked up and transferred to the global focussing component. Step (1) and (2) will be repeated for the modules "Physical Examination" and "Laboratory Test". For conciseness, for them we only describe focussing and results.

(3) LF The LF focusses the knowledge packets "Blood Pressure Measurements", "Basic Parameters", and "Vegetative Symptoms" inside the module "Physical Examination".

Output of the results of the module "Physical Examination":
> overweight, hypertension

(4) LF The LF focusses the knowledge packets "Serum Laboratory Tests", "Blood Count", "Urine Laboratory Test", and "Urine Sediment" inside the module "Laboratory Tests".

Output of the results of the module "Laboratory Test":
> creatinemia greatly increased, creatinine clearance decreased,
> blood-urea increased, serum uric acid increased,
> blood leucocyte count greatly increased, haemoglobin decreased,
> glucose greatly increased, urine leucocyte count increased.
> hypothesis: suspicion of (non acute) kidney disease.
> explanation: suspicion of kidney disease because of greatly increased
> creatinemia,
> decreased creatinine clearance and a slight proteinaemia; non acute
> because there are no indications of acute symptoms.

What to do now? This hypothesis is to vague to serve as a diagnosis and new patient data are not available. Therefore an alternative way should be looked for in the strategy plan of the GF. The plan provides consulting the module "Diagnostic Procedures" first.

(5) **GF** The GF focusses the module "Diagnostic Procedures" and sends it the relevant patient data and the inferred hypothesis.

(6) **LF** For reasons given below, the LF focusses the relevant part of knowledge inside the module "Diagnostic Procedures" and inside the "Anatomical Models" module.

By means of the present vague hypothesis of a kidney disease, the module suggests a kidney sonography as a first search test. To get better results in case of a possible kidney stenosis, the more specific packet "Brightness Scan" is chosen. For the interpretation of the findings, morphological knowledge is necessary. The relevant part of the library module "Anatomical Models" is determined by granularity considerations: The field of view is restricted to the kidney and its neighbors.
Except for the kidney, the foundation level lies at organs as such. For the kidney itself, it is calculated from spatial and tissue resolution of sonography. Thus knowledge about, e.g., normal size and thickness of kidney, pelvis, cortex, and marrow is focussed, but none about microscopic structures.

User-input   The sonographical findings show a cirrhosis of the right kidney but no engorged kidney.

Using the morphological knowledge, the degree of kidney damage is deduced from observed kidney sizes.

(7) **LF** The results of the sonographical findings are transferred to the querying module. The module focusses first the packet "Pattern Interpretation" according to the global task "Hypothesis Generation". At last a pattern regarding the new patient data is built.

Output of the results of the module "Diagnostic Procedure":
> manifest kidney damage in form of a cirrhosis of the right kidney
> but no engorged kidney.
> pattern: cirrhosis of the right kidney, creatinemia greatly increased,
> frequent pyelitis, urine leucocyte count increased.

(8) **GF** Together with the relevant patient data the interpreted pattern will be transferred to the focussed module "Diagnosis Generation".

(9) **LF** The focussed packet which considers data from "Patient History", "Laboratory Test" and "Diagnostic Procedure" together attempts to generate a hypothesis considering the built pattern.

Output of the results of the module "Hyothesis Generation":
> diagnosis: chronical pyelonephritis.
> explanation: pyelonephritis: because of frequent pyelitis in the past;
> chronical because of cirrhosis of the right kidney ......

Before the inferred hypothesis will be displayed to the user, it is verified by the module "Hypothesis Verification". This module contains knowledge about competitive nosographies. After verification of the inferred hypothesis, the global plan for generating a hypothesis is exhausted and a new global plan for generating a therapy will be instantiated.

5 Summary and Outlook

In this paper, we explained our principles for a knowledge-level modularization of a complex (medical) knowledge base and, in particular, showed how their application permits to focus on restricted parts of knowledge.

Based on a model of the overall reasoning process, the knowledge base is decomposed into knowledge modules highly independent from each other, active one at a time. These modules are subdivided into knowledge packets according to specificity and granularity. Focussing such a packet makes knowledge elements outside of it invisible to the inference engine. Whereas *global* focussing activates a module, *local* focussing narrows focus further down to packets or subpackets. Both modules and packets contain associated control knowledge subdivided in KADS-like layers and linked by a layer shift during local focussing. Independent representation and granularity choices in different parts of the knowledge base are made possible by packet interfaces, a common interface handler and a central communication control component. The interplay of knowledge partition, dynamic focussing and the architecture components was illustrated by an authentic medical case.

The system is not in actual use yet; testing covers the entire span of renal hypertension. It relies on the users' competence for weighing evidence; we believe this issue to be rather independent of knowledge structuring.

A problem still consists in determining the useful size of packets. The main criterion is their cohesion: further subdivision should either seem unnatural or lead to crumbs not worth focussing. Sometimes, concurrent organization principles are conceivable, e.g., knowledge about blood and urine parameters may be grouped according to medium or else according to disturbances they give hints at (leading to groups such as kidney profile that contain parameters of blood as well as of urine). In this case, our approach has been to use the "simple" organization according to medium for the basic knowledge (usual physiological range of the parameters) and to keep knowledge about the kidney profile synopsis in a further packet. For optimal packet organization, careful analysis of the domain and of possible interactions is necessary. Sometimes more specific knowledge should be taken into account before more general knowledge has been tried unsuccessfully, especially when special cases admit particularly simple solutions. Criteria for removal seem of minor importance for the moment as the main benefit lies in activating relevant knowledge only.

To conclude, we have found the described approach of knowledge-level modularization greatly useful, especially with respect to an incremental knowledge base development. Though we have worked out modularization principles in the context of a medical domain, we expect their application to yield equally good or better results in other domains, especially when a domain is less strongly interconnected than our domain of hypertension.

References

1. Antoniou, G. & Wachsmuth, I.: Structuring and modules for knowledge bases: motivation for a new model. Knowledge-Based Systems 7 (1), 49-51 (1994)
2. Bocionek, S.: Modulare Regelprogrammierung. Braunschweig: Vieweg (1990)
3. Bylander,T. & Chandrasekaran, B.: Generic Tasks for Knowledge-Based Reasoning: the "Right" Level of Abstraction for Knowledge Acquisition. International Journal of Man-Machine Studies 26, 231-243 (1987)
4. Clancey, W.J.: The Epistemology of a Rule-Based Expert System – a Framework for Explanation. Artificial Intelligence 20 , 215-251 (1983)
5. Clare, M.: When Information Engineering Meets Knowledge Management. Proceedings AAAI Workshop Modelling in the Large, Washington (1993)

6. Davis, R.: Generalized Procedure Calling and Content-Directed Invocation. SIGPLAN Notices 12, 8, 45-54 (1977)
7. Ginsberg, M.L.: Knowledge Interchange Format: The KIF of Death. AI Magazine 12 (3), 57-63 (1991)
8. Heller, B. & Schlegelmilch, S.: Modularization of Knowledge: A Competence-Oriented Approach. Proc. AAAI Workshop Modelling in the Large, Washington (1993)
9. Hobbs, J.R.: "Granularity," IJCAI-85, pp. 432-435 (1985)
10. Lenat, D.B. & Guha, R.V.:. Cyc: a midterm report. AI magazine 11 (3), 32-59 (1990)
11. McCarthy, J.: Notes on Formalizing Context. IJCAI-93, pp. 555-560 (1993)
12. Heller, B., Meyer-Fujara, J. & Schlegelmilch, S.: HYPERCON: Ein Konsultationssystem zur Hypertonie auf Basis modular organisierter Wissensbestände. KI-94 Anwenderkongreß (1994)
13. Neches, R. et al.: Enabling technology for knowledge sharing. AI Magazine 12 (3), 37-56 (1991)
14. Newell, A.: The Knowledge Level. Artificial Intelligence 18, 1-20 (1982)
15. Pan, J.Y.-C., Tenenbaum, J.M. & Glicksman, J.: A framework for knowledge-based computer-integrated manufacturing. IEEE Trans. Semiconductor Manufacturing 2(2), 33-46 (1989)
16. Prerau, D.S. et al.: Maintainability techniques in developing large expert systems. IEEE Expert 5 (3), 71-79 (1990)
17. Reinder, M., Bredeweg, B.: Strategic Reasoning as a Reflective Task. In IMSA '92 International Workshop on Reflection and Meta-level architecture (1992)
18. Soloway, E. & Bachant, J. & Jensen, K.: Assessing the Maintainability of XCON-in-RIME: Coping with the problems of a VERY Large Rule-Base. AAAI-87 (1987)
19. Wachsmuth, I. & Gängler, B.: Knowledge Packets and Knowledge Packet Structures. In O. Herzog & C.-R.Rollinger (eds.): Text Understanding in LILOG: Integrating Computational Linguistics and Artificial Intelligence, Berlin: Springer (1991), pp. 380-393
20. Wachsmuth. I. & Heller, B. & Meyer-Fujara, J.: HYPERCON: Modulare Wissensbasen für Hypertonie-Konsultation. Research Proposal, University of Bielefeld, Faculty of Technology (1992)
21. Wachsmuth. I. & Meyer-Fujara, J.: Adressing the Retrieval Problem in Large Knowledge Bases (Summary). Proc. 3rd Conf. Computational Intelligence (CI-90), Milano (1990)
22. Wielinga, B. & Schreiber, A. Th. & Breuker, J.: KADS: a modeling approach to knowledge engineering. Knowledge Acquisition 4, 5-53 (1992)
23. Yourdon, E. & Constantine, L.L.: Structured Design – Fundamentals of a Discipline of Computer Program and Systems Design. Englewood Cliffs: Prentice-Hall (1979)

Program Verification Techniques as a Tool for Reasoning about Action and Change*

Witold Lukaszewicz   Ewa Madalińska-Bugaj

Institute of Informatics, Warsaw University
Banacha 2, 02-097 Warsaw, POLAND
emails: witlu@mimuw.edu.pl, ewama@mimuw.edu.pl

Abstract. We apply Dijkstra's semantics for programming languages to formalize reasoning about action and change. The basic idea is to view an action A as a transformation which to each formula β assigns a formula α, with the intention that α represents the set of all initial states such that execution of A begun in any one of them is guaranteed to terminate in a state satisfying β.

The major strength of our approach is that it is very simple and computationally effective when compared with other proposals. Yet, it properly deals with a broad class of action scenarios. In particular, both temporal prediction and postdiction reasoning tasks can be solved without restricting initial or final states to be completely specified.

1 Introduction

Reasoning about action and change is one of the most important topics in the AI research. The earliest, but still very influential approach to formalizing this kind of inference is *situation calculus* [8]. In its classical form, the approach involves providing explicit axioms describing effects of each possible action. These axioms are of two kinds: *action axioms* specifying facts that change after performing the action, and *frame axioms* indicating facts that persist when the action takes place.

The main drawback of the classical situation calculus is that the number of frame axioms may be very large. To deal with this problem, called the *frame problem*, non-monotonic versions of situation calculus have been considered.

---

*This research was supported by the ESPRIT Basic Research Action No. 6156 - DRUMS II and by the KBN Grant 2 2041 92 03.

The basic idea of these proposals is to replace the frame axioms by a single non-monotonic rule stating that facts persist in the absence of evidence to the contrary. Unfortunately, as Hanks and McDermott ([3]) have shown, applying the existing non-monotonic formalisms to the frame problem often leads to unintended models (or unintended extensions) in addition to the intended ones, so that some desired conclusions cannot be derived (see [3], for a detailed discussion).

The paper of Hanks and McDermott had enormous impact on the field of reasoning about action, and a large number of new non-monotonic solutions to the frame problem have been proposed. One of the most interesting approaches was introduced in [5] and then investigated in [6], and [7]. This proposal combines an extended situation calculus with ordinary circumscription.

A very interesting approach to the problem of formalizing knowledge about dynamically changing worlds has been recently proposed by Sandewall [9, 10]. The major strength of Sandewall's work is that it provides a very general framework to systematic study of logics of action and change. As a part of this framework, a number of types of preferential entailments are introduced and proven to be correct for particular classes of action scenarios. Sandewall employes a kind of temporal logic as a basis.

All non-monotonic approaches to the problem of formalizing reasoning about action suffer a serious technical problem, typical for non-monotonic formalisms in general: they are difficult to compute. Actually, in Lifschitz' papers, the fact that some conclusion can be derived from a given action scenario is usually formulated as a proposition and provided with a formal proof. In Sandewall's system, which uses the preferential entailment technique as the reasoning method, the computation of preferred models is also a non-trivial task.

An obvious similarity between actions and commands in programming languages, and between action scenarios and programs, suggests that it may be fruitfull to formalize reasoning about action and change employing methods which have been introduced to reason about programs. In the paper, we show that a number of action scenarios can be properly dealt with in the framework of Dijkstra's semantics for programming languages [2]. The major advantage of this approach is its simplicity and computational effectiveness, when compared with other proposals.

To simplify the discussion, we restrict ourselves to deterministic actions here.[1] However, we admit complex inference patterns by allowing to reason about statements combining propositions referring to various points of a given action scenario.

The paper is organized as follows. Section 2 is a brief introduction to Dijkstra's semantics for a simple programming language. In section 3, we provide a general procedure to define action languages using Dijkstra's methodology, illustrate this procedure by specifying a simple "shooting" language, and introduce a notion of an *action scenario*. Section 4 specifies the kind of reasoning we are

---

[1] Actions with random effects can also be dealt with, but they require some additional mechanisms. This problem will be discussed in a future paper.

interested in, and provides a simple method of realizing this type of inference. In section 5, we illustrate this method by analyzing a number of examples, well-known from the AI literature. Finally, in section 6, we provide concluding remarks and discuss the future work.

2 Introduction to Dijkstra's semantics

We start our discussion by providing a brief introduction to Dijkstra's semantics for a very simple programming language which plays an important role in our further discussion.

The basic idea of Dijkstra's approach is the following. For each command S and each formula α, which intuitively describes the desired result of executing S, there is defined another formula, denoted by $wp(S, \alpha)$, that represents the set of all states such that the execution of S begun in any one of them is guaranteed to terminate in a state satisfying α. In other words, $wp(S, \alpha)$ may be viewed as the *weakest precondition* which, if satisfied before performing S, assures that S terminates in a state satisfying α. As an example, consider the assignment command $i := i + 1$ and the formula $i \leq 1$. Clearly,

$$wp(i := i + 1, i \leq 1) = (i \leq 0)$$

for if $i \leq 0$, then execution of $i := i + 1$ terminates with $i \leq 1$, whereas if $i > 0$, execution of $i := i + 1$ cannot achieve $i \leq 1$.

2.1 List of commands

The considered language consists of *skip* command, *multiple assignment* to simple variables, *alternative* command and *sequential composition* of commands.[2] Semantics of these commands is specified as follows.

1. **The *skip* command.** This is the "empty" command in that its execution does not change the computation state. The semantics of *skip* is thus given by

   $$wp(skip, \alpha) = \alpha.$$

2. **The *multiple assignment* command.** This command is of the form $x_1, \ldots, x_n := e_1, \ldots, e_n$, where $x_1, \ldots, x_n$ are distinct simple variables and $e_1, \ldots, e_n$ are expressions. The effect of the command is to simultaneously replace values of all variables in the left part of the command with values of the expressions given in the right part. The semantics of this command is given by

   $$wp(x_1, \ldots, x_n := e_1, \ldots, e_n, \alpha) = \alpha[x_1 \leftarrow e_1, \ldots, x_n \leftarrow e_n]$$

---

[2] The programming language specified here is simpler than that provided in Dijkstra (1976) in two respects. Firstly, we ignore iterative commands which are not needed for our purpose. Secondly, alternative commands we use are fully deterministic.

where $\alpha[x_1 \leftarrow e_1, \ldots, x_n \leftarrow e_n]$ is obtained from α by simultaneously replacing all free occurrences of $x_1, \ldots, x_n$ by $e_1, \ldots, e_n$, respectively.

3. **The** *sequential composition* **command.** This command is of the form $S_1; S_2$, where S_1 and S_2 are any commands. It is executed by first executing S_1 and then executing S_2. Its semantics is given by

$$wp(S_1; S_2, \alpha) = wp(S_1, wp(S_2, \alpha)).$$

4. **The** *alternative* **command.** This command is of the form

   if B **then** S_1 **else** S_2

   where B is a Boolean expression and S_1, S_2 are any commands. The semantics of the alternative command is given by

$$wp(\textbf{if } B \textbf{ then } S_1 \textbf{ else } S_2, \alpha) = (B \supset wp(S_1, \alpha)) \land (\neg B \supset wp(S_2, \alpha)).$$

The above definition of $wp(\textbf{if } B \textbf{ then } S_1 \textbf{ else } S_2, \alpha)$ should be quite obvious. The conjuncts assure that the execution of S_1, if B is true, or of S_2, if $\neg B$ is true, terminates in a state satisfying α.

The following result will be useful.

Theorem 1   For any command S and any formula α, $wp(S, \alpha)$ holds before executing S iff α holds after performing S.

Proof   The left to right implication is obvious. To prove the right to left implication, assume to the contrary that the execution of S begun in a state, say s, where $wp(S, \alpha)$ is false, terminates with α true. The falsity of $wp(S, \alpha)$ in s implies that the execution of S begun in s may result in a state where α is false. Thus, since α was observed to be true after performing S, S must be non-deterministic. On the other hand, all the commands of the considered language are deterministic. A contradiction. ∎

3 Action languages and action scenarios

In this section, we provide a general procedure to specify action languages using Dijkstra's semantics, illustrate the procedure by defining a simple "shooting" language and introduce a notion of an action scenario.

To define an action language one proceeds in three steps.

(1) The first step is to choose the underlying logic in which the effect of actions will be represented. For the shooting language we take the classical propositional logic with two sentential symbols: a and l, standing for *alive* and *loaded*, respectively. To be in accord with the AI terminology, these symbols will be referred to as *fluents*.

(2) The next step is to provide action symbols representing the actions under consideration. In the shooting language we have three such symbols: *load* (a gun), *wait*, and *shoot* (a turkey). The intention is that *load* makes the gun loaded, *wait* does not cause any changes in the world, and *shoot* makes the gun unloaded and the turkey dead, provided, of course, that the gun was loaded before.

(3) The final step is to define Dijkstra-style semantics for the choosen actions. To perform this step for the shooting language, it suffices to note that the considered actions can be easily translated into the programming language specified in the previous section. More specifically[3], *load* corresponds to the assignment command $l := T$, *wait* is just the *skip* command, whereas *shoot* is translated into the alternative command

if l **then** $a, l := F, F$ **else** *skip*.

Given the above translations, we can easily provide the chosen actions with Dijkstra-style semantics:

- $wp(load, \alpha) = \alpha[l \leftarrow T]$
- $wp(wait, \alpha) = \alpha$
- $wp(shoot, \alpha) = (l \supset wp(a, l := F, F, \alpha)) \wedge (\neg l \supset wp(skip, \alpha))$ which can be reduced to $(l \supset \alpha[a \leftarrow F, l \leftarrow F]) \wedge (\neg l \supset \alpha)$.

The objects we shall be primarily interested in are *action scenarios*. These are expressions of the form

$$
\begin{aligned}
&\{\alpha\} \\
&A_1; \\
&\vdots \\
&A_n \\
&\{\beta\}
\end{aligned}
$$

where α and β are formulae and $A_1, \ldots, A_n$ are actions. The scenario has the following intuitive interpretation: α is observed in the *initial situation*, then the actions $A_1, \ldots, A_n$ are sequentially performed, and then β is observed to hold in the *final situation*.[4] If α or β are equivalent to T, they will be omitted. In the sequel, α and β will be referred to as the *initial observation* and the *final observation*, respectively. In the plain text, scenarios will be written in the form $\{\alpha\}\ A_1; \ldots; A_n\ \{\beta\}$ or simply $\{\alpha\}\ S\ \{\beta\}$, where S is to be understood as a sequence of actions.

---

[3]In what follows, T and F stand for the constant propositions *True* and *False*, respectively.
[4]It should be emphasized that α must not be regarded as the condition guaranteeing β after performing $A_1, \ldots, A_n$. α and β are nothing more than facts that have been observed in the initial and the final situation.

Example 1 (Yale Shooting Scenario) Below there is the famous Yale Shooting Scenario [3].

$$\{a \wedge \neg l\}$$
$$load;$$
$$wait;$$
$$shoot.$$

∎

4 Reasoning about action scenarios

Given a scenario $\{\alpha\}\ A_1; \ldots; A_n\ \{\beta\}$, one may be interested in various reasoning tasks. The simplest one is the following: "Given a formula γ and a non-negative integer k such that $0 \leq k \leq n$, determine whether γ holds after performing the actions $A_1; \ldots; A_k$."[5] We also permit more complex forms of reasoning about an action scenario by allowing to combine propositions from its different points. A typical example of such an inference pattern might be to determine whether the following statement is true: If γ_1 holds after performing the actions $A_1; \ldots; A_k$, then either γ_2 holds after performing $A_1; \ldots; A_l$ or γ_3 holds after performing $A_1; \ldots; A_m$.

To allow complex forms of inference about action scenarios, we specify an auxiliary *query language* in which statements to be derived from a given scenario $\{\alpha\}\ A_1; \ldots; A_n\ \{\beta\}$ will be formulated. To this end, we introduce a special two-place predicate symbol $Holds$, taking a formula (of the base logic) and a sequence of actions $A_1; \ldots; A_k$ $(k \geq 0)$ as its arguments. An expression $Holds(\gamma, A_1; \ldots; A_k)$, called an *atomic query*, has the following interpretation: γ holds after sequentially performing the actions $A_1; \ldots; A_k$. We write $Holds(\gamma, init)$ as an abbreviation for $Holds(\gamma, A_1; \ldots; A_k)$, where k=0. That is, $Holds(\gamma, init)$ states that γ holds in the initial situation. By a *query* we understand any Boolean combination of atomic queries.

Example 1 [continued]   Below there are two queries about the Yale Shooting Scenario.

(1) $Holds(\neg a \wedge \neg l,\ load; wait; shoot)$;

(2) $Holds(a,\ load; wait) \vee Holds(a,\ load; wait; shoot)$.   ∎

Since all actions under the consideration are commands of the programming language specified in section 2, Theorem 1 immediately implies

Theorem 2   For any action scenario $\{\alpha\}\ A_1; \ldots; A_n\ \{\beta\}$, any formula γ and any non-negative integer k such that $0 \leq k \leq n$, γ holds after performing the actions $A_1; \ldots; A_n$ if and only if $wp(A_1; \ldots; A_k,\ \gamma)$ holds in the initial situation.
∎

---

[5] If $k = 0$, this reasoning task amounts to determining whether γ holds in the initial situation.

Consider a scenario

$$SC = \{\alpha\}\, A_1; \ldots; A_n\, \{\beta\} \qquad (1)$$

Since β holds in the final situation, it must be the case (in view of Theorem 2) that $wp(A_1; \ldots; A_n,\ \beta)$ holds in the initial situation. This means that the discription of the initial situation of SC is provided by the formula $\alpha \wedge wp(A_1; \ldots; A_n,\ \beta)$. In what follows, this formula will be called the *description of the initial situation of SC*, and will be denoted by $DIS(SC)$.[6]

Suppose now that q is a query about a scenario (1). We write $q*$ to denote the formula obtained from q by replacing each atomic query $Holds(\gamma,\ A_1; \ldots A_k)$ by $wp(A_1; \ldots A_k,\ \gamma)$. In view of Theorem 2, the statement represented by q is true iff $q*$ is true in the initial situation of SC.

Our discussion leads to the following general method to reason about action scenarios.

> Let $SC = \{\alpha\}\, A_1; \ldots; A_n\, \{\beta\}$ be a scenario and suppose that q is a query about SC. The statement represented by q is true iff $DIS(SC) \vdash q*$, where $\vdash$ is the provability relation of the base logic (in our case $\vdash$ is the provability relation of the classical propositional logic).

Consider a scenario SC of the form $\{\alpha\}\, S$, i.e. a scenario in which the final observation is equivalent to T. Since $wp(S, T)$ is T, for any sequence of actions S, $DIS(SC) = \alpha \wedge T$ which is equivalent to α. We often make use of this fact in the sequel.

5 Examples

In this section we consider a number of scenario examples to illustrate the method introduced in the previous section. These examples are well-known in the AI literature and are regarded as difficult to deal with.

Example 1 [continued] The Yale Shooting Scenario (YSS, for short) is an example of the temporal prediction. We have a description of the initial situation and we are interested in what holds in the final situation. The intended conclusion is that after performing the actions the turkey is dead and the gun is unloaded.

Since YSS is a scenario in which the final observation is T, the description of its initial situation is equivalent to its initial observation. That is

$$DIS(YSS) = a \wedge \neg l.$$

The query we are interested in is

$$q:\ Holds(\neg a \wedge \neg l,\ load; wait; shoot).$$

---

[6]It may happen that $DIS(SC)$ is equivalent to F. This means that the scenario is contradictory, i.e. the final observation is inconsistent with respect to the initial observation. In the sequel, we assume that the considered scenarios are non-contradictory.

We calculate $wp(S, \neg a \wedge \neg l)$, where S stands for $load;\ wait;\ shoot$.[7]

$$
\begin{aligned}
wp(S, \neg a \wedge \neg l) &= wp(load;\ wait;\ shoot, \neg a \wedge \neg l) \\
&= wp(load, wp(wait;\ shoot, \neg a \wedge \neg l)) \\
&= wp(load, wp(wait, wp(shoot, \neg a \wedge \neg l))) \\
&= wp(load, wp(wait, [l \supset (\neg F \wedge \neg F)] \wedge [\neg l \supset (\neg a \wedge \neg l)])) \\
&\equiv wp(load, wp(wait, \neg l \supset (\neg a \wedge \neg l))) \\
&= wp(load, \neg l \supset (\neg a \wedge \neg l)) \\
&= \neg T \supset (\neg a \wedge \neg T) \\
&\equiv T.
\end{aligned}
$$

Thus, $q* = T$. Since $DIS(YSS) \vdash q*$, we conclude that in the final situation the turkey is dead and the gun is unloaded. Note that the result we obtained is even stronger: $\neg a \wedge \neg l$ holds after performing the actions $load$, $wait$ and $shoot$, no matter what holds in the initial situation. This is, of course, according to our intuitions. ∎

Example 2 (Stanford Murder Mystery) Consider the following problem, known in the AI literature as the Stanford Murder Mystery (SMM).[8] The turkey is alive in the initial situation, and after the actions $shoot$ and $wait$ are successively performed, it is dead. The story can be represented by the following scenario:

$$\{a\}$$
$$shoot;$$
$$wait$$
$$\{\neg a\}$$

The question we are interested in is when the turkey died and whether the gun was originally loaded. The intended conclusion is that the gun was loaded in the initial situation and the turkey died during the shooting.

$$
\begin{aligned}
DIS(SMM) &= a \wedge wp(shoot;\ wait, \neg a) \\
&\equiv a \wedge wp(shoot, \neg a) \\
&\equiv a \wedge (l \supset T) \wedge (\neg l \supset \neg a) \\
&\equiv a \wedge (\neg l \supset \neg a) \\
&\equiv a \wedge l.
\end{aligned}
$$

The query we are interested in is

$$q = Holds(l, init) \wedge Holds(\neg a, shoot).$$

$q* = l \wedge wp(shoot, \neg a) = l \wedge (l \supset T) \wedge (\neg l \supset \neg a) \equiv l \wedge (l \vee \neg a)$. Since $DIS(SMM) \vdash q*$, we conclude that the gun was loaded in the initial situation and the turkey died during the shooting. ∎

---

[7]Note the use of the symbols "$=$" and "$\equiv$" during the calculation. We write $X = Y$ if Y is obtained from X by employing the semantics of wp, whereas $X \equiv Y$ indicates that X and Y are logically equivalent.

[8]This example is from (Baker 1989).

Example 3 (Deaf Turkey Scenario) This example, introduced in Sandewall [9], extends the Yale Shooting Scenario. We have two additional fluents: d – standing for *deaf*, and h – standing for *hidden*. The actions are as before, but the meaning of *load* and *shoot* is different. After the execution of *load*, the gun becomes loaded and, in addition, the turkey becomes hidden, provided that it is not deaf. The action *shoot* makes the turkey dead, provided that the gun is loaded and the turkey is not hidden. To provide Dijkstra-style semantics for *load* and *shoot*, note that they can be translated into the commands

    if d **then** $l := T$ **else** $l, h := T, T$

and

    if $l \wedge \neg h$ **then** $l, a := F, F$ **else** $l := F$

respectively. Thus,

- $wp(load, \alpha) = (d \supset \alpha[l \leftarrow T]) \wedge (\neg d \supset \alpha[l \leftarrow T, h \leftarrow T])$

- $wp(shoot, \alpha) = (l \wedge \neg h \supset \alpha[l \leftarrow F, a \leftarrow F]) \wedge (\neg l \vee h \supset \alpha[l \leftarrow F])$.

The Deaf Turkey Scenario (DTS) is given by

    $\{a \wedge \neg h\}$
    load;
    shoot

    $DIS(DTS) = a \wedge \neg h$.

The intended conclusion is that either the turkey is deaf in the initial situation and it is dead in the final situation, or it is not deaf in the initial situation and it is alive in the final situation. We represent this statement by the query

$$q = \begin{array}{l} (Holds(d, init) \wedge Holds(\neg a, load; shoot)) \\ \vee(Holds(\neg d, init) \wedge Holds(a, load; shoot)). \end{array}$$

We leave it to the reader to check that

- $wp(load; shoot, \neg a) \equiv (d \wedge \neg h) \vee \neg a$

- $wp(load; shoot, a) \equiv a \wedge (\neg d \vee h)$.

Thus

$$q* = [d \wedge ((d \wedge \neg h) \vee \neg a)] \vee [\neg d \wedge a \wedge (\neg d \vee h)]$$

which can be reduced to

    $[d \wedge (\neg h \vee \neg a)] \vee [\neg d \wedge a]$.

It is easily verified that $DIS(DTS) \vdash q*$. So, we conclude that the statement represented by the query q holds. ∎

6 Conclusions

We have applied Dijkstra's semantics for programming languages to formalize reasoning about action and change. The presented approach can be employed to represent a broad class of action scenarios, including those where complex inference patterns are required. The major advantage of our proposal is that it is very simple and computationally effective when compared with other approaches directed at formalizing reasoning about action and change.

The actions considered in this paper are very simple in that they are represented by identifiers. In practice, it is often necessary to permit action schemata rather, each representing a class of similar actions applicable for various tuples of individuals. For example, we may have the action schema $Put(x, y)$ with the intended meaning that a block x is to be put on the top of a block y. There is no technical difficulty to admit action schemata in our system, but this topic will be disscussed in a future paper.

The question of implementation is another point of interest. Calculating $DIS(SC)$ and $wp(A_1; \ldots; A_k, \gamma)$, for a given scenario $\{\alpha\}$ $A_1, \ldots, A_n$ $\{\beta\}$, amounts to simple syntactic manipulations on formulae and can be performed very efficiently. The only computational problem is to determine whether a given formula can be derived from the description of the initial situation. This task can be realized by using a theorem prover appropriate for the logic in which the effects of actions are described. For the shooting language all we need is a theorem prover for classical propositional logic. In more complex applications, a theorem prover for first-order logic will be required. In any case, we work in the framework of classical monotonic logic which makes our approach simpler and computationally more efficient when compared with the approaches employing non-monotonic forms of reasoning.

References

1. Baker, A. B., "A Simple Solution to the Yale Shooting Problem", in: *Proc. Principles of Knowledge Representation and Reasoning*", R. J. Brachman, H. J. Levesque, R. Reiter (eds.), Toronto, Canada, 1989, 11-19.

2. Dijkstra E. W., "*A Discipline of Programming*", Prentice Hall, Englewood Cliffs, 1976.

3. Hanks, S., McDermott, D., "Nonmonotonic Logic and Temporal Projection", *Artificial Intelligence*, **33**, 1987, 379-412.

4. Kautz, H. A., "The Logic of Persistence", in: *Proc. AAAI-86*, 1986, 401-405.

5. Lifschitz, V., "Formal Theories of Action: Preliminary Report", in: *Proc. IJCAI-87*, 1987, 966-972.

6. Lifschitz, V., "Formal Theories of Action", in: *Readings in Nonmonotonic Reasoning*, M. Ginsberg (ed.), Morgan Kaufmann Publishers, Palo Alto, CA, 1988, 35-57.

7. Lifschitz, V., Rabinov, A., "Miracles in Formal Theories of Action", *Artificial Intelligence*, **38**, 225-237.

8. McCarthy, J., Hayes, P.J., "Some Philosophical Problems from the Standpoint of Artificial Intelligence", in: B. Meltzer and D. Michie (eds.), *Machine Intelligence* **4**, 1969, 463-502.

9. Sandewall, E., "Features and Fluents: A Systematic Approach to the Representation of Knowledge about Dynamical Systems", Technical Report LITH-IDA-R-92-30, Department of Computer and Information Science, Linköping University, Sweden.

10. Sandewall, E., "The Range of Applicability of Nonmonotonic Logics for the Inertia Problem", in: *Proc. IJCAI-93*, 1993, 738-743.

A Conditional Logic for Updating in the Possible Models Approach

Luis Fariñas del Cerro, Andreas Herzig

Applied Logic Group, I.R.I.T., Université Paul Sabatier
118 Route de Narbonne, F-31062 Toulouse Cedex (France)
email: {farinas, herzig}@irit.fr, FAX: (33) 61 55 62 58

Abstract. In this paper we study Winslett's possible models approach, which is a minimal change semantics where no meta-linguistical information e.g. about preference or entrenchment is involved. Via the Ramsey Test we represent the change operation in the language by a conditional operator. We express minimal change in conditional logics by an axiom

$$C \rightarrow A{>}C \qquad\qquad \text{if A and C do not interfere}$$

where two formulas A and C interfere if they have some propositional variable in common.

Our main results are a complete axiomatization of the possible models approach, a proof procedure based on normal forming, and new complexity results for the case of change restricted to conjunctions or disjunctions of literals.

1 INTRODUCTION

Philosophers have presented various possible worlds semantics for conditional logics. In all of them, a conditional A>C is true in a world w if C holds in all A-worlds that are closest to w. (An A-world is a world where A is true.) They differ by the structures which are employed to compute the closest worlds: In the most general case of selection functions (Chellas 1975) to each formula A there is associated some function f_A that for a given world gives us the set of closest A-worlds $f_A(w)$. [0] In the case of relations (Katsuno Satoh 1991) the closest A-worlds are the minimal elements of a transitive and smooth relation R(w) that is associated to w. Finally, in sphere systems (Lewis 1973) there is a set $(w) of nested spheres[1] around every world w, and the closest A-worlds are those which are in the smallest sphere containing at least one A-world.

In all these logics, several conditions on the respective structures are then defined which correspond to particular axioms one may want to hold. E.g. the axiom A>C $\rightarrow$. A$\rightarrow$C means that w $\in$ $f_A(w)$ whenever w is an A-world. Generally, what is studied by means of these axioms is the interplay between the conditional operator > and the classical connectives, and it is in this sense that these semantics differ. On the other hand, it remains unclear how one can concretely construct these structures. (D. Lewis (1973) has stressed that this had been done deliberately, and that there is no context-independent closeness criterion. We think that this question is worth being re-

---

[0] More precisely, the index of f is the extension $|A|_M$ of A in the possible worlds model M.
[1] Spheres are sets of worlds.

discussed by the people from philosophy, AI and databases.) This criticism applies also to recent ordering-based update formalizations (Katsuno Mendelzon 1991a, 1991b, Grahne 1991): It is far from being practically feasible to write down these orderings.

As a matter of fact, reasoning about change in AI and databases seems to require more precise closeness criterions. Particular instances of the above cited semantics with simple closeness criterions have been proposed as a semantics for database updates (see (Katsuno Mendelzon 1989)). One of the most successful ones has been the Possible Models Approach - PMA for short - as described in (Winslett 1988) (see also Winslett 1990, 1994). There, the closest A-worlds to an actual world w are just those which differ as little as possible from w in what concerns the interpretation of the propositional variables.

A natural question to ask is how this semantics fits in the conditional logic picture. We shall answer this question by axiomatizing the PMA. The syntactical counterpart to the PMA-closeness criterion will be an interference relation between formulas. "A and B interfere" means that A and B have some propositional variable in common. Non-interference of A and B conditions the application of a unique frame axiom:

$$B \;\to\; A{>}B \quad \text{if A and B do not interfere}$$

Basically, the resulting ASSUME logic is an extension of the standard conditional logics with a frame axiom which is sound and complete w.r.t. the PMA.

Our axiomatisation gives also a proof procedure for the PMA: By establishing that ASSUME logic has very strong normal form theorems we are able to prove theorems in a two-step procedure. In a first step formulas are normalized, and in a second step a theorem prover for classical logic can be used. We shall also prove in this paper new complexity results for updates which are restricted to conjunctions or disjunctions of literals.

In the rest of the paper, based on the PMA semantics (section 2) we axiomatize our conditional logic ASSUME (section 3). Then we introduce a very simple normal form (section 4). Using the latter we show that a simple completeness proof (section 5) and a decision procedure (section 6) can be given (in opposition to standard conditional logics). We state two complexity results for restrictions on the type of change formulas.

2 LANGUAGE AND SEMANTICS

In this section we present the semantics of the PMA of (Winslett 1988) in terms of a conditional language. We give some interactions between its notion of minimal change and the classical connectors.

We suppose a language built from a set of propositional variables PVAR with the classical connectives plus a conditional operator >. In the formula A>C, A is called the *change formula*. Note that nested conditional operators as in (A>B)>C are allowed.

As usual, *literals* are propositional variables or negations of propositional variables, and *clauses* are disjunctions of literals. We consider true to be an abreviation of $A \lor \neg A$, and false of $A \land \neg A$. We shall use a function *pvar* which associates to every formula the set of propositional variables appearing in it. For example, pvar(A>(C∧D)) = {A,C,D}.

The central notion of the paper is that of interference: We say that two formulas A and B *interfere* if they have some propositional variables in common, i.e. pvar(A) ∩ pvar(B) ≠ Ø.

Usually, semantics of conditional logics is given in terms of possible world models. In our case, we only need to refer to a single classical interpretation, which we suppose to be a subset of the set of propositional variables PVAR. This may seem somewhat puzzling, because the usual interpretation of the conditional operator refers to other classical interpretations (through the notion of possible worlds). In fact, the effect of the non-interference axioms is so drastic that given a classical interpretation w and a change formula A, we are able to entirely construct the update of w by A, which is a set of classical interpretations that we note w*A.

Definition. Given two interpretations w and v, the *distance* between w and v is defined as the symmetric difference w ∸ v = (w \ v) ∪ (v \ w).

In other words, w ∸ v = {p: either p∈ w and p∉ w', or p∉ w and p∈ w'}. In the sequel an interpretation satisfying A will be called an *A-world*, and the set of A-worlds is noted /A/. The set w*A will be the set of A-worlds whose distance to w is minimal. We simultaneously define the update of w by A and satisfaction of A in w.

Definition. Let w be a classical interpretation and A a formula.

$$w*A = \{v: v \text{ is an A-world, and there is no A-world } J'$$

$$\text{such that } w ∸ v ⊃ w ∸ J'\}$$

w |= A>C if for every v ∈ w*A, v |= C

w |= A if A ∈ PVAR and A ∈ w

For the other connectives, |= is defined as usual.

C is a semantical consequence of A (noted A |= C) if for every A-world w, w |= C. Abusing slightly our notation, we shall write S*A = ∪_{I∈ S} w*A if S is a set of interpretations.

In the possible models approach, the update of KB by A is identified with |KB|*A. (Note that A is always classical there.) It is easy to check that such a semantics satisfies the Ramsey Test:

Fact. KB*A |= C iff KB |= A>C.

In the rest of the section we study Winslett's semantics through the interplay between * and the classical connectives. A subset of the syntactical expression of these properties will re-appear as our axiomatics.

Fact. Let v ∈ w*A.

(0) w ∸ v = Ø iff w |= A iff w*A = {w}

(1) w ∸ v is a subset of pvar(A).

(2) If w ∸ v ≠ ∅ then (w ∸ v) ∩ pvar(A) ≠ ∅

(3) For every B such that A and B do not interfere, (w ∸ v) ∩ pvar(B) = ∅

Proofs.
(0) This follows from the definition of distance and that of non-interference.

(1) Supposing the contrary the distance between w and v would not be minimal (contradicting that v ∉ w*A).

(2) and (3) follow from (0) and (1) respectively.

Property 2.1. Suppose A and B do not interfere, and v ∈ w*A. Then w ⊨ B iff v ⊨ B.
Proof. By (3) of the above fact, the interpretations w and v agree on the variables of B.

Property 2.2. Suppose A and B do not interfere. Then w*A∧B = w*A*B.
Proof. This follows from (3) of the above fact.

Fact. Suppose v ∈ w*A∧B, and w ⊭ A.

(4) (w ∸ v) ∩ pvar(A) ≠ ∅.
Proof. v ∈ |A| ,and w ∉ |A|. By classical logic, w and v cannot agree on every variable of A.

Fact. Suppose A and B do not interfere.
(5) If w ⊨ A then w*A∧B = w*B.
(6) If w⊭ A then w*(A∧B')∨B ⊇ w*B.
Proofs.
(5) First, by Property 2.1 w*A∧B = w*A*B. By (0), w*A = {w}, hence w*A*B = w*B.

(6) Suppose v ∈ w*B. We prove that there is no J' ∈ w*A∧B' which is closer to w than v, establishing thus that v ∈ w*(A∧B')∨B: As w ⊭ A, w ∸ J' ∩ pvar(A) ≠ ∅ by (2) of the above fact. On the other hand, as A and B do not interfere, w ∸ v ∩ pvar(A) = ∅. Hence we can never have w ∸ v ⊃ w ∸ J', and therefore v ∈ w*(A∧B')∨B.

Property 2.3. Suppose A and B do not interfere, and w ⊨ A. Then
$$w*(A∧B)∨B' = w*B∨B'.$$

Proof. w*(A∧B)∨B' is the set of those elements of w*A∧B ∪ w*B' whose distance to w is minimal.[2] As w ⊨ A and A and B do not interfere, by (5) this set is equal to the minimal elements of w*B ∪ w*B'. But the latter is nothing else than w*B∨B'.

Property 2.4. Suppose A and B as well as A and B' do not interfere, and w ⊭ A. Then
$$w*(A∧B)∨B' = (w*B∨B'\|B'|)*A ∪ w*B'.$$

---

2   To see that, suppose v ∈ w*B and v ∉ w*(A∧B)∨B'. The latter means that there is a v' ∈
w*A∧B such that w ∸ v ⊃ w ∸ v'.

Proof. From the right to the left: If $v \in w*B'$, then as $w \not\models A$ and A and B' do not interfere the proof is done by (6) of the above fact. Hence suppose $v \in (w*B \vee B' \setminus |B'|)*A$. This means that there is some $J_B \in w*B \vee B'$ such that $v \in J_B*A$ and $J_B \not\models B'$. Thus $J_B \in w*B$, and there is no $J_{B'} \in v*B'$ closer to w. In other words, for every $J_{B'}$ we have $pvar(B') \supseteq w \div J_{B'}$, and there is some variable $p \in w \div J_{B'}$ such that $p \notin w \div J_B$. Hence (and his is the crucial step) as A and B' do not interfere, by (3) of the above fact we have also that $p \notin w \div v$. This means $v \in w*B*A$, and moreover there is no $J_{B'} \in v*B'$ such that $w \div v \supset w \div J_{B'}$. As A and B do not interfere, by Property 2.2 $v \in w*A \wedge B$, and thus $v \in w*(A \wedge B) \vee B'$ because there is no $J_{B'} \in v*B'$ closer to w.

From the left to the right: Suppose $v \in w*(A \wedge B) \vee B'$. Then either $v \in w*B'$ and we are done, or $v \in w*A \wedge B$, and there is no $J' \in w*B'$ which is closer to w than v. In the latter case $v \in w*B*A$ because A and B do not interfere. This means that there is some $J_B \in w*B \vee B'$ such that $v \in J_B*A$ and $J_B \not\models B'$. Hence $v \in (w*B \vee B' \setminus |B'|)*A$.

Property 2.5. Let $B \vee C$ a clause. If $w \not\models B \vee C$ then $w*B \vee C = w*B \cup w*C$.

3   AXIOMATICS

In the style of (Chellas 1975) we give the following inference rules and axiom schemes for the conditional logic *ASSUME*, based on some axiomatization of classical propositional logic.

(RCEA)
$$\frac{A \leftrightarrow B}{A>C \leftrightarrow B>C}$$

(RCK)
$$\frac{B_1 \wedge B_2 \wedge ... \wedge B_n \ .\rightarrow \ C}{A>B_1 \wedge A>B_2 \wedge ... \wedge A>B_n \ .\rightarrow \ A>C}$$

(ID) $A>A$

(CA) $A>C \wedge B>C \ .\rightarrow (A \vee B)>C$

(literal consistency) $\neg(A>\neg A)$ if A is a literal

(non-interference1) $C \rightarrow A>C$ if A and C do not interfere

(non-interference2) $(A \wedge B)>C \leftrightarrow A>(B>C)$ if A and B do not interfere

(non-interference3) $A \rightarrow. ((A \wedge B) \vee B')>C \leftrightarrow (B \vee B')>C$
if A and B do not interfere

(non-interference4) $\neg A \rightarrow. ((A \wedge B) \vee B')>C \leftrightarrow (B'>C \wedge (B \vee B')>(B' \vee (A>C)))$
if A and B, and A and B' do not interfere

We recall that A and B interfere if $pvar(A) \cap pvar(B) \neq \emptyset.$[3] The first four axioms are standard. Thus, ASSUME logic is build on the system CK (Nute 1980, Chellas 1985) which contains just the inference rules (RCEA) and (RCK). The last axioms deal with interference. In (literal consistency), it is important that "false" is not in the set of propositional variables. The rest of the axioms approximate the requirements of the non-interference postulate. (non-interference1) is our frame axiom. (non-interference2) to (non-interference4) account for the interplay between non-interference and the classical connectives.

Fact. The following formulas are derivable in ASSUME logic.

(1) $A>(C \wedge D) \ . \rightarrow . \ A>C \wedge A>D$

(2) $A>C \wedge A>D \ . \rightarrow . \ A>(C \wedge D)$

(3) $A>true$

(4) $A>C \ \rightarrow . \ A \rightarrow C$

(5) $A \wedge C \ . \rightarrow \ A>C$

(6) $false>A$

(7) $A \ \rightarrow . \ C \leftrightarrow A>C$

(8) $(A \vee B)>C \ \rightarrow . \ A \vee (B>C)$ if A and B do not interfere

(9) $(A \vee B)>C \ \leftrightarrow . \ ((A \vee B) \wedge C) \vee (A>C \wedge B>C)$ if A and B do not interfere

(10) $\neg(A>false)$ if A is a literal

(11) $A>C \rightarrow \neg(A>\neg C)$ if A is a literal

Proofs.
(1) to (3) By (RCK). In the literature, these formulas are called respectively (CM), (CC), (CN).

(4) and (5) By (non-interference3), putting true for B and false for B' (or, more precisely, $p \vee \neg p$ for B and $p \wedge \neg p$ for B', for some porpositional variable not occurring in B or B').[4]

(6) By ID, false>false. As false $\leftrightarrow . \ A \wedge \neg A$, by (RCEA) false>(A $\wedge \neg$A). By (CM), false>A.

(7) By (MP) and (CS).

---

3 It is tempting to formulate non-interference of two formulas A and C in terms of logical independence by "A $\wedge$ C, A $\wedge \neg$C, $\neg$A $\wedge$ C and $\neg$A $\wedge \neg$C are all consistent". But then axiom (non-interference1) would not be valid due to the following counterexample: Let C be $p \wedge q \ . \vee . \ \neg p \wedge r$, and let A be $\neg q$. C and A non interfering, $(p \wedge q) \vee (\neg p \wedge r) \ . \rightarrow . \ \neg q>((p \wedge q) \vee (\neg p \wedge r))$ would be a theorem. Let us show that this formula would not be valid: Let w an interpretation such that w $\models$ p and w $\models$ q. (Hence w $\models$ C). Changing w by $\neg$q leads to a v such that v $\models$ p and v $\models \neg$q. Hence w $\not\models$ C and v $\not\models$ C $\rightarrow$ A>C.

4 In the literature, these formulas are called respectively (MP) or (weak centering), and (CS) or (strong centering). In this sense, (non-interference3) can be seen as a generalized centering axiom.

(8) As A and B do not interfere, $\neg A \rightarrow .$ $(A \lor B) > C \leftrightarrow (B > C \land B > (B \lor A > C))$ follows from (non-interference4), putting true for B and B for B'. Then it is enough to apply (ID) and classical tautologies.

(9) The left-to-right-direction follows from (8) and (4). From the right to the left: First, $(A \lor B) \land C . \rightarrow . (A \lor B) > C$ by (5). Second, $A > C \land B > C \rightarrow (A \lor B) > C$ by (CA).

(10) and (11) follow from (literal consistency).

4 NORMAL FORMING

In this section we show that every clausal change formula is equivalent in ASSUME to a classical formula. This will be used to prove completeness as well as to give a proof procedure. The following properties will be useful to put formulas in normal form.

Property 4.1. Suppose A and B and A and B' do not interfere. Then the following equivalence is derivable in ASSUME.

$$((A \land B) \lor (\neg A \land B') \lor B'') > C . \leftrightarrow .$$
$$(A \land (B \lor (\neg A \land B') \lor B'') > C) \lor (\neg A \land ((A \land B) \lor B' \lor B'') > C$$

Proof. It is sufficient to apply (non-interference3) twice.

Property 4.2. Suppose A and B, and A and B' do not interfere. Then the following equivalence is derivable in ASSUME.

$$((A \land B) \lor B')) > C \leftrightarrow . (A \land (B \lor B') > C) \lor (\neg A \land B' > C \land (B \lor B') > (B' \lor (A > C)))$$

Proof. This follows from (non-interference3) and (non-interference4).

These properties permit to eliminate change formulas which are not literals. We use that every classical formula is classically equivalent to a formula of either the form $(A \land B) \lor (\neg A \land B') \lor B''$ or of the form $(A \land B) \lor B'$ such that A and B and A and B' do not interfere.[5] Then we can apply the above equivalences.[6] Every resulting change formula will be less complex than the original one. Iterating this process we obtain formulas with only literals as change formulas.

The next property will permit to distribute change literals over conjunction and disjunction. Thus (supposing that the formulas are in negation normal form, i.e. there are only literals in the scope of negations) we can produce formulas where the conditional operator > does not govern conjunction and disjunction any longer.

---

[5] One might e.g. apply the following algorithm: First transform the change formula into disjunctive normal form. Then choose a propositional variable p and put the formula into the form $(p \land B) \lor (\neg p \land B') \lor B''$, or $(p \land B) \lor B' \lor B''$, or $(\neg p \land B) \lor B' \lor B''$, such that p and B, and p and B' do not interfere. (Factorizing p "as much as possible" is useful for efficiency reasons.)

[6] Various optimizations seem to be possible and will be exploited in future work. An immediate improvement is e.g. to combine both equivalences.

Property 4.3. Let L a literal. Then $L>(B \wedge C) \leftrightarrow L>B \wedge L>C$.

Proof. This is a consequence of (RCK).

Property 4.4. Let L a literal. Then $L>(B \vee C) \leftrightarrow L>B \vee L>C$

Proof. From the right to the left: This is warranted by by (RCK).

From the left to the right by (literal consistency): $L>(B \vee C)$ implies $\neg(L>(\neg B \wedge \neg C))$. Then the latter is equivalent to $\neg(L>\neg B \wedge L> \neg C)$ by Property 4.3. Then the required formula follows again by Property 4.3 and (literal consistency).

   Thus we obtain formulas where sequences of literal change formulas govern literals. The next theorem will allow us to eliminate the conditional operator entirely from the formulas.

Property 4.5. Let L be a literal. Then following equivalences are derivable in ASSUME logic.

(1)	$L>L'$	$\leftrightarrow$	true	if $L = L'$
(2)	$L>L'$	$\leftrightarrow$	false	if $L = \neg L'$ or $L' = \neg L$
(3)	$L>L'$	$\leftrightarrow$	L'	if $pvar(L) \neq pvar(L')$

Proofs. These are immediate consequences of (ID), (literal consistency) and (non-interference1), respectively (Fariñas Herzig 1988).

   All these properties lead us to the following important

Normalization Theorem. In ASSUME, every change formula is equivalent to a classical formula.

Proof. Let A an ASSUME formula. There is at least one subformula B>C of A. First use Property 2.0 in order to factorize some propositional variable from B. Hence B is equivalent ot some B'. Then apply Properties 4.1 and 4.2 in order to decompose B'>C. All the change formulas coming from that process contain strictly less propositional variables than B. Iterating this we obtain literal change formulas. Then applying Properties 4.3, 4.4, and 4.5 we eliminate all of them, getting a formula A' which has one conditional less than A. In this manner we can obtain a classical formula.

   A simpler normal form can be obtained when the change formulas are restricted to *clauses* or *conjunctions of literals*. Thus we improve considerably the complexity bound for the general case of Winslett's possible worlds approach as given in (Eiter Gottlob 1992), answering at the same time an open question from the latter.

Property 4.6. Let $L_1 \wedge ... \wedge L_n$ a conjunction of literals. Then the following equivalences are derivable in ASSUME.

(1)	$(L_1 \wedge ... \wedge L_n)>C \leftrightarrow$	true	if there are L_i, L_j such that $L_i = \neg L_j$
(2)	$(L_1 \wedge ... \wedge L_n)>C \leftrightarrow$	$L_1>(...>(L_n>C)...)$	

Proofs. (1) follows from (ID). (2) follows from (non-interference2).

Example. The formula $p \to (q \land \neg(p \land q)) > (q \land \neg p)$ is by (RCEA) equivalent to the formula $p \to (q \land \neg p) > (q \land \neg p)$, which is equivalent to $p \to q > (\neg p > (q \land \neg p))$ by Property 4.6. As again by Property 4.6, $\neg p > (q \land \neg p) \leftrightarrow \neg p > q \land \neg p > \neg p \leftrightarrow q \land \text{true}$, the latter is equivalent to $p \to q > q$, which is on its turn equivalent to $p \to \text{true}$.

It is easy to see that in the case of conjunctions of literals normal forming can be done in linear time:

Theorem. If every clausal change formula A is a conjunctions of literals, normalization is in $O(n)$, where n is the number of symbols in A.

The case of clauses is slightly more complex. We use the following fact:

Property 4.7. Let $L_1 \lor ... \lor L_n$ a clause. Then following equivalence is derivable in ASSUME.

$$(L_1 \lor ... \lor L_n) > C \leftrightarrow \quad ((L_1 \lor ... \lor L_n) \land C) \lor (L_1 > C \land ... \land L_n > C)$$

Proof. It is sufficient to prove that for every clause $A \lor B$, the following equivalence is derivable:

$$(A \lor B) > C \leftrightarrow \quad ((A \lor B) \land C) \lor (A > C \land B > C)$$

From the right to the left, the proof can be done by (CA) and (CS). From the left to the right: First, as $A \lor B$ is a clause either there are two contradictory literals in it and $(A \lor B) > C \leftrightarrow \text{true} > C \leftrightarrow (A \lor B) \land C$, or there are clauses A', B', D which pairwisely have no propositional variable in common such that $A \leftrightarrow A' \lor D$ and $B \leftrightarrow B' \lor D$. Then by (RCEA), $(A \lor B) > C$ is equivalent to $(A' \lor D \lor B') > C$. Now (disjunctive non-interference) can be applied twice, yielding first $A' > C \land (D \lor B') > C$ .v. $A' \lor D \lor B'$ and then $A' > C \land ((D > C \land B' > C) \lor ((D \lor B') \land C))$ .v. $A' \lor D \lor B'$. The latter is classically equivalent to $A' > C \land D > C \land B' > C$ .v. $A' \lor D \lor B'$, which on its turn by (CA) implies that $(A' \lor D > C) \land (D \lor B' > C)$ .v. $A' \lor D \lor B'$. The latter together with the premiss entails by (MP) $(A' \lor D \lor B') \land C$ .v. $(A' \lor D) > C \land (D \lor B') > C$.

Example. Let the formula $A = p \land q \land r .\to (\neg p \land (p \lor \neg q \lor \neg r)) > r$. By (RCEA) the conditional is equivalent to $(\neg p \land (\neg q \lor \neg r)) > r$. By Property 4.2, the latter is equivalent to the formula $\neg p \land (\neg q \lor \neg r) > r$ .v. $p \land \text{false} > r \land (\neg q \lor \neg r) > (\text{false} \lor \neg p > r)$. Now by Property 4.7, $(\neg q \lor \neg r) > r$ is equivalent to $(\neg q \lor \neg r) \land r$ .v. $\neg q > r \land \neg r > r$, which is $\neg q \land r$ by Property 4.5. Hence A is equivalent to $p \land q \land r .\to. (\neg p \land \neg q \land r) \lor (p \land \neg q \land r)$, i.e. $p \land q \land r .\to. \neg q \land r$. As this is not valid in classical logic, A is not a theorem of ASSUME either.

It is easy to see that in the case of clausal change formulas normal forming can be done in quadratic time:

Theorem. Let A a formula A without "$\leftrightarrow$" such every change formula is a clause. Then normalization is in $O(n^2)$, where n is the number of symbols in A.

5 SOUNDNESS AND COMPLETENESS

In order to establish *soundness* we must prove that the axioms of ASSUME are valid, and that the inference rules preserve validity. The case of most of the axioms is clear. The validity of (non-interference1) to (non-interference4) is guaranteed respectively by Properties 2.1 to 2.4. *Completeness* can be proved using the fact that every formula is equivalent to a classical formula: Every formula A which is valid in ASSUME has its normal form A' valid in ASSUME (because of soundness). As A' is a classical formula, it is also valid in classical logic. Through the completeness of classical logic, A' is also a theorem of classical logic. As the axiomatics of ASSUME contains that of classical logic, A' is a theorem of ASSUME. Thus A is a theorem of ASSUME, too, via the normalization theorem.

6 IMPLEMENTING UPDATES WITH ASSUME

The normalization theorem furnishes a tool for performing automated deduction in ASSUME logic. Here a spectrum of possibilities appears, depending on how the normalization theorem is used.

It can be used globally: In a first step we transform the formula KB $\rightarrow$ A>C into an equivalent classical one, and then a classical proof method can be used. As normalization is generally exponential this is not very efficient (except when the change formulas are clauses or conjunctions of literals).

In the other extremity, we may use a lazy normalization, in other words we use the normalizsation theorem only when it is necessary to go on with the deduction.

Example (Winslett 1988). Let two knowledge bases KB1 = {p,q} and KB2 = {p, p$\rightarrow$q}. KB1 and KB2 are equivalent. Thus updating by $\neg$q should have the same effect on KB1 as on KB2, i.e. KB1*$\neg$q should be equal to KB2*$\neg$q. This is indeed the case: We have KB1 $\vdash$-ASSUME $\neg$q>(p$\land\neg$q) as well as KB2 $\vdash$-ASSUME $\neg$q>(p$\land\neg$q).

7 CONCLUSION

We have defined a conditional logic ASSUME for reasoning about change, and we have given a proof procedure.

In the semantics we have the minimality notion proposed in (Winslett 1988). It is a particular case of that in (Katsuno Mendelzon 1991b, Grahne 1991), where the notion of minimality is expressible by any orderings on worlds.

Due to its syntactical flavour, our proof procedure for the PMA seems to us more attractive than that described in (Chou Winslett 1991, Winslett 1994) : In the latter approach, updates are computed on a model-by-model basis. This amounts to enumerate the models of the knowledge base (in fact the minimal models) and to do each time the update on the model. Similar to (Del Val 1992) in our method the result of an update is essentially computed by proving theorems in classical logic. This permits to use the whole power of the existing technology in classical theorem proving resulting from 30 years of research in that area. Del Val's method is not in terms of a conditional operator, but in terms of an update operator. Although he claims it to be a syntactical characterization of the PMA, it still has a model-based flavour: In the axiomatization formulas are supposed to be in normal form, and there is a function Diff(.,.) that computes the difference between two conjunctions of literals, which is very close to the computation of the difference between two worlds in the semantics.

We are aware that that the theoretical complexity of the known change operations is desperately high (Eiter Gottlob 1992). One hope is that often updates can be limited to be conjunctions or disjunctions of literals, for which we have found new complexity results.

ACKNOWLEDGEMENTS

We owe our thanks to a lot of people who through discussions and comments (hopefully) contributed to make the previous versions of the paper clearer and more readable. Among those are Nicolas Asher, Gabriella Crocco, Robert Demolombe, Didier Dubois, Joachim Hertzberg, Philippe Lamarre, Pierre Marquis, Alberto O. Mendelzon, Bernhard Nebel, and the participants of the LogIn'92 colloquium in Konstanz, in particular David Makinson and Karl Schlechta.

REFERENCES

B.F. Chellas (1975), *Basic conditional logic.* J. of Philos. Logic, 4, pp 133-53.

T.S. Chou & M. Winslett (1991), *Immortal: A model-based belief revision system.* Proc. KR'91.

A. Del Val (1992), *Computing knowledge base updates.* Proc. KR'92.

Th. Eiter & G. Gottlob (1992), *On the complexity of propositional knowledge base revision, updates, and counterfactuals.* Journal of AI 57, pp. 227-270.

L. Fariñas del Cerro & A. Herzig (1988), *An automated modal logic for elementary changes.* Non-Standard Logics for Automated Reasoning (ed. P Smets, A, Mandani, D. Dubois & H. Prade). Academic Press, pp 63-79.

G. Grahne (1991), *Updates and Contrafactuals.* Proc. KR'91.

H. Katsuno & A.O. Mendelzon (1989), *A unified view of propositional knowledge base updates.* Proc. IJCAI'89.

H. Katsuno & A.O. Mendelzon (1991), *Propositional knowledge base revision and minimal change.* Journal of AI 52, 263-294.

H. Katsuno & A.O. Mendelzon (1991), *On the Difference between Updating a Knowledge Base and Revising it.* Proc. KR'91.

H. Katsuno & K. Satoh (1991), *A unified view of consequence relation, belief revision and conditional logic.* Proc. IJCAI'91.

D. K. Lewis (1973), *Counterfactuals.* Blackwell, Oxford.

M. Winslett (1988), *Reasoning about actions.* Proc. AAAI'88, pp 89-93.

M. Winslett (1990), *Updating Logical Databases.* Cambridge Tracts in Theoretical Computer Science. Cambridge University Press.

M. Winslett (1994), *Updating Logical Databases.* Handbook of Logic in AI (ed. D. Gabbay, A. Galton, C. Hogger), Oxford University Press, to appear.

Probabilistic Justification of Default Reasoning

Gerhard Schurz

Institut für Philosophie, Abtlg. Logik und Wissenschaftstheorie
Universität Salzburg, A-5020 Salzburg, Austria

Abstract. A probabilistic justification of default reasoning is given which is based on ε-semantics. Whenever a consequence is derived from a default law and a fact in the presence of further facts, a default assumption is generated claiming that these further facts are probabilistically irrelevant. Each extension E_i of a knowledge base **K** (in Reiter's sense) corresponds to a set of default assumptions D_i generated by E_i. It is proved that if Reiter's original definition is modified, then for each extension E_i, D_i will be ε−consistent with **K**, and E_i will contain exactly those sentences which are ε-entailed by **K** plus D_i. As a result, we obtain a method of calculating lower probability bounds of the consequences in E_i from the default assumptions D_i and the given (nonextreme) lower probability bounds associated with the default laws. Finally, a method of deriving one single and preferred extension E is introduced which is based on a solution of the problem of collective defeat and is probabilistically justified in the same way.

1 Introduction

Default reasoning is reasoning from uncertain laws, so-called *default laws*, like

(1)   "Birds normally can fly"   formalized as: $Bird(x) \Rightarrow Can\text{-}Fly(x)$

($\Rightarrow$ for uncertain implication). It is based on the observation that from the uncertain law (1) plus the instantiated antecedent Bird(tweety) ("Tweety is a bird") we are allowed to derive the instantiated consequent Can-Fly(tweety) *only* as long as *nothing else* is derivable from our *knowledge base* **K** which implies that Can-Fly(tweety) is false, i.e. that Tweety is an 'exceptional' bird w.r.t. flying. For instance, if we *also* know Penguin(tweety) and the strict law Penguin(x) $\rightarrow$ Can't-Fly(x) ($\rightarrow$ for material implication), then the detachment from (1) is no longer allowed. Thus, inference from default laws is *nonmonotonic*: additional knowledge may make previously derived concequences underivable.

Various different reasoning systems of nonmonotonic reasoning have been developed – nonmonotonic logic [9], default reasoning [15, 13, 5], defeasible reasoning [10, 17] – but the problems seem to be still greater than the success which has been reached [cf. 14]. The most important task is to give clear criteria for the *justification* of default reasoning systems, which presupposes a clear definition of the *correctness* of a nonmonotonic inference. In deductive logic, correctness coincides with *truth-preservation*: if the premises are true, then the conclusion is *certainly* true. But what is – or better: *should* be – *preserved* in a nonmonotonic inference? One most plausible suggestion is *probability*: given the premises are true, then the conclusion is true with high probability (in the statistical sense). The practical reason for this demand is clear: if the demand is satisfied, and the assumptions of an *expert system* <L,F> are true or at least highly probable, then the expert system applied to a representative sample of applications will produce correct predictions in a high percentage of cases, and hence will be *reliable* (similarly argues Adams [1, ch. III, §4]).

Unfortunately, to establish a satisfactory connection between default reasoning and probability theory is rather difficult. This paper is one more step in this direction. I base the following considerations on ε-semantics developed by Adams [1] and suggested by Pearl [11, ch. 10.2] as the basis for a probabilistic foundation of nonmonotonic reasoning. First some *terminology*. In what follows, x (y...) stand for sequences of individual variables ($<x_i|i\leq n>$ for some $n\geq 1$) and a (b...) for sequences of individual constants; Ax (Bx...) are open formulas of the first order language $\mathcal{L}$ containing the variables in x free; Aa is the closed formula resulting from Ax by substituting a_i for x_i ($1\leq i\leq n$). Formulas of the form Aa are also called 'facts'. ('Proper' facts have to be quantifier-free; but we don't need this assumption). A default law has the form Ax⇒Bx (note that ⇒ is *not* an expression of $\mathcal{L}$). A knowledge base is a tuple K = <L,F> with L a finite set of default laws and Fa finite set of facts. "⊢" stands for logical (first order) inference, and $\vdash_i$ stands for (indexed) notion(s) of nonmonotonic inference.

ε-semantics interprets default laws Ax⇒Bx as high conditional probability statements of the form $p(Bx/Ax) \geq 1-\varepsilon$, for ε a small but nonzero number. For purposes of application the probabilities are assumed to be *statistical* ones. For instance, the default law (1) above is interpreted as the claim that the percentage of animals which can fly among all birds is very high. There is no theoretical need to specify the actual (empirically true) probability value because ε-semantics is based on limit considerations. For practical purposes, however, the actual probability values or at least their lower bounds (estimated by experts in some reliable way) are very important. Fortunately, theorem 1 below will allow us to apply ε-semantics to those actual probability values.

As in Goldszmidt et al [7, p. 647], we extend the usual definition of conditional probability by putting $p(Bx/Ax)=1$ if $p(Ax)=0$; this simplifies several definitions. The following definitions are basis of ε-semantics. A set L of default laws is called *ε-consistent* iff (if and only if) convergence of the associated conditional probabilities arbitrarily close to 1 is consistent with probability theory – more exactly, iff for every (arbitrarily small) ε>0 there exists a probability distribution p such that $p(Bx/Ax)\geq 1-\varepsilon$ for every default law Ax⇒Bx ∈ L [cf. 1, p. 51; 11, p. 487].[1] L *ε-entails* a default law Cx⇒Dx, in short L $\vdash_\varepsilon$ Cx⇒Dx, iff probability theory implies that conditional probability associated with the conclusion goes arbitrarily close to 1 if the conditional probabilities associated with the premises in L are going sufficiently close to 1 – more exactly, iff for every (arbitrarily small) δ>0 there exists an ε>0 such that for all probability dis-

---

[1]   Adams excludes conditionals with inconsistent antecedents [1, p. 46] and restricts p to 'proper' distributions, where $p(Ax)>0$ for Ax⇒Bx ∈ L holds.

tributions p satisfying $p(Bx/Ax) \geq 1-\epsilon$ for all $Ax \Rightarrow Bx \in L$, $p(Dx/Cx) \geq 1-\delta$ holds [1, p. 57; 11, p. 484]. The definition of ϵ-entailment of factual conclusions Ca is given by: $<L,F> \vdash_\epsilon Ca$ iff $L \vdash_\epsilon Fx \Rightarrow Cx$, where Fx stands for the conjunction of *all* the facts in F with constants a replaced by variables x [cf. 11, ch. 10.22]. This is nothing but the old 'principle of total evidence' for direct inferences: the (subjective) probability which a knowledge base $<L,F>$ conveys to a particular fact Ca is identified with the (statistical) probability of Cx conditional to the *total* fact-knowledge [cf. Carnap 4, p. 211; 2, p. 563]. For sake of simplicity we do not introduce a separate set of deterministic laws **Ld** of the form $Ax \rightarrow Bx$, with associated probabilities $p(Bx/Ax)=1$, though such an enrichment could easily be embedded into our framework.[2]

Does ϵ-semantics yield the intended justification of default reasoning? Two arguments seem to speak against that. *First*, ϵ-semantics deals with extreme probabilities, arbitrarily close to 1, but in practical applications (e.g., expert systems) we reason with high but nonextreme probabilities [cf. 11, p. 494f]. For instance, a medical expert system typically tells us that the probability of a desease, given certain symptoms, is is high, say ≥ 0.9 or ≥ 0.95, but not arbitrarily close to 1. Fortunately, this argument is *not* a really serious objection because of the following theorem [cf. 1, p. 57, Th. 3.1]:

Theorem 1 (Adams): If $\{L_1,...,L_n\} \vdash_\epsilon Fx \Rightarrow Cx$, and p is a probability distribution associating the conditional probability $1-\epsilon_i$ with each L_i $(1 \leq i \leq n)$, then $p(Cx/Fx) \geq 1 - (\epsilon_1+...+\epsilon_n)$.

Three remarks are appropriate. *First*, theorem 1 does, of course, *not* presuppose that the facts in F are probabilistically independent – it holds for every probability distribution. *Second*, in special cases, lower bounds higher than $1 - (\epsilon_1+...+\epsilon_n)$ are calculable from probability theory, but on the cost of more computational effort. *Third*, we may assume that $\{L_1,...,L_n\}$ contains only those default laws in L on which the proof of $Fx \Rightarrow Cx$ (with help of the rules stated below) did *depend*. This gives an easy way to calculate lower probability bounds of the conclusions of an expert system from (high but nonextreme) lower probability bounds associated with its default laws, just by summing up the uncertainties ϵ_i of the laws L_i *used* in the proof of the conclusion, *provided* $<L,F>$ *ϵ-entails Ca*. Of course, it must be presupposed that the lower probability bounds associated with the laws in L are probabilistically consistent. We will assume slightly more, namely that *L is ϵ-consistent:* this is a reasonable condition which implies probabilistic consistency for any nonextreme lower bounds and can easily be decided by theorem 2.

Some further definitions: A default law $Ax \Rightarrow Bx$ is *nontrivial* if Ax is logically consistent; a set Γ of default laws is nontrivial if it contains at least one nontrivial default law. $Ax \Rightarrow Bx$ is verified [falsified] by a (propositional) truth valuation v if $v(Ax)=1$ and $v(Bx)=1$ [$v(Ax)=1$ and $v(Bx)=0$, respectively]. The following theorem is crucial for deciding ϵ-consistency.

---

2   We have then to understand $\vdash$ as logical derivability from **Ld** and consistency as consistency w.r.t. **Ld**. Truth valuations (cf. theorem 3) have to be restricted to those verifying **Ld**. Cf. also [6, p. 71].

Theorem 2: [Adams 1, p. 52, th. 1]: **L** is ε-consistent iff for every nontrivial subset Γ ⊆ **L** there exists a truth valuation falsifying no element of Γ and verifying at least one element of Γ.

The *really serious* problem of ε-semantics – and this is the *second* argument – is that ε-entailment is much *weaker* than the typical entailment relations of default reasoning. The following theorem is the core of Adams' results [1, p. 61f, th. 4; cf. also 6, p. 71; 11 p. 485]:

Theorem 3 (Adams): *(3.1)* If **L** is finite, then **L** ε-entails A⇒B iff A⇒B is derivable from **L** by the following rules of inference:

(L):	Infer A⇒B from A ⊢ B	(Logical Inference)
(C)	Infer A⇒C from A⇒B, A∧B⇒C	(Cautious Cut)
(M)	Infer A∧B⇒C from A⇒B and A⇒C	(Cautious Monotonicity)
(∨)	Infer A∨B⇒C from A⇒C and B⇒C	(Disjunction)
(L*)	Infer A⇒B from C⇒D, ⊬ ¬C and C ⊢¬D	(Logical Contradiction)

(3.2): The following inference rules are derivable:

(∧)	Infer A⇒B∧C from A⇒B and A⇒C	(Conjunction)
(LE)	Infer B⇒C from ⊢A↔B and A⇒B	(Left Logical Equivalence)
(RW)	Infer A⇒C from A⇒B and B ⊢ C	(Right Weakening)

L has to be finite because ε-entailment is noncompact [1, p. 52]. Default laws derivable from an ε-consistent finite **L** are always derivable *without* (L*).[3] It follows from theorem 3 that ⊢ε is monotonic w.r.t. **L** (<L,F> ⊢ε C, L ⊆ L* implies <L*,F> ⊢ε C). It is, of course, not monotonic w.r.t. **F**.

These inference rules alone (though reasonable and safe[4]) are too weak as a basis for default reasoning, because they do not allow *the default moves* which are *characteristic* for nonmonotonic reasoning – namely to infer Ba from Aa ∈ **F** and Ax⇒Bx ∈ **L** as long as *nothing else* is known in **K** which implies ¬Ba. For example, Can-Fly(tweety) is inferred from **K** = <{Bird(x)⇒Can-Fly(x)}, {Bird(twee-ty), Female(tweety)}> because **K**'s additional fact Female(tweety) does not imply ¬Can-Fly(tweety) via other default laws in **L** – it is *irrelevant* for the conclusion Can-Fly(tweety). But this inference is *not* allowed in ε-semantics: <{Ax⇒Bx}, {Aa,Ca}> ⊬ε Ba, because Ax⇒Bx does not ε-entail Ax∧Cx⇒Bx. (This is the reason why ε-semantics, in *distinction* to default reasoning, is monotonic w.r.t. **L**). So, what we need for a probabilistic justification of default reasoning are *additional probabilistic irrelevancy assumptions* which correspond to these 'default moves'.

Goldszmidt et al [7; cf. also 11, ch. 10.2.3) and in a similar way Bacchus et al [2] overcome this problem as follows. Instead of referring to *all* probability distributions p with p(Bx/Ax)≥1–ε for all Ax⇒Bx ∈ **L** (in the definition of ε-entailment), they pick out just one single probability distribution p*. In the maximal entropy approach of [11, ch. 10.2.3] and [7, p. 648f], p* is that probability

---

3   ...whence Geffner/Pearl [6, p. 71] and Pearl [11, p.485] omit this rule. Adams has two further rules [p. 60f]: his (R2) is derivable (see our theorem 3.2, (LE), cf. also [6, p. 72]); his (R1) is superfluous.

4   They correspond exactly to the basic axioms of cumulative logic after [8].

distribution (among those satisfying the ε–constraints) which yields *maximal entropy*; in [2, p. 565f] it is that which gives *equal* probability to all possible worlds compatible with what is known in the knowledge base. In [2, p. 568] it is proved that both approaches are equivalent for monadic languages. This justification does its job insofar Ba is now derivable from Ax⇒Bx and Aa even in the presence of irrelevant additional facts. One problem of both approaches is their high computational complexity [cf. 11, p. 493]. The other problem is that their additional assumptions are *unnecessarily* strong. Why *should* one make the – rather improbable – assumption that the real world's entropy is maximal (among all possible and knowledge-compatible worlds) – if *all* what one needs to derive Ba from Ax⇒Bx and Aa∧Ca is to asume that Cx is probabilistically irrelevant for Bx, given Ax? I think, the assumption of these two approaches is even *too* strong. For instance, it validates contraposition Ax⇒Bx |~ ¬Bx⇒¬Ax as a correct inference [7, p. 652], which intuitively is not generally correct on various reasons, for instance, because it does *not* preserve high probability [cf. 11, p. 847]. Another undesired result is that sometimes inferrability depends on how (logically equivalent) default laws are formulated [7, p. 651]. In particular, if nonextreme probabilities are associated with the default laws the approach implies too strong results, since the fixed probability distribution p* will imply a definite probability value for every formula of the language.

I what follows I give a *minimal* probabilistic justification of default reasoning, making only those probabilistic assumptions which directly correspond to default moves. Whenever a default reasoning system (with inference relation |~) infers a conclusion Ba from a law Ax⇒Bx ∈ L and an already derived antecedent Aa, it has *implicitly* assumed that the (remainder) facts in F are probabilistically irrelevant for Aa – i.e. that p(Bx/Ax) and p(Bx/Ax∧Fx) are approximately equal – hence, it has made the implicit assumption Fx∧Ax ⇒ Bx, which I call a *default assumption* (in distinction from the default laws in L), and say that Fx∧Ax ⇒ Bx has been *generated* by this inference step. The (nonextreme) lower probability bound associated with Ax⇒Bx is associated also with the default assumption Fx∧Ax⇒Bx. This idea is similar to the relevance-based approach of Geffner/Pearl [6], who add irrelevance assumptions to knowledge bases; but their approach remains syntactical and gives no ε-semantical justification. Our main questions of the next section will be: *First*, provided L is ε–consistent, is the set of implicit default assumptions D generated by a default reasoning system during the production of an extension of <L,F> always ε–consistent with L – and if no, under which conditions? Of course, the ε-consistency of L∪D is a *minimal* condition for regarding the generated default assumptions as justified. *Second*, can a correspondence be established between some relevant default reasoning system (|~) such that <L,F> |~ Aa iff Aa is ε–entailed by <L∪D,F>?

2 Multiple Extensions and Generated Default Assumptions

Default laws Ax⇒Bx correspond to Reiter's *normal* defaults of the form (Aa: MBa / Ba) [15, p. 95]. How are the nonmonotonic consequences of a knowledge base defined? According to the basic idea underlying [15] and [16], one may derive nonmonotonic consequences as long as the resulting consequence set remains consistent. If a set of consequences derived in this manner is *maximal*, i.e. if every consequence derivable from it is contained in it, it is called an *extension* of the knowledge base. Each consistent normal default theory has an extension [15, p. 95, th. 3.1], but as is-well known, there may be *multiple* extensions. To illustrate it by an example, assume

(2) L = {Quaker(x)⇒Pacifist(x), Conservative(x)⇒¬Pacifist(x)}
       F = {Quaker(nixon), Conservative(nixon)}

If we detach first Pacifist(nixon) from the first law and its instantiated antecedent, we obtain $F \cup$ {Pacifist(nixon)} (plus classical consequences) as an extension in which the second law is 'blocked'. If we detach first ¬Pacifist(nixon) from the second law and its instantiated antecedent, we obtain $F \cup$ {¬Pacifist(nixon)} (plus classical consequences) as a second extension, in which the first law is 'blocked'.

Let C range over sets of fact-like $\mathcal{L}$-formulas, and Cn(C):={A|C⊢A} denote the classical closure of C. C is consistent iff p∧¬p ∉ Cn(C). Then, we may define the notion of an extension as follows.

Definition 1: Let K = <L,F> be a fixed knowledge base.
(1.1) <L,C> ⊢ Aa *iff* for some Bx⇒Ax ∈ L, (i) Ba ∈ Cn(C) and (ii) ¬Aa ∉ Cn(C).
(1.2) For f:ω⊤̄$\mathcal{L}$ [f(i) := A_i] any enumeration of $\mathcal{L}$'s formulas, we define: (i) C_0 = Cn(F), (ii) C_{i+1} = Cn($C_i \cup \{A_{i+1}\}$) if <L,C_i> ⊢ A_{i+1}, else C_{i+1} = C_i, finally (iii) C_f = ⋃{C_i|i∈ ω}.
(1.3) C_f is called an *F-extension* of K iff for each Aa with <L,C_f> ⊢ Aa, Aa ∈ C_f holds. We write E_f := $E_f(K)$ for a C_f which is an F-extension of K.

It is easily seen that this definition of an F-extension of K is equivalent to Reiter's definition of K-extensions for normal defaults (see p. 95, proof for Th. 3.1). It is also clear that each $E_f(K)$ is consistent, provided F is consistent. Definition 1 takes into consideration that not any formula enumeration f will produce an extension. For example, if L = {Ax⇒Bx, Bx⇒Cx}, F = {Aa}, and Ca comes before Ba in the enumeration, then Ca will not be derived after Ba has been derived because it never appears once again in the enumeration. So, in this case C_f will not be closed under ⊢. On the other hand, every extension will be produced by *some* formula enumeration. That such an enumeration exists is important for the following. Also note that the inference relation ⊢ satisfies reflexivity and cut, but as a result of multiple extensions, *neither* cautious monotonicity nor conjunction.

For each step i in which some A_ia was added to C_i with help of Bx⇒A_ix ∈ L, the default assumption generated by step i is generally defined as Fx∧Bx⇒A_ix. If Ba is a fact in F, this is logically equivalent with Fx⇒A_ix. In the example (2) above, the default assumption generated while producing the first extension is Quaker(x)∧Conservative(x) ⇒ Pacifist(x); that generated while producing the second extension is Quaker(x)∧Conservative(x) ⇒ ¬Pacifist(x).

Let D_f denote the set of all default assumptions generated in deriving the extension E_f (of a given <L,F>). We call $L \cup D_f$ the L-extension of K corresponding to E_f. For the (most liberal) definition of ⊢ in def. 1, $L \cup D_f$ will *not* always be ε-consistent. Consider the example

(3) $L = \{Ax \Rightarrow Bx, Cx \Rightarrow \neg Bx, Cx \Rightarrow Ax\}$
        $F = \{Aa, Ca\}$
        Illustration: "Ax" for "x is an Adult", "Bx" for "x is employed", "Cx" for
        "x is a student".

$\langle L,F \rangle$ has two F-extensions, $E1 = \{Aa,Ca,Ba\}$ and $E2 = \{Aa,Ca,\neg Ba\}$ (plus classical consequences), with the corresponding sets of generated default assumptions $D1 = \{Ax \wedge Cx \Rightarrow Bx\}$ and $D2 = \{Ax \wedge Cx \Rightarrow \neg Bx\}$. Only $L \cup D2$ is ε-consistent, while $L \cup D1$ is ε-inconsistent, since $Ax \wedge Cx \Rightarrow \neg Bx$ is ε-entailed by $Cx \Rightarrow \neg Bx$ and $Cx \Rightarrow Ax$ via (M). Hence, by theorem 1, E1 is an example where def. 1 of an extension leads to probabilistically *incorrect* results: E1 contains Ba though $p(Bx/Fx)$ must be *low* given the conditional probabilities of the laws are high.

The example is a case of the well-known *specifity* rule: Ca gives more specific information than Aa about a since almost all C's are A's but not vice versa, hence the law $Cx \Rightarrow \neg Bx$ is *preferred* over $Ax \Rightarrow Bx$. Several recent approaches to default reasoning include this specifity rule as a means for selecting 'preferred' extensions [cf. 13, 5, 10, 17; see 16 for applications to explanation]. It is important to observe, however, that ε-semantic does not give a general validation of the specifity rule, but only in the case where there are no further irrelevant facts. Take for example L as above and put $F = \{Aa,Ca,Da\}$. In our example, "Da" may mean "a is male". Then $Ax \wedge Cx \wedge Dx \Rightarrow Bx$ is again ε-consistent with $L := \{Ax \Rightarrow Bx, Cx \Rightarrow \neg Bx, Cx \Rightarrow Ax\}$, whence Ba is ε-entailed by F together with an ε-consistent L-extension of K via the default assumption $Ax \wedge Cx \wedge Dx \Rightarrow Bx$.

To obtain the intended probabilistic justification of default reasoning, we must eliminate probabilistically incorrect extensions. We can do that simply by redefining the start set in def. 1 as follows:

Definition 1*: $\langle L,F \rangle \vdash^* A$ is defined as in def. 1 except that the start set C_0 is defined as: $C_0 := C_\varepsilon(K) := \{Aa \in \mathcal{L} | \langle L,F \rangle \vdash_\varepsilon Aa\}$.

If the start set contains all ε-consequences of $\langle L,F \rangle$, we can prove that the standard process of forming a maximal consistent extension will generate only default assumptions which are ε-consistent with L. The proof proceeds through several lemmata. Γ, Δ range over *finite* sets of default laws. $\vdash_0$ means inference of propositional logic.

Lemma 1: (Adams 1, p. 58, th. 3.5): $\Gamma \cup \{Ax \Rightarrow Bx\}$ is ε-inconsistent iff $\Gamma \vdash_\varepsilon Ax \Rightarrow \neg Bx$.

Lemma 2: If Γ is ε-consistent, then: $\Gamma \vdash_\varepsilon Ax \Rightarrow Bx$ iff there exists some subset $\Delta := \{A_i x \Rightarrow B_i x | i \leq n\} \subseteq \Gamma$ such that: (a) $\bigvee \{A_i x | i \leq n\} \wedge \bigwedge \{A_i x \rightarrow B_i x | i \leq n\} \vdash_0 Ax \wedge Bx$, and (b) $Ax \wedge \neg Bx \vdash_0 \bigvee \{A_i x \wedge \neg B_i x | i \leq n\}$. – *Proof:* From Adams' lemma about 'yielding' in the 'proof of 4.1' [1, p. 61] and propositional logic.

If $D = Fx \wedge Ax \Rightarrow Bx$, we define $D^* := Fx \Rightarrow Bx$ and call D^* the *reduced* default assumption corresponding to D. We define $D_f^* := \{D^* | D \in D_f\}$.

Lemma 3. (3.1): If Aa $\in$ E_f(<L,F>) (according to def. 1*), then <L$\cup$D$_f$> $\vdash_\varepsilon$ Fx$\Rightarrow$Ax. *(3.2):* L$\cup$D$_f$ and L$\cup$D$_f$* are ε-interderivable.

Proof: (3.1): Straightforward induction on step numbers i in def. 1*. *(3.2)* For each Fx$\wedge$Ax$\Rightarrow$Bx $\in$ D$_f$, Aa$\in$ E$_f$, whence Fx$\Rightarrow$Ax is ε-entailed by L$\cup$D$_f$ by lemma (3.1). From Fx$\Rightarrow$Ax and Fx$\wedge$Ax$\Rightarrow$Bx, Fx$\Rightarrow$Bx is ε-inferrable by (C); and vice versa, Fx$\wedge$Ax$\Rightarrow$Bx is ε-inferrable from Fx$\Rightarrow$Bx and Fx$\Rightarrow$Ax by (M).

Lemma 4: Let D* be a finite set of reduced default assumptions of the form Fx$\Rightarrow$Bx and let L$\cup$D* be ε-consistent. Then: L$\cup$D* $\vdash_\varepsilon$ Fx$\Rightarrow$Ax *iff* L $\vdash_\varepsilon$ Fx$\Rightarrow$($\wedge$X $\rightarrow$ Ax), for X a subset of {Bx | Fx$\Rightarrow$Bx $\in$ D*} ($\wedge$X the conjunction of X's elements).

Proof: From right to left: For each Bx $\in$ X, Fx$\Rightarrow$Bx is in D*; hence D* $\vdash_\varepsilon$ Fx$\Rightarrow\wedge$X by ($\wedge$). Thus, L$\cup$D* $\vdash_\varepsilon$ Fx$\Rightarrow$($\wedge$X$\rightarrow$Ax)$\wedge\wedge$X by ($\wedge$), from which L$\cup$D* $\vdash_\varepsilon$ Fx$\Rightarrow$Ax follows by (RW). *From left to right:* By lemma 2, L$\cup$D* $\vdash_\varepsilon$ Fx$\Rightarrow$Ax iff there exists some finite subsets L' := {A$_i$x$\Rightarrow$B$_i$x|i$\leq$n} of L and D' := {Fx$\Rightarrow$C$_i$x|i$\leq$m} of D* such that:

(a) ($\vee${A$_i$x|i$\leq$n}$\vee$Fx) $\wedge$ ($\wedge${A$_i$x$\rightarrow$B$_i$x|i$\leq$n} $\wedge$ (Fx$\rightarrow\wedge${C$_i$x|i$\leq$m})) $\vdash_0$ Fx$\wedge$Ax

(b) Fx$\wedge\neg$Ax $\vdash_0$ $\vee${A$_i$x$\wedge\neg$B$_i$x|i$\leq$n} $\vee$ $\vee${Fx$\wedge\neg$C$_i$x|i$\leq$m}.

From (a) we obtain by propositional logic:

(a') ($\vee${A$_i$x|i$\leq$n}) $\wedge$ $\wedge${A$_i$x$\rightarrow$B$_i$x|i$\leq$n} $\vdash_0$ (Fx$\rightarrow\wedge${C$_i$x|i$\leq$m}) $\rightarrow$ (Fx$\wedge$Ax)), and since (p$\rightarrow$q)$\rightarrow$(p$\wedge$r) is logically equivalent with p$\wedge$(q$\rightarrow$r), we obtain:

(a'') ($\vee${A$_i$x|i$\leq$n}) $\wedge$ $\wedge${A$_i$x$\rightarrow$B$_i$x|i$\leq$n} $\vdash_0$ Fx $\wedge$ ($\wedge${C$_i$x|i$\leq$m}$\rightarrow$Ax).

Propositional transformation of (b) gives us:

(b') Fx$\wedge\wedge${C$_i$x|i$\leq$m}$\wedge\neg$Ax $\vdash_0$ $\vee${A$_i$x$\wedge\neg$B$_i$x|i$\leq$n}.

From (a'') and (b') we conclude, by applying lemma 2 again, that L $\vdash_\varepsilon$ Fx $\Rightarrow$ ($\wedge${C$_i$x|i$\leq$m}$\rightarrow$Ax). Q.E.D.

We prove now that each F-extension of <L,F> corresponds to an ε-consistent extension of L by default assumptions.

Theorem 4: Let E$_f$ be an F-extension of <L,F> according to def. 1*, and D$_f$ the corresponding set of generated default assumptions. Then: If L is ε-consistent, then L$\cup$D$_f$ is ε-consistent.

Proof: By lemma 3, it suffices to show that L$\cup$D$_f$* is ε-consistent. Let D$_{f,n}$* be the set of default assumptions generated in all steps i$\leq$n. We prove, by induction on n, that L$\cup$D$_{f,n}$* will be ε-consistent for each n. Assume by ind. hyp. that L$\cup$D$_{f,n}$* is ε-consistent, and that Fx$\Rightarrow$Ax [A = A$_{n+1}$] is added in step n+1. Since D$_{f,n}$* is finite, we have by lemma 1 that L$\cup$D$_{f,n+1}$* := L$\cup$D$_{f,n}$* $\cup${Fx$\Rightarrow$Ax} is ε-inconsistent iff L$\cup$D$_{f,n}$* $\vdash_\varepsilon$ Fx$\Rightarrow\neg$Ax. By lemma 4 this holds iff L $\vdash_\varepsilon$ Fx $\Rightarrow$ ($\wedge$X$\rightarrow\neg$Ax), for X a finite set of consequents of default assumptions in D$_{f,n}$*. Whenever a new default assumption is generated in step i, its instantiated consequent Ca is taken into C$_i$; so X[a] will be logically entailed by and hence be contained in C$_n$. ($\wedge$X[a]$\rightarrow\neg$Aa) is in C$_0$ and hence also in C$_n$, whence $\neg$Aa must be contained in C$_n$. But according to def 1*, this contradicts the assumption that Fx$\Rightarrow$Ax is added in step n. So L$\cup$D$_{f,n+1}$* is ε-consistent. – It remains to show that $L \cup D_f{}^*$ is ϵ-consistent. Since L is finite, $D_f{}^*$ must be finite, too (for, each $D \in D_f{}^*$ corresponds uniquely to a law in L). So for some n, $D_f{}^* = D_{f,n}{}^*$; so $L \cup D^*$ is ϵ-consistent. Q.E.D.

We are finally able to prove that each F-extension of $<L,F>$ has the intended probabilistic justification via the L-extension $L \cup D_f$.

Theorem 5: For any F-extension E_f of $<L,F>$: $Aa \in E_f$ *iff* $<L \cup D_f, F> \vdash_\epsilon Aa$.
Proof: Again we may replace D_f by $D_f{}^*$ (lemma 3). *From left to right:* By lemma (3.1). *From right to left:* Assume $<L \cup D_f{}^*, F> \vdash_\epsilon Aa$, hence $L \cup D_f{}^* \vdash_\epsilon Fx \Rightarrow Ax$, and so $L \vdash_\epsilon Fx \Rightarrow (\wedge X \to Ax)$ for some (finite) set of consequents of default assumptions in $D_f{}^*$ (lemma 4). So $X[a]$ is in E_f (argued as for theorem 4), and $\wedge X[a] \to Aa$ is C_0 and thus also in E_f, whence Aa will be in E_f. Q.E.D.

Observe that in order to derive $Fx \Rightarrow Ax$ by the rules of ϵ-entailment, only the default assumptions in D_f are needed, but not the laws. So we obtain as a corollary from theorem 5:

Corollary 1: For any F-extension E_f of $<L,F>$: $Aa \in E_f$ *iff* $<D_f, F> \vdash_\epsilon Aa$.

Recall that every default assumption in D_f corresponds to a law used in the production of the extension, and that the conditional probability $p(Bx/Ax \wedge Fx)$ associated with a default assumption results from the conditional probability $p(Bx/Ax)$ associated with the corresponding default law $Ax \Rightarrow Bx$ plus the corresponding probabilistic irrelevancy assumptions saying that $p(Bx/Ax)$ is approximately equal $p(Bx/Ax \wedge Fx)$. If we combine theorem 5 and corollary 1 with theorem 1, the significance for nonextreme probability values in practical applications gets cashed out in the following corollary 2.

Corollary 2: If $\{1-\epsilon_1, ..., 1-\epsilon_n\}$ are nonextreme lower probability bounds associated with the laws *used* in the ϵ-proof of $A \in E_f$ from $<L,F>$, then $1-(\epsilon_1 + ... + \epsilon_n)$ is a lower bound of $p(Ax/Fx)$, which follows by probability theory from the conditional probabilities associated with these laws plus the corresponding probabilistic irrelevancy assumptions. (*Proof:* Th.s 1 and 5, Cor. 1).

It is not difficult to implement the content of corollary 2 into an expert system based on default laws. With hardly any computational effort this system would be able to tell the user, for each of its predictions, its exact lower probability bound following from default laws and irrelevancy assumptions. Herein I see the practical significance of this result.

3 Choosing a Single Extension: The Problem of Collective Defeat

The specificity rule is a basic tool for ordering conflicting laws (and their respective default assumptions) w.r.t. their plausibility [cf. 3, §5.4]. Given $L = \{Ax \Rightarrow Bx, Cx \Rightarrow \neg Bx, Cx \Rightarrow Ax\}$ and $\{Aa, Ca\} \subset F$ (F may contain further facts), then the default assumption $Cx \wedge Fx \Rightarrow \neg Bx$ is *preferred* over $Ax \wedge Fx \Rightarrow Bx$. This rule has its justification in the following *preservation principle* for irrelevance: Fx is considered as irrelevant for a default law $Ax \Rightarrow Bx$ *only* if every formula Cx inferrable from Fx via L [hence $<L,F> \vdash Ca$] can be considered as irrelevant for $Ax \Rightarrow Bx$, too – i.e., if for no such Cx, L ε–entails $Ax \wedge Cx \Rightarrow \neg Bx$. In the above example this is violated because L ε–entails $Ax \wedge Cx \Rightarrow \neg Bx$. One may conjecture that a *single* extension can be produced as follows: if two laws are in conflict and one is more specific than the other, we prefer the more specific one, *else* both laws are 'blocked'. Hence, if $L = \{Ax \Rightarrow Bx, Cx \Rightarrow \neg Bx\}$ and $\{Aa, Ca\} \subseteq F$ – as in the example (2), possibly with some further irrelevant facts – we derive nothing, since there is no priority between the conflicting laws. Is this enough to produce a single consistent extension?

The answer is *no*, because of the problem of *collective defeat* (so-called after Pollock [12]). Here, the consequents of *more than two* laws taken together are inconsistent, but no proper subset of them is inconsistent. Consider the following example:

(4) $L = \{A_1 x \Rightarrow B_1 x, A_2 \Rightarrow B_2 x, C_1 \Rightarrow D_1 x, C_2 \Rightarrow (D_1 x \rightarrow \neg(B_1 x \wedge B_2))\}$
   $F = \{A_1 a, A_2 a, C_1 a, C_2 a\}$.
   Illustration: A_1 = evidence for being married (B_1), A_2 = evidence for being a priest (B_2), C_1 = evidence for being catholic (D_1), C_2 = evidence that the person obeys the law

According to above proposal, the instantiated consequents of all four laws will be inferrable, but the result $\{B_1 a, B_2 a, D_1 a, D_1 a \rightarrow \neg(B_1 a \wedge B_2 a)\}$ is logically inconsistent. An (extreme) example of collective defeat is the lottery-paradox.

Like Pollock [12, p. 493] I think that in such a case none of the four consequents should be inferrable, because together they are inconsistent and there is no reason to prefer one of the four laws over another one. Of course, *if* there is such a reason, then the collective defeat is 'undercutted'. An axiomatization of default reasoning which produces a single extension and takes care of the problem of collective defeat is given in Schurz [17]. It is based on the axiomatization technique of Nute's default reasoning [10], which produces not only the formulas derivable from $<L,F>$ but simultaneously (in a separated list) all those which are not derivable (similar as PROLOG's negation-by-failure). Presupposing such an axiomatization, the definition is as follows. $C_\varepsilon(K)$ is again the starting point for deriving the single extension. A *collectively defeating* K-set is a set $\{A_i a | i \leq n\}$ of instantiated antecedents of laws $A_i x \Rightarrow B_i x$ in L such that the corresponding set of instantiated law consequents $\{B_i a | i \leq n\}$ is inconsistent with $C_\varepsilon(K)$, though no proper subset of $\{B_i a | i \leq n\}$ is inconsistent with $C_\varepsilon(K)$.

Definition 2: (2.1): Ba is *less specific* than Aa w.r.t. L iff $<L, \{Aa\}> \vdash Ba$.
(2.2): $K := <L,F> \vdash Ca$ *iff* (1) either $Ca \in C_\varepsilon(K)$ or (2) there exists $Dx \Rightarrow Cx \in L$ with $<L,F> \vdash Da$ *and* for each collectively defeating K-set $\{Da\} \cup \{A_i a | i \leq n\}$ it holds that *either* (2a) $K \nvdash A_i a$ for some $i \leq n$, *or* (2b) some element of $\{Da\} \cup \{A_i a | i \leq n\}$ is less specific w.r.t. L than another one, but Da is not less specific w.r.t. L than any other element in $\{A_i a | i \leq n\}$.

Hence, whenever $\langle L,F \rangle \vdash Aa$, $Ax \Rightarrow Bx \in L$ but Aa is member of a collectively defeating $\langle L,F \rangle$-set each of which members is $\langle L,F \rangle$-inferrable, then the inference of Ba is blocked except that the collective defeat is undercutted in the sense of clause 2b. Our final task is to give the probabilistic justification of the inference relation of def. 2. Assume a knowledge base $K := \langle L,F \rangle$, let $E_K := \{Aa| K \vdash A\}$ be its unique F-extension (according to def. 2) and D_K the corresponding L-extension of default assumptions generated during the derivation of E_K. We show that given L is ε-consistent, then $L \cup D_K$ will be ε-consistent (theorem 6), and $\langle L \cup D_K, F \rangle \vdash_\varepsilon Aa$ iff $Aa \in E_K$ will hold (theorem 7).

Theorem 6: Assume $K = \langle L,F \rangle$. If L is ε-consistent, then $L \cup D_K$ is ε-consistent.

Proof: We proceed be induction on the derivation of E_K (def. 2). $D_K = \{D_1,...,D_n\}$ is finite (cf. th. 4); assume $1,...,n$ is the ordering in which the D_i were generated. Let E_i be the set of all consequences derived before D_{i+1} was generated. By the ind. hyp., $L \cup D_i := \{D_1,...,D_i\}$ is ε-consistent; we have to show that $L \cup D_i \cup \{D_{i+1}\}$ is ε-consistent, with $D_{i+1} := Fx \wedge Ex \Rightarrow Gx$, $Ex \Rightarrow Gx \in L$ and $Ea \in E_i$. If not, then by lemma 1 (and because $Fx \wedge Ex \Rightarrow Gx$ is ε-equivalent in $L \cup D_i$ with $Fx \Rightarrow Gx$, lemma 3), $L \cup D_i \vdash_\varepsilon Fx \Rightarrow \neg Gx$; and so by lemma 4, $L \vdash_\varepsilon F \Rightarrow (\wedge X \rightarrow \neg Gx)$, for $X := \{B_1 x,...,B_m x\}$ a (finite) set of consequents of default assumptions in D_i. Each $B_i a$ is in E_i, and so by def. 2 there must be laws $A_i x \Rightarrow B_i x$ in L and $A_i a$ must be in E_i for each $i \leq n$. But then, $\{A_i a| i \leq m\} \cup \{Ea\}$ is a collectively defeating set, since $\{B_i a| i \leq m\} \cup \{Ga\}$ is inconsistent with $\wedge X[a] \rightarrow \neg Ga$, which is in $C_\varepsilon(K)$ (and we choose X so that no subset of $\{B_i a| i \leq m\} \cup \{Ga\}$ is inconsistent with $\wedge X[a] \rightarrow \neg Ga$). Since all elements of $\{B_i a| i \leq m\}$ are in E_i, it must hold according to clause (2b) of def. 2 that some element of $\{A_i a| i \leq m\} \cup \{Ea\}$ is less specific (than some other one), though no element of $\{A_i a| i \leq m\}$ is less specific. Hence Ea must be the element of $\{A_i a| i \leq m\} \cup \{Ea\}$ which is less specific, and thus, by clause (2b) of def. 2, Ga is not inferrable and D_{i+1} is not generated, contradicting the assumption. Q.E.D.

Theorem 7: $Aa \in E_K$ iff $\langle L \cup D_K, F \rangle \vdash_\varepsilon Fx \Rightarrow Ax$ iff $\langle D_K, F \rangle \vdash_\varepsilon Fx \Rightarrow Ax$
Proof: As for theorem 5 and corollary 1.

As an important corollary (corollary 3), we obtain the consistency guarantee for E_K – which, in distinction to the previous def. 1*, is not obvious from the def. 2. Corollay 2 about nonextreme probability values holds as before.

Corollary 3: E is logically consistent. – *Proof:* By theorems 6 and 7.

References

1. E. W. Adams: The Logic of Conditionals. Dordrecht: Reidel 1975.
2. F. Bacchus et al: Statistical Foundations for Default Reasoning. In: Proc.13th IJCAI 1993, Vol I, pp. 563-569.
3. G. Brewka: Nonmonotonic Reasoning. Logical Foundations of Commonsense. Cambridge: Cambridge University Press.

4. R. Carnap: Logical Foundations of Probability. 2nd ed. Chicago: Univ. of Chicago Press 1962.

5. J.P. Delgrande: An Approach to Default Reasoning Based on a First-Order Conditional Logic: Revised Report. Artificial Intelligence 36, 63 - 90 (1988).

6. H. Geffner/J. Pearl: A Framework for Reasoning with Defaults. In: H.E. Kyburg et al (eds.): Knowledge Representation and Defeasible Reasoning. The Netherlands: Kluwer 1990, pp. 69-87.

7. M. Goldszmidt et al: A Maximum Entropy Approach to Nonmonotonic Reasoning. In: Proc. Nat. Conf. on AI (AAAI-90) 1990, pp. 646-652.

8. S. Kraus, D. Lehmann and M. Magodor: Nonmonotonic Reasoning, Preferential Models and Cumulative Logics. Artificial Intelligence 44, 167 - 207 (1990).

9. D. McDermott/J. Doyle: Non-Monotonic Logic I. Artificial Intelligence 13, 41-72 (1980).

10. D. Nute: Basic Defeasible Logic. In: L. Farinas del Carro/M. Pentonnen (eds.): Intentional Logics for Programming. Oxford: Oxford University Press 1992, pp. 125 - 154.

11. J. Pearl: Probabilistic Reasoning in Intelligent Systems. Santa Mateo: Morgan Kaufmann 1988.

12. J. L. Pollock: Defeasible Reasoning. Cognitive Science 11, 481-518 (1987).

13. D. Poole: A Logical Framework for Default Reasoning. Artificial Intelligence 36, 27-47 (1988).

14. D. Poole: The Effect of Knowledge on Belief: Conditioning, Specifity and the Lottery Paradox in Default Reasoning. Artificial Intelligence 49, 281-307 (1991).

15. R. Reiter: A Logic for Default Reasoning. Artificial Intelligence 13, 81-132 (1980).

16. G. Schurz: Erklärungsmodelle in der Wissenschaftstheorie und in der Künstlichen Intelligenz. In: H. Stoyan (ed.): Erklärung im Gespräch - Erklärung im Mensch-Maschine-Dialog.Informatik Fachberichte 310, Berlin: Springer 1992, pp. 1-42.

17. G. Schurz: Defeasible Reasoning Based on Constructive and Cumulative Rules. In: R. Casati/B. Smith/G. White (eds.): Philosophy and the Cognitive Sciences. Vienna: Hölder-Pichler-Tempsky 1994.

A Prioritized Contextual Default Logic: Curing Anomalous Extensions with a Simple Abnormality Default Theory

Gerson Zaverucha

COPPE, Universidade Federal do Rio de Janeiro
Programa de Engenharia de Sistemas e Computação
Caixa Postal 68511
211945-970 Rio de Janeiro, Brazil
E-mail: gerson@cos.ufrj.br

Abstract. In Reiter's Default Logic (DL), semi-normal defaults are needed to give priorities to defaults to eliminate anomalous extensions. However, Morris' example with the same pattern of the Yale Shooting Problem has demonstrated that the use in DL of McCarthy's simple abnormality formalism with semi-normal default rules (henceforth called a simple abnormality default theory) still gives rise to an anomalous extension. In this paper, we present a modified version of DL called Prioritized Contextual Default Logic (PCtDL). In this logic a context is used to give priority to a default deriving another default's exception condition and therefore the non-normal part of the justification of a semi-normal default rule is treated differently from its normal part. PCtDL eliminates the possibility of anomalous extensions in both problems without however sacrificing the use of the simple abnormality theory. We also give some basic properties of PCtDL (like joint consistency) and present a possible worlds semantics, with respect to which it is shown to be sound and complete. In some ways, our result is akin to McCarthy's Prioritized Circumscription (although in the YSP other forms of circumscription were used to solve it, like Lifschitz's Pointwise Circumscription). Likewise, the preference criterion used in Brewka's Cumulative Default Logic (with filters), CDL_F, albeit similar to ours, still results in an anomalous extension when applied to the aforementioned problems.

1 Introduction

Reiter's Default Logic (DL) [34] is one of the most widely used and investigated formalisms for default reasoning. Several variants of DL have been proposed in the literature to deal with some counterintuitive feature: Lukaszewicz's Justified Default Logic (JDL) [18], Brewka's Cumulative Default Logic (CDL) [6] and Schaub's (and also Delgrande's [9]) Constrained Default Logic (CoDL) [36].

Besnard and Schaub [3] developed Contextual Default Logic (CtDL), a unifying framework for default logics which extends the notion of a default rule and supplies each extension with a context. The intuitive idea of a context is basically the set of assumptions made to build an extension. They have shown that all the aforementioned logics can be embedded in CtDL and that they mainly differ in the way they deal with an implicit (as in DL) or an explicit (as in JDL and CoDL) underlying context.

An adequate treatment of priorities is a central issue in nonmonotonic reasoning. Reiter and Criscuolo [32] argued for the use of semi-normal defaults in DL to give priorities between defaults to eliminate anomalous extensions. To obtain the appropriate semi-normal default theory is part of the task of getting an adequate axiomatization of the problem in DL.

McCarthy [22] suggested, using Circumscription (see [17]), that it would be nice to have a fixed circumscription policy of minimizing the abnormality predicates with all other predicates as variables. So the general facts would include the abnormality predicates while the specific facts would not involve them. McCarthy called such a theory, *a simple abnormality theory*. Although this formalization was simple and intuitive, unfortunately McCarthy has shown that it was too weak because of conflicts in the minimization and therefore developed Prioritized Circumscription.

Morris [23] presented an example, where time played no role, which had the same pattern of the well-known Yale Shooting Problem [15]. He showed that their formalization in DL using a simple abnormality theory with semi-normal default rules (henceforth called a *simple abnormality default theory*), still gave rise to an anomalous extension. Pequeno [26] pointed out that the reason for such anomalous behavior was that DL treats the exception condition contained in the non-normal part of the justification of a semi-normal default rule in the same way it treats the normal part. As a matter of fact, the notation using conjunction to link them makes it impossible to distinguish the different roles they play. To deal with this problem, Pequeno developed the logic Inconsistent Default Logic (IDL) having as a base logic a paraconsistent logic LEI [25, 26].

Marek and Truszczynski [20, theorem 3.2] have shown that any DL theory can be represented as a semi-normal default theory. Since Morris has shown, in both problems, that the anomalous extension could be eliminated using non-normal defaults, we can use Marek and Truszczynski translation and convert Morris' non-normal default theory into a semi-normal default theory. But this is achieved sacrificing the simple abnormality theory, by extending the underlying language and by introducing new default rules. Marek and Truszczynski have pointed out that the new semi-normal DL theory may be much larger than the original one.

In this paper, we present a modified version of DL called Prioritized Contextual Default Logic (PCtDL), where a context is used to give priority to a default deriving another default's exception condition. As in IDL, the non-normal part of the justification of a semi-normal default rule is treated differently from its normal part, but it still keeps classical logic as its base logic. PCtDL eliminates the possibility of anomalous extensions in both aforementioned problems without however sacrificing the use of the simple abnormality theory.

We also give some basic properties of PCtDL (like joint consistency) and present a possible worlds semantics, with respect to which it is shown to be sound and complete. Besnard and Schaub [2] developed a uniform semantical framework in terms of Kripke structures, which was used to compare the existing default logics. Our semantics is based on their framework and similarly, PCtDL can be compared to the various default logics.

In some ways, our result is akin to McCarthy's Prioritized Circumscription (although in the YSP other forms of circumscription were used to solve it, like Lifschitz's Pointwise Circumscription). Likewise, a similar prioritization seems to be intended by Brewka in [6]. Although computationally attractive, Brewka has pointed out that semi-monotonicity destroys part of the additional expressiveness of semi-normal defaults. DL and IDL, are not semi-monotonic but CDL, JDL, CoDL and also Theorist are all semi-monotonic (see [35]). Brewka presented an example where it is crucial that the logic is not semi-monotonic. To deal with that example, he developed CDL$_F$ modifying CDL by adding filters on extensions keeping the ones which were *priority preserving*. This notion is closely associated with the priority in PCtDL " ... we have to treat consequents and justifications differently: if there is a default *d* inapplicable with respect to an extension E, but only because its consequent contradicts the justifications of applied defaults, then we know that this default should have been applied and simply reject E." (pp. 195). But when CDL$_F$ is applied to the aforementioned problems it still gives rise to an anomalous extension.

In the next section, we briefly review DL and apply it to some examples presented in the literature that shows some of its problems. In section 3, we first introduce McCarthy's simple abnormality formalism through some examples using Circumscription and its translation in DL, the simple abnormality default theory; then we present Morris's example (and the YSP) and its solution using Marek and Truszczynski's translation. In section 4 we define PCtDL, give some basic properties and see how it deals with the examples of the previous sections. In section 5 we briefly review Besnard and Schaub's possible worlds semantics for DL, then we present a possible worlds semantics for PCtDL and show its soundness and completeness theorem. Finally in section 6 we give some conclusions and point out some future work.

2 Background

We will briefly introduce Reiter's Default Logic (DL) [34] (see [4, 7, 11, 18, 19, 28 and 35] for a thorough discussion), one of the most widely used nonmonotonic formalisms, which augments classical logic with default rules .

Definition 2.1 A *default* is any expression of the form: $A: B_1 ,..., B_k / C$

where A, the *pre-requisite*, $B_1 ,...., B_k$, the *justifications*, and C, the *consequent*, are first-order formulae. A default is called *open* iff at least one of its constituents formula contains a free-variable; otherwise, it is called *closed*. ♦

Definition 2.2 A *default theory* is a pair (W, D), where W is a set of first-order sentences, called *facts*, and D is a set of defaults. A default theory is said to be *open* iff it contains at least one open default; otherwise, it is said to be *closed*. ♦

Definition 2.3 A default rule is *normal* if is of the form A : B / B; a default theory is *normal* iff all of its defaults are normal. A default rule is *semi-normal* if it is of the form $A : B \wedge C / C$; similarly, a default theory is *semi-normal* iff all of its defaults are semi-normal. ♦

Default rules induce extensions of an initial set of facts.

Definition 2.4 Let T = (W, D) be a closed default theory over a first-order language L. For any set of sentences $S \subseteq L$, let $\Gamma(S)$ be the smallest sets of sentences from L satisfying the following properties:

(1) $W \subseteq \Gamma(S)$,

(2) $\Gamma(S)$ is deductively closed, i.e., $Th(\Gamma(S)) = \Gamma(S)$,

(3) for any A: B_1, ..., $B_k / C \in D$, if $A \in \Gamma(S)$, and $\neg B_1 \notin S$,..., $\neg B_k \notin S$, then $C \in \Gamma(S)$.

A set of sentences $E \subseteq L$ is an *extension* of T iff $\Gamma(E) = E$. ♦

Theorem 2.1 If T = <W, D> is a closed default theory, then a set E of sentences is an extension of T iff $E = U_{i=0}^{\infty} E_i$, where

$E_0 = W$, and for i ≥ 0

$E_{i+1} = Th(E_i) \cup \{C \mid (A : B_1, ..., B_k / C) \in D$, where $E_i \vdash A$ and $\neg B_1 \notin E,..., \neg B_k \notin E\}$

Normal default theories have many properties, among them:

Theorem 2.2 (Existence of extensions) Every closed normal default theory has an extension.

Theorem 2.3 (Semi-monotonicity) Let D and D_1 be sets of closed-normal defaults such that $D_1 \subseteq D$. Let E_1 be an extension of $T_1 = (W, D_1)$ and suppose that $T = (W, D)$. Then T has an extension E such that $E_1 \subseteq E$.

Some problems of DL have been pointed out in the literature. For example, Poole [29] argued for the "commitment to assumptions", that is the joint consistency of an extension with the justifications of all applying default rules.

Example 2.1 Joint consistency (Poole's Broken-arms example [29])

: Usable(x) $\wedge$ ¬Broken(x) / Usable(x)

Broken (Leftarm) $\vee$ Broken(Rightarm)

There is only one extension with Usable(Leftarm) and Usable(Rightarm) although it was assumed ¬Broken (Leftarm) and ¬Broken(Rightarm) and it is a fact that one of them is Broken. ♦

Another problem, pointed out by Makinson [21], is that DL is not cumulative (see [10]). Intuitively cumulativity [13] says that adding a theorem to a set of premises does not change the derivable formulas.

Example 2.2 Cumulativity (Makinson's example [21])

: P / P

P ∨ Q: ¬P / ¬P

From these defaults (W = { }) we get the single extension Th({P}). This extension contains P ∨ Q; but adding it to the premises give rise to an additional extension Th({¬P, Q}) where P is not inferred. ♦

To deal with the two aforementioned examples Brewka [6] developed Cumulative Default Logic (CDL).

Although normal defaults have many nice properties, unfortunately they are not sufficient for practical applications. As shown by Reiter and Criscuolo [33], semi-normal defaults are needed to give priorities between defaults to eliminate anomalous extensions. Although a general semi-normal default theory may not have an extension, *plain ordered* (see [1, 11, 4]) theories always have an extension. Reiter's semi-normal default theory also lack the semi-monotonicity property but, although computationally it is a very desirable property, it destroys the additional expressiveness of semi-normal defaults.

Example 2.3 (Brewka [6])

1) Student: ¬Married / ¬Married
2) Adult: Married ∧ ¬Student / Married
3) Beard: Student / Student
4) Beard: Adult / Adult
5) Beard

There is only one extension, as expected, E = Th({Beard, Student,¬Married}). From (5) and (4) we have (6) Adult; from (5) and (3) we have (7) Student, which blocks (2). From (7) and (1) we get (8) ¬Marrried. The exception condition to (2), (7) Student, is derived by default. If we apply the rules in a different order we still get the same extension. From (5) and (4) we get (6). Applying (2) we get (temporarily) (9) Married; but (3) is still applicable and so we get (7), which blocks the application of (2). As Brewka [5, pp.195] has pointed out *it is crucial* that (3) overrides the semi-normal default (2) and not vice-versa, i.e., *that the logic is not semi-monotonic.* From (7) and (1) we get (8) ¬Marrried. ♦

Since CDL is also semi-monotonic, to deal with the above example Brewka developed CDL_F modifying CDL by adding filters on extensions keeping the ones which were *priority preserving.*

Definition 2.5 (Brewka [6, pp.195]) Let E be a CDL extension of (W, D). E is called *priority preserving* if for no A: B / C ∈ D\GD(E): A ∈ Form(E), {B, C} ∪ Form(E) is consistent, and {C} ∪ Form(E) ∪ Supp(E) is inconsistent.

3 A Simple Abnormality Default Theory

McCarthy [22] suggested, using Circumscription, that it would be nice to have a fixed circumscription policy of minimizing the abnormality predicates with all other predicates as variables. So the general facts would include the abnormality predicates while the specific facts wouldn't involve them. He called such a theory, *a simple abnormality theory.* Unfortunately he has shown that this was not enough because of conflicts in the minimization.

Example 3.1

1) Bird(x) ∧ ¬Ab1(x) → Fly(x)
2) Bird(Tweety)

3) Penguin(x) → Bird(x)
4) Penguin(x) ∧ ¬Ab2(x) → ¬ Fly(x)
5) Penguin(Sam)

Applying the above circumscription policy, we are not able to infer ¬Fly(Sam) nor Fly(Sam), only their disjunction. Notice that because of (3) a penguim inherit all the properties of birds and that is the reason for getting the above disjunction.

Translating to DL:

1) Bird(x): Fly(x) ∧ ¬Ab1(x) / Fly(x)
2) Bird(Tweety)
3) Penguin(x) → Bird(x)
4) Penguin(x):¬ Fly(x) ∧ ¬Ab2(x) / ¬ Fly(x)
5) Penguin(Sam)

We get two extensions: from (5) and (3), we have Penguin(Sam) and together with (1), we have Fly(Sam); the other extension, from (5) and (4), we have ¬Fly(Sam). To prevent the inheritance of flying we explicitly state:

6) Penguin(x)→ Ab1(x), called by McCarthy a *cancellation of inheritance axiom*.

So now Circumscription gives only the intuitive answer ¬Fly(Sam), and in DL the anomalous extension is eliminated.   ◆

Example 3.2 McCarthy [22]:

1) ¬ Ab1(x) → ¬ Fly(x)
2) Bird(x) → Ab1(x)
3) Bird(x) ∧ ¬Ab2(x) → Fly(x)
4) Canary(x) ∧ ¬Ab3(x) → Bird(x)
5) Canary(Tweety)

McCarthy argues that (4) allows the possibility that "canary" be used in the sense of old-gangster movies. Its intent is that canary inherit all bird's properties unless it's Ab3. Since we are going to minimize the Ab predicates, it is expected that canary inherit the property of flying and thus Fly(Tweety). Unfortunately, applying the same circumscription policy the question is left undecided because Tweety can either be Ab1 or Ab3: together axioms (4) and (2) imply (6) Canary(x) → Ab1(x) ∨ Ab3(x). In example 3.1 a similar situation happened, but there we wanted to prevent inheritance while the objective here is to inherit. McCarthy's solution was to develop Prioritized Circumscription.

Translating to DL, we have *the simple abnormality default theory*:

1) : ¬ Fly(x) ∧ ¬ Ab1(x) / ¬ Fly(x)
2) Bird(x) → Ab1(x)
3) Bird(x): Fly(x) ∧ ¬Ab2(x) / Fly(x)
4) Canary(x): Bird(x) ∧ ¬Ab3(x) / Bird(x)
5) Canary(Tweety)

We have only one extension: from (5) and (4), we have Bird(Tweety) and with (3) we have Fly(Tweety) which together with (2), we have Ab1(Tweety). If we apply (1) first, we can still apply (4) and with (2) we have Ab1(Tweety), which blocks (1).   ◆

Therefore DL solves the above problem, but Morris gave the following example.

Example 3.3 (Morris [23])

1) Animal(x): ¬Fly(x) ∧ ¬Ab1(x) / ¬Fly(x)
2) Wing(x) → Ab1(x)
3) Wing(x) → Fly(x)
4) Bird(x) → Animal(x)
5) Bird(x) : Wing(x) ∧ ¬Ab2(x) / Wing(x)
6) Bird(Tweety)

The intuitive extension: from (6) and (5), we have Wing(Tweety) and with (2) we have Ab1(Tweety), which blocks the applicability of (1), and with (3) we have Fly(Tweety). The exception condition to (1), Wing(Tweety), is derived by default.

From (6) and (4), we have Animal(Tweety). Applying (1), we have ¬Fly(Tweety) and from the contrapositive of (3), we have ¬Wing(Tweety). This blocks the application of (5). Therefore there is an anomalous extension where Tweety is a wingless bird.   ♦

We point out that even CDL_F cannot deal with the above problem (and also with the next one). The anomalous extensions is also priority preserving (see Definition 2.5), since default (5) ∈ (D \ GD(E)) but it violates the condition (({B, C} ∪ Form(E)) is consistent for {Wing(Tweety), ¬Ab2(Tweety)} ∪ Th({Bird(Tweety), Animal(Tweety), ¬Wing(Tweety), ¬Fly(Tweety)}) is inconsistent.

Example 3.4 Yale Shooting Problem [15] (see Morris[23])

1) Holds(Alive, S_0)
2) Holds(Loaded, res(Load, s))
3) Holds(Loaded, s) → ¬Holds(Alive, res(Shoot, s))
4) Holds(Loaded, s) → Ab(Alive, Shoot, s)
5) Holds(f, s): Holds(f, res(e, s)) ∧ ¬Ab(f, e, s) / Holds(f, res(e, s))
S_1 = res(Load, S_0), S_2 = res(Wait, S_1), S_3 = res(Shoot, S_2)

For convenience, we instantiate some facts and defaults:

(2') Holds(Loaded, S_1)
(3') Holds(Loaded, S_2) → ¬Holds(Alive, res(Shoot, S_2))
(4')Holds(Loaded, S_2) → Ab(Alive, Shoot, S_2)
(5') Holds(Loaded, S_1): Holds(Loaded, S_2) ∧ ¬Ab(Loaded, Wait, S_1) / Holds(Loaded, S_2)
(5") Holds(Alive, S_2): Holds(Alive, S_3) ∧ ¬Ab(Alive, Shoot, S_2) / Holds(Alive, S_3)

The intuitive extension arises from (1) by applying (5) we have (6) Holds(Alive, res(Load, S_0)). From (2) we have (2') Holds(Loaded, res(Load, S_0)) and applying (5') we have (7) Holds(Loaded, res(Wait, S_1)) and from (6) and (5) we have (8) Holds(Alive, res(Wait, S_1)). From (7) and (4') we have (9) Ab (Alive, Shoot, res(Wait, S_1)), which blocks the applicability of (5") , and from (7) and (3') we have (10) ¬Holds(Alive, res(Shoot,res(Wait, S_1)). The exception condition to (5"), (7) Holds(Loaded, res(Wait, S_1)), is derived by default.

The anomalous extension: we similarly also get (6) and (2'). Now from (6) applying (5) we also get (8); from (8) and (5") we get (11) Holds(Alive, S_3). From (11) and (3') by contraposition we get (12) ¬Holds(Loaded,res(Wait, S_1)). So the gun gets mysteriously unloaded while waiting! So now (5') is no longer applicable!   ♦

Remark 3.1 a) the examples 3.3 and 3.4, as Morris has shown have the same pattern; b) the examples 2.3, 3.3 and 3.4 above, all have a similar problem: the exception condition to a default is derived by default.

Morris has shown that examples 3.3 and 3.4 could be solved using non-normal defaults.

Example 3.3 revisited

1) Animal(x): ¬Ab1(x) / ¬Fly(x)
2) Wing(x) → Ab1(x)
3) Wing(x) → Fly(x)
4) Bird(x) → Animal(x)
5) Bird(x) : ¬Ab2(x) / Wing(x)
6) Bird(Tweety)

The anomalous extension is eliminated (now, ¬Wing(Tweety) does not block the application of (5)).

Marek and Truszczynski [20, theorem 3.2] have shown that any DL theory can be represented as a semi-normal default theory. But this is achieved by extending the underlying language and the introduction of new default rules. They have pointed out that the new semi-normal DL theory may be much larger than the original one. Using their technique, where C_1 and C_2 are new constants introduced in the language:

1) $Animal(x): \neg Ab1(x) \wedge C_1 / C_1$

2) $Wing(x) \rightarrow Ab1(x)$
3) $Wing(x) \rightarrow Fly(x)$
4) $Bird(x) \rightarrow Animal(x)$
5) $Bird(x): \neg Ab2(x) \wedge C_2 / C_2$
6) $Bird(Tweety)$
7) $C_1: / \neg Fly(x)$
8) $C_1: / Wing(x)$ ◆

We argue that this axiomatization is very unnatural and we will show in the next section that is possible to keep the simple abnormality theory and still eliminate the anomalous extension.

4 A Prioritized Contextual Default Logic

In this section, we present a modified version of DL called Prioritized Contextual Default Logic (PCtDL). In this logic a context is used to give priority to a default deriving another default's exception condition and therefore the non-normal part of the justification of a semi-normal default rule is treated differently from its normal part. We also give some basic properties of PCtDL (like joint consistency) and see how it deals with the examples of the previous sections.

The general PCtDL default rule is of the form: $\alpha: \beta \mid \gamma / \beta$. A PCtDL theory is a pair (W, D), where W is a set of formulas and D is a set of PCtDL default rules.

Definition 4.1 Let (W, D) be a closed PCtDL theory. For any pair of sets of sentences (S,T), let $\Gamma(S, T)$ be the pair of smallest sets of sentences (S', T') such that
(1) $W \subseteq S'$;
(2) S' is deductively closed, i.e., Th(S') = S';
(3) for any $\alpha: \beta \mid \gamma / \beta \in D$, if $\alpha \in S'$, ($\neg\beta \notin S$ or ($\neg\beta \notin Th(W)$ and $W \cup \{\beta\} \vdash \neg t_i$ for
some $t_i \in T$)) and $S \cup T \nvdash \neg\gamma$ then $\beta \in S'$ and $\gamma \in T$.
A pair of sets of sentences (E, C) is a prioritized contextual extension of (W, D) iff $\Gamma(E, C) = (E, C)$. E is the extension and C is its context.   ◆

Remark 4.1 a) Notice that in an extension the condition in italic is never satisfied since it is incompatible with the condition $S \cup T \nvdash \neg\gamma$, for $t_i = \gamma$; b) C is connected with the set of assumptions (justifications) J in Lukaszewicz's Default Logic [17]. ◆

We now give some basic properties of PCtDL.

As in DL, a more intuitive characterization of an extension is obtained.

Theorem 4.1 If (W, D) is a closed PCtDL default theory and E and C be sets of sentences, then a set (E, C) of sentences is a prioritized contextual extension of (W, D) iff

$(E, C) = (\bigcup_{i=0}^{\infty} E_i, \bigcup_{i=0}^{\infty} C_i)$, where

$E_0 = W$ and $C_0 = \{ \}$, and for $i \geq 0$

$E_{i+1} = Th(E_i) \cup \{\beta \mid \alpha: \beta \mid \gamma / \beta \in D$, where $E_i \vdash \alpha$ and ($\neg\beta \notin E$ or ($\neg\beta \notin Th(W)$ and
$W \cup \{\beta\} \vdash \neg t_i$ for some $t_i \in C_i$) and $E \cup C \nvdash \neg\gamma\}$

$C_{i+1} = C_i \cup \{\gamma \mid \alpha: \beta \mid \gamma / \beta \in D$, where $E_i \vdash \alpha$ and ($\neg\beta \notin E$ or ($\neg\beta \notin Th(W)$ and
$W \cup \{\beta\} \vdash \neg t_i$ for some $t_i \in C_i$) and $E \cup C \nvdash \neg\gamma\}$ ◆

Corollary 4.2 A closed PCtDL default theory (W, D) has an extension (E, C) where E is inconsistent iff W is inconsistent. ◆

Corollary 4.3 If a closed PCtDL default theory (W, D) has an extension (E, C) where E is inconsistent then this is its only extension. ◆

Corollary 4.4 If a closed PCtDL default theory (W, D) has an extension (E, C) where E is inconsistent then C is the empty set. ♦

We can characterize PCtDL extensions by means of their generating default rules.

Definition 4.2 Let (E, C) be a PCtDL extension of $T = (W, D)$. The set of generating default rules for (E, C) wrt T is defined as

$$GD(E, T) = \{\alpha : \beta \mid \gamma / \beta \in D \mid \alpha \in E, E \cup C \nvdash \neg\beta \text{ and } E \cup C \nvdash \neg\gamma\}.$$

The set $\text{Justifg}(GD(E, T)) = \{\gamma \mid \alpha : \beta \mid \gamma / \beta \in GD(E, T)\}$ and

$\text{Conseq}(GD(E, T)) = \{\beta \mid \alpha : \beta \mid \gamma / \beta \in GD(E, T)\}$. ♦

Theorem 4.2 Let (E, C) be a PCtDL extension of $T = (W, D)$. We have
  $E = \text{Th}(W \cup \text{Conseq}(GD(E, T)))$,
  $C = \text{Justifg}(GD(E, T))$. ♦

Theorem 4.3 (Groundedness) Let (E, C) be a PCtDL extension of $T = (W, D)$. Then there exists an enumeration $<d_i>i \in I$ (integers) of $GD(E, T)$ such that for $i \in I$

$$W \cup \text{Conseq}(\{d_0, ..., d_{i-1}\}) \vdash \text{Prereq}(d_i). \quad ♦$$

One important property which holds in DL only for normal theories is the orthogonality of extensions: two different extensions are always contradictory to each other. In PCtDL we have

Theorem 4.4 (Weak Orthogonality) Let $T = (W, D)$ be a PCtDL default theory. If (E, C) and (E', C') are distinct PCtDL extensions of T, then $(E \cup C) \cup (E' \cup C')$ is inconsistent. ♦

Theorem 4.5 Let $T = (W, D)$ be a normal default theory and E a set of sentences. Then E is a DL extension of T iff $(E, \varnothing)$ is a PCtDL extension of T. ♦

Remark 4.2 Neither every PCtDL extension is a DL extension since DL does not have the joint consistency property nor every DL extension is a PCtDL extension since the extension may not be a prioritized one and also PCtDL has the joint consistency property. ♦

We now apply PCtDL to the examples of the previous sections.

Example 2.3 revisited

1) Student: ¬Married / ¬Married
2) Adult: Married | ¬Student / Married
3) Beard: Student / Student
4) Beard: Adult / Adult
5) Beard

There is only one extension, as expected, $(E = \text{Th}(\text{Beard, Student,}\neg\text{Married}), C = \{ \})$. From (5) and (4) we have (6) Adult; from (5) and (3) we have (7) Student, which blocks (2). From (7) and (1), we get (8) ¬Marrried. If we apply the rules in a different order we still get the same extension. From (5) and (4) we get (6). Applying (2) we get (temporarily) (9) Married; but (3) is still applicable and so we get (7), which blocks the application of (2). We also could have formalized this example using a simple abnormality theory (obtaining similar results). ♦

Example 3.3 revisited

1) Animal(x): ¬Fly(x) | ¬Ab1(x) / ¬Fly(x)
2) Wing(x) → Ab1(x)
3) Wing(x) → Fly(x)
4) Bird(x) → Animal(x)
5) Bird(x) : Wing(x) | ¬Ab2(x) / Wing(x)
6) Bird(Tweety)

From (6) and (4), we have Animal(Tweety). Applying (1), we have ¬Fly(Tweety) and from the contrapositive of (3), we have ¬Wing(Tweety). Now, this does not block the application of (5) for ¬Wing(Tweety) ∉ Th ({(2)-(4), (6)}) and {(2)-(4), (6)} ∪ {Wing(Tweety)} ⊢ Ab1(Tweety). Therefore we have Wing(Tweety) and with (2), we have Ab1(Tweety) which blocks the application of (1). Therefore the anomalous extension is eliminated. ♦

Example 3.4 revisited

1) Holds(Alive, S_0)
2) Holds(Loaded, res(Load, s))
3) Holds(Loaded, s) → ¬Holds(Alive, res(Shoot, s))
4) Holds(Loaded, s) → Ab(Alive, Shoot, s)
5) Holds(f, s): Holds(f, res(e, s)) ∧ ¬Ab(f, e, s) / Holds(f, res(e, s))
S_1 = res(Load, S_0), S_2 = res(Wait, S_1), S_3 = res(Shoot, S_2)

For convenience, we instantiate some facts and defaults:

(2') Holds(Loaded, S_1)
(3') Holds(Loaded, S_2) → ¬Holds(Alive, res(Shoot, S_2))
(4')Holds(Loaded, S_2) → Ab(Alive, Shoot, S_2)
(5') Holds(Loaded, S_1): Holds(Loaded, S_2) ∧ ¬Ab(Loaded, Wait, S_1) / Holds(Loaded, S_2)
(5") Holds(Alive, S_2): Holds(Alive, S_3) ∧ ¬Ab(Alive, Shoot, S_2) / Holds(Alive, S_3)

From (1) by applying (5), we have (6) Holds(Alive, res(Load, S_0)). From (2) we have (2') Holds(Loaded, res(Load, S_0)). From (6) applying (5) we get (8)Holds(Alive, res(Wait, S_1)); from (8) and (5") we get (11) Holds(Alive, S_3). From (11) and (3'), by contraposition, we get (12) ¬Holds(Loaded,res(Wait, S_1)). But now (5') is applicable, for ¬Holds(Loaded,res(Wait, S_1)) ∉ Th ({(1)-(4)}) and {(1)-(4)} ∪ {Holds(Loaded,res(Wait, S_1)) } ⊢ Ab(Alive, Shoot, S_2). Therefore, we have (7) Holds(Loaded, res(Wait, S_1)) and with (4') we have (9) Ab (Alive, Shoot, res(Wait, S_1)), which blocks the applicability of (5"). From (6) and (5), we have (8) Holds(Alive, res(Wait, S_1)). From (7) and (3'), we have (10) ¬Holds(Alive, res(Shoot,res(Wait, S_1)). Therefore the anomalous extension is eliminated. ♦

Example 2.1 revisited

    : Usable(x) | ¬Broken(x) / Usable(x)
Broken (Leftarm) ∨ Broken(Rightarm)

Now there are two extensions: one with Usable(Leftarm) and assuming ¬Broken (Leftarm), which together with the fact derive Broken(Rightarm) which blocks the applicability of the default for Usable(Rightarm); similarly, we have the other extension with Usable(Rightarm) and assuming ¬Broken(Rightarm), which together with the fact derive Broken (Leftarm) which blocks the applicability of the default for Usable(Leftarm). We also could have formalized this example using a simple abnormality theory (obtaining similar results). ♦

5   A Possible Worlds Semantics

We first briefly review Besnard and Schaub's possible worlds semantics for DL, then in section 5.2 present a possible worlds semantics for PCtDL and show its soundness and completeness theorem.

5.1   Besnard and Schaub's Possible Worlds Semantics

Besnard and Schaub [2] developed a uniform semantical framework in terms of Kripke structures, which was used to compare the existing default logics. We present their semantics for DL.

We use m to denote Kripke structures (henceforth called K-models), M to denote classes of K-models, and to denote the modal logic K entailment relation.

Definition 5.1 Let d = α : β / γ. Let M and N be distict classes of K-models. We define M >$_d$ N iff M = {m ∈ N | m ⊨ γ ∧ □γ ∧ ◇β} and (1) N ⊨ α and (2) N ⊭ □¬β ♦

Definition 5.2 Given a set of default rules D, the strict partial order >$_D$ amounts to the union of the strict partial orders >$_d$ as follows. M >$_D$ N iff there exists an enumeration

$<d_i>i \in I$ of some $D' \subseteq D$ such that $M_{i+1} >_{di} M_i$ for some sequence $<M_i>i \in I$ of subclasses

of N satisfying $N = M_0$ and $M = \bigcap_{i \in I} M_i$. ◆

Definition 5.3 We define the class of K-models associated with W as

$M_W = \{m \mid m \vDash \gamma \land \Box\gamma, \gamma \in W\}$ and refer to $>_D$-maximal classes above M_W as the *preferred* classes of K-models wrt (W, D). ◆

Although DL does not employ explicitly a context (or constraints), we can define

Definition 5.4 The context C with respect to a set of formulas E is defined as $C_E = \{\beta \mid \alpha : \beta / \gamma \in D, \alpha \in E, \neg\beta \notin E\}$. ◆

Theorem 5.1 (Soundness and Completeness) Let (W, D) be a default theory. Let M be a class of K-models and E be a deductively closed set of formulas such that

$$M = \{m \mid m \vDash E \land \Box E \land \Diamond C_E\}.$$

Then, E is a consistent extension of (W, D) iff M is a $>_D$-maximal non-empty class above M_W. ◆

5.2 A Possible Worlds Semantics For PCtDL

Similarly to definition 5.1 we define,

Definition 5.1 Let $d = \alpha : \beta \mid \gamma / \beta$ and C_i be a set of formulas. Let M and N be distict classes of K-models. We define $M >_d N$ iff $M = \{m \in N \mid m \vDash \beta \land \Box\beta \land \Box\gamma\}$ and

(1) $N \vDash \alpha$ and

(2) $(N \nvDash \Box\neg\beta$ or $(M_W \nvDash \Box\neg\beta$ and $M_W \cup \{\beta\} \vDash \Box\neg g$ for some $g \in C_i)$) and

(3) $N \nvDash \Box\neg\gamma$. ◆

The order $>_D$ is defined analogously to defintion 5.2. Moreover C_i is the current set of justifications $(\gamma) \in D$ in the enumeration. Therefore

Theorem 5.2 (Soundness and Completeness) Let (W, D) be a PCtDL default theory. Let M be a class of K-models, E be a deductively closed set of formulas and C a set of formulas such that

$$M = \{m \mid m \vDash E \land \Box E \land \Box C\}.$$

Then, (E, C) is a consistent PCtDL extension of (W, D) iff M is a $>_D$-maximal non-empty class above M_W. ◆

Example 3.3 revisited

$M_0 = M_W \vDash Bird(Tweety) \land Animal (Tweety) \land \Box Bird(Tweety) \land \Box Animal (Tweety)$
$C_0 = \emptyset$

We have that $M_1 >_{(1)} M_W$

$M_1 = \{m \in M_W \mid m \vDash \neg Fly(Tweety) \land \Box\neg Fly(Tweety) \land \Box\neg Ab1(Tweety)\}$

and (1) $M_W \vDash Animal (Tweety)$, (2) $M_W \nvDash \Box Fly(Tweety)$ and (3) $M_W \nvDash \Box Ab1(Tweety)$.
$C_1 = \{\neg Ab1(Tweety)\}$

We have that $M_2 >_{(5)} M_1$

$M_2 = \{m \in M_1 \mid m \vDash Wing(Tweety) \land \Box Wing(Tweety) \land \Box\neg Ab2(Tweety)\}$

and (1) $M_1 \vDash Bird(Tweety)$,

2) $M_1 \vDash \Box\neg Wing(Tweety)$ but

$(M_W \nvDash \Box\neg Wing(Tweety)$ and $M_W \cup \{Wing(Tweety)\} \vDash \Box Ab1(Tweety))$,

3) $M_W \nvDash \Box Ab2(Tweety)$

$C_2 = \{\neg Ab1 \, (\text{Tweety}), \neg Ab2 \, (\text{Tweety})\}$ ♦

We see that M_2 is empty because $M_2 \vDash \Box \text{Fly}(\text{Tweety}) \wedge \Box \neg \text{Fly}(\text{Tweety})$. Therefore the anomalous extension is eliminated. If we enumerate the defaults in the reverse order we get the intuitive extension.

6 Conclusions

By differentiating the non-normal part of the justification from the normal part of a semi-normal default rule and by using a context to give priority to a default deriving another default's exception condition, Prioritized Context Default Logic (PCtDL), is able to solve, still using a simple abnormality default theory, some important problems discussed in the literature. PCtDL is not semi-monotonic, has the weak orthogonality, groundedness and the joint consistency properties and cumulativity can be achieved by using Schaub's [36] technique of lemma generation. Unfortunately, like seminormal DL theories, the existence of extensions cannot be guaranteed but, as in DL, plain ordered theories always have an extension. PCtDL has a possible worlds semantics with respect to which it is shown to be sound and complete.

Brewka [5] criticized DL for not having the specificity principle [31, 24, 36] built-in. He developed a method of automatically generating priorities that model the specificity principle into a variant of DL. Delgrande and Schaub [8] also addressed the problem of specificity where the priorities obtained from system Z is expressed into a semi-normal DL theory. But specificity is not the only one preference criteria. As pointed out by Prakken [31] and also by Gordon [14], in legal reasoning there are other priority criteria: authority, where a Federal Authority has preference over a Local Authority, time of enactment, where a more general rule has priority over a more specific rule if it was created more recently, etc. It would be interesting to see whether these two approaches can solve Morris example and the YSP still using a simple abnormality default theory.

As future works, we would like to develop a proof-procedure for PCtDL. It would be interesting to modify Poole's Theorist, by strengthening its constraint, so that PCtDL (prerequisite-free) could be mapped into it. We also would like to investigate the relationship between PCtDL and Prioritized Circumscription.

Acknowledgements
We would like to thank Tarcisio Pequeno, João Carlos da Silva and Sheila Veloso for many useful discussions, and also Valmir Barbosa and the anonymous referees for valuable comments and suggestions. The author is partially financially supported by the Brazilian National Research Council (CNPq), grant number 30.0282/90.7.

References

1. G. Antoniou, G. , E. Langetepe, V. Sperschneider: New proofs in default logic theory. 1993, Draft.
2. P. Besnard, T. Schaub: Possible worlds semantics for default logics. Fundamenta Informaticae. Forthcoming
3. P. Besnard, T. Schaub: A context-based framework for default logics. Proceedings of the AAAI-93, pp.406-411.
4. P. Besnard: An introduction to default logic. Springer Verlag 1989.
5. G. Brewka: Adding priorities and specificity to default logic. GMD report, Bonn 1993.
6. G. Brewka: Cumulative Default Logic - in defense of nonmonotonic inference rules. Artificial Intelligence 50 1991, pp. 183-205.
7. G. Brewka: Nonmonotonic Reasoning - Logical Foundations of Commonsense. Cambridge Tracts in Theoretical Computer Science 12, Cambridge University Press 1991.
8. J. P. Delgrande, T. Schaub: On using system Z to generate prioritized default logic. Proc. of

Dutch / German Workshop on Nonmonotonic Reasoning Techniques and Their Applications, eds. Brewka, G and Witteveen, C. Aachen 1993.

9. J. P. Delgrande, W. K. Jackson: Default Logic revisited. Proc. Second International Conference on Principles of Knowledge Representation and Reasoning, Boston 1991.

10. J. Dix: Default Theories of Poole-Type and a Method for Constructing Cumulative Versions of Default Logic. Proceedings of ECAI92, ed. Bernd Neumann, John Wiley & Sons 1992. pp. 289-293.

11. D. W. Etherington: Reasoning with Incomplete Information, Pitman, London 1988.

12. D. M. Gabbay: Labelled Deductive Systems. 1st draft Sept 1989, 6th draft Feb 91. To appear as a book with OUP.

13. D. M. Gabbay: Theoretical Foundations for Nonmonotonic Reasoning in Expert Systems. Logics and Models of Concurrent Systems, Ed. by K. Apt, Springer-Verlag 1985, pp. 439-459.

14. M. T. Gordon: The Pleadings Game: Formalizing Procedural Justice 1993.

15. S. Hanks, D. McDermott: Nonmonotonic logic and temporal projection. Artificial Intelligence 33 1988 pp.379-412.

16. A. Hunter: A conceptualization of preferences in non-monotonic proof theory. In JELIA-92, Berlin, LNCS, Springer.

17. Lifschitz, V. Circumscription. Handbook of Logic in Artificial Intelligence, eds. Gabbay, D., Hogger, C. and Robinson, J. eds. Vol III. Oxford University Press 1994.

18. W. Lukasziewicz: Nonmonotonic Reasoning: formalization of commonsense reasoning. Ellis Horwood 1990.

19. W. Marek, M. Truszczynski: Nonmonotonic logic: context dependent reasoning. Springer Verlag 1993.

20. W. Marek, M. Truszczynski: Normal form results for default logics. Nonmonotonic and Inductive Logic, eds. Brewka, G. , Jantke, K. P. and Schmitt, P. H., LNAI 659, Springer Verlag 1993, pp.153 -174.

21. D. Makinson: General patterns in non-monotonic reasoning. Handbook of Logic in Artificial Intelligence, eds. Gabbay, D., Hogger, C. and Robinson, J. eds. Vol III. Oxford University Press 1994.

22. J. McCarthy: Applications of circumscription to formalizing commonsense knowledge. Artificial Intelligence 28, 1986, pp. 89-116.

23. Morris, P. H. The anomalous extension problem in default reasoning. Artificial Intelligence 35 1988, pp.383-399.

24. D. Nute: Basic Defeasible Logic . Intensional Logics for Programming, eds. Farinas del Cerro and Pentonnen, OUP 1991.

25. T. Pequeno, A.R.V. Buchsbaum: The Logic of Epistemic Inconsistency. Proc. KR 1991.

26. T. Pequeno: A Logic for Inconsistent Nonmonotonic Reasoning. Technical Report 90/6 Department of Computing, Imperial College, London 1990.

27. J. Pollock: Defeasible Reasoning. Cognitive Science 11 1987, pp. 481-518.

28. D. L. Poole: Default Logic. Handbook of Logic in Artificial Intelligence, eds. Gabbay, D., Hogger, C. and Robinson, J. eds. Vol III. Oxford University Press 1994.

29. D. L. Poole: What the lottery paradox tells us about default reasoning. Proc. First International Conference on Principles of Knowledge Representation and Reasoning (KR) 1989, pp.333-340.

30. D. L. Poole: A logical framework for default reasoning. Artificial Intelligence 36 1987, pp.27-47.

31. D. L. Poole: On the comparison of theories: preferring the most specific explanation. Proceedings of IJCAI 1985, Los Angeles, pp 144-147.

32. H. Prakken: Logical tools for modelling legal arguments, PhD thesis, VU Amsterdam 1993.

33. R. Reiter, G. Criscuolo: Some representational issues in default reasoning. J. Computers and Maths. with Appls. (Special issue on computational linguistics) 9, 1983, pp. 1-13.

34. R. Reiter: A logic for default reasoning. Artificial Intelligence 13, 1980, pp. 81-132.

35. T. Schaub: Considerations on default logics. Dissertation, TH Darmstadt 1992.

36. T. Schaub: On constrained default theories. Proceedings of ECAI92, ed. Bernd Neumann, John Wiley & Sons 1992, pp. 304-308.

37. G. Simari, R. Loui: A mathematical treatment of defeasible reasoning and its implementation. Artificial Intelligence 53, 1992.

Incorporating Specificity into Circumscriptive Theories

James P. Delgrande[1] and Torsten H. Schaub[2]

[1] Simon Fraser University, Burnaby, B.C., Canada V5A 1S6, jim@cs.sfu.ca
[2] IRISA, Campus de Beaulieu, 35042 Rennes cedex, France, torsten@irisa.fr

Abstract. We describe an approach whereby specificity notions are introduced into circumscriptive theories. In this approach, a default theory is initially given as a set of strict and defeasible conditionals. By making use of a theory of default conditionals, here given by System **Z**, we isolate minimal sets of defaults with specificity conflicts. From the specificity information intrinsic in these sets, a propositional theory is specified. By circumscribing a set of "abnormality" propositions, one obtains a nonmonotonic reasoning system in which specificity information is appropriately handled. This notion of specificity subsumes that of property inheritance, and so in this approach a bird will fly (by default) whereas a penguin will not. This work differs from previous work in specifying priorities in circumscription, in that priorities are obtained from information intrinsic in a set of conditionals, rather than assumed to exist a priori. This paper extends earlier work in hybrid non-monotonic reasoning systems: First, in this previous work specificity issues were addressed with respect to Default Logic. Second, we here augment the approach to allow strict as well as default knowledge.

1 Introduction

A fundamental difference between reasoning in mathematics and commonsense reasoning is that the former deals with universal rules, while the latter employs general rules admitting exceptional cases. In mathematical reasoning, exceptions are explicitly listed in the antecedent of a rule, for instance, "if $n \neq 0$ then $f(n) = \frac{1}{n}$". In real life, however, we use rules like "birds fly" that allow arbitrary exceptions. For example, penguins and ostriches don't fly; the same applies to newborn birds. Since it is impossible to list all exceptional conditionals, or all exceptional individuals, any approach to formalizing commonsense reasoning has to incorporate the notion of an "exception".

Circumscription [13] is one of the best known and most-widely used approaches to formalizing commonsense reasoning. However, unlike e.g. default logic [18], circumscription deals with theories expressed in classical logic. In circumscription, exceptions to general rules are captured by means of so-called abnormality sentences, expressed here as ab.[3] Accordingly, a rule such as "birds fly" is represented by an implication $B \land \neg ab \supset F$. This expresses the fact that a bird that is not abnormal flies. However, given only that B is true, there is no way to derive $\neg ab$ in classical logic, and so we cannot derive F. The role of circumscription is to provide formal means for concluding that things are as normal as possible—that is, the number of abnormal things is as small as possible. In this

---

[3] Circumscription is usually phrased in a first-order framework, and so would make use of abnormality *predicates*. Here for simplicity we deal with propositional circumscription.

way, circumscription allows us to conclude that birds are normal, provided that they cannot be shown to be abnormal. Formally, this is expressed by means of a circumscription axiom that is added to a given set of formulas representing a world description. This axiom (very roughly) states that the number of abnormalities is as small as possible. That is, given B in the above example, the circumscription axiom allows us to nonmonotonically assume $\neg ab$; and from this we can conclude F.

Unfortunately, the basic approach to circumscription does not always allow for intuitively expected commonsense conclusions. As observed by McCarthy in [14], circumscription does not respect the notion of *specificity*. Specificity is a fundamental principle in commonsense reasoning, according to which more specific defaults are preferred over less specific ones. Consider an example where birds fly, penguins are birds, penguins don't fly, and birds have wings. We can write this informally as:

$$B \to F, \; P \Rightarrow B, \; P \to \neg F, \; B \to W \tag{1}$$

where $\to$ is used for a defeasible conditional and $\Rightarrow$ is used as a strict conditional. In a circumscriptive theory, we could write this as: [4]

$$B \wedge \neg ab_1 \supset F, \; P \supset B, \; P \wedge \neg ab_2 \supset \neg F, \; B \wedge \neg ab_3 \supset W.$$

From this theory, given that P is true, one would want to conclude $\neg F$ by default. Intuitively, being a penguin is a more specific notion than that of being a bird, and, in the case of a conflict, we would want to use the more specific default. However, circumscription does not allow for concluding $\neg F$. For example, given the above theory together with the fact that P is true, we minimise abnormalities by circumscribing the abnormality sentences ab_1, ab_2, and ab_3. However, as we will see in Section 4, by circumscribing these sentences we obtain only that $ab_1 \equiv \neg ab_2$ along with $\neg ab_3$ are true; hence we can conclude nothing about F. The difficulty here is that being a penguin is a more specific notion that being a bird, and so we would want to assert that being normal with respect to being a penguin should take precedence over being normal with respect to being a bird when there is a conflict. Hence, intuitively, we would want the result of circumscribing to yield $\neg ab_2$, from which we can conclude $\neg F$. However, this is an issue that is independent of the approach of circumscription; in circumscription, one simply wishes to minimise the number of sentences in some set assumed to be true.

One possible solution is to specify a priority ordering on sentences that are to be minimised [12]. However this possibility complicates the machinery of circumscription. More importantly, it leaves open the question of how this ordering was derived. In this paper we develop a means of "automatically" adding specificity to a circumscriptive theory. This is accomplished by extending and adapting an existing approach for "hybrid" default reasoning [5]. This approach involved the compilation of a default theory, expressed as a set of defeasible conditionals, into a default theory in Default Logic [18], in which specificity information was appropriately dealt with. In Section 3 we describe how specificity information may

---

[4] We distinguish different types or aspects of abnormality by using a set of abnormality propositions ab_1, ab_2, ...

be obtained from a set of (strict and defeasible) conditionals. In Section 4 we show how our approach may be used to obtain circumscriptive theories in which specificity constraints are enforced. Section 6 gives a brief conclusion along with an overview of related work, including our original approach.

2 The Form of Default Theories

We take knowledge about the world, expressed in a knowledge base Δ, to be divided into two sets:

R : Background knowledge, or facts or rules which are assumed to be applicable in every domain.

W : Contingent knowledge, or facts which are true in the case under considera-tion, and which may vary from case to case.

This is essentially the difference between necessary and contingent knowledge in modal logics, or between probabilistic knowledge and conditioning knowledge in probabilistic reasoning systems [15]. Background knowledge is in turn considered to consist of two sets:

R_N: Necessary implications, or rules which must be true in any setting.

R_D: Default knowledge, or rules that are usually true, but allow exceptions.

This division is found in the various *conditional* approaches in Artificial Intelli-gence to default reasoning, such as [6, 7, 2, 9] and less directly in [11]. So the background knowledge will be taken as comprising a *default theory*. The back-ground knowledge may also be taken as providing a *generic world description*. Elements of W are formulas of classical propositional logic. Elements of R_N are formulas of the form $\alpha \Rightarrow \beta$ while elements of R_D are formulas of the form $\alpha \rightarrow \beta$, where α and β are propositional formulas. This means that neither connective $\Rightarrow$ nor $\rightarrow$ allows nested occurrences. Note too that we reserve $\supset$ for classical (material) implication.

So a knowledge base Δ is of the form $\Delta = \langle\langle R_N, R_D\rangle, W\rangle$, where $\langle R_N, R_D\rangle$ represents generic world knowledge, comprised of a set of strict conditionals R_N and a set of defeasible (exception-allowing) conditionals R_D. Our initial example can now be represented as:

$$\langle\{P \Rightarrow B\}, \{B \rightarrow F,\ B \rightarrow W,\ P \rightarrow \neg F\}\rangle.$$

Thus penguins must be birds, and this conditional admits no exceptions. Again, given that P is true (i.e. $W = \{P\}$), one would want to conclude $\neg F$ by default.

3 Obtaining Specificity Information

In System **Z** a set of rules R representing default conditionals is partitioned into an ordered list of mutually exclusive sets of rules $R_0, \ldots, R_n$. Lower ranked rules are considered more normal (or less specific) than higher ranked rules. Here we describe an extension to System **Z** incorporating strict conditionals; for simplicity we refer to this extension as System **Z**, too.[5] We begin with a *generic*

---

[5] Note that this extension differs from that of [9], where strict and default conditionals are arbitrarily mixed in the ordering.

world description $\langle R_D, R_N \rangle$. Again, $R_D = \{r \mid \alpha_r \rightarrow \beta_r\}$ is a set of defeasible conditionals and $R_N = \{r \mid \alpha_r \Rightarrow \beta_r\}$ is a set of strict conditionals,[6] where each α_r and β_r are propositional formulas over a finite alphabet.

A central notion is that of *toleration*:

Definition 1. Let $\langle R_N, R_D \rangle$ be a generic world description. A defeasible rule $\alpha \rightarrow \beta$ is tolerated by $R_D \cup R_N$ iff $\{\alpha \wedge \beta\} \cup \{\gamma_r \supset \delta_r \mid r \in R_D\} \cup \{\gamma_r \supset \delta_r \mid r \in R_N\}$ is satisfiable.

We assume in what follows that for every non-empty $R' \subseteq R_D \cup R_N$, some $r' \in R'$ is tolerated by $R' - \{r'\}$. Using this notion of tolerance, a so-called **Z**-*ordering* on the rules in $R_D \cup R_N$ is defined:

1. Find all rules in R_D tolerated by $R_D \cup R_N$, and call this subset R_0.
2. Next, find all rules tolerated by $(R_D - R_0) \cup R_N$, and call this subset R_1.
3. Continue in this fashion until all rules have been accounted for.
4. For the least n such that $R_D = \bigcup_{i=1}^{n} R_i$, set $R_{n+1} = R_N$.

In this way, we obtain a partition $(R_0, \ldots, R_n, R_{n+1})$ of $R_D \cup R_N$, where $R_i = \{r \mid r$ is tolerated by $(R_D - R_0 - \ldots - R_{i-1}) \cup R_N\}$ for $1 \le i \le n$ and $R_{n+1} = R_N$. A set of rules R is called *trivial* iff its partition consists only of a single set of rules. For our initial set of rules in (1), we obtain the following **Z**-ordering, where the necessary rules are given by the highest layer R_2 since they admit no exceptions, and so are "minimally falsifiable":

$$R_0 = \{B \rightarrow F, B \rightarrow W\}, \qquad R_1 = \{P \rightarrow \neg F\}, \qquad R_2 = \{P \Rightarrow B\}. \qquad (2)$$

Note that the procedure treats the connectives $\rightarrow$ and $\Rightarrow$ both as $\supset$. Also, observe that necessary rules can never occur in R_0 provided that there are default rules. In this way, necessary rules are always more specific than default rules.

From this point, [16] defines a ranking on models, determined by which rules are falsified in the model; subsequently a notion of default inference is obtained. These considerations need not concern us here, since it is just the ordering that we make use of.[7] In fact, we gather information extracted from certain **Z**-orderings in order to (ultimately) generate a circumscriptive theory: A **Z**-ordering provides specificity information, and so for example, tells us that $P \rightarrow \neg F$ is more specific than $B \rightarrow F$. However, we do not use the full **Z**-ordering (since it may introduce unwanted specificities), but rather we determine minimal sets of rules that conflict, and use these sets to sort out specificity information.

Consider our initial example (1), expressed as a **Z**-ordering in (2). First we locate the minimal sets of conditionals having a non-trivial **Z**-ordering. In our example this set $C = C_0 \cup C_1 \cup C_2$ consists solely of:

$$C_0 = \{B \rightarrow F\}, \qquad C_1 = \{P \rightarrow \neg F\}, \qquad C_2 = \{P \Rightarrow B\}.$$

Any such set is called a *minimal conflicting set* of defaults. Such a set has a non-trivial **Z**-ordering, but for any subset there is no non-trivial **Z**-ordering. What

---

[6] Note that this approach allows for an arbitrary strict formula α to be encoded as $\top \Rightarrow \alpha$. However it is convenient to represent strict knowledge using conditionals.

[7] Indeed, System **Z** as a whole is too strong for our requirements (see [5]).

this in turn means is that if all the rules in such a set are jointly applicable, then, one way or another there will be a conflict.[8] Formally, we have:

Definition 2. Let R be a set of rules. $C \subseteq R$ is a minimal conflicting set in R iff C has a non-trivial Z-ordering and any $C' \subset C$ has a trivial Z-ordering.

Observe that adding new rules to R cannot alter or destroy any existing minimal conflicting sets. That is, for sets of rules R and R', where $C \subseteq R \subseteq R'$, we have that if C is a minimal conflicting set in R then C is a minimal conflicting set in R'. As shown in [5], each such minimal conflicting set C must consist of a binary or (with strict conditionals) a ternary partition; furthermore the rules in the set C_0 are less specific than those in C_1 or C_2. Consequently, if the rules in C_1 (and C_2) are applicable, then we would want to insure that some rule in C_0 was blocked.

It turns out that there are different ways in which we can select rules to block default inferences. However, we choose the selection criterion so that it is independent of the default theory in which the rules are embedded. Thus, if we wish to block the default $B \to F$ in the case of P in default theory R, then we will also want to block this rule in any superset R'. We do this as follows: For a minimal conflicting set C, we select those defaults that actually conflict and hence cause the non-triviality of C. The rules selected in this way constitute the *minimal conflicting rules* and *maximal conflicting rules* respectively. In our example, we obtain the rules $B \to F$ and $P \to \neg F$. Then, the minimal conflicting rules constitute the candidates to be blocked. Formally:

Definition 3. Let $C = (C_0, C_1, C_2)$ be a minimal conflicting set. A conflicting core of C is a pair of least non-empty sets $(min(C), max(C))$ where

1. $min(C) \subseteq C_0$,
2. $max(C) \subseteq C_1 \cup C_2$,
3. $\{\alpha_r \wedge \beta_r \mid r \in max(C) \cup min(C)\} \models \perp$.

The rules $B \to F$ and $P \to \neg F$ yield the conflicting core $(\{B \to F\}, \{P \to \neg F\})$.

4 Adding specificity to circumscription

Circumscription was introduced by John McCarthy in [13, 14] as an approach to formalizing diverse nonmonotonic aspects of commonsense reasoning. This is accomplished by "logical minimization". That is, a formula α follows from a theory W by circumscription, if α is true in all models of W that are minimal in a certain sense. In applications to default reasoning, circumscription is used to minimize "abnormalities" of default rules. For this purpose, the language is enriched by certain abnormality propositions like ab. Following this general principle, we transform a set of default rules into a set of implications. That is, for a generic world description $\langle R_N, R_D \rangle$, we define

$$R_N^* = \{\alpha_r \supset \beta_r \mid \alpha_r \Rightarrow \beta_r \in R_N\};$$
$$R_D^{ab} = \{\alpha_r \wedge \neg ab_r \supset \beta_r \mid \alpha_r \to \beta_r \in R_D\}.$$

As an example, consider the following generic world description:

---

[8] If the rules were represented as normal default rules in default logic for example, one would obtain multiple extensions.

$$R_N = \{B \Rightarrow F\} \qquad\qquad R_D = \{P \rightarrow B, \; P \rightarrow \neg F\}. \qquad (3)$$

For R_D, we obtain:

$$R_D^{ab} = \{B \wedge \neg ab_1 \supset F, \; P \wedge \neg ab_2 \supset \neg F\}. \qquad (4)$$

The strict rules in R_N become $R_N^* = \{B \supset F\}$. Now, the set of rules in $R_N^* \cup R_D^{ab}$ can be seen as a description of our birds scenario in (3) in standard propositional logic. However, we also want to express that things are considered as normal as possible—provided that there is no evidence to the contrary. This assumption is formally accomplished by circumscribing a world description: Let W be a propositional formula, and $P \dot\cup Z$ a partition of all atoms in W. The circumscription of P in W while varying Z is defined as (cf. [13, 12])

$$Circum(W; P; Z) = W \wedge (\forall P', Z' (W[P/P', Z/Z'] \wedge (P' \supset P) \supset (P \supset P'))).$$

In this formula, P' and Z' are disjoint sets of new propositional variables corresponding to the ones in P and Z. That is, $P' = \{p' \mid p \in P\}$ and $Z' = \{z' \mid z \in Z\}$. The formula $W[P/P', Z/Z']$ denotes the result obtained by replacing in W all occurrences of variables in $P \cup Z$ by their counterparts in $P' \cup Z'$. $(P' \supset P)$ and $(P \supset P')$ abbreviate $\bigwedge_{p \in P}(p' \supset p)$ and $\bigwedge_{p \in P}(p \supset p')$, respectively. The net result is that the circumscription axiom asserts that the number of atoms in P that are true is as small as possible. Furthermore, in achieving this minimisation, the truth values of atoms in Z are allowed to vary. The semantical underpinnings for circumscription are given by minimal models. We denote interpretations as sets of atoms. For interpretations M and N, we define $M \leq_{(P;Z)} N$ if $M \cap P \subseteq N \cap P$. Then, according to [12], M is a model of $Circum(W; P; Z)$ iff M is minimal among all models of W with respect to $\leq_{(P;Z)}$.

Consider our birds example along with the fact P. The models of P, R_N^*, and R_D^{ab} are the following:

$$\{P, B, F, ab_1, ab_2\}, \; \{P, B, ab_1, ab_2\}, \; \{P, B, F, ab_2\}, \; \{P, B, ab_1\} \qquad (5)$$

Circumscribing the propositions ab_1 and ab_2 while varying B, F, P amounts to reasoning with respect to those models in (5) that have the fewest abnormality propositions. In fact, there are two such minimal models, $\{P, B, ab_1\}$ and $\{P, B, F, ab_2\}$. As a consequence, we cannot conclude much more than from the original world description in (3). That is, we have

$$Circum(\{P\} \cup R_N^* \cup R_D^{ab}; \{ab_1, ab_2\}; \{B, F, P\}) \models B \wedge P \wedge ab_1 \equiv \neg ab_2.$$

In particular, we cannot derive ab_1, ab_2, or F, nor their negation. This shortcoming was observed in [14]. For fixing this problem, McCarthy introduced a prioritized version of circumscription by assuming that abnormality propositions are a priori assigned different priorities. We take up this approach in Section 5.

We address the lack of specificity by specifying axioms reflecting the precedence of more specific rules over less specific rules. We accomplish this by taking advantage of the specificity information provided by minimal conflicting sets. This information is encoded by means of specificity axioms that express precedences among default rules conflicting because of differing specificity.

Definition 4. Let $\langle R_N, R_D \rangle$ be a generic world description. Let $\langle C^i \rangle_{i \in I}$ be the family of all minimal conflicting sets in $R_N \cup R_D$. We define

$$R_D^{sp} = \{\neg \bigwedge_{r' \in R_r} (\alpha_{r'} \supset \beta_{r'}) \supset ab_r \mid r \in R_D\} \tag{6}$$

where $R_r = \{r' \in max(C^i) \mid r \in min(C^i)$ for $i \in I \}$.

This definition provides a *circumscription policy* for specificity using standard circumscription, rather prioritized circumscription [14] (see below). Observe that rules like $\neg \bigwedge_{r' \in R_r}(\alpha_{r'} \supset \beta_{r'}) \supset ab_r$ have the form of inheritance cancellation axioms as described in [14]. Note that necessary rules can be discarded in the formation of antecedents of specificity axioms, since they constitute true sentences in the world description obtained by adding R_N^*. Consequently, a specificity axiom is tautological if R_r consists of necessary rules only. We detail the effect of specificity axioms below.

Consider our birds example in (3). As required in Definition 4, we associate with each default rule a set of less specific, conflicting default rules extracted from the minimal conflicting sets. For the default rules R_D in (3), this yields the following sets of default rules according to the specification of R_r in Definition 4:

$$R_{B \to F} = \{P \to \neg F\} \qquad\qquad R_{P \to \neg F} = \emptyset$$

The first set expresses the fact that $P \to \neg F$ is more specific than $B \to F$, while the second equation tells us that there is no more specific (conflicting) default rule than $P \to \neg F$. According to Definition 4, we thus obtain for the default rules R_D in (3) the following specificity axiom:

$$R_D^{sp} = \{\neg(P \supset \neg F) \supset ab_1\}. \tag{7}$$

We have omitted the tautology obtained in the case of $P \to \neg F$.

Our construction yields the following classical theory in propositional logic when applied to our generic world description in (3):

$$R_N^* \cup R_D^{ab} \cup R_D^{sp} = \{P \supset B, B \wedge \neg ab_1 \supset F, P \wedge \neg ab_2 \supset \neg F, \neg(P \supset \neg F) \supset ab_1\}. \tag{8}$$

Together with the contingent fact P, these rules have the following models:

$$\{P, B, F, ab_1, ab_2\}, \ \{P, B, ab_1, ab_2\}, \ \{P, B, ab_1\} \tag{9}$$

In contrast to the models in (5), we now have only a single minimal model, namely $\{P, B, ab_1\}$. Hence, circumscription allows for concluding P, B, ab_1, and $\neg F$, $\neg ab_2$ from the transformed world description.

One might wonder why we compose specificity axioms by taking entire rules and not merely their antecedents. This would amount to considering the rule $P \supset ab_1$ instead of the one given in (7). Interestingly, $P \supset ab_1$ is the inheritance cancellation axiom suggested in [14]. Let us illustrate this by the following theory constituting a minimal conflicting set:

$$C_0 = \{A \to \neg B, C \to \neg D\} \qquad\qquad C_1 = \{A \wedge C \to B \vee D\}.$$

This minimal conflicting set comprises two less specific conflicting rules, a situation frequently encountered in multiple inheritance networks. Applying the transformations in (4) and (6) yields:

$$R_D^{ab} = \{A \wedge \neg ab_1 \supset \neg B, \ C \wedge \neg ab_2 \supset \neg D, \ A \wedge C \wedge \neg ab_3 \supset B \vee D\}$$

$$R_D^{sp} = \{\neg(A \wedge C \supset B \vee D) \supset ab_1, \ \neg(A \wedge C \supset B \vee D) \supset ab_2\}. \tag{10}$$

Given $\{A, C, D\}$, we observe a single "abnormality minimal" model of the resulting world description, namely $\{A, C, D, ab_2\}$. In this way, an appropriate circumscription allows us to conclude $\neg B$. This amounts to applying the first default $A \to \neg B$. Now, let us replace the specificity axioms in (10) by

$$R_D^{ic} = \{A \wedge C \supset ab_1, \ A \wedge C \supset ab_2\}$$

according to the putative recipe described above. Now, we obtain for the world description built on the facts $\{A, C, D\}$ *two* "abnormality minimal" models, $\{A, C, D, ab_1, ab_2\}$ and $\{A, B, C, D, ab_1, ab_2\}$. Consequently, we cannot derive $\neg B$. Given $\{A, C, D\}$ there is, however, no reason why the default $A \rightarrow \neg B$ should not apply. This shows that our approach is advantageous over plain blocking conditions. Another advantage of our construction is that it allows for an elegant alternative formulation for incorporating specificity, as we will see next.

Observe that the last two implications in (8) can be put together to: $P \wedge (\neg ab_2 \vee \neg ab_1) \supset \neg F$. This indicates that we can alternatively modify the more specific rules instead of adding axioms referring to the least specific ones. As a general result, the next definition provides us with an alternative but more compact translation of default rules along with their specificity information into classical logic:

Definition 5. Let $\langle R_N, R_D \rangle$ be a generic world description. Let $\langle C^i \rangle_{i \in I}$ be the family of all minimal conflicting sets in $R_N \cup R_D$. We define

$$R_D^\star = \{\alpha_r \wedge \left(\neg ab_r \vee \bigvee_{r' \in R'_r} \neg ab_{r'}\right) \supset \beta_r \mid r \in R_D\}$$

where $R'_r = \{r' \in min(C^i) \mid r \in max(C^i) \text{ for } i \in I \}$.

This transformation unifies the ones given in (4) and (6). This is accomplished by slightly extending transformation (4) in the case of more specific conflicting default rules. To this end, we extend the abnormality condition of more specific default rules by disjoining the abnormality propositions of the less specific default rules. This yields for our generic world description in (3) the following set of strict rules:

$$R_N^\star \cup R_D^\star = \{P \supset B\} \cup \{B \wedge \neg ab_1 \supset F, \ P \wedge (\neg ab_2 \vee \neg ab_1) \supset \neg F\}.$$

This result should be compared with the one obtained in (8).

Note that R'_r reverses the roles of $min(C^i)$ and $max(C^i)$ in the specification of R_r in Definition 4. Also, it is interesting to observe that more specific necessary rules remain unaffected by the previous translation. This corresponds to the fact that necessary rules can be discarded in the formation of antecedents of specificity axioms in (6).

The next theorem tells us that both constructions are in fact equivalent:

Theorem 6. *Let $\langle R_N, R_D \rangle$ be a generic world description. Then, $R_N^\star \cup R_D^{ab} \cup R_D^{sp}$ is logically equivalent to $R_N^\star \cup R_D^\star$.*

Now, let us further study the effect of our approach by means of a general but simple example. Consider a generic world description comprising two conflicting rules r and r' and suppose that r is more specific than r'. Hence, we have $R'_r = \{r'\}$ and we obtain in turn

$$\alpha_r \wedge (\neg ab_r \vee \neg ab_{r'}) \supset \beta_r \quad \text{and} \quad \alpha_{r'} \wedge \neg ab_{r'} \supset \beta_{r'} \ .$$

Our intended interpretation is that r is preferable over r' (because of specificity) whenever r and r' are both potentially "applicable". Assume that β_r and $\beta_{r'}$ are not jointly satisfiable, since r and r' conflict. Then, the first default takes precedence over the second one whenever both antecedents, α_r and $\alpha_{r'}$, are derivable. This is so because of the following reasons: Clearly, $\{\alpha_r, \alpha_{r'}, \beta_r, \beta_{r'}\}$ is no "abnormality minimal" model, since β_r and $\beta_{r'}$ are not jointly satisfiable. Also, $\{\alpha_r, \alpha_{r'}, ab_r, \beta_{r'}\}, \{\alpha_r, \alpha_{r'}, ab_r, \beta_r\}, \{\alpha_r, \alpha_{r'}, ab_r\}, \{\alpha_r, \alpha_{r'}, ab_{r'}, \beta_{r'}\}, \{\alpha_r, \alpha_{r'}, ab_{r'}\}$ are not "abnormality minimal" models, since they either falsify $\alpha_r \wedge (\neg ab_r \vee \neg ab_{r'}) \supset \beta_r$ or $\alpha_{r'} \wedge \neg ab_{r'} \supset \beta_{r'}$. Finally, there remain three candidates satisfying a single abnormality proposition:

$$\{\alpha_r, \alpha_{r'}, ab_r, \beta_r, \beta_{r'}\}, \ \{\alpha_r, \alpha_{r'}, ab_{r'}, \beta_r, \beta_{r'}\}, \ \{\alpha_r, \alpha_{r'}, ab_{r'}, \beta_r\}.$$

In fact, these three models are "abnormality minimal". Since all of them satisfy β_r, they prefer the more specific default r over r'.

Importantly, both transformations are consistency-preserving.

Theorem 7. *Let $\langle R_N, R_D \rangle$ be a generic world description such that $R_N^* \cup \{\alpha_r \supset \beta_r \mid \alpha_r \rightarrow \beta_r \in R_D\}$ is satisfiable. Then, $R_N^* \cup R_D^*$ is satisfiable.*

Clearly, the same result applies to our initial approach using the rules in $R_N^* \cup R_D^{ab} \cup R_D^{sp}$. Moreover, consistency is also preserved when applying circumscription to specificity-integrating world descriptions:

Theorem 8. *Let $\langle \langle R_N, R_D \rangle, W \rangle$ be a world description such that $W \cup R_N^*$ is satisfiable. Then, $Circum(W \cup R_N^* \cup R_D^* ; \{ab_r \mid r \in R_D\}; Z)$ is satisfiable, where Z is the set of all propositional variables in (W, R_N, R_D).*

Thus, unlike standard default logic and autoepistemic logic in which one might obtain incoherent theories [5], the transformation given for circumscription cannot render an original theory incoherent.

Finally, Theorem 8 provides us with a compact summary of our approach. That is, we start from knowledge bases of the form $\langle \langle R_N, R_D \rangle, W \rangle$. Next, we treat the generic part of such a world description by means of techniques developed in Section 3 for isolating minimal sets of default rules with specificity conflicts. Then, we take the initial world description along with the determined specificity information obtained in the previous step and translate it into a classical theory in propositional logic, namely $W \cup R_N^* \cup R_D^*$. In a final step, we compute the resulting conclusions by circumscribing the introduced abnormality propositions while varying all propositions in the original world description.

5 Discussion and Related Work

McCarthy [14] addressed the lack of specificity in circumscription by introducing *prioritized circumscription*. This approach has been further developed in [12]. The idea is to partition the circumscribed propositions into priority layers. For this, a set of propositions P is partitioned into disjoint subsets $P_1 \dot\cup \ldots \dot\cup P_n$ where the propositions in P_i should take priority over those in P_{i+1}. For computing the result of prioritized circumscription, Lifschitz shows in [12] that any prioritized circumscription, written $Circum(W; P_1 > \ldots > P_n; Z)$, can be expressed as a conjunction of ordinary circumscriptions. That is, $Circum(W; P_1 > \ldots > P_n; Z)$ is equivalent to $\bigwedge_{i=1}^n Circum(W; P_i; P_{i+1} \cup \ldots \cup P_n \cup Z)$. In this way, a prioritized circumscription becomes a sequence of ordinary circumscriptions where propositions in a higher layer are "minimized" while all propositions in a lower layer are varied. This process is iterated over all layers in the partition of P.

In our simple birds example, we could give the abnormality proposition of the more specific default rule, ab_2, priority over the one of the less specific rule, ab_1. This yields

$$Circum(\{P\} \cup R_N^* \cup R_D^{ab} \,;\, \{ab_2\} > \{ab_1\} \,;\, \{B, F, P\}) =$$
$$Circum(\{P\} \cup R_N^* \cup R_D^{ab} \,;\, \{ab_2\} \,;\, \{ab_1, B, F, P\})$$
$$\wedge\; Circum(\{P\} \cup R_N^* \cup R_D^{ab} \,;\, \{ab_1\} \,;\, \{B, F, P\}) \qquad \models P \wedge B \wedge \neg F.$$

Observe however that such an approach works only if the partial order induced by specificity can be pressed into a "layered format" without introducing unwanted preference relations. For instance, [10] gives partial orders that cannot be represented in "layered format". For similar reasons one usually refrains from mapping a full Z-ordering onto "layered structures" in default reasoning systems (see [5]). Finally, the iterated format used for computing prioritized circumscription amounts to a treatment of specificity on the metalevel, rather than producing an object level theory, as in our approach.

Grosof [10] extends prioritized circumscription for dealing with partial orders. In this way, his approach allows for formalizing partial orders representing specificity information. There are however some important differences to our approach. First, [10] describes default rules with specificity in terms of an extended prioritized circumscription, while we deal with the basic approach to circumscription. Second, it is (to our knowledge) yet unknown how and if this extended prioritized circumscription is reducible to iterated ordinary circumscriptions. Hence this approach remains outside the basic circumscriptive machinery. Consequently, it is impossible to apply, for instance, techniques for transforming circumscription in first-order or even propositional logic (see [12]). Observe that, in contrast, we deal with a single basic circumscriptive theory that allows for applying the aforementioned techniques along with existing implementations of circumscriptive theorem provers [8].

Specificity per se is specifically addressed in [17], although it has of course appeared earlier. Instead of System Z, we could have as easily used an approach described in [11] for example; however specificity, as it appears in System Z is particularly straightforwardly describable. Other approaches are too weak to be useful here. For example conditional entailment [7] does not support full inheritance reasoning.

[5] describes a hybrid approach to nonmonotonic reasoning which addresses the problem of specificity in default logic [18]. One begins with a set of rules that express default conditionals, and produces a default theory expressed in default logic, where conflicts arising from differing specificities are resolved. As above, minimally conflicting sets of rules are located. Consider the minimal conflicting set: $\{B \rightarrow F,\ P \rightarrow B,\ P \rightarrow \neg F\}$. In a second step, the derived specificity information is used to produce a set of default rules in default logic from the rules in such a way that specificity is suitably handled. For the previous rules we would obtain the theory

$$\frac{B : F \wedge \neg P}{F},\ \frac{B : W}{W},\ \frac{P : B}{B},\ \frac{P : \neg F}{\neg F}.$$

Now, given that P is true, this default theory allows us to conclude $\neg F$ in default logic. A limitation of the previous approach is that it does not allow for the incorporation of strict rules. So, for example, the approach does not allow for the assertion that penguins must be birds, or penguins are *necessarily* birds.

The approaches of [3, 1, 4] deal with specificity in default logic. We note however that these approaches obtain specificity by requiring modifications to default logic. [3] deals with compiling a full Z-ordering into (prioritised) default logic. [1] addresses specificity in terminological reasoners. [4] has adopted the idea of minimal conflicting sets described here, but in a more restricted setting.

6 Conclusion

We have presented an approach for automatically generating a classical propositional theory wherein specificity, or priorities, among defaults are handled. Generic background knowledge is expressed by sets of strict and default conditionals. By appeal to a theory of defaults, here System **Z**, specificity conflicts are isolated into minimal conflicting sets. Using these minimal conflicting sets, a classical propositional theory is generated. Provably, once the *ab* sentences are circumscribed, we obtain a propositional theory wherein specificity is appropriately handled. The extension of this approach to universally quantified first-order default theories is straightforward.

The choice of circumscription as a target formalism rather than, for example, default logic or autoepistemic logic, has several benefits. Foremost, we work largely within classical logic: a classical theory is generated; there is a circumscriptive step minimising *ab* sentences, after which one has a classical knowledge base. Circumscription itself has several rather nice features: we don't have the notion of "extension" to be concerned with; also circumscription is cumulative. Furthermore computational properties of circumscription are well-studied [12, 8].

Compared to other approaches using circumscription, we avoid the need of any explicit form of "prioritisation". Furthermore, priorities are generated from a given default theory, rather than being required a priori. Among other things, this approach has yielded a more comprehensive form of "inheritance cancellation" axioms, appropriate for multiple inheritance systems. The approach can be seen then as a general method to encode partial orders in circumscription on the object level. Consequently, other partial orders (as suggested in [10] for example) would be amenable to the same treatment.

Acknowledgments We would like to thank Y. Moinard and the referees for their helpful comments. The first author was a visitor at York University and the University of Toronto while this work was being carried out. The first author also acknowledges support from the Natural Science and Engineering Research Council of Canada grant A0884, as well as the Institute for Robotics and Intelligent Systems (IRIS) in the Canadian Networks of Centres of Excellence Program. The second author was supported by the Commission of the European Communities under grant no. ERB4001GT922433.

References

1. F. Baader and B. Hollunder. How to prefer more specific defaults in terminological default logic. In *Proc. IJCAI-93*, pages 669–674, Chambéry, Fr., 1993.
2. Craig Boutilier. *Conditional Logics for Default Reasoning and Belief Revision*. PhD thesis, Department of Computer Science, University of Toronto, 1992.
3. Craig Boutilier. What is a default priority? In *Canadian Conference on AI*, Vancouver, B.C., 1992.
4. G. Brewka. Adding priorities and specificity to default logic. Manuscript, 1993.
5. J. P. Delgrande and T. Schaub. A general approach to specificity in default reasoning. In *Fourth International Conference on Principles of Knowledge Representation and Reasoning*, Bonn, Germany, May 1994.
6. J.P. Delgrande. A first-order conditional logic for prototypical properties. *Artificial Intelligence*, 33(1):105–130, 1987.
7. Hector Geffner and Judea Pearl. Conditional entailment: Bridging two approaches to default reasoning. *Artificial Intelligence*, 53(2-3):209–244, 1992.
8. M. Ginsberg. A circumscriprive theorem prover. *Artificial Intelligence*, 39:209–230, 1989.
9. Moisés Goldszmidt. *Qualitative Probabilities: A Normative Framework for Commonsense Reasoning*. PhD thesis, Department of Computer Science, University of California, Los Angeles, 1992.
10. B. Grosof. Generalizing prioritization. In J. A. Allen, R. Fikes, and E. Sandewall, editors, *Proceedings of the Second International Conference on the Principles of Knowledge Representation and Reasoning*, pages 289–300, San Mateo, CA, April 1991. Morgan Kaufmann.
11. S. Kraus, D. Lehmann, and M. Magidor. Nonmonotonic reasoning, preferential models and cumulative logics. *Artificial Intelligence*, 44(1-2), 1990.
12. V. Lifschitz. Computing circumscription. In *Proc. IJCAI-85*, pages 121–127, Los Angeles, 1985.
13. J. McCarthy. Circumscription – a form of non-monotonic reasoning. *Artificial Intelligence*, 13:27–39, 1980.
14. J. McCarthy. Applications of circumscription to formalizing common-sense knowledge. *Artificial Intelligence*, 28:89–116, 1986.
15. J. Pearl. Probabilistic semantics for nonmonotonic reasoning: A survey. In *Proc. KR-89*, pages 505–516, Toronto, May 1989. Morgan Kaufman.
16. J. Pearl. System Z: A natural ordering of defaults with tractable applications to nonmonotonic reasoning. In *Proc. of the Third Conference on Theoretical Aspects of Reasoning About Knowledge*, pages 121–135, Pacific Grove, Ca., 1990.
17. D. Poole. On the comparison of theories: Preferring the most specific explanation. In *Proc. IJCAI-85*, pages 144–147, 1985.
18. R. Reiter. A logic for default reasoning. *Artificial Intelligence*, 13:81–132, 1980.

Coherent choice and epistemic entrenchment (Preliminary report)

Hans Rott

University of Konstanz, Department of Philosophy
P.O. Box 5560, 78434 Konstanz, Germany
pirott@nyx.uni-konstanz.de

Abstract. Belief revision has recently been modelled with the help of the notion of epistemic entrenchment (Gärdenfors and Makinson, *TARK* 1988, and Rott, *JoLLI* 1992). This paper offers a systematic justification of the postulates for entrenchment by interpreting entrenchment in terms of the general theory of rational choice. A translation is specified from conditions for entrenchment into conditions for choice, and vice versa. The relative strengths of the postulates are studied, and connections with related work are discussed.

1   Introduction

The notion of the *epistemic entrenchment* has recently attracted quite some attention in the AI community. It was introduced, first under the name "epistemic importance", by Peter Gärdenfors [7, 8]. He specified two possible "origins" of epistemic entrenchment: an *information-theoretic appoach* and a *paradigm approach*. However, neither of these approaches squares well with the logical constraints which are placed on entrenchment relations in the later and more mature work of Gärdenfors and Makinson [10]. Although it is now known how epistemic entrenchment can be put to work technically, the problem of providing a *systematic justification of the postulates for entrenchment relations* is still largely unresolved. The present paper offers a solution to this problem which is faithful to the literal meaning of the term "entrenchment".

We follow the philosophical strategy of reducing logical principles to abstract principles of rationality for decisions and actions which we consider to be more fundamental than the former. The standard theory of epistemic entrenchment [10, 21] is interpreted in terms of the general theory of rational choice, and the following questions are being addressed. Are the usual postulates for entrenchment justified by principles of rational choice? Do the latter principles, or the mere interpretation of entrenchments in terms of choice, impose interesting additional constraints on entrenchment relations? Conversely, which principles of rational choice can be retrieved from the entrenchment postulates, and what is their status in the theory of choice?

2 Basic Principles

The following considerations presuppose a propositional language that contains at least the binary connective '∧' for conjunction. No other connectives will be needed for our discussion. An *epistemic state*, or a *knowledge base*, will be represented by the set K of sentences which are believed or accepted by an agent in that epistemic state (in the knowledge base). *Revision* and *contraction functions* are used for the representation of changes of belief. The general format is this: ⟨old knowledge base, set to retract⟩ ⟼ new knowledge base. The retract set S consists of the set of sentences *at least one of which* has to be given up. The *pick contraction* of K with respect to S, denoted $K \dot{-} \langle S \rangle$, is the minimal (most economic) contraction of the belief set K that is necessary in order to discard at least one of element of S. It is left to the agent's decision which element(s) of S is (are) best to give up.

We assume in this paper that the beliefs of an agent are closed under conjunction:

$$\{\phi_1, \ldots, \phi_n\} \subseteq K \text{ iff } \phi_1 \wedge \ldots \wedge \phi_n \in K \qquad \text{(CCl)}$$

Call two sentences *variants* iff they are accepted in exactly the same epistemic states. We are interested only in ∧-*variants*. From (CCl), we can infer that ∧ satisfies associativity, commutativity, ∧-contraction and ∧-expansion, which allows us to delete parentheses. Conjunctions show a set-like behaviour which we call the *variability of conjunctions*. Our second assumption says that ∧-variants as inputs lead to identical belief states:

$$\text{If } \phi \text{ and } \psi \text{ are } \wedge\text{-variants, then } K \dot{-} \phi = K \dot{-} \psi \qquad \text{(CEq)}$$

The next principle we are going to invoke connects rational contractions with an underlying relation of epistemic entrenchment.

$$\phi < \psi \text{ iff } \psi \in K \dot{-} \langle \{\phi, \psi\} \rangle \qquad \text{(Def <)}$$

This is to express the following idea: ψ is more firmly entrenched in K than ϕ iff the agent would keep ψ when facing with the need to give up (at least) one of ϕ and ψ.

Our last two principles concern the contractions which are referred to in (Def<). In pick contractions the goal is to retract at least one of a set of sentences from a given knowledge base K, i.e., to see to it that $S \not\subseteq Cn(K \dot{-} \langle S \rangle)$. We know from (CCl) that in order to retract one element of $\{\phi_1, \ldots, \phi_n\}$, it is necessary and sufficient to give up $\phi_1 \wedge \ldots \wedge \phi_n$. Intuitively, the latter task seems even *identical* with the former:

$$K \dot{-} \langle \phi_1, \ldots, \phi_n \rangle = K \dot{-} (\phi_1 \wedge \ldots \wedge \phi_n) \qquad \text{(Def} \langle \dot{-} \rangle)$$

Finally, pick contractions present by their very nature problems of rational choice. For any non-empty set of sentences S, the agent must make a decision which sentences of S to give up in $K \dot{-} \langle S \rangle$. He must retract at least one element of S, but may in the case of ties of course retract several of them at the same time. In order to get these restrictions started, we presuppose that $S \not\subseteq Cn(\emptyset)$). We now introduce the device of a *choice function* γ such that for every $\phi \in S$,

$$\phi \in \gamma(S) \ \text{ iff } \ \phi \notin K \dot{-} \langle S \rangle \qquad (\text{Def}\gamma)$$

In the theory of rational choice, S is called the *issue* or the *menu*, and $\gamma(S)$ is called the *choice set* of S (with respect to γ). As usual for choice functions, it is required here that $\emptyset \neq \gamma(S) \subseteq S$. Intuitively, γ picks the elements of S which are *best to withdraw* from K, or *least secure* in S. If both ϕ and ψ, say, are in $\gamma(S)$, this means that the agent suspends judgment on *both* ϕ and ψ because no decision can be reached as to which of them is worse. We restrict ourselves to the case of finite S's in order to ensure that $(\text{Def}\langle \dot{-} \rangle)$ is applicable.

The connections established by our basic principles are summarized in Fig. 1. It is only the structure imposed on pick contractions by the vertical part of the scheme which will enable us to get an efficient translation process in the horizontal part.

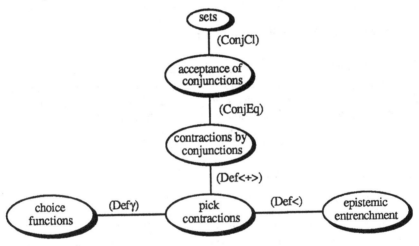

Fig. 1. Connecting choice and entrenchment

3 Translations

The general argument to be used in our translations is this:

$\phi_1 \wedge \ldots \wedge \phi_n < \psi_1 \wedge \ldots \wedge \psi_m$

iff $\psi_1 \wedge \ldots \wedge \psi_m \in K \dot{-} \langle \phi_1 \wedge \ldots \wedge \phi_n, \psi_1 \wedge \ldots \wedge \psi_m \rangle$	by (Def<)
iff $\psi_1 \wedge \ldots \wedge \psi_m \in K \dot{-} ((\phi_1 \wedge \ldots \wedge \phi_n) \wedge (\psi_1 \wedge \ldots \wedge \psi_m))$	by $(\text{Def}\langle \dot{-} \rangle)$
iff $\forall j \leq m \colon \psi_j \in K \dot{-} (\phi_1 \wedge \ldots \wedge \phi_n \wedge \psi_1 \wedge \ldots \wedge \psi_m)$	by (CCl), (CEq)
iff $\forall j \leq m \colon \psi_j \in K \dot{-} \langle \{ \phi_1, \ldots, \phi_n, \psi_1, \ldots, \psi_m \} \rangle$	by $(\text{Def}\langle \dot{-} \rangle)$
iff $\forall j \leq m \colon \psi_j \notin \gamma(\{ \phi_1, \ldots, \phi_n, \psi_1, \ldots, \psi_m \})$	by (Defγ)

In short, we have for any two finite sets of sentences S and S' with $S - S' \neq \emptyset$ that $\bigwedge S < \bigwedge S'$ iff $S' \cap \gamma(S \cup S') = \emptyset$.

3.1 From Entrenchments to Choices

The translation process is described by the above argument read from the top to the bottom. It is actually ambiguous, due to the possibility of leaving some conjunctions unbroken. We insist, however, that the standard translation must break up every conjunction into its "atomic" parts. But we are not dealing with real atoms here. For the translation of axiom schemata below, we must keep in mind that all sentential metavariables may be instantiated by conjunctions. Hence $\phi \wedge \psi < \chi$, say, must not be converted simply into $\chi \notin \gamma(\{\phi,\psi,\chi\})$, but instead into the more general $S'' \cap \gamma(S \cup S' \cup S'') = \emptyset$, where ϕ, ψ and χ are thought of as the conjunctions of the elements of S, S' and S'', respectively.

3.2 From Choices to Entrenchments

The translation process is described by the above argument read from the bottom to the top. Due to the variability of conjunctions, however, the translation process is *essentially* ambiguous. The fully general formulation is a little complicated. Let $S'_1 \cup \ldots \cup S'_k = S'$ and S_i be such that $S_i \cup S'_i = S \cup S'$, for every $i \leq k$. Then $S' \cap \gamma(S \cup S') = \emptyset$ iff for every i, $\bigwedge S_i < \bigwedge S'_i$.

3.3 Admissible Relations

Which relations $<$ over the set of all sentences in our language can possibly qualify as entrenchment relations? Our basic principles limit the field of candidate relations considerably. First, we get the condition of *substitutivity of variants*:

If ϕ and ψ are $\wedge$-variants, then $\phi < \chi$ iff $\psi < \chi$, and $\chi < \phi$ iff $\chi < \psi$ (SV)

When considering some $\gamma(S)$ we presuppose that S is finite and $S \not\subseteq Cn(\emptyset)$. Recall that the concept of a choice function requires that $\gamma(S)$ be a *non-empty* subset of S. By the above translation, this means that

$$\phi_1 \wedge \ldots \wedge \phi_n \not< \phi_i \tag{NE}$$

The ambiguity in the translation of conditions of epistemic entrenchment into choice conditions is irrelevant for our concerns. On the other hand, the ambiguity involved in the converse direction is important. This is because entrenchment relations take account of the internal structure of the sentences related. We are thus presented essentially with a many-one translation. Many conditions on the side of epistemic entrenchment correspond to exactly one condition on the side of rational choice. For this reason some nontrivial necessary conditions on entrenchment relations are to be imposed. Our aim is to make the entrenchment relation $<$ consistently translatable into (and a consistent translation of) a choice function γ. The key idea is the following condition which embodies in a nutshell the connection between *entrenchment and choice*:

$$\phi < \psi \wedge \chi \quad \text{iff} \quad \phi \wedge \psi < \chi \text{ and } \phi \wedge \chi < \psi \tag{E\&C}$$

Clearly, (E&C) is a necessary condition for translatable relations $<$, because both the left-hand side and the right-hand side of (E&C) translate into (and are translations of) $\{\psi, \chi\} \cap \gamma(\{\phi, \psi, \chi\}) = \emptyset$. Now let $S_1' \cup \ldots \cup S_k' = S'$ and S_i such that $S_i \cup S_i' = S \cup S'$, for every $i \leq k$. It can be verified that

$$\bigwedge S < \bigwedge S' \quad \text{iff} \quad \bigwedge S_i < \bigwedge S_i' \text{ for every } i$$

The right-hand side is the fully general translation for $S' \cap \gamma(S \cup S') = \emptyset$. Our standard translation and (E&C) suffice for deriving it.

Given (SV) and (E&C), (NE) is equivalent to the asymmetry of $<$. We call an arbitrary relation $<$ between sentences *admissible* (for the representation of entrenchments) if and only if it is asymmetric and satisfies (SV) and (E&C). Only admissible relations can qualify as relations of epistemic entrenchment.

4 Postulates

4.1 Postulates for Coherent Choice

The constraint (E&C) was placed on a relation $<$ since there are different ways of encoding the choices determined by γ *in one and the same issue S*. More constraints will be imposed on entrenchment relations when coherence conditions connecting choices *in different issues (of different cardinality)* are respected. The following discussion is based on a set of postulates for choice functions which are well-known in the literature on rational choice and which play—with one slight modification—a central role in the model theory of belief revision in [23].

$$\text{If } S \subseteq S', \text{ then } S \cap \gamma(S') \subseteq \gamma(S) \tag{I}$$

$$\bigcap_{i \leq k} \gamma(S_i) \subseteq \gamma(\bigcup_{i \leq k} S_i) \tag{II}$$

$$\text{If } S \subseteq S' \text{ and } \gamma(S') \subseteq S, \text{ then } \gamma(S) \subseteq \gamma(S') \tag{III}$$

$$\text{If } S \subseteq S' \text{ and } \gamma(S') \cap S \neq \emptyset, \text{ then } \gamma(S) \subseteq \gamma(S') \tag{IV}$$

Condition (I) is Sen's Property α and sometimes called "Chernoff"; (II) is a finite version of Sen's Property γ, also called "expansion axiom"; (III) is sometimes called "Aizerman's axiom"; (IV) is Sen's Property $\beta+$, also known as "Dual Chernoff". Notice that (IV) implies both (II) and (III). As there are many relations $<$ satisfying (I) – (IV), this set of postulates is consistent.

A relation $<$ is called *modular* iff $\phi < \psi$ entails that either $\phi < \chi$ or $\chi < \psi$, for every χ. Modularity and asymmetry jointly entail transitivity. A choice function γ is called *(transitively, modularly) rationalizable* iff there is a (transitive, modular) preference relation $<$ such that for all S,

$$\gamma(S) = \{\phi \in S : \text{there is no } \psi \in S \text{ such that } \psi < \phi\}$$

The following facts have been common knowledge in the theory of rational choice at least since Sen [25].

Observation 1 *Let γ be a choice function which can take all finite subsets of a given domain as arguments.*
(a) γ is rationalizable iff it is rationalizable by the preference relation defined by

$$\phi < \psi \ \ \text{iff} \ \ \psi \notin \gamma(\{\phi, \psi\}) \tag{$*$}$$

(b) γ is rationalizable iff it satisfies (I) and (II);
(c) γ is transitively rationalizable iff it satisfies (I), (II), and (III);
(d) γ is modularly rationalizable iff it satisfies (I) and (IV).

Condition ($*$) is a typical definition of "revealed preferences" which are widely used in the theory of choice and preference. It is the asymmetric version of the "base preferences" originating with H. Uzawa and K. Arrow. Condition ($*$) above can be obtained by conjoining (Def$<$) with (Defγ). Epistemic entrenchment is just a certain kind of revealed preference. It is more general insofar as it can take combinations (i.e., conjunctions) of elements rather than only single elements as arguments. The objects between which to choose possess an internal structure.

4.2 Postulates for Epistemic Entrenchment

Essentially the following set of postulates is advocated as a set of conditions suitable for capturing the notion of epistemic entrenchment in Rott [21], where a corresponding set of postulates for belief revision is specified.

$$\phi \not< \phi \tag{EE1}$$
$$\text{If } \phi < \psi \wedge \chi, \text{ then } \phi < \psi \tag{EE2$\uparrow$}$$
$$\text{If } \phi < \psi, \text{ then } \phi \wedge \chi < \psi \tag{EE2$\downarrow$}$$
$$\text{If } \phi < \psi \text{ and } \phi < \chi, \text{ then } \phi < \psi \wedge \chi \tag{EE3$\uparrow$}$$
$$\text{If } \phi \wedge \psi < \psi, \text{ then } \phi < \psi \tag{EE3$\downarrow$}$$

If we add the postulate of virtual connectivity or modularity,

$$\text{If } \phi < \psi, \text{ then } \phi < \chi \text{ or } \chi < \psi \tag{EE4}$$

we get essentially the concept of epistemic entrenchment as originally introduced by Gärdenfors and Makinson [10]. We refer to relations satisfying (EE1) – (EE3$\downarrow$)

as *generalized* relations of epistemic entrenchment, and to those satisfying in addition (EE4) as *standard* relations of epistemic entrenchment. Modularity is a very powerful condition. It corresponds to the condition of Rational Monotony—postulate ($\dot{-}8$) in the AGM nomenclature—in the theory of belief revision. For the theory of epistemic entrenchment, it has the following consequences:

Observation 2 *Suppose the relation $<$ satisfies (EE1) and (EE4). Then (a) $<$ satisfies (EE2$^\uparrow$) iff it satisfies (EE2$^\downarrow$); (b) if $<$ satisfies (EE3$^\uparrow$), then it satisfies (EE3$^\downarrow$); if $<$ is asymmetric and satisfies (EE3$^\downarrow$), then it also satisfies (EE3$^\uparrow$).*

Relations of epistemic entrenchment *with comparability* can thus be characterized, e.g., by postulates (EE1), (EE2$^\uparrow$), (EE3$^\uparrow$) and (EE4). There are also minimality and maximality conditions in [10] which correspond to the following constraints on γ:

$$\gamma(S) = S - K \text{ iff } S - K \neq \emptyset \qquad \text{(Minimality)}$$

$$\gamma(S) \cap Cn(\emptyset) = \emptyset \text{ , unless } S \subseteq Cn(\emptyset) \qquad \text{(Maximality)}$$

These conditions relate γ to K and Cn and are thus not purely structural conditions of rational choice.

5 The Postulates Translated

5.1 From Coherent Choice to Epistemic Entrenchment

We wish to see whether some widely accepted coherence criteria for choices are already taken account of by the usual requirements for epistemic entrenchment relations. By (non-trivial) application of the translation specified in Section 3.2, we get the following constraints on entrenchment relations.

$$\text{If } \phi < \psi, \text{ then } \phi \wedge \chi < \psi \qquad \text{(EI)}$$
$$\text{If } \phi \wedge \psi < \chi, \text{ then } \phi < \chi \text{ or } \psi < \chi \qquad \text{(EII)}$$
$$\text{If } \phi \wedge \psi < \chi \text{ and } \phi \wedge \chi < \psi, \text{ then } \phi < \chi \qquad \text{(EIII)}$$
$$\text{If } \phi \wedge \psi < \chi \text{ and } \psi \not< \phi \wedge \chi, \text{ then } \phi < \chi \qquad \text{(EIV)}$$

Relations satisfying—at least some interesting selection from—the postulates (EI) – (EIV) can be taken to exhibit features of rational choice.

5.2 From Epistemic Entrenchment to Coherent Choice

By (straightforward) application of the translation specified in Section 3.1 , we get the following constraints on choice functions.

$$S \cap \gamma(S) \neq \emptyset \qquad \text{(CC1)}$$

$$\text{If } (S \cup S') \cap \gamma(S \cup S' \cup S'') = \emptyset, \text{ then } S' \cap \gamma(S' \cup S'') = \emptyset \quad (CC2^\uparrow)$$

$$\text{If } S \cap \gamma(S \cup S') = \emptyset, \text{ then } S \cap \gamma(S \cup S' \cup S'') = \emptyset \quad (CC2^\downarrow)$$

$$\text{If } S' \cap \gamma(S \cup S') = \emptyset \text{ and } S'' \cap \gamma(S \cup S'') = \emptyset,$$
$$\text{then } (S' \cup S'') \cap \gamma(S \cup S' \cup S'') = \emptyset \quad (CC3^\uparrow)$$

$$\text{If } S \cap \gamma(S \cup S \cup S') = \emptyset, \text{ then } S \cap \gamma(S \cup S') = \emptyset \quad (CC3^\downarrow)$$

$$\text{If } S \cap \gamma(S \cup S') = \emptyset, \text{ then } S \cap \gamma(S \cup S'') = \emptyset$$
$$\text{or } S'' \cap \gamma(S' \cup S'') = \emptyset \quad (CC4)$$

6 Implications

We now study the relative strength of the postulates for choice and entrenchment.

6.1 Implications between Choice Postulates

Observation 3 *(a) (CC1) holds for every choice function γ; (b) ($CC2^\uparrow$) is equivalent with (III); (c) ($CC2^\downarrow$) is equivalent with (I); (d) ($CC3^\uparrow$) follows trivially from ($CC2^\downarrow$); (e) ($CC3^\downarrow$) is trivially satisfied; (f) (CC4) implies (IV), and follows from the conjunction of (I) and (IV).*

Part (d) of Observation 3 shows that although ($EE2^\uparrow$) is logically independent from ($EE2^\downarrow$) in the theory of epistemic entrenchment, the translations are not. Part (e) tells us that although ($EE3^\downarrow$) in non-trivial, its translation is. The explanation for these surprising facts is that *given the admissibility of* $<$, ($EE3^\uparrow$) is just a weakening of ($EE2^\downarrow$), and ($EE3^\downarrow$) does not add anything new. Together with Observation 1, parts (c) and (f) of Observation 3 reveal *a new axiomatization of modularly rationalizable choice functions*: A choice function is rationalizable by a modular preference relation iff it satisfies ($CC2^\downarrow$) and (CC4).

6.2 Implications between Entrenchment Postulates

We know from the previous section and the translatability of choice conditions into conditions for entrenchment relations that certain equivalences must hold between the original conditions set up in [10] and [21] and the ones derived from coherent choice. Still it is instructive to study in detail the interrelations at the level of entrenchment relations.

Observation 4 *(a) (NE) follows from (EE1) and ($EE3^\uparrow$); (b) (E&C) follows from ($EE2^\uparrow$), ($EE2^\downarrow$), ($EE3^\uparrow$) and ($EE3^\downarrow$); (c) (EI) is identical with ($EE2^\downarrow$); (d) (EII) follows from (EE1), ($EE3^\uparrow$) and (EE4); (e) (EIII) follows from ($EE2^\uparrow$), ($EE2^\downarrow$), ($EE3^\uparrow$) and ($EE3^\downarrow$); (f) (EIV) follows from ($EE2^\downarrow$), ($EE3^\downarrow$) and (EE4).*

Observation 5 *(a) (EE1) follows from (NE); (b) (EE2↑) follows from (E&C) and (EIII); (c) (EE2↓) is identical with (EI); (d) (EE3↑) follows from (E&C) and (EI); (e) (EE3↓) follows from (EIII); (f) (EE4) follows from (E&C), (EI), (EIII) and (EIV).*

For admissible relations $<$, (EIV) implies both (EII) and (EIII), just as (IV) implies (II) and (III). Thus asymmetry, (SV), (E&C), (EI) and (EIV) provide an *alternative axiomatization of epistemic entrenchment*.

7 Conclusion and Related Work

Let us summarize the major results of the previous sections in non-technical terms, thereby answering the questions asked in the introduction:

• The entrenchment postulates (EE1), (EE2↓), (EE3↑) and (EE3↓), translated into constraints on the choice of retractible sentences, are satisfied by all rationalizable choice functions. In addition, (EE2↑) is satisfied by all transitively rationalizable choice functions, and (EE4) is satisfied by all modularly rationalizable choice functions.

• The choice postulates (I) and (III), translated into constraints on the entrenchment of sentences, as well as the general admissibility constraints imposed by the interpretation of entrenchment in terms of choices, are satisfied by all generalized relations of epistemic entrenchment. In addition, the choice postulates (II) and (IV) are satisfied by all standard relations of epistemic entrenchment.

• All admissible relations $<$ satisfying the choice postulates (I) and (III), translated into constraints on the entrenchment of sentences, are generalized relations of epistemic entrenchment. If $<$ in addition satisfies (IV), translated into a constraints on the entrenchment of sentences, it is a standard relations of epistemic entrenchment.

In a companion paper [24], we study the correspondences between choice postulates and systems of nonmonotonic reasoning which are based on choices or preferences between default assumptions or expectations. It turns out that (I) corresponds to the condition "Or", (II) to a weakened form of Disjunctive Monotony, (III) to Cumulative Monotony, and (IV) to Rational Monotony. (For all these terms, see [6, 13, 16, 17].) It is interesting that seen from the present perspective, Disjunctive Monotony is at least as plausible as Cumulative Monotony.

The focus of the present paper has been the concept of epistemic entrenchment (or that of an "expectation ordering" [11]). However, we gave no material explanation where the entrenchment relations might come from. What we have attempted to give is rather a theoretical explanation or justification of *the logical constraints* for such relations. We now briefly discuss alternative ways of doing this.

First of all, we note that in the literature one can distinguish *qualitative-relational* from *quantitative-numerical* approaches, with the obvious connection that $\phi < \psi$ (where '$<$' is epistemic entrenchment) iff $Ent(\phi) < Ent(\psi)$ (where '$<$' is the usual less-than relation over ordinal or real numbers). More importantly, we can also distinguish comparative-necessity based approaches from comparative-possibility based approaches, with the connection $\phi < \psi$ iff $\neg\phi \prec \neg\psi$, or $Ent(\phi) = Plaus(\neg\phi)$ (see, e.g., [11, Appendix A2]). Here $\neg\phi \prec \neg\psi$ is to be understood as saying that $\neg\phi$ is closer to one's present beliefs, or *more* plausible, than $\neg\psi$, and similarly, smaller *Plaus*-values signify a higher plausibility. Epistemic entrenchment is perhaps the best known example of the former kind, while various people are working in the second framework, for instance, Lewis, Spohn, Grove, and Freund. In much of the work of Dubois and Prade the connection between comparative necessity and possibility is carefully discussed.

There have been several attempts to give a natural derivation of relations of comparative necessity or possibility. (In the following, we mean by an ordering a *weak* ordering in which ties are permitted.) Firstly, one can derive an ordering of propositions from an ordering of models. The basic idea is best expressed in terms of comparative possibility and says that $Plaus(\phi) = \inf\{Plaus(\omega) : \omega$ satisfies $\phi\}$. The usual logical constraints on comparative possibility are then automatically satisfied. This idea can be traced back at least to David Lewis' [14] construction of comparative possibilities out of comparative similarities and Lofti A. Zadeh's [27] construction of a possibility measure out of a possibility distribution. The latter approach has been turned into a powerful research program by Dubois and Prade and their collaborators (see, e.g., [2, 5]). The former approach has been extended and modified by Grove [12] and Spohn [26], and also—as we now know with the benefit of hindsight—in the research paradigm of Alchourrón, Gärdenfors and Makinson [1, 8, 11, 19]. Here the necessity-like concept of epistemic entrenchment has been constructed from a preference relation of maximal non-implying subsets (which in turn stand in a 1-1-correspondence to the non-models) of the current belief set. A more general model-theoretic characterization of comparative possibility without connectivity has been given by Freund [6]. Except for a limiting case condition for logical truths, his postulates for "preferential preorderings" are exact duals of the postulates for generalized epistemic entrenchment of Rott [21].

Secondly, one can draw on syntactical constructions starting from arbitrary (partial) orderings of the sentences in a belief base. Here one can distinguish a *positive* and a *negative* idea. The first one, suggested for the first time by Dubois and Prade [4], judges the entrenchment of ϕ according to the weakest elements in any proof set for ϕ. A more general version of this idea without connectivity assumptions has independently been used in [20]. The second one, suggested in Rott [22], judges the entrenchment of ϕ according to the most conservative or economical way to discard ϕ. It has been shown that in the context of prioritized belief bases this relation is identical with the relation studied in the present paper (*minimal change* vs. *competitive interpretation* of epistemic entrenchment [22]), and that it can be used to approximate prioritized base contractions in the style of Nebel [18]. It is not difficult to show that the negative idea leads to a (proper) extension of epistemic entrenchment relation < obtained from formalizing the positive idea. However, the usual way of applying epistemic entrenchment relations [10, 21] does not lead to very good results in the context of belief bases (as opposed to belief *sets* which are closed under Cn), since they suffer from what Benferhat *et al.* [2] call the "drowning effect".

Thirdly, entrenchment relations have been reconstructed from contraction behaviour over full belief sets (Gärdenfors and Makinson [10, 21]). This is evidently very close the the approach followed in this paper, but the crucial and strong AGM postulates $(K \dot{-} 7)$ and $(K \dot{-} 8)$ are not as systematically motivated as the criteria studied in rational choice theory.

Finally, we mention that the decision-theoretic or choice-theoretic framework has already been systematically employed in belief revision and nonmonotonic reasoning by Lindström [15] and Rott [23]. There, however, preferences and choices are considered on the model-theoretical level, and no relations between sentences are considered. Correspondingly, problems of conceptualization, postulates for contractions, and methods of proof are quite different. Perhaps the first author to point out the relevance of the theory of choice and its economic sense of rationality for belief revision was Doyle [3], who however used preferences over *sets* of sentences and did not study the implications of criteria of rational choice for the logic of belief change.

References

1. Alchourrón, Carlos, Peter Gärdenfors and David Makinson: 1985, "On the logic of theory change: Partial meet contraction functions and their associated revision functions", *Journal of Symbolic Logic* 50, 510–530.
2. Benferhat, Salem, Claude Cayrol, Didier Dubois, Jérôme Lang and Henri Prade: 1993, "Inconsistency management and prioritized syntax-based entailment", in R. Bajcsy (ed.), *Proceedings of the 13th International Joint Conference on Artificial Intelligence*, Morgan Kaufmann, San Mateo, Ca, 640–645.
3. Doyle, Jon: 1991, "Rational belief revision: Preliminary report", in J. Allen, R. Fikes and E. Sandewall (eds.), *Principles of Knowledge Representation and Reasoning: Proceedings of the 2nd International Conference*, Morgan Kaufmann, San Mateo, Ca., 163–174.
4. Dubois, Didier, and Henri Prade: 1987, "Necessity measures and the resolution principle", *IEEE Transactions on Systems, Man and Cybernetics* 17, 474-478.
5. Dubois, Didier, and Henri Prade: 1991, "Epistemic entrenchment and possibilistic logic", *Artificial Intelligence* 50, 223–239.
6. Freund, Michael: 1993, "Injective models and disjunctive relations", *Journal of Logic Programming* 3, 231–247.
7. Gärdenfors, Peter: 1984, "Epistemic importance and minimal changes of belief", *Australasian Journal of Philosophy* 62, 136–157.

8. Gärdenfors, Peter: 1988, *Knowledge in Flux: Modeling the Dynamics of Epistemic States*, Bradford Books, MIT Press, Cambridge, Mass.

9. Gärdenfors, Peter (ed.): 1992, *Belief Revision*, Cambridge University Press, Cambridge.

10. Gärdenfors, Peter, and David Makinson: 1988, "Revisions of knowledge systems using epistemic entrenchment", in M. Vardi (ed.), *Theoretical Aspects of Reasoning About Knowledge*, Morgan Kaufmann, Los Altos, pp. 83–95.

11. Gärdenfors, Peter, and David Makinson: 1994, "Nonmonotonic Inference Based on Expectations", *Artificial Intelligence* 65, 197–245.

12. Grove, Adam: 1988, "Two modellings for theory change", *Journal of Philosophical Logic* 17, 157–170.

13. Lehmann, Daniel, and Menachem Magidor: 1992, "What does a conditional knowledge base entail?", *Artificial Intelligence* 55, 1–60.

14. Lewis, David: 1973, *Counterfactuals*, Blackwell, Oxford.

15. Lindström, Sten: 1991, "A semantic approach to nonmonotonic reasoning: Inference operations and choice", Department of Philosophy, University of Uppsala, Uppsala Prints and Preprints in Philosophy, Number 6.

16. Makinson, David: 1990, "General patterns in nonmonotonic reasoning", in D.M. Gabbay a.o. (eds.), *Handbook of Logic in Artificial Intelligence and Logic Programming, Vol. II: Nonmonotonic and Uncertain Reasoning*, Oxford UP, Oxford, to appear.

17. Makinson, David, and Peter Gärdenfors: 1991, "Relations between the logic of theory change and nonmonotonic logic", in A. Fuhrmann and M. Morreau (eds.), *The Logic of Theory Change*, Springer LNCS 465, Berlin etc., pp. 185–205.

18. Nebel, Bernhard: 1992, "Syntax-based approaches to belief revision", in [9], pp. 52–88.

19. Rott, Hans: 1991, "Two methods of constructing contractions and revisions of knowledge systems", *Journal of Philosophical Logic* 20, 149–173.

20. Rott, Hans: 1992, "On the logic of theory change: More maps between different kinds of contraction function", in [9], pp. 122–141.

21. Rott, Hans: 1992, "Preferential belief change using generalized epistemic entrenchment", *Journal of Logic, Language and Information* 1, 45–78.

22. Rott, Hans: 1992, "Modellings for belief change: Prioritization and entrenchment", *Theoria* 58, to appear.

23. Rott, Hans: 1993, "Belief contraction in the context of the general theory of rational choice", *Journal of Symbolic Logic* 58, 1426–1450.

24. Rott, Hans: 1994, "Nonmonotonic logic = monotonic logic + choice", Manuscript, University of Konstanz, June 1994.

25. Sen, Amartya K.: 1971, "Choice functions and revealed preference", *Review of Economic Studies* 38, 307–317.

26. Spohn, Wolfgang: 1988, "Ordinal Conditional Functions", in William L. Harper and Brian Skyrms (eds.), *Causation in Decision, Belief Change, and Statistics*, vol. II, Reidel, Dordrecht, 105–134.

27. Zadeh, Lofti A.: 1978, "Fuzzy sets as a basis for a theory of possibility", *Fuzzy Sets and Systems* 1, 3–28.

A Note on Tableaux of Logic of Paradox *

Zuoquan Lin   Wei Li
Computer Science Department
Shantou University, Shantou 515063, P.R. China
zqlin%stumis@hkucnt.hku.hk
and
Computer Science Department
BUAA, Beijing 100083, P.R. China

Abstract

The logic of paradox LP proposed by Priest [1979] is one of paraconsistent logics. One of the motivations behind paraconsistent logic, namely LP, is that it should not be the case that everything follows from a single contradiction. It must pay a price , however, that some classical inferences would be invalid in LP. In Priest's recent invention, the logic of minimal paradox LP_m can overcome the drawback, such that paraconsistent logic would be equivalent to classical logic when there is not direct effect of a contradiction. Although some proof theories for LP were introduced, there has not yet been a satisfactory proof theory for LP_m. We will propose a sound and complete tableaux for LP_m in this article.

1   Introduction

The *logic of paradox LP* proposed by Priest [1979] is one of well-known paraconsistent logics in the literature (*cf.*, [14]). We say that a theory is *inconsistent* if it contains both A and $\neg A$ for some proposition A. A theory is   *trivial* if it contains every proposition. *Paraconsistent logics* are those logics in which an inconsistent theory can be nontrivial. One of the motivations behind paraconsistent logic, namely LP, is that it might get rid of triviality, *i.e.*, it should not be the case that everything follows from a single contradiction. Therefore, paraconsistent logic can be used as a tool for formalizing reasoning in the presence of inconsistency.

As a paraconsistent logic, LP can indeed localize contradictions and obtain nontriviality. It must, however, pay a price: some inferences that are classically valid are not valid in LP, so that it would be too weak to permit interesting

---

*The work is supported in part by National Hi-Tech 863 Project, in part by National Key Project of Fundamental Research Climbing Program and in part by Natural Science Foundation of China.

conclusions [13]. In Priest's recent invention [13], the logic of *minimal* paradox LP_m provided as a *nonmonotonic* extension of LP, among other things, can overcome the drawback. Interestingly, LP_m by introducing nonmonotonicity into LP can overcome the weakness problem of the paraconsistency. LP_m is nonmonotonic in a sense that the inconsistency is *minimal*. This is because the *minimally inconsistent models* of an enlarging set of premises would be changed so that some previous conclusions could be withdrawn when facing with new information .[1] LP_m has some nice properties from which it is considered interesting in formalizing commonsense reasoning with incomplete and inconsistent knowledge [9].

Originally, LP was defined as a semantic entailment of paraconsistent logic. In [7], a reasoning method based on resolution was provided as a satisfactory proof procedure for LP. The method can be easily rewritten as a so-called *mated* tableaux for LP. Essentially the same idea was first used in [3,4] as a proof theory for first-degree entailment of relevance logic [1]. [2] Similarly, a sequent calculus can also be provided for LP as pointed out in [13]. Also, LP_m was originally defined in semantic way. As pointed out in [12], there was an open problem of how to provide a satisfactory proof theory for LP_m. In [8], an attempt to revise mated tableaux for LP to fit LP_m failed as pointed out by the author himself, [3] and the problem was left open and challenge.

In this paper we will provide a *minimal* tableaux as a satisfactory proof theory for LP_m. Firstly, we present another tableaux, *signed tableaux*, for LP by modifying the procedure of *analytic tableaux* in [15]. [4] In spirit, our signed tableaux method is similar to mated tableaux one for LP [7,8] in that classical tableau rules are remained and the closed conditions of tableaux are modified to fit the paraconsistency. Then, we will propose a *minimal tableaux* for LP_m based on signed tableaux for LP. In order to capture the minimality of LP_m by tableaux we must modify the construction of signed tableaux to eliminate the *redundant* branches of of the non-minimally inconsistent models in the tableaux. Technically, our minimal tableaux method is similar to those of the literature [6] and [10] to capture nonmonotonicity, but different in a significant sense to capture paraconsistency. The tableaux are sound and complete with respect to the semantics of LP and LP_m, respectively.

The rest of the paper is organized as follows. In Section 2, we review the semantics of LP and LP_m. In Sections 3 and 4, we present the sound and complete tableaux for LP and LP_m, respectively. We make some remarks about related works in the concluding section. The proof of the sound and complete

---

[1]However, the logic LP_m is not well suitable for dealing with the reasoning with incomplete information in the sense of the motivation of nonmonotonic formalism. In [9], the logic of *circumscriptive* paradox was provided as a significant extension of LP_m which remains the nice properties of LP_m and has the ability of circumscription for nonmonotonic reasoning.

[2]There existed some quite tableau systems for other paraconsistent logics differently in spirit, for instance, the calculi C_n introduced by da Costa in the literature [2].

[3]Personal communication, 1992.

[4]Notice that (signed) tableaux has been frequently used as proof procedure for non-classical logics. As we will see in this paper, the method we used is very different from other ones for non-classical logics. It seems that we do not need to list much literatures on tableaux.

theorems of the tableaux with respect to the semantics of LP and LP_m are presented in the appendix.

2   Semantics of LP and LP_m

Throughout this paper, we suppose L as a propositional language, and the (well-formed) formulas are defined as usual. An evaluation π assigns to each atomic proposition p in L one of the following three values: 0, 1 or 01. We say that p is *true* under π if $\pi(p) = 1$ or $\pi(p) = 01$; and p is *false* under π if $\pi(p) = 0$ or $\pi(p) = 01$. Thus LP is one kind of three-valued semantics in which under an evaluation, some proposition may be *both true and false*.

Under an evaluation, truth values can be extended conventionally to non-atomic propositions as follows: [5]

1. $\neg A$ is true iff A is false; $\neg A$ is false iff A is true.

2. $A \vee B$ is true iff either A or B is true; $A \vee B$ is false iff both A and B is false

3. $A \wedge B$ is true iff both A and B are true; $A \wedge B$ is false iff either A or B is fasle.

And other connectives are defined in the standard way, *e.g.*, $A \rightarrow B$ is defined by $\neg A \vee B$.

We will write $\pi(A) = 1$ if A is *true but not false* under π; $\pi(A) = 0$ if A is *false but not true* under π; and $\pi(A) = 01$ if A is *both true and false* under π. In the following, we say that an evaluation π is a *model* of a formula A (a set S of formulas) if A (every member of S) is *true* under the evaluation .

The *semantic entailment* of LP is defined in the standard way.

Definition 1 *Let S be a set of formulas and A a formula. A is a semantic consequence of S, written as $S \models_{LP} A$, iff A is true in all models of S.*

The properties of logic LP can be easily seen by the following example.

Example 1. Let p and q be two different atomic propositions. It is easy to see that $p \wedge \neg p \models_{LP} p$; but $p \wedge \neg p \not\models_{LP} q$, for under the evaluation π such that $\pi(p) = 01$ and $\pi(q) = 0$, $p \wedge \neg p$ is true (actually it is both true and false) but q is not true.

One of the motivations behind paraconsistent logic is that we should not allow everything to follow from a single contradiction. Thus LP get rid of the triviality of classical logic, and as a paraconsistent logic, it indeed in a sense localizes contradictions. It has, however, paid a price: if A is a classically

---

[5]It is easy to illustrate truth tables of the semantics of LP according to the following definition that are actually the same as Kleene's strong three-valued logic.

consistent formula and B follows from A in classical logic, then B may not follow from A in LP. Obviously, *reductio ad absurdum* fails in LP. Exactly, what fails is the disjunctive syllogism: $A, \neg A \vee B / B$, for taking an evaluation π that makes A both true and false and B false only. In fact, the disjunctive syllogism is the only classically valid inference to fail for LP in the sense that if it is added into LP then LP collapses into classical logic [12]. It might be thought that if the disjunctive syllogism fails then the system of inference is too weak to permit reasonable conclusions [13]. The logic of *minimal* paradox LP_m, among other things, can overcome the drawback.

Notice that to obtain a LP counter example to the disjunctive syllogism we must render the situation inconsistent by making some formula both true and false. Thus it is natural to take consistency as a default assumption. LP_m extends LP based on the intuition that normally contradictions are rare, and we assign a truth value that is both true and false (01) to a proposition only when we are forced to do so, that is, only when the proposition is a contradiction. In fact, LP_m is based on the idea of nonmonotonic logic as a kind of *minimally inconsistent* entailment.[6]

Definition 2 *Let S be a set of formulas. A evaluation π of S is minimally inconsistent* (mi) *iff there is no other model π' of S such that $\pi' \prec \pi$, where the partial order $\prec$ is defined over evaluations in the following way: let π and π' be two evaluations, $\pi' \prec \pi$ iff for any atomic proposition p, if $\pi'(p) = 01$ then $\pi(p) = 01$, and there is an atomic proposition q such that $\pi(q) = 01$ but $\pi'(q) \neq 01$.*

Intuitively, $\pi' \prec \pi$ iff π contains more contradictions than π' does, and the *mi*-models are those in which the contradictions would be minimal. Semantically, we can define the semantic entailment of LP_m, written as $\models_{LP_m}$, as follows.

Definition 3 *Let S be a set of formulas and A a formula, $S \models_{LP_m} A$ iff A is true in all* minimally inconsistent models *of S.*

The properties of the logic LP_m can also be seen by the following example.

Example 2. Let p and q be two different atomic propositions. It is easy to see that $p, \neg p \vee q \models_{LP_m} q$, for the evaluation π that makes $\pi(p) = 01$ would not be a *mi*-model (actually there is only one *mi*-model π that makes both $\pi(p) = 1$ and $\pi(q) = 1$); but $\neg p \vee q, p, p \wedge \neg p \not\models_{LP_m} q$, for under the evaluation π such that $\pi(p) = 01$ and $\pi(q) = 0$, $p \wedge \neg p$ is true and q is not true.

It is clear that LP_m is nonmonotonic from the example. LP_m has some nice properties. It can give all classical consequences if the premises are consistent. This can be proved by noting that the *mi*-models of consistent premises are exactly classical models, that is, there are no assignments of 01 to any proposition of consistent premises. Moreover, LP_m still validates the disjunctive syllogism

---

[6]There is much literature on the topic of nonmonotonic logic (*cf.*, [5][9]).

even in some inconsistent situations. For example, $p, \neg p \lor q, r \land \neg r \models_{LP_m} q$. That is, LP_m validates all classical inferences except where inconsistency would make them naturally doubtful anyway [13]. The set of logical truths of LP_m is exactly that of classical logic. In the other words, LP_m is equivalent to classical logic when there is not direct effect of a contradiction.

Another interesting property of LP_m is that there is no greater danger of collapse into triviality with $\models_{LP_m}$ than with $\models_{LP}$ [13]. That is, for any formula S, if there is a minimally inconsistent model of S, then $S \models_{LP} A$ is true for every A iff $S \models_{LP_m} A$ is true for every A. Furthermore, LP_m has the well-founded property. That is, if π is a model of S then there is a minimal model π' with respect to the partial order $\prec$ [9].

Notice that LP_m is nonmonotonic only in a sense that the inconsistency is minimal. As pointed out in [9], LP_m is not enough to capture the reasoning with incomplete information as motivated in nonmonotonic logic. However, it is interesting to note that nonmonotonicity yields a solution to the weakness of paraconsistent logic.

3 Tableaux for LP

From the examples of LP we have seen that by allowing a proposition to be *both true and false*, LP destroys the triviality of classical logic: a contradiction does not imply everything. From the viewpoint of proof theory, we can get rid of the trivial problem to invalidate the proof that everything follows from a single contradiction in classical logic anyway. Perhaps the simplest way is by using the rule of *reductio ad absurdum*. According to this rule, for any formula A, A entails B iff we can infer a contradiction from $A \land \neg B$. Thus if A already is contradictory, then certainly for any B we can infer a contradiction from $A \land \neg B$; therefore A implies B. As mentioned above, *reductio ad absurdum* fails in LP. But, as presented in [3] and [7], one way to invalidate the proof of triviality is to restrict the rule of *reductio ad absurdum* as: A entails B iff we can infer a contradiction from A and $\neg B$ by *using some relevant information from B*.

The rule of *reductio ad absurdum* is just the basis of analytic tableaux [15]. We have seen in LP, the central point of paraconsistency is that if A contains a single contradiction $p \land \neg p$, then it could only infer either the contradiction $p \land p$ or the propositions p or $\neg p$ concerning the aspects of the contradiction, and not infer anything. If we would invalidate that any B followed from a single contradiction A, we could render the closed conditions of the tableaux by using the relevant information from B, *i.e.*, to check whether B is the aspects of the contradiction or not, such that B follows from A only if it is concerning with p and/or $\neg p$. With this idea of using some relevant information from B in mind, we can formulate the proof procedure by remaining the standard rules of tableaux for classical logic but modifying the closure definition of the tableaux to get rid of the triviality. One way of formalizing the rule of *restricted* reduction to absurdity is to split the tree of tableaux T for $A \land \neg B$ into two trees t_1 and t_2 of tableaux for A and $\neg B$ respectively, and define *mated* tableaux to arrive on (*cf.*, [7]). Another way to do so is by using *signed* tableaux as we will do in the following way.

Definition 4 *We introduce two symbols T (for true) and F (for false) in* L. *A signed formula has the form $T\psi$ or $F\psi$, where $\psi \in L$. We extend an evaluation π to signed formulas as follows: for every formula A,*

1. $\pi(TA) = 1$ *iff* $\pi(A) = 1$; $\pi(TA) = 01$ *iff* $\pi(A) = 01$
2. $\pi(FA) = 1$ *iff* $\pi(\neg A) = 1$; $\pi(FA) = 01$ *iff* $\pi(\neg A) = 01$.

In the other words, $\pi(TA) = true$ iff $\pi(A) = true$, and $\pi(FA) = true$ iff $\pi(\neg A) = true$. Notice that we extend LP evaluation to signed formulas similar to the way of classical logic [15]. In the following, we say that a *signed literal* is a signed formula in which the objective formula of symbols T or F is an atomic proposition or negation of an atomic proposition.

Definition 5 *A tableau is a tree whose nodes are formulas. Let ψ be a set of signed formulas. The* signed *tableaux for ψ are defined inductively according to the following rules:*

1. *The tableau with ψ as its only node is a signed tableau for ψ.*
2. *Let* T *be a signed tableau for ψ, and b a branch of* T.
   - (a) *If $T\neg\neg\alpha$ is a node of b, then the tableau obtained from* T *by extending b to $T\alpha$ is also for ψ; If $F\neg\neg\alpha$ is a node of b, then the tableau obtained from* T *by extending b to $F\alpha$ is also for ψ;*
   - (b) *If $T(\alpha \vee \beta)$ is a node of b, then the tableau obtained from* T *by adding $T\alpha$ and $T\beta$ as two children of b's leaf is also for ψ; If $F\neg(\alpha \vee \beta)$ is a node of b, then the tableau obtained from* T *by adding $F\neg\alpha$ and $F\neg\beta$ as two children of b's is also for ψ.*
   - (c) *If $T\neg(\alpha \vee \beta)$ is a node of b, then the tableau obtained from* T *by extending b to $T\neg\alpha$ and $T\neg\beta$ is also for ψ; If $F(\alpha \vee \beta)$ is a node of b, then the tableau obtained from* T *by extending b to $F\alpha$ and $F\beta$ is also for ψ.*
   - (d) *If $T(\alpha \wedge \beta)$ is a node of b, then the tableau obtained from* T *by extending b to $T\alpha$ and $T\beta$ is also for ψ; If $F\neg(\alpha \wedge \beta)$ is a node of b, then the tableau obtained from* T *by extending b to $F\neg\alpha$ and $F\neg\beta$ is also for ψ.*
   - (e) *If $T\neg(\alpha\wedge\beta)$ is a node of b, then the tableau obtained from* T *by adding $T\neg\alpha$ and $T\neg\beta$ as two children of b's leaf is also for ψ; If $F(\alpha \wedge \beta)$ is a node of b, then the tableau obtained from* T *by adding $F\alpha$ and $F\beta$ as two children of b's is also for ψ.*

Similarly, other connectives can be defined in the standard way. We say that a formula is *marked* when a rule is applied to it; otherwise, a formula is said *non-marked*.

Definition 6 *A branch b of a signed tableau* T *is complete iff non-marked formulas in b are signed literals, that is, every rule that can be used to extend b has been applied at least once. A signed tableau* T *for ψ is complete iff every branch of* T *is complete.*

Definition 7 *A branch b of a signed tableau* T *is closed iff one of the following conditions holds:*

1. *for some formula A, TA ∈ b and FA ∈ b;*

2. *for some formula A, FA ∈ b and F¬A ∈ b.*

A signed tableau T *is closed iff every branch of* T *is closed.*

Comparing with the standard tableaux for classical logic, if we add a condition that a branch contains TA and $T\neg A$ is closed into the avove definition, then the tableaux are *refutation* complete about classical logic in the sense that for any signed formula ψ, ψ is contradictory iff there is a tableau for ψ such that every branch of the tableaux is closed. Therefore, according to the rule of *reductio ad absurdum*, A entails B iff we can draw a tableau for TA and FB such that every branch of the signed tableau is closed.

As mentioned above, one way to obtain a paraconsistent logic is by restricting the rule of *reductio ad absurdum*. In the case of LP, we only need to weak the closed conditions as defined above. This leads to the following sound and complete theorem of signed tableaux with respect to the semantics of LP.

Theorem 1 *Let S be a set of formulas and A a formula. $S \models_{LP} A$ iff the signed tableaux for TS and FA are closed.*

The proof of this theorem will be given in the appendix.
We write $S \vdash_{LP} A$ to denote that the tableaux for TS and FA are closed. [7]

Example 1 (Continued). Let p, q be as in Example 1. It is easy to check that $p \wedge \neg p \vdash_{LP} p$, for the tableau for $T(p \wedge \neg p)$ and Fp has only a branch $\{Tp, T\neg p, Fp\}$ which is closed; ; but $p \wedge \neg p \not\vdash_{LP} q$, for the tableau for $T(p \wedge \neg p)$ and Fq has only a branch $\{Tp, T\neg p, Fq\}$ which is not closed.

4 Tableaux for LP_m

As noted in Section 2, LP_m is a kind of minimal entailment. In order to capture LP_m by tableaux, having to prove that A is minimally entailed by S we might modify the construction of the signed tableaux to eliminate the branches of *non-minimally-inconsistent models* of S. LP_m can be captured by the minimality of eliminating the *redundant* branches over *complete* signed tableaux.

Let t be a complete branch of a tableau. We write $\Pi(t) = \{Tp|p$ is an atomic proposition, $Tp \in t$ and $T\neg p \in t\}$.

---

[7] Perhaps the reader could describe the procedure clearly by expoiting the tree-like structure of signed tableaux.

Definition 8 *A branch b of signed tableau* T *is* redundant, *iff b is complete and there is another complete branch b' of* T *such that* $\Pi(b') \subset \Pi(b)$. *We say that a non-redundant branch of a signed tableau is a* minimal branch *of the tableau. The* minimal tableaux T_m *for* ψ *is taken from the signed tableaux* T *for* ψ *by eliminating every redundant branch of* T.

Definition 9 *A signed tableaux* T *for* ψ *is* minimally closed *iff every non-redundant branch of* T *is closed, that is, the minimal tableaux* T_m *for* ψ *is closed.*

Parallel to Theorem 1, we have the following sound and complete theorem of minimal tableaux with respect to the semantics of LP_m.

Theorem 2 *Let S be a set of formulas and A a formula.* $S \models_{LP_m} A$ *iff the signed tableaux for TS and FA is minimally closed.*

Again the proof of this theorem will be given in the appendix.

We write $S \vdash_{LP_m} A$ to denote that the minimal tableaux for TS and FA is closed.

Example 2 (Continued). Let p, q and r be as in Example 2 . It is easy to check that $p, \neg p \vee q \vdash_{LP_m} q$, since there are two branches in which $b_1 = \{Tp, T\neg p, Fq\}$ is redundant and $b_2 = \{Tp, Tq, Fq\}$ is closed; $p, \neg p \vee q, p \wedge \neg p \not\vdash_{LP_m} q$, since non-redundant one of two branches $b_1 = \{Tp, T\neg q, Fq\}$ is not closed (the other branch $b_2 = \{Tp, Tq, T\neg p, Fq\}$ is redundant because $T(b_1) \subset T(b_2)$); and $p, \neg p \vee q, r \wedge \neg r \vdash_{LP_m} q$, since there are two branches, the one $b_1 = \{Tp, T\neg p, Fq, Tr, T\neg r\}$ is redundant and the other $b_2 = \{Tp, Tq, Fq, Tr, T\neg r\}$ is closed.

5 Concluding Remarks

In summary, LP, as a paraconsistent logic, destroys the triviality for formalizing reasoning in the presence of inconsistency, but it invalidates some classical inferences that seem too weak to permit reasonable conclusions. The logic of minimal paradox, LP_m, as a nonmonotonic extension of paraconsistent logic, among other things, can overcome the drawback of LP with some nice properties in a significant way. Actually, most paraconsistent logics have the properties similar to LP. Therefore the technique of LP_m can be applied to extend other paraconsistent and relevance logics and obtain the nice properties similar to LP_m. In particular, the signed tableaux for the first-degree entailment of relevance [1] based on a four-valued semantics can be obtained by slightly changing the closed conditions of the tableaux. Futhermore, the minimal tableaux developed in this paper can also be used as satisfactory proof theories for some paraconsistent and nonmonotonic logics. For example, [9] provides the semantics of logic LP_c by combining LP with the ability of circumscription for nonmonotonic reasoning, which is *truly* paraconsistent and nonmonotonic. The minimal tableaux for LP_c can be obtained by slightly modifying the definition of redundant branches.

The main results of this paper can be straightforwardly extended into first-order case. It is not difficult to obtain the signed tableaux for first-order LP and its sound and complete theorems. The minimal tableaux for first-order LP_m can also be defined. Surprisingly, we could also obtain the sound and complete theorems of the minimal tableaux for first-order LP_m. Notice that the sound and complete theorems of the minimal tableaux for circumscription is only partially correct in first-order case. This is due to the nonmonotonicity of LP_m is weaker than most nonmonotonic logics, and hence LP_m has the well-founded property. Therefore we hope to obtain better results for first-order LP_m than the case of nonmonotonic logic, and shed some new lights on the applications of LP_m in formalizing commonsense reasoning in the future.

Appendix: Proofs of Theorems

Theorem 1 Let S be a set of formulas and A a formula. $S \models_{LP} A$ iff $S \vdash_{LP} A$, i.e., the signed tableaux T for TS and FA are closed.

Proof. Suppose that T is a signed tableau for TS and FA which is closed. We prove that $S \models_{LP} A$. Let π be a model of S. We need to prove that π is also a model of A. Suppose otherwise, π is not a model of A, then $\pi(\neg A) = 1$, and $\pi(FA) = 1$. Since T is a signed tableau for TS and FA and $\pi(FA) = 1$, it is straightforward to see that there is a branch b of complete T such that π is a model of every formulas and $\pi(FA) = 1$ in b by induction on the construction of T. But this is impossible because by the definition of closure, either there might be some atomic proposition p such that $Tp \in b$ and $Fp \in b$, and hence $\pi(Tp) = 1$ and $\pi(Fp) = 1$ in b, or else there might be some atomic proposition p such that $Fp \in b$ and $F\neg p \in b$, and hence $\pi(Fp) = 1$ and $\pi(F\neg p) = 1$ in b, this is a contradiction. From the contradiction we conclude that π must be a model of A.

Conversely, suppose that $S \models_{LP} A$. We prove that there is a signed tableau T for TS and FA such that T is closed. We claim that T is closed. Suppose otherwise, then there is a branch b of complete T such that b is not closed. Construct an evaluation π as follows: for any atomic proposition p,

1. if $Tp \cup Fp \in b$, then $\pi(p) = 01$,

2. if $Tp \in b$ but $T\neg p \notin b$, then $\pi(p) = 1$,

3. if $Fp \in b$ but $F\neg p \notin b$, then $\pi(p) = 0$,

4. otherwise, assign $\pi(p)$ indifferently.

It is straightforward to see that π is a model of every formulas (including S), and for any formula ψ (including $\neg A$), $\pi(\psi) = 1$ by induction on the complexity of formulas. Thus π is a model of S, but is not a model of A, a contradiction with the assumption $S \models_{LP} A$, and we conclude that T must be closed.

As a corollary to the proof, we have the following simple proposition.

Corollary 1 Let S be a set of formulas. $S \models_{LP} A$ for every formula A iff for any complete signed tableau T of TS, any atomic proposition p, and any branch b of T, both Tp and $T\neg p$ are in b.

Theorem 2 Let S be a set of formulas and A a formula. $S \models_{LP_m} A$ iff $S \vdash_{LP_m} A$, *i.e.*, the signed tableaux T for TS and FA is minimally closed.

Proof. Suppose there is a signed tableau T for TS and FA such that T is minimally closed. We prove that $S \models_{LP_m} A$. Let π be a minimally inconsistent model of S. We need to prove that π is a model of A. Suppose otherwise, π is not a model of A, then $\pi(\neg A) = 1$, and $\pi(FA) = 1$. Since T is a signed tableau for TS and FA and $\pi(FA) = 1$, it is straightforward to see that there is a branch b of complete T such that π is a model of every formulas in b by induction on the construction of T. We claim that b is not closed. Otherwise, as in the case of Theorem 1, this is impossible because by the definition of closure, either there might be some atomic proposition p such that $Tp \in b$ and $Fp \in b$, and hence $\pi(Tp) = 1$ and $\pi(Fp) = 1$ in b, or else there might be some atomic proposition p such that $Fp \in b$ and $F\neg p \in b$, and hence $\pi(Fp) = 1$ and $\pi(F\neg p) = 1$ in b, this is a contradiction. We claim that b is not redundant. Otherwise, for some atomic proposition $p \in b$, we have another branch b' of T such that $\Pi(b') \subset \Pi(b)$. Defining an evaluation π' as follows: for any atomic proposition p,

1. if $Tp \cup T\neg p \in b'$, then $\pi'(p) = 01$,

2. if $Tp \in b'$ but $T\neg p \notin b'$, then $\pi'(p) = 1$,

3. if $Fp \in b'$ but $F\neg p \notin b'$, then $\pi'(p) = 0$,

4. otherwise, assign $\pi'(p)$ indiffrently.

It is straightforward to see that π' is a model of S by induction on the complexity of formulas. If $\pi'(p) = 01$ then $Tp \cup T\neg p \in b'$, but since $\Pi(b') \subset \Pi(b)$ we have $Tp \cup T\neg p \in b$ and hence $\pi(p) = 01$. By $\Pi(b') \subset \Pi(b)$ there is an atomic proposition q such that $Tq \cup T\neg q \in b$ but $Tq \cup T\neg q \notin b'$. We have $\pi(q) = 01$ but $\pi'(q) \neq 01$, and $\pi' \prec \pi$, contadicting the supposed minimality of π. From the contradictions we have that every tableau T for TS and FA contains a branch b which is neither closed nor redundant, and conclude that π must be a model of A.

Conversely, suppose that $S \models_{LP_m} A$. We prove that there is a signed tableau T for TS and FA such that T is minimally closed. We claim that T is minimally closed. Suppose otherwise, then there is a branch b of complete T such that b is neither closed nor redundant. Since b is not closed, we construct an evaluation π as follows: for any atomic proposition p,

1. if $Tp \cup T\neg p \in b$, then $\pi(p) = 01$,

2. if $Tp \in b$ but $T\neg p \notin b$, then $\pi(p) = 1$,

3. if $Fp \in b$ but $F\neg p \notin b$, then $\pi(p) = 0$,

4. otherwise, assign $\pi(p)$ indifferently.

It is straightforward to see that π is a model of every formulas (including S), and for any formula ψ (including $\neg A$), $\pi(\psi) = 1$ by induction on the complexity of formulas. Thus π is a model of S, but is not a model of A. We claim that π must be minimal. For otherwise, there is a model π' of S such that $\pi' \prec \pi$. Then there is a branch b' of complete T such that π' is a model of every formulas in b'. Let $Tp \cup T\neg p \in b'$ then $\pi'(p) = 01$, and this implies $\pi(p) = 01$ for $\pi' \prec \pi$, and hence $Tp \cup T\neg p \in b$. Similarly, there is an atomic proposition q such that $\pi(q) = 01$ but $\pi'(\neg q) \neq 01$, and hence we have $Tq \cup T\neg q \in b$ but $Tq \cup T\neg q \notin b'$. Thus we have proven that $\Pi(b') \subset \Pi(b)$. contradicting the hypothesis that b is not redundant. Therefore, π is a minimally inconsistent model of S, but is not a model of A , a contradiction with the assumption of $S \models_{LP_m} A$. We conclude that T must be minimally closed.

As a result of Theorem 1 and Theorem 2, we also prove the following *reassurance theorem* announced in [13] without proof.

Theorem 3 For a set of formulas S, if there is a minimally inconsistent of S, and $S \models_{LP} A$ is true for every A iff $S \models_{LP_m} A$ is true for every A. That is, there is no more danger of collapsing into triviality with $\models_{LP_m}$ than with $\models_{LP}$.

Proof. It is easy to see that we only need to prove that if there exists a minimally inconsistent model of S, and $S \models_{LP_m} A$ is true for any formula A, then $S \models_{LP} A$ is also true for every formula A. This is also straightforward by Corollary 1 and Theorem 2.

Acknowledgement

This note was written as a revision from Lin [1989] which was pointed out to fail to capture LP_m by the tableaux. The author would like to thank Fangzhen Lin for giving me such a challenging problem.

References

[1] Anderson. R and Belnap. N, *Entailment*, Vol. 1, (Princeton, 1975)

[2] da Costa. N and Alves. E, *A Semantic Analysis of the Calculi C_n*, Notre Dame J. of Formal Logic 15 (1977),621-630

[3] Dunn. M, *Intuitive Semantics for First-Order Entailments and 'Coupled Tree'*, Philosophical Studies, 29 (1976), 149-168

[4] Dunn. M, *A Sieve for Entailments*, J. of Philosophical Logic, 9 (1980), 41-57

[5] Ginsberg. M (Ed.), *Readings in Nonmonotonic Reasoning*, (Morgan Kaufmann, 1987)

[6] Hintikka. J, *Model Minimization – An Alternative to Circumscription*, J. of Automated Reasoning, 4 (1988)

[7] Lin. F, *Reasoning in the Presence of Inconsistency*, Proceedings of AAAI-87, (Morgan Kaufmann, 1987), 139-143

[8] Lin. F, *Tableau Systems for Logic of Paradox*, draft, 1989

[9] Lin. Z, *Circumscription in a Paraconsistent Logic*, Proceedings of Canadian Artificial Intelligence Conference, Banff, Alberta, 1994

[10] Olivetti. N, *Tableaux and Sequent Calculus for Minimal Entailment*, J. of Automated Reasoning 9 (1992), 99-139

[11] Priest. G, *Logic of Paradox*, J. of Philosophical Logic, 8 (1979), 219-241

[12] Priest. G, *Consistency by Default*, Technical Report, Automated Reasoning Project, Austrialian National University, 1988

[13] Priest. G, *Reasoning about Truth*, Artificial Intelligence, 39 (1989), 231-244

[14] Priest. G et al. (Eds.), *Paraconsistent Logic: Essays in the Inconsistency*, (Philosophia Verlag, 1989)

[15] Smullyan. M, *First-Order Logic*, (Springer Verlag, 1968)

When nonmonotonicity comes from distances

Nicholas Asher and Jérôme Lang

IRIT, Université Paul Sabatier
118, route de Narbonne
F-31062 Toulouse Cedex, France
E-mail: asher,lang@irit.fr

Abstract. We propose a methodology for defining nonmonotonic inference relations, involving distances (in a non-topological meaning) between "labels", each label being associated with a logical theory. Our framework is motivated by applications to spatial reasoning (reasoning by proximity) and taxonomic reasoning, though it also applies to temporal reasoning (degradation of persistence). We propose several ways of defining nonmonotonic inference relations from distances.

1 Introduction

In the literature of nonmonotonic reasoning, and, analogously, belief revision, it has been widely recognized that most nonmonotonic inference relations have or impose an underlying *ordering structure* on worlds, or sets of worlds (e.g. [14], [15], [11]). Now, ordering relations are also used (in a more syntactical way - they are called then *priorities*) in syntax-based default reasoning (e.g. [17] [3] [1] [16]); and more generally, orderings and priorities are exploited in other nonmonotonic formalisms, in belief revision (e.g. [10]'s epistemic entrenchment relations), in updating formalisms, in logic programming, etc.

One major question which is often unanswered is *where do these orderings and priorities come from?* Two answers are given in the literature:

- orderings come from the user. In this case, they usually represent uncertainty: some statements are more reliable than others.
- orderings derive from a knowledge base consisting in a set of default rules $\alpha_i \mathrel{\vdash} \beta_i$ (or equivalently from a set of conditional statements $\alpha_i \rightarrow \beta_i$) which determines a nonmonotonic inference relation. In Rational Closure [15] and in System-Z [18], defaults are automatically ranked according to their *specificity* and this ranking induces a rational inference relation.

In this paper, we propose an alternative way to induce orderings, and consequently an alternative way to derive inference relations. Here, orderings come directly from *pseudo-distances*[1]. These pseudo-distances can apply to time points, points of space, sources, situations, classes, and other types of things. To induce nonmonotonic inferences from distances, we "reason by *proximity*, which is a sort of *extrapolation* process. Consider for instance a time-stamped knowledge base, i.e. a set of formulas, each formula being indexed by the time point when it was put in the knowledge base: it is clear that the more recent the information, the more certain we are that it is still holding, and thus the more priority it should be assigned (provided that the given formulas encode fluents[2] which generally tend to persist). As a second example, consider a knowledge base consisting in observations at different points of a given region. Suppose that we do not know whether a given formula holds at

---

[1] We avoid using the word *distance* which evokes the topological definition; our pseudo-distances are not necessarily defined on a completely ordered scale, they are not necessarily symmetrical, nor necessarily satisfy the triangle inequality.

[2] A fluent is a proposition whose truth value changes with time.

a point x. To find out, we may consider points *close* to x at which information is known; the closer y is to x, the more pertinent is the information at y to x. We then extrapolate for x. The general principle behind these examples is that distances between "labels" (time points, points in the space etc.) play the role of priorities: the closer the labels, the higher the priority. Thus, from a labelled (temporal, spatial etc.) knowledge base we will define a set of nonmonotonic inference relations–one for each label. Our examples will focus on temporal, spatial, and taxonomic reasoning. We first develop the basic formalism and supply it with a modal semantics. Then we propose three different ways of defining nonmonotonic inference relations from pseudo-distances: *projection* (which is intuitive and easy to compute, but which sometimes gives unintended results), *radial accumulation* (which gives a rational inference relation when the distance is complete) and prioritized syntax-based entailment.

2 Labelled pseudo-metric structures

2.1 Labels and pseudo-distances

The general structure we have in mind is the following. We have a collection of knowledge items, i.e. formulas labelled by something indicating the location of the observation, or when it was put in the knowledge base, etc. This set of "labels" will be equipped with a kind of metric.[3] From now on, $\mathcal{L}$ denotes a propositional language whose formulas are denoted by greek letters φ, ψ etc. $\top$ and $\perp$ denote respectively tautology and contradiction, $\vdash$ classical entailment and $Cn(S)$ the set of all logical consequences of the set of formulas S.

Definition 1 (label structure) *A label structure is a pair $\langle X, d \rangle$ where X (the label set) is a nonempty set and d (the pseudo-distance on X) is a mapping from $X \times X$ to a (completely or not) ordered set U_d (the distance scale) with a minimal element denoted 0, verifying $\forall y \in X, d(x,y) = 0$ iff $x = y$.*

From d we induce the collection of pre-ordering relations (i.e. reflexive and transitive relations) $\leq_x, x \in X$, defined by: $\forall x, y, z \in X$, $y \leq_x z$ iff $d(x,y) \leq d(x,z)$. Intuitively, $y \leq_x z$ means that y is closer to x than z. If U_d is completely ordered, then all $\leq_x$ are complete preorderings. In this case, d and $\langle X, d \rangle$ are both said to be *complete*. $y <_x z$ will be an abbreviation for $y \leq_x z$ and not ($z \leq_x y$). Note that we have $\forall y \in X, x \leq_x y$ and $\forall y \in X, y \leq_x x \Leftrightarrow x = y$.

As illustrations, we will explain each new definition with respect to *spatial* structures. However, the reader should keep in mind that the framework is much more general. As a simple example of a label structure, we consider the discretized portion of 2-dimensional space $\{(x,y),\ x = 0, 1, 2, 3,\ y = 0, 1, 2, 3\}$ equipped with the distance $d((x,y),(x',y')) = |x - x'| + |y - y'|$. The distance scale is obviously $U_d = \{0, 1, ..., 6\}$.

Definition 2 (labelled formula, labelled knowledge base) *Let $\langle X, d \rangle$ be a label structure. If φ is a formula of $\mathcal{L}$ and Y is a non-empty subset of X then $Y : \varphi$ is a labelled formula, meaning that φ holds at every label of Y. When Y is a singleton we will note $y : \varphi$ instead of $\{y\} : \varphi$.*

A labelled knowledge base LKB is a finite set of labelled formulas.

The theory at label x induced by LKB, denoted by $Cn_x(LKB)$ is the logical closure of the set of all formulas $Y_i : \varphi_i$ in LKB such that $x \in Y_i$. The logical closure of LKB, denoted $Cn(LKB)$ is the collection of closed theories $\{Cn_x(LKB), x \in X\}$.

---

[3] So far no internal operation on the set of labels is needed, and so our framework has thus far very little to do with [9]'s labelled deductive systems.

Note that, in practice, LKB may contain punctual *observations* $y_i : \varphi_i$ as well as *constraints* holding at every label $X : \varphi_j$.

We say that a labelled knowledge base is consistent iff it is consistent at every label, i.e. if all theories $Cn_x(LKB)$ are consistent. In this paper, we restrict our attention to consistent labelled knowledge bases only.[4] H being a consistent labelled theory, $H(x)(= Cn_x(LKB))$ will denote the theory at label x; thus $H = \{H(x)|x \in X\}$.

Example: let $\langle X, d \rangle$ be the discrete spatial structure as defined above, and $LKB = \{X : \neg(r \wedge s); \ \{(0,1),(0,2)\} : r \vee s; \ (1,0) : \neg s; (1,3) : \neg r; \ (3,0) : \neg r \wedge \neg s; \ \{(2,2),(3,2)\} : r\}$ (where r and s stand respectively for raining and snowing). LKB is depicted by Figure 1. The induced labelled theory contains, for example, $\neg s$ at label $(3,2)$.

x \ y	0	1	2	3
0		$r \vee s$	$r \vee s$	
1	$\neg s$			$\neg r$
2			r	
3	$\neg r \wedge \neg s$		r	

and everywhere: $\neg(r \wedge s)$

Figure 1: a spatial example of a labelled knowledge base

2.2 Examples of labelled pseudo-metric structures

- $X = [t_{min}, t_{max}]$ is a linear time scale (discrete or continuous) and labels are time points; $d(x,y) = |x - y|$.
- X is still a time scale but $d(x,y) = (sign(x-y), |x-y|)$, with $(s, \alpha) \leq (s', \alpha')$ iff $s = s'$ and $\alpha \leq \alpha'$, or $\alpha = 0$. This non-complete, non-symmetrical pseudo-distance considers past and future separately.
- X is a region of a n-dimensional Euclidean space, and labels are points (of the Euclidean plan, of space, ...); d is the Euclidean distance of X.
- X is still a region of a n-dimensional Euclidean space, but $d(x,y)$ is the vector **xy**, with the ordering $\mathbf{u} \leq \mathbf{v}$ iff $\mathbf{u} = k.\mathbf{v}$ with $0 \leq k \leq 1$.
- X is a set of *sources*; a source being closer to another if it generally behaves the same way, give the same information, has the same opinion etc.). The actual situation may be considered as a distinguished source s_0.
- $X = 2^S$ where S is a set of *hypotheses*; d can be the symmetric difference between subsets of S (the ordering on U_d being set inclusion), or the cardinality of the symmetric difference. A label, i.e. a set of hypotheses, corresponds to a "situation" or a "configuration". Thus, applying our methodology here consists roughly in completing the context of an environment by adding what is true in the "closest" environments.
- X is a taxonomic graph (the labels being classes or types of situations), d is a distance between classes - given with the graph. Applying our methodology here means that if a property of an object is not known, one extrapolates from the most similar classes (the closest w.r.t d). This gives rise to a kind of reasoning by analogy.

2.3 A modal view of pseudo-metric structures

It is possible to give our labelled structures a modal interpretation.[5] Since the knowledge at a label is generally not complete, each label will be associated not with a single world but with a set of worlds:

---

[4] This restriction to consistent knowledge bases assumes that we get first rid of punctual inconsistencies (by any method - there are many in the literature). A discussion of this point is beyond the scope of this paper.

[5] This section is not necessary for understanding most of the rest of the paper.

Definition 3 (pseudo-metric model) *A pseudo-metric model for a pseudo-metric structure* $\langle X, d \rangle$ *is a 4-uple* $M = \langle W, m, C, \mathcal{O} \rangle$ *where* W *is a set of worlds,* m *a classical meaning function on worlds (i.e.* $\forall w \in W$, $m(w) \subseteq \mathcal{L}$); C *is an equivalence relation on* W, *and* $\mathcal{O} = \{\leq_w, w \in W\}$ *is a collection of reflexive and transitive relations verifying* $\forall w' \in W, w \leq_w w'$.

The relation C defines clusters of worlds (one cluster for each label). Now, a consistent labelled theory whose atomic formulas and subformulas define a sublanguage of $\mathcal{L}$, $\mathcal{L}_H$ L induces a "biggest" labelled pseudo-metric model defined as the collection of all maximal consistent sets of $\mathcal{L}_H$ formulas that make all the formulas labelled at x in H true, for all $x \in X$. Note that several duplicate worlds (i.e. mapped identically by m) may appear in different clusters, since they may be possible at different labels. We will assume that these are distinguished by indices. Lastly, the preordering $\leq_w$ is the transposition of $\leq_x$. Formally:

Definition 4 *The pseudo-metric model* M_H *associated with the consistent labelled theory* H *on* $\langle X, d \rangle$ *is the tuple* $M = \langle W*, m, C, \mathcal{O}* \rangle$ *where:* $W* = \bigcup \{D(x) : x \in X\}$, $D(x) = \{w_x | w_x$ *is a maximal consistent set of* $\mathcal{L}_H$ *formulas that includes* $H(x)\}$ *(duplicate worlds being distinguished by the label* x*), and* $\mathcal{O}* = \{\leq_w \mid \leq_w$ *is reflexive and transitive on* $W*$ *and if* $w \in C(x)$, $w' \in C(y)$ *and* $w'' \in C(z)$ *then* $w' \leq_w w''$ *iff* $y \leq_x z\}$.

In the example of figure 1, for example, $C((0,0)) = \{r\bar{s}, \bar{r}s, \bar{r}\bar{s}\}$, $C((0,1)) = \{r\bar{s}, \bar{r}s\}$, etc.

We have the following property: w being any world in $C(x)$, $\varphi \in H(x) \Leftrightarrow w \models \Box\varphi$ (φ is known at x). Since this is true for each $w \in C(x)$ we will note $C(x) \models \Box\varphi$. $\Box$ is from S5 since C is an equivalence relation. The structure (W, m, C) enables us to draw *monotonic* conclusions. $\mathcal{O}$ will then enable nonmonotonic conclusions; namely we will define a nonmonotonic inference relation $\alpha \hspace{1mm}\mid\hspace{-3mm}\sim_{H,x}\beta$ for each $x \in X$. To a class c of nonmonotonic inference relations induced by distances there will be a conditional operator $\Rightarrow^c$ such that $\alpha \hspace{1mm}\mid\hspace{-3mm}\sim_{H,x}^{c}\beta$ iff $M_H, C(x) \models \alpha \Rightarrow^c \beta$.

3 Extrapolation by projection

We now propose to draw nonmonotonic conclusions at a given label, using the following intuitive principle: our background knowledge being represented by H, then φ nonmonotonically entails ψ at label x iff at the closest labels where φ is known to hold and the truth value of ψ is determined, then this truth value is TRUE. To guarantee that these *closest labels* exist, we have to add an extra assumption:

Definition 5 (smooth labelled theories) *A consistent labelled theory* H *is smooth iff* $\forall x \in X, \forall \varphi \in \mathcal{L}$, *for any infinite* $\leq_x$-descending chain $\{z_i\}_{i \geq 1}$ *such that* $\forall i, \varphi \in H(z_i)$, *then* $\exists \bar{z} \in X$ *such that* $\bar{z} = \lim_{i \to \infty} z_i$ *and* $\varphi \in H(\bar{z})$.

We will only consider subsequently smooth labelled theories. This constraint is easily fulfilled, of course if X is finite or if H associates a non-trivial theory to only a finite number of labels. It is also fulfilled also if $\langle X, d \rangle$ is a topological metric space and $\forall\varphi$, the set of labels where φ is true is topologically closed.[6] In the rest of the Section, H is a smooth consistent labelled theory.

Definition 6
$Known_H(\varphi) = \{x \in X | \varphi \in H(x)\}$; $Det_H(x, \varphi) = Known_H(\varphi) \cup Known_H(\neg\varphi)$

Thus, $Known_H(\varphi)$ is the set of labels where φ is known to be true (w.r.t. H) and $Det_H(\varphi)$ is the set of labels where φ has a determined truth value. Now, ψ is inferred

---

[6] Note that this last condition is fulfilled if H is the logical closure of a labelled knowledge base $LKB = \{Y_i : \varphi_i, i = 1...n\}$ such that all Y_i's are topologically closed.

nonmonotonically from φ given H iff φ implies logically ψ [7] or ψ holds at all closest labels where φ is known to be true and ψ is determined:

Definition 7 (projection inference relation)
$\varphi \mathrel{\vdash\mkern-9mu\sim} _{H,x}^{PROJ} \psi$ iff $\varphi \vdash \psi$ or $Min(\leq_x, Known(\varphi) \cap Det_H(\psi)) \subseteq Known(\psi)$

In the simple case where $\varphi = \top$ (which is frequent in practice) the definition reduces to $\top \mathrel{\vdash\mkern-9mu\sim} _{H,x}^{PROJ} \psi$ iff $Min(\leq_x, Det_H(\psi)) \subseteq Known(\psi)$.

We can see a similarity between the definition of projection entailment and preferential entailment where one looks if ψ holds in all preferred φ-worlds; here we are dealing with *clusters of worlds* instead of worlds, and one looks if ψ holds in all closest (preferred) "φ-clusters" where ψ has a determined truth value.[8]

An immediate and important property of $\mathrel{\vdash\mkern-9mu\sim} _{H,x}^{PROJ}$ is that it preserves what is already known in the labelled theory H:

Proposition 1 *if $\psi \in H(x)$ then $\mathrel{\vdash\mkern-9mu\sim} _{H,x}^{PROJ} \psi$*

Proposition 2 *Let $\Rightarrow^P$ be the conditional operator defined by $M, w \models \varphi \Rightarrow^P \psi$ iff $\forall w' \leq_w$-minimal such that $M, w' \models \Box\varphi \wedge (\Box\psi \vee \Box\neg\psi)$, then $w' \models \psi$. Then $\varphi \mathrel{\vdash\mkern-9mu\sim} _{H,x}^{PROJ} \psi$ iff $M_H, f(x) \models \varphi \Rightarrow^P \psi$.*

The Example in Figure 1 and *PROJ*:
• at label $(1,1)$, nothing else than the constraint $\neg(s \wedge r)$ is known for sure; the closest label where s is determined is $(1,0)$ (at distance 1), therefore $\mathrel{\vdash\mkern-9mu\sim} _{H,(1,1)}^{PROJ} \neg s$. Now, the closest labels where r is determined are $(1,3)$ and $(2,2)$ (at distance 2) but they disagree about its truth value. Therefore, neither r nor $\neg r$ is inferred (from $\top$) at $(1,1)$.
• at label $(1,2)$ we get $\mathrel{\vdash\mkern-9mu\sim} _{H,(1,2)}^{PROJ} r \vee s$ (the closest labels where $r \vee s$ is determined are $(0,2)$ and $(2,2)$) and $\mathrel{\vdash\mkern-9mu\sim} _{H,(1,2)}^{PROJ} \neg s$ (the closest label where s is determined is $(2,2)$). However we cannot infer r nor $\neg r$ since the closest labels where r is determined, i.e., $(1,3)$ and $(2,2)$, disagree on r.

This last example shows that $\mathrel{\vdash\mkern-9mu\sim} _{H,x}^{PROJ}$ does not satisfy the (And) property since $\mathrel{\vdash\mkern-9mu\sim} _{H,(1,2)}^{PROJ} r \vee s$, $\mathrel{\vdash\mkern-9mu\sim} _{H,(1,2)}^{PROJ} \neg s$ and however $\mathrel{\not\vdash\mkern-9mu\sim} _{H,(1,2)}^{PROJ} r$ [9] and thus is not even a *basic* consequence relation in the sense of [11]. However, projection entailment is rather easy to compute and we think it might be adequate in some simple cases. In the next section we propose another definition which is generally more satisfactory.

4 Extrapolation by radial accumulation in the complete case

We assume $\langle X, d \rangle$ is complete (the general case is not considered in this paper for lack of space) and propose now a second inference relation consisting intuitively in gathering together the pieces of information attached to the labels inside *spheres* around x; one considers first the smallest sphere $\{x\}$, and then larger and larger spheres, until we can prove one of the formulas we look for.

---

[7] this condition is needed to ensure that $\perp \mathrel{\vdash\mkern-9mu\sim} _{H,x}^{PROJ} \psi$, and thus to guarantee supraclassicality [11].
[8] The alternative definition $\varphi \mathrel{\vdash\mkern-9mu\sim} _{H,x}^{PROJ} \psi$ iff $\varphi \vdash \psi$ or $Min(\leq_x, Known(\varphi)) \subseteq Known(\psi)$ would be too cautious: take for instance $\varphi = \top$, then $Min(\leq_x, Known(\top)) = \{x\}$ and thus $\mathrel{\vdash\mkern-9mu\sim} _{H,x}^{PROJ} \psi$ iff $\psi \in H(x)$ (i.e., $\mathrel{\vdash\mkern-9mu\sim} _{H,x}^{PROJ}$ would be reduced to its monotonic part).
[9] More intuitively, although there is a close label where $r \vee s$ is known and another close label where $\neg s$ is known, there is no close label where both are known together; in other terms, projection does not allow for using in a proof formulas known at different labels

Definition 8 (spheres and theories around a label) *Let H be a labelled theory, x a label, φ a formula and $\rho \in U$.*

$S(x,\rho) = \{y \in X | d(x,y) \leq \rho\}$

$Th(x,\rho,H) = Cn(\bigcup_{y \in S(x,\rho)} H(y))$

To avoid problems with infinite descending chains of spheres, we add:

Definition 9 *A labelled theory H is s-smooth iff for any descending chain $\{\rho_i\}_{i \geq 1}$ such that $\forall i, \; \varphi \in Th(x,\rho_i,H)$, then $\varphi \in Th(x,\bar{\rho},H)$ where $\bar{\rho} = \lim_{i \to \infty} \rho_i$*

Proposition 3 *if $\mathcal{L}$ is finite then H is s-smooth iff it is smooth.*

Let H be a s-smooth labelled theory.

Definition 10 $Rad(x,\varphi,H) = Min\{\rho \in U, \varphi \in Th(x,\rho,H)\}$

It is worth noticing that $\varphi \mapsto Rad(x,\varphi,H)$ is a kind of necessity function [10] (see for instance [7]), which is expressed by the following proposition:

Proposition 4 *(i) $Rad(x,\top,H) = 0$*
(ii) $Rad(x,\perp,H) > 0$
(iii) $Rad(x,\varphi \wedge \psi,H) = max(Rad(x,\varphi,H), Rad(x,\psi,H))$

The proof is immediate. Note that (ii) comes from the consistency of $H(x)$.

Definition 11 (radial inference relations) [11]
$\varphi \mathrel{\vdash\mkern-9mu\sim} {}^{RAD}_{H,x} \psi$ iff $\varphi \vdash \psi$ or $Rad(x,\varphi \to \psi,H) < Rad(x,\varphi \to \neg\psi,H)$

For $\varphi = \top$ we get $\mathrel{\vdash\mkern-9mu\sim} {}^{RAD}_{H,x} \psi$ iff $\vdash \psi$ or $Rad(x,\psi,H) < Rad(x,\perp,H)$, thus ψ is nonmonotonically inferred at x iff the smallest sphere around x proving ψ is contained in the smallest inconsistent sphere around x.

Proposition 5 $\mathrel{\vdash\mkern-9mu\sim} {}^{RAD}_{H,x}$ *is a comparative inference relation[12].*

The proof just consists in proving that the relation $<_{x,H}$ defined on $\mathcal{L} \times \mathcal{L}$ by $\alpha \leq_{x,H} \beta$ iff $Rad(x,\alpha) \geq Rad(x,\beta)$ is an expectation ordering ([11]) [13]. Then, since the definition given for $\mathrel{\vdash\mkern-9mu\sim} {}^{RAD}_{H,x}$ coincides with Gärdenfors and Makinson's definition, hence the result.
Note that $\mathrel{\vdash\mkern-9mu\sim} {}^{RAD}_{H,x}$ also preserves H too:

Proposition 6 *if $\psi \in H(x)$ then $\mathrel{\vdash\mkern-9mu\sim} {}^{RAD}_{H,x} \psi$*

Previous results on connections between comparative inference relations and conditional logics [2][8][4] imply that the conditional operator $\Rightarrow^R$ associated to $\mathrel{\vdash\mkern-9mu\sim} {}^{RAD}$ is the $\Rightarrow$ of Lewis' conditional logic VA (whose semantics is expressed with systems of nested spheres), or alternatively, expressed with ranked clusters of worlds, of the logic CO [2]. The underlying complete preordering relation R on the set of worlds is defined by: vRw iff $Min\{\rho, v \not\models Th(x,\rho,H)\} \leq Min\{\rho, w \not\models Th(x,\rho,H)\}$.

---

[10] A necessity function is a mapping from $\mathcal{L}$ to $[0,1]$ such that $N(\top) = 1$, $N(\perp) < N(\top)$ and $N(\varphi \wedge \psi) = min(N(\varphi), N(\psi))$. The only difference betwen N and Rad is that the scale $([0,1], \leq)$ has been replaced by $([0,+\infty], \geq)$ or any other complete ordered scale.

[11] equivalently, $\varphi \mathrel{\vdash\mkern-9mu\sim} {}^{RAD}_{H,x} \psi$ iff $\varphi \vdash \psi$ or $Rad(x,\varphi \to \psi,H) < Rad(x,\neg\varphi,H)$.

[12] A comparative inference relation [11] is a rational inference relation [15] which satisfies moreover Consistency Preservation).

[13] this is intuitively obvious knowing the links between expectation orderings and necessity functions [7], and Rad being a necessity-like function.

The Example of Figure 1 and RAD:

- Consider the label $(1,1)$. Nothing other than the constraint $\neg(r \wedge s)$ is known for sure, so $\rho = 0$ does not give anything interesting. The labels at the distance $\rho = 1$ are $(0,1), (2,1)$, $(1,0)$ and $(2,0)$. Thus we have $Th((1,1), 1, H) = Cn(\{\neg s, r \vee s\})$. As to $Th((1,1), 2, H)$, it is inconsistent. Thus we have $\not\hspace{-0.3em}\sim^{RAD}_{H,(1,1)} r \wedge \neg s$.

- Consider the label $(1,2)$. We have $Th((1,2), 1, H) = Cn(\{r \vee s, \neg r, \neg s\})$ which is inconsistent, therefore radial accumulation does not enable any non-trivial inference at $(1,2)$. Remember that at this label the projection inference relation was less cautious. The results of the application of radial accumulation to the example is depicted on Figure 2.

x \ y	0	1	2	3
0	r	r	$r \vee s$	s
1	$\neg s$	r		$\neg r$
2	$\neg r \wedge \neg s$	r	r	
3	$\neg r \wedge \neg s$	$\neg s$	r	r

Figure 2: radial accumulation applied to the spatial example (cf Fig.1)

A generalisation of RAD to the general (non-complete) case would define a preferential inference relation. We omit a discussion of this for lack of space.

5 Extrapolation by syntax-based entailment

Syntax-based approaches to nonmonotonic reasoning (see [17]) consider each formula of the knowledge base as an independent piece of information; they often make use of priorities ([3], [17], [1], [16]) without specifying where these priorities come from. Our methods for defining priorities based on distances can be combined with the usual methods for defining a syntax-based inference relation, especially the definition proposed in [17], [3], and *lexicographic entailment*, proposed in [1] and [16]. As argued in [1], these inference relations avoid the *drowning effect*, in contrast to radial accumulation. In order to apply distance based priorities in this case, however, we have to assume that the number of possible distance values is finite, due to the fact that there must be a finite number of priority levels.

6 Selected applications

6.1 Temporal reasoning

Although our first motivation was directed towards applications in spatial reasoning, our approach also has some relevance to temporal reasoning, in particular the persistence problem. Roughly, the persistence problem consists in extrapolating the truth value of fluents at some time points where it is unknown. The intuitive idea of our approach in the temporal domain is that our belief in the persistence of properties gradually grows weaker and weaker as time continues. Traditional approaches to persistence (see [19] for a critical survey) do not use this gradual notion; thus in the case where a fluent φ is known to be true at t_0 and false at a later time point t_1 (nothing else being known), skeptical approaches do not conclude anything about φ within (t_0, t_1), which is too cautious, and chronological approches such as [20] conclude that φ changes its truth value at the last possible time point (i.e. at t_1). In contrast, our approach extrapolates the truth value of φ to TRUE(resp. FALSE) at time-points close to t_0 (resp. t_1). Now, it is clear that our basic approach, used alone, cannot handle examples with laws about explicit changes (updates, actions, ...) such as the Yale Shooting Problem. The latter cannot be even represented in our language; our approach applies only to problems of pure persistence without causality. The next step toward a treatment of "realistic" temporal (whose technical details are beyond the scope of this paper) would consist in integrating distance-based persistence in the minimization criterion to select the preferred models in a given framework for handling changes with preferential entailment (for instance Sandewall's approach [19]).

Besides traditional approaches, we know two gradual approaches to persistence. Dean and Kanazawa's [5] probabilistic projection extrapolate a probabilistic persistence function, and it may be considered as the probabilistic counterpart of the application of our work to temporal reasoning. It is discussed in [6], where a more qualitative, possibilistic approach is proposed. Such approaches have the advantage of potentially solving another problem that affects the application of our distance based inference relations to temporal reasoning (as well as that of many others) All of the latter treat the persistence of all fluents in the same way. While we could separate totally persistent fluents such as *dead* from usual fluents (simply in the closure phase of the labelled knowledge base: the labelled theory must be such that if we know *dead* at t_0, then we know *dead* at any later time point), we cannot express the fact that fluents persist in different ways: for instance, *married* usually persists longer than *asleep*; some fluents are periodic, for instance $red - traffic - light$; some fluents may even be chaotic, i.e. they do not tend at all to persist.

6.2 Spatial reasoning (reasoning by proximity)

Our original motivation was to treat the persistence of properties over spatial regions. In the persistence of properties over spatial boundaries without known boundaries, agronomists and others have used, though not formally defined or studied, pseudo-metric based systems of inference. They have not attempted a formal study of persistence principles of the kind we have pursued here. The only work we know on this subject is [13]: the authors point out that some notions used in temporal reasoning transfer to spatial reasoning and they define then *spatial persistence*; they use distances for relaxing a spatial constraint satisfaction problem (using a fuzzy model). But their framework is not oriented towards deduction; it is oriented towards finding a solution. Nevertheless, the underlying ideas are related to ours.

For us, spatial reasoning corresponds to *nonmonotonic reasoning by proximity*: we extrapolate by taking account of the closest points of the space. Here is a plausible example of such reasoning having to do with weather. For example, if a pilot is making a trip from A to B and he asks for weather at three stations along his route and the weather briefer tells him: Station 1 rain, Station 2 no report, Station 3 rain, the pilot and the weather briefer will extrapolate concerning station 2's weather from the reports given at stations 1 and 3. If station 2 is between stations 1 and 3, then both RAD and PROJ will allow us to infer RAIN at station 2. To be sure this is not the only sort of information that the pilot might consider; he might have special knowledge of the terrain at station 2 that would override or defeat this inference—for example, the fact that station 2 is in a deep desert valley where the weather is usually much better than at stations 1 and 3).

In spatial reasoning as in temporal reasoning, we should not treat the persistence of spatial propositions completely uniformly; some tend to "persist through space" more than others. Further, in addition to our relations *PROJ* and *RAD*, we would like to investigate more empirical, more quantitative but perhaps more realistic inference relations for space. Finally, we should exploit geometrical reasoning in performing the logical closure giving H within our distance based account of persistence; for instance, if we want to delimit an object which we know to be, say, convex, we can deduce many facts from a few punctual observations. Object boundaries will obviously affect persistence of spatial propositions.

6.3 Taxonomic reasoning

Distance based nonmonotonic inference relations also have a natural application in taxonomic reasoning, though we know of no work in AI other than our own in this area. Fields like classification theory, however, have used distance based reasoning, though again the formal study of inference relations based on distances have not been studied. One simple application of $PROJ$ and RAD in taxonomic domain concerns a classification task. Consider, for instance, the problem of classifying a particular mushroom as being of a given type. Our "space" is in this case a space of features rather than physical distances. We propose two different ways to define such distances.

Feature distances

The label set X is now a conceptual net with nodes labelled by concepts $C_1, ..., C_n$ or by individuals $a_1, ..., a_m$. With each node is also associated a list of features. The labelled theory consists in specifying which features are associated to which nodes. The features give rise to a number of natural distance metrics between nodes. One, for instance, comes from the Jaccard Index (let $F_1, ... F_p$ denote the different features): $d(x, y) = \frac{|\{F_i : F_i \in H(x) \cap H(y)\}|}{|\{F_i : F_i \in H(x) \cup H(y)\}|} - 1$

With these preliminaries in mind, we return to the categorization example. We are interested in categorizing a particular object a_0 with features $F_1, ..., F_n$. In our example, a_0 might be a particular mushroom whose type we are trying to identify. Types of mushrooms (cepes, girolles, amanitas, etc.) also are nodes in our feature space. We will suppose that each type node is exclusive so (so for instance $\neg(cepe \wedge girolle)$ holds at all nodes. Suppose now using the Jaccard measure that the closest nodes to a_0 at which $cepe$ is either true or false make $cepe$ true. Then by the projection inference relation, we conclude $\mathrel{\vdash}\, ^{PROJ}_{H,a_0} cepe$, i.e. $cepe$ is true at a_0. Another way to employ the distance based inference relations in taxonomic reasoning is to extrapolate particular properties about a_0 that are not known from the original inspection. Continuing our example above, if $cepe$ is the closest node to a_0 at which the property "edible" is determined, then $\mathrel{\vdash}\, ^{PROJ}_{H,a_0} edible$.

Distances based on counting individuals

Taxonomic reasoning is usually thought to verify a specificity property like the following. If A strictly implies B and A's by default are not C's and B's are by default C's, then given that we know that something is an A and a B, then we by default infer that it is not C. To capture inheritance, we need a different kind of distance metric than the one constructed using the Jaccard Index. We fix a model M, captueing the" real world" extensional (i.e. cardinality and membership) relations between individuals and types in our conceptual space. Then a metric appropriate to the verification of the specificity property with both the projective and the radial methods is familiar from conditional probability:

$$d(C_i, C_j) = \frac{|\{x | M \models C_i(x)\}|}{|\{x | M \models C_i(x) \wedge C_j(x)\}|} - 1 = \frac{1}{Prob(C_j | C_i)} - 1$$

Note that we have $d(C_i, C_j)$ is minimal (and equals 0) iff $C_i \subseteq C_j$ and maximal (and equals $= \infty$) iff $C_i \cap C_j = \emptyset$.

As an example of specificity reasoning, consider the network of nodes in which we have Penguin (p), Bird (b), Flying-animals (fa) and Non-flying-animals (nfa) as nodes, with an assignment of extensions to these types in a model as one would expect (i.e. that model the real world or at least our expectations about the real world). As all penguins are birds, we have $d(p, b) = 0$. If the model is as we expect, then $d(p, nfa) < d(p, fa)$ (or equivalently $Prob(nfa|p) > Prob(fa|p)$), and $d(b, fa) < d(b, nfa)$. Now we would like to reason about what happens if we know that something is a penguin. Using any of the proposed inference relations and the previous distance, we get that $\mathrel{\vdash}\, _{H,p} \neg fly$ since the closest node to p where fly is determined is nfa where fly is false.

It may be that nonmonotonic reasoning in general and taxonomic reasoning in particular uses a variety of measures are used; we select the appropriate measure because it is suited to a particular task. Hence, the distances based on the Jaccard index and on conditional probability might be suited to different taxonomic reasoning tasks.

7 Conclusion

We have proposed a general principle for defining several nonmonotonic inference relations from distances with applications to temporal, spatial and taxonomic reasoning. This methodology is an alternative way to define already known nonmonotonic inference relations (e.g., the comparative inference relation): here our premises do not include a set of conditional assertions or default rules as in most approaches, but a set of temporally or spatially indexed data (among other possibilities). It should be possible to use our approach to show how many formalisms already studied from a theoretical point of view apply in this way to spatially and temporally indexed data. As to complexity results for our nonmonotonic inference relations, some results can be directly taken from [12] and [17], and for the projection inference relation, the associated decision problem is obviously in Δ_2^P).

References

1. Salem Benferhat, Claudette Cayrol, Didier Dubois, Jérôme Lang and Henri Prade, *Inconsistency management and prioritized syntax-based entailment*, Proceedings of IJCAI'93,640-645.
2. Craig Boutilier, *Conditional logics for default reasoning*, PhD thesis, University of Toronto, 1992.
3. Gerd Brewka, *Preferred subtheories: an extended logical framework for default reasoning*, Proceedings of IJCAI'89, 1043-1048.
4. Gabriella Crocco and Philippe Lamarre, *On the connection between nonmonotonic inference relations and conditional logics*, Proceedings of KR'92, 565-571.
5. Thomas Dean and Keiji Kanazawa, *A model for reasoning about persistence and causation*, Computational Intelligence, 5(3): 142-150.
6. Dimiter Driankov and Jérôme Lang, *Possibilistic decreasing persistence*, Proceedings of Uncertainty in AI'93, 469-476.
7. Didier Dubois and Henri Prade, *Epistemic entrenchment and possibilistic logic*, Artificial Intelligence 50:223-239, 1991.
8. Luis Fariñas del Cerro, Andreas Herzig and Jérôme Lang, *From ordering-based nonmonotonic reasoning to conditional logics*, Artificial Intelligence 66, 375-303, 1994.
9. Dov Gabbay, *Labelled Deductive Systems*, Technical Report, Centrum für Informations und Sprachverarbeitung, Universität München.
10. Peter Gärdenfors and David Makinson, *Revision of knowledge systems using epistemic entrenchment*, Proceedings of TARK'88.
11. Peter Gärdenfors and David Makinson, *Nonmonotonic reasoning based on expectations*, Artificial Intelligence.
12. Georg Gottlob, *Complexity results for nonmonotonic logics*, Journal of Logic and Computation 2 (3), 397-425, 1992.
13. Hans Werner Guesguen and Joachim Hertzberg, *Spatial persistence*, Proceedings of the Ijcai Workshop on Temporal and Spatial Reasoning (Chambéry, 1993), 11-34.
14. Sarit Kraus, Daniel Lehmann and Menahem Magidor, *Nonmonotonic reasoning, preferential models and cumulative logics*. Artificial Intelligence 44 (1990), 167-207.
15. Daniel Lehmann and Menahem Magidor, *What does a conditional knowledge base entail?*, Artificial Intelligence 55 (1992), 1-60.
16. Daniel Lehmann, *Another perspective on default reasoning*, Technical Report 92-12, Hebrew University of Jerusalem, 1992.

17. Bernhard Nebel, *Belief revision and default reasoning: syntax-based approaches*, Proceedings of KR'91, 417-428.
18. Judea Pearl, *System Z: a natural ordering of defaults with tractable applications to default reasoning*, Proceedings of TARK'90, 121-135.
19. Erik Sandewall, *Features and fluents: a systematic approach to the representation of knowledge about dynamical systems*, Technical Report LiTH-IDA-R-92-30, Dept of Computer and Information Science, Linköping University, 1992.
20. Yoav Shoham, *Chronological ignorance: experiments in nonmonotonic temporal reasoning*, Artificial Intelligence 36 (1988), pp. 279-331.

Rigid Unification by Completion and Rigid Paramodulation*

Gérard Becher[1] and Uwe Petermann[**2]

[1] LAIAC Université de Caen, 14032 Caen Cedex (France)
Net: becher@univ-caen.fr
[2] FB IMN, HTWK Leipzig, Postfach 66, D-04251 Leipzig (F.R.G.)
Net: uwe@imn.th-leipzig.de

Abstract. This paper addresses the problem of computing complete sets of rigid-E-unifiers, initially introduced by Gallier, Narendran, Plaisted and Snyder who gave a proof of its NP-completeness. Our algorithm is based on completion and on a variant of basic paramodulation named rigid paramodulation. The crucial point of the algorithm is to ensure a constant orientation of the rules during the completion and the paramodulation process. This is achieved by defining *minimal* substitutions and proving that we can restrict our attention to such substitutions. This restriction allows us to use total term orderings because we don't need stability. We claim that our decision procedure becomes simpler. We prove soundness, completeness and termination of our algorithm.

Keywords
Automated deduction, equality, rigid E-unification, completion.

1 Introduction

In this paper we describe an algorithm for computing complete sets of rigid-E-unifiers. Rigid E-unification is necessary for building-in equality into proof calculi like the connection method [4], the model elimination method [16] or the matrix method [1]. Rigid E-unifiers were initially defined by W. Bibel [4] under the name *eq-unifiers*. J. Gallier et al. [9] introduced the notion of rigid E-unification for the problem of finding eq-unifiers. Given a set E of equations, a substitution θ is a rigid-E-unifier of a set of equations S iff for every equation $u \approx v \in S$, θu and θv are congruent modulo θE.

Example 1. Let $E = \{\, gfx \approx z, fgy \approx z \,\}$ and let $S = \{\, fx \approx gy \,\}$. The substitution $\theta = \{\, x/gz, y/z \,\}$ is a rigid E-unifier of S, since $\theta(fx) = fgz$ and $\theta(gy) = gz$ are congruent modulo $\theta E = \{\, gfgz \approx z, fgz \approx z \,\}$.

The non-deterministic rigid E-unification procedure given in [9] relies on critical pair completion techniques. One of its main drawbacks is the necessity to guess (and to backtrack over) certain orderings on the terms (the *order assignments*). Due to the high complexity of that guess, the method is quite difficult to implement and seems to be rather a proof of NP-completeness than a practical

---

* Supported by a grant of the French-German PROCOPE-project.
** Supported in part by a grant of the Alexander von Humboldt-Stiftung and the Alfried Krupp von Bohlen und Halbach-Stiftung.

algorithm. This and some other attempts to design rigid E-unification algorithms will be discussed in section 8. We describe a rule-based algorithm where the application of the rules is restricted by a set of constraints. The notion of constraints is tailored in order to prune the search space and to ensure the termination. We combine a completion based approach with a variant of basic narrowing [12] called rigid paramodulation. Rigid paramodulation is incomplete in general. Therefore, we complete the set of equations E until rigid paramodulation is applicable. The crucial point of the algorithm is to ensure a constant orientation of the rules during the completion and the paramodulation phases. We achieve this by defining *minimal* substitutions and proving that we can restrict our search to such substitutions. Like in [7] and in contrast to [9], we don't need to require the stability of the ordering which we use to orient the equations. Therefore we avoid the problem of guessing order assignments and our decision procedure becomes simpler. Most of the results in this paper are stated without proof. The proofs can be found in the extended version of the paper [2].

2 Preliminaries

First-order logic Throughout this paper, $T_\Sigma(X)$ denotes the free Σ-algebra over a set of variables X. Syntactic equality between terms of $T_\Sigma(X)$ is expressed by $s \equiv t$. If t is a term and α an address in t, then by $t|_\alpha$ we denote the subterm occurring at that address. We write $t[s]_\alpha$ (or simply $t[s]$) whenever $t|_\alpha \equiv s$. By $t[\alpha \leftarrow s]$ we denote the term obtained by substituting $t|_\alpha$ by s in t. An *equation* is an atomic formula of the form $u \approx v$. Equations are unoriented, oriented equations are denoted by $u \to v$. A *substitution* is a mapping from the set of variables into the set of terms which is almost everywhere equal to the identity. The *domain* of a substitution θ is denoted by $\mathcal{D}(\theta)$. The *composition* $\sigma\theta$ of substitutions σ and θ is the substitution which assign to every variable x the term $\sigma(\theta(x))$. We write $\sigma \leq \theta$ to express that σ is more general than θ.

Term orderings The following notions may be found in [6]. A binary relation $\succ$ on a set of terms has the *subterm property* if for each term $t[s]$, $t[s] \succ s$ holds. A strict ordering $\succ$ on a set of terms is a *simplification ordering* if it is monotonic w.r.t. the term structure and has the subterm property. If the set of variable and function symbols is finite, then every simplification ordering on $T_\Sigma(X)$ is well-founded. Throughout this paper, we use a simplification ordering denoted by $\succ$ which is total on $T_\Sigma(X)$. Such orderings exist for every signature Σ but are not stable by instantiation. There is no matter which ordering is chosen and in fact one can even run the algorithm without fixing this choice[3]. Since we never take variants of equations, the set of variable (and function) symbols that we consider in a given problem is always finite. Thus $\succ$ is necessarily well-founded.

---

[3] The following simplification ordering is intended throughout all examples in the paper : $s \succ t$ iff $size(s) > size(t)$ or else ($size(s) = size(t)$ and $root(s) >_a root(t)$) or else ($size(s) = size(t)$ and $root(s) = root(t)$ and $args(s) \succ_{lex} args(t)$), where $>_a$ is the alphabetical ordering on symbols and variables and $\succ_{lex}$ is the lexicographic ordering induced by $\succ$ on the tuples of arguments of s and t.

Rigid E-Unifiers We use three equivalent notations (and definitions) to express that a substitution is a rigid-E-unifier of a (set of) pairs of terms. The first notation is similar to that used in [11] : if E and S are sets of equations over $T_\Sigma(X)$, then we write $\theta E \vdash \theta S$ to denote that θS is an equational consequence of θE where the variables in θE and θS are treated as constants. An idempotent substitution θ is a rigid E-unifier of S iff $\theta E \vdash \theta S$. Gallier *et al.* use the following binary relation : if t and s are two terms, then $t \cong_{\theta E} s$ iff there is some equation $l \approx r \in E$ s.t. $t \equiv t[\theta l]_\alpha$ and $s \equiv t[\alpha \leftarrow \theta r]$. The reflexive and transitive closure $\stackrel{*}{\cong}_{\theta E}$ of $\cong_{\theta E}$ is a congruence relation over $T_\Sigma(X)$. Given any two terms u and v, a substitution θ is a rigid E-unifier of u and v iff $\theta u \stackrel{*}{\cong}_{\theta E} \theta v$. Finally, we introduce the three relations $\leftrightarrow_\theta$, $\leftrightarrow_E$ and $\leftrightarrow_{E,\theta}$ defined between terms by : *i)* $u \leftrightarrow_\theta v$ iff $\theta u \equiv \theta v$; *ii)* $u \leftrightarrow_E v$ iff $E \vdash u \approx v$ and *iii)* $\leftrightarrow_{E,\theta} = (\leftrightarrow_\theta \cup \leftrightarrow_E)$ respectively. We denote by $\stackrel{*}{\leftrightarrow}_\theta$, $\stackrel{*}{\leftrightarrow}_E$ and $\stackrel{*}{\leftrightarrow}_{E,\theta}$ the reflexive and transitive closures of these three relations. Obviously, these are congruence relations over $T_\Sigma(X)$ and we say that θ is a rigid E-unifier of u and v iff $u \stackrel{*}{\leftrightarrow}_{E,\theta} v$. The following proposition expresses the equivalence of these definitions :

Proposition 1. *Let E be any set of equations, let θ be an idempotent substitution and let u and v be any two terms. The following assertions are equivalent :*
(i) $u \stackrel{*}{\leftrightarrow}_{E,\theta} v$; *(ii)* $\theta E \vdash \theta u \approx \theta v$; *(iii)* $\theta u \stackrel{*}{\cong}_{\theta E} \theta v$.

It can be noticed that the relations $\stackrel{*}{\cong}_{\theta E}$ and $\stackrel{*}{\leftrightarrow}_{E,\theta}$ are *not equal*[4], but it is easy to see that $\stackrel{*}{\cong}_{\theta E} \subseteq \stackrel{*}{\leftrightarrow}_{E,\theta}$. Another subtlety is the difference between $\stackrel{*}{\leftrightarrow}_{\theta E}$ and $\stackrel{*}{\leftrightarrow}_{E,\theta}$. It can be proved that $\stackrel{*}{\leftrightarrow}_{\theta E} \subseteq \stackrel{*}{\leftrightarrow}_{E,\theta}$ but the converse is not true in general[5].

A pre-ordering relation on substitutions

Definition 2. *Let E be a set of equations and let σ and θ be two substitutions. We say that $\sigma \sqsubseteq_E \theta$ iff $\mathcal{D}(\sigma) = \mathcal{D}(\theta)$ and for all x, $\sigma x \stackrel{*}{\leftrightarrow}_{E,\theta} \theta x$ holds.*

The relation $\sqsubseteq_E$ is reflexive and transitive. It is in general not a symmetric relation. The relation $\sqsubseteq_E$ is a preorder on the set of substitutions. In [9], J. Gallier *et al.* use the same symbol with another definition[6]. However, for idempotent substitutions, both definitions are equivalent, as stated by the next lemma.

Lemma 3. *Let E be a set of equations and let σ and θ be two substitutions with the same domain. If σ and θ are idempotent, then the three following assertions are equivalent (a) $\forall x$ $\sigma x \stackrel{*}{\leftrightarrow}_{E,\theta} \theta x$; (b) $\forall x$ $\theta E \vdash \sigma x \approx \theta x$; (c) $\forall x$ $\sigma x \stackrel{*}{\cong}_{\theta E} \theta x$.*

The relation $\sqsubseteq_E$ induces an equivalence relation on the set of substitutions.

Definition 4. *For substitutions σ and θ let $\sigma =_E \theta$ iff $\sigma \sqsubseteq_E \theta$ and $\theta \sqsubseteq_E \sigma$.*

Lemma 5. *If $\sigma =_E \theta$, then the congruences $\stackrel{*}{\leftrightarrow}_{E,\sigma}$ and $\stackrel{*}{\leftrightarrow}_{E,\theta}$ are identical.*

---

[4] For every term t, for example, $t \stackrel{*}{\leftrightarrow}_{E,\theta} \theta t$ holds, but not (in general) $t \stackrel{*}{\cong}_{\theta E} \theta t$
[5] Take $E = \{ a \approx b \}$ and $\theta = \{ x/a \}$. Then $x \stackrel{*}{\leftrightarrow}_{E,\theta} a$ but not $x \stackrel{*}{\leftrightarrow}_{\theta E} a$.
[6] Gallier's definition is most close to that in point c) of lemma 3

3   Overview of the method, introductory example

The whole process can be decomposed in two phases : a completion phase and a paramodulation phase. In each phase, an equation in E can only be used after orientation w.r.t. the solution θ and a given simplification ordering $\succ$. An equation $l \approx r$ is well-oriented iff $\theta l \succ \theta r$. In a first time, all equations of E are oriented in both directions. Further, the orientations which are incompatible with the current knowledge about θ and $\succ$ are eliminated. Whenever an equation is used with a certain orientation, this orientation is recorded in a so-called *constraints set*. At every moment, the constraints set C must remain *satisfiable*, that is there must exist a substitution θ and a simplification ordering $\succ$ such that $\theta l \succ \theta r$ for all $l \to r \in C$. Oriented equations $l \to r$ such that $C \cup \{ l > r \}$ is unsatisfiable are systematically eliminated[7]. We give here a complete example of the indeterministic process which computes a rigid E-unifier of a set S although some details will be explained only further in the paper. In each step, the set E contains unoriented equations while the oriented ones are in R.

- Completion phase
  - **Initial problem.**
    $E = \{ ga \approx a, fgy \approx a, kz \approx y \}$; $R = \emptyset$; $S = \{ ky \approx z, ggy \approx fy \}$;
    $C = \emptyset$; $\theta = \emptyset$
  - **Orient + Delete:** Orient the equations in E and eliminate impossible orientations.
    $E = \emptyset$; $R = \{ ga \to a, fgy \to a, kz \to y, y \to kz \}$;
    $S = \{ ky \approx z, ggy \approx fy \}$; $C = \emptyset$; $\theta = \emptyset$
  - **Complete:** Overlap ga and gy, guessing $\theta(gy) = \theta(ga)$. Replace $fgy \to a$ by the unoriented critical equation $fa \approx a$. Record the two oriented equations which have been used. Instantiate the whole problem (replace y by a).
    $E = \{ fa \approx a \}$; $R = \{ ga \to a, kz \to a, a \to kz \}$;
    $S = \{ ka \approx z, gga \approx fa \}$; $C = \{ ga > a, fga > a \}$; $\theta = \{ y/a \}$
  - **Orient + Delete.**
    $E = \emptyset$; $R = \{ fa \to a, ga \to a, kz \to a \}$; $S = \{ ka \approx z, gga \approx fa \}$;
    $C = \{ ga > a, fga > a \}$; $\theta = \{ y/a \}$
  - **Trivial:** Delete from S equations with sides being congruent modulo $E \cup R$.
    $E = \emptyset$; $R = \{ fa \to a, ga \to a, kz \to a \}$; $S = \{ ka \approx z \}$;
    $C = \{ ga > a, fga > a \}$; $\theta = \{ y/a \}$
- Paramodulation phase
  - **Paramodulate:** Overlap ka and kz, guessing that $\theta(kz) = \theta(ka)$. Replace in S ka by a. Record the oriented equation which has been used.
    $E = \emptyset$; $R = \{ fa \to a, ga \to a, kz \to a \}$; $S = \{ a \approx z \}$;
    $C = \{ ga > a, fga > a, kz > a \}$; $\theta = \{ y/a, z/a \}$
  - **Trivial:** Eliminate the equations of S whose sides (once instantiated) are congruent modulo $\theta(E \cup R)$.
    $E = \emptyset$; $R = \{ fa \to a, ga \to a, kz \to a \}$; $S = \emptyset$;
    $C = \{ ga > a, fga > a, kz > a \}$; $\theta = \{ y/a, z/a \}$

---

[7] Choosing a particular simplification ordering can drastically improve this elimination step.

4 Minimal vs. irreducible rigid E-unifiers

Definition 6. For a set of equations E, an idempotent substitution θ is E-*reducible* iff for some variable $x \in \mathcal{D}(\theta)$, equation $l \approx r \in E$ and subterm θl of θx hold $\theta l \succ \theta r$ and $l \not\equiv x$. It is E-irreducible iff it is *not* E-reducible.

The irreducibility of unifiers is necessary to ensure the completeness of Rigid Paramodulation (see section 5). Let us discuss now an example which shows that we need in fact an even stronger property of unifiers, their minimality.

Example 2. Consider the set of equations $E = \{ fgfx \approx a, gy \approx g^2 fa \}$ and the substitution $\theta = \{ x/fg^2fa, y/f^2g^2fa \}$. The orientations of the equations w.r.t. θ and $\succ$ are as follows : $fgfx \to a$, $gy \to g^2 fa$ and so θ is E-irreducible. If we decompose θ in $\lambda\mu$, with $\lambda = \{ x/fg^2fa \}$ and $\mu = \{ y/fx \}$, then we obtain using μ the critical equation $fg^2fa \approx a$ which is oriented as $fg^2fa \to a$. Let E' be $\mu E \cup \{ fg^2fa \approx a \}$. As a matter of a fact, λ is E'-reducible, yielding $\lambda' = \{ x/a \}$. This means that $\theta' = \lambda'\mu$ is less than θ, although equivalent in the sense that the congruences modulo θE and $\theta' E$ are identical. The major problem is now that the orientation of the equations may have changed: $gy \approx g^2 fa$ is oriented as $gy \to g^2 fa$ w.r.t. θ and $\succ$, but as $g^2 fa \to gy$ w.r.t. θ' and $\succ$.

Reorientations can arise because the ordering $\succ$ is not stable by substitution. Consequently our procedure may not terminate. In order to avoid reorientations, we will require that, for every decomposition of θ in $\lambda\mu$, λ is (μE)-irreducible. Substitutions meeting this requirement are called E-*minimal* substitutions.

Definition 7. If E is a set of equations, an idempotent substitution θ is E-*minimal* w.r.t a set of variables X iff for every idempotent substitution $\mu \leq \theta$ it is true that : for every $x \in \mathcal{D}(\theta) \setminus \mathcal{D}(\mu)$, θx is the least element (w.r.t. $\succ$) of the set $\{ t \in T_\Sigma(X) \mid t \equiv \theta t, t \overset{*}{\leftrightarrow}_{E,\mu} \theta x \}$.

In fact, here is the main improvement relatively to Gallier's method : simplification orderings can be chosen total on $T_\Sigma(X)$, whereas the reduction orderings used in other methods are *not* total, and thus necessitate the guess of their extension. Indeed, E-minimality is a stronger property than E-irreducibility.

Lemma 8. *If θ is E-minimal, then θ is E-irreducible.*

We prove now that we can always restrict our attention to E-minimal unifiers.

Proposition 9. *Let E be any set of equations. For every substitution θ, there is an E-minimal substitution θ' such that $\theta' =_E \theta$, that is the congruence $\overset{*}{\leftrightarrow}_{E,\theta'}$ is exactly the same as the congruence $\overset{*}{\leftrightarrow}_{E,\theta}$.*

Definition 10. Let E and S be two finite sets of equations over $T_\Sigma(X)$, a set U of substitutions is a *complete set of rigid E-unifiers* of S iff for all $\sigma \in U$, *i*) σ is idempotent and $\mathcal{D}(\sigma) \subseteq \text{Var}(E) \cup \text{Var}(S)$; *ii*) σ is a rigid E-unifier of S ; *iii*) for every rigid E-unifier φ of S, there is some $\sigma \in U$ and some E-minimal θ such that $\sigma \leq \theta$ and $\theta =_E \varphi$.

The next lemma allows to restrict paramodulating into a variable x to the application of a rule $x \to r$, strengthening the corresponding result in [9].

Lemma 11. *If θ is E-irreducible, and if one can find $x \in \mathcal{D}(\theta)$ such that θx is reducible by some equation $l \approx r \in E$, with $\theta l \succ \theta r$, then $l \equiv x$ and $x \notin Vars(r)$.*

The following lemma justifies the definition of Rigid Paramodulation in section 5 as variant of *basic* paramodulation. This means that the paramodulation steps are based on the set of occurrences in the initial problem. Thus, it is unnecessary to apply the computed substitution during the process.

Lemma 12. *Let E be a set of equations and let θ be an E-irreducible substitution. Let $l \approx r$ be an equation in E and let A be any term such that θA is reducible by $\theta l \approx \theta r$, where $\theta l \succ \theta r$ at position α. Then α is in the domain of A, that is $\theta A \equiv \theta A[\theta l]_\alpha \equiv \theta(A[\alpha \leftarrow l])$*

Proof. Suppose that α is not in the domain of A. Then there exists a variable $x \in Vars(A)$ such that θl is a proper subterm of θx, which is in contradiction with E-irreducibility of θ.

Below, we define the closure of a set of equations E w.r.t. a substitution θ. In section 5, we show that this property together with the E-irreducibility of θ entails completeness of Rigid Paramodulation for the rigid E-unification problem.

Definition 13. *Let E be a set of equations and let θ be any substitution. The associated rule system $R_{E,\theta}$ is defined by : $R_{E,\theta} = \{\, l \rightarrow r \mid l \approx r \in E, \theta l \succ \theta r \,\}$.* The relation $\rightarrow_{\theta E}$ is defined on $T_\Sigma(X)$ by: $u \rightarrow_{\theta E} v$ iff there exists $l \rightarrow r \in R_{E,\theta}$ s.t. $u \equiv u[\theta l]_\alpha$ and $v \equiv u[\theta r]_\alpha$. $\xrightarrow{*}_{\theta E}$ denotes its reflexive. and transitive closure.

Definition 14. *Let E be a set of equations and θ a substitution. If $l \rightarrow r$ and $l' \rightarrow r'$ are two rules in $R_{E,\theta}$, a θ-critical equation is an equation of the form $l[\gamma \leftarrow r'] \approx r$ where $\theta(l|_\gamma) \equiv \theta l'$.*

Note that in the above definition, the subterm $l|_\gamma$ may be a variable x. However, if this is the case and if we suppose that θ is E-irreducible, then θx is reducible by $l' \approx r'$ and by lemma 11 we can conclude that $l' \equiv x$ and $x \notin Vars(r)$.

Definition 15. *A set of equations E is θ-closed iff it contains all its θ-critical equations.*

Proposition 16. *Let θ be an idempotent substitution, let E be a θ-closed set of equations. If θ is E-irreducible, then $\rightarrow_{\theta E}$ is confluent.*

Definition 17. *A constraint is a formula of the form $u > v$, where u and v are terms. A constraint $u > v$ is satisfied by a substitution θ and a simplification ordering $\succ$ iff $\theta u \succ \theta v$. A set of constraints C is satisfiable iff there exist a simplification ordering $\succ$ over $T_\Sigma(X)$ and a substitution θ such that each $u > v$ in C is satisfied by θ and $\succ$.*

Note that a set of constraints can be seen as a conjunction of constraints. A set of constraints can be unsatisfiable, whereas each of its elements is satisfiable.

Example 3.
- Every couple $(\theta, \succ)$ satisfies the constraints $fa > a$ and $gf(x,a) > gx$.
- The constraints $ga > gf(a,x)$ and $x > gx$ are unsatisfiable.

- Constraints $gx > gb$ and $gb > ggx$ are separately satisfiable, but the set $\{gx > gb, gb > ggx\}$ is unsatisfiable.
- The set $\{ga > x, x > a\}$ is unsatisfiable if a and g are the unique symbols in the signature. However it is satisfiable if one allows to extend the signature by new symbols. Beckert [3] names this *weak satisfiability*.

It has been proven in [5] that the satisfiability of a set of constraints is decidable according to the fact that the required simplification ordering is a *lexicographic path ordering*. Nevertheless, the decision procedure given by H. Comon is of high complexity. With the same restriction ($\succ$ interpreted by a lexicographic path ordering), B. Beckert gives in [3] a simpler procedure for checking the weak satisfiability of a constraint. Finally, D. Plaisted gives in [19] a way to check weak satisfiability in polynomial time without any requirement on the interpretation of the simplification ordering. His method relies on the termination of an associated ground rule system, which can be checked in polynomial time. We adopt here indiscriminately the test of D. Plaisted or the test of B. Beckert or any other one which is doable in polynomial time[8]. Doing so, it is clear that we will retain some orientations which are in fact incoherent and lose some time in exploring dead-ends. But, the test will be quite faster and we prove finally that weak satisfiability is sufficient to ensure termination of our process.

5 Rigid Paramodulation

In this section, we give a set of transformation rules which can be used to compute rigid E-unifiers under the θ-closure and the E-irreducibility hypothesis. We prove correctness, completeness and termination of this process. Let a *state* be a tuple (C, E, R, S, φ) constituted by a set of constraints C, a set of equations E, a rule system R (oriented equations), a system of equations S (to be unified); an idempotent substitution φ. A *state* is *solved* if S is empty. By Rigid Paramodulation (in short RP, we mean any sequence of applications of the rules defined in figure 1 according to the pattern $(O|D|T)^*(D|P|T)^*(U|T)^*$ where O, D, P, T and U denote respectively the rules Orient, Delete, Paramodulate, Trivial and Unify. We write $\mathcal{E} \overset{RP}{\Longrightarrow} \mathcal{E}'$ whenever $\mathcal{E}'$ results from $\mathcal{E}$ by any sequence of RP. Note that the rule *Unify* can itself be decomposed in some more primitive rules, which compute a m.g.u. of the terms A and B. Such a rule system can be found for example in [13]. The rule *Trivial* allows to eliminate quickly terms which are already rigid E-unified by φ. For that sake, one can either use a congruence closure algorithm ([17]) or better compute the initial congruence with this algorithm and then maintain it by merging classes as one goes along in the paramodulating process. Usually, paramodulating into a variable is forbidden in order to prune the search space. When looking for rigid E-unifiers, we cannot avoid that, but it is possible to restrict it severely by requiring then to use a *degenerate* equation whose left hand side is this variable. The substitutions are not applied to the problem. This is characteristic for basic paramodulation.

---

[8] In the example of section 3, we delete for example the orientation $y \rightarrow kz$, since the constraint $y > kz$ is unsatisfiable w.r.t. the simplification ordering indicated in footnote 3 (due to size of the terms).

Orient: $\dfrac{(\mathcal{C}, E \cup \{l \approx r\}, R, S, \varphi)}{(\mathcal{C}, E, R \cup \{l \to r,\; r \to l\}, S, \varphi)}$	**Delete:** $\dfrac{(\mathcal{C}, E, R \cup \{l \to r\}, S, \varphi)}{(\mathcal{C}, E, R, S, \varphi)}$ if $\varphi(\mathcal{C} \cup \{l > r\})$ is unsatisfiable

Paramodulate: $\dfrac{(\mathcal{C}, E, R \cup \{l \to r\}, S \cup \{A \approx B\}, \varphi)}{(\mathcal{C} \cup \{l > r\}, E, R \cup \{l \to r\}, S \cup \{A[\alpha \leftarrow r] \approx B\}, \mu\varphi)}$

if $\mu = \mathrm{mgu}(\varphi(A|_\alpha), \varphi l)$, $\mu\varphi(\mathcal{C} \cup \{l > r\})$ is satisfiable
and $\varphi(A|_\alpha)$ not a variable or $\varphi(A|_\alpha) \equiv \varphi l$

Trivial: $\dfrac{(\mathcal{C}, E, R, S \cup \{A \approx B\}, \varphi)}{(\mathcal{C}, E, R, S, \varphi)}$ if $A \overset{*}{\leftrightarrow}_{BUR,\varphi} B$	**Unify:** $\dfrac{(\mathcal{C}, E, R, S \cup \{A \approx B\}, \varphi)}{(\mathcal{C}, E, R, S, \mu\varphi)}$ if $\mu = \mathrm{mgu}(\varphi A, \varphi B)$

Fig. 1. The set RP of Rigid Paramodulation rules

Theorem 18. *If there exists a sequence of Rigid Paramodulation steps which leads from a state $(\mathcal{C}_0, E_0, R_0, S_0, \theta_0)$ to the state $(\mathcal{C}_k, E_k, R_k, \emptyset, \theta_k)$, then θ_k is a rigid E-unifier of the system S_0 where E is the set of unoriented rules in $E_0 \cup R_0$.*

The following lemma is used to derive theorem 20.

Lemma 19. *Let E and S be two sets of equations and let θ be an idempotent substitution such that $\theta E \vdash \theta S$. Let R be a rule system such that $R \supseteq R_{E,\theta}$. Let $\mathcal{C}$ be a set of constraints satisfied by $(\theta, \succ)$. Let ρ be a substitution such that $\rho S = S$, $\rho \mathcal{C} = \mathcal{C}$, $\rho R = R$. If E is θ-closed and θ is E-irreducible, then there exists a finite sequence of Paramodulate steps : $(\mathcal{C}, \emptyset, R, S, \rho) \overset{RP}{\Longrightarrow} (\mathcal{C}', \emptyset, R, S', \varphi\rho)$ where $\rho S' = S'$, $\varphi \leq \theta$ and S' is syntactically unifiable by θ.*

Theorem 20. *Let E and S be two sets of equations and let θ be a an idempotent substitution such that $\theta E \vdash \theta S$. If E is θ-closed and θ is E-irreducible, then there is a finite $\mathcal{RP}$ sequence $(\emptyset, E, \emptyset, S, id) \overset{RP}{\Longrightarrow} (\mathcal{C}, E, R, \emptyset, \sigma)$ s.t. $\sigma \leq \theta$ and $\sigma E \vdash \sigma S$.*

Lemma 21. *Let R be a finite set of oriented equations. Let $(\mathcal{C}_i, t_i)_{i \geq 0}$ be a sequence defined as following: (i) $\mathcal{C}_0$ is any set of constraints ; (ii) t_0 is any term in $T_\Sigma(X)$; (iii) for all $i \geq 0$, there is some rule $l_i \to r_i \in R$ and some position α_i in t_i such that $t_i \equiv t_i[l_i]_{\alpha_i}$, $t_{i+1} = t_i[\alpha_i \leftarrow r_i]$, $\mathcal{C}_{i+1} = \mathcal{C}_i \cup \{l_i > r_i\}$. If for all $i \geq 0$, $\mathcal{C}_i$ is weak satisfiable, i.e., if for all i there is a substitution θ_i (defined on some extended signature Σ_i) and a simplification ordering $\succ_i$ on $T_{\Sigma_i}(X)$ such that for each $l > r$ in $\mathcal{C}_i$, $\theta_i l \succ_i \theta_i r$, then the sequence $(\mathcal{C}_i, t_i)_{i \geq 0}$ is terminating.*

Corollary 22. *Every sequence of Rigid Paramodulation steps is finite.*

6 Rigid Unification

In this section, we consider arbitrary rigid E-unifiers and arbitrary sets of equations. Without the hypothesis that E is θ-closed and θ is E-irreducible, we can no longer hope that the Rigid Paramodulating procedure is complete.

Example 4. Let $E = \{f(a, b) \approx a, a \approx b\}$, $S = \{f(x, x) \approx x\}$ and $\theta = \{x/a\}$. $\theta E \vdash \theta S$ holds but neither $\mathcal{RP}$ nor syntactic unification steps apply to S.

In order to overcome this problem, the set of equations may be completed first. For this purpose we introduce the completion rule. The set RU is obtained by adding to the set RP the rule *Complete* described in figure 2. By rigid unification we mean any sequence of applications of the rules in RU according to the pattern $(O|D|T|C)^*(D|P|T)^*(U|T)^*$, where C, O, D, P, T and U denote respectively the rules Complete, Orient, Delete, Paramodulate, Trivial and Unify. We write $\mathcal{E} \overset{RU}{\Longrightarrow} \mathcal{E}'$ whenever $\mathcal{E}'$ results from $\mathcal{E}$ by some sequence of RU.

Complete: $\dfrac{(C, E, R \cup \{l \to r, l' \to r'\}, S, \varphi)}{(C', \mu(E \cup \{l[\gamma \leftarrow r'] \approx r\}), \mu(R \cup \{l' \to r'\}), \mu S, \mu\varphi)}$

if $\mu = \mathrm{mgu}(l|_\gamma), l)$, $C' = \mu(C \cup \{l > r, l' > r'\})$ is satisfiable

and either $l|_\gamma$ is not a variable or $l|_\gamma \equiv l$

Fig. 2. The completion rule.

Proposition 23. *For all sets of equations E and S and idempotent E-minimal substitution θ, let $\{(E^k, \theta^k, S^k)\}_{k \geq 0}$ be the sequence starting with (E, θ, S) and defined by: For every $k \geq 0$, if $l[\gamma \leftarrow r'] \approx r$ is a θ^k-critical equation of E^k,*

- *$\mu^k = \mathrm{mgu}(l|_\gamma, l')$. Since $\mu^k \leq \theta^k$, we can write θ^k as $\lambda^k \mu^k$*
- *$E^{k+1} = \mu^k E^k \backslash \{\mu^k l \approx \mu^k r\} \cup \{\mu^k l[\gamma \leftarrow \mu^k r'] \approx \mu^k r\}$*
- *$\theta^{k+1} = \lambda^k$*
- *$S^{k+1} = \mu^k S^k$*

This sequence is always finite. For some finite $p \geq 0$ the set E^p contains all its θ^p-critical equations. At this stage, E^p is θ^p-closed and θ^p is E^p-irreducible.

Lemma 24. *Let E and S be two sets of equations and let θ be an idempotent substitution such that $\theta E \vdash \theta S$. Let R be a rule system such that $R \supseteq R_{E,\theta}$. Let C be a set of constraints satisfied by $(\theta, \succ)$. Let φ be a substitution such that $\varphi \leq \theta$ and $\varphi S = S$, $\varphi C = C, \varphi R = R$. If θ is E-minimal, then there exists a finite sequence of Complete, Orient and Delete steps : $(C, \emptyset, R, S, \varphi) \overset{RU}{\Longrightarrow} (C', \emptyset, R', S', \varphi')$ with $\theta = \theta'\varphi'$, $\varphi'C' = C'$, $\varphi'R' = R'$, $\varphi'S' = S'$ and $\theta'E' \vdash \theta'S'$, θ' is E'-irreducible and E' is θ'-closed, where $E' = \{l \approx r \mid l \to r \in R'\}$.*

Theorem 25. *For every idempotent rigid E-unifier ψ of a set of equations S there is a finite Rigid Unification sequence $(\emptyset, E, \emptyset, S, id) \overset{RU}{\Longrightarrow} (C, E, R, \emptyset, \sigma)$ and an E-minimal substitution θ such that $\sigma \leq \theta$, $\theta =_E \psi$ and $\sigma E \vdash \sigma S$.*

Lemma 26. *Let $(C_i)_{i \geq 0}$ be a sequence of sets of constraints such that for all $i \geq 0$, C_i is weak satisfiable and $C_i \subseteq C_{i+1}$. Let $\triangleright$ be the binary relation on terms defined by $s \triangleright t$ iff there is some $n \geq 0$ and some constraint $a > b \in C_n$ such that $s \equiv s[a]_\alpha$ and $t \equiv s[\alpha \leftarrow b]$. The transitive closure of $\triangleright$, written $\blacktriangleright$, is a well-founded ordering on $T_\Sigma(X)$.*

Proof. $\blacktriangleright$ is irreflexive since a simplification ordering $\succ$ satisfying the constraints is monotonic and transitive. $\succ$ contains the homeomorphic embedding $\geq_h$. [6, 18]. This and Kruskal's theorem [15] imply the well-foundedness of $\blacktriangleright$.

Theorem 27. *Every sequence of rigid unification is terminating.*

7 Computing complete sets of rigid unifiers

Below we describe an algorithm which takes as input two sets of equations E and S, and returns as output a complete set of rigid E-unifiers of S. The algorithm consists in applying exhaustively the rules of RU with the following strategy :

- Each application of the *Orient* rule is followed by a maximal number of applications of the *Delete* rule.
- Each application of the *Complete* or the rule *Paramodulate* is preceded by a maximal number of applications of the rules *Trivial*, *Orient* and *Delete*.

The algorithm can be seen as the juxtaposition of three sequences : a completion sequence, a paramodulation sequence and an unification sequence.

Its correctness follows from the correctness of RU. Its completeness is a consequence of the completeness of RU and of the fact that the order in which the *Delete* and *Trivial* steps are performed is irrelevant. The algorithm terminates because every sequence of RU is finite and there are only finitely many rules applicable at a given moment whereas the number of possible applications of each one is bounded. Furthermore, due to the decidability of the constraints satisfiability test, of the congruence closure test and of the syntactic unification test, each application of a rule is done in finite and even polynomial bounded time. Given two sets E and S of equations, the output of the algorithm is a (finite) complete set of rigid E-unifiers of S (cf. theorem 25 and definition 10).

8 Related works

The method of Gallier et al. The problem of computing a rigid E-unifier of a pair of terms u and v has been investigated first by J. Gallier *et al.* in [10]. They observed that D. Kozen ([14]) showed that the problem is NP-complete if the equations in E are ground. Thus, the general rigid E-unification problem is NP-hard. In [9] J. Gallier *et al.* prove that it is in NP.

1. J. Gallier's method is more a proof of NP-completeness rather than a practical algorithm, since the guess of order assignments is very indeterministic. The main advantage of our method is that we don't need any guess of an order assignment. We claim that our method is easier implementable.

2. Each completion step in Gallier's method involves a non empty substitution. So, the number of steps is strictly limited by the number of variables in the problem, whereas we can do a lot of completion or paramodulation steps with empty substitutions. We have to pay this price for avoiding the guess of order assignments. Gallier's procedure invokes a reduction algorithm running in time $O(n^3)$ ([8]) after each completion step. We achieve the same result allowing "ground" completion steps. The complexity of our method becomes less clear, but we conjecture that its global complexity is not greater.

3. Due to a technical trick Gallier's method does not need paramodulation. The NP-completeness proof becomes simpler due to uniform treatment of equations and dis-equations. But it is not quite evident that this leads to any gain in an implementation.

J. Goubault's method. J. Goubault proposes a rule-based method where rules affect congruence classes. The congruence closure algorithm has been enriched in order to hold certain information for triggering the applicability of rules. However, in order to achieve completeness the method contains a highly non-deterministic rule called, nomen est omen, the "guess rule". Unfortunately, the algorithm contains a bug, since it is possible that it ends with success even when there are no solutions as proved by the following counter-example : if one starts with the initial problem $E = \{ x \approx fy \}$, $F = \{ y \approx fx \}$ then the problem has an obvious solution, that is $\{ y/fx \}$ and the given algorithm will find it. But the problem $E = \emptyset$, $F = \{ x \approx fy, y \approx fx \}$ which is very close to the previous one has by evidence no solution. Unfortunately, Goubault's algorithm will work on this problem and find the following "solved form" : $\{ E_\square, \emptyset, B_\square \}$ where $E_\square = \{ x \approx fy, y \approx fx \}$ and $B_\square = \{ x, y \}$. This bug suggests that one cannot merge simply the equations in E and those which occurs as a result of unification, but one have to check the existence of an idempotent solution by an effective occurs check on the variables. In our method, we are on the safe side because we apply substitutions. Gallier et al. are on the safe side too because they put the triangular form of the unifiers computed for critical pairs into the problem representation. J. Goubault simulates an occurs check, but unfortunately he gave a wrong definition of the set $EssVar_E$ of "forbidden" variables[9].

B. Beckert's method. B. Beckert generalizes in his master thesis the E-unification problem to the so-called *mixed* E-unification problem, where variables may occur which are treated rigid as well as others which are universally quantified. The method which is part of a tableaux based prover is completion-based and uses constrained terms and constrained rules (that is terms and oriented equations which can only be used under a given condition). Unfortunately, due to the nature of the mixed problem, which is undecidable, the termination of the process is not proved, even in the case where all variables are treated rigid.

9 Prospectives

The rigid E-unification problem is in fact a restricted form of the *simultaneous* rigid E-unification problem, which is more general : given a family $(E_i, S_i)_{0 \leq i \leq n}$, where E_i and S_i are sets of equations, the question is to find a substitution θ s.t. for all i, $\theta E_i \vdash \theta S_i$. For the applications of rigid E-unification to theorem proving the simultaneous problem is the crucial problem to be solved. The known procedures for rigid E-unification cannot be generalized immediately to those solving the simultaneous problem. In [9], such a generalization is described. Unfortunately, the proof of the method relies on the wrong assumption that one can always restrict the search to substitutions which are *minimal* (in Gallier's sense) in each problem. For example the following simultaneous rigid E-unification problem $(E_1 = \{ x \approx c \},\ S_1 = \{ gb \approx gc \})$, $(E_2 = \{ a \approx b \},\ S_2 = \{ f(a,b) \approx f(x,a) \})$, $(E_3 = \{ f(a,b) \approx f(b,a) \},\ S_3 = \{ f(a,b) \approx f(x,a) \})$ has only one simultaneous rigid E-unifier $\theta = \{ x/b \}$. But if $b \succ a$ then for variable x occurring in S_2 the value θx is θE_2-reducible. Therefore θ is not minimal for

---

[9] Another definition which corrects the bug has been proposed by J. Goubault.

the second problem. With this observation the decidability of the simultaneous rigid unification problem became again an open question. Recently J. Goubault communicated that the problem is DEXPTIME-complete. Nevertheless, it remains the intriguing open problem whether for the purpose of theorem proving with equality it is sufficient to decide this problem in less complex special cases.

Acknowledgment. We wish to thank Patrice Enjalbert, Françoise Debart and Heinrich Herre for many helpful discussions and for their encouragements.

References

1. P. Andrews. Theorem Proving via General Matings. *J.ACM*, 28(2):193–214, 1981.
2. G. Becher and U. Petermann. Rigid E-Unification by Completion and Rigid Paramodulation. Technical report, Cahiers du LAIAC (n. 22) Univ. of Caen, 1993.
3. B. Beckert. Ein vervollständigungsbasiertes Verfahren zur Behandlung von Gleichheit im Tableaukalkül mit freien Variablen. Master's thesis, Karlsruhe (TH), 1993.
4. W. Bibel. *Automated Theorem Proving*. Vieweg, 1st edition, 1982.
5. H. Comon. Solving inequations in term algebras. In C. S. P. IEEE, editor, *Proceedings, LICS*, Philadelphia, 1990.
6. N. Dershowitz. Termination of Rewriting. *Journal of Symbolic Computation*, 3(1&2):69–116, February/April 1987.
7. D. J. Dougherty and P. Johann. An Improved General E-Unification Method. *Journal of Symbolic Computation*, 14:303–320, 1992.
8. J. Gallier, P. Narendran, D. Plaisted, S. Raatz, and W. Snyder. An Algorithm for finding Canonical Sets of Ground Rewrite Rules in Polynomial Time. *Journal of the A.C.M.*, 40:1–16, January 1993.
9. J. Gallier, P. Narendran, D. Plaisted, and W. Snyder. Rigid E-unification: NP-Completeness and Applications to Equational Matings. *Information and Computation*, pages 129–195, 1990.
10. J. Gallier and W. Snyder. Complete Sets of Transformations for General E-Unification. *Theoretical Computer Science*, 67:203 – 260, 1989.
11. J. Goubault. A Rule-Based Algorithm for Rigid E-Unification. In *3rd Kurt Gödel Colloquium '93*, volume 713 of *LNCS*. Springer-Verlag, 1993.
12. J.-M. Hullot. Canonical Forms and Unification. In *Proceedings CADE*, pages 318–334. Springer-Verlag, 1980. Lecture Notes in Artificial Intelligence 87.
13. J.-P. Jouannaud and C. Kirchner. Solving Equations in Abstract Algebras: A Rule-based Survey of Unification. *Computational Logic. Essays in Honour of Alan Robinson*, pages 257–321, 1991.
14. D. Kozen. Positive first-order logic is NP-complete. *IBM Journal of Research and Development*, 4:327–332, 1981.
15. J. Kruskal. Well Quasi Ordering, the Tree Problem and Vazsonyi's conjecture. *Transactions of the American Mathematical Society*, 95:210–225, 1960.
16. D. W. Loveland. Mechanical Theorem Proving by Model Elimination. *JACM*, 15(2), 1978.
17. G. Nelson and D. C. Oppen. Fast Decision Procedures Based on Congruence Closure. *Journal of Association for Computer Machinery*, 27(2), April 1980.
18. D. A. Plaisted. A simple non-termination test for the Knuth-Bendix method. In *Proc 8th CADE, LNCS 230*, pages 79–88. Springer, 1986.
19. D. A. Plaisted. Polynomial Time Termination and Constraint Satisfaction Tests. In *Rewriting Techniques and Applications*, pages 405–420, Montreal, June 1993.

Unification in a Sorted λ-Calculus with Term Declarations and Function Sorts

Michael Kohlhase*

FB Informatik, Universität des Saarlandes, 66041 Saarbrücken, Germany
+49-681-301-4627   kohlhase@cs.uni-sb.de
http://js-sfbsun.cs.uni-sb.de/pub/www

Abstract. The introduction of sorts to first-order automated deduction has brought greater conciseness of representation and a considerable gain in efficiency by reducing search spaces. This suggests that sort information can be employed in higher-order theorem proving with similar results. This paper develops a sorted λ-calculus suitable for automatic theorem proving applications. It extends the simply typed λ-calculus by a higher-order sort concept that includes term declarations and functional base sorts. The term declaration mechanism studied here is powerful enough to subsume subsorting as a derived notion and therefore gives a justification for the special form of subsort inference. We present a set of transformations for sorted (pre-) unification and prove the nondeterministic completeness of the algorithm induced by these transformations.

1 Introduction

In the quest for calculi best suited for automating logic on computers, the introduction of sorts has been one of the most important contributions. Sort techniques consist in syntactically distinguishing between objects of different classes and then assigning sorts (specifying the membership in some class) to objects and restricting the range of variables to particular sorts. Since a good part of the set membership and subset information can be coded into the sorted signature, sorted logics lead to a more concise representation of problems and proofs than the unsorted variants. The exploitation of this information during proof search can dramatically reduce the search space associated with theorem-proving and make the resulting sorted calculi much more efficient. In the context of first-order logic sort information has been successfully employed by C. Walther [21], M. Schmidt-Schauß [19], A. Cohn [6], C. Weidenbach [22] and others.

On the other hand there is an increasing interest in deduction systems for higher-order logic, since many problems in mathematics are inherently higher-order. Current automated deduction systems for higher-order logic like TPS [2] are rather weak on the first-order fragment, which is in part due to the fact that many of the advances of first-order deduction (like sorted calculi) have not yet been transported to higher-order logic. Thus the question about the behavior of higher-order logic under the constraints of a full sorted type structure is a natural one to ask, in particular since calculi in this system promise the development of more powerful deduction systems for real mathematics. G. Huet proposed the

---

* This work was supported by the Deutsche Forschungsgemeinschaft in SFB 314 (D2)

study of a sorted version of higher-order logic in an appendix to [7]. The unification problem in extensions of this system have since been studied by Nipkow and Qian [16] and by Pfenning and the author [14]. Furthermore typed λ-calculi with order-sorted type structures have been of interest in the programming language community as a theoretical basis for object-oriented programming and for more expressive formalisms for higher-order algebraic specifications [18, 4, 3, 17].

Here we present a λ-calculus $\Sigma\mathcal{T}$ that differs from the abovementioned in that we do not consider function restriction as a "built-in" of the system, since we take the mathematical intuition that functions have uniquely specified domains seriously. Consequently our subsort relation is not covariant in the domain sort (this principle semantically corresponds to implicit function restriction). Furthermore the term declaration mechanism is much more powerful than the declaration schemas proposed in those logical systems. This paper is an extension of the results presented in [8, 9]. This subsystem of $\Sigma\mathcal{T}$ only allows signatures consisting of constant declarations and thus treats the interaction of functional base sorts and extensionality in isolation. In contrast to this subsystem the powerful mechanism of term declarations in $\Sigma\mathcal{T}$ allows a straightforward specification of many mathematical concepts (cf. Example 2.8). This paper also corrects an earlier attempt [11] to solve the problem. We have corrected the relevant definitions of [11] and with these were able to prove all the results claimed there. For details and proofs we refer the reader to [12].

In the following we will shortly motivate the primary features of $\Sigma\mathcal{T}$. In unsorted logics the only way to express the knowledge that an object is a member of a certain class of objects is through the use of unary predicates, such as the predicate $N_{\iota\to o}$ in the formulae ($N2_\iota$), i.e. "2 is a natural number", or $\neg(NPeter_\iota)$, i.e. "Peter is not a natural number". This leads to a multitude of unit clauses ($S_{\iota\to o}A$) in the deduction that only carry the sort information for A. Since quantification is unrestricted in unsorted logics, the restricted quantification has to be simulated by formulae like $\forall X_\iota.(NX_\iota) \Rightarrow (\geq_{\iota\to\iota\to o} X_\iota 0_\iota)$. This approach is unsatisfactory because inter alia the derivation of the nonsensical formula (NPeter) $\Rightarrow$ ($\geq$ Peter 0) is permitted, even though ($\geq$ Peter 0) can never be derived because of $\neg(NPeter)$. Sorted logics remedy this situation by assigning sorts to constants and variables and by restricting quantification to sorts. Furthermore formulae have to meet certain (sort) restrictions to denote meaningful objects.

In typed λ-calculi the idea of declaring sort information is very natural, as all objects are already typed, which amounts to a – very coarse – division of the universe into classes. The type system is merely refined by considering the sorts as additional base types. For example the last formula above would read $\forall X_N.(\geq X0)$, where $\geq$ is a binary relation on N and 0 is of sort N in the signature. Sorting the universe of individuals gives rise to new classes of functions, namely functions, where domains and codomains are just the sorts. In addition to this essentially first-order way of sorting the function universes, the classes of functions defined by domains and codomains can be further divided into subclasses that we represent by base sorts of functional type. As an example for the sort restrictions on formulae consider the application $(\mathbf{AB})$. Here, there must be sorts A and B, such that $\mathbf{A}$ is of sort A, $\mathbf{B}$ is of sort B and B is a subsort of the domain sort of A. The sort of the application (AB) is defined to be the codomain sort of A.

In ΣT we relax the implicit condition that only the sorts of constants and variables can be declared, and allow declarations of the form $[\forall \Gamma.A::A]$ called term declarations, where A can be an arbitrary formula of appropriate type and Γ is a variable context. The idea of term declarations is that there can be sort information within the structure of a term, if the term matches a certain schematic term (a term declaration).

Consider for instance the addition function, which we (semantically) would like to have the sort $N \times N \to N$ where N is the sort of natural numbers. If we also have a sort for the even numbers E, then we might want to specify that the expression $[+aa]$ is an even number, even if a is not. This information can be formalized by declaring the term $[+X_N X_N]$ to be of sort E using a term declaration. We might also want to give the addition function the sort $E \times E \to E$, however since we insist that terms have unique domain sorts, we cannot declare this directly in the signature. Closer inspection of the semantics behind our example reveals that it is consistent with our program to declare the restriction of the addition function to the even numbers has codomain in the evens, which we can legally do with a term declaration $[\forall [X::E], [Y::E]. + XY::E]$.

In this expressive system term declarations of the form $[\forall [X::A].X::B]$ entail that A is a subsort of B and induce the intended subsort ordering on the set of sorts.

2 Sorted λ-Calculus

We assume the reader to be familiar with the syntax and semantics of simply typed λ-calculus $(\Lambda^{\to})$ [5, 1]. The set T of types $(\alpha, \beta, \gamma \ldots)$ is built up from a set BT of *base types* by closure under $\to$. We assume a set of typed constants $\overline{\Sigma} := \bigcup_{\alpha \in T} \overline{\Sigma}_\alpha$ and a countably infinite set V_α of variables for each type $\alpha \in T$. Well-formed formulae are built up from variables and constants as *applications* and *λ-abstractions* in the usual way.

Another mathematical notion which will play a great role in this paper is that of a *partial function* $\Phi: A \longrightarrow B$. With this we will mean a relation $\Phi \subseteq A \times B$, such that for all pairs (a, b) and (c, d) in Φ we have $a \neq c$. For partial functions that can be presented by a finite set of pairs (e.g. substitutions or variable contexts), we will often use a notation like $\Phi := [b^1/a^1], \ldots, [b^n/a^n]$ if $\Phi = \{(a^1, b^1), \ldots, (a^n, b^n)\}$. Furthermore, if Ψ is that partial function, such that $\Psi(a) = b$ but $\Psi(c) = \Phi(c)$ for all $c \neq a$, then we will denote Ψ by $\Phi, [b/a]$. If the restrictions of Φ and Ψ to $\mathbf{Dom}(\Phi) \cap \mathbf{Dom}(\Psi)$ are identical, then we say that they *agree* $(\Phi \| \Psi)$. In this case $\Phi \cup \Psi$ is again a partial function.

Definition 2.1 (Sort System) A *sort system* is a quintuple $(\mathcal{S}, BS, \mathfrak{r}, \mathfrak{d}, \tau)$, where BS is a finite set of symbols, called *base sorts* and the *set of sorts* $\mathcal{S}$ is the closure of BS under $\to$. We will denote sorts with symbols like A, B, C, D and have $B \to A \in \mathcal{S}$, whenever $A, B \in \mathcal{S}$. The functions $\mathfrak{r}, \mathfrak{d}$ and τ specify the sorts of the *codomain*, *domain* and the *type* of a sort and we require that $\tau(A) = \tau(\mathfrak{d}(A)) \to \tau(\mathfrak{r}(A))$ for all sorts $A \in \mathcal{S}$. The type $\tau(A) \in T$ is called the *type of the sort* A. We will denote the set of sorts of type α with

$\mathcal{S}_\alpha$, call a sort $A \in \mathcal{S}_{\alpha \to \beta}$ a *functional sort* and denote the set of functional sorts by $\mathcal{S}^f$ (non-functional sorts by $\mathcal{S}^{nf}$). Note that the sets BS and $\mathcal{S}^{nf}$ are in general distinct (see example 2.8). Furthermore let $\ln(A) := 0$, iff $A \in BS$ and $\ln(A \to B) := 1 + \ln(B)$. We will use the shorthands $\mathfrak{r}^i(A)$ and $\mathfrak{r}^i(A)$ defined by

$$\mathfrak{r}^0(A) = A \quad \mathfrak{r}^{i+1}(A) = \mathfrak{r}(\mathfrak{r}^i(A)) \qquad \mathfrak{d}^0(A) = A \quad \mathfrak{d}^{i+1}(A) = \mathfrak{d}(\mathfrak{r}^i(A))$$

It will be important that the signatures over which our well-sorted terms are built "respect function domains,", *i.e.* that for any term A and any sorts A and B of A, the identity $\mathfrak{d}(A) = \mathfrak{d}(B)$ holds. The proof that signatures indeed satisfy this property depends on the consistency conditions for valid signatures, given in terms of the equivalence relation **Rdom**, where A **Rdom** B, iff $\mathfrak{d}^i(A) = \mathfrak{d}^i(B)$ for all $i \leq k$, such that $\mathfrak{r}^k(A)$ and $\mathfrak{r}^k(B)$ are of the same base type.

Next, we will introduce the concept of well-sortedness for formulae. A term A will be called *well-sorted* with respect to a signature Σ and a context Γ, if the judgment $\Gamma \vdash_\Sigma A{::}A$ is derivable in the inference system ΣT. Here the context gives local sort information for the variables, whereas the signature contains sort information given by term schemata (the term declarations). One of the difficulties in devising a formal system with term declarations is that the signature needed for defining well-sortedness in itself contains terms that have to be well sorted. Therefore we need to combine the inference systems for the judgment $\vdash_{sig} \Sigma$ (Σ is a a valid signature) and that for well-sortedness ($\Gamma \vdash_\Sigma A{::}A$) into one large system ΣT. Another difficulty is that we also have to treat a sorted $\beta\eta$-conversion judgment $\Gamma \vdash_\Sigma A =_{\beta\eta} B$ in ΣT, since we want $\beta\eta$-conversion to be sort preserving.

Definition 2.2 (Variable Context) Let X_α be a variable and A a sort, then we call a pair $[X{::}A]$ a *variable declaration* for X, iff $\tau(A) = \alpha$. We call a finite set of variable declarations a *(variable) context* ($\vdash_{ctx} \Gamma$), if it is a partial function *i.e.* $\Gamma \subseteq V_\alpha \times \mathcal{S}_\alpha$. Note that with our convention for partial functions we have $\Gamma(X) = A$ for $\Gamma := \Gamma', [X{::}A]$, even if $\Gamma'(X) = B$.

Definition 2.3 (Well-Sorted Formulae and Valid Signatures) For a fixed signature Σ and a context Γ we say that a formula A *is of sort* A, iff the judgment $\Gamma \vdash_\Sigma A{::}A$ is derivable in the following inference system.

$$\frac{\vdash_{sig} \Sigma \quad \vdash_{ctx} \Gamma \quad \Gamma(X) = A}{\Gamma \vdash_\Sigma X{::}A} \qquad \frac{[\forall \Delta.A{::}A] \in \Sigma \quad \vdash_{sig} \Sigma \quad \Delta \subseteq \Gamma}{\Gamma \vdash_\Sigma A{::}A}$$

$$\frac{\Gamma \vdash_\Sigma A{::}A \quad \Delta \vdash_\Sigma B{::}\mathfrak{d}(A) \quad \Gamma \| \Delta}{\Delta \cup \Gamma \vdash_\Sigma (AB){::}\mathfrak{r}(A)} \qquad \frac{\Gamma, X{::}B \vdash_\Sigma A{::}A}{\Gamma \vdash_\Sigma (\lambda X_B.A){::}B \to A}$$

$$\frac{\Gamma \vdash_\Sigma A{::}A \quad \Gamma \vdash_\Sigma B{::}B \quad \Gamma \vdash_\Sigma A =_{\beta\eta} B}{\Gamma \vdash_\Sigma B{::}A}$$

The following inference rules define the the judgment $\vdash_{sig} \Sigma$ by specifying that it is legal to add term declarations to valid signatures, if either they are the first declarations for new constants, or if the formula **A** is well-sorted and the new sort **A** respects function domains.

$$\frac{\vdash_{sig} \Sigma \quad c \notin \Sigma \quad c \in \overline{\Sigma}_\alpha \quad \mathsf{A} \in \mathcal{S} \quad \tau(\mathsf{A}) = \alpha}{\vdash_{sig} \Sigma, [c::\mathsf{A}]}$$

$$\frac{\Gamma \vdash_\Sigma \mathsf{A}::\mathsf{A} \quad \Sigma \vdash \mathsf{A} \ \mathbf{Rdom} \ \mathsf{B}}{\vdash_{sig} \Sigma, [\forall \Gamma.\mathsf{A}::\mathsf{B}]}$$

$$\vdash_{sig} \emptyset$$

Finally let $\Gamma \vdash_\Sigma \mathsf{A} =_{\beta\eta} \mathsf{B}$ be the congruence judgment induced by the reduction judgment.

$$\frac{\Gamma \vdash_\Sigma \mathsf{A}::\mathsf{A}}{\Gamma \vdash_\Sigma (\lambda X_{\eth(\mathsf{A})}.\mathsf{A}X) \to_\eta \mathsf{A}} \qquad \frac{\Gamma, [X::\mathsf{B}] \vdash_\Sigma \mathsf{A}::\mathsf{A} \quad \Delta \vdash_\Sigma \mathsf{B}::\mathsf{B} \quad \Gamma \| \Delta}{\Gamma \cup \Delta \vdash_\Sigma (\lambda X_{\mathsf{B}}.\mathsf{A})\mathsf{B} \to_\beta [\mathsf{B}/X]\mathsf{A}}$$

In the definition of sorted η-reduction we have taken care to identify the *supporting sort* $\eth(\mathsf{A})$ of **A** (which will turn out to be unique in theorem 2.4), since the formula $(\lambda X_{\mathsf{B}}.\mathsf{A}X)$ denotes the restriction of the function **A** to sort **B**, if **B** is a subsort of $\eth(\mathsf{A})$ and can therefore not be equal to **A**.

It is easy to see that the judgments defined above respect well-typedness, *i.e.* that the information described by $\Sigma\mathcal{T}$ merely refines the type information. In particular sorted $\beta\eta$-conversion is a sub-relation of typed conversion. As a direct consequence sorted $\beta\eta$-reduction is terminating. The confluence result depends on the following theorem

Theorem 2.4 *If* $\Gamma \vdash_\Sigma \mathsf{A}::\mathsf{A}$ *and* $\Gamma \vdash_\Sigma \mathsf{A}::\mathsf{B}$, *then* **A Rdom B**.

In fact the formal system $\Sigma\mathcal{T}$ is designed to capture informal mathematical practice, where functions have unique domains associated with them.

If we only have one base sort per base type, then the set of well-sorted formulae is isomorphic to the set of well-typed formulae, therefore $\Sigma\mathcal{T}$ is a generalization of $\Lambda^\to$. It is an important property of our system, that any valid signature is *subterm-closed*, that is each subterm of a well-sorted term is again well-sorted. This fact is natural, since it does not make sense to allow ill-formed subexpressions in well-formed expressions.

Definition 2.5 Let Γ and Δ be variable contexts, then we call a substitution σ a Σ-*substitution* ($\sigma \in \mathbf{wsSub}(\Sigma, \Delta \to \Gamma)$), iff the judgment $\Gamma \vdash_\Sigma \sigma::\Delta$ is derivable in the following inference system.

$$\frac{}{\emptyset \vdash_\Sigma \emptyset::\emptyset} \qquad \frac{\Gamma \vdash_\Sigma \sigma::\Delta \quad \Gamma' \vdash_\Sigma \mathsf{A}::\mathsf{A} \quad \Gamma \| \Gamma' \quad X \notin \mathbf{Dom}(\Gamma)}{\Gamma \vdash_\Sigma \sigma, [\mathsf{A}/X]::\Delta, [X::\mathsf{A}]}$$

Let $\Gamma \vdash_\Sigma \sigma::\Delta$. We can show that if $\Xi \cup \Delta \vdash_\Sigma \mathsf{A}::\mathsf{A}$, then $\Xi \cup \Gamma \vdash_\Sigma \sigma(\mathsf{A})::\mathsf{A}$ and furthermore $\mathbf{Dom}(\Delta) = \mathbf{Dom}(\sigma)$ and $\mathbf{Dom}(\Delta) \cap \mathbf{Dom}(\Gamma) = \emptyset$. Thus Σ-substitutions are idempotent and their application conserves sets of sorts. As a consequence we can show that if $\Gamma \vdash_\Sigma \mathsf{A} =_{\beta\eta} \mathsf{B}$, then **A** and **B** have the same set of sorts. Thus the fundamental operations of sorted higher-order deduction systems do not allow the formation of ill-sorted terms from well-sorted ones. This will ensure that such systems never have to handle ill-sorted terms, even intermediately.

Let $\Gamma \vdash_\Sigma X{::}\mathsf{B}$ but $\Gamma(X) = \mathsf{A}$ (we abbreviate this by $\Gamma \vdash_\Sigma \mathsf{A} \leq_\Sigma \mathsf{B}$), then for all formulae $\Gamma \vdash_\Sigma \mathsf{A}{::}\mathsf{A}$ we also have $\Gamma \vdash_\Sigma \mathsf{A}{::}\mathsf{B}$, since $\Gamma \vdash_\Sigma [\mathsf{A}/X]X{::}\mathsf{B}$. This is just the situation that is captured with the notion of sort inclusion in traditional sorted logics, where the subsort relation is the smallest partial ordering that contains a set of subsort declarations. The subsort relation plays such a central role in these systems that they are collectively called "order-sorted". Since subsorting is a derived relation in $\Sigma\mathcal{T}$ (cf. theorem 2.7), we do not have to treat it in our meta-logical development. On the object level (and for computation) however it is a useful notion to employ, since it allows to specify taxonomic hierarchies of sorts, which play a great role in intuitive mathematics.

In contrast to the first-order systems the subsort relation is not finite, even with a finite set of base sorts. Thus the relation cannot be pre-computed in advance. On the other hand it is not clear, whether the sort-checking problem is decidable (in fact this problem can be seen to be equivalent to the higher-order matching problem, where decidability is known only for restricted classes of formulae), which is another reason for limited practical usefulness of the full subsorting relation. One way out of this situation is to approximate the subsort relation by a sub-relation computed from a finite set of subsort declarations with certain induction principles.

Definition 2.6 (Sort Inclusion) Let $\mathcal{R}$ be a binary relation on sorts, such that $[X{::}\mathsf{A}] \vdash_\Sigma X{::}\mathsf{B}$, whenever $\mathcal{R}(\mathsf{A}, \mathsf{B})$, then we call $\mathcal{R}$ an *approximation of the subsort relation in Σ*. We will call term declarations of the form $[\forall X_\mathsf{A}.X{::}\mathsf{B}]$ *subsort declarations* and abbreviate them with $[\mathsf{A} \leq \mathsf{B}]$. The following inference system is called the $\Sigma\mathcal{T}$ *subsort inference system for $\mathcal{R}$*

$$\frac{\mathcal{R}(\mathsf{A}, \mathsf{B}) \quad \vdash_{sig} \Sigma}{\Sigma \vdash \mathsf{A} \leq_\mathcal{R} \mathsf{B}} \qquad \frac{\vdash_{sig} \Sigma}{\Sigma \vdash \mathsf{A} \leq_\mathcal{R} \mathsf{A}} \qquad \frac{\vdash_{sig} \Sigma}{\Sigma \vdash \mathsf{A} \leq_\mathcal{R} \mathfrak{d}(\mathsf{A}) \to \mathfrak{r}(\mathsf{A})}$$

$$\frac{\Sigma \vdash \mathsf{A} \leq_\mathcal{R} \mathsf{B} \quad \Sigma \vdash \mathsf{B} \leq_\mathcal{R} \mathsf{C}}{\Sigma \vdash \mathsf{A} \leq_\mathcal{R} \mathsf{C}} \qquad \frac{\Sigma \vdash \mathsf{A} \leq_\mathcal{R} \mathsf{B}}{\Sigma \vdash \mathsf{C} \to \mathsf{A} \leq_\mathcal{R} \mathsf{C} \to \mathsf{B}}$$

We will call the relation $\mathcal{R}^\leq$ defined by $\mathcal{R}^\leq(\mathsf{A}, \mathsf{B})$, iff $\Sigma \vdash \mathsf{A} \leq_\mathcal{R} \mathsf{B}$ is the *ordering relation for $\mathcal{R}$*. For a given, valid signature Σ we will denote subsorting judgment for the subsort declarations simply with $\Sigma \vdash \mathsf{A} \leq \mathsf{B}$.

Theorem 2.7 *If $\mathcal{R}$ is an approximation of the subsort relation of Σ, then the relation $\mathcal{R}^\leq$ is also an approximation.*

The subsort judgment interacts with well-sorted formulae by the classical *weakening rule*, which allows to weaken the sort information.

$$\frac{\Gamma \vdash_\Sigma \mathsf{A}{::}\mathsf{A} \quad \Sigma \vdash \mathsf{A} \leq_\mathcal{R} \mathsf{B}}{\Gamma \vdash_\Sigma \mathsf{A}{::}\mathsf{B}}$$

As a consequence of Theorem 2.7 we can see that if $\mathcal{R}$ is an approximation of the subsort relation in Σ, then the weakening rule is admissible in $\Sigma\mathcal{T}$. Furthermore we have $\mathbf{A}\ \mathbf{Rdom}\ \mathbf{B}$ whenever $\Sigma \vdash \mathbf{A} \leq_{\mathcal{R}} \mathbf{B}$. In particular $\tau(\mathbf{A}) = \tau(\mathbf{B})$ in this situation and therefore, the sets $\{\mathbf{A} \in \mathcal{S} \mid \tau(\mathbf{A}) = \alpha\}$ are mutually incomparable.

Example 2.8 Let $\mathcal{BS} := \{\mathbf{R}, \mathbf{C}, \mathbf{D}, \mathbf{P}\}$ where the intended meaning of $\mathbf{R}$ is the set of real numbers, that of $\mathbf{C}$ and $\mathbf{D}$ the sets of continuous and differentiable functions and finally that of $\mathbf{P}$ the set of polynomials. Therefore the types have to be $\tau(\mathbf{R}) = \iota$, $\tau(\mathbf{C}) = \tau(\mathbf{D}) = \tau(\mathbf{P}) = \iota \to \iota$ and $\mathfrak{r}(\mathbf{C}) = \mathfrak{d}(\mathbf{C}) = \mathbf{R}, \ldots$ In this example we want to model a taxonomy for elementary calculus, so let Σ be the set containing the subsort declarations $[\mathbf{P} \leq \mathbf{D}], [\mathbf{D} \leq \mathbf{C}]$, and the term declarations

$$[\lambda X_{\mathbf{R}}.X::\mathbf{P}],\ [\lambda X_{\mathbf{R}}.Y_{\mathbf{R}}::\mathbf{P}],\ [\lambda X_{\mathbf{R}}. + (F_{\mathbf{P}}X)(G_{\mathbf{P}}X)::\mathbf{P})],\ [\lambda X_{\mathbf{R}}. * (F_{\mathbf{P}}X)(G_{\mathbf{P}}X)::\mathbf{P}]$$

for polynomials and furthermore $[\partial::\mathbf{D} \to \mathbf{C}], [\partial::\mathbf{P} \to \mathbf{P}]$ for the differentiation operator ∂, then it is easy to check that Σ is a valid signature. We can see that we have coded a great deal of information about polynomials and differentiation into the term declarations of Σ. Note that up to (elementary arithmetic) any polynomial is indeed of sort $\mathbf{P}$. The practical advantage of this formalization of elementary algebra is that this can be used in the unification during proof search in refutation calculi and thus considerably reduce the search for proofs.

3 Structure Theorem and General Bindings

The key tool for the investigation of well-sorted formulae will be the structure theorem which we are about to prove. The principal difficulty of $\Sigma\mathcal{T}$ is that the property of well-sortedness is highly non-structural, which makes the classical deduction methods, such as unification that analyze the structure of formulae difficult. The structure theorem recovers structural properties of well-sorted formulae by linking the sort information (the existence of certain term declarations) with structural information about normal forms.

Theorem 3.1 (Structure Theorem) *Let* $\mathbf{A}$ *be a well-sorted formula with long head normal form* $[\lambda\overline{X^k}.h\overline{U^n}]$ *and* $\Gamma \vdash_\Sigma \mathbf{A}::\mathbf{A}$. *Furthermore let* Ξ^j *be the variable context* $[X^1::\mathfrak{d}(\mathbf{A})], \ldots, [X^j::\mathfrak{d}^j(\mathbf{A})]$ *and* $l = \mathbf{ln}(\mathbf{A})$, *then*

1. h *is a variable with* $\Gamma, \Xi^k(h) = \mathbf{B}$, *such that* $\mathfrak{r}^n(\mathbf{B}) = \mathfrak{r}^k(\mathbf{A})$, $\Gamma, \Xi^k \vdash_\Sigma$ $\mathbf{U}^i::\mathfrak{d}^i(\mathbf{B})$ *for* $1 \leq i \leq n$.
2. *there is a term declaration* $[\forall\Delta.\mathbf{B}::\mathbf{B}] \in \Sigma$, *a* Σ-*substitution* θ *and well-sorted formulae* $\mathbf{D}^i$, *such that*
    (a) $\Gamma \vdash_\Sigma \mathbf{A} =_{\beta\eta} (\lambda\overline{X^l_{\mathfrak{d}^l(\mathbf{A})}}.\theta(\mathbf{B})\overline{\mathbf{D}^m})$, *where* $m := l + \mathbf{ln}(\tau(\mathbf{B})) - \mathbf{ln}(\tau(\mathbf{A})) \geq 0$.
    (b) $\Gamma, \Xi^l \vdash_\Sigma \theta::\Delta$, $\Gamma, \Xi^l \vdash_\Sigma \mathbf{D}^i::\mathfrak{d}^i(\mathbf{B})$ *for all* $i \leq m$ *and* $\mathfrak{r}^m(\mathbf{B}) = \mathfrak{r}^l(\mathbf{A})$.
    (c) *If* h *is a constant, then* $\mathbf{head}(\mathbf{B}) = Z \in \mathbf{Dom}(\theta)$ *and* $\mathbf{head}(\theta(Z)) = h$ *or else* $\mathbf{head}(\mathbf{B}) = h$.
    (d) $\mathbf{dp}(\mathbf{D}^i) < \mathbf{dp}(h\overline{U^n})$ *and* $\mathbf{dp}(\theta) < \mathbf{dp}(h\overline{U^n})$.

Here the depth of a substitution θ *is the maximum of the* $\mathbf{dp}(\theta(X))$ *for all* $X \in \mathbf{Dom}(\theta)$ *and the depth of a formula is the depth of the corresponding tree.*

One of the key steps in sort computation and unification is solving the following problem: given a sort A and an atom C, find the most general well-sorted formula of sort A that has head C. Such formulae are called general bindings of sort A for the head C. In $\Sigma\mathcal{T}$, this problem requires a more careful investigation than in $\Lambda^{\rightarrow}$. For instance consider a context Γ, such that $\Gamma(Z) = B \rightarrow B$, $\Gamma(X) = \Gamma(Y) = B$ and $\Gamma(W) = A$ and Σ consists of the following term declarations $[A \leq B]$, $[a::A]$, $[b::B]$, $[f::(B \rightarrow B \rightarrow B)]$, $[\forall[X::B]\langle faX)::A]$, $[\forall[X::B]\langle fXb)::A]$ then the most general formulae with the head f and sort B is fXY, of sort A are faX and fXb and finally of sort $(B \rightarrow A)$ are $\lambda X_B.fa(ZX)$ and $\lambda X_B.f(ZX)b$. In $\Lambda^{\rightarrow}$ these general bindings are unique and consist only of the head and of variables. In order-sorted type-theory each term declaration, that has the appropriate head and meets certain conditions will contribute a general binding.

Definition 3.2 (General Binding) For the definitions of general bindings we have two possibilities, corresponding to the two cases of the structure theorem. The first (classical) one obtains the sort information from the head variable, whereas the second one obtains the sort information from a term declaration. Let Γ be a context and A and B be sorts, such that

1. $l = \ln(A)$ and $m = l + \ln(\tau(A)) - \ln(\tau(B)) \geq 0$
2. $\tau^m(B) = \tau^l(A)$
3. $\mathbf{V}^i = (H^i X^1 \ldots X^l)$, where H^i are variables not in $\mathbf{Dom}(\Gamma)$
4. $\mathcal{H} := [H^1::\overline{\partial^l(A)} \rightarrow \partial^1(B)], \ldots, [H^m::\overline{\partial^l(A)} \rightarrow \partial^m(B)],$

then the formula $G := (\lambda X^1_{\partial^1(A)} \cdots X^l_{\partial^l(A)}.h\mathbf{V}^1 \ldots \mathbf{V}^m)$ is called a *general binding of sort A and head h* if $h = X^j$ or $h \in \mathbf{Dom}(\Gamma)$ and $\Gamma(h) = B$. We call $\mathcal{H}$ the *context of variables introduced for G*.

Let $[\forall\overline{[Y^t::C^n]}.B::B] \in \Sigma$ and A, B and $\mathbf{V}^i$ as above and furthermore

5. $\mathbf{W}^i := (K^i X^1 \ldots X^l)$, where K^i are variables not in $\Gamma \cup \mathcal{H}$
6. $\mathcal{K} := [K^1::\overline{\partial^l(A)} \rightarrow C^1], \ldots, [K^t::\overline{\partial^l(A)} \rightarrow C^t]$
7. $B' = [\overline{\mathbf{W}^t/Y^n}]B$ and $h := \mathbf{head}(B')$

then the formula $G := (\lambda X^1_{\partial^1(A)} \cdots X^l_{\partial^l(A)}.B'\mathbf{V}^1 \ldots \mathbf{V}^m)$ is called a *general binding of sort A and head h*. In this case the context of variables introduced for G is $\mathcal{H} \cup \mathcal{K}$. Now we define the set $\mathcal{G}^h_A(\Sigma, \Gamma, \mathcal{C})$ to be the set of all general bindings of sort A and head h and introduced context $\mathcal{C}$. If the head of G is bound, then we call G a *projection binding*, if h is a variable in $\mathbf{Dom}(\Gamma)$ or a constant *imitation binding* and if $h \in \mathbf{Dom}(\mathcal{K})$ (G is induced by a flexible term declaration in this case), then we call G a *general weakening binding of sort A*. We will denote the set of all such bindings with $\mathcal{W}_A(\Sigma, \Gamma, \mathcal{C})$.

It is easily verified that $\Gamma, \mathcal{C} \vdash_\Sigma G::A$ and $\mathbf{head}(G) = h$, provided that $G \in \mathcal{G}^h_A(\Sigma, \Gamma, \mathcal{C})$, which explains the naming in the definition above. The following theorem is a consequence of the structure theorem and the basis of the unification transformations given below.

Theorem 3.3 (General Binding Theorem) *Let* $A = \lambda\overline{X^k}.h\overline{U^n}$ *be a long* $\beta\eta$-*normal form with* $\Gamma \vdash_\Sigma A::A$, *then there exists a general binding* $G \in \mathcal{G}^h_A(\Sigma, \Gamma, \mathcal{C}) \cup \mathcal{W}_A(\Sigma, \Gamma, \mathcal{C})$ *and a* Σ-*substitution* $\rho \in \mathbf{wsSub}(\mathcal{C} \rightarrow \Gamma, \Sigma)$, *such that* $\mathbf{dp}(\rho) < \mathbf{dp}(A)$ *and* $\mathcal{C}, \Gamma \vdash_\Sigma \rho(G)=_{\beta\eta} A$.

4 Unification

Building upon the notion of general bindings we give a set of transformations for (pre-)unification, which we will prove correct and complete with the methods of [20].

Definition 4.1 (Unification Problem) A *unification problem* is a formula in the language $\mathcal{E} ::= \mathbf{A} \doteq \mathbf{B} \mid \exists[X::\mathsf{A}]\mathcal{E} \mid \forall[X::\mathsf{A}]\mathcal{E} \mid \mathcal{E}_1 \wedge \mathcal{E}_2 \mid \top$. In order to simplify the presentation of the algorithm, we assume that all unification formulae are in $\exists\forall$-form $\mathcal{E} := \exists\Gamma\forall\Delta.\mathcal{E}'$. Each formula is equivalent to one in this form by raising [15]. We call a Σ-substitution θ, such that $\Gamma \vdash_\Sigma \theta::\Delta$ and $\Gamma \vdash_\Sigma \theta(\mathbf{A})=_{\beta\eta}\theta(\mathbf{B})$ for all pairs $\mathbf{A} \doteq \mathbf{B}$ in $\mathcal{E}'$ a Σ-unifier for $\mathcal{E}$ and we will denote the set of Σ-unifiers of $\mathcal{E}$ with $\mathbf{wsU}(\Sigma, \mathcal{E})$. We call a subset $\Psi \subseteq \mathbf{wsU}(\Sigma, \mathcal{E})$ a *complete set of Σ-unifiers of $\mathcal{E}$*, iff for all $\theta \in \mathbf{wsU}(\Sigma, \mathcal{E})$ there is a $\sigma \in \Psi$ that is more general than θ, *i.e.* there is a Σ-substitution ρ, such that $\Gamma \vdash_\Sigma \sigma(X)=_{\beta\eta}\rho(\theta(X))$ for all $X \in \mathbf{Dom}(\Delta) = \mathbf{Dom}(\sigma)$. If the singleton set $\{\sigma\}$ is a complete set of unifiers of $\mathcal{E}$, then we call σ a *most general unifier* for $\mathcal{E}$.

Note that Σ-unifiability does not entail that both formulae of a pair have identical sets of sorts, since these sets may grow as more term declarations become applicable with instantiation. Nevertheless Σ-unifiable pairs must have the same types and furthermore the sorts must obey the **Rdom** relation.

Definition 4.2 (Σ-Solved Form) A unification problem $\mathcal{E} := \exists\Gamma\forall\Delta.\mathcal{E}'$ is in Σ-*solved form* if all of its pairs are in solved form, *i.e.* of the form $X \doteq \mathbf{A}$, such that $\Gamma(X) = \mathsf{A}$, $\Gamma \vdash_\Sigma \mathbf{A}::\mathsf{A}$, neither X nor any $Y \in \mathbf{Dom}(\Delta)$ is free in $\mathbf{A}$, and X is not free elsewhere in $\mathcal{E}$. These conditions are sufficient to ensure that $\sigma_\mathcal{E} = [\mathbf{A}^1/X_1,\ldots,\mathbf{A}^n/X_n]$ is a most general unifier for $\mathcal{E}$ provided that $\mathcal{E}$ is in solved form with matrix $X^1 \doteq \mathbf{A}^1 \wedge \ldots \wedge X^n \doteq \mathbf{A}^n$

Definition 4.3 ($\mathcal{SIM}$: Simplification of Σ-Unification Problems)

$$\frac{\exists\Delta.\forall\Upsilon.(\lambda X_\mathbf{A}.\mathbf{A}) \doteq (\lambda Y_\mathbf{A}.\mathbf{B})}{\exists\Delta.\forall\Upsilon, [X::\mathsf{A}].\mathbf{A} \doteq [X/Y]\mathbf{B}} \qquad \frac{\exists\Delta.\forall\Upsilon.(\lambda X_\mathbf{A}.\mathbf{A}) \doteq \mathbf{B} \quad \Gamma \vdash_\Sigma \mathbf{B}::\mathsf{B} \quad \partial(\mathbf{B}) = \mathsf{A}}{\exists\Delta.\forall\Upsilon, [X::\mathsf{A}].\mathbf{A} \doteq (\mathbf{B}X)}$$

We apply these rules with the understanding that the operators $\wedge$ and $\doteq$ are commutative and associative, that trivial pairs may be dropped and that vacuous quantifications can be eliminated from the prefix. It is easy to see that these simplifications conserve the sets of Σ-unifiers.

Definition 4.4 ($\Sigma\mathcal{UT}$: Transformations for Σ-Unification)
Let $\Sigma\mathcal{UT}$ be the system $\mathcal{SIM}$ augmented by the following inference rules

$$\frac{\exists\Delta.\forall\Upsilon.h\overline{U^n} \doteq h\overline{V^n} \wedge \mathcal{E} \quad h \in \overline{\Sigma} \cup \mathbf{Dom}(\Delta) \cup \mathbf{Dom}(\Upsilon)}{\exists\Delta.\forall\Upsilon.U^1 \doteq V^1 \wedge \ldots \wedge U^n \doteq V^n \wedge \mathcal{E}}$$

together with the following rules where **G** is a general binding of sort **A** in $\mathcal{G}^h(\Sigma, \Delta, \mathcal{C}) \cup \mathcal{G}^j(\Sigma, \Delta, \mathcal{C}) \cup \mathcal{G}^w(\Sigma, \Delta, \mathcal{C})$

$$\frac{\exists \Delta . \forall \Upsilon . F\overline{U} \doteq h\overline{V} \wedge \mathcal{E} \quad \Delta(F) = \mathbf{A}}{\exists \Delta \cup \mathcal{C} . \forall \Upsilon . F \doteq G \wedge [G/f](F\overline{U} \doteq h\overline{V} \wedge \mathcal{E})} \quad *$$

$$\frac{\exists \Delta . \forall \Upsilon . F\overline{U} \doteq h\overline{V} \wedge \mathcal{E} \quad \Delta(F) = \mathbf{A} \quad \Delta(h) = \mathbf{B}}{\exists \Delta \cup \mathcal{C} . \forall \Upsilon . F \doteq G \wedge [G/F](F\overline{U} \doteq h\overline{V} \wedge \mathcal{E})} \quad **$$

Just as in $\mathcal{SIM}$ leave the associativity and commutativity of $\wedge$ and $\doteq$ implicit. Note that the concept of a weakening transformation for unification is new to $\Sigma\Lambda^\rightarrow$, where we use term declarations to model subsorting. We have combined it with the classical imitation (**G** has head h) and projection (**G** is a projection binding) transformations (see [20]) into $*$. This set of rules is used with the convention that all formulae are eagerly reduced to β-normal form.

Since we have captured the relevant features of $\Sigma\mathcal{T}$ in the structure and general binding theorems (both of which are nearly trivial in $\Lambda^\rightarrow$), we can now use the standard techniques (cf. [20, 9]) to soundness and completeness.

Theorem 4.5 (Completeness Theorem for $\Sigma\mathcal{UT}$) *For any well-sorted unification problem $\mathcal{E}$ and any $\theta \in \mathbf{wsU}(\Sigma, \mathcal{E})$, there is a sequence of transformations in $\Sigma\mathcal{UT}$, such that $\mathcal{E} \vdash_{\Sigma\mathcal{UT}} \mathcal{E}'$, where $\mathcal{E}'$ is in Σ-solved form and $\sigma_{\mathcal{E}'} \preceq_{\beta\eta} \theta[\mathbf{Free}(\mathcal{E})]$.*

As for unification in $\Lambda^\rightarrow$, the rule $**$ gives rise to a serious explosion of the search space for unifiers. Huet's solution to this problem was to redefine the higher-order unification problem to a form sufficient for refutation purposes: For the pre-unification problem flex-flex pairs are considered already solved, since they can always be trivially solved by binding the head variables to special constant functions that identify the formulae by absorbing their arguments.

However in $\Sigma\mathcal{T}$ the solution to the flex-flex problem is not as simple as in the unsorted case, since the heads of flex-flex pairs can be variables of functional base sorts **A**. In this case flex-flex-pairs are not solvable independently of their arguments, since in general the constant functions needed for absorbing the arguments are not of sort **A**. Our solution to this problem is to modify the definition of pre-solved pairs and to keep the guess rule, but restrict its application to the problematic flex-flex cases. Furthermore Σ-pre-unification only makes sense for regular signatures, where formulae have a unique least sort (with respect to the full subsort relation). Consider the non-regular signature given by $\mathcal{S} := \{\mathbf{A}, \mathbf{B}\}$, $\tau(\mathbf{A}) = \tau(\mathbf{B}) = \alpha$, $\overline{\Sigma} := \{c_\alpha\}$ and $\Sigma := \{[c::\mathbf{A}], [c::\mathbf{B}]\}$. The Σ-substitution $[c/X], [c/Y]$ is a Σ-unifier of the pair $\exists[X::\mathbf{A}], [Y::\mathbf{B}].X \doteq Y$, but it can only be found by applying some kind of $**$ transformation. Therefore we will only consider regular signatures for pre-unification.

Definition 4.6 Let **A** be a flexible formula with $\beta\eta$-normal form $\lambda\overline{X}.F\overline{U}^n$ and $\Gamma(F) = \overline{\mathbf{A}^n} \rightarrow \mathbf{B}$, then we call **A** *functionally flexible with target sort* **B**. Let $=^p$ be the least congruence relation on well-sorted formulae that contains $=_{\beta\eta}$ and all functional flexible pairs. Let $\mathcal{E} := \exists\Gamma\forall\Delta.\mathcal{E}'$ be an equational system, then a

Σ-substitution σ is called a Σ-pre-unifier of the pair $\mathbf{A} \doteq \mathbf{B} \in \mathcal{E}'$, iff $\Gamma \vdash_\Sigma \sigma{::}\Delta$ and $\Gamma \vdash_\Sigma \sigma(\mathbf{A}) =^p \sigma(\mathbf{B})$. We denote the set of Σ-pre-unifiers by $\mathbf{wsPU}(\Sigma, \mathcal{E})$.

Definition 4.7 (Pre-Solved Form) Let $\mathcal{E} := \exists \Gamma \forall \Delta . \mathcal{E}'$ be an equational system, then we call a formula $F\overline{\mathbf{U}^k \overline{Y}}$ *functionally flexible in* $\mathcal{E}$ *with target sort* $\mathbf{B}$, iff $\Gamma(F) = \overline{\mathbf{A}^k} \to \mathbf{B}$ and $Y^i \in \mathbf{Dom}(\Delta)$. A pair in $\mathcal{E}'$ is in Σ-*pre-solved form* in $\mathcal{E}$, iff it is in solved form, or if it is a pair of functionally flexible formulae with identical target sorts.

This definition is tailored to guarantee that Σ-pre-unifiers can always be extended to Σ-unifiers by finding trivial unifiers for the flexible pairs and that equational problems in Σ-pre-solved form always have most general unifiers. Therefore an equational system $\mathcal{E}$ is Σ-pre-unifiable, iff it is Σ-unifiable.

Definition 4.8 ($\Sigma\mathcal{PT}$:Transformations for Σ-Pre-Unification) We define the set $\Sigma\mathcal{PT}$ of *transformations for well-sorted pre-unification* by modifying the $\Sigma\mathcal{UT}$ rules for decomposition and the rule $*$ by requiring that they may not be performed on a pair $\mathbf{A} \doteq \mathbf{B}$, if $\mathbf{head}(\mathbf{A}) \in \mathbf{Free}(\mathbf{A})$, and restricting $**$ to the case, where the variable it acts on is the head of a flexible pair that is not functionally flexible.

With these definitions we obtain a completeness result for $\Sigma\mathcal{PT}$ similar to 4.5 with the same methods, since most of the technical difficulties are encapsulated in the general binding theorem. In fact these methods can also be extended to yield a Σ-unification algorithm for higher-order patterns (cf. [12]).

5 Conclusion and Further Work

We have presented a sorted version $\Sigma\mathcal{T}$ of $\Lambda^\rightarrow$ that incorporates the notions of functional base sorts and term declarations, which is a a good basis for the development of higher-order automated theorem provers, since it greatly enhances the practical expressive power of $\Lambda^\rightarrow$ as a logic system. We have studied the subtle interactions of functional base sorts, function restriction and extensionality, and of term declarations with sorted β-conversion. We have presented correct and complete sets of transformations for unification and pre-unification in $\Sigma\mathcal{T}$, which form the basis of a sorted higher-order resolution calculus described in [13].

In first-order predicate logic, the introduction of term declarations has been a major step to the development of dynamic sorted logics [22], where variables are restricted to sorts, but where the sorts can also be treated as unary predicates in the logic; thus the signature is no longer fixed across the deduction, as sort information can appear in the deduction process. Extensions of these ideas have been utilized to formalize and mechanize a general first-order Kleene logic for partial functions [10]. In both systems the resolution rule always uses sorted unification with respect to the signature specified by the current state of the proof. Since predicates are primary objects of type theory, a generalization of the methods in [22, 10] may yield very powerful calculi for mechanizing mathematics and in particular analysis, which was the original motivation for the research reported in this paper.

References

1. Peter B. Andrews. *An Introduction to Mathematical Logic and Type Theory: To Truth Through Proof.* Academic Press, 1986.
2. Peter B. Andrews, Eve Longini-Cohen, Dale Miller, and Frank Pfenning. Automating higher order logics. *Contemp. Math,* 29:169–192, 1984.
3. Kim B. Bruce and Giuseppe Longo. A modest model of records, inheritance and bounded quantification. *Information and Computation,* 87:196–240, 1990.
4. Luca Cardelli. A semantics of multiple inheritance. In G. Kahn and G. Plotkin D.G. MacQueen, editors. *Semantics of Data Types,* volume 173 of LNCS. Springer Verlag, 1984.
5. Alonzo Church. A formulation of the simple theory of types. *Journal of Symbolic Logic,* 5:56–68, 1940.
6. A. G. Cohn. Taxonomic reasoning with many-sorted logics. *Artificial Intelligence Review,* 3:89–128, 1989.
7. Gérard P. Huet. *Constrained Resolution: A Complete Method for Higher Order Logic.* PhD thesis, Case Western Reserve University, 1972.
8. Patricia Johann and Michael Kohlhase. Unification in an extensional lambda calculus with ordered function sorts and constant overloading. SEKI-Report SR-93-14, Universität des Saarlandes, 1993.
9. Patricia Johann and Michael Kohlhase. Unification in an extensional lambda calculus with ordered function sorts and constant overloading. In Proc. CADE'94, *LNCS,* Springer Verlag, 1994.
10. Manfred Kerber and Michael Kohlhase. A mechanization of strong Kleene logic for partial functions. In Proc. CADE'94, *LNCS* Springer Verlag, 1994.
11. Michael Kohlhase. Unification in order-sorted type theory. In Proc. LPAR'92, pages 421–432, volume 624 of *LNAI.* Springer Verlag, 1992.
12. Michael Kohlhase. *Automated Deduction in Order-Sorted Type Theory.* PhD thesis, Universität des Saarlandes, 1994. to appear.
13. Michael Kohlhase. Higher-order order-sorted resolution. Seki Report SR-94-01, FB Informatik, Universität des Saarlandes, 1994.
14. Michael Kohlhase and Frank Pfenning. Unification in a λ-calculus with intersection types. In Proc. ILPS'93, pages 488–505. MIT Press, 1993.
15. Dale Miller. Unification under a mixed prefix. *Journal of Symbolic Computation,* pages 321–358, 1992.
16. Tobias Nipkow and Zhenyu Qian. Reduction and unification in lambda calculi with subtypes. In Proc. CADE'92 volume 607 of *LNCS,* pages 66–78, 1992. Springer Verlag.
17. Benjamin C. Pierce. *Programming with Intersection Types and Bounded Polymorphism.* PhD thesis, Carnegie Mellon University, 1991.
18. Zhenyu Qian. *Extensions of Order-Sorted Algebraic Specifications: Parameterization, Higher-Functions and Polymorphism.* PhD thesis, Universität Bremen, 1991.
19. Manfred Schmidt-Schauß. *Computational Aspects of an Order-Sorted Logic with Term Declarations,* volume 395 of *LNAI.* Springer Verlag, 1989.
20. Wayne Snyder. *A Proof Theory for General Unification.* Birkhäuser, 1991.
21. Christoph Walther. *A Many-Sorted Calculus Based on Resolution and Paramodulation.* Pitman, London. Morgan Kaufman Publishers, Inc, 1987.
22. C. Weidenbach. Unification in sort theories and its applications. MPI-Report MPI-I-93-211, MPI Informatik, Saarbrücken, 1993.

Goal oriented equational theorem proving using team work[*]

Jörg Denzinger, Matthias Fuchs
Department of Computer Science, University of Kaiserslautern
Postfach 3049, 67653 Kaiserslautern
Email: {denzinge, fuchs}@informatik.uni-kl.de

Abstract. The team work method is a concept for distributing automated theorem provers by activating several experts to work on a problem. We have implemented this for pure equational logic using the unfailing Knuth-Bendix completion procedure as basic prover. In this paper we present three classes of experts working in a goal oriented fashion. In general, goal oriented experts perform their job "unfair" and so are often unable to solve a given problem alone. However, as team members in the team work method they perform highly efficiently, as we demonstrate by examples, some of which can only be proved using team work.

1 Introduction

The Knuth-Bendix completion procedure ([KB70]), improved to unfailing completion in [BDP89], is known to be quite efficient for proving that a given equation $s = t$ is a logical consequence of a set E of equations. Its main advantage is that it has strong simplification capabilities to keep the relevant information as small as possible. But, from the theorem proving point of view, it has the disadvantage of not being goal oriented. In principle, it generates all logical consequences of E until $s = t$ is generated. This results in a huge search space.

There are some general methods to deal with this problem. One can apply special strategies and heuristics for determining the next inference step and so guide the search. The strategies are based on statistic measures while the heuristics can also use semantic measures (see [De93] and [AD93]). There are also some proposals for explicit goal-directed search (see [Bl86] and [CH93]), but these attempts were not very successful due to the following facts:

- intermediate results needed for the proof were not found,
- goals with almost no structure did not provide enough information for guiding the search,
- fixed sequences of inferences were repeated very often,
- completeness results under reasonable conditions were hard to establish.

We believe that it is hard to solve these problems by using one fixed search strategy or heuristic. Instead we believe that some progress can be achieved by following different search strategies in parallel in such a way that important intermediate results or intermediate system states can be exchanged and so some cross-fertilization becomes possible.

---

[*] This work was supported by the "Forschungsschwerpunkt Deduktion" of the DFG

Our team work method to distribute automated theorem provers allows this cross-fertilization. We implemented it for unfailing completion as basic prover. There is a fixed schedule (set up by a supervisor) to activate a team of experts, to let them work independently (thus competing), then to exchange their most important results (to cooperate) and to start a new round. There are theoretical results ([AD93]) that allow for using "unfair" experts (which may be unable to find solutions alone) without losing completeness of the whole system. This allows us to incorporate into a team goal oriented experts which are typically unfair. Either these experts produce valuable results to shorten the search process of the team or their results are simply forgotten.

In this paper we present three goal oriented experts which proved to be highly efficient in experiments. We describe them in detail, discuss how they work and demonstrate their power by examples. We present problems that we could not solve without these goal directed experts but which were easy to solve using them. One of these experts even proved to perform highly efficiently as standalone prover. We compare our results with those produced (or sometimes not produced) by other well known provers, i.e. Otter 3.0 and REVEAL.

2 Equational deduction by completion

Equational theorem proving is concerned with the following problem:

Input: A set E of equations and a goal $s = t$ over a fixed signature sig
Question: Is $s = t$ a logical consequence of E ?

As usual, $sig = (F, \tau)$ consists of a set F of function symbols and a function τ denoting the arity of the elements of F. We denote by $\mathrm{Term}(F, V)$ the set of terms over F and a set V of variables and by $\mathrm{Term}(F)$ the set of ground terms. If s is a term and p a position in s then s/p denotes the subterm of s at position p and the term $s[p \leftarrow t]$ results from s by replacing s/p with t. A *reduction ordering* $\succ$ on $\mathrm{Term}(F, V)$ is a well-founded partial ordering on $\mathrm{Term}(F, V)$ that is compatible with substitutions and the term structure.

The completion procedure is based on two basic inference steps: (1) generation of critical pairs (paramodulation) and (2) simplification of terms (demodulation) according to a fixed reduction ordering. To explain this, let $l_1 = r_1$ and $l_2 = r_2$ be two equations with no variables in common, let p be a position in l_1 such that l_1/p is no variable and $\sigma = \mathrm{mgu}(l_1/p, l_2)$ exists. If neither $\sigma(r_1) \succ \sigma(l_1)$ nor $\sigma(r_2) \succ \sigma(l_2)$ then $(\sigma(r_1), \sigma(l_1[p \leftarrow r_2]))$ is a *critical pair* of these equations. We denote by $CP(E_0)$ the set of critical pairs induced by the equations in E_0 wrt. $\succ$. If s is a term, $l = r$ an equation and σ a substitution such that $s/p \equiv \sigma(l)$ and $\sigma(l) \succ \sigma(r)$, then $s \Rightarrow s[p \leftarrow \sigma(r)]$. We call $\Rightarrow = \Rightarrow_{E_0}$ the *rewrite relation* of E_0 wrt. $\succ$. We call s reducible if $s \Rightarrow t$ for some term t. We call t a *normal form* of s if $s \Rightarrow^* t$ and t is irreducible. Here $\Rightarrow^*$ denotes the reflexive and transitive closure of $\Rightarrow$. An equation $l = r$ is *interreduced* if l and r are irreducible.

In order to simplify notations and to save comparisons of terms wrt. $\succ$, we split the set E_0 of equations into the set $R = \{\, l \rightarrow r \mid l = r \text{ in } E_0, l \succ r \,\}$ of rules (orientable equations) and the set $E = \{\, l = r \mid l = r \text{ in } E_0, \text{ neither } l \succ r \text{ nor } r \succ l \,\}$ of unorientable equations.

We now describe our basic prover. It takes as input a set E_0 of equations, a goal $s = t$ and a reduction ordering $\succ$. It works on three sets: the set R of rules, the set E of unorientable equations and the set CP of critical pairs that are unprocessed. Initially, both R and E are empty and $CP = E_0$. Now the basic prover consists of the following loop.

basic prover:
while CP is not empty and the normal forms of s and t are not identical do
- choose an equation u' = v' from CP.
- let u and v be the normal forms of u' and v'.
- if not $u \equiv v$ then
  - if either $u \succ v$ or $v \succ u$ then
    - let l be max(u,v) and r be min(u,v).
    - interreduce R and E with $l \rightarrow r$.
    - $R := R \cup \{ l \rightarrow r \}$.
    - let CPnew be the set of critical pairs of $l \rightarrow r$ and R and $l \rightarrow r$ and E.
  else
    - interreduce R and E with u = v.
    - $E := E \cup \{ u = v \}$.
    - let CPnew be the set of critical pairs of u = v and R and u = v and E.
  - $CP := CP \cup CPnew$.

There is one basic point of indeterminism within this prover: How to select the equation u' = v' from CP to be processed next. The way how this indeterminism is fixed determines the search for the proof by the prover. This allows one to integrate different search strategies and heuristics into the prover and so to realize different experts (see below). A search plan that guarantees to find a proof if there is one (i.e. a "fair" plan, see [BDP89] and [AD93]) will in the following be called a strategy while unfair search plans are heuristics. A general way to describe a strategy or heuristic is to define for each equation u = v in CP a value or weight (an integer) val(u = v) and to select the equation u = v in CP with minimal weight to be processed next. Ties are broken arbitrarily. We give some standard strategies by defining val as already used in [Hu80]. Here $|s|$ denotes the length of the term s. By val(u = v) = $|u| + |v|$ we get the smallest sum strategy and by val(u = v) = $MAX\{|u|,|v|\}$ the smallest maximum strategy. In the following, we will refer to these strategies as standard strategies, because they do not use any interpretations of symbols and can therefore be used without changing parameters for all possible examples.

3 The team work method

The team work method (see [De93], [AD93]) is a general approach to distribute theorem proving procedures. It has been inspired by human project teams and has been used to distribute equational theorem proving by completion. A proof system based on team work models human project teams by use of multiple processes running on different processors.

A *team* consists of a single supervisor and a number of experts, each accompanied by a referee evaluating his work. Usually each expert is working on a problem without communication with the other team members. Only at *team meetings* scheduled by the supervisor results are exchanged.

The *supervisor* is selecting the experts to work on a given problem, initially by judging their previous successes on related problems, later by using the referees' evaluation of their performance in dealing with the given problem. Also he determines the lengths of the working phases of the experts between the team meetings.

The *referees* are evaluating the achievements of the different experts. Their assessments are used for selecting a new team and important results (from their respective experts) during the team meetings.

The *experts* are the members of the team working directly on the problem. In our case each of them is using the completion algorithm as described in section 2. They differ in the methods used to choose the next critical pair. At team meetings, the system, i.e. the sets R, E and CP, of the best expert is chosen as the basis for further work. As only one system survives completely, the experts are competing for the best result.

However, competition is only one aspect of the team work method. The second important element is the cooperation between the experts. Cooperation is achieved by integrating outstanding results from inferior experts (as chosen by their referees) into the system of the best expert. This is accomplished by the supervisor during the team meetings, before he presents a new and updated problem description to the experts for the next working phase. In our case of a completion based theorem prover the outstanding results - rules and equations - are handled as new critical pairs to be processed immediately.

It is important to note that most of the results generated by the inferior experts are dropped or *forgotten*. We believe that one of the reasons for the success of team work is this feature of forgetting that avoids blowing up the search space. Furthermore, it allows the use of very specialized selection heuristics for critical pairs that are only capable of generating a few of the necessary results to prove a goal. But these results are generated as early as possible without many unnecessary steps. Our heuristics based on goal similarity are members of this category of experts.

Note that one can prove the completeness of the team work method under relatively weak conditions (see [AD93] for the definition of *team-fairness*). These conditions allow one to have unfair experts in the team (even as winner of a round), one only has to guarantee that in an infinite computation infinitely often a team-fair expert becomes the winner of a competition round. This is easy to achieve, since for example experts following the smallest sum strategy or the smallest maximum strategy are team-fair. For this reason one can activate unfair experts frequently (and design special experts for different proof stages) without losing completeness for the whole team.

4 Goal oriented selection heuristics for completion

In this section we present two kinds of goal oriented heuristics. As explained in section 2, these heuristics are used to select the next equation in CP to be processed by the basic prover. So they each define an expert.

4.1 The structural complexity expert occnest

Our heuristics based on structural complexity derive from the measures proposed in [AA90] to guide the search in a completion based prover. The measures of a term t in [AA90] are based on the occurrences of a function symbol f in t, see the function occ(f,t) defined below as one example. This defines a value of an equation and this value is combined in a lexicographic way with other measures on the equation. According to the order induced by these measures the smallest equation is selected to be processed next. In this way the measures act as a sequence of filters.

Our experiments showed that these sequences of filters define an ordering that is not smooth enough. The combination of different values can be improved by using an arithmetic combination instead of a lexicographic one. We propose the combination of the following values: (1) $\phi(t)$, which is a modified length of t, (2) occ(f,t), which denotes the number of occurrences of f in t and (3) nest(f,t), which is equal to the maximum number of consecutive occurrences of f on a branch of t, when t is presented as a tree. (2) and (3) lead to a value for each element of F. The combination of these values will define our goal oriented heuristic occnest(u=v). We make this precise.

Definition 1. Weight of a term, occ, nest

a) The weight $\phi(t)$ of a term t is recursively defined by
   $\phi(t) = 1$, if t is a variable,
   $\phi(t) = 2 + \phi(t_1) + ... + \phi(t_n)$, if $t \equiv f(t_1,...,t_n)$.
b) The number of occurrences occ(f,t) is recursively defined by
   occ(f,t) = 0, if t is a variable,
   occ(f,t) = occ(f,t_1) + ... + occ(f,t_n), if $t \equiv g(t_1,...,t_n)$, f$\not\equiv$g,
   occ(f,t) = 1 + occ(f,t_1) + ... + occ(f,t_n), if $t \equiv f(t_1,...,t_n)$.
c) The nesting nest(f,t) is recursively defined by
   nest(f,t) = 0, if f is a constant
   nest(f,t) = hnest(f,t,0,0), if f is not a constant, where
      hnest(f,t,cur,abs) = MAX({cur,abs}),
         if t is a variable or a constant,
      hnest(f,t,cur,abs) = MAX({hnest(f,t_i,0,MAX({cur,abs})) | $1 \leq i \leq n$}),
         if $t \equiv g(t_1,...,t_n)$, f$\not\equiv$g,
      hnest(f,t,cur,abs) = MAX({hnest(f,t_i,cur+1,abs) | $1 \leq i \leq n$}),
         if $t \equiv f(t_1,...,t_n)$

We will use $\phi(t)$ as the basic value of a term t and occ(f,t) and nest(f,t) for refinements to express the structure of t. Next we extend occ and nest to equations u = v by occ(f,(u,v)) := MAX({occ(f,u) , occ(f,v)}) and nest(f,(u,v)) := MAX({nest(f,u) , nest(f,v)}).

Finally we define the value occnest(u=v) according to the following idea: We start with the weight of the equation u = v and modify it by a penalty to describe the difference of the structural complexity of u = v and the goal s = t. There are several ways to combine these values. One easily sees that it is reasonable to add the penalty in the form of a factor. This factor has to be at least 1; this is ensured by using the function $\psi(x) = 1$, if $x \leq 0$; $\psi(x) = x + 1$, else. To be flexible, we also allow a set $D \subseteq F$ to describe which operators f in F should contribute to the value occnest(u=v).

Definition 2. occnest
Let $u = v$ be a critical pair and $s = t$ the goal. Let furthermore $D \subseteq F$, where F is the set of all function symbols of *sig*. We define for all $f \in F$:

$m_f := 1$, if $f \notin D$,
$m_f := \psi(\text{occ}(f,(u,v)) - \text{occ}(f,(s,t))) * \psi(\text{nest}(f,(u,v)) - \text{nest}(f,(s,t)))$, otherwise.

Then we have :

$$occnest(u = v) = (\phi(u) + \phi(v)) * \prod_{f \in F} m_f.$$

Clearly, there are many other ways to define structural complexity and to relate the complexity of the goal $s = t$ to that of an equation. We have experimented with occnest and present some experimental results in section 5.

4.2 Experts based on goal similarity .
There are many ways to define the notion "similarity". They differ in the operations under which the objects to compare should be similar. In this section we are interested in the similarity of two equations with respect to the basic operations of completion, namely reduction and generation of critical pairs. Therefore we want to say that two equations are *similar* if they can be transformed into each other by means of several reductions or the generation of several critical pairs. Note that this definition depends on all other rules and equations that are known to be valid.

Now, if we know that an equation and a goal are similar with respect to this criterion then we already have the proof of the goal. Therefore we have to relax this criterion such that we try to estimate the possibility that such a proof can be found. This relaxation should lead to a function measuring similarity that only needs to know the two equations to compare and not any other rules and equations. We developed such functions by means of matching and weighting superfluous parts of terms.

In the following we will make this idea more precise. Because we have two basic operations, we also have two similarity functions, **Goal-in-CP** and **CP-in-Goal**. They weight equations according to their similarity to a given (ground) goal. First we need to define the similarity of a term u to a goal term s.

Definition 3. Similarity of terms
Let s be a ground term (goal term) and u a term.
CP-in-Goal-Similarity sim_{CGp} at position p with substitution σ is defined by
$\text{sim}_{CGp}(u,s,\sigma,p) = \phi(s) - \phi(s/p)$, if $\sigma(u) \equiv s/p$
$\text{sim}_{CGp}(u,s,\sigma,p) = \infty$, otherwise.

CP-in-Goal-Similarity sim_{CG} with substitution σ is
$\text{sim}_{CG}(u,s,\sigma) = \text{MIN}_p(\text{sim}_{CGp}(u,s,\sigma,p))$.

Goal-in-CP-Similarity sim_{GCp} at position p with substitution σ is defined by
$\text{sim}_{GCp}(u,s,\sigma,p) = \phi(u) - \phi(u/p)$, if $\sigma(u/p) \equiv s$ and $\phi(u/p) \geq$ min-struct,
$\text{sim}_{GCp}(u,s,\sigma,p) = \infty$, otherwise.

Goal-in-CP-Similarity sim_{GC} with substitution σ is
$\text{sim}_{GC}(u,s,\sigma) = \text{MIN}_p(\text{sim}_{GCp}(u,s,\sigma,p))$.

The reason for introducing the parameter *min-struct* is to prevent sim_{GC} from using positions in terms that are variables or terms of the form $f(x_1,...,x_n)$ which would be similar to all goals resp. all goals with top-level symbol f. By choosing min-struct $\geq$ n+3 this can be achieved (see the definition of ϕ).

If we want to extend our two similarity notions to an equation u = v and a goal $s = t$ then we encounter the following three cases (note that equations are symmetric, so that u and v can be exchanged; we use sim for either sim_{GC} or sim_{CG}):

I. There is a σ, such that $\text{sim}(u,s,\sigma) < \infty$ and $\text{sim}(v,t,\sigma) < \infty$.
II. There is a σ, such that either $\text{sim}(u,s,\sigma) < \infty$ or $\text{sim}(v,t,\sigma) < \infty$.
III. There is no σ, such that $\text{sim}(u,s,\sigma) < \infty$ or $\text{sim}(v,t,\sigma) < \infty$.

It is obvious that case I is the most desirable of these three. In order to achieve a distinction between these cases while nevertheless describing each critical pair with one value, we use in the following definition two factors, namely *single-match* and *no-match*, that are greater than 1. These factors can be considered as handicaps for the cases II and III. In our implementation we use single-match = 5 and no-match = 50 as default.

Definition 4. Goal-in-CP , CP-in-Goal
Let u=v be a critical pair and $s = t$ be the goal.
$\quad$ CP-in-Goal(u=v,s=t) = MIN_σ ($\text{sim}_{CG}(u,s,\sigma) + \text{sim}_{CG}(v,t,\sigma)$,
$\qquad\qquad\qquad\qquad\qquad$ $\text{sim}_{CG}(u,t,\sigma) + \text{sim}_{CG}(v,s,\sigma)$),
$\qquad$ if there are σ with respect to case I.
$\quad$ CP-in-Goal(u=v,s=t) = MIN_σ ($\text{sim}_{CG}(u,s,\sigma) + \phi(t)$,
$\qquad\qquad\qquad\qquad\qquad$ $\text{sim}_{CG}(u,t,\sigma) + \phi(s)$,
$\qquad\qquad\qquad\qquad\qquad$ $\text{sim}_{CG}(v,s,\sigma) + \phi(t)$,
$\qquad\qquad\qquad\qquad\qquad$ $\text{sim}_{CG}(v,t,\sigma) + \phi(s)$) $*$ single-match,
$\qquad$ if there are σ with respect to case II.
$\quad$ CP-in-Goal(u=v,s=t) = $(\phi(u) + \phi(v)) *$ no-match, otherwise.

$\quad$ Goal-in-CP(u=v,s=t) = MIN_σ ($\text{sim}_{GC}(u,s,\sigma) + \text{sim}_{GC}(v,t,\sigma)$,
$\qquad\qquad\qquad\qquad\qquad$ $\text{sim}_{GC}(u,t,\sigma) + \text{sim}_{GC}(v,s,\sigma)$),
$\qquad$ if there are σ with respect to case I.
$\quad$ Goal-in-CP(u=v,s=t) = MIN_σ ($\text{sim}_{GC}(u,s,\sigma) + \phi(v)$,
$\qquad\qquad\qquad\qquad\qquad$ $\text{sim}_{GC}(u,t,\sigma) + \phi(v)$,
$\qquad\qquad\qquad\qquad\qquad$ $\text{sim}_{GC}(v,s,\sigma) + \phi(u)$,
$\qquad\qquad\qquad\qquad\qquad$ $\text{sim}_{GC}(v,t,\sigma) + \phi(u)$) $*$ single-match,
$\qquad$ if there are σ with respect to case II.
$\quad$ Goal-in-CP(u=v,s=t) = $(\phi(u) + \phi(v)) *$ no-match, otherwise.

As in the case of occnest, the heuristics Goal-in-CP and CP-in-Goal choose the critical pair with the resp. lowest value.

As we stated before presenting the definitions, we want to define similarity of critical pairs to the goal with respect to the operations reduction and generation of critical pairs. Goal-in-CP measures the similarity with respect to the generation of critical pairs and CP-in-Goal with respect to reductions. It is obvious that both heuristics based on similarity are highly specialized. Although there are some examples that can be proved using one of these heuristics working alone, their effectiveness lies in their use in teams. The general idea is that other experts generate a situation in which there are critical pairs that can be classified into case I or II for one of the heuristics. Then this heuristic is very often capable of finishing the proof very fast (see next section).

5 Experiments

The problems the lack of goal orientation causes for completion can be best observed when one is trying to prove several theorems in a fixed domain of interest. The known (non-goal oriented) selection strategies for critical pairs generate for each theorem exactly the same sequence of steps as for other theorems that appear later in the enumeration done by the strategy. Even worse, if there are equations that are suspected to be unnecessary for obtaining a proof for a theorem then the consequences of these equations will nevertheless be generated. This is the reason why one is interested in goal orientation, because such equations (and their successors) would not be considered if the goal were taken into account.

We have chosen the domain of *lattice ordered groups* (see [KK74]) for our examples. After a short introduction to this domain, we will first demonstrate that our goal oriented heuristics, namely occnest, can solve many examples very fast, even several examples where standard strategies have tremendous difficulties.

For each theorem prover and nearly each domain there are theorems that are beyond the limits of the prover. This is also the case for our goal oriented heuristics and the lattice ordered groups. But we will demonstrate that the use of team work enables us to reach beyond the limits of all our sequential experts. We were able to improve run times significantly for problems that can be solved sequentially and even to prove theorems that could not be proved neither by any of our experts working alone nor the respected provers REVEAL ([CA94]) or Otter 3.0 ([Mc94]). We will also give a few examples from other domains where team work in combination with goal oriented heuristics has been successful.

Lattice ordered groups combine the axioms of two mathematical structures, namely lattices and groups. So, we encounter for many theorems the problem mentioned above, that not all axioms are needed for a proof. In order to axiomatize lattice ordered groups we need the group operator f of arity 2, its neutral element 1 and the inverse operator i. A lattice is based on a partial ordering $\leq$ and two binary functions l and u, the greatest lower bound and the least upper bound of two elements. The two functions l and u can be used to get rid of the partial ordering $\leq$ with the help of the definition

$x \leq y$ iff $l(x,y) = x$ or $x \leq y$ iff $u(x,y) = y$.

So, we get the following equational axiomatization for lattice ordered groups:

$$f(f(x,y),z) = f(x,f(y,z)) \qquad f(1,x) = x \qquad f(i(x),x) = 1$$
$$l(l(x,y),z) = l(x,l(y,z)) \qquad l(x,y) = l(y,x) \quad l(x,x) = x$$
$$u(u(x,y),z) = u(x,u(y,z)) \qquad u(x,y) = u(y,x) \, u(x,x) = x$$
$$f(x,l(y,z)) = l(f(x,y),f(x,z)) \quad u(x,l(x,y)) = x \, f(l(x,y),z) = l(f(x,z),f(y,z))$$
$$f(x,u(y,z)) = u(f(x,y),f(x,z)) \, l(x,u(x,y)) = x \, f(u(x,y),z) = u(f(x,z),f(y,z))$$

In Table 1 and Table 2 we use the theorems listed below. As there are two ways to eliminate $\leq$, we derive two problem sets, one using the operator l, denoted by the suffix .a, and one using the operator u, denoted by the suffix .b. As usual, the theorems must be negated and skolemized, conditions are added to the set of axioms. (More theorems can be found in [Fu94].)

Problems:

mono1: $f(x,z) \leq f(y,z)$, if $x \leq y$
p1: $f(i(z),f(x,z)) \leq f(i(z),f(y,z))$, if $x \leq y$
p3: $f(x,z) \leq f(y,w)$, if $x \leq y$, $z \leq w$
p6: $1 \leq f(i(x),f(y,x))$, if $1 \leq y$
p9: $l(x,f(y,z)) = l(x,z)$,
      if $1 \leq x$, $1 \leq y$, $1 \leq z$, $1 = l(x,y)$

mono2: $f(z,x) \leq f(z,y)$, if $x \leq y$
p2: $x \leq y$, if $i(y) \leq i(x)$
p4: $1 \leq f(x,y)$, if $1 \leq x$, $1 \leq y$
p10: $i(u(x,y)) = l(i(x),i(y))$
p8: $l(x,f(y,z)) \leq f(l(x,y),l(x,z))$,
      if $1 \leq x$, $1 \leq y$, $1 \leq z$

The run-times given below were obtained on SUN-ELC workstations, the team runs on a network of two such workstations.

Table 1 compares for most of the examples the run-time of occnest with the run-time of the best standard strategy (see section 2). It shows that goal orientation as defined by occnest is able to solve most of the examples dramatically faster than the standard strategies. Even several examples that took over 3 hours run-time with the standard strategies (and were therefore stopped, because we set this as time limit) can be solved in less than 5 seconds.

Example	occnest	std. strategy	Example	occnest	std. strategy
mono1.a	0.045	45.639	mono1.b	0.045	46.668
mono2.a	0.030	43.995	mono2.b	0.030	44.917
p1.a	0.272	—	p1.b	0.281	—
p3.a	4.135	—	p3.b	2.547	—
p4.a	1.840	32.437	p4.b	1.712	9.263
p6.a	0.388	—	p6.b	0.157	160.049
p9.a	19.568	209.102	p9.b	50.953	207.176

Table 1: run-time comparison occnest *vs* standard strategies (in seconds)

But there are examples that also occnest can not solve alone. Table 2 shows that most of these examples can be solved (quite fast!) using team work and our goal oriented heuristics. We want to mention that the best (and only) sequential heuristic that was able to prove p2.a was Goal-in-CP, showing that also our heuristics based on goal similarity can solve examples working alone, but only very few. Therefore we did not include these heuristics in Table 1.

352

Example	team	goal heuristic used in team	best seq. heuristic	REVEAL	Otter 3.0
p2.a	5.413	occnest	79.516	591.06	17
p2.b	5.381	occnest	—	592.08	16
p8.b	56.837	Goal-in-CP	—	—	sos-empty
p9.a	8.659	occnest	19.568	—	sos-empty
p9.b	8.440	occnest	50.953	—	sos-empty
p10	23.203	Goal-in-CP	—	—	—

Table 2: run-time comparison team *vs* sequential experts *vs* REVEAL *vs* Otter 3.0 (in seconds)

Table 2 shows that team work enables us to prove more examples than our sequential system can. In order to show that the reason for this is not a weak implementation of unfailing completion we tried to prove these examples using the REVEAL 1.0-system and using the new Otter 3.0-system. Because both systems allow various parameter adjustments, we used the default settings of REVEAL and the auto-mode of Otter. One should note that REVEAL allows completion modulo the theory AC (which is not the case for Otter or our system) and the run-times reported in Table 2 were obtained using AC-completion. Without AC-completion REVEAL was not able to prove any of the examples of Table 2. Otter's very sophisticated auto-mode encountered several problems while trying to prove examples p8.b, p9.a and p9.b. Otter restrained itself to only generating critical pairs that had a limited size which resulted in emptying the set-of-support list and therefore in termination without success.

The teams we used consisted of two experts, a standard strategy and a goal oriented heuristic. For the domain lattice ordered groups occnest and Goal-in-CP were useful (as indicated by the column 'goal heuristic used ...'). Table 3 shows that in other domains also CP-in-Goal was useful, and there are even examples (namely luka3) that can be proved using a team consisting of goal oriented heuristics only.

Example	team	goal heuristic used in team	best seq. heuristic
bool5b	72.859	Goal-in-CP	—
ra2	125.373	CP-in-Goal	227.876
sa2	10.745	Goal-in-CP	—
herky3	6.811	occnest	16.091
luka3	81.680	Goal-in-CP, CP-in-Goal	—

Table 3: run-times for teams using goal oriented heuristics in other domains

Example bool5b states that in a boolean ring the associativity axioms are redundant (using an LPO!). Example ra2 is taken from [LW92], sa2 from [BH93] and herky3 from [Zh93]. Example luka3 uses the axiomatization of the propositional calculus given in [AD93] to prove that $(not(x) \rightarrow not(y)) \rightarrow (y \rightarrow x)$.

In order to explain the success of our goal oriented heuristics we used the proof presentation tools developed in [DS94]. An analysis of the runs with which the results of Table 1 were obtained showed that the better performance of occnest is due to a faster selection of the results needed for a proof. Although our analysis showed that occnest also does select many critical pairs that are not needed in the proof the ratio between needed and not needed pairs is much higher than that of standard strategies.

The even bigger success of team work can be explained by two typical behaviours our teams showed. Teams in which occnest is a team member show the characteristic that in most team meetings occnest is rated as the best expert. Due to the general problem that there are examples that need equations for a proof that a goal oriented heuristic does not rate good although they are in the list of critical pairs, occnest alone can not find a proof (or needs quite some time for it). But in combination with a standard strategy, that does rate these equations good and therefore allows a referee to judge the impact of these equations on the problem, success can be achieved.

Teams that use Goal-in-CP or CP-in-Goal show a different behaviour. In the first team meetings the used goal similarity heuristic generates nothing useful. Also in the later team meetings the standard strategy expert gets better ratings by the referees. Nevertheless, there is always a team meeting after which the goal similarity heuristic, using the system of the other expert, can finish the proof. As mentioned earlier, this is exactly the behaviour we did want to achieve with Goal-in-CP and CP-in-Goal.

6 Related Work

A first attempt to develop goal oriented equational deduction was documented by Bläsius in [Bl86]. The general idea was to start with the two sides of the goal and then to use the given equations to reduce the difference (in the term structure) of these two terms. This was repeated until an equational chain between the terms was constructed. But the few examples where this approach was useful can be proved easily by completion (without goal orientation). Without a concept for reduction one could observe that many steps were repeated very often. Moreover, there are many examples where a proof can only be found using equations that do not reduce the difference between the sides of the goal, but instead increase the difference before all differences can be reduced by other equations.

The approach of Cleve and Hutter has to face similar problems (see [CH93]). Although they introduce several notions of difference between terms, they are bound to reduce with each step at least one of them. As we know at the moment of no implementation, no comparisons of this approach to completion or to our work are possible. The lack of a concept for redundancy elimination (i.e. term rewriting) in their approach seems to favour completion.

The measure approach of [AA90] was already presented in section 4. Here we want to point out our modifications, namely the new measure nest and the combination of various measures and ϕ into one selection function.

Finally, the approach by Socher (see [So91]) tries to incorporate the goal into the inference rules of completion. Although this set of inference rules can be shown to be complete, the practical problem which inference rule to use next remains. It is not clear whether the standard selection strategies have the same success for these inference rules as in the case of completion.

7 Conclusion

We presented several goal oriented selection heuristics for critical pairs that can be used to incorporate goal orientation into equational deduction by unfailing completion. The heuristics ranged from methods comparing statistical aspects of goal and critical pairs to methods applying similarity criteria.

The team work method for distributing deduction processes allowed us to combine these goal oriented heuristics with standard selection strategies. This resulted in a system that combines the advantage of working goal oriented and thus reducing the search space with the advantages of completion, namely minimal representation of the actual problem state and the generation of strong rules. Even completeness of this combination can be ensured. So, none of the known disadvantages of goal oriented equational deduction remain.

We demonstrated the success of our approach with many examples from the domain lattice ordered groups and also with examples from other domains. The important observation was that the distributed system is able to prove several examples that can neither be proved by goal oriented heuristics nor by other selection strategies working alone.

References

[AA90] Anantharaman, D. ; Andrianarievelo, N.: *Heuristical criteria in refutational theorem proving*, Proc. DISCO '90, LNCS 429, 1990, pp. 184-193.

[AD93] Avenhaus, J. ; Denzinger, J.: *Distributing equational theorem proving*, Proc. 5th RTA, Montreal, LNCS 690, 1993, pp. 62-76.

[BDP89] Bachmair, L., Dershowitz, N., Plaisted, D.A.: *Completion without Failure*, Coll. on the Resolution of Equations in Algebraic Structures, Austin (1987), Academic Press, 1989.

[BH93] Bonacina, M.P. ; Hsiang, J. : *The clause diffusion methodology for distributed deduction*, Proc. DISCO '92, LNCS 722, 1993, pp. 272-287.

[Bl86] Bläsius, K.H.: *Equality reasoning based on graphs*, Ph.D. thesis, University of Kaiserslautern, 1986.

[CA94] Chalin, J. ; Anantharaman, S. et al. : *REVEAL - a user's guide*, Tech. rep. LIFO.94-12, University of Orleans, 1994.

[CH93] Cleve, J. ; Hutter, D. : *Guiding equational proofs by attribute functions*, SEKI-Report SR-93-15, University of Saarbrücken, 1993.

[De93] Denzinger, J.: *Teamwork : A method to design distributed knowledge based theorem provers (in German)*, Ph.D. thesis, University of Kaiserslautern, 1993.

[DS94] Denzinger, J. ; Schulz, S.: *Analysis and Representation of Equational Proofs Generated by a Distributed Completion Based Proof System*, SEKI-Report SR-94-05, University of Kaiserslautern, 1994.

[Fu94] Fuchs, M.: *The application of goal-oriented heuristics for proving equational theorems via the unfailing Knuth-Bendix completion procedure. A case study: lattice ordered groups*, SEKI-Report SR-94-02, University of Kaiserslautern, 1994.

[Hu80] Huet, G.: *Confluent Reductions: Abstract Properties and Applications to Term Rewriting Systems*, J. of ACM 27, No. 4, 1980, pp. 798-821.

[KB70] Knuth, D.E. ; Bendix, P.B.: *Simple Word Problems in Universal Algebra*, Computational Algebra, J. Leech, Pergamon Press, 1970, pp. 263-297.

[KK74] Kokorin, A.I. ; Kopytov, V.M. : *Fully ordered groups*, Halsted Press, 1974.

[LW92] Lusk, E. ; Wos, L. : *Benchmark problems in which equality plays the major role*, Proc. CADE-11, LNAI 607, 1992, pp. 781-785.

[Mc94] McCune, W.W.: *OTTER 3.0 Reference manual and Guide*, Tech. rep. ANL-94/6, Argonne National Laboratory, 1994.

[So91] Socher, R.: *A Goal Oriented Strategy Based on Completion*, Tech. rep. TR#91/18, SUNY at Stony Brook, 1991.

[Zh93] Zhang, H.: *Automated proofs of equality problems in Overbeek's competition*, JAR 11, 1993, pp. 333-351.

The Hardest Random SAT Problems

Ian P. Gent
Department of Artificial Intelligence
University of Edinburgh
80 South Bridge
Edinburgh EH1 1HN, United Kingdom
I.P.Gent@edinburgh.ac.uk

Toby Walsh
IRST, Loc. Panté di Povo, Trento &
DIST, University of Genoa, Genoa
Italy
toby@irst.it

Abstract. We describe a detailed experimental investigation of the phase transition for several different classes of satisfiability problems including random k-SAT, the constant probability model, and encodings of k-colourability and the independent set problem. We show that the constant probability model has been prematurely dismissed in favour of the random k-SAT model. We also show that for each of these problem class the conventional picture of easy-hard-easy behaviour is inadequate. In each of the problem classes, although median problem difficulty shows an easy-hard-easy pattern, there is also a region of very variable problem difficulty. Within this region, we have found problems orders of magnitude harder than those in the middle of the phase transition. These extraordinary problems can easily dominate the mean problem difficulty. We report experimental evidence which strongly suggests that this behaviour is due to a "constraint gap", a region where the number of constraints on variables is minimal while simultaneously the depth of search required to solve problems is maximal. We also report results suggesting that better algorithms will be unable to eliminate this constraint gap and hence will continue to find very difficult problems in this region. Finally, we report an interesting correlation between these variable regions and a peak in the number of prime implicates. We predict that these extraordinarily hard problems will be of considerable use in analysing and comparing the performance of satisfiability algorithms.

1 Introduction

Many randomly generated NP-hard problems display a phase transition as some order parameter is varied, and as the problems go from being almost always soluble to being almost always insoluble [2]. This phase transition is often associated with problems which are *typically* hard to solve. In this paper, we show that with several different classes of satisfiability problems including random

3-SAT, the phase transition is indeed associated with problems which are typically hard *but* there are also regions in which problems are usually easy but sometimes extraordinarily hard. We postulate that this behaviour occurs when problems are "critically constrained". That is, when search must proceed to great depths because of the absence of easily observable constraints. We confirm this experimentally by demonstrating the existence of a "constraint gap" for the Davis Putnam procedure, the best known complete procedure for satisfiability. The constraint gap occurs in regions where most problems are satisfiable, and the ratio of constraint propagations to search branching reaches a sharp minimum, while the depth of search reaches a corresponding maximum. We predict that similar regions of very variable problem difficulty will be found with many other NP-hard problems besides satisfiability. The extraordinarily hard problems found in these regions may be of considerable use in analysing and comparing the performance of algorithms for NP-hard problems.

2 Satisfiability

Satisfiability (or SAT) is the problem of deciding if there is an assignment for the variables in a propositional formula that makes the formula true. We will consider SAT problems in conjunctive normal form (CNF); a formula, Σ is in CNF iff it is a conjunction of clauses, where a clause is a disjunction of literals, and a literal is a negated or un-negated variable. SAT is of considerable practical interest as many AI tasks like constraint satisfaction, diagnosis and planning can be encoded quite naturally in SAT. It is also of considerable theoretical interest as it is the archetypical NP-hard problem.

procedure DP(Σ)
    if Σ empty **then return** satisfiable
    if Σ contains an empty clause **then return** unsatisfiable
    (*Tautology*) **if** Σ contains a tautologous clause c **then return** DP($\Sigma - \{c\}$)
    (*Unit propagation*) **if** Σ contains a unit clause c **then**
        return DP(Σ simplified by assigning truth value which satisfies c)
    (*Pure literal deletion*) **if** Σ contains a literal l but not the negation of l **then**
        return DP(Σ simplified by assigning truth value which satisfies l)
    (*Split*) **if** DP(Σ simplified by assigning a variable arbitrarily) is satisfiable
        then return satisfiable
        else return DP(Σ simplified by assigning variable opposite value)

Fig. 1. The Davis-Putnam Procedure

A standard procedure for determining satisfiability is due to Davis and Putnam [4] (see Figure 1). To simplify a set of clauses with respect to a partial truth assignment, we delete each clause that is satisfied by the partial truth assignment, and in every other clause delete any literals that contradict the partial truth assignment. Note that the Davis-Putnam procedure is non-deterministic since the literal used by the split rule is unspecified. As in previous studies (*eg.* [12, 6]), we will split upon the first literal in the first clause. We call this variant of the Davis-Putnam procedure "DP". Despite its simplicity, with efficient implementation and good heuristics for choosing literals to split on, the Davis-Putnam procedure is still the best complete procedure for satisfiability [5].

3   Constant Probability Model

In the constant probability model, given N variables, each of the 2N possible literals is included in a clause with probability p. Our experiments use a variant of the constant probability model proposed in [9] and since used in other experimental studies [12, 6]. In this problem class, empty and unit clauses are discarded and replaced by longer clauses since the inclusion of empty or unit clauses typically makes problems easier. We call this the "CP" model. In all our experiments, as in [12, 7], we choose p so that $2Np = 3$ and the mean clause length remains approximately constant as N varies. In [7], we show that the position of the phase transition occurs at fixed L/N when L is the number of clauses and $2Np$ is kept constant.

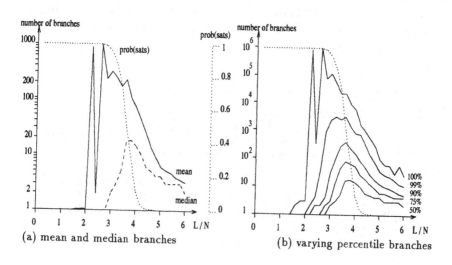

(a) mean and median branches   (b) varying percentile branches

Fig. 2. random CP problems tested using DP, N= 150. Note log scales

In Figure 2 (a) we plot the mean and median number of branches used by DP for the CP model at N = 150.[1] The number of branches is the number of leaf

[1] From L/N = 0.2 to 6 in intervals of 0.2 we tested 1000 problems at each point.

nodes in the search tree, and is an indication of problem difficulty. The dotted line indicates the observed probability that problems were satisfiable. Despite the log scale, there is a very considerable difference between mean and median performance. The worst case mean of 1,009 branches occurs at $L/N = 2.6$ in a mostly satisfiable region, whilst the worst case median of just 18 branches occurs at $L/N = 3.8$ in the middle of the phase transition. Problem difficulty in the mostly satisfiable region was very variable. Figure 2 (b) gives a break-down in percentiles for the number of branches used from 50% (median) up to 100% (worst case). The worst case was 981,018 branches at $L/N = 2.6$, while at $L/N = 3.8$, the point of worst median performance, the worst case was just 8,982 branches, two orders of magnitude smaller. Comparison of Figure 2 (a) and (b) clearly shows that worst case behaviour is responsible for almost all the features seen in the mean in mostly satisfiable region. These graphs show that the CP model can generate hard instances, and that Mitchell *et al.*, by focusing on the median, smaller problem sizes, and a simplified version of DP, were premature to dismiss the CP model in favour of random 3-SAT [12].

In [6], we show that similar behaviour for CP is observed with better splitting heuristics, though variable and difficult behaviour is not apparent till larger N. In §5 we show that non-heuristic refinements to the Davis-Putnam procedure also appear unable to eliminate this behaviour. This suggests that the occurrence of extraordinarily hard problems in highly satisfiable regions is of great importance to the understanding of the hardness of satisfiability problems.

4   Constraint Gap

In the Davis-Putnam procedure, the split rule is the only rule which gives rise to exponential behaviour. The other rules simplify the problem and do not branch the search. For instance, the unit and pure rules take advantage of constraints to commit to particular truth assignments. The poor performance of Davis-Putnam thus arises due to a large number of splits compared to unit propagations and pure literal deletions. We conjecture therefore that both the unit and pure rules will be of less importance in the mostly satisfiable region.

In Figure 3 (a) we plot the mean ratio of pure literal deletions to splits, of unit propagations to splits and of the sum of pure literal deletions and unit propagations to splits for CP at N=150. Since the split rule is merely formalised guessing, the last of these ratios indicates the number of variable assignments that can be deduced for each guess during search. To avoid division by zero, we exclude the trivial problems which tend to occur at small L/N which are solved with no splits. Such problems can be solved in polynomial time using a simple preprocessing step which exhaustively applies the unit and pure rules. The minimum in the mean ratio of the sum of units and pures to splits is 11.0 and occurs at $L/N = 2.4$, close to the region of most variable problem difficulty.

These graphs confirm that the unit and pure rules are not effective in the region of very variable problem difficulty. There appears to be a "constraint gap" in this region. That is, the unit and pure rules are often unable to identify

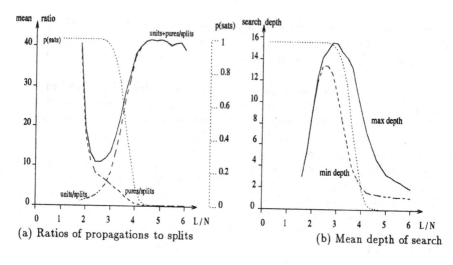

(a) Ratios of propagations to splits

(b) Mean depth of search

Fig. 3. random CP problems tested using DP, N= 150.

any constraint on the truth assignments. We are thus forced to use the split rule extensively. This would suggest that the depth of search (*i.e.* the depth of nesting of split rule applications) would also peak in this region. In Figure 3 (b), we plot the mean minimum, and mean maximum depth of search. The peak of the minimum depth is 13.4 at L/N = 2.6, while the peak of maximum depth is 15.6 at L/N = 2.8. This coincides closely with the minimum in the ratio of the sum of units and pures to splits, and with the position of the variable region. For unsatisfiable problems, a peak in minimum search depth corresponds to an exponentially larger peak in problem difficulty, as all branches must be searched to at least the minimum depth of the tree. We confirmed this be plotting the logarithm of problem difficulty for unsatisfiable problems alone. This was approximately proportional to mean minimum search depth.

A very interesting question is whether the constraint gap occurs with incomplete procedures which can only solve *satisfiable* problems. One such procedure is GSAT [13]. Although we have investigated this point experimentally, we have as yet failed to find any strong evidence for variable behaviour or for a constraint gap in experiments, for instance, on CP at N = 150. Procedures like GSAT do not necessarily explore the whole search space, and so may avoid the exponential growth in search discussed above. Variable behaviour may, however, exist for such procedures but only at larger N.

5   Binary Rule

There are other constraints which might be expected to narrow or even remove this constraint gap. For instance, one of the major features of the CP model which distinguish it from other problem classes like random k-SAT (see next section) is the variable length of clauses, and, in particular, the large numbers of binary clauses. Since there exists a linear time algorithm for the satisfiability of binary clauses [1], we have augmented DP with the following rule:

(Binary) if the binary clauses of (Σ simplified with the literal l set to *True*) are unsatisfiable then set l to *False*.

This rule has a non-deterministic choice of literal; this may affect the number of pure, unit or binary rules applied but *not* the number of splits.

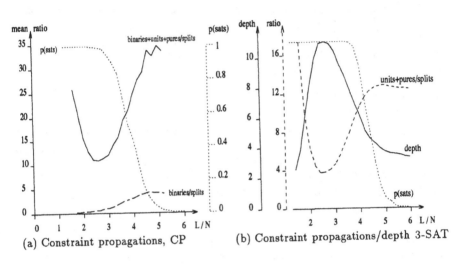

(a) Constraint propagations, CP   (b) Constraint propagations/depth 3-SAT

Fig. 4. CP using DP+(Binary), and random 3-SAT using DP for N= 50

In Figure 4 (a) we plot the mean ratios of the number of applications of the binary rule to splits and of the sum of the unit, pure and binary rules to splits for CP at N=50 (the efficiency of our implementation prevented us using a larger N). As in §3 we fix $2Np = 3$. [2] The binary rule allows a significant number of unsatisfiable problems to be solved without search, and as before these are omitted from the figure, accounting for some noise at large L/N. The ratios of unit and pure rule propagations to splits are similar to those in Figure 3 (a). Note that there are comparatively few applications of the binary rule compared to splits[3] and, like the unit rule, the utility of the binary rule increases with L/N. Although the binary rule reduces search significantly (the peak mean number of branches goes down from approximately 6 to 1.31), it does not appear to be

---

2 From L/N = 0.2 to 6 in intervals of 0.2 we tested 1000 problems at each point.
3 This may be affected by our implementation, in which the binary rule is only applied if the computationally cheaper pure and unit rules fail.

very effective in the variable region. This suggests that the binary rule will not eliminate the constraint gap nor variable behaviour. Indeed, we found tentative evidence of variability. At $L/N = 2.6$, one problem needed 75 branches, almost 3 times more than the next worse case over the whole experiment. The minimum value for the ratio of all propagations to splits also occurred at $L/N = 2.6$, and was 10.8. Given the change in problem size and procedure, it is surprising that this value is so close to the value of 11.0 observed in §4.

We also implemented a restricted version of the binary rule which just determines the satisfiability of the binary clauses and does not simplify on any of the literals. Although this restricted rule is less expensive, it appears to be of little use in reducing search; for CP at $N=100$, $2Np = 3$, it closed at most 20% of branches at large L/N but less than 3% of branches in the region of the constraint gap. It had little affect on mean behaviour. It remains to be seen if other constraints (eg. those on Horn or near Horn clauses) can be used to overcome the constraint gap, but we see no reason to expect this to be possible.

6 Random k-SAT

Although the constant probability model has been the focus of much theoretical study (see for example [10]), most recent experimental work has been on the phase transition of random 3-SAT [12, 3, 11]. A problem in random k-SAT consists of L clauses, each of which has exactly k literals chosen uniformly from the N possible variables, each literal being positive or negative with probability $\frac{1}{2}$.

We have observed a very similar constraint gap in 3-SAT to that seen for CP. In Figure 4 (b) we plot the mean ratio of propagations to splits and the mean minimum search depth for 3-SAT problems at N=50.[4] Again we omit problems solved by constraint propagation alone. The ratio of propagations to splits is very similar to Figure 3 (a), and reaches a minimum of 3.7 at $L/N = 2.4$. The graph of minimum search depth is very similar to Figure 3 (b), and reaches a maximum of 11.1 at $L/N = 2.6$. The graphs clearly illustrate the inverse relationship between search depth and constraint propagation, and the existence of a constraint gap away from the phase transition.

To date, we do not have conclusive evidence that the very variable behaviour described in §3 is found with random k-SAT. However, given the existence of a constraint gap, it is likely that the behaviour is present, but is just more difficult to observe than in CP. Crawford and Auton, for instance, have observed some problems in an otherwise easy region of random 3-SAT for $L/N \approx 2$ that were as hard as the hard problems from the phase transition where $L/N \approx 4.3$ [3]. To investigate this further, we compared 100,000 problems from 3-SAT at N = 50 and L/N set to 2 and 4.3 with a simplified version of the DP used in previous studies [12, 6] in which the pure rule is omitted. Remarkably, while problems at $L/N=2$ were typically very easy, one problem was nearly 60 times harder than

---

4 From $L/N = 0.2$ to 6 in intervals of 0.2 we tested 1000 problems at each point.

the worst case at L/N=4.3. Yet this one problem was the only problem which needed more than 1000 branches to solve at L/N = 2, compared to 21 such problems at L/N = 4.3. Further details of the number of branches searched are given below.

L/N	Prob(sats)	median	mean	s.d.	worst case
2.0	1	1	2.34	313	98,996
4.3	0.566	125	146	124	1,670

Although tentative, the evidence presented here of variable behaviour at L/N $\approx$ 2 is certainly consistent with the constraint gap observed in Figure 4 (b).

7 k-Colourability

Another way of randomly generating SAT problems is to map random problems from some other NP-hard problem into SAT. For example, the k-colourability (kCOL) of random graphs can be easily mapped into SAT. Given a graph, G the k-colourability problem is to assign one of k labels to each vertex of G so that adjacent vertices carry different labels. For a graph with n vertices and e edges, our encoding of kCOL into SAT uses $n.k$ variables. We generate random graphs to encode into SAT by choosing e edges from the $n.(n-1)/2$ possible uniformly at random. We use $\chi(n, e)$ to denote graphs drawn from this class.

In Figure 5 (a) we plot the breakdown in percentiles for the number of branches used by DP for encodings of 3-colourability for 1000 problems taken from $\chi(n, e)$ with $n = 40$ and $e/n = 0.5$ to 4 in steps of 0.1. The worst case was 2,905,011 branches at $e/n = 1.6$, while at $e/n = 2.4$, the point of worst median performance, the worst case was just 4,139 branches, 3 orders of magnitude smaller. As with the other random problem classes, median problem difficulty shows a simple easy-hard-easy pattern through the phase transition. Very similar behaviour for k-colourability was observed by Hogg and Williams using two special purpose colouring algorithms [8]. We again observed a constraint gap for this problem class, closely correlated with the variable region. For example, the maximum depth of search reached a peak at $e/n = 1$.

8   Independent Set

Our final problem class is constructed by mapping the independent set problem (ISET) into SAT. Given an integer k and a graph (V, E), the independent set problem is to find a subset $S \subseteq V$ of size k such that all vertices of S are independent (not connected to each other). This is closely related to the clique problem since (V, E) has an independent set of size k iff $(V, \overline{E})$ has a clique of size k where $\overline{E}$ is the complement of E. For a graph with n edges, our encoding into SAT uses $n.k$ variables. As before, we use random graphs from $\chi(n, e)$.

In Figure 5 (a) we plot the breakdown in percentiles for the number of branches used by DP for encodings of the independent set problem for 1000

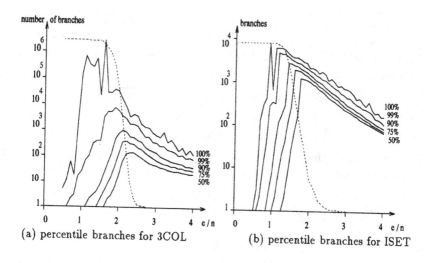

(a) percentile branches for 3COL   (b) percentile branches for ISET

Fig. 5. Encodings of two NP-hard problems into SAT

problems taken from $\chi(n,e)$ with $k = 6$, $n = 12$ and $e/n = \frac{1}{12}$ to 4 in steps of $\frac{1}{12}$. As before, the worst case performance is found in the region of typically underconstrained and satisfiable problems. The worst problem required 8,209 branches at 11 edges. By comparison, median problem difficulty shows a simple easy-hard-easy pattern through the phase transition. The peak median is 1,241 branches at 21 edges, where the worst case was 3,246 branches. We do not yet have conclusive evidence that the constraint gap occurs with this problem class as the ratio of all propagations to splits is within 10.6 ± 0.5 from 2 to 26 edges. Although the variable behaviour is not quite as dramatic as in our previous experiments, it does fit well the pattern identified in this paper. We conjecture therefore that variable behaviour will become more obvious with increasing n.

9 Prime Implicates

In an empirical study of the phase transition for random 3-SAT, Crawford and Auton found a secondary peak in problem difficulty in a region of high satisfiability [3]. Subsequently during a talk at AAAI-93, Crawford and Schrag observed that the number of prime implicates for random 3-SAT appears to peak in the same region, and suggested that the two phenomenon might be related.

A clause D is an *implicate* of a set of clauses C iff C implies D. D is a *prime* implicate iff it is an implicate and there is no other implicate E of C such that E implies D. Since an unsatisfiable set of clauses has a single prime implicate, the empty clause, the number and length of the prime implicates is not of help in understanding the difficulty of unsatisfiable problems. In Figure 6 (a) and (b) we

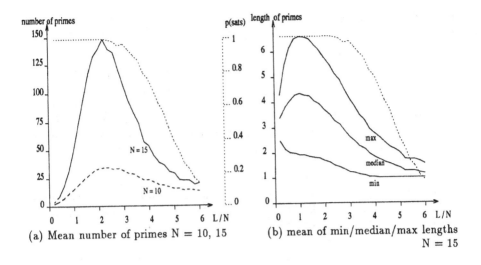

(a) Mean number of primes N = 10, 15

(b) mean of min/median/max lengths N = 15

Fig. 6. Numbers and lengths of Prime Implicates in CP

therefore plot the mean number of prime implicates and their mean minimum, median and maximum length for satisfiable problems generated by the CP model for N=10 and 15. As before, we fix $2Np = 3$. Computational limits prevented us from using larger N.

The peak mean number of prime implicates occurs at L/N = 2.2 for N= 15, and at 2.4 at N= 10. This corresponds closely to the region of very variable problem difficulty seen in §3, the constraint gap identified in §4, and the maximum in the depth of search. We expected the length of the prime implicates to be related to the difficulty of SAT problems since a branch closes if and only if it contains the negations of all the literals of one of the prime implicates. The solution depth and problem difficulty should therefore depend on the length of the prime implicates. Figure 6 (b) suggests, however, that if there is a correlation between the length of prime implicates and problem difficulty then it is not as direct as that with the number of prime implicates.

10 Related Work

Hogg and Williams have observed extremely variable problem difficulty for graph colouring using both a backtracking algorithm based on the Berlaz heuristic and a heuristic repair algorithm [8]. They found that the hardest graph colouring problems were in an otherwise easy region of graphs of low connectivity. The median search cost, by comparison, shows the usual easy-hard-easy pattern through the phase transition.

In an empirical study of the phase transition for random 3-SAT and the CP model using the Davis-Putnam procedure, Mitchell *et al.* noted that the mean is influenced by a very small number of very large values [12]. Their study therefore concentrated solely on the median as they felt that "it appears to be a more informative statistic". Our results suggest that the *distribution* of values is, in fact, of considerable importance in understanding problem difficulty, and that the median alone provides a somewhat incomplete picture.

In another empirical study of random 3-SAT using a tableau based procedure, Crawford and Auton observed a secondary peak in mean problem difficulty in a region of high satisfiability [3]. However, they noted that this peak did not seem to occur with the Davis-Putnam procedure and speculated that it was probably an artifact of the branching heuristics used by their procedure. Subsequently, as mentioned before, Crawford and Schrag have suggested that this peak might be related to the number of prime implicates. Our results suggest that this secondary peak also occurs with the Davis-Putnam procedure, but that it requires larger problems and larger sample sizes to be demonstrated convincingly.

11   Conclusions

We have performed a detailed experimental investigation of the phase transition for four different classes of randomly generated satisfiability problems. With each problem class, the median problem difficulty displays an easy-hard-easy pattern with the hardest problems being associated with the phase transition. We have shown, however, that the "conventional" picture of easy-hard-easy behaviour is inadequate since the distribution of problem difficulties has several other important features. In particular, all the problem classes have a region of very variable problem difficulty where problems are typically underconstrained and satisfiable. Within this region, we have found problems orders of magnitude harder than problems in the middle of the phase transition. With some problem classes, this behaviour is more easily observable than in others. For example, we found it much easier to observe this behaviour with an encoding of 3-COL into SAT and with the CP model than with random 3-SAT or an encoding of ISET.

We have presented evidence that these very hard problems arise because of a "constraint gap"; that is, in this region, there are few constraints on the assignment of truth values to variables, requiring us occasionally to search through exponentially many possible truth assignments. As a consequence, the depth of the search tree also peaks in this region. We have also shown that this gap cannot be eliminated even if we take advantage of extra constraints (*eg.* those on the binary clauses). Finally, we have suggested that the appearance of these very hard problems is related to the number of prime implicates which peaks in this region. Given the wide range of problem classes that exhibit this very variable and sometimes extraordinary hard problem difficulty, this behaviour should be of considerable importance for the analysis of algorithms for satisfiability. In addition, our connection of this variable behaviour with a constraint gap should help researchers identify the hardest regions of other randomly generated problems for SAT and other NP-hard problems.

Acknowledgements

This first author was supported by a SERC Postdoctoral Fellowship and the second by a HCM Research Fellowship. We thank Alan Bundy, Pierre Lescanne, Bob Constable, and the members of the Mathematical Reasoning Group at Edinburgh (supported by SERC grant GR/H 23610), the Eureca group at INRIA-Lorraine, and the Department of Computer Science at Cornell University, for their constructive comments and for rather a lot of CPU cycles.

References

1. B. Aspvall, M.F. Plass, and R.E. Tarjan. A linear-time algorithm for testing the truth of certain quantified Boolean formulas. *Information Processing Letters*, 8:121–123, 1979.
2. P. Cheeseman, B. Kanefsky, and W.M. Taylor. Where the really hard problems are. In *Proceedings of the 12th IJCAI*, pages 163–169. International Joint Conference on Artificial Intelligence, 1991.
3. J.M. Crawford and L.D. Auton. Experimental results on the crossover point in satisfiability problems. In *Proceedings of the Eleventh National Conference on Artificial Intelligence*, pages 21–27. AAAI Press/The MIT Press, 1993.
4. M. Davis and H. Putnam. A computing procedure for quantification theory. *J. Association for Computing Machinery*, 7:201–215, 1960.
5. O. Dubois, P. Andre, Y. Boufkhad, and J. Carlier. SAT versus UNSAT. In *Proceedings of the Second DIMACS Challenge*, 1993.
6. Ian P. Gent and Toby Walsh. Easy problems are sometimes hard. Research Paper 642, Dept. of Artificial Intelligence, Edinburgh, June 27 1993.
7. I.P. Gent and T. Walsh. The SAT phase transition. Proceedings of ECAI-94, 1994.
8. T. Hogg and C. Williams. The Hardest Constraint Problems: A Double Phase Transition. Technical report, Dynamics of Computation Group, Xerox Palo Alto Research Center, 1993. PARC Preprint.
9. J. N. Hooker and C. Fedjki. Branch-and-cut solution of inference problems in propositional logic. *Annals of Mathematics and Artificial Intelligence*, 1:123–139, 1990.
10. Paul Walton Purdom Jr. and Cynthia A. Brown. The pure literal rule and polynomial average time. *SIAM Journal of Computing*, 14(4):943–953, November 1985.
11. T. Larrabee and Y. Tsuji. Evidence for a Satisfiability Threshold for Random 3CNF Formulas. Technical Report UCSC-CRL-92-42, Baskin Center for Computer Engineering and Information Sciences, University of California, Santa Cruz, 1992.
12. David Mitchell, Bart Selman, and Hector Levesque. Hard and easy distributions of SAT problems. In *Proceedings, 10th National Conference on Artificial Intelligence*. AAAI Press/The MIT Press, July 12-16 1992.
13. Bart Selman, Hector Levesque, and David Mitchell. A new method for solving hard satisfiability problems. In *Proceedings, 10th National Conference on Artificial Intelligence*. AAAI Press/The MIT Press, 1992.

Formal Methods for Automated Program Improvement*

Peter Madden
Max-Planck-Institut fuer Informatik
Im Stadtwald, D-66123 Saarbruecken, Germany

Abstract: systems supporting the manipulation of non-trivial program code are complex and are at best semi-automatic. However, formal methods, and in particular theorem proving, are providing a growing foundation of techniques for automatic program development (synthesis, improvement, transformation and verification). In this paper we report on novel research concerning: (1) the exploitation of synthesis proofs for the purposes of automatic program optimization by the transformation of proofs, and; (2) the automatic synthesis of efficient programs from standard equational definitions. A fundamental theme exhibited by our research is that mechanical program construction, whether by direct synthesis or transformation, is tantamount to program verification plus higher-order reasoning.

§1 Introduction

There is a growing interest in the use of formal methods, and in particular automatic theorem proving, for program development (for example, synthesis, improvement, transformation and verification). Systems supporting the manipulation of non-trivial programs are, however, complex and are at best semi-automatic. In this paper we report on novel research concerning the exploitation of synthesis proofs for the purposes of automatic program improvement. The research takes two different, but related, approaches: program improvement by transforming formal synthesis proofs, and; program improvement by synthesizing efficient programs from equational definitions that correspond to less efficient programs. This research has direct applications regarding the improvement of the quality of software produced through automatic programming. Our approach has numerous advantages over more traditional approaches to program optimization which we shall address in the subsequent sections.

Although some of the research has been documented in previous publications, [18, 20], we have since reconstructed and considerably extended the systems reported there in. This paper represents an up to date account of our research. New features of our research documented within this paper include the use of higher-order variables to delay choices concerning the identification of recursive data-types for optimized programs, and the systemization of meta-level control strategies. We also highlight a common theme that links the transformation and synthesis aspects of the research: namely, that (automatic) program generation can be viewed as a higher-order verification process.

§1.1 Formal Methods and Automated Reasoning
As computer programs play an increasingly important role in all our lives so we must depend more and more on techniques, preferably automatic, for ensuring the high quality (*efficiency* and *reliability*) of computer programs. By *efficient* we mean that a program is designed to compute a task with minimum overhead and with maximum space and time efficiency. By *reliable* we mean that a program is ensured, or guaranteed in some sense, to compute the desired, or specified, task.

The most promising technique being developed for the automatic development of high quality software are *formal methods*. Applications of formal methods in software engineering depend critically on the use of automated theorem provers to provide improved support for the development of safety critical systems. Potentially catastrophic consequences can derive from the failure of computerized systems upon which human lives rely such as medical diagnostic systems, air traffic control systems and defence systems. The failure last year of the computerized system controlling the London Ambulance Service provides an example of how serious software failure can be. Formal methods are used to provide programs with, or prove that programs have, certain properties: a

---

*Some of the research reported in this paper was carried out when the author was an SERC Post-Doctoral Research Fellow within the *Mathematical Reasoning Group* at the Department of Artificial Intelligence, Edinburgh University. Acknowledgements are due to Ian Green, Jane Hesketh, Alan Smaill and, in particular, to Alan Bundy. The author also wishes to thank three anonymous *KI-94* referees for feedback on this paper.

program may be proved to *terminate*; two programs may be proved equivalent; an inefficient program may be *transformed* into an equivalent efficient program; a program may be *verified* to satisfy some specification (i.e. a program is proved to compute the specified function/relation); and a program may be *synthesized* that satisfies some specification.

The research described herein addresses both the reliability and efficiency, as well as the automatability, aspects of developing high quality software using formal methods. We describe novel theorem proving techniques for both automatic program optimization and automatic program synthesis. In both cases the *target* program is a significant improvement on the *source* (the efficiency criteria), and is guaranteed to satisfy the desired program specification (the reliability criteria).

In the remainder of this section we provide some background to the proofs as programs paradigm. §§ 2 concerns the application of formal methods – specifically theorem proving – for automatic, and correctness preserving, program improvement. We first, in §§ 2.1, describe the automatic source to target *transformation* of synthesis proofs yielding inefficient programs into synthesis proofs that yield efficient programs. Secondly, in §§ 2.2, we describe program improvement through the automatic *synthesis* of efficient programs from standard equational definitions.

§ 1.2 Background: *Proofs as Programs Paradigm*

Exploiting the *Proofs as Programs Paradigm* for the purposes of program development has already been addressed within the AI community [13, 9]. Constructive logic allows us to correlate computation with logical inference. This is because proofs of propositions in such a logic require us to construct objects, such as functions and sets, in a similar way that programs require that actual objects are constructed in the course of computing a procedure. Historically, this correlation is accounted for by the *Curry-Howard isomorphism* which draws a duality between the inference rules and the functional terms of the λ-calculus [10, 14].

Such considerations allow us to correlate each proof of a proposition with a specific λ-term, λ-terms with programs, and the proposition with a specification of the program. Hence the task of generating a program is treated as the task of proving a theorem: by performing a proof of a formal specification expressed in constructive logic, stating the *input-output* conditions of the desired program, an algorithm can be routinely extracted from the proof. A program specification can be schematically represented thus:

$$\forall inputs,\ \exists output.\ spec(inputs, output)$$

Existential proofs of such specifications must establish (constructively) how, for any input vector, an output can be constructed that satisfies the specification.[1] Thus any synthesized program is guaranteed correct with respect to the specification. Different constructive proofs of the same proposition correspond to different ways of computing that output. By placing certain restrictions on the nature of a synthesis proof we are able to control the efficiency of the target procedure. Thus by controlling the form of the proof we can control the efficiency with which the constructed program computes the specified goal. Here in lies the key to both synthesizing efficient programs, and to transforming proofs that yield inefficient programs into proofs that yield efficient programs.

§ 2 Program Improvement by Formal Methods

This section addresses program improvement by:

1. the optimization of programs through the transformation of synthesis proofs (§§ 2.1), and;
2. the synthesis of efficient programs, from standard equational definitions, using meta-level proof planning strategies called *proof-plans* (§§ 2.2).

In both case the program improvement is completely automatic. Regarding 1. a source proof, together with any source lemmas, form the input to the system. Regarding 2. the source equational definitions form the input to the system. The output in both cases corresponds to a complete target proof from which an improved program can be routinely extracted. Moreover, the resulting program is guaranteed to satisfy the operational criteria specified in the root node (goal) of the proofs.

In both cases meta-variables are employed to circumvent difficult procedural choices during the program construction process. The two approaches differ in the application of the meta-variables since how they are employed depends on characteristics of the kind of optimization required of the target program. The approaches also differ in the means by which the meta-variables are instantiated.

---

[1]Thus constructive logic *excludes* pure existence proofs where the existence of *output* is proved but not identified.

In 1. a source proof is used to create explicit target definitions and then meta-variables are used in the construction of recursive definitions. The instantiation of the meta-variables is aided by further analyses of the induction steps in the source proof. In 2. we use meta-variables to actually formulate both our explicit definition and recursive definitions. The automatic proof planning technique is used to instantiate the meta-variables through higher-order unification.

§2.1 Program Optimization by Proof Transformation

The Proof Transformation System, henceforth PTS, has the desirable properties of *automatability*, *correctness* and mechanisms for *reducing the transformation search space*, and various *control mechanisms* for guiding search through that space. As far a the author is aware, the PTS is the only working system that accomplishes automatic program optimization through proof transformation. We summarize the benefits of this approach below.[2]

Knowledge of theorem proving, and in particular automatic proof guidance techniques, can be brought to bear on the transformation task. The proof transformations allow the human synthesizer to produce an elegant source proof, without clouding the theorem proving process with efficiency issues, and then to transform this into an opaque proof that yields an efficient target program.

The proofs are in a sequent calculus and proved within the OYSTER proof refinement system [6].[3] OYSTER is a theorem prover for intuitionalist type theory, a higher order, constructive, typed logic based on Martin Löf Type Theory [22]. The main benefit of using such a logic is that, recalling §§1.2, it combines typing properties with the properties of constructivism, such that we can both correlate the propositions of the λ-calculus with specifications of programs and correlate the proofs of the propositions with how the specification is computed. The main benefit of using a sequent calculus notation, as opposed to that of any of the numerous natural deduction systems, is that at any stage (node) during a proof development, all the dependencies (assumptions and hypotheses) required to complete that proof stage are explicitly presented. This provides an analysis of the calling structure of the programs synthesized. Such analyses are not present within normal program code. To exploit such information usually requires additional, and expensive, mechanisms such as the production and analyses of (symbolic) dependency graphs [24, 8].

Synthesis proofs differ from straightforward programs in that more information is formalized in the proof than in the program: a description, or *specification*, of the task being performed; a *verification* of the method; and an account of the *dependencies* between facts involved in the computation. Thus, synthesis proofs represent a *program design record* because they encapsulate the reasoning behind the program design by making explicit the procedural commitments and decisions made by the synthesizer. This extra information means that proofs lend themselves better to *transformation* than programs since one expects that the data relevant to the transformation of algorithms will be different and more extensive than the data needed for simple execution.

A key feature of our approach consists in the transformation of the various induction schemas employed in OYSTER synthesis proofs. Of particular importance to inducing recursion in the extracted algorithm is the employment of *mathematical induction* in the synthesis proofs: to each form of induction employed in the proof there corresponds a dual form of recursion [2]. Such dualities offer the user a handle on the type, and efficiency, of recursive behaviour exhibited by the extracted algorithm.

By having a specification present, the PTS ensures that all transformed proofs yield programs that are correct with respect to that specification. Traditional program transformation systems have no such formal specification and this this means there is no immediate means of checking that the target program meets the desired operational criteria. Because of the induction-recursion duality, we can also guarantee that the target will be an optimization of the source program. Thus target programs are guaranteed to compute the input-output relation specified originally for the source, and guaranteed to do so more efficiently.

There are two applications of the PTS corresponding to the way in which inductive proofs are transformed in order to optimize recursive programs: firstly, recursive programs are improved by transforming the induction schemas employed in the source proofs into *logically equivalent* schemas that yield more efficient recursion behaviour[4]. Secondly, whilst retaining the dominant induction,

---

[2]C.A.Goad investigates program *specialization* by proof pruning operations in [16].

[3]OYSTER is the Edinburgh Prolog implementation, and extension, of NuPRL; version "nu" of the *Proof Refinement Logic* system originally developed at Cornell [9].

[4]By logically equivalent induction schemas we mean that the associated induction theorems are inter-derivable. This guarantees that any two proofs satisfying the same complete specification but differing only in which of the two schemas employed are *functionally* equivalent.

the PTS can improve a program by transforming nested inductions into single inductions. Due to space constraints we shall concentrate on the first application, and give only a brief account of the second.

- **Transformation of induction schemas:** source to target transformations of the first kind transform the recursion schemata of source programs. Although the individual syntheses have much in common, in particular the general shape exhibited by the majority of inductive proofs, the main difference between the source and target proofs are the induction schemata employed, and the existential instantiations (witnesses) employed at the induction proof cases. The PTS exploits the induction-recursion duality by transforming a source proof induction schema into a target schema that yields a more efficient recursion schema. To illustrate the process we shall consider the optimization of a program, f, for computing the Fibonacci numbers as a simple example. We consider three types of induction rule that can be employed in proofs of the following specification, S, for Fibonacci:[5]

$$S. \quad \forall input, \exists output. \ f(input) = output$$

In TABLE 1 we show the (uninstantiated) induction schema corresponding to the induction rule employed, where P is some property on natural numbers and all variables are universally quantified (s is the successor, or $+1$, function). Note that such rules are presented upside down, with the goal sequent appearing at the bottom. This reflects the goal-directed nature of the sequent calculus. Also shown, in the second and third rows, are the complexity and recursive data-type of the λ-function constructed through the inductive proof. Finally, in the fourth row, we show the left hand side of the function's definition (i.e. the data-type used for computing the Fibonacci numbers) and the right hand side (i.e. the recursion and terminating branches of the definition). The standard definition for Fibonacci appears in the first, course-of-values, column.

course-of-values	stepwise ($+1$)	divide-and-conquer	
$\dfrac{((y<z)\to P(y))\vdash P(z)}{\vdash P(x)}$	$\dfrac{\vdash P(0) \quad P(y)\vdash P(s(y))}{\vdash P(x)}$	$\dfrac{\vdash P(0) \quad P(y)\vdash P(y+y) \quad P(z)\vdash P(s(z+z))}{\vdash P(x)}$	
exponential	linear	logarithmic	
natural number	tuple	matrix	
f_n	$\langle f_n, f_{n-1}\rangle$	$\begin{bmatrix} f_{n+1} & f_n \\ f_n & f_{n-1}\end{bmatrix}^n$ (abbrv. to $\mathcal{M}$)	
1 $\quad n=0;$	$\langle 1,1\rangle \quad n=0;$	1	$n=0;$
1 $\quad n=1;$		$\mathcal{M}^{n+2}\times\mathcal{M}^{n+2}$	$even(n);$
$f_{n-1}+f_{n-2} \quad n\geq 2.$	$\langle f_{n-1}+f_n, f_n\rangle \quad n\geq 1.$	$\mathcal{M}^{n+2}\times\mathcal{M}^{n+2}\times\mathcal{M}$	$odd(n).$

TABLE 1: RELATION BETWEEN SOURCE AND TARGET PROOFS AND FUNCTIONS

Program optimization through proof transformation consists in transforming a source induction proof to a target proof whose induction schema has a more efficient associated complexity. The pre- and post-conditions of the transformation correspond to the induction schema, and the recursive data-type, of the source and target proofs. Thus, the post-conditions of the exponential to linear transformation are precisely the pre-conditions for the linear to logarithmic transformation. This illustrates how, by "dove-tailing" each of the source to target transformations, depicted in TABLE 1, the passage from an exponential procedure to a logarithmic one, with linearization as an intermediary optimization, is performed automatically through proof transformation (and with the correctness guarantee afforded by the specification language).

Although uniform in strategy, individual inductive proofs will usually differ regarding the following procedural commitments made during the synthesis component of a proof: (i) the choice of induction schema employed; (ii) the type of object introduced at the induction step (e.g. natural number, list, tuple), and; (iii) the witness (existential instantiation) of the object. These commitments are responsible for constructing the recursion schemata and the recursive data types of the target procedures. By incorporating general rules that associate (i) and (ii) with the kind of recursive behaviour desired of the target algorithm, and analysing the definitions of, and dependency information in, the source proofs to identify (iii), the PTS is able to construct the target proofs automatically.

---

[5]The Fibonacci function, f is initially defined through lemmata corresponding to the course-of-values definition given in TABLE 1, column 1:

base lemmas: $fib(0) = s(0);$ $\quad fib(s(0)) = s(0);$

step lemma: $\forall x, \exists y, \exists z.\big((x\neq 0)\wedge(x\neq s(0))\wedge fib(s(x))=y \wedge fib(x)=z\big) \to fib(s(s(x))) = y+z.$

We shall use the *linearization* of the Fibonacci function for the purposes of explanation (i.e. the transformation of course of values induction to stepwise induction). The PTS linearization procedure is, in fact, our adaptation to the proofs as programs paradigm of the unfold/fold *tupling* technique for "merging" repeated (sub)computations, [7, 8].

The most natural way to synthesize a procedure for computing the Fibonacci numbers is to employ the course-of-values induction to S. This is because it directly mirrors the course-of-values recursion exhibited by the standard Fibonacci definition. The corresponding schema, TABLE 1, will be instantiated as follows:

$$\frac{H \colon (\forall z, \forall y.((y < z) \to \exists n'.f(y) = n') \vdash \exists n''.f(z) = n''}{C \colon \vdash \forall x, \exists n.f(x) = n}.$$

The proof of the induction conclusion, C, requires identifying a witness for n. This is obtained by: eliminating on the induction hypothesis, H, twice:[6] first with a value for y of $x - 1$, and subsequently with a value of $x - 2$. The resulting constructs for f_{x-1} and f_{x-2} appear as two new hypotheses. The values of these new and hypotheses are then added to obtain a witness for n, i.e. $\vdash \forall x, f(x) = f(x - 1) + f(x - 2)$

By employing course-of-values induction, and eliminating on the hypothesis twice, we obtain a program such that in order to calculate $fib(n)$ one must first calculate $fib(n - 1)$ and $fib(n - 2)$. Each of these sub-goals leads to another two recursive calls on fib and so on. In short the computational tree is exponential where the number of recursive calls on fib approaches 2^n. The automatic linearization of such procedures involves constructing a target tuple (as shown in TABLE 1) whose elements act as accumulating parameters. The accumulators are used to build up the output as the recursion is entered, so that nothing remains to be done as the recursion exits. This cuts down considerably on the space requirements of a procedure call.

In order to identify a target (tuple) definition, the PTS observes how many times the induction conclusion C appeals to the hypothesis H, and how many applications, namely 2, of the induction constructor/destructor function the proof employs when eliminating on the induction hypothesis in order to synthesize constructs for the induction witnesses. This completely identifies an *explicit* definition, $\mathcal{G}$, for the auxiliary recursive procedure through which Fibonacci can be defined:[7]

$$\mathcal{G} \colon \quad \forall n, \exists u, \exists v.g(n) = \langle u, v \rangle, \quad \text{where} \quad \langle u, v \rangle = \langle f(n+1), f(n) \rangle.$$

The provision of such explicit definitions, where the target is defined in terms of the source, generally constitute the well known *eureka* step in unfold/fold transformations, and are notoriously difficult to automate [7]. The unfold/fold strategy is motivated by the observation that significant optimization of a (declarative) program generally implies the use of a new recursion schema. This process usually depends on the *user* providing the requisite explicit target definition (in our example: $\mathcal{G}$). The strategy then proceeds to evaluate the recursive branches of the target definition, primarily through unfolding with the source definitions, until a fold (match) can be found with the explicit definition.

Within the context of proof transformation, the PTS exploits the source proof to automatically form such definitions. Every new hypothesis formed as result of eliminating on previous hypotheses is recorded in the sequent calculus proof notation. This provides the kind of information usually associated with symbolic dependency graphs and used, for example, in the semi-automatic construction of unfold/fold tuple definitions [8, 24]. The PTS constructs the explicit definitions completely automatically without appealing to the user, or requiring the considerable over-head required in the formation and analyses of dependency graphs.

The explicit definition, $\mathcal{G}$, is automatically applied as a sub-goal of S. This will produce, in addition to $\mathcal{G}$, a trivial justification sub-goal that the function specified by S can be constructed from that specified by the sub-goal: the variable *output* in S is witnessed by v from the body of the $\mathcal{G}$. In effect, the justification sub-proof provides us with a definition for Fibonacci in terms of the auxiliary function g:

$$f(n) = v \quad \text{where} \quad g(n) = \langle \_, v \rangle$$

---

[6] A feature of the goal-directed proofs is that elimination rules have the effect of introducing an existential instantiation in the hypotheses of sequents.

[7] In practice, tuples are represented as conjunctions within the OYSTER system. So a tuple $\langle A, B, C \rangle$ is represented as $A \wedge B \wedge C$. Hence we avoid the charge that (program) tupling techniques rely heavily on any ad hoc requirements to introduce tuples (memo tables or similar objects).

Thus, an advantage of using specification proofs is that at the target proofs completion the PTS ensures that the auxiliary program, corresponding to the sub-proof of $\mathcal{G}$, computes the function specified by the $\mathcal{G}$, *and* by performing the justification goal we ensure that the complete program construction, corresponding to the whole proof, computes $\mathcal{S}$.

To synthesize the auxiliary function, g, the PTS applies *stepwise*, or +1, induction to $\mathcal{G}$ so as to construct the dual stepwise recursion. In other words, the PTS constructs a recursive definition through an inductive proof of the explicit definition $\mathcal{G}$. The base case, $g(0)$, evaluates to $\langle 1, 1 \rangle$ by using symbolic evaluation with the base definitions for Fibonacci. At the step case of the induction the PTS is required to provide a definition for the recursive step in terms of the hypothesis (i.e. $g(n + 1)$ in terms of $g(n)$). A characterizing feature of such tupling proofs is that the recursive definition will consist of some, as of yet unknown, function(s) applied to the tuple components, u and v, of the induction hypothesis. Hence , using upper-case to represent meta-variables, at the induction step of the target proof, the PTS formulates a partially identified definition for the recursive step of g in terms of the hypothesis (we omit the quantifiers for the remainder of this section):

$$ g(n + 1) = \langle M_1(u, v), M_2(u, v) \rangle, \text{ where } \langle u, v \rangle = g(n). $$

The induction step proof then proceeds as in FIG 1 until, by a process of unfolding with the source and target definitions, all references to the source function, f, have been removed from the developing target recursive branch (essential if we wish to eliminate the source inefficiency). Once this stage has been reached, the PTS *could* use higher-order unification to instantiate M_1 to $\lambda u, v.u + v$, and M_2 to $\lambda u, v . u$.

$$ g(n + 1) = \langle M_1(u, v), M_2(u, v) \rangle, \text{ wh. } \underbrace{\langle u, v \rangle = g(n)}; $$

unfold g **unfold g;** source $\mapsto$ target

$$ \langle f(n + 2), f(n + 1) \rangle = \langle M_1(u, v), M_2(u, v) \rangle, \text{ wh. } \underbrace{\langle u, v \rangle = \langle f(n + 1), f(n) \rangle}; $$

unfold f source $\mapsto$ target

$$ \langle (f(n + 1) + f(n)), f(n + 1) \rangle = \langle M_1(u, v), M_2(u, v) \rangle, \text{ wh. } \langle u, v \rangle = \langle f(n + 1), f(n) \rangle; $$

fertilize $(u/f(n + 1),\ v/f(n))$

$$ \langle u + v, u \rangle = \langle M_1(u, v), M_2(u, v) \rangle; $$

instantiation $M_1 = \lambda u, v.u + v$ and $M_2 = \lambda u, v . u.$

$\dfrac{rhs = lhs}{\text{source} \mapsto \text{target}}$ signifies that $rhs = lhs$ obtained by analysis of source to identify:

(1) the tuple size, and; (2) the constituent data structures.

FIG 1: SYNTHESIS COMPONENT OF TARGET PROOF CONSTRUCTION (INDUCTION STEP ONLY)

However, the PTS avoids any need for higher-order matching, and the associated control problems, by providing general *mapping mechanisms* which abstract information from the induction branches of the source proof. This information is then used to instantiate the target meta-variables. The general mapping mechanisms are described in detail in [17].

Regarding our current example, the procedure is quite simple: the first component of the r.h.s tuple (corresponding to the induction conclusion) results from *substituting* the *target* induction hypothesis tuple components, u and v, for those in the *source* induction step. Hence the first component is $u + v$ (i.e. M_1 is instantiated as $\lambda u, v.u + v$). No higher-order matching, or unification, procedures are required since the dominant function of the first tuple component will always be that employed at the induction step of the source (where the number of tuple elements corresponds to the number of source proof eliminations on the induction hypothesis). The second component results from a direct one on one mapping of the first component, u, of the *target* induction hypothesis (i.e. $M_2 = \lambda u, v . u$).

The λ program construction extracted from the target proof is shown below. (We have necessarily simplified the notation. For details on the OYSTER extraction process *cf.* [6]).

$$ \lambda x.(\lambda tuple.(sub(\langle u, v \rangle, [\sim, x, x]))).(step_{+1}(x, \langle s(0), s(0) \rangle, [\bar{x}, \langle u, v \rangle, \langle u + v, u \rangle]))) $$

The solution for *Fibonacci* corresponds to v in the extract (i.e., the second argument of the first tuple component). The *substitution* function, sub, substitutes the second element of the tuple (the desired output v) for x in the root node specification. The $step_{+1}$ function, corresponding to the application of stepwise induction, will automatically build the dual recursion schema into the extract term being synthesized. The application of the $step_{+1}$ induction constructs a triple where the first member, x, names the induction candidate: the argument over which the recursion is defined. The second member, $\langle s(0), s(0)\rangle$, corresponds to the construction of the base case output. The third member is a further triple and corresponds to the induction step shown in FIG 1: $\bar{x}$ denotes the induction variable, and $\langle u, v\rangle$ denotes the constructive evidence for the induction hypothesis. The induction conclusion, $\langle u + v, u\rangle$, is composed from the elements, u and v, of the hypothesis.

The form, or shape, of refinement proofs means that *folding* is not a necessary requirement in order to introduce a recursion into the developing equations. This is because the proof synthesis is driven by the heuristic requirement of matching induction hypothesis with induction conclusion, i.e., *fertilization* (we shall say more concerning fertilization in §§ 2.2). This can be achieved purely by unfolding both sides of the induction step until both head and body match (*cf.* FIG 1). By unfolding terms on *both* sides of the induction conclusion we gradually remove the induction term from the conclusion. This bi-directional rewriting has advantages over the more traditional program derivations, such as [7, 8], wherein re-writing is restricted to the body of the equations: most notably, we avoid the control problems of directing sequences of unfolds toward a fold. The bi-directional search toward the fertilization step significantly reduces the search space.

The verification component of the proof will mirror the synthesis component:

$$g(n + 1) = \langle u + v, u\rangle, \quad where \ \langle u, v\rangle = g(n);$$

$$\textbf{unfold } g \qquad\qquad \textbf{unfold } g;$$

$$\langle f(n + 2), f(n + 1)\rangle = \langle u + v, u\rangle, \quad where \ \langle u, v\rangle = \langle f(n + 1), f(n)\rangle;$$

$$\textbf{unfold } f \qquad\qquad \textbf{fertilize } (u/f(n + 1), v/f(n));$$

$$\langle (f(n + 1) + f(n)), f(n + 1)\rangle = \langle (f(n + 1) + f(n)), f(n + 1)\rangle.$$

FIG 2: VERIFICATION COMPONENT OF TARGET PROOF CONSTRUCTION

An observation is that the essential difference between the synthesis (FIG 1) and verification (FIG 2) components of the target construction is that the former uses meta-variables (simply compare the first lines of each figure). A common theme of our work within the proofs as programs paradigm is that program synthesis/transformation is tantamount to program verification plus meta-variables. That is, we recast first-order synthesis proofs as higher-order verification proofs, and in doing so circumvent eureka steps concerning the identification of recursive data-types. We see a further illustration of this theme in §§ 2.2.

The verification strategy of induction proofs invariably follows the same procedure of applying refinement rules that consist primarily of unfolding the recursive branches with the equational definitions that define the function computed by the extract program. Indeed, the induction strategy is uniform enough to be systemized as a meta-level proof plan, with pre- and post-conditions. So once the PTS has automatically made the target proof procedural commitments corresponding to (i) - (iii), by an analysis of the source proof, then verification is automatically performed through the use of an induction proof plan. We shall return to proof plans in more detail in §§ 2.2. A much more in-depth description of the processes involved, and of the implementation, are provided in [17].

As indicated in TABLE 1, the PTS can automatically optimize linear procedures to logarithmic procedures through proof transformation. This is done using the method of *matrix multiplication* and replacing the *stepwise* induction employed in the source proof by a target *divide-and-conquer* induction. Full details are available in [19].

• **Transformation of nested inductions:** nested inductions are often employed when synthesizing *auxiliary recursive functions*, that is, functions which in computing a self-recursive call must appeal to some other function, either directly or indirectly.[8]

A nested induction may lead to inefficiency since for each of the recursive passes induced by the outermost induction, the program will have to fully recurse on the innermost recursive schema

---

[8]The nesting may be indirect since the structure introduced for the step case of an induction may well correspond to the application of an extract term from another proof which itself employs stepwise/list induction.

induced by the innermost induction. Thus the average time efficiency of such programs will be a multiple of the time efficiencys associated with the two inductions. So for example, the recursive definition of the following schematic function f_1:

$$f_1(n) = f_2(f_3(n), f_1(n-1))$$

contains both an auxiliary function call, $f_3(n)$, and a self-recursive call, $f_1(n-1)$. Each time a recursive call is made on f_1, the program must fully recurse down the schema associated with f_3. Proofs wherein a nested (stepwise) induction is applied at the step case of the outermost induction may, for example, yield a λ program construction of the following (schematic) form:

$$\lambda x.\ step_{+1}(x, \phi_0, [\bar{x}, \phi_{H_{ind}}, \lambda \bar{x}.\ step_{+1}(\bar{x}, \phi_0, [\bar{\bar{x}}', \phi'_{H_{ind}}, \phi'_C])])),$$

where in order to evaluate the step case of the outermost +1 stepwise induction on x, with induction parameter $\bar{x}$, the program must evaluate a nested induction on $\bar{x}$. The terms $\phi_0, \phi_{H_{ind}}, \phi_C$ denote, respectively, the induction base, hypothesis and conclusion constructs. A prime, ', demarcates the nested induction constructs from those of the outer induction. Optimizations on such extract terms are performed through "merging" the innermost induction with the outermost induction. This is achieved by removing the innermost induction and introducing a tuple structure at the cases of the remaining induction. This yields a target construction of the following schematic form:

$$\lambda x.\lambda tuple.\ step_{+1}(x, \langle \phi_0^1, ..., \phi_0^n \rangle, [\bar{x}, \langle \phi_{H_{ind}}^1, ..., \phi_{H_{ind}}^n \rangle, \langle \phi_C^1, ..., \phi_C^n \rangle])$$

where there is a single stepwise induction, on the same variable x. In this case, the induction schema cases are satisfied through the evaluation of a tuple, of fixed size n, at the base and step branches. In effect the remaining induction tabulates the computation associated with the innermost induction removed from the source.

As with application 1, the PTS analyses the dependency information in the source proofs to obtain explicit definitions and to instantiate meta-variables [17].

The PTS is capable of combining the different kinds of induction transformation such that, for example, course-of-values (exponential) definitions that employ auxiliary functions can be optimized to stepwise (linear) definitions with a single induction (single recursion schema). The PTS is also capable of performing more esoteric induction transformations involving schemas such as divide-and-conquer induction (cf. TABLE 1), two step induction, and induction based on the construction of numbers as products of primes [17].

§ 2.2 Program Optimization by Proof Synthesis

The Mathematical Reasoning Group, at the Edinburgh University Department of AI, has achieved considerable success regarding the automation of inductive theorem proving using a meta-level control paradigm called 'proof planning' [3]. A proof planning system, CLAM, is able to prove a large number of inductive theorems automatically [5]. Proof plans are formal outlines of constructive proofs and provide a means for expressing, in a meta-language, the common patterns that define a family of proofs [4, 21]. A tactic expresses the structure of a proof strategy at the level of the inference rules of the object-level logic. Proof plans are constructed from the tactic specifications called *methods*. Using a meta-logic, a method captures explicitly the preconditions under which a tactic is applicable.

This section reports on the most recent application of CLAM: the use of proof plans to control the (automatic) synthesis of efficient functional programs, specified in a standard equational form, $\mathcal{E}$, by using the proofs as programs principle [21]. The goal is that the program extracted from a constructive proof of the specification is an optimization of that defined solely by $\mathcal{E}$. Thus the theorem proving process is a form of program optimization allowing for the construction of an efficient, *target*, program from the definition of an inefficient, *source*, program. Our main concern lies with optimizing the recursive behaviour of programs through the use of proof plans for inductive proofs. Thus again we exploit the duality between induction and recursion (which forms one aspect of the *Curry-Howard isomorphism*).

The main difference from the proof transformation approach to program improvement, §§ 2.1, is that there is no source proof to guide the construction of the target (only source definitional equations). Hence this is a process of synthesis rather than transformation. We again employ meta-variables, except in this case a proof planning technique called *middle-out reasoning* is used to instantiate them through higher-order reasoning. In fact, we view program synthesis as the combination of verification and middle-out reasoning [15]. Middle-out reasoning is a technique that allows us to solve the typical eureka problems arising during the synthesis of efficient programs by allowing the planning to proceed even though certain object-level objects are unknown (e.g. identification of induction schema, recursive types etc.) Subsequent planning then provides the necessary information which, together with the original definitional equations, allows for the instantiation of such meta-variables through higher-order unification procedures.[9]

A further property of program improvement through proof planning is that the nature of the optimization is controlled by placing certain restrictions on the proof. We illustrate one such restriction in the following example.

A Simple Example To illustrate program improvement by proof planning we use a simple example of the synthesis of tail-recursive programs from naïve definitions using the *tail-recursive proof plan* (TRPP) [21].[10]

Consider the following example of a *naïve*, $length_n$, and a *tail recursive*, $length_t$, definition for the *length* function, where $length_t$ is defined in terms of the auxiliary accumulator function $length_2$:

naïve definition	tail recursive definition
$length_n(nil) = 0;$ $length_n(h :: t) = 1 + length_n(t).$	$length_t(l) = length_2(l, 0)$ $length_2(nil, a) = a$ $length_2(h :: t, a) = length_2(t, 1 + a)$

TABLE 2: NAÏVE DEFINITION AND TAIL RECURSIVE DEFINITIONS FOR $length$

The key initial step to the TRPP is to provide an *explicit* target definition by specifying the *tail recursive* algorithm in terms of the *naïve* algorithm. This is depicted on the left hand side of TABLE 3 where we show the schematic form of such explicit definitions, together with the particular instance, (1), for our current example: the specification goal for synthesizing $length_t$.

	preconditions	postconditions
schem.	$\vdash \forall x, \forall \vec{y}, \exists z.\ z = f_n(x, \vec{y})$	$\vdash \forall x, \forall \vec{y}, \forall a, \exists z.\ z = M(f_n(x, \vec{y}), a)$
inst.	$\vdash \forall x, \exists z.\ z = length_n(x)$ (1)	$\vdash \forall x, \forall a, \exists z.\ z = M'(length_n(x), a)$ (2)

TABLE 3: PRE- AND POST- CONDITIONS OF ACCUMULATOR GENERALIZATION

There is no eureka involved with forming such explicit definitions: for any function, f, under consideration all that is stated is that for any input, x, and any additional vectors, $\vec{y}$, that there exists some output, z, equal to $\lambda x. f(n)$.[11]

The next stage is for the TRPP to introduce an accumulator into the function being synthesized through a generalization procedure. This is done by making a call to a (sub)proof plan for *accumulator generalization*. The pre-condition of accumulator generalization is satisfied by a schematic equational form of which (1) is an instance. The post-condition of the generalization is shown on the right hand side: the pre-conditional form is *generalized* through the introduction of a meta-variable M to produce the post-conditional form. In the majority of transformation systems the identification of M is a *eureka* step. The tail-recursive generalization strategy removes the *eureka* step and identifies M automatically through *middle-out* reasoning. In the case of $length_t$ the post-condition is (2) and we shall show how M is automatically instantiated as $\lambda uv. u + v$ through the proof of (2).

Having applied generalization, the proof of (1) is now cashed out in terms of:

- a *synthesis* goal, proving (2), and;

- a *justification* goal, proving that (2) $\vdash$ (1). (i.e. that the new goal entails the original theorem.)

The justification goal is, in fact, a second post-condition of the TRPP and establishes that the new goal entails the original theorem.[12] So the justification goal will, in effect, provide us with a definition

---

[9]λ-*Prolog*, [23], is used for the higher-order unifications and has been interfaced with the CLAM system. An indefinite number of unifications may be produced by such an algorithm if no means of selecting suitable choices is present. Details of such selection criteria, and of the algorithm itself, are provided in [12].

[10]The examplified application of the TRPP is adequate to illustrate the middle-out reasoning methodology. However, since it's original implementation it has been extended to cover a broader range of optimizations such as deforestation and fusion [21].

[11]The trivial instantiation of z, i.e. $f(x)$, is prevented by placing a restriction on the proof that f is not a term of the witness for z.

[12]This is directly analogous to where a justification sub-goal is produced during the PTS transformation of a source proof by cutting in a new sub-goal specifying a target definition (cf. §§2.1).

of the tail-recursive function, $length_t$, in terms of the auxiliary accumulator function, $length_2$, synthesized via the synthesis goal.

A characterizing feature of the TRPP is the restriction that the witnesses of the two existential quantifiers, one in the induction hypothesis and one in the induction conclusion, should be identical. This restriction ensures that we force the value of the function before the recursion is entered (determined by the induction hypothesis) to be the same as the value as the recursive call is exited (determined by the induction conclusion) — i.e. the function synthesized is tail recursive [26].

To continue the illustration we must explain a bare minimum of technical terminology. As mentioned in §§ 2.1, the verification stages of an inductive proof invariably involve a process whereby formulae are "unpacked" - or *unfolded* - by replacing terms by suitably instantiated definitions. The proliferation of this process such that recursive terms are gradually removed from the recursive branches — by the repeated unfolding of induction terms — is part of the (heuristic) process known as *rippling* (following [1]). The goal of the rippling proof-plan is to reduce the induction step case to terms which can be unified with those in the induction hypothesis. As mentioned in §§ 2.1, this unification is called *fertilization*. Fertilization is facilitated by the fact that the induction conclusion is structurally very similar to the induction hypothesis except for those function symbols which surround the induction variable in the conclusion. These points of difference are called *wave-fronts*. Thus, the remainder of the induction conclusion – the *skeleton* – is an exact copy of the hypothesis. Wave fronts consist of expressions with holes — *wave holes* — in them corresponding to sub-terms in the skeleton. Returning to our example, having generalized the specification goal, (1), to produce the higher-order sequent (2), the TRPP must next satisfy the synthesis goal of proving (2). This is done by applying the *induction* proof plan, again as a sub-proof plan, to produce the **step case** sequent (3). By convention, wave-fronts are annotated by placing them in boxes, and the wave-holes are underlined:[13]

$$\forall a, \exists z.\, z = M(length_n(t), a) \quad \vdash \quad \forall a, \exists z.\, z = M(\boxed{1 + \underline{length_n(t)}}, a) \tag{3}$$

Rippling applies special structural rewrite rules, *wave-rules*, so as to remove the difference (wave-fronts) from the conclusion, thus leaving behind the skeleton and allowing fertilization to take place. Wave rules are schematic rewrites — hence they employ meta-variables — and are *automatically* formed, by the proof planning mechanism, from recursive definitions and semantic laws. For example, the wave rule below is formed from the recursive branch, shown in TABLE 2, of $length_n$:

$$length_n(\boxed{X :: \underline{Y}}) \quad \Rightarrow \quad \boxed{1 + \underline{length_n(t)}} \tag{4}$$

So by matching and then applying the current sequent against the available (wave) rules, the meta-variable in (3) is instantiated at the step case of the induction. Briefly, after rippling on (3), using wave-rule (4), we obtain:

$$\forall a, \exists z.\, z = M(length_n(t), a) \quad \vdash \quad \forall a, \exists z.\, z = M(\boxed{1 + \underline{length_n(t)}}, a) \tag{5}$$

By using higher-order matching with the applicable wave-rules, the meta-variable M is instantiated to $\lambda u, v.u + v$ through applying the following wave-rule formed from the law of commutativity of $+$:

$$\boxed{(\underline{U + V})} + W \quad \Rightarrow \quad V + \boxed{(U + \underline{W})} \tag{6}$$

i.e. the result of the applying wave rule (6) to (5) is the following sequent:

$$\forall a, \exists z.\, z = length_n(t) + a \quad \vdash \quad \forall a, \exists z.\, z = length_n(t) + \boxed{1 + \underline{a}} \tag{7}$$

Fertilisation can now take place: a in the induction hypothesis is instantiated to $1 + a$ from the induction conclusion. Such an instantiation effects our tail-recursive restriction: that the witnesses of the two existential quantifiers should be identical. This step is perfectly legitimate since the a's on either side of the sequent are bounded by *distinct* universal quantifiers.

The **base case** sequent is as follows:

$$\vdash \forall a, \exists z.\, z \;=\; M(length_n(nil), a) \tag{8}$$

M is instantiated to $\lambda x, y.x + y$, from the step case, and following symbolic evaluation, using the base definitions of $+$ and $length_n$, (8) is refined to:

---

[13]There are additional annotations which further direct the rippling process. We omit these in this paper. For full details *cf.* [4].

$$\vdash \quad \forall a, \exists z.\ z = a \qquad\qquad (9)$$

A further, and very simple, application of middle-out reasoning strips the universal quantifier and introduces a meta-variable for the base witness, which is subsequently instantiated to a by tautology.

Analysis of the proof so far, specifically (7) and (9), provides the recursive and terminating branches of the auxiliary $length_2$ function (*rhs* of TABLE 2). However, the TRPP must still satisfy the justification obligation. The justification proof will provide a definition for $length_t$ in terms of $length_2$, and requires proving the sub-goal:

$$\forall x, \forall a, \exists z.\ z = length_n(x) + a \quad \vdash \quad \forall x, \exists z.\ z = length_n(x) \qquad (10)$$

The solution to (10) again involves middle-out reasoning: briefly, any universal quantified variables in the conclusion are identified with counterparts in the hypothesis – in this case x. Following the introduction of the universally quantified variables, x, a meta-variable A is inserted for a into the hypothesis:

$$\forall x, \exists z.\ z = length_n(x) + A \quad \vdash \quad \forall x, \exists z.\ z = length_n(x) \qquad (11)$$

Symbolic evaluation instantiates the meta-variable to 0, and the resulting hypothesis can be matched (fertilized) with the conclusion. This completes the proof. The witness 0, for A, provides the definition of $length_t$ in terms of $length_2$ (i.e. $length_t(l) = length_2(l, 0)$).

Rippling has numerous desirable properties. A high degree of control is achieved for applying the rewrites since the wave-fronts in the rule schemas must correspond to those in the instance. This leads to a very low search branching rate which, together with the further search reduction afforded by the proof restrictions, enables the automation of the synthesis process. Rippling is guaranteed to terminate since wave-front movement is always propagated in a desired direction toward some end state (a formal proof of this property is presented in [4]).

Further Applications We have found this approach to program improvement to be very promising. This is demonstrated by the success we have had in expressing, in addition to tail-recursive transformation, a wide variety of well-known, but disparate, program improvement techniques within the proof planning framework. For example, constraint-based transformation, generalization, fusion and tupling can be seen as proof planning [21]. Each of these types of optimization have characteristic features which are used to determine how higher-order meta-variables are employed in the specification goals. These applications also extend the simple tail-recursive syntheses in that the wave-rules themselves may contain second-order meta-variables as well as the sequents to which they apply. We have also extended the work of Wadler, [25] and later Chin, [8], to encompass a larger class of functions that can be usefully optimized using the influential *deforestation technique* [21].

We believe that middle-out reasoning will play an increasingly important role in theorem proving, since it allows us to address important problems like choosing induction schemata and existential witnesses (which correlate with recursion schemata and recursive data types).

§3 Conclusion

We have illustrated the fact that formal methods in general, and theorem proving in particular, provide a foundation for automated reasoning. We have described two novel implemented techniques for the automatic generation of high quality (efficient and reliable) software using the proofs as programs paradigm. Program improvement by transformation is achieved through the transformation of typed proofs in a constructive logic. The synthesis of efficient programs from standard equational definitions is achieved through the use of (meta-level) proof-planning techniques. A common theme of the research is the maxim that program construction can be automated through higher-order verification proofs.

Well known eureka steps concerning the identification of target definitions are circumvented by: in the transformational approach, using higher-order meta-variables and extracting information from source proofs in order to instantiate them, and; in the synthesis approach, using meta-variables in a technique called middle-out reasoning to delay procedural commitments until subsequent theorem proving provides the requisite instantiations. In both case the meta-variables are employed according to characteristics of the type of optimization desired.

Both the transformation and synthesis techniques satisfy the desirable properties for automatic programming systems: correctness, generality, automatability and the means to guide search through the transformation space.

References

[1] R. Aubin. Some generalization heuristics in proofs by induction. In G. Huet and G. Kahn, editors, *Actes du Colloque Construction: Amélioration et vérification de Programmes*. Institut de recherche d'informatique et d'automatique, 1975.

[2] R.S. Boyer and J.S. Moore. *A Computational Logic*. Academic Press, 1979. ACM monograph series.

[3] A. Bundy. The Use of Explicit Plans to Guide Inductive Proofs. In R. Luck and R. Overbeek, editors, *CADE9*. Springer-Verlag, 1988.

[4] A. Bundy, A. Stevens, F. van Harmelen, A. Ireland, and A. Smaill. Rippling: A heuristic for guiding inductive proofs. *Artificial Intelligence*, 62:185–253, 1993.

[5] A. Bundy, F. van Harmelen, J. Hesketh, and A. Smaill. Experiments with proof plans for induction. *Journal of Automated Reasoning*, 7:303–324, 1991.

[6] A. Bundy, F. van Harmelen, C. Horn, and A. Smaill. The Oyster-Clam system. In M.E. Stickel, editor, *10th International Conference on Automated Deduction*, pages 647–648. Springer-Verlag, 1990. Lecture Notes in Artificial Intelligence No. 449.

[7] R.M. Burstall and J. Darlington. A transformation system for developing recursive programs. *Journal of the Association for Computing Machinery*, 24(1):44–67, 1977.

[8] W.N. Chin. *Automatic Methods for Program Transformation*. PhD thesis, Imperial College, 1990.

[9] R.L. Constable, S.F. Allen, H.M. Bromley, et al. *Implementing Mathematics with the Nuprl Proof Development System*. Prentice Hall, 1986.

[10] H.B. Curry and R. Feys. *Combinatory Logic*. North-Holland, 1958.

[11] C. A. Goad. Automatic construction of special purpose programs. In D.W. Loveland, editor, *6th International Conference on Automated Deduction*, pages 194–208. Springer-Verlag, 1982. Lecture Notes in Computer Science, vol. 138.

[12] J.T. Hesketh. *Using Middle-Out Reasoning to Guide Inductive Theorem Proving*. PhD thesis, University of Edinburgh, 1991.

[13] C. Horn and A. Smaill. Theorem proving with Oyster. In Proceedings of the IMA Unified Computation Laboratory, Stirling. Springer Verlag, 1990.

[14] W.A. Howard. The formulae-as-types notion of construction. In J.P. Seldin and J.R. Hindley, editors, *To H.B. Curry; Essays on Combinatory Logic, Lambda Calculus and Formalism*, pages 479–490. Academic Press, 1980.

[15] I. Madden, P. Green. *Optimization = Verification + Middle-Out Reasoning*. Research Paper, Dept. of Artificial Intelligence, University of Edinburgh, 1993. Extended abstract in Proceedings of *Workshop on Automated Theorem Proving*, IJCAI-93.

[16] P. Madden. The specialization and transformation of constructive existence proofs. In N.S. Sridharan, editor, *Proceedings of the Eleventh International Joint Conference on Artificial Intelligence*. Morgan Kaufmann, 1989.

[17] P. Madden. *Automated Program Transformation Through Proof Transformation*. PhD thesis, University of Edinburgh, 1991.

[18] P. Madden. Automatic Program Optimization Through Proof Transformation. In D. Kapur, editor, *CADE11*, pages 446–461. Springer Verlag, 1992. Lecture Notes in Computer Science No. 607.

[19] P. Madden. Linear to logarithmic optimization via proof transformation. Research paper 416, Max-Planck-Institute für Informatik, 1994.

[20] P. Madden and A. Bundy. General techniques for automatic program optimization and synthesis through theorem proving. In *The Proceedings of the EAST-WEST AI CONFERENCE: From Theory to Practice - EWAIC'93*, September 1993.

[21] P. Madden and I. Green. A general technique for automatic optimization by proof planning. In *Proceedings of Second International Conference on Artificial Intelligence and Symbolic Mathematical Computing (AISMC-2)*, King's College, Cambridge, England, August 1994. To Appear.

[22] Per Martin-Löf. *Intuitionistic Type Theory*. Bibliopolis, Naples, 1984. Notes by Giovanni Sambin of a series of lectures given in Padua, June 1980.

[23] D. Miller and G. Nadathur. An overview of λProlog. In R. Bowen, K. & Kowalski, editor, *Proceedings of the Fifth International Logic Programming Conference/ Fifth Symposium on Logic Programming*. MIT Press, 1988.

[24] A. Pettorossi. A powerfull strategy for deriving programs by transformation. In *ACM Lisp and Functional Programming Conference*, pages 405–426, 1984.

[25] P. Wadler. Deforestation: Transforming Programs to Eliminate Trees. In *Proceedings of European Symposium on Programming*, pages 344–358. Nancy, France, 1988.

[26] S.S. Wainer. Computability - logical and recursive complexity, July 1989.

Adapting Methods to Novel Tasks
in Proof Planning*

Xiaorong Huang, Manfred Kerber, Michael Kohlhase, Jörn Richts

Fachbereich Informatik, Universität des Saarlandes
66041 Saarbrücken, Germany
{huang|kerber|kohlhase|richts}@cs.uni-sb.de
WWW: http://js-sfbsun.cs.uni-sb.de/pub/www/

Abstract. In this paper we generalize the notion of method for proof planning. While we adopt the general structure of methods introduced by Alan Bundy, we make an essential advancement in that we strictly separate the declarative knowledge from the procedural knowledge. This change of paradigm not only leads to representations easier to understand, it also enables modeling the important activity of formulating meta-methods, that is, operators that adapt the declarative part of existing methods to suit novel situations. Thus this change of representation leads to a considerably strengthened planning mechanism.

After presenting our declarative approach towards methods we describe the basic proof planning process with these. Then we define the notion of meta-method, provide an overview of practical examples and illustrate how meta-methods can be integrated into the planning process.

1 Introduction

There has been growing concern in the automated theorem proving community that general purpose machine oriented procedures like resolution might have reached their limits in practice. Therefore the old discussion of the merits of a human-oriented vs. a machine oriented approach to automated theorem proving has been revived by researchers like Alan Bundy. In response to his request for a "science of reasoning" [3] a string of systems and theories that aim at combining human-oriented deduction methods with sophisticated planners have been proposed.

A central concept of knowledge based reasoning in mathematics and proof planning is that of a *method*. A method contains a piece of knowledge for solving or simplifying problems or transforming them into a form that is easier to solve. Therefore methods can be quite general such as finding proofs by a case analysis or complete induction, or the advice to expand definitions. On the other hand, domain specific methods are also very common, for instance, a clearly described proof sketch for proving a theorem by diagonalization or Bledsoe's k-parameter technique for proving the completeness of resolution calculi.

During his academic training a mathematician has to accumulate lots of methods. This body of methods is the reasoning repertoire which together with the factual knowledge, to a great extent forms his technical knowledge. Another

---

* This work was supported by the Deutsche Forschungsgemeinschaft, SFB 314 (D2)

equally important knowledge source of a mathematician is his ability to adapt existing methods to suit a new situation. Much of this discussion can already be found in George Pólya's analysis of mathematical reasoning "How to Solve It" [12], where he gives hundreds of examples for methods that mathematicians have to learn. Some of these have been stated very explicitly, others are very general and are largely illustrated with the help of examples only. Allen Newell [11] discussed the relevance of Pólya's heuristics very intensively, although he did not achieve a formalization. While specific methods have been widely implemented as so-called tactics in deduction systems like LCF [6] or Nuprl [4], and extended to methods in Alan Bundy's approach of proof planning [2], no adequate solution to the important problem of adapting methods to novel situations has been found so far. In this paper we propose an extension of Bundy's framework in order to attack precisely this question.

Alan Bundy views methods essentially as a triple consisting of a tactic, a precondition, and a postcondition. There the tactic is a piece of program code that can manipulate the actual proof in a controlled way. The precondition and the postcondition form a specification of the deductive ability of the tactic, formulating declaratively the applicability condition of the tactic and a description of the proof status after its application. This has been an essential progress compared with a mere tactic language because within this framework it is now possible to develop proof plans with the help of the declarative knowledge in the preconditions and postconditions. Following a one-sided approach relying on procedural knowledge only, the OYSTER-CLAM system developed by Bundy's group, still has however a severe drawback: the adaption of methods to other problems is almost impossible, because that would require the transformation of programs – tactics are just programs – which is known to be a very hard problem in practice.

To remedy this shortcoming our notion of method separates the procedural and the declarative knowledge in the tactic part.

2 General Framework

The work in this paper should be understood in the setting of a computational model that casts the entire process of theorem proving, from the analysis of a problem up to the completion of a proof, as an *interleaving process* of proof planning, method application and verification. In particular, this model ascribes a reasoner's reasoning competence to the existence of methods together with a planning mechanism that uses these methods for proof planning. Since only planning with methods and meta-methods accounts for the creative behavior of our approach, we will not elaborate on the verification phase in this paper.

The theorem proving process is centered around a partial proof tree, which accommodates concepts like *proof sketches*, *proof plans*, and *proofs* by providing various levels of certainty for justifications of proof nodes. Concretely the system follows the paradigm of a blackboard architecture, where all system components have access to the central data-structure of the blackboard, which in our case includes the current proof tree, the proof history, the method base, and a database of mathematical definitions, theorems, and proofs [8].

2.1 Methods

The concept of a method is central to the reasoning process, since methods are the basic units which make up proof plans and are carried out to obtain the proof by bridging the gap between premises and conclusions. The body of methods constitutes the basic reasoning repertoire of a reasoner, it is constantly adapted and enriched with increasing experience.

There was a long and heated debate in AI as to whether knowledge should be represented procedurally or declaratively. For both positions, arguments were put forward from psychological and computational perspectives with respect to, among others, flexibility, computational efficiency, and communicability. It has been realized that both forms of knowledge are necessary to simulate intelligent behavior. We believe it is plausible that both aspects play an important role in human theorem proving and in implementing human-oriented deduction systems. Therefore tactics in our methods have two parts, a declarative and a procedural one that interprets the declarative part. Usually in concrete methods the procedural part will be a standard procedure.

Generalizing the tactic part of a method from a procedure (in Bundy's framework) to a pair containing both a procedure and a piece of declarative knowledge is significant. By discerning the declarative part of tactics, it is now possible to formulate meta-methods that adapt the declarative part of existing methods and thus come up with novel methods. In a framework where a tactic only consists of procedural knowledge, we would in effect be confronted with the much more difficult problem of program synthesis. Our framework is cast so general that it accommodates both a small set of general purpose procedures which operate by applying pieces of domain-specific declarative knowledge, and an open-end set of special purpose reasoning procedures, in which knowledge needed is already implicitly incorporated.

We define a *method* to be a 6-tuple with the following components:
- *Rating*: A function evaluating the appropriateness of applying this method.
- *Premises*: A list of lines which are used to prove the conclusions.
- *Constraints*: Conditions that must hold before the method can be applied.
- *Conclusions*: A list of lines which are proved by this method.
- *Declarative content*: A piece of declarative knowledge used by the *rating* and the *procedural content*. We currently only deal with proof schemata.
- *Procedural content*: Either a standard procedure *interpreting* the piece of declarative knowledge, or a special purpose inference procedure.

Viewed within a planning framework, the method structure can be partitioned into different logic units as illustrated in figure 1. The *premises*, the *constraints*, and the *conclusions* slots together specify whether a method is applicable in a particular proof state. The *rating* is a procedure that evaluates the declarative content of the method, the proof history, and the planning state to give an estimation of the probability of a significant contribution of this method. Thus the rating is a central part of the heuristic mechanism that guides the search for plans (for an example of a rating-driven proof planning system see [13]).

While the specification contains all necessary information for the planner, the *declarative content* and the *procedural content* slots *together* play the role of

Method

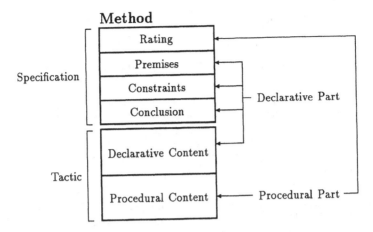

Fig. 1. The Structure of Methods

a so-called *tactic* which is a pure procedure in systems like Nuprl [4] or Bundy's framework for proof planning [3]. For the purposes of this paper it suffices to think of the declarative content as a proof schema with meta-variables, and of the procedural content as a LISP, C, or PROLOG procedure that takes this schema as an argument. The possibilities range from the case where the procedure is an interpreter that matches the proof schema and inserts it into the current proof tree with the meta-variables bound to a situation where the procedure completely ignores the proof schema and constructs new lines purely procedurally. The latter subcase is what can be found in [2]. We only insist that the value of the procedure is a subproof tree that can be integrated into the current partial proof tree.

2.2 Proof Planning with Methods

To give an account of the proof planning process itself, we first remember that the goal of proof planning is to fill gaps in a given partial proof tree by forward and backward reasoning. In our framework we follow a STRIPS-like planning paradigm [5], where the planning operators correspond to the methods. Thus from an abstract point of view the planning process is the process of exploring the search space of *planning states* that is generated by the *planning operators* in order to find a complete *plan* (that is a sequence of instantiated planning operators) from a given *initial state* to a *terminal state*.

Concretely a *planning state* is a subset of lines in the current partial proof that correspond to the boundaries of a gap in the proof. This subset can be divided into *open lines* (that must be proved to bridge the gap) and *support lines* (that can be used to bridge it). The *terminal state* is reached when there are no more open lines. In the planning process new open lines enter the planning state as subgoals by backward reasoning from existing open lines and new support lines by forward reasoning from existing support lines. In order to achieve this with a uni-directional planning mechanism, the planning direction must be independent of the reasoning direction.

The key feature of our approach is that the planning operators are directly derived from the specifications of the methods. However, the specification only

---

Method `def-i` (Definition Introduction)
Premises   `Definition:` $\forall \overline{x}\bullet P(\overline{x}) \Leftrightarrow \Psi_{\overline{x}}$
           $\oplus$ `expanded-line:` $\Psi_{\overline{t}}$
Conclusions $\ominus$ `defined-line:` $P(\overline{t})$

Method `def-e` (Definition Elimination)
Premises   `Definition:` $\forall \overline{x}\bullet P(\overline{x}) \Leftrightarrow \Psi_{\overline{x}}$
         $\ominus$ `defined-line:` $P(\overline{t})$
Conclusions $\oplus$ `expanded-line:` $\Psi_{\overline{t}}$

Fig. 2. The specification of the methods `def-i` and `def-e`

gives a static description (viewed from the completed proof) of the method which is inadequate for the dynamic behavior needed in proof planning. Statically a method derives its *conclusions* from its *premises*. Dynamically, it is important to declare which lines in the specification have to be present in the planning state for the method to be applicable (we will call them *required* lines), and which are constructed by the method. We will do this by labeling the latter lines which will be inserted into the planning state by the label "$\oplus$". Additionally it is useful to specify that some of the required lines will not be used again by the planner. We will mark such lines with a "$\ominus$". Note that the required lines consist of the unmarked ones and those that are marked with "$\ominus$". This labeling in effect determines the direction (forward vs. backward) of reasoning of the method. In order to illustrate these labels, figure 2 shows the specification of two simple methods. These methods are only a simplified version of a more general class of methods applying assertions (definitions and theorems). For a study of this class which approximates basic proof steps encountered in informal mathematical practice see [7].

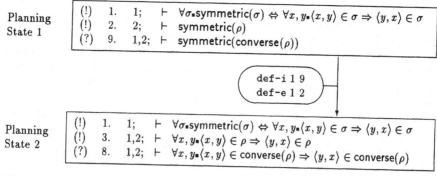

Fig. 3. Using `def-i` and `def-e` in the planning process

Figure 3 shows an example of effect of the methods `def-e` and `def-i` on the planning state. In planning states we mark open lines by "?" and support lines by "!". The method `def-i` applies a definition for the predicate P to an open line and `def-e` applies it to a supporting line. It is obvious that in both methods the line of the definition is required when applying these methods because it is not sensible to "guess" a definition[2]; furthermore this line must not be deleted since it might be used more than once. Therefore Definition has no label. Clearly in both methods defined-line must be a required line and expanded-line can be constructed by the methods (and therefore is labeled with "⊕"). Furthermore defined-line in def-i (and analogously in def-e) is useless after the application because an open line must be proved only once.

In figure 4 we give an abstract view of the planning algorithm. In this algorithm matching must consider the distribution of labels in order to apply the planning operators in the correct direction. In particular an open line in the planning state can only be matched against a line from the *conclusions* slot; similarly support lines can only be matched against *premises*. During the matching of the required lines (in steps 1.(b) and 1.(c)) and the evaluation of the constraints (step 1.(d)) all meta-variables should have been bound to terms without meta-variables (in fact we consider this as one of the applicability conditions). Therefore the new lines of step 4.(a) can be constructed by simply instantiating the meta-variables. The new lines in the *premises* slot are inserted as open lines while the lines from the *conclusions* slot become support lines.

---

1. Find all applicable methods
   - (a) Select a line L from the planning state.
   - (b) Select a method M with a required line that *matches* L.
   - (c) *Match* every required line in M with a line in the planning state.
   - (d) Evaluate the *constraints* of M.
2. Calculate the ratings of Methods
3. Select the best method $\widetilde{M}$ (this is the choice point for backtracking)
4. Apply the planning operator to the planning state
   - (a) *Insert* the new lines *constructed* by $\widetilde{M}$.
   - (b) Delete the lines marked with a "⊖" in $\widetilde{M}$ from the planning state.

Fig. 4. The planning algorithm

Once a complete proof plan is found, all methods in the proof plan are successively applied. Note that such a method application phase need not lead to a complete proof of the problem at hand, since we do not require methods to be sound ·or complete with respect to their specifications. Furthermore the proof segments inserted by the methods may still contain open lines (see e.g. the hom1-1 method) that define further gaps that still have to be closed by the proof planner. Therefore the verification phase may result in a recursive call to the planner or in backtracking. While the first possibility calls for a refinement of the plan found and can be used to model hierarchical planning, the latter rejects the plan and calls the proof planner in order to find a different plan.

Now that we have understood the basic framework, we have a look at the slightly more complex, related example of the hom1-1 method (see figure 5). Its proof strategy can informally be described by: *If f is a given function, P a defined predicate and the goal is to prove $P(f(c))$, then show $P(c)$ and use this*

---

[2] This could be sensible at a more sophisticated level of proof planning. However, this "guessing" should be implemented by a different method in order to clearly separate it from simply applying a definition.

to show $P(f(c))$. The very idea is that f is a homomorphism for the property P and that f can be "rippled out" (compare [2, 9]). Note that line 5 is an open line that does not occur in the specification and therefore does not enter the planning state. This leads to an abstraction in the planning process (i.e. there is less information in the planning state): since line 5 is not considered by the planner, after completing the plan it will be inserted into the proof tree as an open line by the application of the tactic of hom1-1. This will result in a recursive call of the planner in the following verification phase.

Method: hom1-1	
rating	rating-hom1-1
prem	1, 2, $\oplus$3
constr	—
conc	$\ominus$6
dec-cont	1. 1; $\vdash$ $\forall x.\text{Formula}_f$ (J1) 2. 2; $\vdash$ $\forall x_\bullet P(x) \Leftrightarrow \Psi_x$ (J2) 3. 1,2; $\vdash$ $P(c)$ (J3) 4. 1,2; $\vdash$ Ψ_c (def-e 2 3) 5. 1,2; $\vdash$ $\Psi_{f(c)}$ (OPEN 1 4) 6. 1,2; $\vdash$ $P(f(c))$ (def-i 2 5)
proc	schema-interpreter

Fig. 5. The hom1-1 method

For example, to prove that the converse relation of a binary relation ρ is symmetric (formally: symmetric(converse(ρ))), the method hom1-1 can be applied by substituting converse, symmetric, and ρ for the meta-variables f, P, and c, respectively. While in figure 3 we filled the gap between symmetric(ρ) and symmetric(converse(ρ)) which were both existing lines, in this example the method hom1-1 proposes symmetric(ρ) as a new line which can be used to prove symmetric(converse(ρ)) together with the definitions of symmetric and converse. If the plan can be completed (by proving the new open line 3 with some additional information about ρ) the proof resulting from the application of the tactic hom1-1 would look like in figure 6.

1. 1; $\vdash$ $\forall \sigma_\bullet \forall x, y_\bullet \langle x, y \rangle \in \text{converse}(\sigma) \Leftrightarrow \langle y, x \rangle \in \sigma$				(J1)
2. 2; $\vdash$ $\forall \sigma_\bullet \text{symmetric}(\sigma) \Leftrightarrow \forall x, y_\bullet \langle x, y \rangle \in \sigma \Rightarrow \langle y, x \rangle \in \sigma$				(J2)
3. 1,2; $\vdash$ symmetric(ρ)				(J3)
4. 1,2; $\vdash$ $\forall x, y_\bullet \langle x, y \rangle \in \rho \Rightarrow \langle y, x \rangle \in \rho$				(def-e 3 2)
5. 1,2; $\vdash$ $\forall x, y_\bullet \langle x, y \rangle \in \text{converse}(\rho) \Rightarrow \langle y, x \rangle \in \text{converse}(\rho)$				(OPEN 1 4)
6. 1,2; $\vdash$ symmetric(converse(ρ))				(def-i 2 5)

Fig. 6. The proof resulting from the application of the tactic hom1-1

Let us have a look at the justifications in this proof fragment. Justifications J1 and J2 are found by the matching procedure when applying the planning operator of hom1-1, J3 will be inserted by the remaining proof plan. The justifications of lines 4 and 6 stand for the subproofs generated by the applications of the tactics of these methods, whereas the justification of line 5 defines a new gap with support lines containing lines 1 and 4.

3   Extending the Reasoning Repertoire by Meta-Methods

It is one of the main features contributing to the problem solving competence of mathematicians that they can extend their current problem solving repertoire by adapting existing methods to suit novel situations (see [12] for mathematical reasoning and [14] for general problem solving). By adopting a declarative approach for formulating methods, we propose a way to mechanize some aspects of this procedure. In the rest of this paper, the emphasis is laid on the notion of meta-method and a description of classes of meta-methods, while the integration of meta-methods in the planning process is largely left to further research.

3.1   Definition of Meta-Methods

The isolation of the declarative part of tactics makes it feasible to formulate meta-methods adapting existing methods. To achieve the same effect, in a framework where tactics consist only of procedural knowledge, we would be confronted with the much more difficult problem of adapting procedures.

A *meta-method* consists of:[3]

- A *body*: a procedure which takes as input a method, and possibly further parameters (in particular the current state of proof planning) and generates a new method with the same procedural part (see figure 1).
- A *rating*: a procedure which takes as input a method, the current state of proof planning and the proof history. It estimates the contribution of the application of the meta-methods to the solution of the current problem.

We illustrate this definition with the help of the hom1-1 method in figure 5. This method simplifies a problem by generating an intermediate goal, where a *unary* function symbol is eliminated. Suppose we are facing the similar problem of proving that the intersection of symmetric relations is itself a symmetric relation. A variant of hom1-1 is needed, which handles a *binary* function symbol (i.e. "∩") in a similar way.

```
Meta-Method add-argument(M,F)
Rating     add-argument-rating
Procedure add-argument-proc
```

Fig. 7. Meta-Method: add-argument

In the following we illustrate how the meta-method add-argument (figure 7) generates a binary version hom1-2 (figure 8) from the unary version hom1-1 (figure 5). While hom1-1 is applicable to situations with a unary predicate constant P and a unary function constant f, hom1-2 handles situations with a unary

---

[3] In general, a more complete specification will be necessary for more complex problems where meta-level planning is necessary for the generation of a new method.

Method: hom1-2	
rating	`rating-hom1-1`
prem	1, 2, $\oplus$3, $\oplus$4
constr	—
conc	$\ominus$8
dec-cont	1. 1; $\vdash$ $\forall x, y.\text{Formula}_g$ (J1) 2. 2; $\vdash$ $\forall x \bullet P(x) \Leftrightarrow \Psi_x$ (J2) 3. 1,2; $\vdash$ $P(c)$ (J3) 4. 1,2; $\vdash$ $P(d)$ (J4) 5. 1,2; $\vdash$ Ψ_c (def-e 2 3) 6. 1,2; $\vdash$ Ψ_d (def-e 2 4) 7. 1,2; $\vdash$ $\Psi_{g(c,d)}$ (OPEN 1 5 6) 8. 1,2; $\vdash$ $P(g(c,d))$ (def-i 2 7)
proc	`schema-interpreter`

Fig. 8. The `hom1-2` method

predicate constant P and a binary function constant g. Note that P, f, and g are meta-variables standing for object constants.

The meta-method `add-argument` takes as input a method M and a unary function or predicate constant F used in M. This meta-method is supposed to add an argument to the key constant symbol F, the modified constant is called F'. The rating procedure yields the value zero if F does not occur in M, an average value if F does not occur in the premises and conclusions of M. It produces a high value if F is a key symbol of the method M.

The procedure `add-argument-proc` creates a method M' by carrying out the following modification on the declarative part of M:

- replace $F(x)$ by $F'(x, y)$ and augment the corresponding quantifications,
- replace $F(a)$ by $F'(a, b)$ (b has to be a new meta-variable),
- if a occurs in a proof line, but not in a term $F(a)$, a copy of this line will be inserted into the proof schema, replacing a by b (in the example line 4 is copied from 3).

Let us reiterate the crucial advantage of separating the procedural and the declarative knowledge: the procedural part of M can be taken over for the new method.

```
1.  1;   ⊢ ∀ρ, σ•∀x, y•⟨x, y⟩ ∈ (ρ ∩ σ) ⇔ ⟨x, y⟩ ∈ ρ ∧ ⟨x, y⟩ ∈ σ      (J1)
2.  2;   ⊢ ∀σ•symmetric(σ) ⇔ ∀x, y•⟨x, y⟩ ∈ σ ⇒ ⟨y, x⟩ ∈ σ            (J2)
3.  1,2; ⊢ symmetric(ρ)                                               (J3)
4.  1,2; ⊢ symmetric(σ)                                               (J4)
5.  1,2; ⊢ ∀x, y•⟨x, y⟩ ∈ ρ ⇒ ⟨y, x⟩ ∈ ρ                             (def-e 2 3)
6.  1,2; ⊢ ∀x, y•⟨x, y⟩ ∈ σ ⇒ ⟨y, x⟩ ∈ σ                             (def-e 2 4)
7.  1,2; ⊢ ∀x, y•⟨x, y⟩ ∈ (ρ ∩ σ) ⇒ ⟨y, x⟩ ∈ (ρ ∩ σ)                (OPEN 1 5 6)
8.  1,2; ⊢ symmetric((ρ ∩ σ))                                         (def-i 2 7)
```

Fig. 9. The proof resulting from the application of the tactic `hom1-2`

In figure 9 it is shown how the `hom1-2` method simplifies the problem of showing that the intersection of two symmetric relations is symmetric too. Analogously a method `hom2-1` (for handling a unary function symbol and a binary predicate symbol) can be obtained by applying `add-argument` with the arguments `hom1-1` and P.

3.2 Proof Planning with Meta-Methods

Meta-methods can be incorporated into the planning algorithm of figure 4. To do this, firstly it must be possible to interrupt the planning with methods, in order to create a new method with meta-methods. In our approach this is done when all applicable methods yield a rating below a certain threshold. The harder question is the choice of a meta-method and a method for the current situation. We believe that there can hardly be any general answer and we have to rely on heuristics. In an interactive proof development environment like Ω-MKRP [8] the user might want to make this choice himself. Therefore our main emphasis lies in the task of offering the user heuristic support for this choice. Even more challenging would be an automation, of course. A trivial answer would be to apply all existing meta-methods on all existing methods and then choose the applicable one with the highest rating. Such a procedure can be fairly expensive with a large knowledge base. The first heuristics for choosing a method to adapt we will investigate are listed below:

- Organize methods in a hierarchy of mathematical theories and prefer methods that belong to the same theory as the current problem or whose theory is close to that of the problem in the hierarchy.
- Use general conflict solving strategies like those of OPS5 [1], for instance, favor the methods and meta-methods with the most specific specification.
- Take only non-applicable methods with the highest rating[4].

Naturally only successful methods generated in a short-term memory are integrated into the permanent base of methods. Another way to reduce the cost of the operation would be to create only the specification of the methods to be generated, select one for application and create the tactic part by need.

3.3 Classes of Meta-Methods

Clearly the success of the approach outlined in this paper critically depends on the body of meta-methods that is at the disposal of the planner. In order to get an idea of the range of possible meta-methods, consider the following classes.

Generalization This type of meta-methods is designed to generalize an existing method to extend the class of problems it can solve.
- Precondition analysis: a new method may be produced by generalizing or even removing some of the lines in the specification.
- Syntactic abstraction: this type of meta-methods abstracts a given method by replacing terms satisfying certain conditions with corresponding meta-variables.

---

[4] This presupposes sophisticated rating functions, which yield meaningful ratings even if the method in question is not applicable.

- Semantic abstraction: this type of meta-methods produces more abstract methods by capturing the nature of an existing method. For example, a meta-method `fixpoint-freeness` can abstract a concrete method solving the Cantor problem. It recognizes that the very idea of the method is based on the fixpoint-freeness of a function.

Syntactical adaption At least two types of gaps require syntactical adaptions of methods. In the first case, the problem to be solved is basically the same as the one a method is designed to solve, but the original is not applicable due to a different formulation. In the second case, some non-trivial syntactical adaption is necessary in order to solve a related but different problem.

- Change of formulation: Many mathematical concepts are logically identical, in certain sense. For example, sets can be viewed as predicates, and predicates as special functions that yield only boolean values.
  - `set-to-predicate` generates methods by either replacing formulations concerning sets by formulations concerning predicates, or in the opposite direction.
  - `predicate-to-function` and `set-to-function` are similar to `set-to-predicate`.
- Change of syntactical structure:
  - `add-argument` (illustrated in detail in this section).
  - `connective-to-quantifier` generating a method handling problems containing universal quantifiers from a methods containing the logic connective $\wedge$.

For more high-level procedures like learning and analogical reasoning further classes of meta-methods are necessary, for instance, a meta-method that creates new methods by isolating interesting parts in a method.

4 Conclusion

The advanced problem solving competence of a mathematician relies mainly on his ability to adapt problem solving knowledge to new situations where existing methods are not directly applicable. Up to now this has not received enough attention in the field of automated theorem proving. In this paper we have proposed a refined proof planning approach in order to mechanize parts of this ability. It is our conviction that in the proof planning framework this is only possible with declaratively represented knowledge. Therefore we have defined a new structure for representing methods which supports the separation of the knowledge into a declarative and a procedural part.

Since methods describe the planning operators (represented in the "specification") as well as the deduction procedures (represented in the "tactic"), the separation of the declarative and the procedural knowledge is necessary in the specification and in the tactic as well. In order to perform the adaption of methods, we have introduced the new notion of a meta-method. We have specified a proof planning process based on methods and meta-methods. The approach has not only proved to be useful on the investigated examples, but also offers the possibility to formalize analogical reasoning [10] and the basis for learning of methods. Currently we are implementing these ideas in order to gain new experiences from the experiments and to concentrate on the important point of heuristic control through the ratings.

Acknowledgments

We would like to thank Jörg Denzinger, Erica Melis, Arthur Sehn, and Inger Sonntag for many fruitful discussions about proof plans, which inspired and clarified many of the ideas presented here.

References

1. L. Brownston, R. Farrell, E. Kant, and N. Martin. *Programming Expert Systems in OPS5 – An Introduction to Rule-Based Programming*. Addison-Wesley, Reading, Massachusetts, USA, 1985.
2. A. Bundy. The use of explicit plans to guide inductive proofs. In *Proc. of 9th International Conference on Automated Deduction*, pages 111–120. Springer, 1988.
3. A. Bundy. A science of reasoning: Extended abstract. In *Proc. of 10th International Conference on Automated Deduction*, pages 633–640. Springer, 1990.
4. R. Constable et al. *Implementing Mathematics with the Nuprl Proof Development System*. Prentice Hall, New Jersey, 1986.
5. R. E. Fikes and N. J. Nilsson. STRIPS: A new approach to the application of theorem proving to problem solving. *Artificial Intelligence*, 2:189–208, 1971.
6. M. Gordon, R. Milner, and C. Wadsworth. *Edinburgh LCF: A Mechanized Logic of Computation*. LNCS 78. Springer, 1979.
7. X. Huang. Reconstructing proofs at the assertion level. In *Proc. of 12th International Conference on Automated Deduction*. Springer, 1994.
8. X. Huang, M. Kerber, M. Kohlhase, E. Melis, D. Nesmith, J. Richts, and J. Siekmann. Ω-MKRP – a proof development environment. In *Proc. of 12th International Conference on Automated Deduction*. Springer, 1994.
9. D. Hutter. Guiding induction proofs. In *Proc. of the 10th International Conference on Automated Deduction*, pages 147–161. Springer, 1990.
10. E. Melis. Change of representation in theorem proving by analogy. SEKI-Report SR-93-07, Fachbereich Informatik, Universität des Saarlandes, Saarbrücken, Germany, 1993.
11. A. Newell. The heuristic of George Polya and its relation to artificial intelligence. In R. Groner, M. Groner and W. F. Bishof, editors, Methods of Heuristics, Lawrence Erlbaum, Hillsdale, New Jersey, USA, 195-243.
12. G. Pólya. *How to Solve it*. Princeton Univ. Press, 1945.
13. I. Sonntag and J. Denzinger. Extending automatic theorem proving by planning. SEKI-Report SR-93-02 (SFB), Fachbereich Informatik, Universität Kaiserslautern, Kaiserslautern, Germany, 1993.
14. K. VanLehn. Problem solving and cognitive skill acquisition. In M. I. Posner, editor, *Foundations of Cognitive Science*, chapter 14. MIT Press, 1989.

Using Charts for Transfer in MT

Jan W. Amtrup

University of Hamburg, CS Dept., Natural Language Division, Vogt-Kölln-Str. 30,
D-22527 Hamburg. email: amtrup@informatik.uni-hamburg.de

Abstract. We present an adaption of chart-parsing techniques to the application of transfer in machine translation. The resulting flexibility enables the investigation of several architectural features when integrating a transfer stage into an incremental, interactive architecture.

The architecture for an automatic interpreting system capable of translating spontaneously produced dialogue contributions has to obey several restrictions concerning the overall design and the conception of individual components. The features include *incrementality, component interaction*, and — if possible — *time synchronicity* and *parallelization*. It is highly desirable for a transfer module to follow these restrictions in order to augment system usability and behaviour.

Charts have mainly been used for parsing. The ability to store incompletely analyzed constituents as well as the great flexibility implemented by means of an *agenda* enable chart parsing mechanisms to investigate several choices of parsing and search strategies.

We adapted the chart schema for transfer to benefit from these properties. *Active edges* correspond to partially translated source language constituents, the fundamental rule combines two partial translations to form a more complete one thus yielding a tree of transfer edges rooted at every inactive analysis edge. The result is a twodimensional structure of time and solved transfer equations. Transfer rules are formulated within a typed feature structure formalism and carry out structural transfer on a syntactic level.

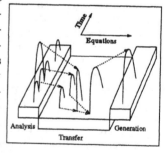

The main features of the approach are: Translations can be *reused*, they don't have to be reanalyzed from scratch when backtracking. The transfer mechanism works *incrementally*, which enables implementation of e.g. left-to-right strategies or best-first approaches. In principle, there are no barriers which prevent interaction between modules to reduce ambiguity, which is an ultimate goal of an incremental, interactive architecture. It is also possible to parallelize the transfer stage using well-known techniques from chart parsing.

A first experimentation system using Lisp and CLOS has been built. Subsequent work will concentrate on the integration of a more elaborate transfer concept into an architectural prototype which follows the architectural lines as indicated above.

A New Frame For Common-Sense Reasoning –
Towards Local Inconsistencies

Matthias Baaz   Karin Hörwein*

Technische Universität Wien, Austria

Consistency checks cause the computational intractability of first order approaches to nonmonotonic reasoning and, more, they are not essential for modeling human reasoning patterns, whence we should try to move beyond them.

To keep the effect of inconsistencies local we introduce the calculus **LP** together with nonlogical axiom sequents. (**LP** corresponds to a variant of the classical Gentzen-style sequent calculus **LK** with the restriction that there is at most one formula one the left hand side of the sequent arrow.) We obtain the following theorem:

Theorem[2]: $\vdash_{LP} \mathcal{A} \wedge \neg \mathcal{A} \to \mathcal{B}$ and $\nvdash_{LP} \to \mathcal{B}$ implies that $\mathcal{B}$ contains a predicate symbol that is connected via use within an axiom sequent with another predicate symbol occuring in $\mathcal{A}$.

The corresponding Kripke-style semantics for **LP** support the default character of common-sense reasoning. A statement is *false* in our momentary world iff it is *false* in all future worlds. As a consequence every statement has the feature of a hypothesis.

LP can be embedded into modal logic in a dual way to intuitionistic logic **LJ**: Define the modal operator $\Diamond$, such that a formala $\Diamond F$ is *false* at a vertex k iff $\mathcal{F}$ is *false* at all vertexes $l \geq k$ (within each world the evalutation of the classical connectives is truthfunctional). We can therefore define a modal extension **LK**^{m} of **LK** and a translation of **LK**-sequents to **LK**^{m}-sequents such that **LP** $\vdash S$ iff **LK**$^m \vdash S^m$.

This allows us to express the idea of Clarke and Gabbay[3] of defining consistency by truth in a possible world within classical logic instead of intuitionistic logic. It holds that $\nvdash_{LK^m} \Diamond(\Diamond F \wedge \Diamond \neg \Diamond F) \to \Diamond G$, for an arbitrary sentence G having no predicate in common with F, since $\nvdash_{LP} F \wedge \neg F \to G$.

(We can understand the propositional part of **LK**^{m} as a characterization of consistency statements in the sense of a provability logic which is based on the classical propositional calculus together with the axioms: $A \supset cons_T(A)$, $cons_T(cons_T(A)) \supset cons_T(A)$, $cons_T(A \vee B) \supset (cons_T(A) \vee cons_T(B))$ and the rule: $A \supset B \vdash cons_T(A) \supset cons_T(B)$.)

---

* Current address: TU-Wien, Karlsplatz 13/E185-2, A-1040 Wien/Austria; phone: +43(1)58801-4103; email: baaz@logic.tuwien.ac.at, karin@logic.tuwien.ac.at

2 M. Baaz, K. Hörwein, *Semantics for LP*, Techn. Report TU-E1182/1852/BH94-1, TU-Wien, Vienna, 1994.

3 M. R. B. Clarke, D. M. Gabbay, *An Intuitionistic Basis for Non-Monotonic Reasoning*, in *Non-Standard Logics for Automated Reasoning*, Academic Press, 1988.

Prioritized Transitions for Updates

Marie-Odile Cordier[1] and Pierre Siegel[2]

[1] IRISA, Campus de Beaulieu, 35042 RENNES Cedex, France, cordier@irisa.fr
[2] LIM, place Victor Hugo, 13331 MARSEILLE, France, siegel@gyptis.univ-mrs.fr

An update operation presupposes that one can predict how the world changes along time. In the absence of a predictive model of evolution, the common sense law of inertia is usually used and justifies the minimal change approach to the frame problem. Instead of relying on an implicit modeling of persistence, we propose to use an *explicit* modeling of the expected evolution. A first step in that direction was already proposed in [1]. Its major flaw is its inability to respect the model-driven principle which was shown to be crucial in an update context (see for example [3]). In this paper [2], we propose a new model-driven semantics of the update operation which can take into account an explicit transition model. It extends the semantics defined in [4] for the Possible Model Approach by allowing an explicit expression of persistence. The transition model provides a more powerful and flexible way to represent how the world tends to change along time. It can moreover be stressed that non only persistence information but also default and transition rules can be expressed in this transition model. It can then be used to represent evolutive systems as required for example in a monitoring or diagnosis context.

The paper is structured as follows : we begin by showing on a motivating example the main issues of the update operation and we point out the flaws of our [1] proposal. The transition model is presented in section 3. The semantics of the update operation is defined in section 4 and illustrated by examples in section 5. We show in section 6 how the relation between PMA and preferential models highlighted in [4] can be extended to take into account an explicit transition model. In the last section, we conclude by comparing our approach to the related ones more precisely.

References

1. Marie Odile Cordier and Pierre Siegel. A temporal revision model for reasoning about world change. In Bernhard Nebel, Charles Rich, and William Swartout, editors, *Principles of Knowledge Representation and Reasoning (KR'92)*, pages 732–739. Morgan Kaufmann, 1992.
2. Marie Odile Cordier and Pierre Siegel. Prioritized transitions for updates. *Internal Report IRISA/LIM*, 1994.
3. Hirofumi Katsuno and Alberto O. Mendelzon. On the difference between updating a knowledge base and revising it. In *Principles of Knowledge Representation and Reasoning (KR'91)*, pages 387–394, 1991.
4. Marianne Winslett. Sometimes updates are circumscription. In *Proceedings of the IJCAI Conference*, pages 859–863, Detroit, 1989.

An Optimal Bidirectional Search Algorithm

Jürgen Eckerle

Institut für Informatik, Universität Freiburg
Rheinstr. 10–12, 79104 Freiburg, Germany
E-Mail: {eckerle}@informatik.uni-freiburg.de

Abstract. Several optimality theorems hold for the A^* algorithm, one important says: A^* dominates every other admissible heuristic search algorithm assumed that the underlying heuristic function is monotone. An analogous result is proved for the bidirectional case. A bidirectional heuristic search algorithm, named OBDS, is presented which is admissible and dominates every other admissible bidirectional heuristic search algorithm B assumed that the underlying heuristic function is bi-monotone.
keywords: search, heuristic search, bidirectional search, optimality

1 Summary

This paper aims to improve the theoretival understanding of bidirectional search which is not as well understood as the unidirectional search (e. g. A^*) by now.

A *state space* corresponds with a weighted graph where nodes represent problem states and arcs operations transforming one state into a successor state (Γ denotes the successor operator). We use a heuristic estimate $h(x, y)$ of the minimal weight of a path from state node x to y. The heuristic h is called (1) *admissible*, if $h(x, y)$ is always an optimistic estimation and (2) *bi-monotone* if h is monotone in both components (i. e. $h(x', y) + c(x, x') \geq h(x, y), x' \in \Gamma(x)$ and $h(x, y') + c(y, y') \geq h(x, y), y' \in \Gamma^{-1}(y)$). According the usual conventions let us name $OPEN_s$ and $OPEN_t$ the set of horizon nodes rooted at the start node s and t, respectively. We evaluate the elements of $OPEN_s$ by $f_s(x) = g_s(x) + min(\{h(x, v) + g_t(v) | v \in OPEN_t\})$ and that of $OPEN_t$ by f_t (analogously defined).

We present a best-first (with respect to f_s and f_t) algorithm OBDS which is admissible (i. e. always finds an optimal solution provided there is one) and proves the following optimality theorem:

Theorem: *Let G be a state space graph, h a bi-monotone heuristic on G and B be an admissible bidirectional heuristic search algorithm. Then there is a decision procedure for OBDS such that OBDS expands only a subset of state nodes expanded by B, i. e. OBDS dominates B.*

The complete article is available by ftp (anonymous) with internet-adress *fidji.informatik.uni-freiburg.de* in the directory */ftp/papers/eckerle/optbid.ps*.

Learning to Discriminate Phases in Gas–Liquid Flow

Bogdan Filipič[1,2], Iztok Žun[2] and Matjaž Perpar[2]

[1] Artificial Intelligence Laboratory, Department of Computer Science,
Jožef Stefan Institute, Jamova 39, 61000 Ljubljana, Slovenia
E-mail: *Bogdan.Filipic@ijs.si*
[2] Laboratory for Fluid Dynamics and Thermodynamics, Faculty of Mechanical
Engineering, University of Ljubljana, Aškerčeva 6, 61000 Ljubljana, Slovenia

Summary

Discrimination of phases, i.e. substances of different aggregate states, in gas-liquid flow is a sensor data interpretation problem. Probes emitting two-state signals are usually used to detect local phase changes through a property, like conductivity, which is different for the two phases [1]. The probe signal then needs to be processed to obtain a particular flow characteristic. The processing methods typically reconstruct the two-state signal from a probe signal by static application of predefined threshold values. Although adequate to acquire certain flow features, the existing methods may in signal interpretation significantly disagree with expert understanding of the underlying physical phenomena.

To alleviate this problem, a discrimination technique has been introduced that incorporates human expertise into probe signal interpretation [2]. Development of the technique includes three stages: designing a prototype phase discrimination procedure, providing training probe and two-state signals, and tuning procedure thresholds. Unlike the existing procedures, the prototype discrimination procedure relates threshold values to local extrema detected in the input signal, what makes it less sensitive to noise and signal drift. In preparing training signals, a human expert is involved demonstrating his/her phase discrimination skill on a selected probe signal sequence. The resulting expert binary signal serves as a reference for threshold tuning. Phase discrimination procedure thresholds are finally tuned using a genetic algorithm. The optimization is performed so that the resulting phase discrimination procedure generates the binary output as close to the one defined by expert as possible.

The experimental verification on air-water flow under laboratory conditions has shown the new technique is suitable for gas–liquid flow measurements and applicable to various flow regimes appearing in industrial processes.

References

1. Cartellier, A. and Achard, J. L.: Local phase detection probes in fluid/fluid two-phase flows. *Review of Scientific Instruments*, **62** (1991) 279–303.
2. Žun, I., Filipič, B., Perpar, M. and Bombač, A.: Phase discrimination in void fraction measurements via genetic algorithms. Presented at the 30th Meeting of the European Two-Phase Flow Group, Hannover, 1993, paper C3.

Strategies for Semantical Contractions

Jürgen Giesl[1] and Ingrid Neumann[2]

[1] Dept. of Computer Science, Technical University Darmstadt, Alexanderstr. 10,
64283 Darmstadt, Germany, Email: giesl@inferenzsysteme.informatik.th-darmstadt.de
[2] Dept. of Computer Science, University of Karlsruhe, Kaiserstr. 12,
76128 Karlsruhe, Germany, Email: neumann@ira.uka.de

The *Logic of Theory Change* developed by Alchourrón, Gärdenfors and Makinson (AGM) is concerned with the revision of beliefs in the face of new and possibly contradicting information. This nonmonotonic process consists of a contraction and an expansion transforming one set of beliefs into another. Beliefs are represented by consistent deductively closed sets of formulas. To achieve minimal change AGM suggested widely accepted postulates that proper contractions have to fulfill.

In practical applications, e.g. knowledge representation, deductively closed sets of formulas have to be representable in a finite way. Therefore our main interest is in *finite contractions*, i.e. contractions that transform sets of formulas possessing a finite base into finitely representable sets again.

We have formulated a semantical characterization of finite contractions satisfying the AGM-postulates which provides an insight into the true nature of these operations and shows all possibilities to define concrete functions of this kind.

Semantically, a finite contraction of a set Φ by a formula φ means extending the models M of Φ by a set of models of $\neg\varphi$ that has to be uniquely determined by its restriction to a finite subsignature.

Examining the concrete contractions known from literature by this characterization we obtain that they are all defined according to the same semantical strategy: The original set of models M is extended by those models of $\neg\varphi$ that can be obtained by a *"small"* change of M. This strategy results in maintaining those formulas of Φ which belong to the (hopefully maximal) subsignature not affected by that change of M. But as the number of "important" formulas in Φ is not equal for different subsignatures of the same size we argue that this strategy leads to a contraintuitive behaviour[3].

Instead, the syntactical goal of keeping as many important formulas as possible in the contracted set corresponds to the following semantical strategy: M has to be extended by some models I of $\neg\varphi$ such that the *number of "big" changes* of M which result in I is *as large as possible*. Finite contractions defined this way meet the intuitive notion of minimal change.

---

[3] When restricting ourselves to clauses instead of formulas a clause is the more important the less literals it consists of. If Φ is the deductive closure of $\{a, b \vee c\}$ the subsignatures $\{a, c\}$ and $\{b, c\}$ have the same size, but the most important clause of Φ does not belong to the latter one.

Conflicts in the Spatial Interaction of Autonomous Agents

J.S.J.H. Penders

PTT Research P.O. Box 421 2260 AK Leidschendam, The Netherlands

We analyze the interaction among mobile agents, robots in particular. On a terminal cargo is sorted by autonomous agents. Each agent is instructed where to pick up a certain piece of cargo and where to bring it. The agents merely have to perform two elementary behaviours: goal finding and obstacle avoidance. The system will perform "mechanistically", the total of operations and interactions however, is complex. The agents might enter into a mutual conflict of avoiding one another, a *balanced conflict* we call it.

We analyze the interaction and develop a precise description of *spatial conflicts*[1]. The analysis provides a basis for assessing how a particular multi-robot system will perform and how it deals with conflicts. Penders et al. in [2] use conflict development to analyze some specific obstacle avoidance procedures. Obstacle avoidance is important not only for robots, but for ships and aircraft as well.

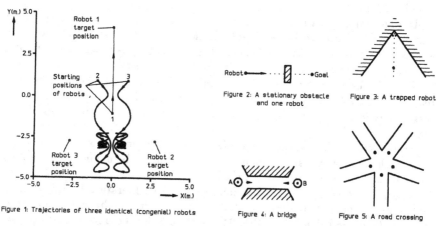

Figure 1: Trajectories of three identical (congenial) robots

Figure 2: A stationary obstacle and one robot

Figure 3: A trapped robot

Figure 4: A bridge

Figure 5: A road crossing

A very typical example of a balanced conflict is given in figure 1. The robots apply a potential field based procedure for goal finding and obstacle avoidance[3]. Figure 2 shows a **stationary** obstacle and one adaptive agent. If the robot does not guide itself away from the baseline it is in a balanced "conflict". In figure 3 the trapped robot is in a balanced conflict too. In severely constrained circumstances balanced conflicts occur in human interaction too. In figure 4 it is impossible for two agents to pass at the same time. Figure 5 shows a road crossing where normal traffic rules are not decisive. Humans solve such conflicts by applying other skills, as boldness for example.

[1] Penders, J.S.J.H., Conflicts in the spatial interaction of Autonomous Agents, PTT Research NT-PU-93-1728.
[2] Penders, J.S.J.H., L. Alboul and P.J. Braspenning, The Interaction of congenial autonomous Robots: Obstacle avoidance using Artificial Potential fields, in: Proc. ECAI-94, Amsterdam 1994..
[3] Wang, P.K.C., Interaction Dynamics of Multiple Mobile Robots with Simple Navigation Strategies, Journal of Robotic Systems, 6(1), pp. 77-101, 1989.

Using Rough Sets Theory to Predict German Word Stress

Stefan Rapp, Michael Jessen, Grzegorz Dogil

Institut für Maschinelle Sprachverarbeitung, Universität Stuttgart, Germany

The location of primary stress in German morphologically simple words is an interesting domain for the application of symbolic machine learning (ML) techniques. It is commonly accepted among phonologists that stress location is predictable from the syllable structure and segmental setup of the last syllables in the word. Using a rough sets based classifier we test some assumptions about the phonological factors underlying stress placement. Whereas phonologists have arrived at these assumptions mostly in a deductive way, machine learning provides the opportunity for corpus-based empirical evaluation.

The words included in our corpus are nouns that are monomorphemic or derived by a nonnative suffix, and they contain more than one non-schwa vowel. They are drawn from a textbook on German word stress and can thus be seen as representative to the stress assignment task. All the words have been transcribed phonetically according to the DUDEN pronouncing dictionary along with syllable boundaries added by the authors. With pronunciation variants the corpus consists of 260 cases (239 different words). Two types of coding have been computationally extracted from the corpus, one being the information commonly used by phonologists, the other a more detailed set of attributes consisting of *presence of syllable onset, vowel height, vowel length, vowel tenseness*, and *number of consonants in syllable coda*. The decision attribute is the location of stress on either the final, the penultimate, or the antepenultimate syllable.

In three experiments we used the rough sets based commercially available ML-Tool DataLogic/R to induce symbolic rules from the attributes. Our first experiment shows that it is valid to concentrate on the last three syllables of the word. Using a *learn = test* scenario we found that for both types of coding the inclusion of information beyond three syllables from the right only makes a negligible contribution to the accuracy of the induced rules. Within a *learn ≠ test* setting, the second experiment demonstrates that the more detailed type of coding yields substantially improved predictive accuracy over the phonological coding. In a third experiment we found that this improvement is due to only the vowel length attributes.

In general, our experiments have demonstrated that ML-techniques are a useful tool in the investigation of current issues in linguistic research.

[1] Pawlak, Z. (1991). *Rough sets: Theoretical Aspects of Reasoning About Data*. Kluwer Academic, Dordrecht, The Netherlands.
[2] Rapp, S. (1994). *Maschinelles Lernen von Aspekten des deutschen Wortakzents*. Diplomarbeit Universität Stuttgart, Fakultät Informatik, to appear.

Graphtheoretical Algorithms and Knowledge-Based Design

Kristina Schaedler[*]

Institute of Computer Science
Martin Luther University of Halle
PO 8
D-06099 Halle
schaedler@informatik.uni-halle.d400.de

Configurations in knowledge-based design systems are often represented as a hierarchical decomposition into sets of their components, where the relations between the components are expressed as additional information in the form of constraints, rules or predicates. However, there are domains where objects cannot be identified without consideration of the relations between their components [2]. As an example there can exist several objects who consist of the same components with different relations between these components. Therefore a decomposition of comfigurations into nets of components and their relations is proposed. Such nets can be modelled by labelled graphs.

The central graphtheoretical algorithms for the handling of graphs in a knowledge-based design system are the search for graph isomorphisms (or automorphisms) and the estimation of the similarity of graphs. The generation of a so called 'canonical representation' (see [1]) of the graphs can be used to find regularities in graphs and increase the performance of operations like search for graph isomorphisms, known or common subgraphs and graph comparison.

Modelling configurations as labelled graphs has the following advantages: It integrates the set of components and their relations into a single data-structure, which can easily exchanged between different programmes and procedures. The information about the relations between the components is interpreted during the generation, the classification and the comparison of the configurations. Graphtheoretical algorithms can be used to detect symmetries and equivalent components in complex configurations. This information reduces the space of possible configurations and, in some cases, the complexity of numerical computations of properties of the configuration by reducing the number of parameters. The inclusion of graphtheoretical algorithms in a knowledge-based design system can increase its ability to cope with complex, regular configuration whose decomposition hierarchy is flat and/or ambiguous. In addition, graphs as a model and representation of configurations are accepted and common in many domains.

References

1. Schädler, K.: Behandlung topologischer Symmetrie mit Kanonisierung. PROKON-Memo August 1993.
2. Schädler, K.: Eine eineindeutige Repräsentation für Konfigurationen. in: Beiträge zum 8. Workshop "Planen und Konfigurieren" SEKI Working Paper SWP-94-01.

[*] Now at: Technical University of Berlin, FB 13, Franklinstr. 28/29, D- 10587 Berlin

Interval Situation Calculus

Eugenia Ternovskaia
*Comput. Center of Russian Academy of Sciences

This paper presents a logical approach to the formalization of qualitative reasoning about processes in an incompletely known world. I take as a basis a variant of the situation calculus which allows representing of concurrent actions and reasoning by default about unspecified changes [1]. My work is founded also on the paper [2] where a general method of (circumscriptive) minimization in theories describing changes has been proposed. The main contributions of this paper is as follows:

- It was shown how to extend the situation calculus to represent processes extending and overlapping in time.

- Branching structure of possible situations inherent in situation calculus is used along with a linear time order.

- Conclusions can be drawn by default about results of a group of concurrent events which includes unspecified ones.

- The solution guarantees that all models corresponding both to assumptions about possible failures to perform one or another event, and to assumptions about what particular events occurred are examined.

- Apparently uncaused changes (*'miracles'*) can be represented as events taking place concurrently with those events which we definitely know as occurring.

These results are provided by elaborating a suitable minimization policy. Thus the approach allows us to reconstruct full qualitative description of a system. The method can be applied both to the reasoning about physical processes, and to a wider class of domains dealing with changes and reasoning about time such as data base evolution and multi-agent systems.

References

[1] M.E.Soutchanski, E.A.Ternovskaia *Logical Theory of Concurrent Actions* In: Soviet J. of Computer and System Sciences, 1993, V.31 (English version).

[2] J.M.Crawford, D.W.Etherington *Formalizing Reasoning About Change: A Qualitative Reasoning Approach.* In: 10th AAAI, 1992, 577-583.

---

*e-mail: eugenia@brokinvest.msk.su After September (tentative): eugenia@ai.toronto.edu

Springer-Verlag
and the Environment

We at Springer-Verlag firmly believe that an international science publisher has a special obligation to the environment, and our corporate policies consistently reflect this conviction.

We also expect our business partners – paper mills, printers, packaging manufacturers, etc. – to commit themselves to using environmentally friendly materials and production processes.

The paper in this book is made from low- or no-chlorine pulp and is acid free, in conformance with international standards for paper permanency.

Author Index

Lecture Notes in Artificial Intelligence (LNAI)

Lecture Notes in Computer Science

Lecture Notes in Artificial Intelligence

This subseries of Lecture Notes in Computer Science reports new developments in artificial intelligence research and teaching, quickly, informally, and at a high level. The timeliness of a manuscript is more important than its form, which may be unfinished or tentative. The type of material considered for publication includes

– drafts of original papers or monographs,

– technical reports of high quality and broad interest,

– advanced-level lectures,

– reports of meetings, provided they are of exceptional interest and focused on a single topic.

Publication of Lecture Notes is intended as a service to the computer science community in that the publisher Springer-Verlag offers global distribution of documents which would otherwise have a restricted readership. Once published and copyrighted, they can be cited in the scientific literature.

Manuscripts

Lecture Notes are printed by photo-offset from the master copy delivered in camera-ready form. Manuscripts should be no less than 100 and preferably no more than 500 pages of text. Authors of monographs and editors of proceedings volumes receive 50 free copies of their book. Manuscripts should be printed with a laser or other high-resolution printer onto white paper of reasonable quality. To ensure that the final photo-reduced pages are easily readable, please use one of the following formats:

Font size (points)	Printing area (cm)	(inches)	Final size (%)
10	12.2 x 19.3	4.8 x 7.6	100
12	15.3 x 24.2	6.0 x 9.5	80

On request the publisher will supply a leaflet with more detailed technical instructions or a TeX macro package for the preparation of manuscripts.

Manuscripts should be sent to one of the series editors or directly to:

Springer-Verlag, Computer Science Editorial I, Tiergartenstr. 17, D-69121 Heidelberg, FRG

ISBN 3-540-58467-6